Comparative Historical Analysis in the Social Sciences

Comparative historical analysis is among the oldest and most distinguished research traditions in the social sciences. Yet recent decades have seen a dramatic proliferation of work in this perspective, often accomplished in a more self-conscious and rigorous fashion than ever before.

This book systematically investigates the past accomplishments and future agendas of contemporary comparative historical analysis. Its core essays explore three major issues: the accumulation of knowledge in the field over the past three decades, the analytic tools used to study temporal processes and historical patterns, and the methodologies available for making inferences and for building theories. The introductory and concluding essays situate the field as a whole by comparing it to alternative approaches within the social sciences.

Comparative Historical Analysis in the Social Sciences will serve as an invaluable resource for scholars in the field, and it will represent a challenge to many other social scientists – especially those who have raised skeptical concerns about comparative historical analysis in the past.

James Mahoney is the Joukowsky Family Assistant Professor of Sociology at Brown University. His 1997 doctoral dissertation was a recipient of the Gabriel Almond Prize of the American Political Science Association and was subsequently revised into his first book, *The Legacies of Liberalism* (2001). Professor Mahoney received a Career Award from the National Science Foundation to pursue his new research.

Dietrich Rueschemeyer is a research professor at Brown's Watson Institute of International Studies. After 35 years of teaching sociology at Brown, he retired as the Charles C. Tillinghast Jr. Professor of International Studies. Rueschemeyer was a Fellow of the Institute of Advanced Study Berlin and of the Swedish Collegium for Advanced Study in the Social Sciences. His books include *Power and the Division of Labour* and *Capitalist Development and Democracy* (with John D. and Evelyne Stephens), winner of the American Sociological Association's 1992 award for the best book in political sociology.

Other Books in the Series

Stefano Bartolini, *The Political Mobilization of the European Left, 1860–1980: The Class Cleavage*
Mark R. Beissinger, *Nationalist Mobilization and the Collapse of the Soviet State*
Carles Boix, *Political Parties, Growth and Equality: Conservative and Social Democratic Economic Strategies in the World Economy*
Catherine Boone, *Merchant Capital and the Roots of State Power in Senegal, 1930–1985*
Michael Bratton and Nicolas van de Walle, *Democratic Experiments in Africa: Regime Transitions in Comparative Perspective*
Valerie Bunce, *Leaving Socialism and Leaving the State: The End of Yugoslavia, the Soviet Union and Czechoslovakia*
Ruth Berins Collier, *Paths Toward Democracy: The Working Class and Elites in Western Europe and South America*
Nancy Bermeo, ed., *Unemployment in the New Europe*
Donatella della Porta, *Social Movements, Political Violence, and the State*
Gerald Easter, *Reconstructing the State: Personal Networks and Elite Identity*
Robert J. Franzese, Jr., *Macroeconomic Policies of Developed Democracies*

Continued on the page following the index

Comparative Historical Analysis in the Social Sciences

Edited by

JAMES MAHONEY

Brown University

DIETRICH RUESCHEMEYER

Brown University

CAMBRIDGE
UNIVERSITY PRESS

CAMBRIDGE UNIVERSITY PRESS
Cambridge, New York, Melbourne, Madrid, Cape Town, Singapore,
São Paulo, Delhi, Dubai, Tokyo, Meixco City

Cambridge University Press
32 Avenue of the Americas, New York, NY 10013-2473, USA

www.cambridge.org
Information on this title: www.cambridge.org/9780521016452

First published 2003
7th printing 2009

A catalog record for this publication is available from the British Library.

Library of Congress Cataloging in Publication Data

Dietrich Rueschemeyer.
p. cm. – (Cambridge studies in comparative politics)
Revised papers generated from two conferences, the first in April 2000 held at the
Watson Institute of International Studies of Brown University, the second in November
2000 at Harvard's Center for European Studies.
Includes bibliographical references and index.
ISBN 0-521-81610-6 – ISBN 0-521-01645-2 (pb.)
1. Social sciences – Research – Methodology. I. Mahoney, James, 1968–
II. Rueschemeyer, Dietrich, 1930– . III. Series.
h61 c524 2002
300'.7'22–dc21 2002024453

ISBN 978-0-521-81610-6 Hardback
ISBN 978-0-521-01645-2 Paperback

To the memory of Roger V. Gould

Contents

Contributors — *page* xi

Preface — xv

Introduction

1 COMPARATIVE HISTORICAL ANALYSIS: ACHIEVEMENTS AND AGENDAS — 3
James Mahoney and Dietrich Rueschemeyer

I Accumulation of Research

2 COMPARATIVE HISTORICAL ANALYSIS AND KNOWLEDGE ACCUMULATION IN THE STUDY OF REVOLUTIONS — 41
Jack A. Goldstone

3 WHAT WE KNOW ABOUT THE DEVELOPMENT OF SOCIAL POLICY: COMPARATIVE AND HISTORICAL RESEARCH IN COMPARATIVE AND HISTORICAL PERSPECTIVE — 91
Edwin Amenta

4 KNOWLEDGE ACCUMULATION IN COMPARATIVE HISTORICAL RESEARCH: THE CASE OF DEMOCRACY AND AUTHORITARIANISM — 131
James Mahoney

II Analytic Tools

5 BIG, SLOW-MOVING, AND... INVISIBLE: MACROSOCIAL PROCESSES IN THE STUDY OF COMPARATIVE POLITICS 177
Paul Pierson

6 HOW INSTITUTIONS EVOLVE: INSIGHTS FROM COMPARATIVE HISTORICAL ANALYSIS 208
Kathleen Thelen

7 USES OF NETWORK TOOLS IN COMPARATIVE HISTORICAL RESEARCH 241
Roger V. Gould

8 PERIODIZATION AND PREFERENCES: REFLECTIONS ON PURPOSIVE ACTION IN COMPARATIVE HISTORICAL SOCIAL SCIENCE 270
Ira Katznelson

III Issues of Method

9 CAN ONE OR A FEW CASES YIELD THEORETICAL GAINS? 305
Dietrich Rueschemeyer

10 STRATEGIES OF CAUSAL ASSESSMENT IN COMPARATIVE HISTORICAL ANALYSIS 337
James Mahoney

11 ALIGNING ONTOLOGY AND METHODOLOGY IN COMPARATIVE POLITICS 373
Peter A. Hall

Conclusion

12 DOUBLY ENGAGED SOCIAL SCIENCE: THE PROMISE OF COMPARATIVE HISTORICAL ANALYSIS 407
Theda Skocpol

Index 429

Contributors

Edwin Amenta is Professor of Sociology at New York University. His interests include political sociology, comparative and historical sociology, social movements, and social policy. He is the author of many articles on these subjects and of *Bold Relief: Institutional Politics and the Origins of Modern American Social Policy* (Princeton University Press, 1998). This book received the 1999 Distinguished Publication Award of the American Sociological Association Section on Political Sociology. Professor Amenta is currently finishing a new book concerning the consequences of social movements tentatively titled *When Movements Matter: The Impact of the Townsend Plan and U.S. Social Spending Challengers.*

Jack A. Goldstone is Professor of Sociology and International Relations at the University of California, Davis. He is the author of the prize-winning *Revolution and Rebellion in the Early Modern World* (University of California Press, 1991) and the editor of *The Encyclopedia of Political Revolutions* (Congressional Quarterly Press, 1998) and *Revolutions of the Late Twentieth Century* (Westview Press, 1991). He has been a Fellow of the Center for Advanced Study in the Behavioral Sciences at Stanford University and has held fellowships from the American Council of Learned Societies, the Research School of Social Sciences at the Australian National University, and the Canadian Institute for Advanced Research. Professor Goldstone is now completing a new monograph titled *Revolutions, Social Movements, and Social Change* (Harvard University Press, forthcoming).

Roger V. Gould taught at the University of Chicago from 1990 to 2000 and then became Professor of Sociology and Political Science at Yale University. He was a Fellow at the Center for Advanced Study in the Behavioral

Sciences and a visiting scholar at the Russell Sage Foundation. Gould's research concentrated on the relation between social network structure and patterns of social conflict, with specific reference to mass protest, elite opposition to state formation, and group violence. His first book, *Insurgent Identities* (University of Chicago Press, 1995), compared urban insurrections in Paris in 1848 and 1871. More recent publications were articles on collective violence in nineteenth-century Corsica and a forthcoming article on the emergence of hierarchy in social networks. At the time of his death, Professor Gould had completed a book on hierarchy and social conflict.

Peter A. Hall is Frank G. Thomson Professor of Government, Harvard College Professor, and Director of the Minda de Gunzburg Center for European Studies at Harvard University. He is President-Elect of the Comparative Politics Section of the American Political Science Association. His book *Governing the Economy: The Politics of State Intervention in Britain and France* (Oxford University Press, 1986) was a recipient of the Woodrow Wilson Award of the American Political Science Association. He has edited *The Political Power of Economic Ideas: Keynesianism across Nations* (Princeton University Press, 1989) and *Varieties of Capitalism: The Institutional Foundations of Comparative Advantage* (Oxford University Press, 2001, with David Soskice). Among Hall's articles are "Political Science and the Three New Institutionalisms" in *Political Studies* (1996, with Rosemary C. R. Taylor) and "Mixed Signals: Central Bank Independence, Coordinated Wage-Bargaining and European Monetary Union" in *International Organization* (1998, with Robert Franzese, Jr.), which received the Gregory Luebbert Prize of the Comparative Politics Section of the American Political Science Association.

Ira Katznelson is Ruggles Professor of Political Science and History at Columbia University and Senior Research Associate at the Centre for History and Economics, King's College, Cambridge University. He also is a Fellow of the American Academy of Arts and Sciences, and he has served as President of the Social Science History Association and the Politics and History Section of the American Political Science Association. Katznelson's many book publications include *Black Men, White Cities: Race, Politics, and Migration in the United States, 1900–1930, and Britain, 1948–1968* (Oxford University Press, 1973), *City Trenches: Urban Politics and the Patterning of Class in the United States* (Pantheon Books, 1981), *Marxism and the City* (Oxford University Press, 1992), and the prize-winning *Liberalism's Crooked*

Circle: Letters to Adam Michnik (Princeton University Press, 1996). He is concluding projects on political knowledge after the period of desolation in the West from the First World War through the Second and on the role of the South in shaping decision making and the fate of ideas during the New Deal–Fair Deal era in the United States.

James Mahoney earned his Ph.D. in the Department of Political Science at the University of California, Berkeley, in 1997, and he now teaches in the Department of Sociology at Brown University. His doctoral dissertation was a recipient of the Gabriel Almond Prize of the American Political Science Association. This work subsequently was revised into his first book publication, *The Legacies of Liberalism: Path Dependence and Political Regimes in Central America* (The Johns Hopkins University Press, 2001). Mahoney received a Career Award from the National Science Foundation to pursue his new research on long-run development and the legacy of colonialism in Spanish America.

Paul Pierson is Professor of Government and Senior Associate of the Center for European Studies at Harvard University. His main teaching and research interests are in the areas of comparative public policy, the contemporary politics of the welfare state, and social theory. He is the author of *Dismantling the Welfare State? The Politics of Retrenchment in Britain and the United States* (Cambridge University Press, 1994); editor of *The New Politics of the Welfare State* (Oxford University Press, 2001); and coeditor of *European Social Policy Between Fragmentation and Integration* (Brookings Institution, 1995). Professor Pierson is currently finishing a book manuscript on the temporal dimensions of social processes tentatively titled *Politics in Time: History, Institutions, and Political Analysis*.

Dietrich Rueschemeyer has taught sociology at Brown University during the past thirty-five years. He is currently a research professor at Brown's Watson Institute for International Studies. Rueschemeyer's book publications include *Lawyers and Their Society: A Comparative Study of the Legal Profession in Germany and in the United States* (Harvard University Press, 1973), *Bringing the State Back In* (Cambridge University Press, 1985, coedited with Peter B. Evans and Theda Skocpol), *Power and the Division of Labour* (Polity Press, 1986), *Capitalist Development and Democracy* (University of Chicago Press, 1992, with John D. Stephens and Evelyne Huber Stephens, winner of the Outstanding Book Award in Political Sociology, American Sociological

Association), and *Participation and Democracy East and West: Comparisons and Interpretations* (M. E. Sharpe, 1998, coedited with Marilyn Rueschemeyer and Björn Wittrock). Rueschemeyer is currently working on a monograph in social theory tentatively titled *Usable Theory: Analytic Tools for Social Research*.

Theda Skocpol is Victor S. Thomas Professor of Government and Sociology at Harvard University, where she also serves as Director of the Center for American Political Studies. Long active in developing methods and agendas for historical and institutional research across disciplines, Skocpol is a member of the American Academy of Arts and Sciences. She served as President of the Social Science History Association in 1996 and will serve as President of the American Political Science Association in 2003. Most prominent among her many books are *States and Social Revolutions: A Comparative Analysis of France, Russia, and China* (Cambridge University Press, 1979), which won two major scholarly awards, and *Protecting Soldiers and Mothers: The Political Origins of Social Policy in the United States* (Harvard University Press, 1992), which won five major awards. Other book publications include *Vision and Method in Historical Sociology* (Cambridge University Press, 1984), *Bringing the State Back In* (Cambridge University Press, 1985, coedited with Peter B. Evans and Dietrich Rueschemeyer), *Social Policy in the United States: Future Possibilities in Historical Perspective* (Princeton University Press, 1995), and *Civic Engagement in American Democracy* (Brookings Institution Press, 1999, coedited with Morris P. Fiorina). Skocpol's current research focuses on states and civil societies, in particular on the development of civic voluntarism in the United States from 1790 to the present.

Kathleen Thelen teaches political science at Northwestern University. She writes on labor politics in the advanced industrial democracies and on historical institutionalism. Her books include *Union of Parts: Labor Politics in Postwar Germany* (Cornell University Press, 1991) and *Structuring Politics: Historical Institutionalism in Comparative Analysis* (Cambridge University Press, 1992, coedited with Sven Steinmo and Frank Longstreth). Recent articles have appeared in *Political Science: The State of the Discipline* (American Political Science Association) and *The Annual Review of Political Science*. Professor Thelen is currently at work on a new book, *How Institutions Evolve*, which traces the origins and evolution of vocational training systems in Germany, Great Britain, Japan, and the United States.

Preface

At the 1998 annual meetings of the American Political Science Association (APSA), David Collier and Paul Pierson convened a dinner meeting to discuss the field of comparative historical analysis. All participants that night were convinced that comparative historical research had made a fundamental contribution to contemporary social science. Yet they all recognized that over the past decade of rapid development and change in the field, scholars had devoted insufficient attention to writing programmatic statements about the substantive contributions, methodological strategies, and theoretical accomplishments of this body of work. The strong conclusion of the discussion was that such a programmatic statement was long overdue.

Upon returning to Brown University after this meeting, James Mahoney began discussions with Dietrich Rueschemeyer about the intellectual excitement surrounding comparative historical research within political science – discussions that ultimately led to the present volume.

From our vantage point in sociology, we sensed not only a similar enthusiasm for comparative historical analysis, but also a real need to take stock of the field as it currently stands. After all, it had been some fifteen years since the publication of the major commentaries that were still held up as defining the state of the art, such as Charles Tilly's *As Sociology Meets History*, Philip Abram's *Historical Sociology*, and Theda Skocpol's edited volume on *Vision and Method in Historical Sociology*. From the APSA discussion alone, it was clear that a great many substantive achievements as well as innovations in theory and method had taken place in the last decade, and surely some effort at systematically reporting these developments was warranted.

Meanwhile, scholars working in other fields *had* taken steps toward spelling out exactly how their research tradition had contributed or could contribute to the social sciences, often in ways that were challenging to comparative historical analysis. For example, Gary King, Robert O. Keohane, and Sydney Verba's *Designing Social Inquiry: Scientific Inference in Qualitative Research* was based on the assumption that statistical researchers have the best tools for pursuing social scientific analysis, and that "qualitative" researchers should seek to emulate these research practices to the degree possible. In *Analytic Narratives*, Robert H. Bates and his coauthors emphasized the advantages of work from the perspective of rational choice theory (especially game theory), and they explored how history through "narratives" could be meaningfully integrated into that tradition. Finally, a collection of essays that were ultimately published as *Beyond the Cultural Turn*, edited by Victoria E. Bonnell and Lynn Hunt, highlighted the distinctive contributions of interpretive and postmodern studies, suggesting that many of the most fruitful efforts at incorporating history into the social sciences had taken place through cultural research.

The existence of these major works advocating alternative kinds of research was another reason why the time seemed ripe to launch a new project examining the achievements and agendas of the contemporary comparative historical tradition. To do justice to this task, a collective effort seemed required. We therefore planned this edited volume, and we invited scholars to participate who had already done important comparative and historical work, and who promised to be active in the field for some time to come. Care was also taken to include both political scientists and sociologists, thereby representing the two disciplines where comparative historical research is most firmly established.

As for the organization of the project, our conversations led us to identify three interrelated issues that eventually became the distinct sections of this book. For the first part, authors were asked to consider the substantive accomplishments and accumulation of knowledge that have occurred in comparative historical analysis. The field has undeniably become a well-established research tradition over the last two or three decades; but what concretely has it taught us about processes and outcomes of interest? Has it achieved intellectual progress on diverse substantive topics? To answer these questions, one set of essays explores the accumulation of knowledge across three specific areas – revolutions, social provision, and democracy and authoritarianism.

The second part of the volume was designed to report on the analytic tools that comparative historical researchers have at their disposal. Although no single theory defines comparative historical analysis, researchers in this tradition do embrace distinctive techniques for studying the social and political world. Among the most important of these are the tools and innovations considered here – theoretical orientations for studying temporal processes, fresh concepts for explaining patterns of institutional change and continuity, new approaches to make sense of social networks, and the latest strategies for linking microlevel preferences with broader social structural forces.

For the third part of the volume, we arranged a set of essays focused on comparative historical methods. The field of comparative historical methodology has in fact grown by leaps and bounds in recent years, and these essays try to synthesize much of this burgeoning literature. This partly entails summarizing the different procedures through which comparative historical researchers make descriptive and causal inferences. It also involves examining the techniques comparative historical researchers have for building theory and for formulating causal propositions, including propositions whose complexity may make them off limits in other research traditions.

Once we had identified the participants and agreed on the basic organizational structure, things moved quickly toward publication. In April 2000, initial drafts of papers were presented at a two-day conference held at the Watson Institute for International Studies of Brown University. An intense and exciting discussion crossed easily the boundaries of substantive review, analytic tools, and issues of method, resulting in stimulating critiques and suggestions. In order to make the most of the momentum generated, the three Harvard colleagues in attendance – Peter Hall, Paul Pierson, and Theda Skocpol – suggested that we hold a follow-up conference at their home university. Especially because of the organizational initiatives of Paul Pierson, this second conference was held in November of the same year at Harvard's Center for European Studies.

That we were able to proceed so quickly is testament to the enthusiasm surrounding the field of comparative historical analysis. Yet it is also testament to the dedication of the scholars whose work appears in this volume. Despite having to carry out the inevitably busy schedules that accompany accomplished academic life, as well as in certain cases navigate through extraordinary personal events that intervened during the course of the project, they conscientiously followed our fast-paced schedule and did so with good cheer. Somewhere between the two formal conferences, the various presentations at other organized meetings, and the frequent e-mail exchanges, we came to identify with one another much more closely than only as a group of scholars interested in the same research tradition. In the last days of our cooperation, we were shocked by the news of the premature death of Roger V. Gould. Comparative historical research has lost one of its most gifted practitioners.

As a collective, we owe our thanks to many organizations and individuals who helped make this book possible. The first conference at Brown University was funded by grants from the Watson Institute for International Studies, the Francis Wayland Collegium for Liberal Learning, and the Lectureships Committee of Brown University. In attendance at this conference were David Collier and Jeff Goodwin, who made valuable comments that helped improve the volume. Thanks also to Matthew Lange, who transcribed the conference discussion, and to Jean Lawlor, who organized affairs in her role as an events manager at the Watson Institute. The follow-up conference at Harvard University was funded by the Center for European Studies, the Center for American Political Studies, and the Weatherhead Center for International Affairs as well as Brown's Watson Institute. Gerardo L. Munck served admirably in his role as discussant. Several other faculty and graduate students from Harvard University raised stimulating questions and made pointed criticisms during the conference. Although we cannot acknowledge them all here, we sincerely appreciate their contribution to this project. For the Harvard event, Lisa Eschenbach of the Center for European Studies expertly took care of all the logistical work.

At Cambridge University Press, Lewis Bateman and Lauren Levin acted as insightful and patient editors. We received excellent and detailed comments from the three reviewers for Cambridge – Laurence Whitehead, Edgar Kiser, and Lars Mjøset. Series editor Margaret Levi deserves our gratitude above all, for she encouraged us to submit the manuscript to Cambridge University Press at an early stage and then provided enthusiastic support through all subsequent stages. This volume was also reviewed at Princeton University Press, and we would like to thank Chuck Myers for all his help, including arranging anonymous reviews from which we benefited. James Mahoney's work on the project was supported in part by a National Science Foundation grant through the Faculty Early Career Development (CAREER) Program. Dietrich Rueschemeyer wishes to thank the Swedish Collegium for Advanced Study in the Social Sciences in Uppsala for the great support it provided during the fall of 2000 when we reviewed and commented on essay drafts and composed the introductory essay. Finally, working on this volume has been a great experience for both of us. We found ourselves in close dialogue with some of the most interesting colleagues in the social sciences, and our own collaboration brought us closer to each other, both as scholars and as friends.

Introduction

PART I

Accumulation of Research

1

Comparative Historical Analysis

ACHIEVEMENTS AND AGENDAS

James Mahoney and Dietrich Rueschemeyer

Comparative historical analysis has a long and distinguished history in the social sciences. Those whom we now regard as the founders of modern social science, from Adam Smith to Alexis de Tocqueville to Karl Marx, all pursued comparative historical analysis as a central mode of investigation. In doing so, they continued a tradition of research that had dominated social thought for centuries. Even when social science began to organize itself into separate disciplines in the early twentieth century, comparative and historical investigation maintained a leading position, figuring prominently in the research of such eminent scholars as Otto Hintze, Max Weber, and Marc Bloch. Only by the mid-twentieth century did other approaches to social knowledge partially eclipse comparative historical research, going so far as to threaten its permanent decline. After some period of neglect, however, recent decades have witnessed a dramatic reemergence of the comparative historical tradition. Although important problems of analytic procedure and methodology remain, this mode of investigation has reasserted itself at the center of today's social sciences.

The revival of comparative historical analysis shows few signs of losing momentum. In the last decade alone, dozens of major new books from this perspective have been published, including many prize-winning analyses.[1]

In addition to the other contributors to this volume, we received helpful comments from Julia Adams, Elisabeth S. Clemens, David Collier, Ruth Berins Collier, Jeff Goodwin, Michael Hechter, Evelyne Huber, Edgar Kiser, Matthew Lange, Lars Mjøset, Gerardo L. Munck, Ann Shola Orloff, Richard Snyder, Sidney Tarrow, Charles Tilly, David Waldner, Laurence Whitehead, and Deborah J. Yashar.

[1] Among the recent comparative historical books that have received prizes organized by sections and committees of the American Political Science Association, the American Sociological Association, and the Social Science History Association are the following: Amenta

These works focus on a wide range of topics, but they are united by a commitment to offering historically grounded explanations of large-scale and substantively important outcomes. Encompassed in this scholarship is a surge of new work on social provision and welfare state development in the United States and Europe[2] and a host of new studies that explore processes of state formation and state restructuring in the regions of Africa, Asia, East Europe, Latin America, and the Middle East as well as in the advanced capitalist countries.[3] In addition, the last decade has seen the publication of important comparative historical books on economic development and industrial policy,[4] racial and ethnic relations and national identities,[5] gender and women's rights,[6] the emergence of democratic and authoritarian national regimes,[7] and the causes and consequences of revolutions in both historical settings and the modern Third World.[8]

This record of research since the 1990s has been accompanied by an increasingly visible place for comparative historical inquiry in the institutions and organizations of the social science disciplines.[9] Articles on comparative historical research appear prominently in social science journals with general readerships as well as those intended for more specialized

1998; Barkey 1994; Clemens 1997; Collier and Collier 1991; Ertman 1997; Goldstone 1991; Haggard and Kaufman 1995; Hall 1986; Luebbert 1991; Markoff 1996; Marx 1998; Orren 1991; Rueschemeyer et al. 1992; Skocpol 1992; Young 1994.

2 See, e.g., Amenta 1998; de Swaan 1988; Esping-Anderson 1990; Hicks 1999; Huber and Stephens 2001; Immergut 1992; Kitschelt et al. 1999; Orloff 1993; Pierson 1994; Skocpol 1992; Steinmetz 1993; Steinmo 1993.

3 See, e.g., Barkey 1994; Bensel 1990; Centeno 2002; Clark 1995; Ekiert 1996; Ertman 1997; Herbst 2000; Silberman 1993; Spruyt 1994; Tilly 1990; Waldner 1999; Young 1994.

4 See, e.g., Carruthers 1996; Chaudhry 1997; Dobbin 1994; Evans 1995; Hopcroft 1999; Itzigsohn 2000; Karl 1997; Roy 1997; Seidman 1994.

5 See, e.g., Brubaker 1992; Calhoun 1997; Hechter 2000; Lustick 1993; Marx 1998; Stinchcombe 1995.

6 See, e.g., Banaszak 1996; Charrad 2001; Htun in press; O'Connor, Orloff, and Shaver 1999.

7 See, e.g., Collier 1999; Collier and Collier 1991; Downing 1992; Haggard and Kaufman 1995; Huber and Safford 1995; Linz and Stepan 1996; Luebbert 1991; Mahoney 2001; Paige 1997; Rueschemeyer et al. 1992; Wood 2000; Yashar 1997.

8 See, e.g., Colburn 1994; Foran 1997; Goldstone 1991; Goodwin 2001; Kimmel 1990; Parsa 2000; Selbin 1993; Wickham-Crowley 1992.

9 In sociology, comparative historical analysis is institutionalized as its own organized section (i.e., the section on comparative and historical sociology) and has strong ties to several other sections, including political sociology. In political science, comparative historical analysis is a major component of the organized sections on comparative politics, politics and history, and states, politics, and policy, as well as the Committee on Concepts and Methods. In history, this tradition is well represented by the Social Science History Association (SSHA) and in the fields of social history and economic history.

audiences.[10] And social science faculty are now often recruited for their expertise in this mode of inquiry, while graduate students are trained to write dissertations explicitly cast as comparative historical studies.

These recent advances derived from earlier developments. By the late 1970s and early 1980s, it was already clear that comparative historical research was experiencing a revival across the social sciences. In her concluding chapter in *Vision and Method in Historical Sociology*, for example, Theda Skocpol (1984a) pointed out that this kind of research was well beyond its days as an isolated mode of analysis carried out by a few older scholars dedicated to the classical tradition. Now, almost two decades later, few observers would deny that comparative historical research is again a leading mode of analysis, widely used throughout the social sciences.

To acknowledge the important place of the comparative historical tradition is not, of course, to suggest an absence of challenging problems for researchers who work in the tradition. For one thing, difficult questions exist about the full scope of empirical issues for which comparative historical studies may be relevant. For example, whether and how studies that focus primarily on microlevel units (e.g., individuals, small groups) can be accommodated within the macro-oriented field of comparative historical analysis remains an open question. Furthermore, some macro topics – such as law and the environment – beckon to be confronted with the tools of comparative historical analysis, but they remain understudied or overlooked in the tradition.[11] Moreover, comparative historical scholars are engaged in not easily resolved disputes over divergent theoretical frameworks, for which the tension between structuralism and culturalism is a major example. And there are still unresolved epistemological issues that arise from the attempt to do justice to historical particularity and at the same time achieve theoretical generalization.

Despite these continuing questions, comparative historical researchers have made major progress toward addressing issues that often were not well

[10] U.S. journals in sociology and political science that frequently publish comparative historical studies include the *American Journal of Sociology*, *Comparative Politics*, *Comparative Social Research*, *Comparative Studies in Society and History*, *Journal of Historical Sociology*, *Political Power and Social Theory*, *Politics and Society*, *Social Science History*, *Sociological Forum*, *Studies in Comparative International Development*, *Studies in American Political Development*, *Theory and Society*, and *World Politics*. Many other excellent area studies journals also regularly publish works in this tradition.

[11] Some comparative historical analysts did address these questions (e.g., Berman 1983, Orren 1991), but even more work needs to be done.

treated in the past. In the area of methodology, these investigators have become highly self-conscious about research design, and the fast-growing field of comparative historical methods has become fertile ground for innovation in the modern social sciences. For example, scholars are now in the midst of exciting research on temporal processes and path dependence,[12] conceptual formation and measurement,[13] and strategies of causal inference ranging from historical narrative and process tracing to Boolean algebra and fuzzy-set analysis.[14] Likewise, sustained engagement with theoretical issues has led comparative historical analysts to major breakthroughs in conceptualizing the kinds of factors that drive macro processes of change. To take one prominent example, these researchers were at the forefront of the scholarly effort to rework the role of states as actors and as institutions, a development that reoriented agendas across the social sciences (including history).[15]

This volume seeks to assess the achievements of comparative historical research over the last thirty years, discuss persistent problems, and explore agendas for the future. In this introductory chapter, we begin that task by delineating the distinctive features of this mode of analysis. We suggest that comparative historical analysis is best considered part of a long-standing intellectual project oriented toward the explanation of substantively important outcomes. It is defined by a concern with causal analysis, an emphasis on processes over time, and the use of systematic and contextualized comparison. In offering this definition, we intentionally exclude other analytical and methodological traits that are often associated with comparative historical analysis but that we do not consider part of its core features. For example, although many comparative historical analyses offer explanations based on social and political structures and their change, the research tradition is not inherently committed to structural explanation or any other single theoretical orientation. Likewise, while most work in the field employs qualitative forms of data analysis, comparative historical analysis is not characterized by any single method of descriptive and causal inference.

[12] See, e.g., Abbott 1990, 1992, 1997; Aminzade 1992; Haydu 1998; Isaac 1997; Mahoney 2000; Pierson 2000a, 2000b; Sewell 1996; Thelen 1999.

[13] See, e.g., Collier and Adcock 1997; Collier and Levitsky 1997; Collier and Mahon 1993; Coppedge 1999; Munck and Verkuilen 2000.

[14] See, e.g., Collier 1993; Dion 1998; George and Bennett in press; Goldstone 1997; Griffin 1992, 1993; Katznelson 1997; Mahoney 1999 and this volume; McKeown 1999; Munck 1998; Ragin 1987, 2000; Rueschemeyer and Stephens 1997; Snyder 2001a; Stryker 1996.

[15] See Skocpol (1985) for an early review of this literature; more recent citations can be found in Migdal, Kohli, and Shue (1994).

A Continued Focus on Big Questions

Although the current outpouring of comparative historical studies began in the 1960s and 1970s,[16] the research tradition has roots that extend back much further in time. As noted initially, comparative historical analysis was the mode of analysis that defined the classics of modern social science, as exemplified by the work of its most important founders.[17] The use of comparative historical techniques by the founders was no accident. Those scholars followed a long-established tradition, but above all they asked questions about the basic contours and evolution of the modern world at a time when pressing issues were raised by the epochal transitions of capitalist commercialization and industrialization in Europe. They found it essential to focus on comprehensive structures and large-scale processes that provided powerful clues to the patterning of social life, both at a macroscopic level and at the level of groups and individuals. Such big processes and structures were – and still are – most appropriately studied through explicit comparisons that transcend national or regional boundaries. In addition, these fundamental processes could not – and cannot – be analyzed without recognizing the importance of temporal sequences and the unfolding of events over time. In basic ways, then, the social analysts who would later be considered the founders of the modern social sciences were unavoidably drawn to comparative historical analysis.

Contemporary researchers who choose to ask "big" questions – that is, questions about large-scale outcomes that are regarded as substantively and normatively important by both specialists and nonspecialists – are often similarly drawn to comparative historical research. As the works cited at the beginning of this essay suggest, there is an affinity between asking big questions and using comparative historical research methods, a fact that has helped to sustain a single tradition from the beginning of modern social science analysis to the present day. Today's comparative historical researchers have renewed this tradition not by simply repeating the emphases and styles of the founders, but by addressing fresh substantive issues

[16] Skocpol (1984a, 1984b) reports on the renewal of comparative historical analysis during this period. Works from that era include the celebrated studies of Anderson 1974a, 1974b; Bendix 1964, 1974, 1978; Eisenstadt 1963, 1978; Lipset and Rokkan 1968; Moore 1966; Tilly 1967, 1975; and Wallerstein 1974.

[17] There was an earlier wave of methodological literature that focused on dissecting the logics of inquiry used by the classical theorists, much of which is cited in Skocpol (1984b, fn. 3, p. 20). More recent contributions include, among many others, Burawoy 1989, Emirbayer 1996, and Kalberg 1994.

and by marshalling novel historical evidence and new methodological tools that have become available over time. Substantive research has expanded to include the themes of our day, ranging from the fall of socialist systems and the reconstitution of welfare states in the face of globalization,[18] to the national and global changes set into motion by information technology and new forms of production,[19] to the recent successes and failures of growth in the countries of Africa, Asia, and Latin America.[20] Furthermore, contemporary scholars continue to raise questions first addressed by the founders that remain of paramount interest today – on topics ranging anywhere from grand sociological studies of the evolution of vast societies[21] to the emergence and the fates of working-class movements across time[22] – but they do so with the aid of methodologies and analytic strategies that help sharpen specific comparisons, bring temporal considerations more systematically into play, and facilitate more rigorous forms of causal assessment.

It is of course true that not all researchers who pose big questions do so from the standpoint of comparative historical analysis.[23] What, then, is distinctive about this tradition's approach to studying big questions? Most basically, comparative historical researchers ask questions and formulate puzzles about specific sets of cases that exhibit sufficient similarity to be meaningfully compared with one another.[24] Comparative historical researchers do not typically seek universal knowledge about all instances of ahistorically constituted populations of cases. For example, Ann Shola Orloff (1993) does not ask what factors might shape the extent of social provision for the elderly across all times and places, but instead inquires about major similarities and sharp divergences in pension policy among Britain, the United States, and Canada during clearly delineated historical periods.

[18] See, e.g., Bunce 1999; Huber and Stephens 2001; Kitschelt 1994; Pierson 2001; Stark and Bruszt 1998.

[19] See, e.g., Castells 1996–8; Piore and Sabel 1984.

[20] See, e.g., Amsden 2001; Deyo 1987; Evans 1995; Gereffi and Wyman 1991; Haggard 1990; Migdal 1988; Pempel 1999; Senghaas 1985; Sikkink 1991; Wade 1990.

[21] See, e.g., Gocek 1996; Lachmann 2000; Mann 1986, 1993; Rueschemeyer 1986.

[22] See, e.g., Katznelson and Zolberg 1986; Kimeldorf 1988; Seidman 1994.

[23] For example, as we discuss later, cross-national statistical researchers or interpretive analysts may ask "big questions," but they do not typically do so in a way that is characteristic of comparative historical research.

[24] See Pierson and Skocpol 2002. "Sufficient similarity" is, of course, defined by the theoretical framework. It may thus encompass cases that from a different point of view may appear to be quite dissimilar. In this sense, a focus on sufficiently similar cases in no way excludes comparisons of highly diverse contexts, including diverse contexts in which similar processes and outcomes take place.

Gregory M. Luebbert (1991) does not attempt to identify the causes of all political-economic regimes in all regions and all eras, but instead seeks to explain the origins of liberalism, fascism, and social democracy specifically in interwar Europe. And Thomas Ertman (1997) asks not what processes have driven statebuilding throughout human history, but instead explores the specific factors that shaped the development of sharply contrasting state-regime complexes in eighteenth-century Western Christendom.

This basic strategy of focusing on important puzzles that apply to particular historical cases is not without its critics, especially among those who seek universalizing knowledge and argue that historically delimited theorizing is fraught with pitfalls. To be sure, the historically delimited questions asked by comparative historical analysts do entail some loss, or better some reduction of ambition, when measured against the goal of fully specified causal propositions that hold across all sociocultural contexts and historical periods. Yet comparative historical analysts continue to ask such questions because of the poverty of universalizing theoretical approaches and because these questions lend themselves to research with significant analytic advantages. From the perspective of the comparative historical tradition, the universalizing programs of the past and present – ranging from structural functionalism and systems theory in the 1960s and 1970s to certain strands of game theory in the 1980s and 1990s[25] – have tended to generate ahistorical concepts and propositions that are often too general to be usefully applied in explanation. In viewing cases and processes at a less abstract level, by contrast, comparative historical analysts are frequently able to derive lessons from past experiences that speak to the concerns of the present. Even though their insights remain grounded in the histories examined and cannot be transposed literally to other contexts, comparative historical studies can yield more meaningful advice concerning contemporary choices and possibilities than studies that aim for universal truths but cannot grasp critical historical details.

It bears emphasis, however, that even as comparative historical studies focus on questions specific to particular historical cases, their concern with explanation often leads to further investigations that go beyond the initial

[25] Included in this group are some of the most famous works of social science analysis of the 1950s and 1960s, such as Easton 1965; Levy 1966; Parsons 1951; and Smelser 1963. For a discussion of the limitations of this kind of work and additional citations, see Skocpol 1984a. For discussions of universalizing forms of game theory (and their alternatives) in contemporary times, see Munck 2001 and Swedberg 2001.

cases. Such efforts at generalization must always take into consideration the "scope conditions" that were used in the initial study to define homogeneous cases appropriate for comparison (i.e., cases for which one would expect a change on a given explanatory variable to have the same average net causal effect). When a particular account is extended to a new context, it will sometimes confirm the original explanation, thereby suggesting its generality and perhaps calling for a refinement in the understanding of scope conditions. More often, attempts at generalization will suggest that an explanation is contingent on complex and variable conditions – conditions that may or may not have been adequately identified in an original scope statement but that can be further specified through the new comparison. In some cases, theoretical generalization may require one to reconceptualize variables on a more abstract level (an option that may be resisted by the more historically minded researchers). But attempts at extension may also reveal that – on current theoretical understanding – the initial account simply does not fit other apparently similar cases, raising basic questions about whether the lack of fit is a product of causal heterogeneity (i.e., the inclusion of new cases that do meet the standard of unit homogeneity) or whether it represents a deficiency in the initial explanation. With all of these possibilities, the analytic orientation of comparative historical inquiry keeps the door open for an examination of the broader implications of studies that ask questions about particular historical cases.

The Distinctive Features of Comparative Historical Analysis

One might be tempted to define comparative historical analysis in a very broad sense, such that the tradition encompasses any and all studies that juxtapose historical patterns across cases. Such an inclusive definition would certainly serve the purpose of illustrating the large scope of this kind of investigation.[26] However, we prefer to reserve the label "comparative historical analysis" for a distinctive kind of research defined by relatively specific characteristics. While not unified by one theory or one method, all work in this tradition does share a concern with causal analysis, an emphasis on processes over time, and the use of systematic and contextualized comparison. In choosing this delimitation, we distinguish comparative historical analysis

[26] In a radical sense, of course, all studies are invariably both historical and comparative. They are historical in that they must make reference to events and processes that happened in the past. They are comparative in that they must inevitably juxtapose two or more observations.

from broader enterprises such as "historical sociology" and "historical institutionalism." These related fields often share with comparative historical research the concern with addressing big questions, but they may do so in ways not fully characteristic of the studies discussed in this volume. For example, the field of historical sociology encompasses comparative historical analysis, but it also includes interpretive and postmodern works that are not part of this tradition (see later). Likewise, all comparative historical works fit comfortably within the field of historical institutionalism, but historical institutionalist works that are not explicitly engaged in systematic comparison do not fall within the field of comparative historical analysis. Hence, we choose to treat comparative historical analysis as one branch within these larger traditions. Our intention is not to stipulate artificial boundaries that prevent the exchange of ideas among scholars working in closely related fields. Rather, we merely seek to recognize a particular kind of research that is treated as its own distinctive scholarly approach by both its practitioners and its critics.

Following emergent usage in the social sciences, then, we see comparative historical analysis as embodying the three features just indicated.[27] First, comparative historical inquiry is fundamentally concerned with explanation and the identification of causal configurations that produce major outcomes of interest. In comparative historical studies, the causal argument is central to the analysis; thus, causal propositions are carefully selected and tested rather than introduced ad hoc as incidental parts of an overall narrative. As such, comparative historical analysis does not include work that explicitly rejects causal analysis or that eschews it in favor of other research goals. For example, scholarship that avoids causal analysis in favor of "interpretive" approaches aimed at uncovering the culturally situated meanings of human behavior is not the kind of research considered in this volume. Likewise, while the "area studies" program of describing historical patterns and illuminating classifications is important

[27] In developing this definition, we have been influenced by the discussions in Collier 1998a; Skocpol 1979, pp. 36–7; 1984a, p. 1; and Skocpol and Somers 1980, pp. 181–3. Skocpol and Somers distinguished three types of comparative history: "macrocausal analysis," "parallel demonstration of theory," and "contrast of contexts." The definition we chose is very close to the first of these (i.e., macrocausal analysis). With this choice we do not, however, mean to suggest that the other two versions of comparative and historical studies are worthless. They are different in character – one more radically leaning toward theoretical generalization, the other virtually rejecting the possibility of theory – but they remain partners in scholarly dialogue.

to comparative historical analysis, these activities are not an end in their own right in the kind of scholarship considered here. Instead, we are concerned with works that attempt to locate the causes of substantively important outcomes. Within this orientation, comparative historical analysts need not embrace any single approach to causal analysis. These researchers in fact draw on a wide range of strategies of causal inference, some of which parallel the multivariate regression techniques used by quantitative researchers and some of which are distinctive to qualitative research (see Munck 1998; Mahoney 1999 and this volume; Ragin 1987, 2000). Practicing comparative historical researchers are thus eclectic in their use of methods, employing those tools that best enable them to address problems at hand.[28]

Second, comparative historical researchers explicitly analyze historical sequences and take seriously the unfolding of processes over time. As Paul Pierson reminds us in his essay in this volume, the events that engage comparative historical researchers – such as social revolutions, the commercialization of agriculture, or state formation – are not static occurrences taking place at a single, fixed point; rather, they are processes that unfold over time and in time (see also Abbott 1990, 1992; Aminzade 1992; Pierson 2000a, 2000b; Rueschemeyer and Stephens 1997; Tilly 1984). As a result, comparative historical analysts incorporate considerations of the temporal structure of events in their explanations. They may, for example, argue that the influence of an event is very much shaped by the duration of the event, as Ruth Berins Collier and David Collier (1991) do when they assess the effects of different "incorporation periods" in Latin America. Likewise, comparative historical researchers may treat differences in the temporal structure of events as major outcomes to be explained, as Charles Tilly (1990) does when he explores why European city-states and federations gave way to modern states at differential rates in Europe. Furthermore, because events are themselves located in time, comparative historical analysts explicitly consider the effects of the timing of events relative to one another. To explain differences in public social spending in Britain and the United States,

[28] This eclecticism may go beyond questions of method and involve also what Peter Hall in his essay calls "ontological" premises, presuppositions that underlie the choice of method. In our attempt to present a collective portrait of comparative historical analysis, we do not explore this – otherwise important – question about the evolution of ontology. More generally, we do not explore here the connections between comparative historical analysis and philosophical "realism," though we believe there are substantial complementarities between the two.

for example, Orloff and Skocpol (1984) argue that it matters a great deal whether bureaucratic reforms came before or after full democratization; similarly, Rueschemeyer (1973) suggests that contrasting features of the legal professions in Germany and the United States were powerfully shaped by the relative timing of bureaucratic rationalization of states and capitalist developments in the economy. Indeed, precisely because events are temporal processes, they may intersect with one another, and the relative timing of that intersection can be of decisive importance.

Finally, comparative historical inquiry is distinctive because its practitioners engage in systematic and contextualized comparisons of similar and contrasting cases. Systematic comparison is, of course, indispensable given the analytic interest in causal analysis. As already suggested, most comparative historical work aims for explanations of important outcomes within delimited historical contexts, usually focusing on a small number of cases. While this approach does not directly aim for universally applicable knowledge, it represents a bargain in which significant advantages are gained. Above all, the approach makes possible a dialogue between theory and evidence of an intensity that is rare in quantitative social research. By employing a small number of cases, comparative historical researchers can comfortably move back and forth between theory and history in many iterations of analysis as they formulate new concepts, discover novel explanations, and refine preexisting theoretical expectations in light of detailed case evidence.

Furthermore, because comparative historical investigators usually know each of their cases well, they can measure variables in light of the broader context of each particular case, thereby achieving a higher level of conceptual and measurement validity than is often possible when a large number of cases are selected. This close inspection of particular cases also allows researchers to explore how variables may have different causal effects across heterogeneous contexts, thereby facilitating what Richard Locke and Kathleen Thelen (1995) call "contextualized comparisons" (see also Ragin 1987, 2000). Moreover, the question of whether and to what extent different cases are independent of each other can be subjected to nuanced examination through the intensive study of cases. For example, Dietrich Rueschemeyer, John D. Stephens, and Evelyne Huber Stephens (1992, pp. 265–7) use their close analysis of the English-speaking islands of the Caribbean, as well as comparisons with other ex-colonial countries around the globe, to show that the existence of democracy in these islands was not primarily due to the influence of the "cradle of democracy," that is, British colonialism, but rather to the character of state–society relations and the overall balance of power within these countries.

The "cases" chosen for comparison vary a great deal. Although nation-states are still the most common units selected, researchers are increasingly exploring federal states or departments within a single country,[29] supranational territories or organizations that encompass multiple nation-states,[30] and informal subnational territories defined by various features such as type of agricultural system or degree of state penetration.[31] And the cases considered need not always refer to territorial boundaries. For example, research comparing social movements and large-scale contention in the comparative historical tradition defines its population in terms of socially constructed groups.[32] Similarly, studies that focus on a single geographic unit may treat periods of time as cases and engage in systematic comparison in this fashion (see Haydu 1998). Thus, the kinds of cases selected correspond to subject matter and problem formulation, not simply to popular geographic categories. State-defined countries are commonly selected because they are often appropriate for macrolevel research questions. This is plain in the three areas of inquiry we consider in Part I of this volume – comparative research on revolutions, social provision, and democratic and authoritarian regimes. For other questions, however, one can and often will do better with other units of comparison.[33]

Conceiving comparative historical analysis as defined by three specific emphases – a concern with causal analysis, the exploration of temporal processes, and the use systematic and contextualized comparison typically limited to a small number of cases – does not encompass all comparative and historical work on large social structures, cultural patterns, and processes of change. Statistical studies that analyze large numbers of countries

29 See, e.g., Clemens 1997; Heller 1999; Kohli 1987; Putnam 1993; Snyder 2001b; Williams 1994.

30 Included here would be the more qualitative strands of the world systems and world society research programs (see, e.g., McMichael 1985; Meyer et al. 1997; Wallerstein 1974, 1980, 1989).

31 See, e.g., Hopcroft 1999; O'Donnell 1993; Paige 1975.

32 Such research includes both classic studies (e.g., Tilly 1967; Tilly, Tilly, and Tilly 1975) and more recent contributions (e.g., McAdam, Tarrow, and Tilly 2001).

33 Regardless of the nature and level of analysis of the cases investigated, it is worth emphasizing that comparative historical researchers do not actually compare these "whole cases" with one another. Rather, they must, of course, select specific aspects of those cases and then systematically evaluate those aspects as variables, not unlike – in this respect – quantitative researchers who work with large numbers of cases (compare to Ragin 1987, p. 52).

are not included, as they select too many cases to easily permit the kind of contextualized comparison that defines comparative historical research. Most interpretive theorists are excluded because they are not centrally concerned with causal analysis. And contributions from history and area studies whose narrative accounts include numerous explanations as well as occasional comparative references are not included if they do not systematically scrutinize their explanatory propositions.[34]

Nevertheless, recent work that does embrace these three dimensions is, in our view, extensive enough and distinctive enough to warrant consideration in its own right. Indeed, we believe that the similar emphases adopted in this large body of work define a group of scholars who increasingly identify with one another – and are identified by other scholars – as a single research community.

The Paradigm Debate in Contemporary Social Science

Ours is a period in which passionate debates about method and approach animate the social sciences. Scholars often forcefully advocate their favored research paradigm and sharply criticize alternatives as inferior. Comparative historical analysts have found themselves in the thick of these disputes, often allying with scholars identified with related approaches that share important emphases, such as historical institutionalism (Hall and Taylor 1996; Katznelson 1997; Pierson and Skocpol 2001; Thelen and Steinmo 1992) or the comparative method tradition (Collier 1993, 1998b). Although the current "paradigm"[35] debate defies easy classification, three

[34] This exclusion will trouble only a few historians, while many will be quite unconcerned. That historians remain largely indifferent to comparative historical analysis actually represents a major unresolved problem of our research tradition, as Sidney Tarrow pointed out in correspondence. Saying this, we again emphasize that our distinctive characterization of comparative historical analysis is not meant to limit communication and exchange between scholars of distinct traditions.

[35] We see "paradigms" as sets of methodological and theoretical commitments that define scholarly communities and often are embodied in model cases of research. Some paradigms are primarily defined by methodology, others more by their theoretical premises; some are loosely structured, others more precisely defined. Rational choice theory, for example, has a precisely defined theoretical core, while comparative historical analysis is primarily defined by methodological commitments. Paradigms and their associated scholarly communities are critical for understanding the dynamics of actual scholarly disputes; but it is important to note that – seen systematically – these disputes may conceal important underlying similarities between paradigmatically defined scholarly communities. Likewise, there may be diversity within each paradigm.

identifiable cleavages involve comparative historical scholarship in significant and illuminating controversies, each of which has played itself out in varying ways from one discipline to the next.

First of all, across the relevant disciplines, methodological disagreements of varying intensities have emerged between qualitative and quantitative approaches. In comparative social science this is represented by disputes between comparative historical researchers and cross-national statistical researchers who work with large numbers of cases.[36] In the late 1960s and early 1970s, when quantitative cross-national research began to be carried out with some frequency, few statistical researchers imagined that comparative historical analysis held much future in the social sciences. Comparative methodologists of the day routinely emphasized the advantages of quantitative methods over small-*N* methods, portraying the latter as only a stepping stone on a path that culminated in the use of powerful statistical tools (e.g., Lijphart 1971, 1975; Smelser 1976). These beliefs were reinforced in the 1970s as important econometric refinements seemed to correct the shortcomings associated with earlier statistical methods. Much optimism abounded about the future of cross-national quantitative research, which seemingly only had to await the creation of data sets appropriate to this kind of research.

Some two decades later, however, it seems less likely that the future of comparative research will soon be dominated by statistical studies of large numbers of cases. Today's methodologists are likely to concede that arriving at reliable inferences using statistical techniques is inherently difficult, and that to date, these techniques have not generated substantive findings in comparative analysis to match the initial optimism that accompanied this kind of research (see Brady and Collier 2002). To be sure, refinements in statistical procedure continue to help analysts overcome the limitations associated with previous rounds of methodological retooling.[37] Likewise, new and better statistics for macroscopic quantitative research are becoming available as real-world changes (e.g., democratization in the Third World) make data collection easier. Nevertheless, in the absence of a plentitude of innovative and compelling findings, today's cross-national

[36] It may not be superfluous to note that quantification may play a quite significant role in the within-case analyses of studies that focus on only a few cross-case comparisons.

[37] Among the most promising innovations are recent methods designed to model temporal processes more effectively. Some recent innovations are discussed in Griffin and van der Linden 1999 and Abbott and Tsay 2000.

statistical researchers usually strike a chord that is a good deal more modest than in the past.[38]

In this intellectual climate, the dialogue between advocates of large-*N* and small-*N* methods appears to be moving in two somewhat contradictory directions. On the one hand, much public discussion focuses on the contribution that each tradition has to make to scholarly knowledge, with analysts acknowledging that there is a place for both in the cycle of research. For example, methodologists report on iterative research programs in which comparative historical research supplements the initial findings of statistical studies, and vice versa (Bennett and George 1998; Collier 1998a; Coppedge 1999). In some areas of research, such complementarity has resulted in significant advances of knowledge (Amenta, this volume). Likewise, excellent works of comparative historical analysis may themselves combine qualitative and quantitative approaches (e.g., Goldstone 1991; Huber and Stephens 2001; Paige 1975; Tilly 1967) or take the results of cross-national statistical research as a point of departure for qualitative comparisons (Rueschemeyer 1991; Rueschemeyer et al. 1992). Given these synergies, some methodologists, not surprisingly, emphasize basic similarities between the two research traditions. For example, in their well-known formulation, Gary King, Robert O. Keohane, and Sydney Verba (1994, p. 4) declare that "the differences between the quantitative and qualitative traditions are only stylistic and are methodologically and substantively unimportant. All good research can be understood – and is indeed best understood – to derive from the same underlying logic of inference."[39]

Yet, on the other hand, real tensions and sharp disagreements continue to exist. Some scholars inspired by the logic of statistical methods remain skeptical that valid causal inferences can be made from a small number of cases

[38] This is true even though since the late 1980s economists have joined political scientists and sociologists in studying economic growth as well as institutional patterns and changes in the cross-national statistical mode of analysis. See Temple (1999) for an overview of the "new growth evidence" based on cross-national statistical research that was stimulated by the new growth theory of the 1980s. Levine and Renelt (1992) offer a skeptical analysis of the robustness of findings derived from partial correlations of economic growth with a range of possible conditioning factors. We thank Louis Putterman for advice on this empirical work in economics.

[39] With regard to King et al.'s (1994) *Designing Social Inquiry*, several observers have pointed out that the book presents a one-sided view in which qualitative researchers should adapt their research practices to those of quantitative researchers, overlooking the ways in which quantitative researchers can benefit by learning about qualitative research techniques. See Munck (1998) for an illuminating discussion. See also Brady and Collier (2002) for a more balanced discussion and a collection of essays on the debate over *Designing Social Inquiry*.

(Goldthorpe 1997; Lieberson 1991, 1994, 1998). Likewise, some analysts have raised concerns about bias in comparative historical analysis resulting from selection on the dependent variable (Geddes 1990) or from the selective use of secondary data sources (Goldthorpe 1991; Lustick 1996). For their part, comparative historical methodologists have attempted to address these criticisms systematically. They have shown that small-N researchers can meet the confidence demands of standard statistical studies in their assessments of necessary and sufficient conditions (Dion 1998; Ragin 2000; see also Braumoeller and Goertz 2000; Mahoney, this volume) and that the use of multiple methods of causal analysis – including various forms of within-case assessment – enables these scholars to effectively probe probabilistic patterns of causation for a small number of aggregate units (George and Bennett in press; Goldstone 1997; Rueschemeyer and Stephens 1997), even though some maintain that significant underlying issues cannot be resolved through the examination of a few cases (Rueschemeyer, this volume). Methodologists have also shown that the specific statistical problem of bias resulting from selection on the dependent variable has been inappropriately applied to many comparative historical studies (Collier and Mahoney 1996; Ragin 2000) and that the use of secondary sources – and now increasingly primary sources – by comparative historical researchers need not result in any systematic error (Mouzelis 1994).[40] Finally, we must note that comparative historical researchers have launched their own telling criticisms of statistical methods. For example, Charles C. Ragin (1997) argues that cross-national statistical researchers routinely violate assumptions of unit homogeneity, fail to consider multiple causal paths to the same outcome, and present inflated error terms or misspecified models stemming from ignorance about particular cases. Likewise, Timothy J. McKeown (1999)

[40] The use of secondary sources by comparative historical researchers is often so thorough that they in effect examine the full "population" of sources, obviating any bias associated with nonrandom selection. Moreover, the validity of many comparative historical arguments does not hinge on a particular reading of the secondary literature; the force and novelty of these arguments typically grow out of the use of systematic comparison and theory, which enables researchers to rely on well-established historical interpretations in their arguments. When comparative historical researchers must adjudicate between rival accounts in the secondary literature, they often are very explicit in reporting how they arrive at particular conclusions (e.g., by examining the use of sources and documentation in the conflicting secondary works). Finally, we hasten to add that some comparative historical researchers now employ undiscovered or underutilized primary materials in their research, making contributions of the sort normally associated with historians (e.g., Bergquist 1986; Chaudhry 1997; Skocpol 1992).

and Alexander L. George and Andrew Bennett (in press) have taken statistical methods to task for their failure to identify causal mechanisms and their limited ability to contribute to theory construction. To our knowledge, statistical researchers have yet to respond systematically to these criticisms.

Turning now to the challenges posed by another paradigm that is becoming increasingly central in political science but is also of some importance in sociology, we consider the debate between advocates of rational choice theory and comparative historical analysis. The use of rational choice theory in macrocomparative research "is clearly still in its infancy" (Bates et al. 2000, p. 296; Goldstone 1999, p. 533), and thus rational choice theorists have not yet generated a large quantity of empirical work in this particular area (for a review see Geddes in press).[41] Nevertheless, in the area of comparative research, rational choice theorists have attracted attention by criticizing the research methods used by comparative historical analysts and by promising an alternative program that might do better in the future.

From the perspective of comparative historical research, it is difficult to evaluate the critiques of rational choice theorists, because these theorists disagree sharply among themselves about what exactly is wrong with this research.[42] For some rational choice theorists, the use of inductive methods is the problem, because these methods lead comparative historical researchers to develop generalizations that apply to only specific times and places. This concern underlies John Goldthorpe's (1991, 1997) contention that comparative historical studies go too far in the direction of idiographic explanation; and it leads Edgar Kiser and Michael Hechter (1991) to proclaim that comparative historical researchers are "antitheoretical," and that the "use of the inductive method in comparative historical research is simply inappropriate" (pp. 3, 13). However, other rational choice scholars insist that induction is a highly appropriate research strategy, and that theoretical generalizations from specific cases are extremely useful (Bates et al. 1998). For these more "pragmatic" rational choice analysts (see Munck 2001), the problem with comparative historical research appears to be its failure to

[41] Indeed, as is by now well known, there is a broader debate over the extent to which rational choice theory has contributed empirical insights to other fields over the last several decades (Bates et al. 2000; Elster 2000; Friedman 1996; Green and Shapiro 1994; see also Geddes 1991; Goldstone 1998; Goldthorpe 1998a; Kiser and Hechter 1998; Munck 2001; Somers 1998).

[42] Rational choice theorists are similarly divided over the usefulness of statistical research. Compare, for example, the views expressed in Goldthorpe 1998b and Laitin 2001.

explicitly or fully develop choice-centric models using assumptions about actor rationality.

Comparative historical researchers view the more orthodox programmatic statements by rational choice theorists with a great deal of skepticism. Like all other previous attempts to employ overarching ahistorical general theories in the social sciences, orthodox rational choice programs have failed to produce lawlike statements or universal propositions that apply to a broad range of cases and times and at the same time deal meaningfully with features of real-world cases that seem of elementary importance. Precisely because of this failure, more pragmatic rational choice theorists have come to accept major emphases long endorsed by comparative historical analysts, such as analytic induction, the use of detailed evidence from particular cases, and the effort to develop midrange generalizations that apply to particular times and places. Unfortunately, however, even more pragmatic rational choice theorists continue to suggest that comparative historical analysts overemphasize history at the expense of theory. For example, they often draw a rigid dichotomy between theory-driven research based on rational choice models and historical studies that rely on mere narrative analysis, and then implicitly or explicitly reduce comparative historical analysis to the latter (Bates et al. 1998; Goldthorpe 1991; Laitin 2002).

Comparative historical researchers have responded to these kinds of criticisms by offering careful discussions of the ways in which they combine theory and history in research. They have repeatedly pointed out that both induction and deduction are valuable components of their work (Goldstone 1997, pp. 112–13; Quadagno and Knapp 1992, p. 493; Ragin 1987, 2000; Rueschemeyer et al. 1992, pp. 36–9; Skocpol 1979, p. 39; Skocpol and Somers 1980, p. 182; Stryker 1996, pp. 310–13; see also Paige 1999). General theories and midrange theories are used explicitly by comparative historical researchers to identify populations of cases appropriate for comparison, formulate orienting concepts, and suggest initial hypotheses about causal processes that may be important. These populations, concepts, and hypotheses may then be refined or rejected in light of historical and comparative evidence from real cases. In the actual practice of research, this dialogue between theory and history typically goes through many iterations before final conclusions are reached.

Given that theory is central to comparative historical analysis, and given that pragmatic rational choice theorists endorse analytic induction and the study of particular cases, one might ask in what respects there is now any significant dispute between the two traditions. Clearly, the division does not revolve around the assumption that actors are rational, since many comparative historical researchers assume that actors behave rationally most of the time. Likewise, the issue is not simply one of micro versus macro levels of analysis, since many rational choice theorists employ highly aggregate actors and refer to quite large processes in their studies, while comparative historical researchers analyze the choices and behavior of specific individuals or reconstruct the conditions under which individuals in specific situations are likely, for instance, to overcome the collective action problem (e.g., Skocpol 1979).

We would suggest that rational choice theorists differ from comparative historical analysts insofar as the former researchers are guided by a single theoretical tradition – rational choice theory – and thereby implicitly reject a pluralistic approach to theory that allows specific research questions and actual historical patterns to help shape the selection of appropriate analytic frameworks. In fact, even pragmatic rational choice theorists are sometimes content to apply the principles of rational choice theory and see little need to pursue detailed, systematic comparison of a small number of cases. This approach diverges from the tradition of comparative historical analysis in that it uses historical cases primarily to illustrate a general theoretical argument or model rather than to develop contextualized concepts and systematically evaluate causal hypotheses (see, e.g., Bates 1981; Levi 1988; North 1966). Yet some scholars who draw on ideas from rational choice theory do pursue systematic and contextualized comparison in an effort to explain specific outcomes in a small number of cases (e.g., Alexander 2002; Jones 2002; Hechter 2000). Finally, there are those rational choice works that juxtapose specific historical cases, but whose strong theoretical orientation may still lead them to use historical information primarily to illustrate a model rather than allow contextualized comparisons to influence hypothesis formation and the systematic testing of alternative explanations (e.g., Bates 1989; Geddes 1994; Laitin 1986; Levi 1997).

A modal tendency toward structural accounts notwithstanding, comparative historical analysts are decidedly pluralistic in their use of overarching theories. Although these scholars can and do draw on choice-centric frameworks in their studies (see, e.g., Collier and Norden 1992), they do not often dwell at length on actor-choice models for their own sake. Nor are they content with abstract assumptions of how actors understand the situations they face. Comparative historical researchers typically give subjective beliefs a more central place, together with "objectively" changing contexts. They – as well as rational choice analysts who take the same tack – introduce an interpretive element into the rational choice agenda in order to stay close to real historical experience.[43] More generally, they do not hesitate to seek guidance from a range of other theoretical traditions, including prominently various strands of "structural" analysis associated with class analytic and conflict theory, state centric theory, social movement theory, international relations theory, identity theory, and network theory. In this overall spectrum, rational choice models are simply one set of tools that comparative historical researchers use to frame specific aspects of their questions and explanations.

Finally, let us consider a third interparadigm debate, one raised by the so-called cultural or linguistic turn in the social sciences. The rise of cultural studies and associated postmodern approaches has been especially notable in history and anthropology, but has also taken place in sociology and political science to some degree (see Dirks 1996; Hunt 1984, 1989; McDonald 1996; Morawska and Spohn 1994; Ortner 1984; Steinmetz 1999). The divisions within the cultural camp are themselves so extensive as to make it difficult to speak of a single research paradigm; here we will focus on those strands of postmodern and interpretive theory that attempt to use comparison and historical analysis to validly answer big questions about the world. We are not concerned with more radical currents that embrace a theoretical nihilism and assume that valid knowledge is inherently illusory.

More mainstream cultural and postmodern theorists still often express disenchantment with social science efforts to formulate universal generalizations and lawlike propositions. A major response of some has been to reject causal analysis as the primary goal of social science analysis and to seek other strategies of enlightenment. For example, Clifford Geertz reflects the sentiments of many interpretive theorists when he asserts that cultural analysis is "not an experimental science in search of law but an interpretive one in search of meaning" (1973, p. 5; see also Rabinow and Sullivan 1987, p. 14). For Geertz and others, one can interpret the contextualized meanings that behaviors have to the participants who perform them without invoking causal laws. For other postmodern theorists, "causal

[43] Gerard Alexander's (2002) analysis of democratic consolidation offers a good example. His parallel testing of hypotheses about complex belief patterns as well as regime preferences of the right throws a fresh and revealing light on the processes underlying constitutional change and stability in Spain before and after the Civil War, in France and Britain before World War I, in France, Britain, Germany, and Italy in the interwar period, and in France, Britain, Germany, and Italy after World War II.

explanation takes a back seat, if it has a seat at all, to the demystification and deconstruction of power" (Bonnell and Hunt 1999, p. 11). Here the goal is to criticize exploitive social relations and emancipate oppressed groups, a task that is again seen as involving something other than a scientific approach to causal analysis.

In contrast to interpretive and postmodern analysts, comparative historical researchers defend the enterprise of causal analysis, though they do not aim for the universalistic kind sought by some rational choice theorists. Indeed, most comparative historical analysts believe that it is difficult to conduct any kind of social science analysis without at least implicitly making causal claims. For example, the work of Geertz and other interpretivists has been shown to be deeply imbued with causal claims (Jones 1998; Mahon 1990; see also Abel 1977).[44] Likewise, a close reading suggests that postmodern theorists are often decidedly ambiguous in their stance toward causal analysis. As Victoria E. Bonnell and Lynn Hunt suggest, while many cultural theorists "do not embrace a strictly scientific understanding of the social sciences," "they have not given up on social or causal explanation" (Bonnell and Hunt 1999, p. 25).

Although some comparative historical researchers are skeptical about too easy invocations of cultural factors in explaining macrosocial developments, virtually all see cultural analysis as important in identifying the character of the social and political structures and developments they study. Moreover, they are in principle open to culturalist explanations as well, as can be seen in recent work in the comparative historical literature on social revolutions (e.g., Foran 1997). Yet they doubt that cultural theorists can effectively pursue their research without adopting an explicit and rigorous approach to causal inference. The reason is twofold. First, causal questioning has the often unrecognized consequence of giving legitimation to focus selectively on certain aspects of a phenomenon rather than others. So does the critique of power that often is a preoccupation of cultural theorists. Yet, for interpretive theorists in the cultural camp, the descriptive project of meaning analysis is less protected against willful selectivity. These analysts are thus vulnerable to the charge that in the face of inevitable selectivity, they lack a basis for focusing on certain aspects of reality as opposed to others.

[44] Social theorists ranging from Max Weber to Alfred Schutz and Jürgen Habermas have stressed that interpretive analysis is not a substitute for causal analysis. For a discussion see Mahon (1990).

The second reason is, of course, that causal claims are actually pervasive in cultural theory, but remain implicit and therefore almost inevitably escape careful scrutiny. Given this reliance on implicit causal claims, how can cultural theorists ever hope to generate valid knowledge without adopting some standards for pursuing causal analysis? This question appears to pose a difficult choice for these theorists as they contemplate the future of their research program. On the one hand, they can more thoroughly embrace a rigorous model of causal analysis, which will enhance the validity of their research and push them in the direction of comparative historical analysis. However, doing so requires losing some of their distinctive "antiscience" identity, an orientation much celebrated in this field. On the other hand, cultural theorists can continue to pursue a research agenda in which causal analysis is used in a nonsystematic and nondisciplined fashion. This option allows these analysts to maintain a distinctively antiscience identity, but it poses real obstacles to their ability to produce valid knowledge about the world. The danger of not taking sides on this issue is that promising young researchers may be steered toward the theoretical nihilism embraced in more extreme forms of postmodern theory.

To conclude this section, we suggest that much scholarly activity in the social sciences – both publicly in articles and books and nonpublicly through exchanges of like-minded colleagues – entails adversarial or perhaps even openly hostile gestures among competing research paradigms. Comparative historical analysts have had a role to play in this process, including by staunchly defending their research methods in the face of quite critical attacks. In acknowledging these realities, however, we do not wish to imply that all participants in this debate embrace a zero-sum understanding of the issues at stake. Leading scholars identified with each of the paradigms considered previously have drawn insights from alternative camps and have explored how other paradigms have strengths that can supplement their main approach of interest. Indeed, several important books have been written in this spirit, including King, Keohane, and Verba's *Designing Social Inquiry: Scientific Inference in Qualitative Research*, Bates et al.'s *Analytic Narratives*, and Bonnell and Hunt's *Beyond the Cultural Turn: New Directions in the Study of Society and Culture*.

We believe that in various ways, comparative historical analysis can gain from dialogue with other paradigms. This is true most basically because, in letting important substantive questions define their research agendas, comparative historical researchers do their best research when they remain open to the use of diverse methodologies and analytic tools. These scholars must always feel free to draw on statistical methods, rational choice models, or cultural variables in their work. At the same time, comparative historical analysts are often well situated to play the role of mediator between rival paradigms. For example, we have indicated how comparative historical research can mediate between cultural analysis, which runs the risk of moving too far in the direction of a speculative understanding of actors' subjectivity and of abandoning causal analysis, and rational choice theory, which runs the opposite risk of ignoring the subjective dimension of actors' behavior and deploying an unrealistic kind of universally valid theory. Similarly, comparative historical analysis can mediate between, on the one hand, the sometimes narrow and technical concerns of statistical researchers with hypothesis testing, and, on the other, the more grandiose concerns of rational choice and cultural researchers with theory construction and weighty normative matters. When interparadigm debates such as these arise, comparative historical analysts often find themselves comfortably situated between the more extreme positions. In these and other ways, we hope that this volume will contribute further to a discussion of how divergent research traditions can be enriched by one another.

Looking Ahead

The essays that follow assess the past contributions, the current state, and the future prospects of comparative historical inquiry. This assessment proceeds in three interconnected parts, focusing on substantive research in comparative historical analysis, the analytic tools suited for recurrent central problems of comparative history, and the methodological issues that arise in this kind of scholarship.

The essays in Part I explore the extent of knowledge accumulation that has taken place across three substantive topics that have been a focus of much comparative historical research: social provision, revolutions, and democracy and authoritarianism. These essays ask the following questions: What have comparative historical researchers learned after roughly three decades of research? To what extent have they developed a cumulative research program in which scholars build on one another's findings? What are the criteria of assessing cumulation? Can we conclude that the scholarly community now knows more than it did three or four decades ago as a result of comparative historical analysis? These questions are important not only because such taking stock of findings is of obvious substantive interest; they are also critical for the broader analytic and methodological assessment of comparative historical analysis: The success or failure of any research program must rest ultimately on its capacity to generate substantively important findings about the world. These essays conclude with reflections on the future agendas suggested by the review of past work.

The essays in Part II explore analytic tools that are of particular importance in comparative historical research. As suggested previously, we do not believe that comparative historical analysts embrace any single theoretical framework. But comparative historical work does adopt distinct analytic tools for studying the world, many of them related to the temporality of large social structures and processes. These essays consider tools, such as models of path dependency and frameworks for understanding institutional persistence, that leave room for joining different theoretical traditions. They probe the effectiveness of certain approaches, such as network analysis, that were first used in other areas of social research in the comparative study of historical patterns and processes. And they ask what analytic tools are most appropriate to deal with the different paces of historical developments – long-term unfoldings, conjunctures of rapid transformation, and combinations of long gestation and swift outcomes or of sudden breaks with long-term consequences.

While Parts I and II on knowledge accumulation and analytical tools touch in various ways on methodological issues, the essays in Part III deal explicitly with these issues. These essays reflect on the choices that comparative historical analysts must make in their research, including choices about the use of a particular strategy of causal assessment or a specific theoretical framework. They ask how strategies of method articulate with fundamental – "ontological" – assumptions about underlying patterns and interrelations of social structures and social processes. They review advances in the methodology of qualitative research. And they consider the different knowledge gains that we can expect from research that seeks to be true to historical particularity and at the same time is oriented toward analytic understanding.

The different contributions in this volume are organized under the three headings of accumulation of research, analytic tools, and issues of method. But these three parts of the volume must not be seen as closed segments. Most essays, while focusing on one set of issues, also reflect on all three of the dimensions, which we consider essential for an assessment of the current state and the future prospects of comparative historical research. The volume closes with an essay by one of the pioneers of the renaissance of comparative and historical inquiry. In the conclusion, Theda Skocpol points toward the "double engagement" of contemporary comparative historical analysis – its pursuit of substantive research on real-world topics while simultaneously involving itself in debates about approach and method – as one of its most distinctive features.

References

Abbott, Andrew. 1990. "Conceptions of Time and Events in Social Science Methods: Causal and Narrative Approaches." *Historical Methods* 23: 140–50.

1992. "From Causes to Events: Notes on Narrative Positivism." *Sociological Methods and Research* 20: 428–55.

1997. "On the Concept of Turning Point." *Comparative Social Research* 16: 85–105.

Abbott, Andrew and Angela Tsay. 2000. "Sequence Analysis and Optimal Matching Methods in Sociology." *Sociological Methods and Research* 29: 3–33.

Abel, Theodore. 1977. "The Operation Called *Verstehen*." Pp. 81–91 in *Understanding and Social Inquiry*, edited by Fred R. Dallmayr and Thomas A. McCarthy. Notre Dame, IN: University of Notre Dame Press.

Alexander, Gerard. 2002. *The Sources of Democratic Consolidation*. Ithaca, NY: Cornell University Press.

Amenta, Edwin. 1998. *Bold Relief: Institutional Politics and the Origins of Modern American Social Policy*. Princeton, NJ: Princeton University Press.

Aminzade, Ronald. 1992. "Historical Sociology and Time." *Sociological Methods and Research* 20: 456–80.

Amsden, Alice. 2001. *The Rise of "the Rest": Challenges to the West from Late-Industrializing Economies*. Oxford: Oxford University Press.

Anderson, Perry. 1974a. *Passages from Antiquity to Feudalism*. London: New Left Books.

1974b. *Lineages of the Absolutist State*. London: New Left Books.

Banaszak, Lee Ann. 1996. *Why Movements Succeed or Fail: Opportunity, Culture, and the Struggle for Women's Suffrage*. Princeton, NJ: Princeton University Press.

Barkey, Karen. 1994. *Bandits and Bureaucrats: The Ottoman Route to State Centralization*. Ithaca, NY: Cornell University Press.

Bates, Robert H. 1981. *Markets and States in Tropical Africa: The Political Basis of Agricultural Policies*. Berkeley: University of California Press.

1989. *Beyond the Miracle of the Market: The Political Economy of Agrarian Development in Kenya*. Cambridge: Cambridge University Press.

Bates, Robert H., Avner Greif, Margaret Levi, Jean-Laurent Rosenthal, and Barry R. Weingast. 1998. *Analytic Narratives*. Princeton, NJ: Princeton University Press.

2000. "The Analytic Narrative Project." *American Political Science Review* 94: 696–702.

Bendix, Reinhard. 1964. *Nation-Building and Citizenship*. New York: Wiley.

1974. *Work and Authority in Industry: Ideologies of Management in the Course of Industrialization*. Berkeley: University of California Press.

1978. *Kings or People: Power and the Mandate to Rule*. Berkeley: University of California Press.

Bennett, Andrew and Alexander George. 1998. "An Alliance of Statistical and Case Study Methods: Research on the Interdemocratic Peace." *APSA-CP: Newsletter of the APSA Organized Section in Comparative Politics* 9:1 (Winter): 6–9.

Bensel, Richard Franklin. 1990. *Yankee Leviathan: The Origins of Central State Authority in America, 1859–1877*. New York: Cambridge University Press.

Bergquist, Charles W. 1986. *Labor in Latin America: Comparative Essays on Chile, Argentina, Venezuela, and Columbia*. Stanford, CA: Stanford University Press.

Berman, Harold J. 1983. *Law and Revolution: The Formation of the Western Legal Tradition*. Cambridge, MA: Harvard University Press.

Bonnell, Victoria E. and Lynn Hunt. 1999. "Introduction." Pp. 1–32 in *Beyond the Cultural Turn: New Directions in the Study of Society and Culture*, edited by Victoria E. Bonnell and Lynn Hunt. Berkeley: University of California Press.

Brady, Henry E. and David Collier, eds. 2002. *Rethinking Social Inquiry: Diverse Tools, Shared Standards*. Lanham, MD, and New York: Rowman & Littlefield.

Braumoeller, Bear F. and Gary Goertz. 2000. "The Methodology of Necessary Conditions." *American Journal of Political Science* 44: 844–58.

Brubaker, Rogers. 1992. *Citizenship and Nationhood in France and Germany*. Cambridge, MA: Harvard University Press.

Bunce, Valerie. 1999. *Subversive Institutions: The Design and the Destruction of Socialism and the State*. Cambridge: Cambridge University Press.

Burawoy, Michael. 1989. "Two Methods in Search of Science: Skocpol versus Trotsky." *Theory and Society* 18: 759–805.

Calhoun, Craig J. 1997. *Nationalism*. Minneapolis: University of Minnesota Press.

Carruthers, Bruce G. 1996. *City of Capital: Politics and Markets in the English Financial Revolution*. Princeton, NJ: Princeton University Press.

Castells, Manuel. 1996–8. *The Information Age: Economy, Society and Culture*. Vols. 1–3. Oxford: Blackwell.

Centeno, Miguel Angel. 2002. *Blood and Debt: War and the Nation-State in Latin America*. University Park: Pennsylvania State University Press.

Charrad, Mourina M. 2001. *States and Women's Rights: The Making of Postcolonial Tunisia, Algeria and Morocco*. Berkeley: University of California Press.

Chaudhry, Kiren Aziz. 1997. *The Price of Wealth: Economies and Institutions in the Middle East*. Ithaca, NY: Cornell University Press.

Clark, Samuel. 1995. *State and Status: The Rise of the State and Aristocratic Power in Western Europe*. Montreal and Kingston: McGill-Queen's University Press.

Clemens, Elisabeth S. 1997. *The People's Lobby: Organizational Innovation and the Rise of Interest Group Politics in the United States, 1890–1925*. Chicago: University of Chicago Press.

Colburn, Forrest D. 1994. *The Vogue of Revolution in Poor Countries*. Princeton, NJ: Princeton University Press.

Collier, David. 1993. "The Comparative Method." Pp. 105–19 in *Political Science: The State of the Discipline II*, edited by Ada Finifter. Washington, DC: American Political Science Association.

1998a. "Comparative-Historical Analysis: Where Do We Stand?" *APSA-CP: Newsletter of the APSA Organized Section in Comparative Politics* 9 (Winter): 1–2, 4–5.

1998b. "Comparative Method in the 1990s." *APSA-CP: Newsletter of the APSA Organized Section in Comparative Politics* 9 (Summer): 1–2, 4–5.

Collier, David and Robert Adcock. 1999. "Democracy and Dichotomies: A Pragmatic Approach to Choices about Concepts." *Review of Political Science* 2: 537–65.

Collier, David and Steven Levitsky. 1997. "Democracy with Adjectives: Conceptual Innovation in Comparative Research." *World Politics* 49: 430–51.

Collier, David and James E. Mahon. 1993. "Conceptual 'Stretching' Revisited: Adapting Categories in Comparative Analysis." *American Political Science Review* 87: 845–55.

Collier, David and James Mahoney. 1996. "Insights and Pitfalls: Selection Bias in Qualitative Research." *World Politics* 49: 56–91.

Collier, David and Deborah L. Norden. 1992. "Strategic Choice Models of Political Change in Latin America." *Comparative Politics* 24: 229–43.

Collier, Ruth Berins. 1999. *Paths Toward Democracy*. New York: Cambridge University Press.

Collier, Ruth Berins and David Collier. 1991. *Shaping the Political Arena: Critical Junctures, the Labor Movement, and Regime Dynamics in Latin America*. Princeton, NJ: Princeton University Press.

Coppedge, Michael. 1999. "Thickening Thin Concepts and Theories: Combining Large *N* and Small in Comparative Politics." *Comparative Politics* 31: 465–76.

de Swaan, Abram. 1988. *In Care of the State: Health Care, Education and Welfare in Europe and the USA in the Modern Era*. New York: Oxford University Press.

Deyo, Frederic, ed. 1987. *The Political Economy of the New Asian Industrialism*. Ithaca, NY: Cornell University Press.

Dion, Douglas. 1998. "Evidence and Inference in the Comparative Case Study." *Comparative Politics* 30: 127–46.

Dirks, Nicholas B. 1996. "Is Vice Versa? Historical Anthropologies and Anthropological Histories." Pp. 17–51 in *The Historic Turn in the Human Sciences*, edited by Terrence J. McDonald. Ann Arbor: University of Michigan Press.

Dobbin, Frank. 1994. *Forging Industrial Policy: The United States, Britain, and France in the Railway Age*. Cambridge: Cambridge University Press.

Downing, Brian M. 1992. *The Military Revolution and Political Change: Origins of Democracy and Autocracy in Early Modern Europe*. Princeton, NJ: Princeton University Press.

Easton, David. 1965. *A Systems Analysis of Political Life*. New York: Wiley.

Eisenstadt, S. N. 1963. *The Political Systems of Empires: The Rise and Fall of Historical Bureaucratic Societies*. New York: Free Press.

1978. *Revolutions and the Transformation of Society*. New York: Free Press.

Ekiert, Grzegorz. 1996. *The State Against Society: Political Crises and Their Aftermath in East Central Europe*. Princeton, NJ: Princeton University Press.

Elster, Jon. 2000. "Rational Choice History: A Case of Excessive Ambition." *American Political Science Review* 94: 685–95.
Emirbayer, Mustafa. 1996. "Durkheim's Contribution to the Sociological Analysis of History." *Sociological Forum* 11: 263–84.
Ertman, Thomas. 1997. *Birth of the Leviathan: Building States and Regimes in Medieval and Early Modern Europe*. Cambridge: Cambridge University Press.
Esping-Andersen, Gøsta. 1990. *The Three Worlds of Welfare Capitalism*. Princeton, NJ: Princeton University Press.
Evans, Peter. 1995. *Embedded Autonomy: States and Industrial Transformation*. Princeton, NJ: Princeton University Press.
Foran, John, ed. 1997. *Theorizing Revolutions*. London: Routledge.
Friedman, Jeffrey, ed. 1996. *The Rational Choice Controversy: Economic Models of Politics Reconsidered*. New Haven, CT: Yale University Press.
Geddes, Barbara. 1990. "How the Cases You Choose Affect the Answers You Get: Selection Bias in Comparative Politics." Pp. 131–50 in *Political Analysis*, vol. 2, edited by James A. Stimson. Ann Arbor: University of Michigan Press.
1991. "Paradigms and Sand Castles in Comparative Politics of Developing Areas." Pp. 45–75 in *Comparative Politics, Policy, and International Relations*, edited by William Crotty. Evanston, IL: Northwestern University Press.
1994. *Politician's Dilemma: Building State Capacity in Latin America*. Berkeley: University of California Press.
in press. *Paradigms and Sand Castles: Theory Building and Research Design in Comparative Politics*. Ann Arbor: University of Michigan Press.
Geertz, Clifford. 1973. *The Interpretation of Cultures: Selected Essays*. New York: Basic Books.
George, Alexander L. and Andrew Bennett. in press. *Case Studies and Theory Development*. Cambridge, MA: MIT Press.
Gereffi, Gary and Donald L. Wyman, eds. 1991. *Manufacturing Miracles: Paths of Industrialization in Latin America and East Asia*. Princeton, NJ: Princeton University Press.
Gocek, Muge. 1996. *Rise of the Bourgeoisie, Demise of Empire: Ottoman Westernization and Social Change*. New York: Oxford University Press.
Goldstone, Jack A. 1991. *Revolution and Rebellion in the Early Modern World*. Berkeley: University of California Press.
1997. "Methodological Issues in Comparative Macrosociology." *Comparative Social Research* 16: 107–20.
1998. "Initial Conditions, General Laws, Path Dependence, and Explanation in Historical Sociology." *American Journal of Sociology* 104: 829–45.
1999. "Analytic Narratives." *American Journal of Sociology* 105: 531–3.
Goldthorpe, John H. 1991. "The Uses of History in Sociology: Reflections on Some Recent Tendencies." *British Journal of Sociology* 42: 211–30.
1997. "Current Issues in Comparative Macrosociology: A Debate on Methodological Issues." *Comparative Social Research* 16: 1–26.
1998a. "Rational Action Theory for Sociology." *British Journal of Sociology* 49: 167–92.

1998b. "The Quantitative Analysis of Large-Scale Data-Sets and Rational Action Theory: For a Sociology Alliance." Pp. 31–53 in *Rational Choice Theory and Large-Scale Data Analysis*, edited by Hans-Peter Blossfeld and Gerald Prein. Boulder, CO: Westview.

Goodwin, Jeff. 2001. *No Other Way Out: States and Revolutionary Movements, 1945–1991*. Cambridge: Cambridge University Press.

Green, Donald P. and Ian Shapiro. 1994. *Pathologies of Rational Choice Theory: A Critique of Applications in Political Science*. New Haven, CT: Yale University Press.

Griffin, Larry J. 1992. "Temporality, Events, and Explanation in Historical Sociology: An Introduction." *Sociological Methods and Research* 20: 403–27.

1993. "Narrative, Event-Structure, and Causal Interpretation in Historical Sociology." *American Journal of Sociology* 98: 1094–1133.

Griffin, Larry J. and Marcel van der Linden, eds. 1999. *New Methods for Social History*. Cambridge: Cambridge University Press.

Haggard, Stephan. 1990. *Pathways from the Periphery: The Politics of Growth in the Newly Industrializing Countries*. Princeton, NJ: Princeton University Press.

Haggard, Stephan and Robert R. Kaufman. 1995. *The Political Economy of Democratic Transitions*. Princeton, NJ: Princeton University Press.

Hall, Peter A. 1986. *Governing the Economy: The Politics of State Intervention in Britain and France*. New York: Oxford University Press.

Hall, Peter A. and Rosemary C. R. Taylor. 1996. "Political Science and the Three New Institutionalisms." *Political Studies* 44: 936–57.

Haydu, Jeffrey. 1998. "Making Use of the Past: Time Periods as Cases to Compare and as Sequences of Problem Solving." *American Journal of Sociology* 104: 339–71.

Hechter, Michael. 2000. *Containing Nationalism*. Oxford: Oxford University Press.

Heller, Patrick. 1999. *The Labor of Development: Workers and the Transformation of Capitalism in Kerala, India*. Ithaca, NY: Cornell University Press.

Herbst, Jeffrey. 2000. *States and Power in Africa: Comparative Lessons in Authority and Control.* Princeton, NJ: Princeton University Press.

Hicks, Alexander. 1999. *Social Democracy and Welfare Capitalism: A Century of Income Security Politics*. Ithaca, NY: Cornell University Press.

Hopcroft, Rosemary L. 1999. *Regions, Institutions, and Agrarian Change in European History*. Ann Arbor: University of Michigan Press.

Htun, Mala. in press. *Democracy, Dictatorship, and Gendered Rights*. Cambridge: Cambridge University Press.

Huber, Evelyne and Frank Safford, eds. 1995. *Agrarian Structure and Political Power: Landlord and Peasant in the Making of Latin America*. Pittsburgh, PA: University of Pittsburgh Press.

Huber, Evelyne and John D. Stephens. 2001. *Development and Crisis of the Welfare State: Parties and Policies in Global Markets*. Chicago: University of Chicago Press.

Hunt, Lynn. 1984. *Politics, Culture, and Class in the French Revolution*. Berkeley: University of California Press.

ed. 1989. *The New Cultural History*. Berkeley: University of California Press.

Immergut, Ellen M. 1992. *Health Politics: Interests and Institutions in Western Europe*. Cambridge: Cambridge University Press.

Isaac, Larry W. 1997. "Transforming Localities: Reflections on Time, Causality, and Narrative in Contemporary Historical Sociology." *Historical Methods* 30: 4–12.

Itzigsohn, José. 2000. *Developing Poverty: The State, Labor Market Deregulation, and the Informal Economy in Costa Rica and the Dominican Republic*. University Park: Pennsylvania State University Press.

Jones, Todd. 1998. "Interpretive Social Science and the 'Native's Point of View': A Closer Look." *Philosophy of the Social Sciences* 28: 32–68.

Jones Luong, Pauline. 2002. *Institutional Change and Political Continuity in Post-Soviet Central Asia: Power, Perceptions, and Pacts*. New York: Cambridge University Press.

Kalberg, Stephen. 1994. *Max Weber's Comparative-Historical Sociology*. Chicago: University of Chicago Press.

Karl, Terry Lynn. 1997. *The Paradox of Plenty: Oil Booms and Petro-States*. Berkeley: University of California Press.

Katznelson, Ira. 1997. "Structure and Configuration in Comparative Politics." Pp. 81–112 in *Comparative Politics: Rationality, Culture, and Structure*, edited by Mark Irving Lichbach and Alan S. Zuckerman. Cambridge: Cambridge University Press.

Katznelson, Ira and Aristide R. Zolberg, eds. 1986. *Working Class Formation: Nineteenth Century Patterns in Western Europe and the United States*. Princeton, NJ: Princeton University Press.

Kimeldorf, Howard. 1988. *Reds or Rackets? The Making of Radical and Conservative Unions on the Waterfront*. Berkeley: University of California Press.

Kimmel, Michael. 1990. *Revolution: A Sociological Interpretation*. Philadelphia: Temple University Press.

King, Gary, Robert O. Keohane, and Sidney Verba. 1994. *Designing Social Inquiry: Scientific Inference in Qualitative Research*. Princeton, NJ: Princeton University Press.

Kiser, Edgar and Michael Hechter. 1991. "The Role of General Theory in Comparative-Historical Sociology." *American Journal of Sociology* 97: 1–30.

1998. "The Debate on Historical Sociology: Rational Choice Theory and Its Critics." *American Journal of Sociology* 104: 785–816.

Kitschelt, Herbert. 1994. *The Transformation of European Social Democracy*. New York: Cambridge University Press.

Kitschelt, Herbert, Peter Lange, Gary Marks, and John D. Stephens, eds. 1999. *Continuity and Change in Contemporary Capitalism*. Cambridge: Cambridge University Press.

Kohli, Atul. 1987. *The State and Poverty in India*. Cambridge: Cambridge University Press.

Lachmann, Richard. 2000. *Capitalists in Spite of Themselves: Elite Conflict and Economic Transitions in Early Modern Europe*. Oxford: Oxford University Press.

Laitin, David D. 1986. *Hegemony and Culture: Politics and Religious Change Among the Yoruba*. Chicago: University of Chicago Press.
2002. "Comparative Politics: The State of the Subdiscipline." In *Political Sciences: The State of the Discipline*, edited by Helen Milner and Ira Katznelson. New York: W. W. Norton.
Levi, Margaret. 1988. *Of Rule and Revenue*. Berkeley: University of California Press.
1997. *Consent, Dissent, and Patriotism*. Cambridge: Cambridge University Press.
Levine, Ross and David Renelt. 1992. "A Sensitivity Analysis of Cross-Country Growth Regressions." *American Economic Review* 82: 942–63.
Levy, Marion J., Jr. 1966. *Modernization and the Structure of Societies*. Princeton, NJ: Princeton University Press.
Lieberson, Stanley. 1991. "Small *N*'s and Big Conclusions: An Examination of the Reasoning in Comparative Studies Based on a Small Number of Cases." *Social Forces* 70: 307–20.
1994. "More on the Uneasy Case for Using Mill-Type Methods in Small-*N* Comparative Studies." *Social Forces* 72: 1225–37.
1998. "Causal Analysis and Comparative Research: What Can We Learn from Studies Based on a Small Number of Cases." Pp. 129–45 in *Rational Choice Theory and Large-Scale Data Analysis*, edited by Hans-Peter Blossfeld and Gerald Prein. Boulder, CO: Westview.
Lijphart, Arend. 1971. "Comparative Politics and the Comparative Method." *American Political Science Review* 65: 682–93.
1975. "The Comparable-Cases Strategy in Comparative Research." *Comparative Political Studies* 8: 158–77.
Linz, Juan J. and Alfred Stepan. 1996. *Problems of Democratic Transition and Consolidation: Southern Europe, South America, and Post-Communist Europe*. Baltimore: Johns Hopkins University Press.
Lipset, Seymour Martin, and Stein Rokkan, eds. 1968. *Party Systems and Voter Alignments: Cross-National Perspectives*. New York: Free Press.
Locke, Richard M. and Kathleen Thelen. 1995. "Apples and Oranges Revisited: Contextualized Comparisons and the Study of Labor Politics." *Politics and Society* 23: 337–67.
Luebbert, Gregory M. 1991. *Liberalism, Fascism, or Social Democracy: Social Classes and the Political Origins of Regimes in Interwar Europe*. New York: Oxford University Press.
Lustick, Ian. 1993. *Unsettled States, Disputed Lands: Britain and Ireland, France and Algeria, Israel and the West Bank-Gaza*. Ithaca, NY: Cornell University Press.
1996. "History, Historiography, and Political Science: Multiple Historical Records and the Problem of Selection Bias." *American Political Science Review* 90: 605–18.
Mahon, James E. 1990. "Interpretive Social Inquiry and Comparative Politics." Manuscript.
Mahoney, James. 1999. "Nominal, Ordinal, and Narrative Appraisal in Macrocausal Analysis." *American Journal of Sociology* 104: 1154–96.
2000. "Path Dependence in Historical Sociology." *Theory and Society* 29: 507–48.

2001. *The Legacies of Liberalism: Path Dependence and Political Regimes in Central America*. Baltimore, MD: Johns Hopkins University Press.

Mann, Michael. 1986. *The Sources of Social Power, Volume I: A History of Power from the Beginning to A.D. 1760*. Cambridge: Cambridge University Press.

1993. *The Sources of Social Power, Volume II: The Rise of Classes and Nation-States, 1760–1914*. Cambridge: Cambridge University Press.

Markoff, John. 1996. *The Abolition of Feudalism: Peasants, Lords, and Legislators in the French Revolution*. University Park: Pennsylvania State University Press.

Marx, Anthony W. 1998. *Making Race and Nation: A Comparison of South Africa, the United States, and Brazil*. Cambridge: Cambridge University Press.

McAdam, Doug, Sidney Tarrow, and Charles Tilly. 2001. *Dynamics of Contention*. Cambridge: Cambridge University Press.

McDonald, Terrence J., ed. 1996. *The Historic Turn in the Human Sciences*. Ann Arbor: University of Michigan Press.

McKeown, Timothy J. 1999. "Case Studies and the Statistical Worldview." *International Organization* 53: 161–90.

McMichael, Philip. 1985. "Britain's Hegemony in the Nineteenth-Century World-Economy." Pp. 117–50 in *States vs. Markets in the World System*. Vol. 8, *Political Economy of the World System Annuals*. Beverly Hills, CA: Sage.

Meyer, John W., John Boli, George M. Thomas, and Francisco O. Ramirez. 1997. "World Society and the Nation-State." *American Journal of Sociology* 103: 144–81.

Migdal, Joel S. 1988. *Strong Societies and Weak States: State–Society Relations and State Capabilities in the Third World*. Princeton, NJ: Princeton University Press.

Migdal, Joel S., Atul Kohli, and Vivienne Shue. 1994. *State Power and Social Forces: Domination and Transformation in the Third World*. Cambridge: Cambridge University Press.

Moore, Barrington, Jr. 1966. *Social Origins of Dictatorship and Democracy: Lord and Peasant in the Making of the Modern World*. Boston: Beacon Press.

Morawska, Ewa and Willfried Spohn. 1994. "'Cultural Pluralism' in Historical Sociology: Recent Theoretical Directions." Pp. 45–90 in *The Sociology of Culture: Emerging Theoretical Perspectives*, edited by Diana Crane. Oxford: Blackwell.

Mouzelis, Nicos. 1994. "In Defense of 'Grand' Historical Sociology." *British Journal of Sociology* 45: 31–6.

Munck, Gerardo L. 1998. "Canons of Research Design in Qualitative Analysis." *Studies in Comparative International Development* 33: 18–45.

2001. "Game Theory and Comparative Politics: New Perspectives and Old Concerns." *World Politics* 53: 173–204.

Munck, Gerardo L. and John Verkuilen. 2000. "Measuring Democracy: Evaluating Alternative Indicators." Paper delivered at the annual meetings of the American Political Science Association, Washington, DC.

North, Douglas C. 1966. *The Economic Growth of the United States, 1790–1860*. New York: W. W. Norton.

O'Connor, Julia S., Ann Shola Orloff, and Sheila Shaver. 1999. *States, Markets, and Families: Gender, Liberalism and Social Policy in Australia, Canada, Great Britain and the United States*. Cambridge: Cambridge University Press.

O'Donnell, Guillermo. 1993. "On the State, Democratization, and Some Conceptual Problems: A Latin American View with Glances at Some Postcommunist Countries." *World Development* 21: 1355–69.

Orloff, Ann Shola. 1993. *The Politics of Pensions: A Comparative Analysis of Britain, Canada, and the United States, 1880–1940*. Madison: University of Wisconsin Press.

Orloff, Ann Shola and Theda Skocpol. 1984. "Why Not Equal Protection? Explaining the Politics of Public Social Spending in Britain, 1900–1911, and the United States, 1880s–1920." *American Sociological Review* 49: 726–50.

Orren, Karen. 1991. *Labor, the Law, and Liberal Development in the United States*. Cambridge: Cambridge University Press.

Ortner, Sherry B. 1984. "Theory in Anthropology since the Sixties." *Comparative Studies in Society and History* 26: 126–66.

Paige, Jeffery M. 1975. *Agrarian Revolution: Social Movements and Export Agriculture in the Underdeveloped World*. New York: Free Press.

1997. *Coffee and Power: Revolution and the Rise of Democracy in Central America*. Cambridge, MA: Harvard University Press.

1999. "Conjuncture, Comparison, and Conditional Theory in Macrosocial Inquiry." *American Journal of Sociology* 105: 781–800.

Parsa, Misagh. 2000. *States, Ideologies, and Social Revolutions*. Cambridge: Cambridge University Press.

Parsons, Talcott. 1951. *The Social System*. Glencoe, IL: Free Press.

Pempel, T. J., ed. 1999. *The Politics of the Asian Economic Crisis*. Ithaca, NY: Cornell University Press.

Pierson, Paul. 1994. *Dismantling the Welfare State? Reagan, Thatcher, and the Politics of Retrenchment*. Cambridge: Cambridge University Press.

2000a. "Increasing Returns, Path Dependence, and the Study of Politics." *American Political Science Review* 94: 251–67.

2000b. "Not Just What, but *When*. Issues of Timing and Sequence in Political Processes." *Studies in American Political Development* 14: 72–92.

ed. 2001. *The New Politics of the Welfare State*. Oxford: Oxford University Press.

Pierson, Paul and Theda Skocpol. 2002. "Historical Institutionalism in Contemporary Political Science."In *Political Science: The State of the Discipline*, edited by Ira Katznelson and Helen Milner. New York: W. W. Norton.

Piore, Michael J. and Charles F. Sabel. 1984. *The Second Industrial Divide: Possibilities for Prosperity*. New York: Basic Books.

Putnam, Robert D. 1993. *Making Democracy Work: Civic Traditions in Modern Italy*. Princeton, NJ: Princeton University Press.

Quadagno, Jill and Stan J. Knapp. 1992. "Have Historical Sociologists Forsaken Theory?: Thoughts on the History/Theory Relationship." *Sociological Methods and Research* 20: 481–507.

Rabinow, Paul and William M. Sullivan. 1987. *Interpretive Social Science: A Second Look*. Berkeley: University of California Press.

Ragin, Charles C. 1987. *The Comparative Method: Moving Beyond Qualitative and Quantitative Strategies*. Berkeley: University of California Press.

1997. "Turning the Tables: How Case-Oriented Research Challenges Variable-Oriented Research." *Comparative Social Research* 16: 27–42.

2000. *Fuzzy-Set Social Science*. Chicago: University of Chicago Press.

Roy, William G. 1997. *Socializing Capital: The Rise of the Large Industrial Corporation in America*. Princeton, NJ: Princeton University Press.

Rueschemeyer, Dietrich. 1973. *Lawyers and Their Society: The Legal Professions in the United States and Germany*. Cambridge, MA: Harvard University Press.

1986. *Power and the Division of Labour*. Stanford, CA: Stanford University Press.

1991. "Different Methods – Contradictory Results? Research on Development and Democracy." *International Journal of Comparative Sociology* 32: 9–38.

Rueschemeyer, Dietrich, Evelyne Huber Stephens, and John D. Stephens. 1992. *Capitalist Development and Democracy*. Chicago: University of Chicago Press.

Rueschemeyer, Dietrich and John D. Stephens. 1997. "Comparing Historical Sequences – A Powerful Tool for Causal Analysis." *Comparative Social Research* 17: 55–72.

Seidman, G. 1994. *Manufacturing Militance: Workers' Movements in Brazil and South Africa, 1970–1985*. Berkeley: University of California Press.

Selbin, Eric. 1993. *Modern Latin American Revolutions*. Boulder, CO: Westview.

Senghaas, Dieter. 1985. *The European Experience: A Historical Critique of Development Theory*. Translated by K. H. Kimmig. Leamington Spa, U.K.: Berg Publishers.

Sewell, William H., Jr. 1996. "Three Temporalities: Toward an Eventful Sociology." Pp. 245–80 in *The Historic Turn in the Human Sciences*, edited by Terrence J. McDonald. Ann Arbor: University of Michigan Press.

Sikkink, Kathryn. 1991. *Ideas and Institutions: Developmentalism in Brazil and Argentina*. Ithaca, NY: Cornell University Press.

Silberman, Bernard S. 1993. *Cages of Reason: The Rise of the Rational State in France, Japan, the United States, and Great Britain*. Chicago: University of Chicago Press.

Skocpol, Theda. 1979. *States and Social Revolutions: A Comparative Analysis of France, Russia, and China*. Cambridge: Cambridge University Press.

1984a. "Emerging Agendas and Recurrent Strategies in Historical Sociology." Pp. 356–91 in *Vision and Method in Historical Sociology*, edited by Theda Skocpol. Cambridge: Cambridge University Press.

1984b. "Sociology's Historical Imagination." Pp. 1–21 in *Vision and Method in Historical Sociology*, edited by Theda Skocpol. Cambridge: Cambridge University Press.

1985. "Bringing the State Back In: Strategies of Analysis in Current Research." Pp. 3–37 in *Bringing the State Back In*, edited by Peter B. Evans, Dietrich Rueschemeyer, and Theda Skocpol. Cambridge: Cambridge University Press.

1992. *Protecting Soldiers and Mothers: The Political Origins of Social Policy in the United States*. Cambridge, MA: Harvard University Press.

Skocpol, Theda and Margaret Somers. 1980. "The Uses of Comparative History in Macrosocial Inquiry." *Comparative Studies in Society and History* 22: 174–97.

Smelser, Neil J. 1963. "Mechanisms to Change and Adjustment to Change." Pp. 32–54 in *Industrialization and Society*, edited by Bert F. Hoselitz and Wilbert E. Moore. The Hague: Mouton.

1976. *Comparative Methods in the Social Sciences*. Englewood Cliffs, NJ: Prentice-Hall.

Snyder, Richard. 2001a. "Scaling Down: The Subnational Comparative Method." *Studies in Comparative International Development* 36: 93–110.

2001b. *Politics after Neoliberalism: Reregulation in Mexico*. Cambridge: Cambridge University Press.

Somers, Margaret R. 1998. "'We're No Angels': Realism, Rational Choice, and Relationality in Social Science." *American Journal of Sociology* 104: 722–84.

Spruyt, Hendrik. 1994. *The Sovereign State and Its Competitors: An Analysis of Systems Change*. Princeton, NJ: Princeton University Press.

Stark, David and Lászlό Bruszt. 1998. *Postsocialist Pathways: Transforming Politics and Property in East Central Europe*. Cambridge: Cambridge University Press.

Steinmetz, George. 1993. *Regulating the Social: The Welfare State and Local Politics in Imperial Germany*. Princeton, NJ: Princeton University Press.

ed. 1999. *State/Culture: State-Formation after the Cultural Turn*. Ithaca, NY: Cornell University Press.

Steinmo, Sven. 1993. *Taxation and Democracy: Swedish, British and American Approaches to Financing the Modern State*. New Haven, CT: Yale University Press.

Stinchcombe, Arthur L. 1995. *Sugar Island Slavery in the Age of Enlightenment: The Political Economy of the Caribbean World*. Princeton, NJ: Princeton University Press.

Stryker, Robin. 1996. "Beyond History versus Theory: Strategic Narrative and Sociological Explanation." *Sociological Methods and Research* 24: 304–52.

Swedberg, Richard. 2001. "Sociology and Game Theory: Contemporary and Historical Perspectives." *Theory and Society* 30: 301–35.

Temple, Jonathan. 1999. "The New Growth Evidence." *Journal of Economic Literature* 37: 112–56.

Thelen, Kathleen. 1999. "Historical Institutionalism and Comparative Politics." *Annual Review of Political Science* 2: 369–404.

Thelen, Kathleen and Sven Steinmo. 1992. "Historical Institutionalism in Comparative Politics." Pp. 1–32 in *Structuring Politics: Historical Institutionalism in Comparative Analysis*, edited by Sven Steinmo, Kathleen Thelen, and Frank Longstreth. Cambridge: Cambridge University Press.

Tilly, Charles. 1967. *The Vendée: A Sociological Analysis of the Counterrevolution of 1793*. New York: Wiley.

ed. 1975. *The Formation of National States in Western Europe*. Princeton, NJ: Princeton University Press.

1984. *Big Structures, Large Processes, Huge Comparisons*. New York: Russell Sage Foundation.

1990. *Coercion, Capital, and European States, AD 990–1990.* Cambridge, MA: Basil Blackwell.
Tilly, Charles, Louise Tilly, and Richard Tilly. 1975. *The Rebellious Century, 1830–1930.* Cambridge, MA: Harvard University Press.
Wade, Robert. 1990. *Governing the Market: Economic Theory and the Role of Government in East Asian Industrialization.* Princeton, NJ: Princeton University Press.
Waldner, David. 1999. *State-Building and Late Development.* Ithaca, NY: Cornell University Press.
Wallerstein, Immanuel. 1974. *The Modern World-System I: Capitalist Agriculture and the Origins of the European World-Economy in the Sixteenth Century.* New York: Academic Press.
1980. *The Modern World-System II: Mercantilism and the Consolidation of the European World-Economy, 1600–1750.* New York: Academic Press.
1989. *The Modern World-System III: The Second Era of Great Expansion of the Capitalist World-Economy, 1730s–1840s.* New York: Academic Press.
Wickham-Crowley, Timothy. 1992. *Guerrillas and Revolution in Latin America: A Comparative Study of Insurgents and Regimes since 1956.* Princeton, NJ: Princeton University Press.
Williams, Robert G. 1994. *States and Social Evolution: Coffee and the Rise of National Governments in Central America.* Chapel Hill: University of North Carolina Press.
Wood, Elisabeth Jean. 2000. *Forging Democracy from Below: Insurgent Transitions in South Africa and Brazil.* New York: Cambridge University Press.
Yashar, Deborah J. 1997. *Demanding Democracy: Reform and Reaction in Costa Rica and Guatemala, 1870s–1950s.* Stanford, CA: Stanford University Press.
Young, Crawford. 1994. *The African Colonial State in Comparative Perspective.* New Haven, CT: Yale University Press.

2

Comparative Historical Analysis and Knowledge Accumulation in the Study of Revolutions

Jack A. Goldstone

A Tale of Two Methods

It is striking that those works on the subject of revolutions that have had lasting influence have been almost exclusively built around comparative case studies. From Crane Brinton's (1938) *The Anatomy of Revolution* to Barrington Moore Jr.'s (1966) *Social Origins of Dictatorship and Democracy* to Theda Skocpol's (1979) *States and Social Revolutions*, this pattern holds true. Even books with widely divergent theoretical perspectives, such as Samuel Huntington's (1968) *Political Order in Changing Societies*, Chalmers Johnson's (1966) *Revolutionary Change*, and Ted Robert Gurr's (1970) *Why Men Rebel* build their arguments around series of brief analytic case accounts, rather than efforts at statistical analysis of large data sets.

This is not because such data sets do not exist. Although it is sometimes argued that revolutions – particularly great social revolutions, such as those of France in 1789 or Russia in 1917 – are too few for formal data analysis, this seems to exaggerate the truth. Jeff Goodwin (2001) lists no fewer than eighteen "major social revolutions" (presumably the most restrictive category of revolutions) from France in 1789 to the collapse of communism in Eastern Europe in 1989. John Foran (1997a), using only a slightly less restrictive definition, lists thirty-one revolutions occurring merely in the Third World since 1900. If we extend the definition to cover not only revolutions but also revolutionary movements, the *Encyclopedia of Political Revolutions* (Goldstone 1998c) lists over 150 cases around the world since the sixteenth century. Studies not merely using cases of revolution, but counting all years during which particular countries experience mass political violence, further push their *n* into the hundreds or thousands.

Nor has there been any lack of effort to undertake the analysis of revolutions using large-N statistical analysis. Gurr (1968) and Feierabend, Feierabend, and Nesvold (1969) sought to develop statistical analyses of the causes of revolutions; Hibbs (1973) used sophisticated recursive time-series models to probe the sources of mass political violence. Muller (1985), Weede (1987), and Midlarsky (1982) used statistical analysis to examine the relationship between inequality and revolutions. Nonetheless, these efforts, far from providing a more solid basis for inference and knowledge accumulation, as some critics of small-N analyses have suggested (Lieberson 1991; Goldthorpe 1997), have themselves failed to provide any cumulative insights. As Mark Lichbach (1989) points out, studies of inequality and revolution have revealed conflicting results. In most statistical studies of revolution, results vary according to the time period and the model specification, so that no consensus emerged. As a result, most of these works are nowadays cited far less frequently than case-study analyses, and the research tradition of large-N statistical studies of revolution has borne modest fruit.

This essay attempts to account for this outcome, showing how comparative and historical analysis of revolutions has led to steady progress and knowledge accumulation. In the following sections, I first consider the logic and methods of comparative historical analysis and point out its advantages for the study of complex events like revolutions. Next, I offer a brief history of the scholarship on revolutions, showing how case-study analyses of revolution have in fact successively built upon prior analyses in rigorous and cumulative fashion, extending the range and detail of theory at the same time that they have deepened empirical knowledge. Finally, I close with a brief compilation of the insights gained from comparative historical analyses of revolution.

The Goals and Inference Methods of Comparative Historical Analysis

Large-N statistical inferences based on normal frequency distributions are designed to answer the following question: Given a large universe of comparable cases, how can we infer the characteristics of those cases – including correlations among hypothesized causes and effects – from a smaller sample? Starting with this problem, concerns about whether the sample is biased, whether it is large enough to distinguish causes from random effects, and whether it is large enough to discern probabilistic relationships are of great importance (Keohane, King, and Verba 1994).

However, this is not the problem addressed by comparative historical analysis (CHA). Analysts using CHA generally face a finite set of cases, chosen against a backdrop of theoretical interests, and aim to determine the causal sequences and patterns producing outcomes of interest in those specific cases. Generalization is certainly a goal, but that generalization is sought by piecing together finite sets of cases, not by sampling and inference to a larger universe.

To offer a homely example, let us say that explorers are surveying a large territory. If they took the large-*N* statistical approach to developing knowledge of that territory, they would have to sample enough locations to provide reliable inferences regarding the territory as a whole. If the territory is fairly homogeneous (or if its main characteristics are distributed in a statistically normal distribution across the territory), such sampling would produce a fairly quick, accurate, and reliable method of determining that territory's main characteristics. If, however, the territory has substantial local variations, and if the explorers are as interested in those variations as in any general characteristics, sampling will be useless. Moreover, as is commonly the case, if the territory has six or seven distinctive zones, then sampling may just produce confusing or inconclusive results, leading observers to imagine a fictitious "average" character that actually obtains nowhere.

By contrast, if the explorers spread out, and each surveys and seeks to understand the character of a different zone, they can put together a map of the entire territory with far greater accuracy than an overall sample would provide. Of course, it takes time, and none of the explorers by themselves would be able to make reliable inferences that extended beyond the zone that they had studied; but together, assembling their distinct maps, they cumulate genuine knowledge of the territory. Indeed, by comparing notes, they may find deep regularities, or relationships among or across different zones, that no statistical averages for the entire territory would reveal (Tilly 1984).

We noted that large-*N* studies of revolutions have, to date, not been terribly fruitful. This strongly suggests that the "territory" we seek to understand in this matter is far from homogeneous. Large-*N* studies that seek to understand the causes of revolution (and nonrevolution) by ignoring the differences between the Soviet Union and Burundi, or between Cuba and Cambodia, and by treating all of these as equivalent "cases," seem bound to founder. Assuming that certain variables have the same effects in all countries, or that specific outcomes are always produced by the same causes, may simply be a wrong starting point.

Charles Ragin (1997) has argued that social phenomena are generally characterized by "causal complexity," in which the same outcome is often produced by varied and different combinations and levels of causes, so that a single set of necessary and sufficient conditions for specific outcomes does not exist. CHA, by starting from the premise that specific cases first need to be thoroughly understood before advancing to seek general patterns, never assumes an identity or equivalence or representativeness of specific cases; instead, the extent of similarity or difference between cases is considered a crucial part of the investigation. CHA does not start out by assuming the existence of, or by seeking, universal causal or other patterns; rather, it assumes that the degree of generality of any particular causal mechanism or pattern is variable and is part of what the investigation needs to determine.

In reply, critics of case study methods would ask (and Goldthorpe [1997] makes this argument): How can such explorers hope to map even one such zone or case without a large number of observations? Changing one large territory into several small ones may reduce the problem of generalizing somewhat, but it does not change the problem of making reliable inferences from limited observations. In particular, establishing causal relationships even for one case still requires a large number of observations. True enough, but once the problem is changed from making inferences about causal relationships in a large universe from a limited sample to tracing the causal pattern or patterns in a small number of cases, new methods may be employed. The most important of these used by CHA are (1) Bayesian analysis, (2) process tracing, and (3) congruence testing. Each of these methods allows practitioners of CHA to move toward their goal of establishing causal relationships in a small and explicitly delimited number of cases as the path to accumulating knowledge.

Bayesian Analysis

While social scientists frequently and explicitly use statistical analysis based on normal distributions, the use of other statistical methods – such as nonparametric and Bayesian statistics – is far more rare (although see Western [2000] for a nicely explicit application of Bayesian statistics in CHA). However, I would argue that CHA implicitly uses Bayesian analysis quite extensively, and it is this approach that makes sense of how even single case studies can be of immense value and influence (McKeown 1999).

"Normal" or "frequentist" statistical analysis presumes a world in which the only prior knowledge one has is a null hypothesis, based on ignorance of causal relationships, and uses data to identify causal relationships that depart from the null hypothesis. In order to establish departures from the null, one needs enough cases to demonstrate that cause A is associated with effect B to a degree that is highly unlikely starting from the assumption of no effect. One or a small number of such associations provides no sure basis for such inferences.

By contrast, CHA rarely starts from ignorance of causal relationships. Quite the contrary; most CHA squarely targets strong prior beliefs about causal relationships. Indeed, what makes case analyses compelling is generally not that they pluck unknown causal relationships from behind a veil of ignorance, but that they are specifically designed to challenge prior beliefs.

A Bayesian approach asks different questions of data than frequentist approaches. The latter approach asks: What data do I need to convince myself that cause A is really connected to effect B and not merely randomly associated with it? Bayesian analysis asks: Given that I have strong prior beliefs about the relationship of A and B, how much would a particular bit of new data shift that belief? If the prior belief is so strong as to be nearly deterministic, then simply one opposing case may cast considerable doubt upon the prior belief.

Let us ponder how the two approaches would view recent trends in scholarship regarding the French Revolution. Allow that scholars (such as Cobban 1964; Taylor 1972; Furet 1981) have uncovered persuasive evidence that the main elite actors in the French Revolution were lawyers, notaries, military officers, government officials, and recently ennobled aristocrats pursuing the ideal of a career open to talents against aristocratic privilege in the state and the army and opposing the monarchy mainly over its desire to raise taxes. However, merchants and bankers – and for that matter policies that assisted the development of private property – played little role. Proponents of a large-*N* statistical approach based on frequentist methods would say: So what? This proves nothing about revolutions in general; how would we have any idea that the same actors would be important in any other revolutions? This case, therefore, is of merely historical interest.

Now consider what this case would mean for a scholar who held a strong prior Marxist belief that revolutions revolve around class conflict, and that the key actors and policies in revolutions against agrarian monarchies should be capitalists and their supporters interested in advancing the gains to be made from private property. Given this prior belief, the findings of Cobban, Taylor, and Furet would be strikingly important. It might still be that the Marxist view held in other cases, but finding that it did not hold in one of the historically most important revolutions (that is, a revolution in one of the largest, most influential, and most imitated states of its day and a frequent exemplar for Marxist theories) would certainly shake one's faith in the value of the prior belief.

CHA thus gains its impact not despite being statistically "faulty" by the standards of frequentist analysis, but because that kind of analysis simply does not apply to the goals and methods of most comparative historical studies. What CHA generally undertakes is the study of a single case or small number of cases with the goal of identifying causal relationships in those cases in order to test (and potentially shake) strong prior beliefs.

Demonstrating the presence of specific causal relationships or patterns within a single case, or a small number of cases, allows CHA to challenge prior beliefs in several ways.

Existence/Absence This shows that causal relationships or patterns are important where they were previously not seen or expected, or are absent where they were previously claimed to be seen or expected. This can also be thought of as the "most likely/least likely" mode of critical case analysis (Przeworski and Teune 1970; Collier 1993). In these analyses, CHA identifies and carefully examines a case where existing theory claims that some pattern or causal relationship is most likely to be found and shows that in fact the claims of that theory cannot be substantiated. Or conversely, CHA identifies and carefully examines a case where theory claims that some pattern or causal relationship is least likely to be found and shows that in fact, contra theory, that case exhibits that pattern.

Convergence/Divergence This shows that cases that theory claims are different in significant ways in fact converge in ways not previously seen or expected or, conversely, that cases that theory claims are essentially similar in fact diverge in ways not previously seen or expected (Collier 1993).

Discrimination/Reconciliation This shows that where existing theories are in conflict, certain cases (or elements of those cases) either discriminate between the two theories or reconcile them by showing how certain aspects of the cases are consistent with one theory while other aspects are consistent with the other.

Many of the most striking and powerful CHA works manage to combine several of these approaches. Theda Skocpol's (1979) work not only showed an unexpected convergence of causes for liberal and communist social revolutions; it also showed systematic divergences between her cases of successful social revolutions and other kinds of revolutionary events (e.g., the English Revolution of 1640, the Japanese Meiji Restoration, and the German Revolutions of 1848). Critics of Skocpol have misunderstood her work greatly by casting it as a study of revolutions in general, as if it were arguing simply from the association of a social revolutionary outcome in a handful of cases with a certain set of variables (or interaction among those variables) that those variables are generally causal to that outcome across a large universe of cases. That would be an unwarrented inference, and Skocpol (1994) explicitly disavowed it.

What astute critics of Skocpol's work have pointed out (Little 1998; Mahoney 1999, 2000a) is that her accomplishment was to demonstrate the existence of certain patterns of events in historically important but disparate cases of revolution – a pattern unseen and unexpected by prior theories. Moreover, she demonstrated that this pattern of events was absent (or differed in various ways) in other kinds of revolutions. By so doing, she greatly shifted our prior beliefs about what were the important causal elements associated with various particular revolutions.

It is not necessary to assume a deterministic world, or to think of this in strict Popperian terms of "refuting" existing theories. It is sufficient to assume a Bayesian perspective that essentially asks: What would you bet that you would find certain conditions in a given case before a CHA of that case, and would you make the same bet after a CHA of that case? If the answer is no, then the CHA has changed the prior belief and made a contribution to our knowledge.

Process Tracing and Congruence Testing

We still need to ask, however, how does CHA persuade scholars to change their prior beliefs? What method of argument or inference provides reliable statements regarding causal relationships in one particular case or set of cases? There are two main approaches used in CHA: process tracing and congruence testing (Bennett and George 1997; George and Bennett 1997).

Process tracing consists of analyzing a case into a sequence (or several concatenating sequences) of events and showing how those events are plausibly linked given the interests and situations faced by groups or individual actors. It does not assume that actions always bring their intended consequences, only that actions are understandable in terms of the knowledge, intent, and circumstances that prevailed at the time decisions were made. Process tracing involves making deductions about how events are linked over time, drawing on general principles of economics, sociology, psychology, and political science regarding human behavior.

For example, in making my argument (Goldstone 1991) that population growth in agrarian bureaucracies led to revolution, I did not proceed by showing that in a large sample of such states there was a statistically significant relationship between population growth and revolution; that would not be possible given the focus on only four main cases (England, France, and the Ottoman and Chinese empires). Rather, I sought to trace out and document the links in the causal chain connecting population growth to revolutionary conflict.

I began by noting that when demand exceeds supply, prices generally rise; thus, population growth in agrarian economies with technically limited growth capability is likely to produce inflation.[1] Drawing on the economic history literature, I documented this association between population movements and price movements over a century or more in each of the four cases. I then pointed out that inflation would wreak havoc with state finances if states have fixed nominal incomes, forcing states to either raise taxes or increase their debts. While many factors influence state finances, including wars and trade, I was able to show that in periods of rising prices, these agrarian bureaucracies were more likely to depend on unsustainable expedients such as selling off assets, imposing forced loans, currency devaluations, defaults, and/or efforts to impose new or unconventional taxes. These expedients not only generally failed to fully restore states' fiscal health; they also imposed burdens on elites or popular groups, leading to potential conflicts.

In regard to elites, I observed that population growth will mean greater competition for elite places at the same time that inflation enriches some elites and groups while eroding the incomes of others; this was documented with evidence on higher rates of social mobility – both upward and downward – among elites during periods of sustained population growth. Thus the state's demands for greater revenue will be addressed to elites who

[1] Of course, overall price inflation, as opposed to relative price shifts, requires an increase in either the velocity or the supply of money. In a separate paper (Goldstone 1984), I showed that if population increase is accompanied by urban growth and craft specialization, the velocity of money will greatly increase. At the same time, states and merchants facing rising nominal prices generally respond by devaluing coinage and extending public and private credit, thus increasing liquidity. The increased demand fueled by population growth is therefore accompanied by increases in the velocity and supply of money.

are themselves in turmoil and divided by heightened up-and-down social mobility. At the same time, urban workers will face falling real wages as rising numbers of workers limit wages, and peasants will be forced to pay higher rents or go landless as increased numbers compete over a fixed supply of land. It was also possible to document patterns of falling real wages and rising rents and landlessness among the peasantry during the periods of population increase.

The combined result of these trends was that as rulers increased demands on elites and popular groups, intraelite competition tended to divide the elites into competing factions, paralyzing the state and often leading some elite factions to seek popular support against the regime. This situation in turn produced opportunities for distressed urban and rural groups to mobilize in protest. In such circumstances, a critical event such as a state bankruptcy, military defeat, or famine – which a healthy state would readily withstand – triggered escalating state–elite, intraelite, and elite–popular conflicts that combined to create a revolution.

This CHA is certainly not made without quantitative analysis or large amounts of statistical data. In fact, I used hundreds of statistical and historical observations regarding prices, wages, rents, population, the fate of families, declarations of support or conflict by leading actors, and sequences of events to demonstrate that in England, France, Turkey, and China from 1500 to 1750 those periods during which population mounted were marked by rising prices, increasing state debts and fiscal difficulties, repeated conflicts over taxes, heightened elite mobility, falling real wages, and growing political tensions. In contrast, those decades in this period in which population stagnated or declined were marked by stable or falling prices, rising state real revenues, sharply reduced elite mobility, rising real wages, and political settlements. However, the data are used primarily to establish the validity of trends and relationships *within* complex cases that are explored in considerable detail, which are then carefully compared for similarities or differences, and not to establish the statistical significance of such trends or relationships across large numbers of relatively unexplored cases.

It is this process tracing, in which hundreds of observations are marshaled to support deductive claims regarding linkages in a causal chain, on which CHA rests, not simply causal inference from associations among macroconditions. Where generalization across cases is gained, it is not in universal generalization to all agrarian bureaucracies at all times (which is neither claimed nor demonstrated), but rather simply in showing that for a finite set of cases, where convergence was not previously expected, a common pattern of causation of state upheavals in fact can be found.

Congruence testing provides the basis for claims regarding "common patterns." Skocpol demonstrated by careful exploration of her cases that the roles of state crisis, elite revolt, and popular mobilization formed nearly the same, or "congruent," patterns in the French, Russian, and Chinese revolutions. In doing so, she overturned the idea that the causal structure of the latter two communist revolutions was different from that of the liberal French Revolution. I showed for Britain, France, the Ottoman Empire, and China that prior to periods of massive rebellion and state overthrow there were extremely similar, or congruent, patterns of sustained population growth, price inflation, state fiscal distress, heightened elite mobility, falling wages, and peasant landlessness. The congruence between the patterns found in the Asian empires with the patterns established for the Western monarchies provides a strong alteration in the prior belief that the Western revolutions and Asian rebellions were different phenomena brought on by different causes and a powerful challenge to the idea that the Western revolutions resulted from social conflicts found only with the rise of Western capitalism.

The goal of congruence testing is therefore not to establish universal generalizations across a broad (and perhaps unconnected) range of cases. Rather, congruence testing uses the fruits of process tracing to challenge and improve our understanding of how *particular cases of interest* are related or different. If our goals are to understand how democratic and communist revolutions were similar or different, to determine if Western revolutions were truly distinct from Asian rebellions, or to examine why military autocracies emerged in some Latin American or European countries and not others, then congruence testing among selected cases can bring us closer to our goals. Such comparative case studies provide solid building blocks for theories of social change and development, allowing us to work toward larger generalizations gradually by incorporating additional cases and patterns.

Both process tracing and congruence testing are generally carried out through what Robin Stryker (1996) has described as "strategic narrative." Strategic narrative differs from a straightforward narrative of historical events by being structured to focus attention on how patterns of events relate to prior theoretical beliefs about social phenomena. Strategic narrative selects its elements in response to a clearly articulated theoretical backdrop and focuses on empirical anomalies relative to such theory. Sometimes such narratives are designed to demonstrate the strict causal connections between elements in a sequence of events (Abbott 1990, 1992; Griffin 1992); sometimes they are designed to demonstrate the impact of contingency or path dependence in producing divergent or unexpected outcomes (Sewell 1996; Haydu 1998; Goldstone 1999; Mahoney 2000b). Either way, the narrative marshals evidence that particular sequences or patterns unfolded in a particular way, for particular reasons, and it relates those data to our confidence in existing theory.

Neither process tracing nor congruence testing provides a means of generalizing to a universe of cases beyond the finite samples. Instead, their goal is to test, challenge, and shift prior beliefs about the cases under examination. Of course, if the prior beliefs are very strong and general, and the results of process tracing and congruence testing shatter those beliefs, they may be extensively modified or changed, to the point where the shift affects people's expectations about other cases as well.

The overall development of CHA in any particular field thus presents a research program (Lakatos 1983) with the following features. At any one time, a finite number of cases deemed to be of interest to a research community are under investigation. Using process tracing, scholars seek to uncover causal sequences that produced the results or cases of interest. Using congruence testing, scholars make claims about the number of cases that "fit" a particular causal sequence or pattern (or "model"). This then sets up strong prior beliefs about which cases are accurately explained by particular models.

The research program can then make progress in several ways. Further congruence testing of additional cases can extend the number of cases that are seen as fitting a particular model. Where the fit is poor, new process tracing in those additional cases may reveal new patterns, leading to revisions of the old model or the need for new models. Moreover, new process tracing in previously analyzed cases may challenge the validity of received models, leading to their revision, modification, or abandonment. Throughout, the process is one of operating on finite numbers of cases chosen to investigate how their analysis shifts prior beliefs (Bayesian inference), not one of sampling cases in order to establish patterns in a general population (standard or "normal" statistical inference). This method remains respectful of the historical context and details of each case, advances generalizations slowly and circumspectly in stages, and does not presuppose a deterministic view of the world. However, it constantly challenges prevailing wisdom by confronting it with empirical details derived from further process tracing of old or new cases and by testing the congruence of those cases against prevailing expectations. CHA is thus capable – in the best scientific sense – of extending and cumulating knowledge while rejecting theories that are inconsistent with empirical evidence.

For the specific field of revolutions, I will show in the following sections that this research program has yielded steady and cumulative progress. A common indictment of theory development in sociology is that it is often a matter of shifting fads – modernization, Marxism, feminism, postmodernism – with little accumulation or greater understanding of the empirical world. Nonetheless, I believe that theories of revolution have made remarkable progress in understanding the causes, processes, and outcomes of revolutions. Naturally, this progress involves controversies, the falsification and abandonment of some theories, and the supersession and incorporation of others. What is important, however, is that these shifts in theory have been driven by the confrontation of theory with empirical events. This confrontation has led to successive modification of theories, the introduction of new concepts, and the development of new approaches. The result is that theories of revolution today address more cases, with more fidelity to historical events, and with a greater grasp of the various elements that comprise revolutions, than ever before.

Definitions of Revolution

We might first ask, what are revolutions? Again, a large-*N* statistical approach would require a universal definition, so that the sample could be consistently coded to reflect "revolution" as a dependent variable (to study causes) or as an independent variable (to study outcomes). However, since CHA does not proceed by sampling and seeking significant associations between variables, but instead by rigorously examining a finite number of cases, revolution can be roughly or even implicitly defined through the initial selection of cases. Then, as the research program develops, additional cases can be examined, and the initial definition modified or expanded according to which features of the cases prove to be of lasting interest. In fact, the definition of revolution has developed over time in response to new empirical information, and to changes in our understanding of the nature and possibilities of revolutionary events.

Throughout most of history, sudden changes in government were treated by historians and political analysts as cyclical phenomena (hence the term "revolution"). These changes might involve cycling through different kinds of regimes (democracy, oligarchy, tyranny), as discussed by Plato and Aristotle. Or these changes might involve an alternation of opposing factions or parties in power, as occurred in the Renaissance Italian city-states and the seventeenth-century British civil wars. Yet by the time of the Enlightenment of the eighteenth century, the notion of continuous improvement had come into wide use, and writers such as Thomas Paine viewed certain changes in government – replacing traditional authorities with new institutions devised by reason – as part of the march of progress. From the time of the American Revolution of 1776, and even more the French Revolution of 1789, revolution came to be associated with the replacement of obsolete governments with newer, more rational regimes. Revolution was henceforth defined as a progressive and irreversible change in the institutions and values that provided the basis of political authority.

The French Revolution of 1789, and even more the Russian Revolution of 1917, also provided the image of popular uprisings and violence against authorities as key aspects of revolution. From 1789 to 1979, the prevailing definitions of revolution thus incorporated three elements: a dramatic and progressive change in a society's values and institutions, mass action, and violence (Huntington 1968; Skocpol 1979).

However, from the 1970s to the 1990s, it became increasingly clear that these definitions were inadequate to the full range of events being studied by scholars of revolutions. The revolution that overthrew the shah of Iran in 1979 featured general strikes and massive street protests in Tehran, Tabriz, Qom, and other major cities, but little or no popular violence against authorities. Such violence as occurred came mainly from the shah's forces firing on protestors or, after the shah had fallen, in the attacks on Bahai, Jews, and those Iranians whose behavior appeared to violate the proscriptions of increasingly strict Islamic authorities (Arjomand 1988). The "people power" revolution that overthrew Ferdinand Marcos in the Philippines in 1986, and the anticommunist revolutions in the Soviet Union and Eastern Europe, showed considerable mass protest but startlingly little violence, to the point where some observers wondered if the latter events should be considered revolutions at all (Garton Ash 1989).

These recent cases prompted scholars to take a second look at the role of violence in historical cases. It was soon recognized that the pattern seen in Iran was not exceptional and that in general far more violence is committed by new revolutionary regimes after seizing power – in order to consolidate their control of society, or in civil wars between revolutionaries and counterrevolutionaries – than is committed by revolutionary actors against authorities before the latter are overthrown. Thus, in the French Revolution, it was the Terror and the actions to crush the counterrevolutionary movements in the Vendée that produced the greatest number of deaths; in the Russian Revolution it was the civil wars and Stalinist purges, not the workers' insurrections or peasant uprisings, that produced the greatest death toll. Revolutions are therefore no longer defined in terms of violence against authorities. Instead, the role of violence in revolutions is now seen as complex and contingent, with old regimes, revolutionary oppositions, and new revolutionary regimes all capable of violence or nonviolence to varying degrees at different times.

In addition, many episodes that scholars study as being revolutionary have not led to the permanent transformation of institutions and values. Efforts to remake society often fall short, and even revolutions that take power sometimes are superseded by restorations of the old order. After the fall of Napoleon, many of the key institutional changes of the French Revolution were overturned. The monarchy was restored, as was the prestige of the nobility and the Catholic Church. Studies of local wealth holding have shown that, despite the revolution's vocal attack on the aristocracy, the families that held leading positions throughout France before the revolution were, in the main, the same families that held leading positions in the 1840s (Forster 1980). The English Revolution of 1640 ended the monarchy, the monopoly of the Church of England, and the House of Lords; yet all were restored in 1660 and kept their power for generations. The European revolutions of 1848 were largely defeated after brief but inspiring bursts of energy. And most of the guerrilla movements in Latin America in the twentieth century, such as the Shining Path movement in Peru and the Farabundo Martí National Liberation Front in El Salvador, though clearly episodes of revolutionary conflict, failed to transform their societies. Thus, success in changing values and institutions, like violence, is now seen as a matter of degree and a contingent outcome in revolutionary events rather than part of the definition.

A more recent definition of revolution guided by these insights focuses on efforts to change values and institutions and on mass action, but without insisting on revolutionary success or violence. In this view, revolutions are "an effort to transform the political institutions and the justifications for political authority in a society, accompanied by . . . mass mobilization and noninstitutionalized actions that undermine existing authorities" (Goldstone 2001, p. 142). This definition includes both successful revolutions and unsuccessful yet clearly revolutionary challenges to state authorities. It excludes both coups and civil wars that change only rulers, not institutions or the structure of political authority (such as most African and Latin American military coups). It also excludes reform movements that achieve changes without mass mobilization or attacks on existing authorities (such as the Prussian Reform Movement of the early nineteenth century, or the American New Deal under Franklin D. Roosevelt). It suggests that the key defining element of revolution is always the attack on authorities' right to rule and mass involvement in that attack; but the level of success and the violence involved are contingent factors to be explained, not assumed as part of the definition.

In short, the very definition of revolutions – a key part of any theory – has changed over time in response to careful case studies of how revolutionary events have unfolded.

The comparative and historical study of revolutions extends from classical times to the present. Accounts of sudden changes in government and regime collapse were collected and analyzed by Plato, Aristotle, Thucydides, Tacitus, Montesquieu, Machiavelli, de Tocqueville, Marx, and Trotsky, among many others. However, it is convenient to focus on the accumulation of knowledge in the twentieth century, beginning with the "natural history" school.

The Natural History of Revolutions

Scholars working from this perspective aimed to study revolutions the way biologists studied natural history (i.e., the history of life), namely, by gathering specimens, detailing their major parts and processes, and seeking common patterns.

These scholars – notably Edwards (1927), Pettee (1938), and Brinton (1938) – compared sequences of events in the English, American, French, and Russian revolutions and traced distinct patterns that reappeared across these cases. They laid out a scheme of events that they believed all major revolutions followed, ranging from causes to outcomes. In brief, they noted that prior to a revolution, the majority of the "intellectuals" – journalists, poets, playwrights, essayists, teachers, members of the clergy, lawyers, and trained members of the bureaucracy – cease to support the regime, write condemnations, and demand major reforms. Just prior to the fall of the old regime, the state attempts to meet this criticism by undertaking major reforms. However, the actual fall of the regime begins with an acute political crisis brought on by the government's inability to deal with some economic, military, or political problem rather than with the action of a revolutionary opposition.

After the old regime falls, even where revolutionaries had united solidly against the old regime, their internal conflicts soon cause problems. While the first group to seize the reins of state usually consists of moderate reformers, who often employ organizational forms left over from the old regime, more radical centers of mass mobilization spring up with new forms of organization (such as the Jacobin clubs in France or the Leninist vanguard parties). These radical groups challenge the moderates, and eventually gather popular support and drive them from power. The great changes in the organization and ideology of a society occur in revolutions not when the old regime first falls, but when the radical, alternative, mass-mobilizing organizations succeed in supplanting the moderates.

However, the disorder brought by the revolution and the implementation of radical control usually result in forced imposition of order by coercive rule, often accompanied by a period of state-imposed terror. The struggles between radicals and moderates and between defenders of the revolution and external enemies frequently allow military leaders to take commanding, even absolute, leadership of the new revolutionary regimes (e.g., Cromwell, Washington, or Napoleon). Eventually, the radical phase of the revolution gives way to a phase of pragmatism and moderate pursuit of progress within the new status quo, but with an enlarged and more centralized state.

The natural history school provided a clear and fairly comprehensive picture of the preconditions, dynamics, and outcomes of the revolutionary process. Not only did this schema fit rather well the cases for which it was developed; it also fit remarkably well cases that arose decades later, such as the Islamic Revolution in Iran in 1979.

However, despite uncovering persistent and recurring patterns in the course of major revolutions, this approach failed to present a convincing reason why revolutions should occur at certain times and places but not others. The defection of the intellectuals, and the initiating political crisis, simply appear as historical contingencies. The fall of the old regime then follows as a matter of course.

Some political scientists and sociologists, however, noted a further temporal pattern in the course of revolutions. They attributed the spread of revolutions through history to the process they called "modernization." In particular, they saw popular discontent with "traditional" regimes bringing conscious efforts to modernize societies by means of revolution.

Modernization and Revolutions

From the 1950s to the 1970s, there was a growing belief that most important features of long-term social change could be explained by focusing on a universal process of transition described as "modernization" (Parsons 1966; Almond 1973). In this view, most societies throughout history have been "traditional" – vesting political authority on the basis of custom and heredity; having economies in which most activity was subsistence-producing, nonmarket, and preindustrial; and with social hierarchies that stressed conformity to traditional values and privileges. In contrast, "modern" societies have political authorities (whether democratic regimes or dictatorships) that are deliberately and recently established to provide efficient and bureaucratic rule, economies that are market-oriented and industrialized, and social hierarchies based on universal citizenship and achievement. Although this transition was sometimes smooth, modernization theorists of revolution argued that often the transition was jarring or uneven, with traditional authorities trying to hang on to power in societies that were already partially modernized; the imbalance then produced a revolutionary situation and attacks on those authorities.

Several different theories of revolution were derived from the basic modernization framework. Chalmers Johnson (1966) suggested that in many developing countries, trade, travel, and communications tended to break down traditional values, while economies and political systems changed far more slowly, leading to a dysfunctional breach between modernizing values and traditional social and political organization. Samuel Huntington (1968) focused more tightly on political demands. He noted that developing countries often provided increased education and participation of their people in the market economy while maintaining a closed, traditional political system. Unless political participation was also expanded, he believed this imbalance would lead to explosive demands for changing the structure of political authority. Ted Robert Gurr (1970) claimed that even if economies were growing and political systems were developing, imbalances could still arise. If people expected still greater change to occur than they actually experienced, they would feel "relative deprivation." This feeling of frustration could lead to demands for still more rapid and extensive changes, fueling a revolutionary transformation of society.

All these theories were variants of a model in which modernizing changes in traditional societies disrupted established patterns and expectations regarding social and political life. This may sound similar to Marx's assertion that economic changes lead to revolutionary class conflicts. However, Johnson, Huntington, and Gurr all eschewed class analysis and argued that economic change had no primacy; changes in values, education, and expectations were part of the social disruption, not merely economic change. These theorists thought more in terms of a conflict between governments and society at large, spurred by unbalanced social change, rather than conflicts among classes, and kept their distance from Marxist theories.

In addition, because modernization theory suggested that there were universal processes of transition that applied to all societies, it seemed an excellent candidate for large-*N*, global statistical studies that could demonstrate a significant association between the strains of transition and political violence. Several such studies were undertaken (Gurr 1968; Feierabend et al. 1969; Hibbs 1973). However, they bore mixed results. It proved nearly impossible to measure the independent variable in a way that would discriminate among competing versions of modernization theory: How do you determine if political violence is associated with a change in people's values, or with a change in their desire for political participation, or with discontent with economic growth relative to their expectations? To get at these issues on a global basis would have required comprehensive opinion polling in every country in the world at a time just prior to their outbreaks of revolution. The large-*N* studies therefore used easier-to-measure proxies for progress toward modernization, such as energy use, industrial output, and consumption. While these studies did show that countries that were "less" modern had higher levels of political violence than countries that were "more" modern, there were three major problems in interpreting these results.

First, it was never completely clear what were the causal mechanisms that linked changes in material conditions and revolution. Was it those individuals who were feeling most "deprived" or most left behind by modern progress who actually created revolutions? Or was it those individuals who had become most modernized in their values and thus were most discontented with still partially traditional institutions? Perhaps revolutions had little to do with values or discontent at all, but were a matter of elite competition for the fruits of growing economic output or the loss of regime leverage over elites as the economic structure of society changed. For the most part, modernization theories paid little attention to which elites, or which popular groups, were most involved in conflict and thus could not answer these questions.

Second, it was not clear that the dependent variable – "political violence" – was the same as revolution. Many countries had high and persistent levels of political violence, but without their governments succumbing to revolution (e.g., Colombia, and South Africa in the 1970s and 1980s). Moreover, some revolutions, such as those in Iran in 1979 and the Philippines in 1986, came about mainly through mass defections from the regime and urban street demonstrations, with relatively brief and mild intervals of political violence producing major changes in government. Furthermore, in some major revolutions, such as the Mexican Revolution of 1911 and the Russian Revolution of 1917, all the major political violence occurred in the civil wars of 1911–20 and 1917–21, *after* the old regime had already been overturned. In these cases, revolutions apparently caused the political violence, rather than the reverse. Huntington (1968) noted that some revolutions involved long periods of guerrilla warfare in the periphery of society before the fall of the old regime, while in other revolutions the central regime experienced a sudden collapse. Clearly, a focus on the correlates of political violence was telling us very little that was useful about the causes, patterns, and dynamics of major revolutions.

Third, a surprising but consistent finding was that the best predictor of political violence was almost always the presence of prior political violence. In other words, some countries – regardless of their level of modernization – were simply more prone to political violence than others. This finding called into question the whole premise that all countries could be treated similarly, with differing levels of political violence varying mainly according to levels of modernization. Instead, it increasingly appeared, even in the work of modernization theorists of revolutions, that different countries were different in important ways and that revolutions themselves were different in how they unfolded, their levels of violence, and which elites and groups were involved.

These points emerged most clearly in the work of two comparative historical scholars whose work – carefully grounded in CHA of specific countries and conflicts – criticized the modernization approach.

Charles Tilly (1973, 1978) went directly after Huntington and Gurr, arguing that popular discontent could never by itself launch a revolution. In stating this, he elaborated on the insights of Leon Trotsky, who had organized and led the Red Army for Lenin's Bolsheviks in the Russian Revolution and who wrote a brilliant, theoretically astute chronicle of the revolution (Trotsky 1959). Trotsky observed that popular misery and frustration never lead to revolution by themselves; if they did, he wrote, the masses would be in revolt at all times and everywhere. As Lenin (1973) insisted, a revolutionary organization was required to channel popular discontent into political grievances and to mobilize the masses for revolutionary action. Trotsky further observed that in the course of a revolution, a critical period of contention occurs between revolutionary forces and the government, during which the government is still in command but is losing popular support, while the revolutionary forces are gaining support and resources but are not yet in power. The resolution of this period of "dual power" is the key to the revolution; only if the revolutionary forces are able to increase their strength and defeat the forces of the government can a revolution triumph.

Tilly (1978) constructed from these observations a more formal theory of revolutionary mobilization and contention. He argued that only when organized contenders emerge, capable of mobilizing popular support against the government and defeating the government for control of society, can revolution occur. Modernization might lead to the emergence of such contenders, but it would not automatically provide for their success. That required action by the contenders to assemble revolutionary forces, to acquire political, military, economic, and other resources to confront the government, and then to defeat it. Only where modernization put this particular sequence in motion would revolution follow.

A further challenge to modernization theories of revolution came from the work of Barrington Moore, Jr. (1966). Moore argued that while modernization might be the fate of all nations, there were in fact several distinct paths to modernization, with very different economic and political outcomes. Moore highlighted a democratic path, founded on liberal revolutions such as those that occurred in England and France; a communist path, founded on Leninist revolutions such as those that occurred in Russia and China; and a fascist path, founded on nationalist revolutions such as those that occurred in fascist Italy, Nazi Germany, and Meiji Japan.

Which path a particular nation took depended, as Marx had insisted, on its pattern of class relations. Yet, while prevailing Marxist theory had simplified those classes into landlords, peasants, workers, and capitalists and postulated a similar historical pattern of class conflict in all societies, Moore argued that patterns of class power and conflict could vary. Tracing out divergent patterns among several cases, Moore showed that the emerging capitalist elite might unite with the older landlord elite in order to suppress the masses and create fascism; in other cases, it might unite with the masses to overturn the landlords and create democratic capitalism; in still others, it might remain so weak that it would be overwhelmed by a popular revolution that created socialism. Which path a country followed depended not only on its initial conditions, which were similar in all his cases circa 1500; it also depended on the precise sequence of events that followed. Where agriculture turned early to capitalist organization and dependence on free wage labor, while industrialization came later, then that labor force could be readily recruited to industry, creating a common interest among wage laborers and industrial employers in opposing political control of the state by landlords. This path led to bourgeois revolutions against aristocratic states, as in England, France, and the United States (where Moore sees the 1860s Civil War as a revolution by Northern industrialists to overturn political control of the national government by Southern planter landlords). Where agriculture continued to rely on coerced labor until industrialization began, industrialists would need to ally with landlords in order to gain access to a labor force, leading to a conservative alliance that would prevent revolutionary mobilization from below, and instead produce fascist regimes, as in Germany, Italy, and Japan. Finally, where industry emerged very late, weak, and highly dependent on the state, while landlords continued to control the state and a coerced rural labor force, revolutionary parties could emerge as the main opponent of the landlords, leading to communist revolutions that would both overturn the landlord regime and seize control of industry, as in Russia and China.

Moore's model of divergent, path-dependent evolution leading to different kinds of revolutions marked several major advances over both natural history and earlier modernization theories. First, Moore incorporated more cases, indeed some cases that many scholars had not treated as revolutionary situations (Nazi Germany, fascist Italy, the United States during the Civil War). Second, his demonstration that class conflicts and alliances were varied and contingent overturned a fixed Marxist view of uniform social and political development, replacing it with a far richer and more flexible view. Third, his demonstration that different kinds of revolutions had to be distinguished not only according to their causes, but also by their different outcomes, laid out multiple trajectories of revolutionary conflict and change, and offered far greater accuracy than theories that pointed only to a modernization or strengthening of state power as the general outcome of revolution.

By the late 1970s, theories that simply equated risks of revolution with transitions to modernization were in retreat. Tilly's mobilization theory gained acceptance as a key element in any explanation of revolutions and other kinds of social protest. Moore had laid down a critical challenge to modernization theory by demonstrating that modernizing revolutions were not all of one sort, but had clearly distinct outcomes reflecting different kinds of transitions to modernity.

However, additional process tracing of further historical cases, and of newly emerging revolutionary conflicts in the Third World, revealed that they had surprisingly little consistency with regard to modernization, indeed perhaps no relationship to modernization at all. The Latin American revolutions of independence, from 1808 to 1825, occurred in countries with few measurable signs of economic or value modernization. More recently, the separatist revolts in the Congo (Zaire) in the 1960s, the Sudanese civil wars, and the Cambodian Revolution occurred in states where modernization seemed to have hardly begun. In contrast, the revolutions to found communism in Cuba and in Eastern Europe after World War II occurred in countries that, compared to most of the world and certainly compared to England in the 1640s or France in 1789, were already quite well modernized. The transition to modernization per se thus seemed to be a weak reed on which to rest any analysis of why revolutions occurred in certain societies at particular times.

Modernization theories of revolution thus were coming under fatal fire. There was a clear need to improve on modernization theory by better specifying the causes of revolutionary situations while also incorporating Tilly's theory of mobilization and Moore's insights regarding the variety of revolutionary outcomes. This challenge was met by the next major step forward in theories of revolution, the social-structural theory of Theda Skocpol.

Social-Structural Theory and Its Critics

In 1979, Theda Skocpol published *States and Social Revolutions*, which was immediately recognized as a landmark in the theory of revolutions. Although it was preceded by several other books that took a somewhat similar approach (Wolf 1970; Paige 1975; Eisenstadt 1978), it was considerably more successful than any other work in resolving the dilemmas in revolutionary theory at the end of the 1970s.

Skocpol did confine her range of coverage in order to improve on the accuracy of her theory and cover a number of distinct elements of the revolutionary process. She chose to focus on the great social revolutions – namely, the French, Russian, and Chinese revolutions. She then compared these cases with other cases of less extensive or less successful revolutionary change: the English Revolution, the German Revolution of 1848, the Prussian Reform Movement, and the Japanese Meiji Restoration. Skocpol also limited her methodological and theoretical range. She worked almost entirely by comparing historical narratives, and focused on revolutions to the exclusion of any other kind of social protest or collective action. Nonetheless, within these bounds, she was able to make powerful advances in exploring new (or heretofore unappreciated) elements of the revolutionary process, and in creating a theory with far greater correspondence to the facts of these great revolutions than was offered by any modernization-based theories.

Skocpol's first step, following the lead of Wallerstein (1974), was to take modernization out of the individual country and move it to the world system as a whole. Skocpol argued that it was not the impact of modernizing change within a country that disturbed political stability; rather, it was international military and economic competition between states at different levels of modernization that created destabilizing pressures. A regime that faced military pressure or economic competition from a neighboring state at a more advanced level of development would have no choice but to seek to increase its own resources by restructuring its financial, military, and economic systems. In Skocpol's cases, eighteenth-century France faced pressure on its trade and colonies from more advanced Britain; tsarist Russia was overwhelmed by German military might; and China had to deal with a long stream of imperialist incursions from European powers and Japan. Skocpol pointed out that if a state in this situation encountered resistance to reform from powerful elites in its own country, this conflict could trigger a political crisis and precipitate a revolution. Oddly, international pressures had remained largely absent from prior theories of revolution. Adding this new element made revolutionary theory correspond better to observed conditions facing states, and at the same time helped resolve the conundrums presented by modernization theories that focused only on internal change.

Skocpol's second innovation was to highlight the conflicts between state rulers and a country's political and economic elites. Prior revolutionary theories had more or less taken for granted that state rulers and national elites would be natural allies. Even in Moore's nuanced accounts of class conflict, the question was which combination of elites would take state power, not how rulers and elites might themselves come into conflict. Elite theories of politics, such as those of Pareto and Mosca, spoke of the rotation of power among different elites, and conflict between them, but not of an autonomous ruler facing off against elite groups. In pointing out that state rulers have their own agendas and resources, and that the need for rulers to raise more resources could come into conflict with elite claims to those resources, Skocpol presented a scarcely appreciated source of revolutionary dynamics. Harking back to Tocqueville, this aspect of her theory of revolutionary processes corresponded far better with the observed conflicts between the French monarchy and the elite *parlements* that led to the calling of the Estates-General in 1789, or with the observed conflicts between the Chinese imperial rulers and the warlords who took over China after 1911, than did any modernization theories.

If conflict between a state's ruler needing to pursue reforms and elites who resisted them could precipitate a crisis, Skocpol nonetheless realized that this would not suffice for a revolution. Following Tilly's mobilization theory, Skocpol argued that an organizational framework was needed that would allow popular groups to take advantage of conflict and crisis at the political center. This could be a Leninist party, as was the case with the Communist Party in China. However, Skocpol also pointed out that where peasants had their own village organizations and leaders, who were accustomed to making decisions for the village on matters such as taxation or the distribution of land, this village structure could form the basis for local rural uprisings. In countries like eighteenth-century France and twentieth-century Russia, strong local peasant villages could therefore act when the political center was paralyzed by conflict, launching rural uprisings that would undermine the political and social orders.

Skocpol thus presented her theory as laying out three conditions in a country's social and political structures that were necessary and sufficient for a great social revolution: international pressure from a more advanced state or states; economic or political elites who had the power to resist state-led reforms and create a political crisis; and organizations (either village or party) that were capable of mobilizing peasants for popular uprisings against local authorities. Countries lacking one of these conditions might have less extensive or unsuccessful revolutionary events, but they could not undergo great social revolutions.

Skocpol did not rest with an analysis of the causes of revolution. She continued to consider the variation in outcomes. She argued that social structure also constrained outcomes. Where the sources of wealth in the economy were widely dispersed (such as land, small shops, and artisanal establishments), no revolutionary regime could seize control of the economy. In such conditions, revolutions would produce new regimes that protected private property (as in England in the 1640s and France in 1789). However, where industrialization had produced great concentrations of economic power in the shape of large factories, electrical power grids, and railroads, a revolutionary regime could (and most likely would) seize those resources in its drive for power, creating a communist regime with the government commanding the economy. Here, differences in the level of modernization drive differences in revolutionary outcomes, respecting Moore's insights while incorporating modernization theory into an account of revolutionary outcomes rather than causes.

Skocpol's three-factor theory of revolutionary causes and her account of outcomes appeared to provide a simple and elegant solution to the problems of prior theory. Even though she covered only a handful of cases, she successfully illuminated new elements – international pressures and state–elite conflicts – that appeared to have wide applicability to other cases. Her treatment of modernization in terms of international competition and constraints on outcomes seemed far more accurate than the claims of prior modernization theories of revolution.

Skocpol's argument that she had specified a set of necessary and sufficient conditions for social revolutions did not rest simply on showing that those causes were present in her major cases. Indeed, as critics of Skocpol have shown (Nichols 1986), her cases in fact are *not* identical with regard to causation. Where France and China faced moderate levels of international pressure and strong resistance to change from domestic elites, Russia faced extremely high levels of pressure in World War I, high enough to disable the government even with very weak resistance from domestic elites. Skocpol granted this; her argument was that she had identified common conditions that, in various combinations, produced the major revolutions of modern history, both liberal and communist (Skocpol 1994). Through process tracing and congruence testing, she had demonstrated that these conditions better explained the details of these major cases than did prior theories.

Skocpol's social-structural theory became the dominant theory of revolutions for the last two decades of the twentieth century. Yet almost as soon as it was published, the theory was challenged by new empirical events. Revolutions in Iran and Nicaragua in 1979, in the Philippines in 1986, and in the communist countries of Eastern Europe and the Soviet Union raised new questions about the causes, processes, and outcomes of revolutions.

The Iranian Revolution soon generated a debate on the applicability of Skocpol's theory (Skocpol 1982). The Iranian state under the shah, far from being pressured by competition from more advanced states, was the most powerful and advanced state in the Persian Gulf region and had the strong and committed support of the world's leading superpower, the United States. Yet the shah's government nonetheless provoked the opposition of almost all sectors of the Iranian elites. While there were economic and political reasons for this opposition, a major role was clearly played by ideological conflict, specifically between the shah's advancing of Westernization and elites defending traditional Islamic practices and laws. Skocpol's theory allowed no role for such ideological roots of state crisis, stating that revolutions are not made, but come as a result of external military or economic pressures. In Iran, the revolution did appear to be made by the opposition, and the state crisis seemed to revolve around the escalation of ideologically motivated conflicts (Kurzman 1996; Rasler 1996; Parsa 2000).

Skocpol's theory of revolutionary mobilization also began to seem deficient in light of new events. The Iranian Revolution had no peasant revolts, whether party-led or based in rural village organizations. The Philippine Revolution also had no peasant revolts – or rather, the revolutionary party that organized rural rebellion played little or no role in driving the dictator Marcos from power. In both Iran and the Philippines it was overwhelmingly urban protestors who provided the popular base for the revolution (Gugler 1982). Shifting attention to urban crowds made it clear that Skocpol had perhaps underestimated the importance of urban protest in her cases of France and Russia, where the critical events in Paris and St. Petersburg were downplayed relative to peasant revolts. Urban revolt was even more undeniably the story of popular protests in the overthrow of communism. Here, neither vanguard parties nor any other formal organizations seemed to play a major role in popular mobilization. Virtually spontaneous protests in Leipzig, Prague, and Moscow, erupting from little more than a public call for protests, grew until the communist regimes lost the heart to suppress them and collapsed (Oberschall 1994a; Opp, Voss, and Gern 1995; Urban, Igrunov, and Mitrokhin 1997).

Finally, Skocpol's theory of structural constraints on revolutionary outcomes seemed incapable of dealing with the emergent and varied patterns of revolutionary change. John Markoff (1996) has established that for one of Skocpol's central cases, the French Revolution, the key outcome of abolishing feudalism was not the result of structural oppositions between the monarchy's interests and that of the revolutionary elite; it was the product of an emerging interaction between bursts of peasant protest and efforts by the revolutionary elite to respond and contain it. This led to more thoroughgoing attacks on elite privileges than either the peasants or elites had demanded or foreseen in July 1789.

The notion of structural constraints on outcomes was also at odds with the wide variety of outcomes of revolutions in the 1970s, 1980s, and 1990s. In Iran, revolutionaries erected an Islamic republic. In Nicaragua, socialist revolutionaries built a state that respected and preserved private property, and where the vanguard Sandinista Party surrendered to democratic elections. In the Philippines, revolution also led to democracy, as it did in Eastern Europe and the Baltic states. Yet in Russia and most of the other Soviet successor states, democracy was shaky or absent; and even though all these states had a high degree of concentration of modern industries, most attempted to create free-market economies and undo state control. It appeared that the ideals and programs of the revolutionary regimes, rather than inescapable structural constraints, were dictating the pattern of revolutionary outcomes (Foran and Goodwin 1993; Selbin 1993).

Despite these difficulties, scholars did not quickly abandon Skocpol's social-structural perspective. The key insights regarding the importance of international influences and state–elites conflicts seemed sound, even if the details of recent events departed somewhat from the pattern of Skocpol's historical cases. The treatment of popular protest, it was believed, could be extended to incorporate urban protests. Thus, scholars worked to extend Skocpol's perspective to cover a variety of additional cases, including Iran and Nicaragua (Farhi 1990), anticolonial revolutions (Goodwin and Skocpol 1989), and guerrilla wars in Latin America (Wickham-Crowley 1992).

Nonetheless, the deficiencies in the social-structural approach grew more apparent, especially with the collapse of communist regimes. In these cases, especially in the central case of the Soviet Union, it was not clear that one could even speak of conflict between state rulers and elites, since there were no independent economic or political elites outside the structure of the communist party-state. Rather, it was cleavages within the party, setting reformist against conservative factions of the military and political elites, that led to the fall of the Soviet regime.

New comparative studies of revolution therefore appeared that departed in various ways from Skocpol's specific structural theory, while still incorporating many of the elements of her approach. I offered analyses of revolutions and large-scale revolts in Europe, the Middle East, and Asia from 1500 to 1800 (Goldstone 1991), in which I argued that international pressures created state crises only if states were already weakened by fiscal strain. Moreover, I pointed out that merely having a conflict between states and elites need not produce a revolution; strong states could overcome elite opposition, while elites that were firmly united against the state could simply insist on a change in rulers or reforms. It was only when elites themselves were severely divided over how to meet those pressures that a paralyzing revolutionary crisis would occur.

Also, while Skocpol had argued that the masses always had reasons to revolt, in these cases both urban and rural protests clearly had roots in declining economic opportunities. In the cities, rising unemployment and falling real wages made workers open to revolutionary mobilization; in rural villages, shortage of land and rising land rents similarly disposed peasants to protest action. Moreover, a formal organization to orchestrate popular action, whether it be a vanguard party or a village communal organization, was not always necessary. What mattered was that popular groups saw the state as vulnerable, and were prompted by elites calling for change and claiming that it was necessary. Popular groups could then call on a wide array of existing social networks – villages, neighborhoods, workplaces, occupational groups, religious congregations – to mobilize for protest action. Work by Glenn (1999), Gould (1995), Osa (1997), Parsa (2000), and Pfaff (1996) made it clear that no one form of formal organization was needed for protest mobilization; rather, a wide variety of formal and informal networks could fulfill that role.

Perhaps the most significant aspect of this comparison of major European revolutions and Asian rebellions was its demonstration of a different pattern of state upheavals than would have been predicted by Skocpol's theory that international pressures from more advanced states on weaker states produced the critical pressures leading to revolutions. Instead, revolutions and major rebellions across Europe and Asia from 1500 to 1800 occurred in states with highly varied levels of capitalist development, across times of both high and low international conflicts, and in waves that followed the pattern of population growth and decline across those centuries. From 1500 to 1650 population increased, and a wave of revolutionary upheavals grew from the late 1500s to the 1660s in

Europe, the Ottoman Empire, and China. From 1650 to 1730, population growth receded and revolutions were rare, despite nearly continuous and widespread international conflicts. But from 1730 to 1850 population growth resumed, and revolutionary conflicts again spread across Europe, the Middle East, and China from the late eighteenth century to the 1840s and 1850s. Showing how population growth could affect the key mechanisms of state crisis, elite conflicts, and popular unrest allowed an explanation of this wave pattern across three centuries. In addition, it extended the coverage of revolutionary theory to new cases of state breakdown, such as regional revolts in the Ottoman Empire and the collapse of the Ming Dynasty.

The structural basis of Skocpol's theory of revolutionary outcomes, as noted previously, also needed revision in light of these cases. The great revolutions in Europe and the major revolts in Asia seemed to have very similar economic and political origins; they all also led to substantial institutional changes. Yet in Europe, these changes were often accompanied by a major shift in values and a condemnation of the old regime as obsolete and in need of replacement; in Asia, these changes were usually accompanied by little or no shift in values and a condemnation of the old regime mainly for its failure to live up to traditional values and ideals. I therefore argued that social-structural conditions alone could not account for the different character of revolutionary outcomes; rather, the revolutionary breakdown of the former regime offers a uniquely fluid situation in which the new revolutionary leadership has choices regarding how to present itself and how to rebuild the social and political orders. The ideology of the new revolutionary regime can therefore be decisive in determining the outcome and trajectory of the postrevolutionary state.

These revisions to Skocpol's approach thus continued the progress of the theory of revolutions. The range of historical cases covered now ranged from the absolutist states of Europe to the great empires of the Middle East and China. The elements of the revolutionary process were now expanded to include international pressures, fiscal strain, intraelite conflict, a wide range of popular protest and mobilization, underlying population pressure on resources, and coordination between opposition elites and popular protest to produce revolutionary situations, as well as the pivotal role of revolutionary ideologies in guiding outcomes. Correspondence to empirical events continued to improve, as various details of state actions, elite conflicts, and popular action could be grounded in revolutionary theory. The ability of that theory to provide an explanation for the wave pattern of revolutionary crises across Eurasia in the late preindustrial period was particularly striking.

Skocpol's emphasis on international factors also opened the way for a major area of research, including works by Eckstein (1982), Walt (1996), Halliday (1999), Armstrong (1993), and Snyder (1999) showing how the origins, development, and outcomes of modern revolutions were affected by international forces and how international relations among states were affected by revolutions. These scholars showed that international economic relations constrained revolutionary outcomes. They also showed that wars and shifts in international alignments were highly likely to follow revolutions, since revolutionary regimes tended to distance themselves not only from old regime domestic policies, but from their international policies and alliances as well.

Yet deficiencies in the theory of revolutions remained. It was highly problematic to apply Skocpol's or my approach, both focused on the dynamics of agrarian bureaucracies, to the revolutions in Eastern Europe and the Soviet Union, where the limits of traditional agrarian economies no longer applied. While I had called for a critical role of ideology in guiding revolutionary outcomes, critics of structural theory further insisted that ideology must be given a far greater role in the origins of revolutions, in shaping the opposition and guiding revolutionary mobilization (Sewell 1985; Foran 1992; Selbin 1993; Emirbayer and Goodwin 1994; Katz 1997; Mahoney and Snyder 1999). In particular, they noted that structural accounts gave far too little role to leadership and conscious decision making by both rulers and revolutionaries. It may have been true, as Skocpol argued, that Lenin's precise designs for communism in Russia could not be implemented. Yet it is hardly credible to go from that observation to theorizing as if Lenin's decisions and actions were wholly irrelevant to the development and outcome of the Russian Revolution. Several scholars therefore undertook important studies of modern revolutions that demonstrated the key role of ideology and leadership at multiple stages in revolutionary processes (Selbin 1993; Foran 1997a; Goodwin 1997; Katz 1997; Parsa 2000).

Finally, an entirely separate line of theorizing regarding revolutions was developing among political scientists using game theory (also called "rational choice analysis"). Instead of studying empirical cases in detail, rational choice analysts created formal mathematical structures whose logic was held to embody the choices faced by actors in revolutionary situations. Oddly, the initial formulation of these formal models predicted that revolutions should not happen at all. Olson (1965) and Tullock (1971) showed that for any individual who contemplated joining in a revolutionary action, the risks and efforts of protest that he or she faced were normally quite considerable, while his or her contribution to the success of that protest was usually small. In fact, for most individuals, their contribution was so modest that the outcome for society – whether or not the revolution succeeded – would likely be the same whether they joined or not. Thus, for any individual, the logical incentives were strongly in favor of not joining a revolutionary protest, as individuals faced substantial risks but were unlikely to change the outcome.

This paradox of collective action was held to show a major deficiency in sociological theories of revolution based on analysis of large-scale national revolutionary trajectories. Without showing how the paradox of collective action was overcome, rational choice theorists accused sociological theorists of offering theories that lacked solid foundations in individual behavior (Kiser and Hechter 1991).

Over the course of the twentieth century, comparative historical studies of revolutions had made enormous strides in identifying the causal patterns behind the major preindustrial revolutions, in explaining their timing and their outcomes. Yet for all its triumphs, the social-structural approach was under severe assault.

Extending Social-Structural Approaches: New Perspectives and New Cases

As has happened before when revolutionary theory based on CHA was confronted with new empirical and theoretical challenges, scholars have delved into new cases of revolutions and reexamined old ones. While it is too soon to identify a new dominant perspective on revolutions, the building blocks for that new perspective are already apparent. Older theorists such as Goldstone, Tilly, Oberschall, and Opp and younger scholars such as Foran, Gould, Lichbach, Goodwin, Wickham-Crowley, and Parsa have used additional case analyses to test prior theories and lay out new principles for understanding a still broader range of revolutionary events.

Let us begin with the challenges posed by rational choice theory. Mark Lichbach (1995) has led the way in showing how the collective action problem can be overcome. He has identified over a dozen different mechanisms by which opposition groups can motivate people to join revolutionary movements, consistent with rational action. Whether through contracts, incentives, prior commitments, or exercising preexisting authority over individuals, opposition movements have a variety of tools available to promote mobilization. The key to these approaches is to realize that individuals do not make isolated choices about whether or not to join revolutionary protests, as the early rational choice theorists suggested. Rather, individuals come to social interaction already bound up in a web of social connections and obligations. It is through building on these extant linkages and commitments that revolutionary mobilization occurs (Opp and Roehl 1990; Goldstone 1994a; Gould 1995).

However, formal models alone have not been persuasive to scholars. Testing of those models in the context of detailed case studies, using process tracing to demonstrate congruence with the predictions of rational choice models, was required to convince analysts of revolution of the value of rational choice approaches (Kiser 1996). These case studies have focused particularly on Eastern Europe (Opp 1989; Kuran 1991, 1995; Oberschall 1994b; Opp, Voss, and Gern 1995) and have shown that mass mobilization was explicable as a "rational" response to a perceived increased opportunity to protest against and overturn the communist regimes. However, as Opp (1999) has argued, this approach involved developing a "thick" rationality, rich in case-study insights of the determinants of people's decision making in those particular cases, to supplement the "thin" rationality of abstract formal models. Indeed, many leading proponents of applying rational choice models to understanding political change now argue in favor of a synthetic approach, using "analytic narratives" that combine insights from both rational choice logic *and* close analysis of specific historical cases (Bates et al. 1998).

Another area in which case studies of revolutionary processes are blending with work in adjacent fields is efforts to link revolutionary theory with theories of social movements. As McAdam, Tarrow, and Tilly (1997) and I (Goldstone 1998a) have pointed out, case-study analyses of major social movements (e.g., McAdam 1982) and of revolutions were in fact converging on similar sets of conditions and processes for protest and revolutions. Social movement theory had argued that protest movements arose when three conditions were conjoined: (1) political opportunities, which are brought by state weakness or intraelite conflicts; (2) active mobilization networks drawing on preexisting social linkages or organizations; and (3) a cognitive framework showing the need for and effectiveness of protest, created by leaders who "frame" the need for protest in a persuasive ideology (Tarrow 1998). The first two of these conditions were, in effect, already part of the theory of revolutions. The last condition, ideology, clearly needed to be brought into revolutionary theory.

The role of ideology, however, is extremely complex and is still being explored. Selbin (1993), in a comparative set of case studies of modern Latin American revolutions (Bolivia, Cuba, Nicaragua, and Grenada), has argued that ideology is linked to leadership, and that effective leadership is needed both to inspire revolutionaries through persuasive ideology and to build and maintain revolutionary institutions. Using the approach of demonstrating divergence among cases that appear similar in light of past theories, Selbin showed that only in Cuba were the revolutionary transformations both institutionalized and consolidated. In each of the other cases, either revolutionary gains were reversed or the revolutionary regime itself failed to become institutionalized. Selbin showed that structural theories are unable to account for this divergence, and that the effectiveness (or lack of effectiveness) of leadership in both sustaining a vision focused on revolutionary goals and building institutions to implement them is crucial to determining revolutionary outcomes. Foran and Goodwin have further shown, in a comparison of revolutionary outcomes in Nicaragua and Iran, that the emergence of democratic characteristics and economic changes are strongly affected by "which set of organized political leaders within the revolutionary coalition is able to consolidate its hold on state power after the overthrow of the old regime" and the "ideological visions of the new revolutionary leadership" (1993, pp. 210–11).

A number of scholars have also used comparative case studies to illustrate the role of ideology in the origins of revolutions. Foran (1997a) and Wickham-Crowley (1992) have argued that almost all societies maintain a stock of ideologies of protest or rebellion from past conflicts with authorities, and that revolutionary leaders need to tap into these memories of conflict experiences in their own societies to construct persuasive and attractive ideologies of rebellion. Wickham-Crowley (1991), Foran (1997a), and Parsa (2000) have argued that it is ideologies that provide the glue for alliances between elites and popular groups. Calhoun (1994) has further pointed out that ideologies carry notions of identity and group commitment, which help sustain and invigorate the social networks that mobilize people for revolutionary action. It is clear that ideologies play so many crucial roles in revolutionary processes that the task of integrating ideology into revolutionary theory is just beginning.

The largest challenge to revolutionary theory is to accurately encompass the major revolutions of the late twentieth century, including anticolonial, nationalist, and antidictatorial revolutions such as those in Cuba, Iran, the Philippines, and the former communist regimes. Here too, theories of revolution have made significant progress, with efforts by many scholars to grapple with different sets of cases.

Foran (1997b), Wickham-Crowley (1992), Goodwin (2001), Goodwin and Skocpol (1989), and Goldstone, Gurr, and Moshiri (1991) have all shown that modern revolutions share common features with the earlier revolutions in agrarian monarchies and empires. Most of those features were already laid out in the social-structural approach. International pressures, state crises, intraelite conflicts, and popular mobilization remain key components in the development of revolutionary situations even in modern regimes. However, these broad factors need to be modified to gain accurate correspondence with the events observed in modern revolutions, and a role needs to be added for ideology as well. Although these scholars overlap to a large degree in identifying the factors important to modern revolutions, they do not agree on precisely which conditions should comprise the core of revolutionary theories.

International pressures, for example, are not sufficiently described in terms of international military or economic competition. Increasingly, direct foreign intervention and support – or withdrawal of that support – are common. In Cuba, Iran, Nicaragua, and the Philippines, the pattern of initial U.S. support for dictators, followed by reduction or withdrawal of that support, contributed to the outbreak of revolutionary conflicts (Halliday 1999; Snyder 1999).

State crisis is also not merely a problem of states running into elite resistance to reforms. In modern states, the relationships between rulers and elites are quite varied. Elites may oppose rulers because of failures of patronage, problems in economic development, exclusion from political power, or lack of progress on nationalist goals. Goodwin (1994, 2001), Goldstone (1994b), Wickham-Crowley (1992), and Snyder (1998), all building on the key work of Dix (1983, 1984), have argued that one type of modern dictatorship – the personalist, or neopatrimonial dictatorship, in which a single individual has amassed great power and gains elite loyalty mainly by dispensing favors and positions – is especially vulnerable to social revolutions. This kind of regime can appear quite strong when the dictator is able to keep elites factionalized and dependent on his favor. Yet when economic or international political pressures weaken the dictator's ability to control the elites, there are no other traditional or institutional supports for his regime. Such regimes can thus fall with remarkable swiftness when they lose elite support. In addition, because the dictator has no established organizations or institutions to enlist and maintain popular support, beyond the repression of the police and military, elites can fairly easily encourage popular opposition if the repressive institutions appear weakened or unwilling to defend the regime. This pattern of neopatrimonial regime collapse can be identified in the revolutions in Cuba (1959), Nicaragua (1979), and Iran (1979), and was expected – and in fact occurred – in the Philippines (1986), Indonesia (1998), and Zaire (1998). In contrast, dictatorships linked to and strongly supported by a particular social group, be it the military, landed elites, industrialists, or a political party organization, are more stable.

The study of modern revolutions has also shown that if intraelite conflicts are necessary to create conditions favorable to revolution, a strong revolutionary movement generally requires cross-class coalitions linking elite and popular groups (Foran 1992, 1997a; Parsa 2000; Goodwin 2001). This is particularly true where revolutionary movements take the form of guerrilla war against the government. For such movements to succeed, the rural guerrillas must find allies among elites and urban groups; otherwise, they remain isolated in rural rebellion (Wickham-Crowley 1991, 1992).

Scholars have demonstrated that even the collapse of communist regimes can be brought within the scope of revolutionary theory. In an analysis of the collapse of the Soviet Union, I have used process tracing to demonstrate the role of causal patterns and sequences familiar from prior revolutions (Goldstone 1998b). International competitive military and economic pressure from the West brought a faction of Soviet elites led by Mikhail Gorbachev to seek major reforms in the communist regime (glasnost and perestroika). However, by the time those reforms occurred, a sharp contraction in Soviet economic growth had already weakened the state's ability to provide continued employment improvement and higher living standards for its population. In addition, the stagnation of professional employment produced a large number of educated elites (technicals) with college degrees who were stuck in blue-collar jobs and excluded from political or economic advancement. A fiscally strapped regime thus faced elites who were divided and distressed over state policy and problems of social mobility.

Economic decline, along with grievous pollution and inefficient health care, had also produced a marked decline in life expectancy since the mid-1970s. Health and safety concerns were particularly strong in those areas with the most polluting and dangerous factories and mines. Urban groups and miners thus became a particular source of popular mobilization against the communist regime.

The technical elites, urban workers, and miners saw Gorbachev's reforms as an opportunity not merely to reform, but to throw out communist control over political and economic life. They supported the reformist faction, led by Boris Yeltsin in Russia and by other nationalist leaders in the Baltic, Caucasus, and Central Asian Soviet republics and pressed for the end of communist control. The key elements in this process – international pressure, state weakness, intraelite conflicts, cross-class coalitions among elite reformers and popular groups facing depressed living conditions, and ideologies of rebellion (democracy and nationalism) that united regime opponents and inspired rebellion – are precisely those found in other major revolutions. As a consequence, I suggested that as in most other major revolutions, struggles for power would likely continue, and in the absence of leaders strongly committed to democracy – an absence felt in most former communist regimes except for a few in Eastern Europe and the Baltics – democracy was not likely to develop, whatever the hopes of Western aid contributors and well-wishers.

Goodwin (2001), in a comparative case study of the anticommunist revolutions in Eastern Europe, further pointed out that differences in the way those revolutions unfolded reflected differences in state structure. Romania's revolution against the neopatrimonial Ceauçescu regime was most like the sudden and violent overthrow of other personalist dictators, while the limited resistance put up by the communist regimes in East Germany and Czechoslovakia meant that these events unfolded more like social protest movements.

A New Synthesis: Focusing on Causes of Stability

While these efforts have shown how revolutionary theory can be modified and applied to explain modern revolutions, they have also created their own problem in the complexity that resulted from the extension of theory to cover more cases. In the course of these efforts, the earlier goal of identifying a short and consistent list of causes that lead to revolution seems to have been lost. For example, while state weakness or crisis is frequently identified as a condition of revolution, what are the causes that produce that condition? Scholars have enumerated such causes as military defeat or competition, economic downturns, excessive state debt or fiscal strain, long-term demographic pressures, uneven or unsuccessful economic development, strains on colonial powers' resources or domestic support, rulers' departures from religious or nationalist principles, foreign interventions, shifts in state resources due to changing export or import prices, ethnic conflicts, erratic or excessive repression by rulers, shifts in international standards for human rights, and harvest failures or other natural disasters (including earthquakes, floods, and droughts), with no two revolutions having precisely the same causes. Similarly, intraelite conflicts may arise from ethnic divisions, political exclusion, state actions that favor a particular group, religious divisions, conflicts over resources or economic development, or shifts in social mobility that produce new elite aspirants or that undermine the continuity of existing elite families.

In short, it has become more difficult to look behind the "conditions" of revolution – such as state crisis or elite conflicts – for concrete historical causes. The latter are simply too diverse, and vary too greatly across cases, to serve as the foundation for a general theory. Moreover, there is a realization that the unfolding of revolutions has emergent properties; once a revolutionary situation has begun, the actions and decisions of rulers and revolutionaries influence further events. Certain mechanisms persist across revolutionary situations (McAdam, Tarrow, and Tilly 2001) – popular mobilization, leadership, ideological framing, building cross-class coalitions, confronting authorities with mass actions – but they may develop in different ways in different cases. Thus, simply listing conditions for revolution does not tell us how revolutions develop, because these conditions combine and concatenate in different ways.

For example, in Russia, intraelite conflict was not important until World War I produced a collapse of the tsar's military; Lenin's and Trotsky's leadership and mobilization of workers then proved critical in the ensuing intraelite struggles for control of the posttsarist state. In Iran, by contrast, the military was never weakened by international conflicts. Rather, intraelite conflicts precipitated protests over the shah's religious policies and alliance with the United States; these protests then led to more constrained U.S. support and a decision by the shah's military to withdraw from defending the shah against mass opposition. In other cases, revolutions develop through guerrilla wars; in still others, through relatively peaceful strikes and protests. A list of the causes of revolution is thus too static to capture the reality of the revolutionary process, in which causal factors occur in different combinations and temporal patterns, interacting with the decisions of rulers and revolutionaries to produce varied revolutionary trajectories. The efforts of scholars to achieve greater accuracy in understanding the causes of revolutions, in an increasing number of cases, thus appear to have succeeded at the expense of parsimony and generality (Przeworski and Teune 1970, pp. 20–3).

I have tentatively suggested (Goldstone 2001) a way out of this impasse by turning the problem of revolutionary causation around. Theories of revolution have generally proceeded on the assumption that states have a huge variety of ways to operate normally but that only a small and particular set of conditions is sufficiently disruptive to produce revolutions. However, more than a century of empirical events and investigations now suggest that may not be so. Instead, it appears that a huge variety of events are involved, in various combinations, in producing different varieties of revolutionary situations. Thus, instead of treating stability as unproblematic and piling up a set of conditions that lead to revolution, I have argued that we may be better served by treating stability as the problem and seeing revolutions as the result of the loss or undermining of the conditions that maintain stability. A small number of conditions may in fact be critical to sustaining state stability, while many different combinations and patterns of causation can undermine these conditions and lead to state breakdown. The different ways this happens will generate different trajectories leading to various processes and outcomes of protest and/or revolution.

The conditions for stability seem fairly easily enumerated by abstracting from and inverting the much longer list of revolutionary conditions. They are (1) rulers (or ruling organizations) that are widely perceived as both effective and just; (2) elites that are unified and loyal to the regime; and (3) popular groups that are able to secure their customary standard of living in a reliable manner. States that meet these conditions are reliably stable; the more states fall short of meeting these conditions, the more likely they are to experience conflict, protest, and revolution.

Departures from the conditions for stability then create situations in which revolutionary leaders can begin to mobilize oppositions and rulers to plan their response. The decisions and actions of rulers and revolutionaries, the particular elite cleavages and groups that are mobilized, the specific ideologies used to generate support, and international reactions then generate the variety in the pattern of protests and revolutions that we observe – some involving guerrilla warfare, some involving the sudden collapse of a state, some occurring in neopatrimonial dictatorships, some in one-party states, some in democracies.

By focusing on the loss or undermining of conditions of stability, revolutionary theory can allow much greater scope for dynamic processes such as leadership, mobilization, and decision making by rulers and revolutionary opponents, and for the interplay of these processes to vary over time. In addition, specifying conditions for stability allows the enormous range of specific concrete factors shown to be important in revolutions – such as military or economic failures, failures to uphold religious or nationalist principles, or excessive or inadequate repression or response to disasters, to name a few – to play a role without having to specify the same set of causal factors as being involved in all revolutions. In this way, the specific factors specified by Skocpol – military pressure that undermines state effectiveness, state reforms that undermine elite unity and support for the state, and village communal organizations facing more onerous taxes and rents – become simply one particular set of conditions undermining state stability. The demographic pressures I had noted in late preindustrial societies, and the ways that personalist dictatorships may decline in effectiveness or forfeit elite loyalty, similarly become special cases subsumed under the broader theory of regime stability. The ineffectiveness of the Weimar regime that led to the Nazi revolution and the weakness of the Chinese imperial court; the elite court–country divisions in seventeenth-century England and in the reformist–conservative blocs in the Communist Party of the Soviet Union in the late twentieth century; the impact of demographic pressures and of commercialized agriculture on peasants across time and space all can be brought into a common framework of factors that undermine the conditions of state stability. When all three of those conditions of stability are simultaneously lost, by whatever means, a revolutionary situation is the result.

Harking back to Weber's view of revolutions as requiring the institutionalization of new values, the process and outcomes of revolutions can then be conceptualized as an ongoing effort to re-create the conditions of stability. Revolutionary leaders use ideological struggles and mobilization to secure elite support for the revolution, while building a stronger state is essential to gain effectiveness for the new revolutionary regime. Securing a stable material existence for the population is often the most difficult condition to meet, and thus it is normal to expect recurrent popular protests as part of the revolutionary process. Indeed, the difficulty of rebuilding stable conditions implies that revolutionary struggles will often last for years, or even for decades, and that the fall of the old regime will generally not, in itself, bring a society to popular prosperity, elite loyalty, and effective and just governance (Stinchcombe 1999).

It is too early to tell if a theory based on conditions of stability will prove able to simplify theories of revolution while comprehending a wide range of cases and aspects of the process of revolutions. However, it appears promising, as is the range of excellent work done on ideology, on revolutions in neopatrimonial states, on guerrilla wars, and on the collapse of communist regimes. Revolutionary theory thus appears well on its way to meeting current challenges.

By focusing on international pressures, state weakness, intraelite conflicts, cross-class coalitions, personalist regimes, ideologies of rebellion, mobilization networks, popular living standards, and revolutionary leadership, CHAs of revolution have moved toward a common explanatory framework covering events ranging from the French Revolution to the collapse of the Soviet Union. This framework has its roots in the insights of the fathers of sociological theory, but it has continually developed over time in response to new events, expanding to incorporate new cases and additional details of the revolutionary process.

Lest we end on too triumphal a note, we should be clear that important further challenges for revolutionary studies remain. Although receiving increasing attention, the role of women and gender issues in revolution has yet to be adequately analyzed (Moghadam 1997; Tétreault 1994; Wasserstrom 1994). Although rational choice theory has offered some guidance, no mathematical formalization of revolutionary processes is widely accepted. And although there are promising starts (Scott 1990; Goodwin 1997), macrolevel theories of revolution still need to be harmonized with social-psychological theories of individual behavior. As in any fruitful field of research, further frontiers beckon.

Knowledge Accumulation in the Study of Revolutions

In this section, I wish to summarize briefly some of the key findings presented by scholars using CHA regarding revolutions. I believe it will be evident that these findings could not have been uncovered by any methods other than careful process tracing and congruence testing of discrete historical cases.

Conjunctural Causation

CHA of revolutions has shown that there is no single set of necessary and sufficient causes that lie behind all revolutions. Rather, revolutions are the result of a conjuncture of distinct causal streams, and the type and development of a revolution depend on the precise combination and components in those causal streams. The key to understanding collapses of authority of a magnitude that can lead to revolution is that they involve the breakdown of authority at several levels in society: state command over elites fails; elite unity or cooperation is sundered; popular acceptance of political authority and/or certain elite privileges is replaced by active rejection.

An enormous range of events and conditions can contribute to such conjunctures. Across varied cases, scholars have identified as frequently important all of the following: international military pressures on state fiscal health and effectiveness; demographic pressures on agrarian economies and traditional status recruitment; elite alienation stemming from political exclusion by personalist dictatorships; elite and popular alienation due to striking repression or cultural and religious deviation by the regime; economic downturns or natural disasters that not only bring great popular distress but are perceived as caused or exacerbated by the regime; the development of cross-class or multiclass coalitions of opposition; the spread of compelling ideologies of opposition rooted in nationalist, religious, or other widespread and popular cultural idioms; the emergence of leadership that is both inspiring and pragmatically effective; and mobilization networks, whether formal or informal, that draw on personal ties and group affiliations to forge oppositional identities.

The complexity of the preceding list is inseparable from the complexity of the events we collectively label revolutions. However, this does not mean that they are so complex as to resist explanation or even fairly straightforward analysis. By abstracting from concrete causes, such as those enumerated in the preceding paragraphs, and focusing on more general conditions that indicate the collapse of state stability, we can arrive at the following list of five key conditions that must arise for a revolutionary episode to begin:[2]

1. A crisis of state authority in which the state is widely perceived by elites and popular groups as both ineffective and unjust.
2. A crisis of elite relationships in which elites become divided, alienated, and polarized into factions that disagree over how to reconstitute state authority.
3. A crisis of popular welfare in which urban and/or rural groups find it difficult to maintain their customary standard of living through accustomed means.

[2] This list is compiled, with considerable abstraction, primarily from the works of Skocpol (1979), Goldstone (1991), Foran (1997a), Goodwin (2001), and Wickham-Crowley (1992).

4. The emergence of an elite–popular coalition to attack the authority of the state.
5. An ideology of opposition that binds elite and popular groups in their attack on the authorities, justifies that attack, and suggests alternative bases for authority.

While the presence of any one or several of these conditions can lead to a political crisis, such as a peasant rebellion, urban uprising, elite revolt or coup, or civil war, *all* of these conditions seem to be required for a truly revolutionary situation to arise.

Variety in Processes and Outcomes

One of the most critical insights of CHAs of revolutions is the need to separate clearly the study of origins, processes, and outcomes of revolutions. The causal origins of revolutions – that is, the factors that undermine the stability of regimes – interact with prior conditions and with actions by states, opposition groups, and international actors to produce contingent and emergent revolutionary processes of coalition formation, revolutionary tactics and confrontations, and factional struggles. These processes of revolutionary conflict can last for decades before a stable outcome is achieved. That outcome, in turn, is highly contingent on the particular leaders, coalitions, ideologies, and experiences that emerge as dominant from the revolutionary process as it unfolds.

We have already mentioned that some revolutions develop slowly out of visibly active revolutionary movements that gradually gain strength, while other revolutions erupt suddenly and unexpectedly from the implosion of the old regime. Each pattern reflects a different combination of causal components. Where states retain considerable elite support and fiscal strength but act unjustly and repressively, revolutionary movements often build on the periphery, awaiting a shift in state strength or external alliances to provide an opportunity for successful rebellion. Led by marginal or dissident elites, they need to battle to win over dominant elites and extend their popular support. This was the pattern in the Cuban, Nicaraguan, and Chinese communist revolutions. Where states are weakening in their material resources and are seen as increasingly ineffective, and where elite defections are widespread, a sudden collapse in state authority may occur, with elites mobilizing popular groups first for reform and then for the overthrow of the regime. This was the pattern in the English, French, Mexican, Russian, and anti-Soviet revolutions.

Both of these patterns can in turn produce a variety of outcomes. Here the ideology of rebellion, the constellation of external and internal struggles facing the revolution, and the character of the revolutionary leadership are critical. Revolutionary leaders who believe in democracy as a chief goal, trumping other aims, appear to be essential to create democratic outcomes. If they have that goal – such as Nelson Mandela in South Africa, the Sandinistas in Nicaragua, or Corazon Aquino in the Philippines – then even counterrevolutionary threats, severe ethnic conflicts, and dire economic conditions do not prevent the construction of democratic institutions. In contrast, leaders who are willing to subordinate building democratic institutions to other goals – whether economic, religious, or military – tend to produce party-states or dictatorships, even facing far lesser threats, as in Ayatollah Khomeini's postrevolutionary regime in Iran.

Other economic and political aspects of revolutionary outcomes are also strongly related to the ideology of the revolutionary leadership, and how that intersects with their experience and the conditions they face. Every revolutionary leadership faces the problem of how to restore stability, which in turn requires effective fiscal and military action by the new regime, gaining the loyalty of elites, and reducing popular grievances. How the leadership frames the solution to these problems often determines the outcome of the regime. Often, heightened centralization and bureaucratization of the new regime compared to the old is necessary for effective mobilization of money and manpower. However, even more important is how the leadership views the faults of the old regime. If the old regime was seen as failed because it departed from past virtues, which now need to be restored, the revolution may have a highly conservative cast, even as it creates new institutions of governance, as for example in Meiji Japan. In contrast, if the old regime was seen as failed because it held tight to old, obsolete, invalid ideals and principles, the revolution will take a radical stance, even if in many respects it simply extends and modifies institutions of the old regime, as in the French and Russian revolutions.

Lastly, it must be noted that many of the processes and outcomes of revolutions are emergent, unknowable until they are produced in reaction to the events of the revolutionary process itself. Many revolutions begin as essentially reformist, only to become radicalized under the failure of moderates to secure stability, or in the heat of battle with counterrevolutionary foreign and domestic foes. For example, Francisco Madero's reformist revolution in Mexico against Porfirio Diaz only led to massive peasant rebellions and civil war because of the imposition of the counterrevolutionary de la Huerta regime. Similarly, in the wake of the moderate New Economic Program in Russia's revolution and Lenin's death, a power struggle arose between those who wished a more radical return to communism and those who sought to continue on a more gradual path to socialism. The victory of the former under Joseph Stalin put the Russian Revolution on a more distinctly communist and authoritarian path.

Conclusion

Revolutions differ profoundly in their concrete causes, their patterns of unfolding, and their outcomes. Moreover, the pattern of development and outcome of a given revolution are emergent properties that depend on events and struggles within the unfolding revolution, and on the actions of particular leaders, international actors, and popular groups. Given this complexity, CHA is an essential method for understanding the range and variety of causal mechanisms involved in revolutions.

Process tracing can reveal those causal mechanisms and how they operate in varied contexts, while congruence testing can demonstrate the similarities and differences among revolutionary events. These methods of CHA have continually confronted prior beliefs about revolutions with new empirical findings, challenging and expanding our views. This process is certain to continue, as it seems unlikely that we have exhausted all the varieties of causation or outcomes that revolutions could produce. Especially with that prospect, CHA will remain crucial to continue the cumulative progress in our knowledge of revolutions and revolutionary movements.

References

Abbott, Andrew. 1990. "Conceptions of Time and Events in Social Science Methods: Causal and Narrative Approaches." *Historical Methods* 23: 140–50.

1992. "From Causes to Events: Notes on Narrative Positivism." *Sociological Methods and Research* 20: 428–55.

Almond, Gabriel A., ed. 1973. *Crisis, Choice, and Change: Historical Studies of Political Development*. Boston: Little, Brown.

Arjomand, Said A. 1988. *The Turban for the Crown: The Islamic Revolution in Iran*. New York: Oxford University Press.

Armstrong, David. 1993. *Revolution and World Order: The Revolutionary State in International Society*. Oxford: Oxford University Press.

Bates, Robert H., Avner Greif, Margaret Levi, Jean-Laurent Rosenthal, and Barry R. Weingast. 1998. *Analytic Narratives*. Princeton, NJ: Princeton University Press.

Bennett, Andrew and Alexander L. George. 1997. "Process Tracing in Case Study Research." Paper presented at the MacArthur Foundation Workshop on Case Study Methods, Belfer Center for Science and International Affairs (BCSIA), Harvard University, October 17–19.

Brinton, Crane. 1938. *The Anatomy of Revolution*. New York: W. W. Norton.

Calhoun, Craig. 1994. *Neither Gods Nor Emperors: Students and the Struggle for Democracy in China*. Berkeley: University of California Press.

Cobban, Alfred. 1964. *The Social Interpretation of the French Revolution*. Cambridge: Cambridge University Press.

Collier, David. 1993. "The Comparative Method." Pp. 105–19 in *Political Science: The State of the Discipline II*, edited by Ada Finifter. Washington, DC: American Political Science Association.

Dix, Robert. 1983. "The Varieties of Revolution." *Comparative Politics* 15: 281–95.

1984. "Why Revolutions Succeed and Fail." *Polity* 16: 423–46.

Eckstein, Susan. 1982. "The Impact of Revolution on Social Welfare in Latin America." *Theory and Society* 11: 43–94.

Edwards, Lyford P. 1927. *The Natural History of Revolutions*. Chicago: University of Chicago Press.

Eisenstadt, S. N. 1978. *Revolution and the Transformation of Societies*. New York: Free Press.

Emirbayer, Mustafa and Jeff Goodwin. 1994. "Network Analysis, Culture and the Problem of Agency." *American Journal of Sociology* 99: 1411–54.

Farhi, Farideh. 1990. *States and Urban-Based Revolution: Iran and Nicaragua*. Urbana and Chicago: University of Illinois Press.

Feierabend, Ivo K., Rosalind L. Feierabend, and Betty A. Nesvold. 1969. "Social Change and Political Violence: Cross-National Patterns. Pp. 606–68 in *Violence in America: Historical and Comparative Perspectives*, edited by Hugh D. Graham and Ted R. Gurr. New York: Praeger.

Foran, John. 1992. "A Theory of Third World Social Revolutions: Iran, Nicaragua, and El Salvador Compared." *Critical Sociology* 19: 3–27.

1997a. "The Comparative-Historical Sociology of Third World Social Revolutions: Why a Few Succeed, Why Most Fail." Pp. 227–67 in Foran 1997b.

ed. 1997b. *Theorizing Revolutions*. London: Routledge.

Foran, John and Jeff Goodwin. 1993. "Revolutionary Outcomes in Iran and Nicaragua: Coalition Fragmentation, War, and the Limits of Social Transformation." *Theory and Society* 22: 209–47.

Forster, Robert. 1980. "The French Revolution and the New Elite, 1800–1850." Pp. 182–207 in *The American and European Revolutions, 1776–1850*, edited by J. Pelenski. Iowa City: University of Iowa Press.

Furet, François. 1981. *Interpreting the French Revolution*. Cambridge: Cambridge University Press.

Garton Ash, Timothy. 1989. "Refolution in Hungary and Poland." *New York Review of Books* 36 (August 17): 9–15.

George, Alexander with Andrew Bennett. 1997. "The Role of the Congruence

Method for Case Study Research." Paper presented at the 38th Annual Convention of the International Studies Association, Toronto, March 18–22.

Glenn, John K. 1999. "Competing Challengers and Contested Outcomes to State Breakdown: The Velvet Revolution in Czechoslovakia." *Social Forces* 78: 187–212.

Goldstone, Jack A. 1984. "Urbanization and Inflation: Lessons from the English Price Revolution of the 16th and 17th Centuries." *American Journal of Sociology* 89: 1112–60.

1991. *Revolution and Rebellion in the Early Modern World*. Berkeley: University of California Press.

1994a. "Is Revolution Individually Rational?" *Rationality and Society* 6: 139–66.

1994b. "Revolution in Modern Dictatorships." Pp. 70–7 in *Revolutions: Theoretical, Comparative, and Historical Studies*, 2nd ed., edited by Jack A. Goldstone. Fort Worth, TX: Harcourt Brace.

1998a. "Social Movements or Revolutions? On the Evolution and Outcomes of Collective Action." Pp. 125–45 in *Democracy and Contention*, edited by Marco Guigni, Doug McAdam, and Charles Tilly. Boulder, CO: Rowman & Littlefield.

1998b. "The Soviet Union: Revolution and Transformation." Pp. 95–123 in *Elites, Crises, and the Origins of Regimes*, edited by Mattei Dogan and John Higley. Boulder, CO: Rowman & Littlefield.

ed. 1998c. *The Encyclopedia of Political Revolutions*. Washington, DC: Congressional Quarterly Press.

1999. "Initial Conditions, General Laws, Path Dependence, and Explanation in Historical Sociology." *American Journal of Sociology* 104: 829–45.

2001. "Toward a Fourth Generation of Revolutionary Theory." *Annual Review of Political Science* 4: 139–87.

Goldstone, Jack A., Ted Robert Gurr, and Farrokh Moshiri, eds. *Revolutions of the Late Twentieth Century*. Boulder, CO: Westview.

Goldthorpe, John H. 1997. "Current Issues in Comparative Macro-Sociology: A Debate on Methodological Issues." *Comparative Social Research* 16: 1–26.

Goodwin, Jeff. 1994. "Old Regimes and Revolutions in the Second and Third Worlds: A Comparative Perspective." *Social Science History* 18: 575–604.

1997. "The Libidinal Constitution of a High-Risk Social Movement: Affectual Ties and Solidarity in the Huk Rebellion, 1946 to 1954." *American Sociological Review* 62: 53–70.

2001. *No Other Way Out: States and Revolutionary Movements, 1945–1991*. Cambridge: Cambridge University Press.

Goodwin, Jeff and Theda Skocpol. 1989. "Explaining Revolutions in the Contemporary Third World." *Politics and Society* 17: 489–507.

Gould, Roger V. 1995. *Insurgent Identities: Class, Community, and Protest in Paris from 1848 to the Commune*. Chicago: University of Chicago Press.

Griffin, Larry J. 1992. "Temporality, Events, and Explanation in Historical Sociology: An Introduction." *Sociological Methods and Research* 20: 403–27.

Gugler, Josef. 1982. "The Urban Character of Contemporary Revolutions." *Studies in Comparative International Development* 17: 60–73.
Gurr, Ted Robert. 1968. "A Causal Model of Civil Strife: A Comparative Analysis Using New Indices." *American Political Science Review* 62: 1104–24.
1970. *Why Men Rebel*. Princeton, NJ: Princeton University Press.
ed. 1980. *Handbook of Political Conflict*. New York: Free Press.
Halliday, Fred. 1999. *Revolution and World Politics*. London: Macmillan.
Haydu, Jeffrey. 1998. "Making Use of the Past: Time Periods as Cases to Compare and as Sequences of Problem Solving." *American Journal of Sociology* 104: 339–71.
Hibbs, Douglas A. 1973. *Mass Political Violence: A Cross-National Causal Analysis*. New York: Wiley.
Huntington, Samuel P. 1968. *Political Order in Changing Societies*. New Haven, CT: Yale University Press.
Johnson, Chalmers. 1966. *Revolutionary Change*. Boston: Little, Brown.
Katz, Mark. 1997. *Revolutions and Revolutionary Waves*. New York: St. Martin's Press.
King, Gary, Robert O. Keohane, and Sidney Verba. 1994. *Designing Social Inquiry: Scientific Inference in Qualitative Research*. Cambridge: Cambridge University Press.
Kiser, Edgar. 1996. "The Revival of Narrative in Historical Sociology: What Rational Choice Theory Can Contribute." *Politics and Society* 24: 249–71.
Kiser, Edgar and Michael Hechter. 1991. "The Role of General Theory in Comparative-Historical Sociology." *American Journal of Sociology* 97: 1–30.
Kuran, Timur. 1991. "Now out of Never: The Element of Surprise in the Eastern European Revolution of 1989." *World Politics* 44: 7–48.
1995. *Private Truths, Public Lies: The Social Consequences of Preference Falsification*. Cambridge, MA: Harvard University Press.
Kurzman, Charles. 1996. "Structural Opportunity and Perceived Opportunity in Social Movement Theory."*American Sociological Review* 61: 153–70.
Lakatos, Imre. 1983. *The Methodology of Scientific Research Programmes*, edited by John Worrall and Gregory Currie. Cambridge: Cambridge University Press.
Lenin, Vladimir Ilich. [1973]. *What Is to Be Done? Burning Questions of Our Movement*. Translation of the 1st ed. of 1902. Peking: Foreign Languages Press.
Lichbach, Mark I. 1989. "An Evaluation of 'Does Economic Inequality Breed Political Conflict?' Studies." *World Politics* 41: 431–70.
1995. *The Rebels' Dilemma*. Ann Arbor: University of Michigan Press.
Lieberson, Stanley. 1991. "Small *N*'s and Big Conclusions: An Examination of the Reasoning in Comparative Studies Based on a Small Number of Cases." *Social Forces* 70: 307–20.
Little, Daniel. 1998. *Microfoundations, Method, and Causation: On the Philosophy of the Social Sciences*. New Brunswick, NJ: Transaction Publishers.
Mahoney, James. 1999. "Nominal, Ordinal, and Narrative Appraisal in Macrocausal Analysis." *American Journal of Sociology* 104: 1154–96.
2000a. "Strategies of Causal Inference in Small-*N* Analysis." *Sociological Methods and Research* 28: 387–424.

2000b. "Path Dependence in Historical Sociology." *Theory and Society* 29: 507–48.
Mahoney, James and Richard Snyder. 1999. "Rethinking Agency and Structure in the Study of Regime Change." *Studies in Comparative International Development* 34: 3–32.
Markoff, John. 1996. *The Abolition of Feudalism*. University Park: Pennsylvania State University Press.
McAdam, Doug. 1982. *Political Process and the Development of Black Insurgency, 1930–1970*. Chicago: University of Chicago Press.
McAdam, Doug, Sidney Tarrow and Charles Tilly. 1997. "Toward a Comparative Perspective on Social Movements and Revolution." Pp. 142–73 in *Comparative Politics: Rationality, Culture, and Structure*, edited by Mark Lichbach and Alan Zuckerman. Cambridge: Cambridge University Press.
2001. *Dynamics of Contention*. Cambridge: Cambridge University Press.
McKeown, Timothy J. 1999. "Case Studies and the Statistical Worldview." *International Organization* 53: 161–90.
Midlarsky, Manus I. 1982. "Scarcity and Inequality: Prologue to the Onset of Mass Revolution." *Journal of Conflict Resolution* 26: 3–38.
Moghadam, Val M. 1997. "Gender and Revolutions." Pp. 137–67 in Foran 1997c.
Moore, Barrington, Jr. 1966. *Social Origins of Dictatorship and Democracy*. Boston: Beacon Press.
Muller, Edward N. 1985. "Income Inequality, Regime Repressiveness, and Political Violence." *American Sociological Review* 50: 47–61.
Nichols, Elizabeth. 1986. "Skocpol on Revolution: Comparative Analysis vs. Historical Conjuncture." *Comparative Social Research* 9: 163–86.
Oberschall, Anthony. 1994a. "Protest Demonstrations and the End of Communist Regimes in 1989." *Research in Social Movements, Conflict, and Change* 17: 1–24.
1994b. "Rational Choice in Collective Protests." *Rationality and Society* 6: 79–100.
Olson, M., Jr. 1965. *The Logic of Collective Action: Public Goods and the Theory of Groups*. Cambridge, MA: Harvard University Press.
Opp, Karl-Dieter. 1989. *The Rationality of Political Protest*. Boulder, CO: Westview.
1999. "Contending Conceptions of the Theory of Rational Action." *Journal of Theoretical Politics* 11: 171–202.
Opp, Karl-Dieter and Wolfgang Roehl. 1990. "Repression, Micromobilization, and Political Protest." *Social Forces* 69: 521–47.
Opp, Karl-Dieter, Peter Voss, and Christianne Gern. 1995. *Origins of a Spontaneous Revolution: East Germany, 1989*. Ann Arbor: University of Michigan Press.
Osa, Maryjane. 1997. "Creating Solidarity: The Religious Foundations of the Polish Social Movement."*East European Politics and Society* 11: 339–65.
Paige, Jeffery M. 1975. *Agrarian Revolution*. New York: Free Press.
Parsa, Misagh. 2000. *States, Ideologies, and Social Revolutions: A Comparative Analysis of Iran, Nicaragua, and the Philippines*. Cambridge: Cambridge University Press.
Parsons, Talcott. 1966. *Societies: Evolutionary and Comparative Perspectives*. Englewood Cliffs, NJ: Prentice-Hall.
Pettee, George S. 1938. *The Process of Revolution*. New York: Harper & Row.

Pfaff, Steven. 1996. "Collective Identity and Informal Groups in Revolutionary Mobilization: East Germany in 1989." *Social Forces* 75: 91–110.

Przeworski, Adam and Henry Teune. 1970. *The Logic of Comparative Social Inquiry*. New York: Wiley-Interscience.

Ragin, Charles C. 1997. "Turning the Tables: How Case-Oriented Research Challenges Variable-Oriented Research." *Comparative Social Research* 16: 27–42.

Rasler, Karen. 1996. "Concessions, Repression, and Political Protest in the Iranian Revolution." *American Sociological Review* 61: 132–52.

Scott, James C. 1990. *Domination and the Arts of Resistance: Hidden Transcripts*. New Haven, CT: Yale University Press.

Selbin, Eric. 1993. *Modern Latin American Revolutions*. Boulder, CO: Westview.

Sewell, William, Jr. 1985. "Ideologies and Social Revolutions: Reflections on the French Case." *Journal of Modern History* 57: 57–85.

1996. "Three Temporalities: Toward an Eventful Sociology." Pp. 245–80 in *The Historic Turn in the Human Sciences*, edited by Terence J. McDonald. Ann Arbor: University of Michigan Press.

Skocpol, Theda. 1979. *States and Social Revolutions*. Cambridge: Cambridge University Press.

1982. "Rentier State and Shi'a Islam in the Iranian Revolution." *Theory and Society* 11: 265–303, with responses by Nikki Keddie, Walter Goldfrank, and Eqbal Ahmed.

1994. *Social Revolutions in the Modern World*. Cambridge: Cambridge University Press.

Snyder, Richard. 1998. "Paths out of Sultanistic Regimes: Combining Structural and Voluntarist Perspectives." Pp. 49–81 in *Sultanistic Regimes*, edited by H. E. Chehabi and J. J. Linz. Baltimore, MD: Johns Hopkins University Press.

Snyder, Robert S. 1999. "The U.S. and Third World Revolutionary States: Understanding the Breakdown in Relations." *International Studies Quarterly* 43: 265–90.

Stinchcombe, Arthur L. 1999. "Ending Revolutions and Building New Governments." *Annual Review of Political Science* 2: 49–73.

Stryker, Robin. 1996. "Beyond History versus Theory: Strategic Narrative and Sociological Explanation." *Sociological Methods and Research* 24: 304–52.

Tarrow, Sidney. 1998. *Power in Movement: Social Movements and Contentious Politics*, 2nd ed. Cambridge: Cambridge University Press.

Taylor, George V. 1972. "Noncapitalist Wealth and the Origins of the French Revolution." *American Historical Review* 67: 956–77.

Tétreault, M. A., ed. 1994. *Women and Revolution in Africa, Asia, and the New World*. Columbia: University of South Carolina Press.

Tilly, C. 1973. "Does Modernization Breed Revolution?" *Comparative Politics* 5: 425–47.

1978. *From Mobilization to Revolution*. Reading, MA: Addison-Wesley.

1984. *Big Structures, Large Processes, Huge Comparisons*. New York: Russell Sage Foundation.

Trotsky, Leon. 1959. *The Russian Revolution*, selected and edited By F. W. Dupee, translated by Max Eastman. New York: Doubleday/Anchor Books.

Tullock, G. 1971. "The Paradox of Revolution." *Public Choice* 1: 89–99.

Urban, M., V. Igrunov, and S. Mitrokhin. 1997. *The Rebirth of Politics in Russia*. Cambridge: Cambridge University Press.

Wallerstein, Immanuel. 1974. *The Modern World System*, Vol. 1. New York: Academic Press.

Walt, Stephen M. 1996. *Revolution and War*. Ithaca, NY: Cornell University Press.

Wasserstrom, Jeffrey N. 1994. "Gender and Revolution in Europe and Asia." *Journal of Women's History* 5: 170–83; 6: 109–20.

Weede, Eric. 1987. "Some New Evidence on Correlates of Political Violence: Income Inequality, Regime Repressiveness, and Economic Development." *European Sociological Review* 3: 97–108.

Western, Bruce. 2000. "Bayesian Thinking About Macrosociology." Estudio/Working Paper 2000/152. Madrid: Juan March Institute.

Wickham-Crowley, Timothy. 1991. *Exploring Revolution: Essays on Latin American Insurgency and Revolutionary Theory*. Armonk, NY: M. E. Sharpe.

1992. *Guerrillas and Revolution in Latin America*. Princeton, NJ: Princeton University Press.

Wolf, Eric. 1970. *Peasant Wars of the Twentieth Century*. New York: Harper.

3

What We Know about the Development of Social Policy

COMPARATIVE AND HISTORICAL RESEARCH IN COMPARATIVE AND HISTORICAL PERSPECTIVE

Edwin Amenta

In 1975, two important quantitative comparative analyses of social policy were published. Harold Wilensky's *The Welfare State and Equality* addressed the differences in social spending efforts among sixty-odd countries in the 1960s and found that the level of economic development and the age of populations accounted for most of the variance in efforts. This study was the best and latest in a series of cross-sectional analyses of countries and American states that suggested that economic and social modernization processes determined social policy (review in Skocpol and Amenta 1986). The second study, David Collier and Richard Messick's "Prerequisites versus Diffusion: Testing Alternative Explanations of Social Security Adoption," examined a similar group of countries, but with a wider time horizon, and addressed the adoption of social insurance policies. Their findings cast serious doubt on the modernization hypothesis, as well as on the strategy of generalizing from studies of many countries on social spending at a single point in time. Just a year earlier, Hugh Heclo had published *Modern Social Politics and Britain and Sweden*, one of the first studies to take a comparative and historical approach to the development of social policy.

Previous versions of this essay were presented at the Conferences on Comparative Historical Analysis, Brown University, April 2000, and at Harvard University, November 2000, and the annual meeting of the American Political Science Association, 2001, San Francisco. My thanks to Ellen Benoit, Chris Bonastia, David Collier, Marshall Ganz, Jack Goldstone, Jeff Goodwin, Roger Gould, Peter Hall, Ira Katznelson, Bonnie Meguid, Gerardo Munck, Paul Pierson, Theda Skocpol, Kathy Thelen, Dietrich Rueschemeyer, and James Mahoney for helpful comments on previous versions of this essay. This work was supported in part by National Science Foundation Grant SBR-9709618.

In the generation since then, we have learned a great deal about social policy – largely through comparative and historical work of the small-*N* variety. On the empirical side, we have learned when various countries adopted social programs, when these programs were expanded or contracted, the forms that social policy has taken, when countries completed their systems of social policy, differences in social spending among countries at different points in time, and which countries have seen significant retrenchment in social policy of what sort. More important, comparative and historical work in this area has built our theoretical knowledge. It has been the source of or contributed to the three main theories of social policy and the welfare state, two of which came in reaction to quantitative research on the modernization thesis. At the same time, the history of social policy in comparative perspective has served as an empirical proving ground for hypotheses based on these theories. In turn, the comparative and historical research has led to the revision of theoretical arguments and has helped scholars to place scope conditions on theoretical generalizations, another way that scholarship can progress. Comparative and historical scholars have developed new methodological approaches, in particular by synthesizing comparative and historical and quantitative techniques in individual projects. Perhaps most important of all, comparative and historical research on social policy has jump-started various lines of research by asking some large questions and identifying empirical puzzles to solve and by deepening the concept of social policy. In transforming our understanding of social policy, these projects have aided theoretical refinement and advanced the research agenda in this area.

Why has there been such great progress? Partly it was because of broad conceptual agreement on what was important to study. In conducting their research, scholars tended to see social policy as lines of state action to reduce income insecurity and to provide minimum standards of income and services and thus to reduce inequalities. State programs that worked in these ways were called "social programs" or sometimes, more hopefully, "welfare state programs," with the whole of these programs known as "social policy."[1] This understanding has anchored empirical analyses. It also mattered that scholars disagreed on the theoretical arguments best suited to explain

[1] States were typically understood as dominant organizations exerting political authority and control over defined territories and their inhabitants. States that devoted most of their fiscal and bureaucratic efforts in these directions were and are considered to be "welfare states." Comparative and historical research centered on explaining differences in the adoption, the form, the extension, and sometimes the retrenchment of major social programs.

social policy while reaching broad agreement on the set of theoretical arguments deemed worth developing and appraising. Scholars focused on a few socioeconomic, political, or institutional arguments, which were often couched as parts of larger theories of the state or of politics. There were also informational preconditions – the ready availability of extensive historical records and comparative data. Finally, scholars as individuals and as a group had an open-minded outlook on methodology and theory. In this area, comparative and historical research engaged in an unusual and fruitful dialogue with quantitative cross-national work. The direction of the progress is due mainly to the relative strengths and weaknesses of comparative and historical approaches, which are well suited for identifying and addressing big questions, employing comparisons to rule out certain answers, appraising the mechanisms of theoretical arguments by tracing over time the processes of policy adoption and development, and developing new theoretical arguments, if weaker in providing strong tests of general hypotheses.

In what follows, I discuss some of the important things we know by way of comparative and historical analyses of social policy and the cumulation of knowledge in this area, including empirical, theoretical, and methodological growth. I also address why we know as much as we know and why the knowledge was able to build. I do this through a sort of comparative and historical approach, comparing over time the comparative and historical analysis of social policy with comparative and historical work in related areas. Mainly this is a theory-building project in the sociology of knowledge. I finish by addressing some new and promising lines of comparative and historical research on social policy and the challenges they face.

Comparative and Historical Causal Research and Its Progress

To ascertain the impact of comparative and historical causal research on the determinants of social policy, one needs to identify it. I see it not as a theory or a specific method or technique, but as an approach that has been undertaken by scholars with varied academic, theoretical, and methodological affiliations and preferences. By "comparative," I mean studies that address the experiences of two or more country cases (Lijphart 1971), but also one-country studies that situate empirical questions in a comparative context or make significant macrolevel comparisons in causal argumentation. Comparative studies do not have to use Mill's methods (Lieberson 1992), have a holistic understanding of the cases (Ragin 1987), or employ system-level variables to explain differences in within-in system relationships

Table 3.1. *Causal Research According to Methodological Approaches*

		Comparative Approach	
		Yes	No
Historical	Yes	Comparative and Historical Research Proper (1)	Historical Only: Historiography; Historical Case Studies (2)
Approach	No	Comparative Only: Cross-National Analyses with Quantitative or Formal Qualitative Methods (3)	Neither: Within-Country Quantitative Work; Present-Oriented Case Studies (4)

(Przeworski and Teune 1970). By "historical," I mean that the investigator situates the study within the relevant historical contexts, takes a sophisticated approach to historiography, thinks seriously about issues of process, timing, and historical trajectories, and gains a deep understanding of the cases.[2] Historical work does not necessarily have to refer back more than fifty years, employ data not created by the researcher (Miriampolski and Hughes 1978), rely on secondary sources (Lustick 1996), take a narrative form, or make causal arguments based on sequences of events (Abbott 1992; Griffin 1992). Finally, to fit, studies have to take causality seriously in a double sense: to attempt to explain important historical differences or trajectories; and to appraise, modify, or produce something theoretically portable – a line of causal argumentation conceptualized so as to apply to other cases or time periods.[3]

Comparative and historical causal analyses in social policy appear in the box at the upper left of Table 3.1. This category, which I am calling "type 1," includes major small-*N* monographs such as Gaston Rimlinger's (1971) *Welfare Policy and Industrialization in Europe, America, and Russia* and Heclo's aforementioned *Modern Social Politics in Britain and Sweden.* Also included here, though, are quantitative and comparative and historical

[2] This term was suggested to me by Peter Hall.

[3] Out of bounds would be what Skocpol and Somers (1980) refer to as "contrast of contexts" or what Charles Tilly (1984) refers to as "individualizing comparisons."

syntheses such as John Stephens's (1979) *The Transition from Capitalism to Socialism* and comparatively informed case studies such as Theda Skocpol's (1992) *Protecting Soldiers and Mothers* (for some additional American examples, see also Katznelson and Pietrykowski 1991; Quadagno 1994; Howard 1997; Lieberman 1998). These studies situate U.S. developments in comparative perspective, employ comparative methods, and employ arguments that could be used outside the U.S. context. Studies without a causal impulse would fall outside Table 3.1, and the causal work that is furthest away from my concerns is situated at the lower right of the table (type 4). This category includes most within-country quantitative work, including testing general hypotheses on experiences of U.S. states or on time series of individual countries, as well as single-country case studies lacking a historical perspective. The most outstanding examples of comparative-only work (at bottom left, type 3) are the many cross-national quantitative articles on social policy expenditures in the post–World War II period.[4] The "historical only" type (2) includes historiography on social policy such as, to take famous American examples, Michael Katz's (1986) *In the Shadow of the Poorhouse* or James Patterson's (1986) *America's Struggle Against Poverty*.

To ascertain what we have learned from comparative and historical research in social policy means to ask, What would be lost if there had been no comparative and historical research in this area? And any answer to the question involves defining scholarly progress. To my way of thinking, an area has progressed if important questions have been identified and addressed and if informed, theoretically meaningful answers have been advanced by way of empirical demonstrations, with scholars using the results to formulate other questions, answering them in sophisticated ways that refine theory and lead to new questions, and so on. In the process, we appraise and develop new theoretical arguments, ascertain the conditions under which they apply or do not, refining theoretical argumentation along the way, and uncover new empirical facts and patterns as a result of new questions and theoretical development. This sort of advancement is not merely a matter of how much work exists on a subject or how frequently it is cited.

[4] In this category I also place cross-national quantitative comparative analysis studies (Ragin 1994) and cross-national work relying mainly on Andrew Abbott's sequence analyses (Abbott and DeViney 1992) – as each methodological technique is based on algorithms that can be employed on preexisting or easily created data sets. These methods could, of course, be employed in work that is broadly comparative and historical (e.g., Wickham-Crowley 1992: conclusion).

The issue may be easier to address by breaking it down into smaller questions: What have been the central gains in empirical knowledge from comparative and historical work on social policy? To what degree has this work added to our theoretical knowledge? Have causal hypotheses been tested extensively by this work in a way that refines them? Has theory been developed by this work, both in creating theory and in extending it? Have scholars deepened their concepts in terms of what is to be explained and employed these concepts to develop or delimit theoretical argumentation? Have scholars built on both the empirical and theoretical knowledge to develop new agendas of research that have promised or achieved progress? Have there been collateral benefits in other areas of scholarship, with new methodological advances made in the area and theoretical argumentation being employed to good effect in other areas?

These questions are not easy to answer either, but any attempt to do so suggests that what we have learned from comparative and historical research in social policy is substantial and cumulative. Important gains have been made in empirical knowledge, much more so than one usually expects in comparative and historical work; the empirical knowledge has built on shared understandings about what is worth knowing and has filled gaps in what scholars want to know. There have been more significant theoretical gains. Comparative and historical research has made important contributions to the development of middle-range theory, devised from more overarching theoretical frameworks, to explain social policy. Theoretical gains have also come from appraising hypotheses on different sets of cases and time periods. Progress has been made especially in ruling out some aspects of broad generalizations and appraising the mechanisms of theoretical argumentation as they play out over time. Through hypothesis-testing, theoretical arguments also have been modified – another important part of building knowledge. Some of the greatest means of advancement in this area, however, have come through the sorts of questions that have been asked in comparative and historical research – questions that are not as easy to devise a suitable answer for in quantitative research – and the progressive development of the research agenda in this area. This development has occurred through the process of asking research questions, advancing increasingly sophisticated and empirically supported answers to them, unearthing new anomalies in the process, leading to new questions, tentative answers, and so on. There have also been some important influences on other areas of study and on the development of methodological techniques. Although these gains have come as a result of a process and although individual projects have produced contributions across the board, let me begin with the empirical progress.

Empirical Contributions of Comparative and Historical Research

According to some standard views, comparative and historical research involves a division of labor in which historians work for social scientists: Historians write monographs centered on specific countries and issues surrounding the development of democracy, the progress of revolutions, and so on. Comparative historical social scientists reconceptualize the problem, ask the large comparative questions – why democracy or revolutions occur here and not there, and so on – scour historiography on several different countries and time periods regarding the surrounding issues, and then produce more comprehensive explanations that account for developments across these countries. In the process, they may dismiss the inessential and sometimes parochial arguments plausible to experts on one country alone. Such efforts, though, may be limited by the data or interpretations of the historiography on which they rely (Lustick 1996), even if scholars employ all extant historiography, as it might include conflicts in data or interpretations.

Social scientists working in the comparative and historical mode on social policy have often diverged from this model. Significantly, they often have gathered key information on which such higher-order analyses have been based and have been able to intervene in primary literature to make and defend their own interpretations. Social policy scholars did much of the initial digging that allowed the comparative questions to be framed and addressed. Also, where needed, comparative and historical scholars have supplemented historiography with their own archival work to fill in gaps in information or to adjudicate among historical interpretations, if needed. To understand how these processes worked and the knowledge gained by them, it is worthwhile to discuss what I call the "consensus on social policy" – the concepts social scientists employed and the typical ways that social policy was made operational in empirical study.

The consensus view was that modern social policy meant state efforts to reduce economic inequality by providing certain floors on income and services and preventing income losses due to certain risks. These perils include growing old and infirm; being injured at work; becoming ill, unhealthy, or disabled; becoming unemployed or underemployed; and being in a family where the principal wage earner or earners are incapacitated or removed by these other risks or where there is no principal wage earner. The connection between inequality and insecurity of income was a close one, because a lack of programs to address risks to income was deemed to be a major cause of inequality and poverty. And, later, it was thought that the absence or destruction of programs to ensure security would increase inequality. Inequality or security typically was understood with reference to households. Research questions and projects were based on this common understanding of social policy. Into the 1990s, comparative and historical analyses of social policy typically focused on two things – the enactment of major social insurance programs and differences in the amount of social spending or "efforts" in social spending (see Skocpol and Amenta 1986; Amenta 1993). The focus of attention was modern social insurance and social assistance programs. The source of the consensus is not entirely clear, but the likeliest suspects are the U.S. Social Security Administration, which collected a great deal of information of use to both comparative historical and quantitative scholars (Rimlinger 1971; Wilensky 1975), and William Beveridge, whose impact went beyond designing what came to be known in Britain as the "welfare state."

This understanding of social policy had considerable appeal. It was easy to make the case that social policy mattered because it was at the center of the tremendous growth of states and changes in the character of many states in the twentieth century. It would be impossible to understand and explain the development of these states without understanding social policy, if only because of the sheer amount of money and bureaucratic effort expended on state old-age programs and health programs – especially in comparison with a century ago. Many states have been converted into welfare states – a pretty great transformation that is of interest to the thinking public as well as to scholars.

This conceptualization of social policy and the rationale for studying it helped to direct the research efforts of comparative and historical scholars. They relied on the research of historians, to be sure, but they also set out to ascertain through governmental records information regarding when social insurance programs were adopted in different countries and when they were expanded to include new segments of the citizenry. In short, they helped to set the parameters by which comparative and historical questions could be asked. The most outstanding examples of historical data collection serving conceptual understanding were the research projects of Peter Flora and associates, including *The Development of Welfare States in Europe and America* (1981) as well as *Growth to Limits* (1986) and the comparative data collection of *State, Economy, and Society in Western Europe, 1815–1975* (1983).

Individual comparative and historical researchers, however, also built our empirical knowledge by supplementing secondary sources and pursuing answers to questions by engaging in primary research. Although Theda Skocpol (1992), for instance, worked from many secondary sources in her study of American social policy through the 1920s, in calling attention to the role of Civil War veterans' benefits in providing substitutes for old-age and disability pensions, she also turned to primary documents, including numerous governmental records, to gain information unavailable in secondary sources, as this information was not collected according to conceptual agreements over the meaning of social policy. By using these primary sources and employing social science understandings of social policy, she was able to provide her own interpretation and analytical history of the development of U.S. social policy rather than relying on the interpretation of historians. Other scholars did the same, avoiding some of the problems of historical and comparative research – relying selectively on the interpretations or data in extant historiography (see the review in Amenta, Bonastia, and Caren 2001).

In their research, Peter Flora and Jens Alber (1981) also famously identified four periods in the development of social insurance programs in Europe and the United States: their adoption around the first decade of the twentieth century, their consolidation in the interwar years, their completion in the immediate postwar period, and their expansion in the decades after the war. It is probably agreed by now that the period comprising the last two decades of the century saw sustained bids to retrench social policy (Mishra 1990; Pierson 1994). This research facilitated the drawing of a group portrait of development of modern social policy over the last century or so for many countries, especially regarding when major programs were adopted. This periodization also proved useful in helping to set empirical research agendas, making it easier for scholars to devise new research questions and advance theory.

Theoretical Advances

Comparative and historical work in social policy has also made great theoretical contributions – probably more extensive than those in comparative and historical work in other subject areas. This is because comparative and historical scholarship in social policy has proposed and developed major middle-range theoretical explanations of social policy, in one case by developing an entire perspective to explain anomalies. Theoretical advancement has also come in part through the testing and rejection of hypotheses and arguments based in modernization theory. The advances here have also included the refinement of theory through the testing of hypotheses by comparing social policy across country cases and tracing historical processes. Theory has also been refined by ascertaining the conditions under which certain causal factors have influences – a process that has gone hand in hand with the conceptual deepening of social policy. Because the work of comparative and historical scholars has often engaged the scholarship of quantitative comparative scholars, and because in some cases comparative historical and quantitative approaches were combined in single works, it is sometimes difficult to sort out the specific contributions of comparative and historical work. Yet it is not impossible to do so, and even by a conservative standard the comparative and historical contribution to theory building and refinement has been substantial.

Influential early work on social policy (e.g., Titmuss 1958; Peacock and Wiseman 1961; Marshall 1963) focused on post–World War II Britain's adoption of comprehensive public social provision and the term "welfare state." These studies, which fall outside my definition of comparative and historical because of their lack of comparative sensibility, argue from one case for the inevitably progressive influence on social provision of the expansion of citizen rights or the social solidarities forged in modern war.

It is perhaps not surprising that by the middle 1970s, the arguments with the best comparative empirical support in explaining the development of social policy were not these British-centered ideas, but theoretical arguments based on modernization and industrialization processes. To simplify, the idea was that economic modernization would cause a series of events, including the aging of the population, the adoption of nuclear families, and increased economic surpluses that would lead to the rise and development of modern social policies everywhere and with it a change in the nature of the state. This line of argumentation mainly emerged in U.S.-centered and comparative quantitative work (see the review in Skocpol and Amenta 1986), though it was developed to some extent as well in comparative and historical work (Rimlinger 1971). These arguments were also tested and found wanting by quantitative researchers, who employed them to explain variation across advanced capitalist democracies in the post–World War II period (see the review in Amenta 1993). But it was left to comparative and historical scholars to develop the historical implications of the arguments (e.g., Flora and Alber 1981; Kuhnle 1981; Orloff and Skocpol 1984) in order to appraise them.

In the last two decades, two main theoretical arguments dominated thinking about comparative social policy, one of them mainly developed by way of comparative and historical work and the other almost entirely so. What might be called "political organizational" arguments hold basically that variation in the mobilization of political groups has determined the fate of social policy. Of these arguments, the best-supported explanation has been the social democratic or power resources thesis, based in Marxian theory. According to it, countries with large, centralized labor movements connected to social democratic political parties that govern political life are the likeliest candidates for extensive redistributive social spending. Although this argument has been stated in various ways, and although several scholars, some comparative and historical and some quantitative, approached similar ideas at around the same time (see the reviews in Shalev 1983; Esping-Andersen and van Kersbergen 1992), this argument received perhaps its most influential treatment in John D. Stephens's (1979) *The Transition from Capitalism to Socialism* – a work that employed both comparative and historical and quantitative approaches. The so-called Piven–Cloward hypothesis (1977), an alternative political argument about the impact of social movements on social policy, has been influential in U.S.-centered and quantitative studies and was developed through work at the borderline of comparative and historical scholarship (see the review in Skocpol and Amenta 1986).

The other main line of argumentation was institutional or state-centered, based on the ideas of Weber and Tocqueville (Skocpol 1985; Thelen and Steinmo 1992; Thelen 1999) and was developed almost entirely from comparative and historical work. The earliest and most extensive version of these arguments appeared in Heclo's (1974) *Modern Social Politics* and in Orloff and Skocpol's (1984) "Why Not Equal Protection?" and was extended in Skocpol's (1992) *Protecting Soldiers and Mothers*. Alternative political institutional arguments have been offered, notably in Ellen Immergut's (1992) *Health Politics* and Sven Steinmo's (1993) *Taxation and Democracy*. To simplify again, these scholars suggest that the adoption and development of social spending policies are encouraged by centralized political institutions and states with greater bureaucratic and financial capacities and are frustrated by fragmented political institutions and incapable states. The argument also specifies the conditions under which state domestic bureaucrats will have influence over policy making and in which directions. These state- or polity-related arguments have been supplemented by other political institutional arguments about the influence of different forms of political party systems on social policy (Amenta 1998; see the review in Amenta et al. 2001). For the most part, this line of argumentation is structural and systemic and helps to explain long-run differences in policy formation and processes across countries.

The development of middle-range theoretical argumentation has gone beyond the creation of theoretical perspectives to the refinement of theoretical argumentation through comparative and historical empirical appraisals and the deepening of the concept of social policy. The social democratic hypothesis was importantly amended and transformed over time by comparative and historical work. From a focus on left-wing or social democratic parties in power, scholars have considered the role of the unified right-wing parties (Castles 1985), farmer–labor political coalitions (Esping-Andersen 1990), expert–labor alliances (Orloff 1993a), and Christian Democratic rule (van Kersbergen 1995). Similarly, the role of business organizations in influencing social policy has been treated in a more sophisticated manner (e.g., Swenson 1996; n.d.), seeking to sort out the conditions under which capitalists oppose or support some versions of social policy. Comparative and historical work has suggested that the role of capitalist support or secondary preferences for policy alternatives may be especially important in later phases of policy development, when policies have been in effect for a long time and have had the opportunity to restructure preferences (see the review in Pierson 2000a), as compared to the finding that capitalist organizations largely opposed social policy in its initial stages (Orloff and Parker 1990; Amenta 1998; Huber and Stephens 2001a). The left-party hypothesis has also been extended in work that addresses social policy in postcommunist Eastern Europe (Cook and Orenstein 1999; Rueschemeyer and Wolchik 1999).

Comparative and historical scholars have also gone on to build more theoretically synthetic or configurational arguments. Some of the more promising of these combine the structural strengths of institutional claims with those based on political identities and action (Skocpol 1992; Amenta 1998; Hicks 1999; Huber and Stephens 2001a; see the review in Amenta et al. 2001). These arguments rely on conjunctural or combinational causation (Ragin 1987; Katznelson 1997), in which different combinations of factors are hypothesized to bring about specific outcomes. Basically, political action is claimed to influence social policy development under some institutional conditions rather than others (Amenta 1998). Sometimes these arguments have been appraised by way of formal qualitative comparative techniques (Hicks, Misra, and Ng 1995; Amenta and Poulsen 1996; Amenta and Halfmann 2000).

These theoretical refinements have come largely through the appraisal of hypotheses in comparative and historical work. In applying empirical tests, there was something like a division of labor between social scientists employing comparative and historical approaches and those employing quantitative cross-national analyses. Social scientists who did historical work often addressed the enactment and expansion of the "big five" social insurance programs – workers' compensation, old-age insurance, unemployment insurance, health insurance, and family allowances (Flora and Heidenheimer 1981) and their growth. There have been numerous case studies and close comparisons of the policy trajectories and fates of a few carefully chosen, economically developed nations (e.g., Rimlinger 1971; Heclo 1974; Stephens 1979; Flora and Heidenheimer 1981; Orloff and Skocpol 1984; Castles 1985; Esping-Andersen 1985, 1990; Baldwin 1990; Immergut 1992; Orloff 1993a; Steinmo 1993; Pierson 1994; Rueschemeyer and Skocpol 1996; Amenta 1998). In these latter studies, economic circumstances were held relatively constant. Divergences in the adoption of policy innovations and in the form of social spending systems have been explained by a range of factors, especially aspects of the state and political institutions such as the form and nature of bureaucracies and party systems.

Comparative and historical studies could do many things that quantitative studies could not in testing hypotheses. For one thing, they can examine the historical processes by which individual programs were adopted. Notably, the explicit or implicit mechanisms of these hypotheses could be given close scrutiny. To take one significant example in the social policy area, it was possible to ascertain whether social democratic parties were responsible for the adoption of initial social programs or whether these programs came in the wake of the campaigns of organized workers for them. The preponderance of this evidence was that social democratic parties did not hold power until after the period of initial adoption – that various sorts of liberal and centrist parties were the ones that enacted these programs (see the review in Amenta 1993). This has led some scholars to develop different arguments about the origins of social policy (Hicks 1999). To take another example, it was possible to ascertain whether the social problems associated with economic modernization brought generic social policy responses, as the modernization theory suggests. In the period between the world wars, however, what constituted a politically important threat to the incomes of citizens varied, and countries took different approaches to protecting citizens from risks to income and employment and had not converged on specific policies to address these risks (Kuhnle 1981; Orloff and Skocpol 1984; Amenta 1998).

More generally, historical sequences could be examined to see whether developments were largely in line with theoretical claims (Rueschemeyer and Stephens 1997). This possibility was aided by the fact that the small-*N* studies often were of the "most similar systems" type (Przeworski and Teune 1970), in which cases were similar on a number of theoretically relevant dimensions. A number of studies (beginning with Orloff and Skocpol 1984) were undertaken to understand why the United States did not move forward in developing specific social programs in crucial historical periods in comparison to countries with similar economic, political, legal, and cultural backgrounds, such as Canada and Britain. Case studies were now often done much differently than the pioneering studies by Titmuss and Marshall. The new studies were implicitly comparative in that policy developments in one country were analyzed with the backdrop of the experience of other countries informing them. That said, hypotheses have not been appraised mainly through a process in which scholars examine whether one or more cases seem to fit or contradict theoretical arguments, as in the literature on democratization and authoritarianism (see Mahoney, this volume), but have typically been appraised across different country cases in various studies that employ paired comparisons and argumentation based on methods like Mill's.

Although Mill's methods and similar ones have cast doubt on the most general claims of some arguments, the main advantage of this type of work has been in appraising hypotheses regarding the mechanisms of theories. It has also been possible through this work to see whether theoretical arguments are consistent with the origins of social policy – which has been difficult for quantitative work to address given the data difficulties. From here, scholars have been able to develop middle-range theory further. And so, comparative and historical work in social policy has exploited the advantages inherent in these sorts of analyses.

Comparative and historical research has some well-known disadvantages in appraising hypotheses, though. It is difficult to give arguments a rigorous test across complete populations of cases, for given the steep knowledge and informational requirements of comparative and historical work it is the rare comparative and historical study that can address the population of the theoretically relevant cases (cf. Ertman 1997). There are often too many hypotheses chasing too few observations, making it difficult to rule out some plausible alternative hypotheses. And case selection is almost never random, with the potential to lead to biases. As I will argue, however, comparative and historical research in this area has worked in a synchronic way with quantitative work to enhance the value of each means of appraising and developing theoretical argumentation.

Conceptual Deepening, Big Questions, and New Research Agendas

Perhaps the greatest advantage of the small-*N* studies and comparatively informed case studies was that they allowed scholars to ask the big questions about the development of social policy, setting off a process in which theories were developed or appraised or both, with theoretical refinements and conceptual deepening in studies leading to new questions to ask. It was possible for comparative and historical researchers to ask why some countries were leaders and laggards in social policy and why some countries had entirely different types of social policies from other countries – questions that were difficult for quantitative researchers to approach given the need for extensive comparable data across populations or large samples. Comparative and historical scholars were also free to rethink what social policy meant and to deepen the concept by exploring its boundaries, dividing it into processes, or lumping social policy development into larger types. In working from but questioning the consensus on the conceptualization and operationalization of social policy and helping to deepening the concept, comparative and historical scholars have aided the progress of theory and research. In this process, comparative and historical scholars have devised new questions and have opened new research agendas, helping to develop and refine theoretical argumentation.

Comparative and historical researchers have asked the big questions about the development of social policy, and they have not been restricted to asking questions only for which there are sufficient data on a population of cases to answer the questions. These questions have included the following: Why did social policy take off when it did, and why did it become so prevalent? Why did some countries lead and why did some others fall behind in different phases of the development of social policy? Why did some states adopt distinctive forms of social policy? By situating the experiences of different countries against the group portraits, comparative and historical scholars brought to light historical anomalies and puzzles to solve. In addressing these questions, these scholars also addressed hypotheses based on larger theoretical arguments, as noted previously, and in their historical research also challenged the focus of social policy research.

One important way that scholars have developed this research agenda and advanced theory is through taking seriously the phases of development in social policy and the possibility that different aspects of social policy had different determinants. From this point of view, because they differ as processes, the adoption of social policy may be determined by different causes than its expansion or its retrenchment. The breaking down of social policy into different processes not only added to our empirical knowledge, but also helped scholars to form plausible research questions. One could examine why one country was a late or early adopter, consolidator, or completer of standard social policy. The comparative work of Orloff (1993a) and Orloff and Skocpol (1984) on the adoption of social policy comes to mind here. Even case studies were informed by this sort of thinking, however. In particular, much has been written about the lateness of the U.S. adoption of standard social policy and the incompleteness of its policy framework. These studies implicitly looked to European welfare states to attempt to explain what made U.S. policy developments so different – with "different" usually understood as backward in some respect (Skocpol 1992; Weir 1992; Quadagno 1994).

This conceptualization reflects back on theory in another way. By breaking social policy into different processes, it is expected that conditions and variables will have a different impact across them. Partisanship may have its greatest effect in the phases of adoption and consolidation, policy feedback has effects in the phases of expansion and retrenchment, and more systemic influences of the state likely have mediating effects all the way through. For instance, it has been argued with regard to the social democratic model that a period of social democratic rule after the establishment of social policy may have less impact than when states have become welfare states. A given term of social democratic rule in the 1990s will thus have a smaller effect than in the 1930s or 1940s, when social policies were being adopted or changed in form (see, e.g., Hicks 1999).

This case for theorizing different processes separately has been made most famously for the retrenchment of social policy. Pierson (1994) has argued convincingly that the retrenchment of social policy constitutes a different process than the adoption of social policy. The basic idea is that cutting back a social policy is a more difficult process than adopting one and depends crucially on processes set in motion by the nature of the policy in question. The argument has been deemed appropriate to explain social policy developments since the 1980s (see also Huber and Stephens 2001a; Swank 2001). By this time, most systems of social spending had been completed and expanded – had become "institutionalized" – and bids to cut them back were taken up in force by many political regimes. Although there were international pressures on all states in this period, it may be useful to consider retrenchment as a recurrent possibility throughout the history of social policy with different determinants when social policy has been established as compared to when it is at an early stage of institutionalization. However one approaches it, this conceptualization of policy suggests that theoretical arguments need to be developed to explain specific processes in social policy.

The conceptualization of different phases of social policy by comparative and historical researchers has had an important impact on social science theory. It has been argued that the initial configuration of social policy influences its future in an important way – that the structure of social policy has important impacts on the politics of social policy and thus on its future (Esping-Andersen 1990; Skocpol 1992; Pierson 1994). From this way of thinking, policies have feedback effects that influence later social politics. This goes back to the distinctions made by Theodore Lowi in the 1960s concerning the politics surrounding distributive and redistributive policies. Programs for poor people make poor programs in that the coalitions that can form behind them are likely to be weak. These arguments were conceptualized in ways that make it possible to construct and appraise theoretically coherent path-dependent arguments (see Abbott 1992; Griffin 1992; Mahoney 2000; Pierson 2000b). Notably, this sort of claim has been made and addressed in work ranging from explaining the origins of social policy (Skocpol 1992) and economic policy (Weir 1992) to work explaining efforts to retrench it (Pierson 1994).

Comparative and historical scholars have been able as well to appraise theoretical arguments by addressing social programs other than the main social programs that are usually summarized in quantitative work. Comparative and historical scholars have noted other state programs that addressed economic inequality or insecurity, and these scholars in turn have examined other state policy responses to basic societal risks to employment, income, and economic security (Weir, Orloff, and Skocpol 1988). These scholars have also recognized that social relations in the modern capitalist and democratic world produce a number of perils to income beyond the standard ones for which states have developed responses. And so, they have explored causal arguments about the determinants of social policy on new empirical terrain.

There has been no shortage of programs offered for analysis by comparative and historical researchers. Among the possibilities were veterans' benefits (Skocpol 1992), education (Heidenheimer 1981; Katznelson and Weir 1985; de Swaan 1988), taxation policy (Steinmo 1993; Howard 1997), housing policy (Pierson 1994; Castles 1998; Bonastia 2000), economic policy (Hall 1986; Weir 1992), drug policies (Benoit 2000), and work programs (Amenta 1998). In each instance, it was argued that the line of state action had important impacts on economic insecurity and inequality and that researchers ignored these policies at their peril.

Indeed, in addressing programs outside the standard boundaries, scholars often argued that an entire country case or set of cases should be reinterpreted. One of the more famous is Skocpol's (1992) claim that Civil War veterans' benefits were more generous than European old-age and disability programs, though restricted to groups other than industrial workers. Others (Steinmo 1993; Howard 1997; Myles and Pierson 1998) argued that taxation expenditures need to be addressed in order to understand social policy. U.S. social policy may not be backward, given the great efforts in this area, but merely different in form. To take my favorite example, I (Amenta 1998) show through the conventional modes of measurement of spending effort that work policies during the New Deal made the United States one of the world's leaders in the late 1930s. Sometimes, however, U.S. policy was seen to be even more backward than was previously thought, as in the case of economic policy (Weir 1992). Reinterpretations were also suggested by analyses of education as social policy (Heidenheimer 1981; Katznelson and Weir 1985) and explorations of home ownership as a possible functional substitute for social insurance programs (Castles 1998; Conley 2000). These studies place social policy in a different light, in addition to showing the distinctiveness of individual cases, and have promoted the asking of new questions.

Comparative and historical research has been important in the development of two other conceptualizations of social policy: ideal types that characterize policies as whole. Building on previous models of social policy, Esping-Andersen's (1990) "welfare state regimes" address social policy's influence on labor-market relations. According to this scheme, the "social democratic" regime, often seen in Nordic countries, is best for workers; it is based on the principles of universalism and "decommodification"; workers are freed from inequality due to the need to take what labor markets offer. Typically seen in continental Europe, the second-best "conservative corporatist" regime is also universal but does not smooth status distinctions between groups and upholds the traditional family, with a male breadwinner bringing home a family wage. The "liberal" welfare regime, the most inferior, is designed to make labor markets run smoothly at the expense of people; public social policy has a small presence and a large means-tested component, and is augmented by private control over areas elsewhere handled by states (see also Castles and Mitchell 1993; Huber and Stephens 2001a). Although these concepts have been contested as guides to historical research, they have been used to good advantage in research on retrenchment over the last two decades, as different configurations of social policy have been shown to pose different possibilities for retrenchment (Pierson 2000c).

New conceptualizations of social policy have also been provided by feminist scholars (reviews in Orloff 1996; Haney 2000; Pierson 2000a), many of whom work in a comparative and historical mode (Skocpol 1992; Pedersen 1993; Sainsbury 1996; O'Connor, Orloff, and Shaver 1999). The main responses have been to modify Esping-Andersen's types or to replace them with gender-based policy regimes. Orloff (1993b), for instance, adopts Esping-Andersen's types, but transforms them by adding new dimensions, including access to paid labor and the ability to establish an autonomous household. Indeed, decommodification may not be helpful for many women, and access to paid work for women, "commodifying" them, often promotes their financial autonomy from men (O'Connor 1993; Orloff 1993b). Thus, policy supporting equal participation in the paid labor force, as through antidiscrimination and comparable worth programs, tends to free women from potentially onerous reliance on men as breadwinners. By contrast, Sainsbury (1996) replaces Esping-Andersen's types with two based on unequal gender relations – the breadwinner and individual models – and employs a number of different dimensions to separate the types. All agree, though, that a focus on the relationship between policy and gender inequality raises difficult issues that differ from those concerning policy and economic inequality. State transfer programs that tend to alleviate economic inequality among households may have little influence on inequalities between sexes or may even reinforce them (see also Esping-Andersen 1999).

Impact on Other Types of Research and Methodology

Comparative and historical research has also had an impact on other types of causal research, including cross-national quantitative and historical work on social policy and work in other areas. Notably, comparative and historical work in social policy has helped to generate theoretical arguments to be tested on larger data sets, just as cross-national quantitative work has provided hypotheses for comparative and historical appraisal. The comparative and historical work has also had an impact on strictly historical work, as historians are using the results of this literature to conceptualize, frame, justify, and develop their own projects. Comparative and historical work has also brought methodological contributions.

Comparative quantitative studies typically addressed the amount of spending on social policy in relation to a country's income or national product – to show how much effort was being put into state initiatives against inequality or insecurity – using the country (or country-year) as the unit of analysis. To summarize ruthlessly, social scientists began with quantitative, cross-sectional studies of all the countries of the post–World War II world (e.g., Cutright 1965; Wilensky 1975) and typically found that socioeconomic "modernization," especially industrialization and the aging of the population, underlay social spending differences. U.S. states, with their large populations and extensive socioeconomic variation, were also used as quantitative laboratories to test these propositions and others with respect to policy innovation and spending (e.g., Dye 1966; Sharkansky and Hofferbert 1969). Soon, however, quantitative scholars began focusing on the postwar experiences of capitalist democracies, which provided theoretical rather than proper-name scope conditions for causal claims; scholars argued that wealthy capitalist democracies would have determinants of social policy that differed from those of other sorts of polities. The most widely supported argument was a version of the social democratic argument. These studies, especially those that pooled cross-sectional and time series data, provided a sufficient number of observations to test hypotheses against one another, and data from the 1960s on were relatively complete in coverage (see the discussion in Amenta 1993).

Quantitative analyses of postwar capitalist democracies have done well to attempt to appraise some aspects of the institutional arguments often seen in the small-*N* historical studies. An influential article by Huber, Ragin, and Stephens (1993) addresses the effects of political or constitutional structures that hinder slim electoral majorities from enacting policy and that abet obstructionism from small groups – taking an insight from institutional theory and attempting to merge it with argumentation concerning the impact of social democratic and Christian Democratic political parties. In my own quantitative collaborations on American policy (e.g., Amenta and Poulsen 1996; Cauthen and Amenta 1996; Amenta and Halfmann 2000), I address hard-to-operationalize statist arguments as well as versions of political ones in examining outcomes deemed important from historical investigations.

This line of research, however, suffered from limitations even in settling the debates about the expansion of social policy in these types of polities. One limitation based on data deficits was that it was difficult to appraise some theories. Given their structural and sometimes more complicated nature, the statist and institutional theories were more difficult to assess than the political ones. Part of the problem is that the relevant data were not readily available, as no international organization was collecting them. Even among the political arguments, it was easier to appraise the ones based on the institutional politics of elections, cabinet formation, and labor movements rather than the information-poor activity of social movements. Even in studies that used the same indicators, researchers debated their meaning, as Hicks and Mishra (1993) and Huber et al. (1993) interpreted economic indicators differently from each other, as well as differently from modernization theorists. More important limitations rested on the type of research and the empirical setting to which it was confined. Very few of these countries developed new and large social spending programs since 1960. Thus this type of research has been unable to address critical phenomena such as the timing and content of innovations in public spending.

There were some important quantitative comparative studies of the early years of social programs (e.g., Collier and Messick 1975; Schneider 1982; Hage, Hanneman, and Gargon 1989) and quantitative work within countries (Wright 1974; Skocpol et al. 1993; Steinmetz 1993; Cauthen and Amenta 1996), but given the less than comprehensive nature of the case coverage and data coverage of hypotheses, work like this was far from definitive. As a result of comparative and historical work, however, quantitative studies have been executed with increasing and considerable historical sophistication. Close attention is paid to time periods. A particularly powerful example of this is Alexander Hicks's *Social Democracy and Welfare Capitalism* (1999), in which comparative quantitative analyses, as well as Boolean qualitative comparative analyses, are employed on different periods of welfare state development. Scholars have done much better in matching theoretical concepts to historically appropriate indicators, especially in what I call "synthetic modes of analysis."

Comparative and historical researchers have made important methodological contributions, notably including true syntheses of quantitative and comparative and historical analyses. By this, I mean something different from King, Keohane, and Verba's (1994) injunction to use different data sets to test the same lines of argument (see also Ragin 1987, pp. 82–4). Studies have been able to address large questions about differences in timing or trajectories or outcomes in social policy by examining a few cases or one case in a comparative context. In these analyses, it is possible to develop and tentatively appraise relatively complex arguments, sometimes involving multiple and conjunctural causation (Ragin 1987), sometimes involving mechanisms of process. Standard quantitative techniques have difficulty in assessing these more complex arguments, much as standard comparative and historical work can provide only rudimentary tests of hypotheses. All the same, some comparative and historical studies have gone on to appraise as far as possible these complex arguments on relevant cross-national data sets or data sets on subunits within a country. By juxtaposing the results of the one to the other, one can then modify the arguments. In social science, most scholars are comfortable with one style of research, and so the willingness and ability of individual scholars in this literature to combine methodological approaches, sometimes in a single work, is remarkable.

The pioneering synthetic work was John Stephens's (1979) *The Transition from Capitalism to Socialism*, in which comparative quantitative studies were augmented with comparative and historical analyses of a few countries. John Myles's (1984/1989) *Old Age in the Welfare State* also has something of this quality. Other examples come from scholars who employ different techniques on the same subject matter across different works (Pampel and Williamson 1989; Skocpol 1992; Skocpol et al. 1993; Williamson and Pampel 1993). In *Bold Relief* (1998), for instance, I appraise a conjunctural institutional politics theory by way of a historical analysis of the United States during the 1930s and 1940s and in comparison with Britain. I also examine historical trajectories in policy across four states and appraise the argument on state-level data sets, whose indicators of social policy are informed by the historical work. In related projects I employ Boolean qualitative comparative analyses, which can address the configurations in the institutional and political arguments (Amenta and Poulsen 1996; Amenta and Halfmann 2000). Evelyne Huber and John Stephens return to the synthetic mode of analysis in their *Development and Crisis of the Welfare State* (2001a), which addresses the rise of welfare states as well as efforts at retrenchment over the last decades. They join pooled time series and cross-sectional regression analyses with detailed case histories of different types of highly developed welfare states in examining the development of social policy over long periods. The latter are used in order to get around the short-term biases in regression analyses and to closely examine critical periods of policy development.

The comparative and historical work on social policy inspired other work that employed other formal qualitative and medium-*N* methodologies, like sequence analyses and Boolean qualitative comparative analysis (Abbott and DeViney 1992; Ragin 1994; Hicks et al. 1995). And although the use of methodological techniques like qualitative comparative analysis and sequence analyses does not in itself make for a comparative and historical study, scholars have been able to explore these analyses on social policy cases because of comparative and historical work. As I suggest later, this sort of work is possible because of a consensus on what is to be explained and the ease with which outcomes and arguments can be operationalized into categorical or sequence variables. And as I noted previously, in some instances these investigations have been influenced by comparative and historical work, even if these scholars were not working in a strictly synthetic way.

Comparative and historical analyses of social policy have also had an impact on standard historiography and one-country studies. To take U.S. examples again, historiography on social policy now frequently locates historical questions about the development of social policy by way of findings and conceptualizations from comparative and historical work. This change can be seen, for instance, by comparing Edward Berkowitz and Kim McQuaid's (1980) *Creating the Welfare State* with its second edition (1988) or with Berkowitz's (1991) *America's Welfare State*. Similarly, U.S.-centered historical classics on social policy, such as Frances Fox Piven and Richard A. Cloward's (1971/1993) *Regulating the Poor*, have been revised by way of reflection on this literature. Recent historical studies of U.S. taxation (Brownlee 1997; Zelizer 1999), for instance, have been influenced by the comparative and historical literature on the welfare state. As a result of this cross-fertilization, it has become difficult to separate out the impact of comparative historical work on this new historiography, as it now often resembles comparative and historical work in its concern to place historical developments in a comparative context in order to explain them.

Since the 1970s we have learned much about social policy through comparative and historical work. In 1975, Harold Wilensky could examine a cross section of nations and argue that processes of industrialization drove social spending. Today no quantitative study would argue that an analysis of a snapshot of a large number of countries could appraise complex theoretical arguments. In the meantime, because of comparative and historical work, there have been many new empirical findings, new theoretical perspectives, empirical appraisals across different cases and time periods, the deepening of the concept of social policy through both aggregation and disaggregation, theoretical refinements due to empirical appraisals and conceptual deepening, and a research agenda that has moved from question to question. What accounts for this progress and greatly increased sophistication?

Why Comparative and Historical Research in Social Policy Was So Productive

To address this question, I place the comparative and historical research on social policy of the 1980s and early 1990s in comparative and historical perspective. That is, I juxtapose it with the research programs that went before and with some current lines of research, and I compare comparative and historical work on social policy with comparative and historical work in related areas. Another political sociology area that I work in – social movements – has received as much attention if not more but has not, I would submit, advanced as far in either comparative and historical or quantitative work. I would also venture to say that the area of social policy has progressed further, and progressed further through comparative and historical work, than the other areas reviewed in this volume. My discussion is speculative, as I have not reviewed in detail the other literatures, and is mainly an exercise in theory building, but for ease of presentation I will state the points as baldly as possible.

The literature on social policy has advanced as far as it has partly because there was relative agreement on what was to be explained, while there was disagreement over the possible explanations. Although the standard definition of social policy was more like an anchor than a fixed standpoint, this sort of consensus about what was to be explained turned everyone's attention in a similar direction. At the same time, scholars tended to disagree about the potential explanations. This situation promotes the testing of hypotheses and the development of middle-range social science theory in the first instance because it gives researchers with attachments to different theoretical perspectives something with which to appraise their arguments. It also provides ways of sharpening arguments as scholars assess how far they go to explain something of agreed-upon importance and to think about why arguments are limited. Having scholars with allegiances to different theoretical arguments ensures a lively debate over the degree and nature of the empirical support. Having an agreement on what is to be explained

Table 3.2. *Research Programs According to Agreement and Disagreement on What Is to Be Explained and the Explanation*

		Explanation	
		Disagreement	Agreement
To Be Explained	Agreement	*Recurrent Appraisals of Alternative Hypotheses*: Social Policy	*Reiterated Hypothesis Testing*:
	Disagreement	*Conceptual Proliferation*:	*Appraisals of Same Hypotheses on New Outcomes*: Social Movement

also helps scholars to locate empirical anomalies and to seek explanations for them.

The different possibilities regarding agreement and disagreement on what is to be explained and potential explanations are outlined in Table 3.2. At the upper left of the table is the situation in which scholars of social policy and the welfare state found themselves during the 1980s and early 1990s. There was relatively high agreement on what was to be explained – the adoption and expansion of major social programs – but relative disagreement among theoretical perspectives. Socioeconomic modernization theories were appraised alongside various Marxian political theories and state-centered or institutional theories. This situation did not preclude others with wholly different perspectives from trying their hand as well. It helped, too, that most of the theoretical arguments made were of the middle-range sort. This situation results in what I am calling "recurrent appraisals of alternative hypotheses." Scholars would be able to find different research sites to appraise and develop arguments. This entertaining of more than one argument may have aided the process by which different scholars moved away from relatively one-sided theoretical arguments – such as strictly social democratic or statist arguments – to more hybrid ones (cf. Orloff and Skocpol 1984 and Skocpol 1992; cf. Stephens 1979 and Huber et al. 1993).

In the area of social movements, by contrast, there is relatively little agreement on what is to be explained, with more substantial agreement on the theoretical perspectives. "Social movement" has no one meaning that scholars rally around. It has been held to refer to everything from a desire in public opinion for change to the creation of specific organizations to redress inequalities among the relatively powerless to the noninstitutional political action engaged in by such groups. Perhaps for this reason, scholars have addressed a wide variety of social movement outcomes, including the timing of the emergence of social movements, resources gained by them, who participates, the numbers of participants, their techniques of protest, the potential results of movements, and so on (reviewed in McAdam, McCarthy, and Zald 1988). Even if one were to say that the emergence of movements is the most important question, because of disagreements in the definition of social movements this is difficult to assess. There is also more or less agreement on the theoretical program advanced by Doug McAdam, John D. McCarthy, and Mayer Zald (1996) that social movement phenomena can be understood and explained by processes of framing, mobilization structures, and political opportunities. Again, the match is not perfect, but in general the situation is one in which the same theoretical arguments are applied to different sets of outcomes to see whether there is an empirical fit. Most of the work in this area is by way of case studies of individual movements or organizations, but there is some comparative and historical work. It is possible to create different sorts of balance sheets here, with the results for a set of hypotheses juxtaposed to different outcomes. Because of the various conceptual and data problems, however, such balance sheets would be more difficult to construct.

A second reason for the progress in social policy was the nature of the consensus on what was to be explained. It was useful in ways that went beyond the advantages of agreement. Social policy was conceptualized in ways that were easy to operationalize but far from simplistic. It could sometimes be studied in an all-or-nothing way, as in the timing of adoption of programs, which is easier to pinpoint than the emergence of a social movement. But there were more variegated ways to bring it down to earth it as well. Scholars focused on a specific set of state activities and programs, with some more important than others given their likely impact on insecurity and inequality. It was deemed important to analyze some specific programs, and it was possible to add up social policy in meaningful ways. The programs were relatively few, making it possible to develop research projects examining them all. But each of the programs had enough going for it so that one could write an entire historical monograph on a specific program – not to mention a quantitative research paper. Having basic agreement on an operationalization of social policy also made it clear when and where one was disagreeing with it – and it was possible to learn from that as well. The concept was sometimes disaggregated or aggregated in other useful ways, as when different processes of social policy or larger ideal types of social policy were examined. I believe that the advantages are more epistemological than ontological – that is, due to the way that the phenomena have been understood than with the nature of the phenomena themselves (cf. Hall, this volume).

Third, a good deal of relevant information about social policy was available. It was not that reams of new data were being collected by researchers – almost all the data were historical in the sense of being gleaned from the data-generating projects of organizations, mainly states and intergovernmental organizations. Abundant relevant historical documents were available, as one would expect with the object of the analysis being state activity, and they probably were more informative than those used in the classic literature on state formation given the great increases in bureaucratization of states in the twentieth century. This wealth of information eased the writing of the high-quality historiography and other secondary sources on which comparative and historical work greatly relies. The ready availability of governmental records also opened the way for social scientists to do their own targeted archival work as needed, without extensive costs. And the data were useful for theoretical purposes as well, because the units of observation were not merely a convenience, an aggregation of activity and relationships within the borders of a given country, but lines of action taken by the state, indicating relationships between the state and citizens. The ability of governments to keep good records and quantitative data matters much, and that may be attested to by the relative lack of comprehensive comparative research on poorer countries (for exceptions, see Pampel and Williamson 1989; review in Skocpol and Amenta 1986).

There were special benefits as well to the variability in the availability in forms of data. Hard and systematic data suitable for quantitative studies existed only for the periods of expansion and retrenchment, while less complete information of this sort was available for the periods of adoption, consolidation, and completion. This led to a division of labor of sorts, as Table 3.3 suggests. Quantitative comparative researchers mainly analyzed data from the 1960s and beyond, and comparative and historical researchers took charge of the first half of the century. The comparative and historical researchers tended to work where the historical perspective had the greatest room to maneuver, and they were more likely to leave more recent developments to those working with quantitative techniques. The relative deficiency of hard data in the earlier period probably prevented the quantitative researchers from preempting the possibilities of historical research. There was a great deal of interesting work as well, however, on the off-diagonal situations noted in Table 3.3, and these studies were often sites of innovation and spurs to analysis of the other variety. Mary Ruggie

Table 3.3. *Research in Social Policy According to Time Period and Methodology*

		Methodology	
		Comparative/Historical	Quantitative/Formal Qualitative
Time Period	Pre–Second World War	*Historical Perspective Expanded*: Most comparative and historical research	*Hard Data Scarce*: Collier and Messick 1975; Schneider 1982; Abbott and DeViney 1992; Hicks et al. 1995; Cauthen and Amenta 1996
	Post-1950	*Historical Perspective Diminished*: Ruggie 1984; Hall 1986; Pierson 1994; O'Connor et al. 1999	*Hard Data Abundant*: Most comparative quantitative work

(1984), for instance, addressed the impact of social policy on gender relations, and Paul Pierson (1994) opened a new line of thinking and research on retrenchment, providing hypotheses addressed later by quantitative researchers. The quantitative article by Collier and Messick (1975) cast great doubt on the modernization thesis with respect to the adoption of social policy and spurred comparative and historical work on this question.

The fourth reason was the open-minded methodological outlook of many of the prominent researchers in the area. The social scientists studying social policy were well versed in debates over comparative and historical methods, and few took a hard line in favor of one over another. Although scholars had preferences for one or another line of work, they rarely denigrated the work of others. Few quantitative researchers derided the work of comparative and historical researchers as soft or lacking in rigor. Few comparative and historical researchers saw the work of the quantitative scholars as simplistic and lacking in depth and validity. The tone was set early on, with Gaston Rimlinger (1971) employing the gold standard of quantitative studies, the measure of social spending "effort," to situate his path-breaking comparative and historical investigations. The willingness and ability of researchers to work in different modes was key. John Stephens, Evelyne Huber, Theda Skocpol, and Gøsta Esping-Andersen were prominent among those scholars proficient in one type of methodology but willing or driven sometimes to employ others. Attempting studies in different modes was not the typical response of most individual scholars in this area, but the research of the one set of scholars was required

Table 3.4. *Comparative and Historical Research Programs According to Presence of Quantitative Work and Its Engagement with Comparative and Historical Research*

		Presence of Quantitative Work	
		Strong	Weak
Engagement with Comparative and Historical Work	Strong	*Synergy*: Social Policy and Welfare State Literature	*Diminished Synergy*: Literature on Revolutions
	Weak	*Synergy Failure*: NA	*Synergy Impossible*: Social Movement Literature

reading for the other. These scholars understood that different approaches had advantages and disadvantages, and instead of accenting the disadvantages in each, scholars exploited the advantages in each to allow greater progress than could be achieved by one or another approach.

Conceptual agreement on social policy, the ability to operationalize it in sophisticated ways, the availability of different types of data to do so, and the willingness of scholars to address both types of analysis – all of this generated a synergy between comparative and historical and comparative quantitative work. The favorable situation faced by those working in social policy is depicted in the upper left part of Table 3.4, which arrays the presence of quantitative work with its engagement with comparative and historical work. Here there was a strong presence of quantitative work and a strong engagement with comparative and historical research. The result is that the advantages of each type of research benefited the other in ways that led to greater achievements than would have been possible on their own.

Other areas of research do not have the same sort of connection between comparative and historical and quantitative work. In the category at the bottom right, where there is little quantitative comparative work and little connection between it and comparative and historical work, synergy of this sort is not possible. I place the recent academic literature on social movements here (see the reviews in McAdam et al. 1988; Guigni 1998). In this instance, the relative lack of quantitative comparative work is due in part to lack of agreement among researchers in this area about what is important to explain. Also, there are no extensive data, perhaps because of the relatively fleeting nature of movement organizations and activity, available to operationalize the most basic understandings of social movements across countries. There have been surveys tapping self-reported participation in different sorts of political action across some countries for a few time periods (Dalton 1988), but these measures do not seem likely to win consensus status among scholars as indicators for the concept of social mobilization. Because of conceptual disagreements and lack of data, no one can say compellingly whether social movements are more present in some countries rather than others or whether they are becoming more important in individual countries over time. For the same reason, the comparative and historical literature is limited – mainly to broad comparisons across countries of the size and impact of individual social movements during the postwar period (e.g., Kitschelt 1986; Kriesi et al. 1995; Banaszak 1996).

In other research areas, it seems possible for there to be some synergy between the different types of work, but with little potential or unrealized potential. Perhaps needless to say, where there is little quantitative comparative work or few prospects for it, there is little chance for this synergy. In the case of revolutions, there is some quantitative work that largely corresponds to the main conceptualizations of revolutions in the literature (see Goldstone, this volume). Yet the possibilities for synergy in this area are diminished, perhaps in part by the standard conceptualization of revolutions as all-or-nothing outcomes or events. The more extensive quantitative comparative literature on collective violence, for which data are available, does not address the same subject. It seems possible that in some areas there may be both quantitative and comparative and historical work, but where researchers miss a chance for synergy by conceptualizing the object of analysis much differently or by paying little attention to one another.

In studying the causes of social policy, scholars doing comparative and historical work have embraced to an unusual degree quantitative, cross-national research as well as the work of historians. The attention has been reciprocated, and research on social policy has been the better for it. New lines of research contesting the old consensus on what was worth explaining in social policy have already produced results. It is not as if there were no room for improvement here, though, as the new ways of conceptualizing social policy have brought more questions than answers. I close with some reflections on this emerging research agenda and suggestions for contributions that comparative and historical research may make. As these lines of research develop, I hope that scholars can reflect back on what worked in the past and learn from it.

Conclusion

One of the reasons that comparative and historical work in social policy has made such dramatic progress is that there was a useful consensus on the understanding of social policy. This consensus has begun to shift in the last decade, leading to important insights and empirical findings and opening up new subjects for study, as scholars have largely answered some questions based on the old consensus and have moved on. But it is worth reflecting back on what has worked in the past, conceptually speaking, to see how new understandings of social policy can be employed or altered to spur further progress.

One way this might be done further is through examining policies and programs outside the usual understanding of social policy. There has been an abundance of comparative and historical work showing that programs other than the standard ones have impacts on poverty or inequality of different sorts, and this research has shed new light on social policies and theoretical claims about them. This work seems well worth pursuing in ways that deepen further the concept of social policy and provide additional opportunities to appraise and refine theory. Some comparative and historical studies (Steinmo 1993; Howard 1997), for instance, make an excellent case for the need to take into account tax expenditures for social purposes in studies of social policy, as these tax breaks are often functional substitutes for spending programs. Yet some work needs to be done to make the idea applicable in other research settings in order to make useful comparisons among tax expenditure policies. Some tax expenditures are doubtfully redistributive, and these should be treated differently from social policy, just as many governmental expenditures have not been considered to be part of social policy. The issue of home ownership has important redistributive consequences, but has been neglected in part because it is difficult to operationalize comparatively. Here some thinking is needed to separate out what is due explicitly to state policy and how to ascertain this. From here, it should be possible to indicate how much these policies matter as compared to the standard transfer programs and services on issues such as the reduction of poverty. This would help to maximize the benefits opened by comparative and historical work on these additional aspects of policy.

The regime conceptualization was developed in work with a comparative and historical sensibility, but might be further followed up in the manner that occurred regarding the adoption of social policy. Comparative historical research can help here to ascertain when different cases sorted themselves out in these directions, as well as to appraise theoretical thinking as to why this happened. However, there has not been as much research on the initial development of the types of welfare states. Esping-Andersen's (1990) hypotheses about the development of the types have not been closely appraised by his own or other research. Given their more recent origins, feminist analyses of the state have had a greater focus on recent developments. It would also be worthwhile to devise comparative and historical research projects to address the question of the long-run development of different gender-based types of social policy.

Social policy regime types have advanced research in social policy but might be made more flexible as previous understandings of social policy. One way to increase the flexibility and usability of the concepts would be to modify the two main types – Esping-Andersen's regimes based on freeing workers from markets and feminist models concerned with the impact of state policy on gender equality. The degree to which states provide equal access to paid labor and ease the possibility of establishing autonomous households, as suggested by Orloff (1993b), and O'Connor (1993), seem like the most fruitful lines for further conceptual development. These dimensions might be employed to build conceptual categories that fall somewhere between policy regimes and individual programs. This sort of conceptualization would be useful for the development of theoretical argumentation that could be appraised by research of the comparative and historical kind as well as the quantitative and formal qualitative sorts.

Regime models like Esping-Andersen's have been helpful in explaining cross-national differences in retrenchment efforts (Pierson 2000c; Huber and Stephens 2001b), and these arguments have begun with the premise that the structure of social policy will influence the potential of any sort of politics. More work along these lines seems promising, with scholars paying careful attention to constructing arguments that have clear and appraisable implications across countries and policies. This is an area where comparative and historical scholars might make theoretical impacts, specifying in comparably appraisable ways the "feedback" arguments that have become so much a part of this literature and employing comparative and historical techniques to assess these arguments.

It may be useful to think of states holistically in different ways, however. Scholars studying the state have focused almost exclusively on social policy. It has been assumed that as social policy dominates and states come more to resemble welfare states, the punishing and disciplining aspects of states will diminish. This is not necessarily true, however. Recent U.S. experience has indicated that increased social spending has gone along not only with reduced military spending, but also with increased efforts toward imprisonment. State conceptualizations and theories may need to address the character of entire states, not merely the aspects of the state that provide services and income protection from risks. Comparative and historical research on social policy is often based on theories of the state and politics and might link up with the literature on state-building by addressing states as such.

I think we should strive to recognize the strengths of different types of research, as scholars in this area have done. If everyone were to take this sort of approach, my task here – sorting out the contributions of comparative and historical research to a given subfield of study – would be unnecessary and probably impossible. Because scholars already work together so well in this field, fortunately the exercise is difficult.

References

Abbott, Andrew. 1992. "From Causes to Events: Notes on Narrative Positivism." *Sociological Methods and Research* 20: 428–55.

Abbott, Andrew and Stanley DeViney. 1992. "The Welfare State as Transnational Event: Evidence from Sequences of Policy Adoption." *Social Science History* 16: 245–74.

Amenta, Edwin. 1993. "The State of the Art in Welfare State Research on Social Spending Efforts in Capitalist Democracies Since 1960." *American Journal of Sociology* 99: 750–63.

1998. *Bold Relief: Institutional Politics and the Origins of Modern American Social Policy*. Princeton, NJ: Princeton University Press.

Amenta, Edwin, Chris Bonastia, and Neal Caren. 2001. "U.S. Social Policy in Comparative and Historical Perspective: Concepts, Images, Arguments, and Research Strategies." *Annual Review of Sociology* 27: 213–34.

Amenta, Edwin and Drew Halfmann. 2000. "Wage Wars: Institutional Politics, the WPA, and the Struggle for U.S. Social Policy." *American Sociological Review* 64: 506–28.

Amenta, Edwin and Jane D. Poulsen. 1996. "Social Politics in Context: The Institutional Politics Theory and Social Spending at the End of the New Deal." *Social Forces* 75: 33–60.

Baldwin, Peter. 1990. *The Politics of Social Solidarity: Class Bases of the European Welfare State 1875–1975*. Cambridge: Cambridge University Press.

Banaszak, Lee Ann. 1996. *Why Movements Succeed or Fail: Opportunity, Culture, and the Struggle for Woman Suffrage*. Princeton, NJ: Princeton University Press.

Benoit, Ellen. 2000. "Controlling Drugs in the Welfare State: American Policy in Comparative, Historical Perspective." Ph.D. dissertation, Department of Sociology, New York University.

Berkowitz, Edward. 1991. *America's Welfare State: From Roosevelt to Reagan*. Baltimore, MD: Johns Hopkins University Press.

Berkowitz, Edward and Kim McQuaid. 1988 [1980]. *Creating the Welfare State: The Political Economy of Twentieth-Century Reform*. Lawrence: University Press of Kansas.

Bonastia, Christopher. 2000. "Why Did Affirmative Action in Housing Fail During the Nixon Era?: Exploring the 'Institutional Homes' of Social Policies." *Social Problems* 47: 523–42.

Brownlee, W. Elliot, ed. 1997. *Funding the Modern American State, 1941–1995: The Rise and Fall of the Era of Easy Finance.* Washington, DC: Woodrow Wilson Center Press and New York: Cambridge University Press.

Castles, Francis G. 1985. *The Working Class and Welfare: Reflections on the Political Development of the Welfare State in Australia and New Zealand.* Sydney and London: Allen & Unwin.

1998. "The Really Big Trade-off: Home Ownership and the Welfare State in the New World and the Old." *Acta Politica* 33: 5–19.

Castles, Francis G. and Deborah Mitchell. 1993. "Worlds of Welfare and Families of Nations." Pp. 93–128 in *Families of Nations: Patterns of Public Policy in Western Democracies*, edited by Francis G. Castles. Aldershot, U.K.: Dartmouth.

Cauthen, Nancy K. and Edwin Amenta. 1996. "Not for Widows Only: Institutional Politics and the Formative Years of Aid to Dependent Children." *American Sociological Review* 61: 427–48.

Collier, David and Richard Messick. 1975. "Prerequisites versus Diffusion: Testing Alternative Explanations of Social Security Adoption." *American Political Science Review* 69: 1299–1315.

Cook, Linda J. and Mitchell Orenstein. 1999. "The Return of the Left and Its Impact on the Welfare State in Russia, Poland, and Hungary." Pp. 47–108 in *Left Parties and Social Policy in Post-Communist Europe*, edited by Linda J. Cook, Mitchell Orenstein, and Marilyn Rueschemeyer. Boulder, CO: Westview.

Conley, Dalton. 2000. *Home Ownership, the Welfare State and Cross-National Poverty Comparisons. Conference on Saving, Intergenerational Transfers, and the Distribution of Wealth.* Presented at the Jerome Levy Economics Institute of Bard College, Annandale-on-Hudson, NY.

Cutright, Phillips. 1965. "Political Structure, Economic Development, and National Social Security Programs." *American Journal of Sociology* 70: 537–50.

Dalton, Russell. 1988. *Citizen Politics in Western Democracies: Public Opinion and Political Parties in the United States, Great Britain, West Germany, and France.* Chatham, NJ: Chatham House.

de Swaan, Abram. 1988. *In Care of the State: Health Care, Education and Welfare in Europe and the USA in the Modern Era.* New York: Oxford University Press.

Dye, Thomas R. 1966. *Politics, Economics, and the Public: Policy Outcomes in the American States.* Chicago: Rand McNally.

Ertman, Thomas. 1997. *Birth of the Leviathan: Building States and Regimes in Medieval and Early Modern Europe.* New York: Cambridge University Press.

Esping-Andersen, Gøsta. 1985. *Politics Against Markets: The Social Democratic Road to Power.* Princeton, NJ: Princeton University Press.

1990. *The Three Worlds of Welfare Capitalism.* Princeton, NJ: Princeton University Press.

1999. *The Social Foundations of Postindustrial Economies.* New York: Oxford University Press.

Esping-Andersen, Gøsta and Kees van Kersbergen. 1992. "Contemporary Research on Social Democracy." *Annual Review of Sociology* 18: 187–208.

Flora, Peter, ed. 1986. *Growth to Limits: The Western European Welfare States since World War II.* New York: Aldine de Gruyter.

Flora, Peter and Jens Alber. 1981. "Modernization, Democratization and the Development of Welfare States in Western Europe." Pp. 37–80 in *The Development of Welfare States in Europe and America*, edited by P. Flora and A. Heidenheimer. New Brunswick, NJ: Transaction Books.

Flora, Peter, Jens Alber, Richard Eichenberg, Jürgen Kohl, Franz Kraus, Winfried Pfenning, and Kurt Seebohm. 1983. *State, Economy, and Society in Western Europe 1815–1975: The Growth of Mass Democracies and Welfare States.* Chicago: St. James.

Flora, Peter and Arnold J. Heidenheimer, eds. 1981. *The Development of Welfare States in Europe and America.* New Brunswick, NJ: Transaction Books.

Giugni, Marco G. 1998. "Was It Worth the Effort? The Outcomes and Consequences of Social Movements." *Annual Review of Sociology* 24: 371–93.

Griffin, Larry. 1992. "Temporality, Events, and Explanation in Historical Sociology: An Introduction." *Sociological Methods and Research* 20: 403–27.

Hage, Jerald, Robert Hanneman, and Edward Gargon. 1989. *State Responsiveness and State Activism.* London: Unwin Hyman.

Hall, Peter A. 1986. *Governing the Economy: The Politics of State Intervention in Britain and France.* New York: Oxford University Press.

Haney, Lynne. 2000. "Feminist State Theory: Comparing Gender Regimes Across Apparatuses." *Annual Review of Sociology* 26: 641–66.

Heclo, Hugh. 1974. *Modern Social Politics in Britain and Sweden: From Relief to Income Maintenance.* New Haven, CT: Yale University Press.

Heidenheimer, Arnold J. 1981. "Education and Social Security Entitlements in Europe and America." Pp. 269–305 in *The Development of Welfare States in Europe and America*, edited by Peter Flora and Arnold J. Heidenheimer. New Brunswick, NJ: Transaction Books.

Hicks, Alexander. 1999. *Social Democracy and Welfare Capitalism: A Century of Income Security Politics.* Ithaca, NY: Cornell University Press.

Hicks, Alexander and Joya Misra. 1993. "Political Resources and the Growth of Welfare in Affluent Capitalist Democracies, 1960–1982." *American Journal of Sociology* 99: 668–710.

Hicks, Alexander, Joya Misra, and Tang Nah Ng. 1995. "The Programmatic Emergence of the Social Security State." *American Sociological Review* 60: 329–49.

Howard, Christopher. 1997. *The Hidden Welfare State: Tax Expenditures and Social Policy in the United States.* Princeton, NJ: Princeton University Press.

Huber, Evelyne, Charles Ragin, and John D. Stephens. 1993. "Social Democracy, Christian Democracy, Constitutional Structure, and the Welfare State." *American Journal of Sociology* 99: 711–49.

Huber, Evelyne and John D. Stephens. 2001a. *Development and Crisis of the Welfare State: Parties and Policies in Global Markets.* Chicago: University of Chicago Press.

2001b. "Welfare State and Production Regimes in the Era of Retrenchment." Pp. 107–45 in *The New Politics of the Welfare State*, edited by Paul Pierson. New York: Oxford University Press.

Immergut, Ellen M. 1992. *Health Politics: Interests and Institutions in Western Europe.* Cambridge: Cambridge University Press.

Katz, Michael. 1986. *In the Shadow of the Poorhouse: A Social History of Welfare in America.* New York: Basic Books.

Katznelson, Ira. 1997. "Structure and Configuration in Comparative Politics." Pp. 81–112 in *Comparative Politics: Rationality, Culture, and Structure*, edited by Mark Irving Lichbach and Alan S. Zuckerman. New York: Cambridge University Press.

Katznelson, Ira and Bruce Pietrykowski. 1991. "Rebuilding the American State: Evidence from the 1940s." *Studies in American Political Development* 5: 301–99.

Katznelson, Ira and Margaret Weir. 1985. *Schooling for All: Class, Race, and the Decline of the Democratic Ideal.* New York: Basic Books.

King, Gary, Robert O. Keohane, and Sidney Verba. 1994. *Designing Social Inquiry: Scientific Inference in Qualitative Research.* Princeton, NJ: Princeton University Press.

Kitschelt, Herbert P. 1986. "Political Opportunity Structures and Political Protest: Anti-Nuclear Movements in Four Democracies." *British Journal of Political Science* 16: 57–85.

Kriesi, Hanspeter, Ruud Koopmans, Jan Willem Duyvendak, and Marco G. Giugni. 1995. *New Social Movements in Western Europe: A Comparative Analysis.* Minneapolis: University of Minnesota Press.

Kuhnle, Stein. 1981. "The Growth of Social Insurance Programs in Scandinavia: Outside Influences and Internal Forces." Pp. 269–305 in *The Development of Welfare States in Europe and America*, edited by Peter Flora and Arnold J. Heidenheimer. New Brunswick, NJ: Transaction Books.

Lieberman, Robert C. 1998. *Shifting the Color Line: Race and the American Welfare State.* Cambridge, MA: Harvard University Press.

Lieberson, Stanley. 1992. "Small *N*'s and Big Conclusions: An Examination of the Reasoning in Comparative Studies Based on a Small Number of Cases." Pp. 105–18 in *What Is a Case?: Exploring the Foundations of Social Inquiry*, edited by Charles C. Ragin and Howard S. Becker. Cambridge: Cambridge University Press.

Lijphart, Arend. 1971. "Comparative Politics and the Comparative Method." *American Political Science Review* 65: 691–3.

Lustick, Ian. 1996. "History, Historiography, and Political Science: Historical Records and Selection Bias." *American Political Science Review* 90: 605–18.

Mahoney, James. 2000. "Path Dependence in Historical Sociology." *Theory and Society* 29: 507–48.

Marshall, T. H. 1963. *Class, Citizenship, and Social Development*. Chicago: University of Chicago Press.

McAdam, Doug, John D. McCarthy, and Mayer N. Zald. 1988. "Social Movements." Pp. 695–737 in *The Handbook of Sociology*, edited by Neil J. Smelser. Beverly Hills, CA: Sage.

1996. "Introduction: Opportunities, Mobilizing Structures, and Framing Processes – Toward a Synthetic, Comparative Perspective on Social Movements." Pp. 1–22 in *Comparative Perspectives on Social Movements: Political Opportunities, Mobilizing Structures, and Cultural Framings*, edited by Doug McAdam, John D. McCarthy, and Mayer N. Zald. New York: Cambridge University Press.

Miriampolski, Hyman and Dana C. Hughes. 1978. "The Uses of Personal Documents in Historical Sociology." *The American Sociologist* 13: 104–13.

Mishra, Ramesh. 1990. *The Welfare State in Capitalist Society: Policies of Retrenchment and Maintenance in Europe, North America, and Australia*. Toronto: University of Toronto Press.

Myles, John. 1989 [1984]. *Old Age in the Welfare State: The Political Economy of Public Pensions*, 2nd ed. Lawrence: University Press of Kansas.

Myles, John and Paul Pierson. 1998. "Friedman's Revenge: The Reform of 'Liberal' Welfare States in Canada and the United States." *Politics and Society*: 25: 443–72

O'Connor, Julia S. 1993. "Gender, Class and Citizenship in the Comparative Analysis of Welfare State Regimes: Theoretical and Methodological Issues." *British Journal of Sociology* 44: 501–18.

O'Connor, Julia S., Ann Shola Orloff, and Sheila Shaver. 1999. *States, Markets, Families: Gender, Liberalism and Social Policy in Australia, Canada, Great Britain and the United States*. Cambridge: Cambridge University Press.

Orloff, Ann Shola. 1993a. *The Politics of Pensions: A Comparative Analysis of Britain, Canada, and the United States, 1880–1940*. Madison: University of Wisconsin Press.

1993b. "Gender and the Social Rights of Citizenship: The Comparative Analysis of Gender Relations and Welfare States." *American Sociological Review* 58: 303–28.

1996. "Gender in the Welfare State. *Annual Review of Sociology* 22: 51–78.

Orloff, Ann Shola and Eric Parker. 1990. "Business and Social Policy in Canada and the United States, 1920–1940." *Comparative Social Research* 12: 295–339.

Orloff, Ann Shola and Theda Skocpol. 1984. "Why Not Equal Protection? Explaining the Politics of Public Social Welfare in Britain and the United States, 1880s–1920s." *American Sociological Review* 49: 726–50.

Pampel, Fred C. and John B. Williamson. 1989. *Age, Class, Politics, and the Welfare State*. Cambridge: Cambridge University Press.

Patterson, James. 1986. *America's Struggle against Poverty*. Cambridge, MA: Harvard University Press.

Peacock, Alan R. and Jack Wiseman. 1961. *The Growth of Public Expenditure in the United Kingdom*. Princeton, NJ: Princeton University Press.

Pedersen, Susan. 1993. *Family, Dependence, and the Origins of the Welfare State: Britain and France, 1914–1945*. Cambridge: Cambridge University Press.

Pierson, Paul. 1994. *Dismantling the Welfare State? Reagan, Thatcher, and the Politics of Retrenchment*. Cambridge: Cambridge University Press.

2000a. "Three Worlds of Welfare State Research." *Comparative Political Studies* 33: 822–44.

2000b. "Path Dependence, Increasing Returns, and the Study of Politics." *American Political Science Review* 94: 251–67.

2000c. "Coping with Permanent Austerity: Welfare State Restructuring in Affluent Democracies." Pp. 410–56 in *The New Politics of the Welfare State*, edited by Paul Pierson. New York: Oxford University Press.

Piven, Frances Fox and Richard A. Cloward. [1971] 1993. *Regulating the Poor: The Functions of Public Welfare*, updated ed. New York: Vintage Books.

Przeworski, Adam and Henry Teune. 1970.*The Logic of Comparative Social Inquiry*. New York: Wiley-Interscience.

Quadagno, Jill. 1987. "Theories of the Welfare State." *Annual Review of Sociology* 13: 109–28.

1994. *The Color of Welfare: How Racism Undermined the War on Poverty*. New York: Oxford University Press.

Ragin, Charles C. 1987. *The Comparative Method*. Berkeley: University of California Press.

1994. "A Qualitative Comparative Analysis of Pension Systems." Pp. 320–45 in *Methodological Advances in Comparative Political Economy*, edited by Thomas Janoski and Alexander Hicks. New York: Cambridge University Press.

Rimlinger, Gaston V. 1971. *Welfare Policy and Industrialization in Europe, America, and Russia*. New York: Wiley.

Rueschemeyer, Dietrich and Theda Skocpol. 1996. *States, Social Knowledge and the Origins of Modern Social Policies*. Princeton, NJ: Princeton University Press.

Rueschemeyer, Dietrich and John D. Stephens. 1997. "Comparing Historical Sequences – A Powerful Tool for Causal Analysis." *Comparative Social Research* 17: 55–72.

Rueschemeyer, Marilyn and Sharon L. Wolchik. 1999. "The Return of Left-Oriented Social Parties in Eastern Germany and the Czech Republic and Their Social Policies." Pp. 109–43 in *Left Parties and Social Policy in Post-Communist Europe*, edited by Linda J. Cook, Mitchell Orenstein, and Marilyn Rueschemeyer. Boulder, CO: Westview.

Ruggie, Mary. 1984. *The State and Working Women*. Ithaca, NY: Cornell University Press.

Sainsbury, Diane. 1996. *Gender, Equality and Welfare States*. Cambridge: Cambridge University Press.

Schneider, Saundra K. 1982. "The Sequential Development of Social Programs in Eighteen Welfare States." *Comparative Social Research* 5: 195–219.

Shalev, Michael. 1983. "The Social Democratic Model and Beyond: Two 'Generations' of Comparative Research on the Welfare State." *Comparative Social Research* 6: 315–51.

Sharkansky, Ira and Richard Hofferbert. 1969. "Dimensions of State Politics, Economics, and Public Policy." *American Political Science Review* 63: 867–78.

Skocpol, Theda. 1985. "Bringing the State Back In: Strategies of Analysis in Current Research." Pp. 3–37 in *Bringing the State Back In*, edited by Peter B. Evans, Dietrich Rueschemeyer, and Theda Skocpol. Cambridge: Cambridge University Press.

1992. *Protecting Soldiers and Mothers*. Cambridge, MA: Harvard University Press.

Skocpol, Theda, Marjorie Abend-Wein, Christopher Howard, and Susan G. Lehmann. 1993. "Women's Associations and the Enactment of Mothers' Pensions in the United States." *American Political Science Review* 87: 686–701.

Skocpol, Theda and Edwin Amenta. 1986. "States and Social Policies." *Annual Review of Sociology* 12: 131–57.

Skocpol, Theda and Margaret Somers. 1980. "The Uses of Comparative History in Macrosocial Inquiry." *Comparative Studies in Society and History* 22: 174–97.

Steinmetz, George. 1993. *Regulating the Social: The Welfare State and Local Politics in Imperial Germany*. Princeton, NJ: Princeton University Press.

Steinmo, Sven. 1993. *Taxation and Democracy: Swedish, British and American Approaches to Financing the Modern State*. New Haven, CT: Yale University Press.

Stephens, John D. 1979. *The Transition from Capitalism to Socialism*. London: Macmillan.

Swank, Duane. 2001. *Diminished Democracy? Globalization, Political Institutions, and the Welfare State in Advanced Market Economies*. New York: Cambridge University Press.

Swenson, Peter. 1996. "Arranged Alliance: Business Interests in the New Deal." *Politics and Society* 25: 66–116.

n.d. "Labor Markets and Welfare States: Employers in the Making of the American and Swedish Systems." Unpublished manuscript, Department of Political Science, Northwestern University.

Thelen, Kathleen. 1999. "Historical Institutionalism in Comparative Politics." *Annual Review of Political Science* 2: 369–404.

Thelen, Kathleen and Sven Steinmo. 1992. "Historical Institutionalism in Comparative Politics." Pp. 1–32 in *Structuring Politics: Historical Institutionalism in Comparative Analysis*, edited by Sven Steinmo, Kathleen Thelen, and Frank Longstreth. New York: Cambridge University Press.

Tilly, Charles. 1984. *Big Structures, Large Processes, Huge Comparisons*. New York: Russell Sage.

Titmuss, Richard. 1958. "War and Social Policy." Pp. 75–87 in Richard Titmuss, *Essays on the Welfare State*. London: Allen and Unwin.

Van Kersbergen, Kees. 1995. *Social Capitalism*. London: Routledge.

Weir, Margaret. 1992. *Politics and Jobs: The Boundaries of Employment Policy in the United States*. Princeton, NJ: Princeton University Press.

Weir, Margaret, Ann Shola Orloff, and Theda Skocpol. 1988. "Understanding American Social Politics." Pp. 3–27 in *The Politics of Social Policy in the United States*, edited by Margaret Weir, Ann Shola Orloff, and Theda Skocpol. Princeton, NJ: Princeton University Press.

Wickham-Crowley, Timothy P. 1992. *Guerrillas and Revolution in Latin America: A Comparative Study of Insurgents and Regimes since 1965*. Princeton, NJ: Princeton University Press.
Wilensky, Harold L. 1975. *The Welfare State and Equality: Structural and Ideological Roots of Public Expenditures*. Berkeley and Los Angeles: University of California Press.
Williamson, John B. and Fred C. Pampel. 1993. *Old-Age Security in Comparative Perspective*. New York: Oxford University Press.
Wright, Gavin. 1974. "The Political Economy of New Deal Spending: An Econometric Analysis." *Review of Economics and Statistics* 56: 30–8.
Zelizer, Julian E. 1999. *Taxing America: Wilbur D. Mills, Congress, and the State, 1945–1975*. New York: Cambridge University Press.

4

Knowledge Accumulation in Comparative Historical Research

THE CASE OF DEMOCRACY AND AUTHORITARIANISM

James Mahoney

Surprisingly little attention has been devoted to thinking about knowledge accumulation in the social sciences. Although many social scientists agree that a basic purpose of their research is to produce cumulative knowledge about the world, they do not often reflect on the nature of such accumulation and how it takes place. Currently, we lack a clear answer to questions such as: What constitutes knowledge accumulation in the social sciences? How can it be measured and compared across different scholarly research programs? What promotes or inhibits knowledge accumulation in the social sciences? One might be inclined to see these questions as raising epistemological issues that cannot be resolved across disparate scholarly communities. However, I shall argue in this essay that most social scientists in fact agree on how to answer these questions, at least implicitly and in broad terms. In attempting to outline this shared position, I seek to initiate a larger discussion about how to study knowledge accumulation in social science analysis.

My immediate goal is to assess the extent of knowledge accumulation that has taken place in the field of comparative historical analysis, a research area that is sometimes criticized as having failed to achieve cumulative knowledge. I limit my discussion to studies of the origins of democratic and authoritarian national regimes. Although this is a relatively specific focus, few scholars would deny that the study of democracy and authoritarianism raises "first-order questions" – that is, "questions that draw people to study social life in the first place, and that are constantly raised anew in the

I thank David Collier, Barbara Geddes, Gerardo Munck, Richard Snyder, Hillel Soifer, and the other contributors to this volume for their helpful comments and suggestions. This material is based upon work supported by the National Science Foundation under Grant No. 0093754.

minds of nonspecialists" (Rule 1997, p. 46). Any program of social research that seeks to make a real claim to scholarly advancement – and ultimately hold the attention of nonspecialists – must make progress in addressing such first-order questions. In the field of comparative historical analysis, a very substantial body of research focuses on the causes of democracy and authoritarianism, and the survey that follows is not designed to be a comprehensive overview. Instead, I concentrate on certain works that I view as particularly salient landmarks in the regime change literature, with much attention being devoted to analyses of Europe and Latin America, the two geographical regions where my own substantive interests fall. In particular, I identify and discuss three major research programs – what I call the Barrington Moore, Guillermo O'Donnell, and Juan Linz and Alfred Stepan research programs. Between them, these programs encompass a good deal of the comparative historical literature on democracy and authoritarianism, including its leading personalities, research findings, and central axes of debate.

In examining these research programs, I am concerned mainly with the issue of whether knowledge accumulation has taken place, especially knowledge about causal processes. While I do offer some discussion of *why* accumulation has or has not occurred, this is not my main interest; I primarily seek only to document the cumulative knowledge that has been generated. Likewise, for the most part, I leave it to others to explore the extent to which scholars working outside of the comparative historical field have produced cumulative knowledge about democracy and authoritarianism. For example, I consider work in the fields of rational choice theory and statistical analysis mainly insofar as it has affected the trajectory of knowledge accumulation in comparative historical analysis.

Defining Knowledge Accumulation

To evaluate knowledge accumulation, it is helpful to reach some consensus on the meaning of "accumulation" and the meaning of "knowledge." Let me begin by discussing accumulation. At a minimum, most scholars will agree that accumulation implies progress in understanding and learning; new and useful knowledge must be produced for accumulation to occur (Cohen 1989, p. 319). Yet, most analysts will also agree that accumulation does not merely entail the introduction of new knowledge or the proliferation of new empirical insights. In this sense, knowledge *accumulation* is not equivalent to knowledge *generation*. Unless the new knowledge grows

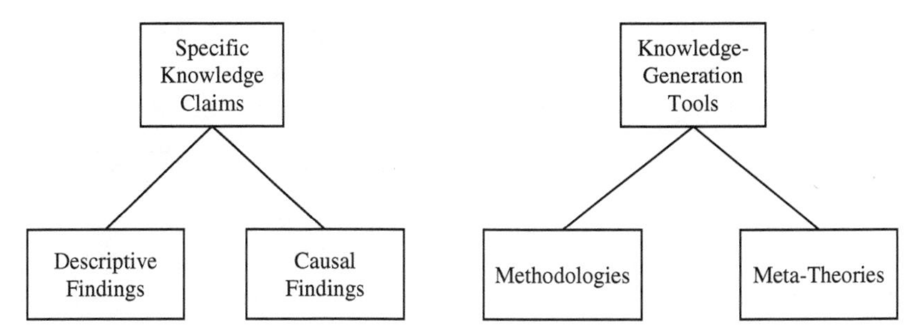

Figure 4.1 Elements of accumulation in a research tradition.

out of preexisting knowledge, its addition to a research program does not signify accumulation (Freese 1980, pp. 18, 41–2; Rule 1997, p. 27). Thus, accumulation occurs when the generation of new knowledge is *dependent on* previously obtained knowledge.[1]

The question of what constitutes knowledge probably cannot be resolved in a fashion that will please all scholars. Here I aim for the more modest goal of identifying certain elements that many social scientists will readily recognize as important components of their work. I highlight four basic elements: descriptive findings, causal findings, methodologies, and meta-theories (see Figure 4.1). The first two of these involve specific knowledge claims offered by practicing social scientists, whereas the second two entail tools developed and used by social scientists for generating knowledge claims. Scholars representing different traditions will disagree about the relative importance of each of these elements. In addition, some scholars, most notably postmodern scholars, may dismiss the relevance of one or

[1] As Lee Freese puts it, "Knowledge is cumulative when the discoveries it yields at one point in time depend upon discoveries made at an earlier point in time" (1980, p. 18). Freese goes on to adopt the strong position that the new knowledge must encompass and supersede earlier knowledge. He therefore concludes that knowledge accumulation "implies that the best knowledge today will be inferior in the future. When it becomes inferior its discoverers assume historical significance only. The soundest measure of whether a body of knowledge is cumulative is the speed with which its principal contributors lose their relevance" (1980, p. 18). I am inclined to disagree that progress must imply that a principal contributor's work is fully superseded by subsequent advances. In many cases, the generation of new knowledge is stimulated by an initial investigator's work, but this new knowledge does not directly challenge or make irrelevant all of the claims found in the initial work. Furthermore, reading early works in an overall trajectory of knowledge development can be useful for stimulating new knowledge claims. For example, many knowledge-generating biologists still find it useful to study the work of Darwin.

more of these items. However, I argue that the elements encompass a good deal of what most practicing social scientists regard as knowledge.

First, descriptive findings about the social world are routinely regarded as one piece of our stock of social science knowledge. These findings include various collections of data, whether qualitative or quantitative, contemporary or historical. The addition of new descriptive material occurs almost continuously in the social sciences as analysts gather more and more data about the world. However, the production of new descriptive knowledge does not necessarily signify *accumulation*, since the new data frequently do not depend on the existence of any prior information. Rather, as is often noted, much of our descriptive information about the social world is fragmented and unconnected. For example, in the recent literature on democracy in developing countries, rapid data collection often has outpaced the ability of analysts to organize findings systematically, such that we now have a great deal of unintegrated information about many countries.

Knowledge accumulation through description is facilitated when scholars classify existing information using well-specified concepts, typologies, and quantitative indexes. These classification apparatuses enable analysts to formulate new and useful knowledge that is systematically related to and dependent on prior knowledge. For instance, as we will see, Juan J. Linz's classification of different types of political regimes was crucial to the accumulation of much descriptive knowledge. As political systems evolved over the years, scholars were able to organize the new information systematically in light of Linz's preexisting regime typology. This development parallels statistical cross-national studies of democratization, where the creation of indexes of democracy has promoted knowledge accumulation by providing scholars with tools for coherently organizing data about democratic freedoms and processes.

Second, findings about causal processes are an essential component of social science knowledge. Some analysts go so far as to say that causal findings are the ultimate point of social science research. Regardless of whether one agrees, it is undeniable that a great deal of scholarly activity is devoted to this end. Yet, one still hears complaints that social scientists fail to build on each other's causal findings. Skeptics are quick to assert that we have much fragmented and uncertain knowledge about causal processes and little integrated and solid knowledge that can provide a reliable guide for explaining events.

When social researchers accumulate knowledge about causal findings, they systematically draw on prior findings in their causal analyses. In doing so, they often pursue two kinds of activities: iterated hypothesis testing and hypothesis elaboration. With *iterated hypothesis testing*, one or more researchers conduct tests of a causal hypothesis (or set of hypotheses) that was previously developed and tested by a different researcher.[2] The new researchers may attempt to replicate the original finding exactly, or they may retest the original hypothesis using new data and cases. Either way, the goal of iterated hypothesis testing is to carefully scrutinize a preexisting hypothesis in order to increase scholarly confidence about its validity. It is worth noting that cumulative research does not depend on the repeated empirical confirmation of a given hypothesis; knowledge progression routinely takes place through the falsification of an initial hypothesis (Cohen 1989, p. 301).

The process of *hypothesis elaboration* occurs when analysts use an initial causal hypothesis as a stepping stone for the development and testing of new hypotheses (see Wagner and Berger 1985, p. 707). For example, scholars may introduce new independent variables that work in conjunction with previously identified ones to better explain the outcome under consideration. Likewise, scholars may extend independent variables used to account for a given outcome to a new set of outcomes, thereby exploring the generality of the initial explanation. Hypothesis elaboration also can take place by more precisely identifying the scope conditions that govern a hypothesis (i.e., more clearly delineating the variables that make up the conditions under which a given hypothesis can be expected to operate). In each of these examples of hypothesis elaboration, an initial hypothesis serves as a springboard for the creation of a new hypothesis that yields additional information about causal patterns.

Descriptive and causal findings are the basic knowledge produced by most practicing social scientists. However, when evaluating the overall knowledge generated by a *research tradition*, such as comparative historical analysis, it is important to consider progress regarding the tools used to formulate descriptive and causal findings. A progressive research tradition should be characterized by accumulation with respect to these tools. Methodology and meta-theory – the third and fourth elements of knowledge specified previously – are important examples of such tools.

[2] This is similar to what Cohen (1989, chap. 15) calls "lateral accumulation," which is marked by the repeated testing of a given knowledge claim, and what Wagner and Berger (1985, pp. 702–4) call "unit theories," in which knowledge accumulation is evaluated by exploring the linkage between a given theory and empirical data.

Methodology encompasses the broad range of procedures analysts use to generate descriptive and causal inferences. Included here are various rules concerning data collection, case selection, variable operationalization, measurement, hypothesis testing, and recording and reporting results. Ultimately, much of methodology is concerned with codifying rigorous procedures for producing valid findings, whether descriptive or causal. By contrast, meta-theory refers to overarching assumptions and orientations that can be used to formulate empirical puzzles and testable hypotheses, and that help analysts frame more specific research questions. Meta-theories suggest orienting concepts, target certain kinds of variables as important, and point to styles of research and explanation. However, they do not entail the specification of any set of directly testable propositions. As we will see, comparative historical scholars working on democracy and authoritarianism have used overarching meta-theoretical orientations such as structuralism and voluntarism extensively.

Cumulative progress in methodological and meta-theoretical development requires that scholars consciously build on one another's work. When this takes place, it may in turn facilitate the generation of knowledge about specific causal and descriptive processes.[3] Much discussion in the philosophy of science has focused on meta-theoretical accumulation through shifts in paradigms or research programs (e.g., Kuhn 1970; Lakatos and Musgrave 1970). Although scholars debate the extent to which these notions can be applied to the social sciences, at a minimum they offer useful heuristics for thinking about meta-theoretical evolution in the field of comparative historical analysis. For example, some scholars have characterized the literature on political regime change as having evolved from a structuralist meta-theory, to a voluntarist meta-theory, to an integrative meta-theory. Regarding methodology, these tools are often well adapted to accumulation, as can be seen clearly in the field of statistics, where recent innovations are highly dependent on earlier developments. In comparative historical analysis, the evolution from J. S. Mill's methods of agreement and difference, to Boolean algebra, to fuzzy-set techniques may signal a similar progression. The accumulation of knowledge with respect to methodology is especially

[3] Knowledge accumulation with respect to meta-theoretical formulation and methodologies makes possible – but does not guarantee – the production of more useful and more reliable substantive knowledge claims. As meta-theories are better elaborated, scholars are better positioned to formulate compelling hypotheses. And as methodologies develop, scholars are more capable of reliably testing their knowledge claims.

notable when the tools are actually used in substantive research. When this takes place, new methodologies may quickly become "indispensable," such that analysts "need to know them" and "cannot afford to do without them" (Rule 1997, pp. 5–6).

It bears emphasis that the descriptive and causal findings produced by knowledge-generating tools always contain an element of uncertainty. No matter how powerful the meta-theoretical or methodological tools, the process of knowledge accumulation does not culminate in the production of claims that are definitively true. Rather, knowledge at any one point in time can always be subsequently called into question. In this sense, readers cannot expect comparative historical analysis – or any other research tradition for that matter – to produce some list of findings that are proven beyond all possible doubt.

The following analysis will explore these criteria of knowledge accumulation, focusing most centrally on *causal findings* about the origins of democratic and authoritarian regimes.[4] I concentrate on this area because many scholars who work in the field – including vocal critics of comparative historical analysis – privilege causal analysis as the ultimate goal of social science research. Critics of comparative historical analysis may concede that the field has accumulated some knowledge with respect to descriptive findings, meta-theoretical formulations, and possibly methodologies. However, they would be less likely to make a similar concession regarding causal findings. Hence, the criterion of causal findings provides a "hard case" for the comparative historical study of democracy and authoritarianism.

The Barrington Moore Research Program

Barrington Moore, Jr.'s *Social Origins of Dictatorship and Democracy: Lord and Peasant in the Making of the Modern World* (1966) is often regarded as the single most important book in the comparative historical research tradition. Yet, from a contemporary perspective, the importance of Moore's work does not rest on the validity of its causal hypotheses concerning the origins of parliamentary democracy, fascist dictatorship, and communist dictatorship. In fact, Moore's specific hypotheses were stated in a relatively vague manner that has made it difficult for subsequent scholars to evaluate his claims

[4] With respect to causal findings, there is also a growing comparative historical literature on the consequences of democratic and authoritarian regimes, and on democratic performance and stability. I do not address these literatures here.

empirically. Moreover, in the process of iterated hypothesis testing, subsequent scholars often have not found empirical support for these hypotheses.

Nevertheless, Moore's work deservedly occupies its leading place in the annals of comparative historical research. For Moore's central contribution was not to end discussion of the origins of dictatorship and democracy definitively, but to inspire subsequent hypothesis elaboration and metatheoretical development on a scale that surpasses nearly any other work in modern social science.

Iterated Hypothesis Testing and the Falsification of Moore's Argument

Moore's full argument cannot be easily outlined. He emphasized the timing of events relative to one another (e.g., the timing of commercial agriculture relative to crises of agrarian states), making it difficult to specify the argument in terms of static variables. Furthermore, he was concerned with the ways in which variables bundled together to affect outcomes and with how institutional and epochal contexts influenced the workings of these variables. As a result, scholars have had difficulty summarizing *Social Origins*, leading to a rather diverse set of interpretations regarding the main arguments of the book (compare, for example, Skocpol 1973; Stephens 1989; and Paige 1997). Nevertheless, despite some confusion about the argument as a whole, there is wide agreement on particular hypotheses that guided the study. Since my concern is with democracy and authoritarianism, I consider here two hypotheses about the establishment of these regime outcomes. These two hypotheses do not encompass all of Moore's argument, but their falsification would call into question important elements of the analysis.

First, Moore argues that a strong bourgeoisie (understood mainly as town people engaged in commerce and industry) was important to the creation of democracy. In particular, democracy developed in France, England, and the United States because the bourgeoisie ultimately avoided becoming the subordinate partner in an alliance with landed elites against the peasantry (Hypothesis 1). This antipeasant alliance was bypassed in Moore's democratic countries because landed elites were weakened or displaced during a revolutionary period in which agriculture and/or politics was transformed (i.e., events surrounding the English Revolution, the French Revolution, and the American Civil War). With this weakening of landed elites, the bourgeoisie was able to fulfill its historic role and establish parliamentary democracy.

Second, in reactionary-authoritarian cases, labor-repressive landlords forged an alliance with the bourgeoisie against the peasants. Specifically, reactionary authoritarianism developed in Japan and Germany because labor-repressive landlords maintained the upper hand in an antipeasant coalition with a bourgeoisie of intermediate strength (Hypothesis 2). In these cases, labor-repressive landlords were not displaced by bourgeois revolutions, and peasants lacked the solidarity structures to successfully lead revolutions from below. As a result, a repressive authoritarianism developed in which landed elites used the state to increase surplus labor from the peasantry during the process of agricultural commercialization.

Numerous comparative historical researchers have directly or indirectly evaluated these hypotheses. The evidence from these subsequent tests does not consistently support Moore's hypotheses (see Tables 4.1 and 4.2). Some of the most powerful challenges have come from scholars who present new data on the original cases analyzed in *Social Origins*.[5] For example, Moore's discussion of England has been called into question because English landlords were among the most politically powerful in Europe until well into the nineteenth century, yet England developed a democratic regime (Skocpol 1973; Stephens 1989).[6] In addition, although much evidence supports Moore's claim that the English bourgeoisie was economically quite strong by the nineteenth century, scholars have raised doubts that the Glorious Revolution can be considered a bourgeoisie revolution, even in the limited sense of furthering bourgeois interests in the distant future (Plumb 1966; Stone 1967). Still other analysts have questioned whether the bourgeoisie ever autonomously pushed forward democracy in the nineteenth century without being pressured by other actors (Stephens 1989, pp. 1032–4; see also Collier 1999, pp. 96–101).

Scholars have also criticized Moore's argument that the American Civil War was crucial to the establishment of democracy. For Moore, the Civil War was a "bourgeois revolution" in which an alliance of Northern

[5] The use of Moore's original cases is important because Moore did not intend his argument to apply to all countries. The scope conditions governing the argument in *Social Origins* were never clearly specified (but see Moore's comments on "smaller countries" on p. xiii).

[6] Moore attempts to get around this problem by asserting that the enclosures allowed the landed upper class to successfully commercialize agriculture and avoid labor-repressive agriculture. Hence, he claims that the usual repressive mechanisms through which landlord political strength translated into authoritarianism do not apply to England. However, Skocpol (1973) raises concerns about the empirical grounds for claiming that England's landed elites were more market-oriented and less labor-repressive than those in other countries.

Table 4.1. *Iterated Hypothesis Testing in the Moore Research Program: Democratic Establishment*

HYPOTHESIS: A strong bourgeoisie that avoids an antipeasant alliance with a labor-repressive landed elite facilitates demmocracy.

	Relationship of New Evidence to Moore's Hypothesis			
	Confirming	Partial Support	Disconfirming	
England			X	Skocpol 1973 J. Stephens 1989 Stone 1967
United States			X	Wiener 1976 Wiener 1978 Bensel 1990
France		X		Skocpol 1979 Huber/Stephens 1995
Sweden		X		Castles 1973 Tilton 1974 J. Stephens 1989
Switzerland	X			J. Stephens 1989
Denmark		X		J. Stephens 1989
Norway		X		J. Stephens 1989
Netherlands		X		J. Stephens 1989 Downing 1992
Belgium		X		J. Stephens 1989
Costa Rica	X			Gudmundson 1995 Paige 1997 Mahoney 2001
Chile			X	Valenzuela 2001 Huber/Stephens 1995
Uruguay		X		Huber/Stephens 1995
Argentina	X			Halperín 1995

industrialists and Western farmers defeated labor-repressive planters from the South. Yet, analysts have pointed out that labor-repressive agriculture was reimposed in the United States after the Civil War, such that the country was not kept off an authoritarian path (Wiener 1976, 1978). Some scholars have gone so far as to assert that the Union victory may have hindered progressive social and political development (Bensel 1990). In any event, several commentators believe that the class coalitional patterns forged during the Civil War were not decisive for democratization, even in the South, and

Table 4.2. *Iterated Hypothesis Testing in the Moore Research Program: Authoritarian Regime Establishment*

HYPOTHESIS: An antipeasant alliance that unites a labor-represive landed elite with a politically subordinate bourgeoisie facilitates authoritarianism.

	Relationship of New Evidence to Moore's Hypothesis			
	Confirming	Partial Support	Disconfirming	
Germany			X	J. Stephens 1989 Luebbert 1991
Japan			X	Skocpol 1973 Huber/Stephens 1995
Austria	X			J. Stephens 1989
Spain		X		J. Stephens 1989 Schatz 2001
Italy		X		J. Stephens 1989
Guatemala	X			Mahoney 2001
El Salvador	X			Paige 1997 Mahoney 2001
Nicaragua			X	Paige 1997 Mahoney 2001
Honduras			X	Mahoney 2001
Brazil	X			Huber/Stephens 1995
Colombia		X		Huber/Stephens 1995
Ecuador			X	Huber/Stephens 1995
Mexico			X	Huber/Stephens 1995
Paraguay			X	Huber/Stephens 1995

that the real push for democracy stemmed from social forces and coalitions quite different from those analyzed by Moore (Rueschemeyer, Stephens, and Stephens 1992, pp. 122–32).

New evidence on the French case is mixed. Moore downplays the direct role of the bourgeoisie in the French Revolution, arguing that the most important effect of the revolution was to destroy seignorial privileges and the political power of the landed elite. These facts are debated, but many scholars suggest that Moore overestimates the weakening of the nobility in the aftermath of the revolution and underestimates the importance of events in the mid-nineteenth century for democratization (Rueschemeyer et al. 1992, pp. 88–90; Huber and Stephens 1995, pp. 214–15). Likewise, Skocpol (1979, p. 332) argues that Moore fails to recognize that the revolution created new state structures that became important *obstacles* to democratization.

Moore's argument about fascism in Germany has also been challenged on numerous empirical grounds. Drawing on more recent historical sources, Stephens (1989, pp. 1044–7) shows that while an alliance between the East Elbian landed upper class, the Junkers, and the industrial bourgeoisie did develop, it was the bourgeoisie – not labor-repressive landed elites – that was the most influential partner in the alliance. This evidence leads Stephens to conclude that Moore overestimates the importance of the bourgeoisie for democracy. Yet while Stephens maintains that labor-repressive landed elites were important to the creation of fascism in Germany, Luebbert (1991, pp. 308–9) calls even this more limited assertion into question. Luebbert presents evidence that landed elites often did not deliver large numbers of peasant votes for fascism, and that support for fascism was strongest in precisely those areas not dominated by landed elites, such as north-central Germany.[7]

Finally, serious questions have been raised about the validity of Moore's argument for Japan. Most basically, scholars have pointed out that Japan lacked an influential and politically powerful class of large landlords (Skocpol 1973; Huber and Stephens 1995, pp. 216–17). Hence, Moore's argument that this class was central to establishing reactionary authoritarianism cannot be sustained. At most, landlords played the relatively passive role of allowing powerful bureaucratic and military elites to seize state power and initiate industrial expansion that ultimately benefited the modern bourgeoisie.

Given that there are empirical limitations with Moore's hypotheses when applied to his own cases, it is not surprising that problems have arisen in subsequent analyses that look at other cases. Two early efforts to apply the Moore thesis that reached contradictory conclusions are Castles' (1973) and Tilton's (1974) analyses of democratization in Sweden. Tilton argues that the reforms of Charles XI in the late seventeenth century undercut the power of the Swedish land elite, and Gustav III prevented a subsequent landed elite–bourgeoisie alliance during the late eighteenth century. Hence, his analysis supports the main thrust of Moore's argument. By contrast, Castles argues that landed elites remained politically powerful despite Charles XI's reforms and, by the early nineteenth century, entered into a political alliance with industrial and bureaucratic elites that strongly resembles Moore's "marriage of iron and rye" leading to authoritarianism.

[7] However, there is evidence that Germany's subsequent transition to democracy can be explained in light of Moore's hypothesis for democratic development (see Bernhard 2001).

Hence, Castles suggests that Sweden should have developed a reactionary authoritarian regime if Moore's argument is correct. Of the two studies, Castles' appears to be based on more systematic evidence.

The most substantial effort to test Moore's hypotheses in light of multiple cases is the work of Rueschemeyer et al. (1992) (see also Huber Stephens 1989; Stephens 1989; and Huber and Stafford 1995). These authors test many different implications of Moore's arguments, reaching nuanced if decidedly mixed conclusions about their validity. Of the interwar authoritarian cases in Europe[8] that were not studied by Moore, Austria appears to provide the most support for Moore's thesis. In Austria, politically powerful and labor-repressive landlords forged an alliance with the crown and the army to oversee a highly authoritarian regime. Moreover, the Austrian bourgeoisie was linked to these landed elites as a subordinate partner (Stephens 1989, p. 1057). By contrast, the onset of authoritarianism in Spain and Italy provides only partial support for Moore's argument. Although landholding was highly concentrated in these cases, the landed upper class was not directly engaged in labor-repressive agriculture and did not assume a politically leading role, as suggested in Moore's coalitional argument of authoritarianism. In addition, the bourgeoisie was not dependent on landed elites in Spain and Italy (Stephens 1989, pp. 1040–1, 1060–1; but see Schatz 2001).

Rueschemeyer et al. (1992) also analyze Moore's thesis in relation to democratization in Denmark, Norway, Sweden, Switzerland, Belgium, and the Netherlands. The evidence from these cases is generally more confirmatory, even though the authors are convinced that other explanatory factors not emphasized by Moore are the most important variables at work. In these countries, labor-repressive landed elites were not powerful enough to lead authoritarian coalitions, while the bourgeoisie – although not necessarily strong – was one important actor in the establishment of democracy. Perhaps the best case for the role of the bourgeoisie in democratization can be made for Switzerland, where early industrialization allowed urban dwellers to play a major part in the charge for democracy (Rueschemeyer et al. 1992, pp. 85–6; see also R. Collier 1999). The alliance between urban middle classes and peasants also was important to early steps of democratization in Denmark and Norway. Likewise, in Belgium and the Netherlands,

[8] Here I focus on Western Europe. For an assessment of Moore's hypotheses in light of Eastern Europe, see Stokes (1989). Stokes finds partial support for Moore's thesis in his analysis of Bulgaria, Hungary, and the Czech lands; he finds little support in the analysis of Romania and Serbia.

the bourgeoisie played a role in a broader coalition of subordinate actors in early suffrage extension and political reforms (R. Collier 1999, chap. 3). Yet, according to Rueschemeyer et al. (1992, pp. 142–3), the bourgeoisie actively resisted the political incorporation of important subordinate groups in these latter four countries. Hence, they conclude that the bourgeoisie's role in furthering democracy was ambiguous, offering only partial support for Moore's hypothesis.

Several scholars have also assessed Moore's hypotheses in relation to the substantial political variation that has characterized the countries of Central America (Gudmundson 1995; Paige 1997; Mahoney 2001). The majority of the evidence for regime outcomes in three of these countries – authoritarianism in Guatemala and El Salvador and democracy in Costa Rica – is supportive of Moore's coalitional argument. In Guatemala and El Salvador, entrenched coffee elites tied to a weaker bourgeois faction in an antipeasant alliance was one important element in the creation and endurance of authoritarianism. Likewise, consistent with Moore, the establishment of democracy in Costa Rica has been linked to the relative absence of labor-repressive agriculture along with the relatively strong position of a commercially based processing elite (i.e., a bourgeoisie). However, the evidence is more problematic for authoritarianism in Nicaragua and Honduras, where landed elites lost most of their political power in the aftermath of episodes of U.S. intervention in the early twentieth century.[9]

Elsewhere in Latin America, Moore's thesis has also received systematic attention (see J. S. Valenzuela [2001], Huber Stephens [1990], and the essays in Huber and Stafford [1995], especially the concluding chapter by Huber and Stephens [1995]). For the first half of the twentieth century in Chile, most analysts agree that democracy was able to develop despite the presence of labor-repressive agriculture and a powerful landed oligarchy (but see J. S. Valenzuela 2001). In Argentina, the bourgeoisie was freed from an alliance with landed elites, and it could be argued to have played an important role in establishing democracy in the early twentieth century (Halperín 1995), though with Uruguay at roughly the same time, the story of initial democratization is more complicated because large landowners actively supported democracy along with an incipient bourgeoisie (Huber and Stephens 1995, p. 201). Of the authoritarian cases in early- and mid-twentieth-century Latin America, only that of Brazil

[9] Nicaragua and Honduras actually correspond more closely to the implicit pattern of development offered in Moore's discussion of India. See Mahoney (2001) for a discussion.

under the Old Republic strongly supports Moore; other countries developed authoritarian regimes without specifically *labor-repressive* landed elites playing a significant role (Paraguay, Ecuador, and Mexico) or playing only a rather small role (Peru and Colombia) (see Huber and Stephens 1995).

Several conclusions from this survey of research are worth underlining. First, with respect to new evidence that has emerged over the last three decades, Moore's *specific* hypotheses about democracy and authoritarianism receive only limited and highly conditional support. Given that superior alternatives to Moore's hypotheses now exist (see later), I believe this new evidence is sufficient to falsify the two hypotheses considered in this section as a general explanation of regime outcomes. Second, the most contradictory evidence has come not from new cases that Moore failed to consider, but from new data on the countries actually analyzed in *Social Origins*. Given all the attention that the small-*N* problem has received from critics of comparative historical analysis, it is revealing that hypothesis falsification in this mode of research can take place through the reanalysis of the original cases. Third, in the effort to reexamine Moore's hypotheses, a great deal of new information about the causes of democracy and authoritarianism has been generated. Even tests of a hypothesis that come up "negative" have much to teach us so long as the hypothesis is theoretically interesting to begin with.

Fourth, Moore's work inspired knowledge accumulation with respect to descriptive categories, especially social class categories. This can be seen by the work of the many scholars who applied Moore's categories to new cases not considered by Moore himself. Moreover, scholars creatively modified Moore's class categories in their subsequent research. For example, Paige's (1997) analysis of the coffee elite of Central America led him to define a new class category – agrarian-bourgeoisie – that combined features of Moore's landlord and bourgeois classes. Likewise, Rueschemeyer et al. (1992) made important refinements in understanding the role of labor repression in the conceptualization of agrarian landlords, modifications that influenced other comparative historical researchers (e.g., Wood 2000, pp. 8–9). Finally, of course, this survey shows that knowledge accumulation through iterated hypothesis testing has taken place on a large scale in the comparative historical literature on democracy and authoritarianism. Although scholars often lament the fact that causal findings are rarely subjected to replication and repeated testing in the social sciences, this charge does not apply to the Barrington Moore research program.

Hypothesis Elaboration and Knowledge Progression

The central contribution of Moore's book was to stimulate a community of scholars to elaborate his hypotheses such that we now have much coherent knowledge about the causes of democracy and authoritarianism. Such hypothesis elaboration has not merely involved ad hoc modifications to Moore's original claims. Rather, the process of reevaluation has led to new hypotheses with many testable implications not considered by Moore. As these new hypotheses have been developed, subsequent investigators have retested them, thereby initiating new processes of iterated hypothesis testing.

Rueschemeyer et al.'s *Capitalist Development and Democracy* is arguably the most important work in this Barrington Moore research program on democracy and authoritarianism. The book is especially interesting because it builds on quantitative research on democracy, using this research as a starting point for a comparative historical argument. In particular, the authors begin with the statistical association between capitalist development and democracy, which has been repeatedly confirmed in the quantitative literature.[10] Through a narrative analysis of historical sequences, their goal is to locate the intervening processes that explain why this correlation exists.

The authors arrive at a number of fruitful modifications to Moore's arguments. Their most basic hypothesis is that capitalist development is correlated with democracy because it alters the relative balance of class power in society.[11] In particular, development tends to strengthen the working class and other subordinate classes while weakening the landed upper class. The authors hypothesize that the working class will typically lead the charge for democracy, though it may need peasant, middle-class, or bourgeois allies to establish democracy successfully. By contrast, in a subtle elaboration of Moore's work, they hypothesize that landed elites dependent on a large supply of cheap labor – not necessarily labor-repressive landlords – will be the most consistently antidemocratic force. The authors test this argument

[10] A recent review of this literature can be found in Bunce (2000). Key early works include Lipset (1959), Cutwright (1963), and Bollen (1979). More recent work suggests that economic development may affect the sustainability of democracy over time rather than the emergence of democracy itself. See Londregan and Poole (1996), Gasiorowski and Power (1998), Przeworski et al. (1996), and Przeworski and Limongi (1997).

[11] In addition to class power, the authors consider the autonomous power of the state and transnational power relations to explain democratization.

by examining an impressive range of advanced capitalist and Latin American countries.

Ruth Berins Collier (1999; see also Bermeo 1997) has recently presented a somewhat more complicated portrait of the specific role of the working class in democratization. On the one hand, Collier emphasizes that the working class has been underestimated in many explanations of contemporary democratization (see also Collier and Mahoney 1997). On the other hand, however, she retests Rueschemeyer et al.'s hypotheses for the nineteenth- and early-twentieth-century cases, finding that the working-class role has been overemphasized for certain countries. She concludes that while democratization is in part a class-based process, it is also a political and strategic process in which parties and elites have a greater role to play than is often acknowledged in the Barrington Moore research program.

Works such as these – along with many other related books and articles by scholars in the Moore tradition (e.g., Huber and Stafford 1995; Paige 1997; Yashar 1997; Skocpol 1998; Wood 2000) – tell us much about the class-based origins of democracy and dictatorship. We now have solid evidence that the power of labor-dependent landed elites – if not labor-repressive landed elites, as Moore hypothesized – is negatively correlated with the establishment and persistence of democracy. For example, in Europe, we know from the work of Stephens (1989) that England is perhaps the only major exception to the inverse relationship between agrarian elite strength and democratic survival during the interwar period. In Latin America, three countries with notably significant democratic histories – Uruguay, Argentina, and Costa Rica – have all been characterized by relatively weak landlords. By contrast, at least before the 1980s, countries with more significant labor-dependent landed elites were generally more authoritarian, including Brazil, Bolivia, Peru, Ecuador, Guatemala, and El Salvador (see Huber and Stafford 1995). The biggest outlier for Latin America is probably Chile, which has a long democratic history but is often viewed as having a powerful labor-dependent landed elite.[12] At the same time, several studies suggest that the influence of landlords in shaping authoritarianism in Latin America must be seen in the light of broader historical sequences involving the formation of political coalitions (e.g., Collier and Collier 1991; Yashar 1997). For example, weak landlords may be successful at preventing

[12] However, divisions in the historiography make it difficult to characterize unambiguously the nature of the Chilean landed elite. See J. S. Valenzuela (2001).

democracy if subordinate classes are unable to form coalitions. Given these overall findings, however, it is fair to say that the weakening of landed elites is currently the most plausible explanation for why capitalist development is associated with the emergence and/or endurance of democracy in cross-national quantitative studies.[13]

We have much knowledge about the role of other classes in democratization. We know, for example, that the bourgeoisie has not played the historically progressive role envisaged by Moore and other Marxist analysts. Likewise, we know that middle-class actors have been far less consistently in favor of democratization than many modernization theorists have suggested (see Rueschemeyer et al. 1992). In general, the bourgeoisie and the middle classes have supported their own political inclusion and, when divided and facing party competition, factions of these classes have sometimes advocated the inclusion of subordinate groups to mobilize political support. However, in many historical and contemporary cases, the bourgeoisie and the middle classes have been unwilling to concede democratic rights to a broad spectrum of society (D. Collier 1979a; Luebbert 1991; Rueschemeyer et al. 1992; Huber and Stafford 1995; Paige 1997; R. Collier 1999). Comparative historical researchers have thus shown that one simply cannot sustain the general claim that the bourgeoisie or the middle classes have been central carriers of democracy, much less necessary for democracy.

We have considerable evidence that the working class was one of several important actors in many historical and contemporary processes of democratization. Likewise, there is good evidence showing that the working class has been a consistently prodemocratic class actor, even if there are important exceptions when the working class adopted an antidemocratic stance (Therborn 1977, 1979; Rueschemeyer et al. 1992; R. Collier 1999). Indeed, we now have an understanding of key variables that shape working-class attitudes toward democracy, including aristocratic privilege (e.g., Bellin 2000). Yet, we also know that democratization has rarely been a triumph from below in which workers and other lower-class groups bear

[13] As Ertman (1998) points out, however, it is sometimes difficult to sustain the argument that direct landlord "agency" was important in preventing democratic establishment or fostering democratic breakdowns. Recent comparative historical work on Latin America suggests that landlord power might be viewed as a "structural" variable that affects democratization primarily by shaping the strategic calculations and agency of other actors, including especially the military. In any case, more research needs to be done to explain the intervening variables through which landed-elite power itself affects democracy.

sole or even primary responsibility. For one thing, as Dahl (1971) suggested, historical processes of democratization often involve many steps in which different classes and actors are influential at different stages. As a generalization for the European cases, one can say that workers and subordinate groups tended to play their most important role in the final stages, while elites had the primary role in the early stages. Overall, the working-class role in Europe tended to be greatest in those historical cases where democracy was established relatively late (e.g., Sweden in 1918, Finland in 1919, Belgium in 1918) and less extensive where it was established earlier (e.g., Switzerland in 1848, Denmark in 1849, Greece in 1864) (R. Collier 1999).

In addition to knowledge about specific class actors, engagement with Moore's hypotheses has led many scholars to develop new insights into the class coalitional bases of regime outcomes. Although these studies do not necessarily offer universalistic arguments that can be applied to all times and places, they teach us much about specific sets of cases. For example, Luebbert's argument about the social class coalitions that produced liberal democracy, social democracy, and fascism in Europe during the interwar period sheds new light on the ways in which political parties shape class coalitional configurations. Although iterated hypothesis testing has called into question some of Luebbert's propositions for specific cases (see Kitschelt 1992; Ertman 1998), there is substantial empirical evidence to support his general argument that (1) alliances between liberal parties and the labor movement before World War I helped facilitate liberal democracy during the interwar period and (2) the decision of farmers' parties to forge alliances with workers' parties or with far-right parties greatly influenced whether social democracy or fascism developed. Among Luebbert's most important modifications to Moore's work are a concern with the way in which political parties mediate the interests and demands of social classes and an emphasis on a broader array of class actors than Moore's landed elites, bourgeoisie, and peasantry.

Other efforts at hypothesis elaboration have involved situating social-class causes in relation to international-systemic causes more thoroughly than was true in *Social Origins*. An important example in this regard is Downing's (1992) work on the origins of democracy and authoritarianism in early modern Europe, in which "every page . . . was written with attention to Barrington Moore's classic study" (p. 241). Despite his debt to Moore, Downing argues that the roots of regime outcomes in modern

Europe rested much more significantly with international warfare and the establishment of domestic military forces than Moore ever suggested. In particular, Downing holds that authoritarianism developed in those European countries that faced significant warfare *and* mobilized extensive domestic resources to finance modern armies; when either of these conditions was absent, democracy was the outcome. Although Downing explores at length the relationship between these variables and the class coalitional factors emphasized by Moore, the main explanation of the book highlights primarily international military pressures. Barrington Moore himself appreciated this difference, writing that Downing's work "takes a big step beyond my *Social Origins of Dictatorship and Democracy.*"[14]

More radical efforts to elaborate the hypotheses offered by Moore – while still accepting his basic research orientation – include a focus on actors and processes in civil society that cannot necessarily be reduced to social classes. In a recent formulation of this position, Ertman (1998) argues that patterns of associational life and political party competition can explain why some Western European countries maintained democracies during the interwar period, whereas others broke down into right-wing authoritarianism. In particular, he suggests that the maintenance of democracy required *both* a highly developed associational landscape *and* well-established parties and party competition. Although this "Tocquevillean" argument certainly moves beyond Moore's hypotheses, Ertman develops it through an explicit dialogue with Moore. The challenge is now for other scholars to assess Ertman's argument through iterated hypothesis testing.

As this analysis suggests, comparative historical researchers have gone well beyond Moore's work to understand the origins of democracy and authoritarianism. In this research, there has been a fruitful interaction between those studies designed to maximize generality and those studies focused closely on a small number of cases. A nice example is Moore's emphasis on landed elites, which was originally developed in relation to a limited range of cases but has subsequently been generalized to a much larger population of countries, including in recent statistical studies (e.g., Vanhanen 1997). Likewise, work focused on a small number of cases has employed insights from statistical studies in order to maximize our understanding of the causal forces at work in particular cases. A good example is Rueschemeyer et al.'s (1992) book, which built on the statistical correlation between capitalist

[14] From the quotation by Moore on the back cover of Downing's (1992) book.

democracy and democracy – originally formulated by Lipset (1959) – to offer a new comparative historical explanation of democracy.

A Note on Meta-Theory and Methodology: Structuralism and Sequence Analysis

There can be no denying the importance of *Social Origins* to the "structural" tradition in the social sciences. Although structuralism has roots going all the way back to Karl Marx and beyond, few scholars were working within this tradition when *Social Origins* was published. Instead, at the time, most scholars either avoided comparative questions about macrosocial development or addressed them from within the confines of natural history approaches and their functionalist theory variants. *Social Origins* offered such a compelling alternative that it reinvigorated an entire structural tradition that now influences scholarly work on a vast array of empirical topics in political science and sociology.

Structuralism is best conceived as a meta-theory, or a general orientation that offers guidelines for formulating hypotheses and understanding social phenomena without embracing any specific testable propositions. At the core of structuralism is the concern with analyzing objective relationships between groups and societies. Structuralism holds that configurations of social relations shape, constrain, and empower actors in predictable ways. Structuralism generally downplays or rejects cultural and value-based explanations of social phenomena. Likewise, structuralism opposes approaches that explain social outcomes solely or primarily in terms of psychological states, individual decision-making processes, or other individual-level characteristics.

Moore's structuralism drew on Marxist political economy in emphasizing class relationships as the driving force of modernization. Among Moore's many innovations was the extension of classical Marxism to the agrarian sector. Over the years, numerous scholars have found this focus on agrarian classes to be useful (e.g., Paige 1975, 1997; Skocpol 1979; Wickham-Crowley 1992; Yashar 1997). At the same time, scholars have extended Moore's emphasis on classes to other kinds of social relationships, including especially state structures and international structures (e.g., Skocpol 1979; Collier and Collier 1991; Rueschemeyer et al. 1992). The new structuralist meta-theory that has emerged emphasizes relationships among classes, relationships between classes and the state, and relationships among states (i.e., class–class, class–state, and state–state relationships). A good many of the explanatory hypotheses in comparative historical research (and now other kinds of macroanalysis) have been derived from the analysis of these relationships.

In addition to the shift toward a structuralist meta-theory, Moore revived a methodological emphasis on historical sequences and timing in comparative historical research. In contrast to commonplace arguments that stressed how the *degree to which* variables are present affects outcomes, Moore explored how the *temporal positions* of variables within sequences also influence outcomes. For Moore, the issue was, as Pierson (2000) puts it, "not just what, but *when*." For instance, Moore argued that the timing of the onset of political crises in agrarian-bureaucratic states relative to agricultural commercialization was of crucial importance. When political crises occurred *after* the development of commercial agriculture, Moore hypothesized that the bourgeoisie would be stronger and thus democracy would be more likely to emerge. By contrast, when political crises occurred *before* commercial agriculture was well established, the lingering strength of agrarian classes would more likely produce an authoritarian outcome. Since the publication of *Social Origins*, nearly all comparative historical scholars have come to theorize about the ways in which the temporal ordering of events and processes can have a significant impact on outcomes. Indeed, we now have a rich and cumulative literature that discusses the methodological issues that arise in such sequence analysis.

The O'Donnell and Linz–Stepan Research Programs

Other highly visible research programs in the field of comparative historical analysis were launched with the seminal work of Guillermo O'Donnell and of Juan J. Linz and Alfred Stepan. The O'Donnell program is similar in meta-theoretical emphases to the Moore program, but it offers a distinctive set of concepts and hypotheses concerning the evolution of political regimes in Latin America. By contrast, the Linz–Stepan program is built on a quite different meta-theoretical foundation, one that lends itself to a focus on leadership, strategic choice, and contingency.

Testing the Bureaucratic-Authoritarian Model

O'Donnell's (1973) theory of the origins of bureaucratic-authoritarian (B-A) regimes in Latin America was influenced by a series of arguments about dependent capitalist development and social and political change in Latin America.[15] His famous *Modernization and Bureaucratic-Authoritarianism: Studies in South American Politics* and related writings grew out of the "dependency theory" tradition. Dependency theory is best conceived as a meta-theory rather than a set of directly testable hypotheses; its advocates have resisted efforts to equate the approach with specific hypotheses about the effects of levels and types of dependency (e.g., Cardoso 1977; Palma 1978). Dependency theory holds that the position of a country in the global capitalist economy greatly affects its development prospects. Countries in the periphery of the global economy are prone to become dependent on "core" countries and experience highly distorted forms of capitalist development. Beyond these generalizations, actual situations of dependency will vary from one society to the next; thus the effects of dependent development must be analyzed in light of the structures of real countries. Doing so requires paying attention to the evolving interrelationship between domestic social groups and classes, the state, and external actors (Cardoso and Faletto 1979; Evans 1979).

O'Donnell advanced the dependency theory tradition by offering a specific argument about the origins of a particularly harsh and technocratic kind of authoritarian regime that emerged in the most economically advanced countries of South America beginning in the 1960s – Brazil in 1964–85, Argentina in 1966–70 and 1976–83, Uruguay in 1973–85, and Chile in 1973–90. To explain how these B-A regimes could emerge despite substantial economic development, O'Donnell focused on three crucial aspects of dependent modernization: industrialization, the political activation of the popular sector, and the growth of technocratic roles in the state and society (see Collier 1979a, pp. 25–8). First, he stressed the problems associated with the "deepening" of industrialization in dependent countries, which involved the challenges of moving from the production of simple consumer goods to the manufacture of intermediate and capital goods. Although light consumer industries could thrive for a period of time under tariff protections and state subsidies, eventually inflation, balance of payments problems, and saturated domestic demand would force policymakers to pursue the production of more advanced capital goods. In doing so, they would likely adopt more market-oriented policies and actively seek foreign investment. Second, during the early and easy phase of light

[15] In particular, O'Donnell was building on the work of scholars such as Fernando Henrique Cardoso and Enzo Faletto, Philippe Schmitter, Alfred Stepan, Thomas Skidmore, Celso Furtado, Torcuato di Tella, and many others. See O'Donnell (1973, p. 53, fn. 2).

industrialization, workers and other popular actors developed substantial political power under the protection of populist state policies. With the introduction of economic crises and orthodox polices, however, these politically activated groups would be prone to carry out strikes and protests, exacerbating ongoing economic and political problems. Third, initial industrialization led to the expansion of technocrats in the private sector and the state, including the military. These preexisting alliances between military and civilian technocrats could promote the formation of a coup coalition that would ultimately establish a repressive B-A regime.

These arguments attracted substantial attention in the mid-1970s, as O'Donnell's theory – originally formulated when only Argentina and Brazil had B-A regimes – seemed to predict correctly the emergence of bureaucratic authoritarianism in Chile and Uruguay as well as its reappearance in Argentina. The predictive aspect of this theory launched efforts at iterated hypothesis testing among scholars, the most serious of which took place with the publication of *The New Authoritarianism in Latin America* (Collier 1979a). David Collier's (1979b) first chapter brought together O'Donnell's various arguments into a single coherent model, offering a clear conceptual framework and a set of hypotheses for other contributors to assess. Subsequent chapters in the volume then rigorously evaluated, refined, and rejected these concepts and hypotheses. As with Moore's work, some of the most important challenges to O'Donnell's model came from analyses that reevaluated the evidence in light of the B-A cases themselves. For example, with respect to the hypothesis about deepening, Hirschman (1979), Serra (1979), and Kaufman (1979) found little support outside of Argentina. Instead, these scholars showed that a concern with deepening industrialization was often of little importance to key political actors inside B-A regimes. Other hypotheses – such as those concerning the role of popular sector protest and technocrats – received mixed support and were subsequently elaborated in fruitful directions through comparisons with additional Latin American countries. For example, subsequent scholars found that the growing political role of the popular sector was one element in the creation of B-A regimes. However, among the Latin American countries, the strength of the popular sector varied a great deal, and not all B-A cases were marked by a powerful popular sector (e.g., Brazil). Other specific hypotheses were more consistently supported by the Latin American countries. This was true with the general verification of O'Donnell's argument that a particularly severe "demands–performance gap" was associated with the onset of bureaucratic authoritarianism in Brazil, Argentina, Uruguay, and Chile.

In the concluding chapter, Collier (1979c) usefully synthesized the volume's findings, providing a kind of "scorecard" for assessing O'Donnell's hypotheses and pointing toward priorities for future research.

Subsequent efforts dedicated to testing O'Donnell's hypotheses evaluated other specific implications of O'Donnell's original model (e.g., Remmer and Merkx 1982; Cammack 1985; Remmer 1989). Most of these analyses, however, used O'Donnell's hypotheses as a point of departure for their own arguments about authoritarianism in Latin America. For example, Munck (1998) used O'Donnell's work as a basis for theorizing about the transition from bureaucratic authoritarianism to democracy in Latin America. In doing so, he emphasized how regimes evolve through a series of life cycle phases (origin, evolution, and transition) and how identifiable variables (degree of cohesion among governing elites, strength of opposition, and institutional arrangements) drive the movement from one phase to the next. Remmer (1989) also built on O'Donnell's model by hypothesizing that exclusionary authoritarian regimes are likely to emerge at relatively low and relatively high levels of socioeconomic modernization, whereas more inclusionary authoritarian regimes are likely to emerge at middle levels of socioeconomic modernization. Remmer's proposed processes for mediating these relationships – such as international integration, political dynamics, and social inequality – were extensions of the O'Donnell model.

O'Donnell did not specify scope conditions in a way that unambiguously defined a set of cases for testing the B-A model. Not surprisingly, disputes subsequently emerged over the extension of the B-A argument to additional cases outside of Latin America. For example, questions arose about whether the argument could be meaningfully tested with evidence from countries such as Turkey and South Korea and from regions such as Southern Europe and Africa (O'Donnell 1973, pp. 92–3; Collier 1979b, pp. 395–7; Mouzelis 1986, pp. 177–81; Im 1987; Richards and Waterbury 1990, p. 359). Most scholars who extended O'Donnell's argument outside of Latin America were not particularly concerned with using new evidence to refute the B-A model. Rather, they drew on the model as a set of sensitizing concepts and orienting hypotheses, finding that O'Donnell's ideas had substantial utility when refined to apply to the new context. In this sense, even though many of the specific hypotheses of O'Donnell's model were called into question with evidence from Latin America, experts on regions other than Latin America were still able to draw fruitfully on the descriptive findings and meta-theoretical orientation proposed by O'Donnell.

In the field of Latin American politics, O'Donnell's work was one important stimulus for Collier and Collier's *Shaping the Political Arena* (1991), which helped crystallize the "critical juncture" approach now used in many comparative historical analyses. In the concluding chapter of *The New Authoritarianism*, D. Collier (1979c) had suggested that the rise and fall of authoritarianism should be seen within the framework of longer cycles of regime change. *Shaping the Political Arena* picked up this theme by arguing that the different ways in which labor incorporation occurred in early- to mid-twentieth-century Latin America had a major impact on events in the post–World War II period. For example, in Brazil, labor incorporation was carried out by the state in the 1930s and early 1940s with the goal of depoliticizing and controlling the labor movement. As a result, by the late 1950s, Brazil was characterized by substantial political polarization and policy immobilism, conditions that directly contributed to the breakdown of democracy and the emergence of military rule in 1964. By contrast, in Venezuela, a political party with the goal of mobilizing and actively promoting the labor movement carried out labor incorporation in the 1930s and 1940s. As a result, by the late 1950s, Venezuela had established a relatively peaceful electoral system marked by competition between two competing parties.

Collier and Collier's argument was sweeping in scope and detail, presenting a fine-grained analysis of eight countries across several decades. The breadth and nuance of this argument have made it difficult for scholars to pursue an iterated hypothesis-testing program. Nevertheless, the critical juncture framework developed in *Shaping the Political Arena* has been explicitly adopted by several scholars working on regime change and party system evolution in Latin America (e.g., Scully 1992; Yashar 1997; Mahoney 2001). These works signal an important intersection between the classic tradition of comparative historical analysis associated with Moore and the political economy and dependency perspectives associated with work on Latin America. It is now difficult or impossible to separate those regime change studies that fall in the Moore tradition from those that fall in the tradition of O'Donnell.

A Voluntarist Meta-Theory: Leadership and Beyond

A quite different research program has its origins in the famous *Breakdown of Democratic Regimes* series edited by Juan J. Linz and Alfred Stepan (1978). This Linz–Stepan program was motivated by a concern with political agency and voluntarism, including an effort to move away from the more "deterministic" structural approaches found within the emerging Moore and O'Donnell research programs. The goal of the series was to incorporate leadership and contingent political choices alongside more structuralist factors such as class conflict. As Linz (1978) explained in the theoretical volume for the *Breakdown* series, "We feel that the structural characteristics of societies . . . constitute a series of opportunities and constraints for the social and political actors." However, he went on to say that "We shall start from the assumption that those actors have certain choices that can increase or decrease the probability of the persistence and stability of a regime. . . . leadership . . . can be decisive and cannot be predicted by any model" (pp. 4, 5). In the case analyses of the *Breakdown* project, the volume's participants developed this voluntaristic theme, underscoring the importance of leadership as the "realm of the non-inevitable" in regime change processes (Stepan 1978; see also A. Valenzuela 1978).

Given this emphasis on political elites and voluntarism, it is hardly surprising that Linz and Stepan were as concerned with *describing* the central elements and modal stages of democratic breakdowns as with *explaining* these events through well-specified independent variables. Much attention focused on the political processes and sequences that characterized democratic breakdowns. For example, Linz (1978) mapped out the characteristic stages through which democratic regimes evolve in the process of breaking down into authoritarian regimes. These stages include decreased regime efficacy and effectiveness, the emergence of "unsolvable" problems, declining levels of overall regime legitimacy, the appearance of powerful disloyal oppositions, the transformation of a loyal opposition into a semiloyal opposition, and, eventually, the overthrow of the democratic regime. Central emphasis was placed on the role of incumbents in carrying out actions that could defuse regime crises, thereby hindering movement to subsequent stages and cutting short the breakdown process. In addition, within the modal pattern of breakdown, much scholarly energy was spent on developing subpatterns, nuances, and variations tailored to particular cases of special interest to Linz (e.g., 1978, pp. 75–6).

Along the way, the Linz–Stepan program also offered, at least implicitly, several hypotheses about the causes of authoritarianism. Many of these hypotheses were grounded in assumptions about the legitimacy of regime systems, with declining legitimacy understood to generate democratic breakdowns. Other hypotheses codified conventional but important understandings about the political trends that preceded a transition to authoritarianism. For example, Linz identified shifts in the electorate toward parties of the extreme right and condemnations of the government by important elites as percipients of democratic breakdown. These hypotheses were less successful at stimulating a focused program of iterated evaluation equivalent to what characterized the Moore and O'Donnell programs. For example, problems arose in establishing measures of legitimacy that were fully independent of regime stability, and scholars did not devote substantial efforts to testing whether the political events identified by Linz were in fact consistently related to regime change.

The comparatively limited cumulative knowledge about causal processes in the Linz–Stepan program is partially balanced by the program's success at stimulating knowledge accumulation through descriptive findings. Perhaps the most basic contribution of the Linz–Stepan program was concept development and regime classification. Linz's (1975) famous work on the defining dimensions of democratic, authoritarian, and totalitarian regimes has influenced countless studies of regime change. His definition of an authoritarian regime – limited pluralism and the absence of an elaborate ideology among governing elites and limited political mobilization within society (1975, p. 264) – remains the most influential in the literature. This definition facilitated the creation of authoritarian subtypes such as bureaucratic authoritarianism, military authoritarianism, and personalistic authoritarianism (i.e., sultanism). These concepts are among the more stable analytic categories in the field, representing crucial foundations for a great deal of scholarly work. Linz's typology also helped scholars formally specify the distinction between authoritarian regimes such as Franco's Spain and totalitarian communist systems such as the Soviet Union; the latter, Linz noted, were marked by monism and an elaborate guiding ideology among governing elites and by high levels of channeled obligatory participation within society.

Perhaps second only to Robert Dahl (1971), Linz was a major founder of the procedural and minimal definition of democracy that has become the consensus currently employed in research on democratization. Linz defined democracy as "legal freedom to formulate and advocate political alternatives with the concomitant rights to association, free speech, and other basic freedoms of person; free and nonviolent competition among leaders with periodic validation of their claim to rule; inclusion of all effective political offices in the democratic process; and provision for the participation of all members of the political community, whatever their political preferences" (1978, p. 5). For many or most scholars today, democracy is understood in similar terms as encompassing contested elections with broad suffrage and the absence of major fraud, along with effective guarantees of civil liberties, including freedom of speech, assembly, and association. Although many comparative historical researchers use this definition to understand democracy as a dichotomous variable, they also routinely employ regime subtypes (e.g., electoral democracy, restrictive democracy, soft authoritarianism) that capture different gradations (see Collier and Levitsky 1997).

As for the voluntarist meta-theory of the Linz–Stepan program, its influence can be readily seen in the "transitions literature" on contemporary democratization. In their now classic study *Tentative Conclusions about Uncertain Democracies*, O'Donnell and Schmitter (1986) extended the anti-structuralist orientation of Linz and Stepan, suggesting that "normal science" may not be appropriate for explaining contemporary democracy in the developing world. These authors likewise followed Linz and Stepan in offering a primarily descriptive approach, one oriented toward identifying the modal pattern through which authoritarian regimes evolve into democracies. When compared to structural explanations, there was a clear shift in focus to elites, pacts, political crafting, and effective leadership – themes that were quickly picked up by other scholars (e.g., Baloyra 1987; Di Palma 1990; Higley and Gunther 1992).[16] As more and more countries became democratic, a large literature emerged that categorized alternative paths to democracy and "modes of transition" for different sets of countries, often drawing distinctions based on the varying roles played by political incumbents and opposition actors (Linz 1981; Share and Mainwaring 1986; Stepan 1986; Karl 1990; Karl and Schmitter 1991).

One can legitimately raise questions about the extent to which the Linz–Stepan program falls within the comparative historical research tradition, as defined in the introduction to this volume. On the one hand, the program has been highly successful at formulating concepts and classification schemes that have become building blocks for research in this field. The program also has used history as a basis for illuminating overall modal patterns of regime change. Yet, on the other hand, comparative historical research is defined by the causal analysis of well-specified outcomes in carefully delineated cases. The Linz–Stepan program has been less focused on

[16] See also Diamond, Linz, and Lipset's (1988–9) edited volumes on *Democracy in Developing Countries*. Although this study incorporates a wide range of variables, it lacks a systematic framework to integrate these variables. As a result, its main value has been to offer rich descriptions of processes in particular cases.

this activity. The transitions literature, in particular, has not been the site of substantial cumulative research about causal findings. As scholars such as Nancy Bermeo (1990), Karen Remmer (1991), and Gerardo Munck (1994) have argued, the voluntarist underpinnings of this work have led many analysts to characterize each transition as unique and unpredictable, while comparatively little effort has been devoted to offering generalizations that might stimulate iterated processes of hypothesis testing. As a result, scholars have not learned as much from one another about causal processes in recent transitions to democracy as was true with research programs grounded in more structural meta-theories.

Over the last few years, two fruitful extensions of the transitions literature have taken place that might underpin more successful research programs in the future. First, scholars from an alternative methodological and analytical orientation – rational choice analysis – have been drawn to the bargaining and negotiation aspects of this literature. In O'Donnell and Schmitter's original formulation, the transition process was portrayed as a four-player game driven by the strategies of regime hardliners and softliners, and opposition maximalists and minimalists. These ideas have been more formally presented using the tools of game theory (e.g., Bova 1991; Colomer 1991). In addition, analysts have used various game theory models to compare and contrast the transition processes across multiple countries (e.g., Przeworski 1991; Cohen 1994; Geddes 1999).

A second promising extension involves efforts to build a bridge between the voluntarist emphases of the transitions literature and the more structural concerns of research in the Moore and O'Donnell programs. Samuel P. Huntington's (1991) *The Third Wave: Democratization in the Late Twentieth Century* attempts such a synthesis by distinguishing between the "causes" of democracy, which correspond to historical and structural factors such as economic development, changes in the global economy, and the spread of international norms, and the "causers" of democracy, which correspond to the regime actors and opposition factions who make key choices during transition periods that produce democratic regimes (see Mahoney and Snyder 1999). Huntington's book offers a remarkably good review of existing structural and process-centered works on democratization, contributing much in its own right to taking stock of current findings. Nevertheless, the book does not offer an explicit mechanism for integrating the diverse findings of the transitions literature and the structuralist literature. As a result, while *The Third Wave* stands out for its bold coverage of vast literatures and cases, it cannot be said to offer a framework that others could use directly to bridge voluntarism and structuralism. Similar remarks can be made about Larry Diamond's (1999) sweeping analysis of democratic transition and consolidation, which extends Huntington's work to the late 1990s and explores democratic endurance and the future of democracy in the developing world.[17]

Stephan Haggard and Robert R. Kaufman's (1995) *The Political Economy of Democratic Transitions* is another interesting example of how more structuralist factors might be brought into the transitions literature. These authors draw on this literature to argue that divisions within authoritarian regimes and defections among key elites can be crucial impetuses to democratization. However, they show that these cleavages usually occur under identifiable and predictable structural conditions, in particular under the conditions of major economic crises (e.g., Argentina, Bolivia, Brazil, Peru, Uruguay, and the Philippines). By contrast, when an economic crisis does not accompany the transition (e.g., Chile, Korea, Turkey, and Thailand), challenges to authoritarian rule are more likely to revolve around political demands for liberalization rather the full modal pattern specified in the transitions literature.[18] While Haggard and Kaufman's arguments have not yet (to my knowledge) been subjected to iterated hypothesis testing, they offer a potentially transportable approach for combining structural context with strategic actor choice.

Other scholars have used political institutional variables as a means to build a bridge between the transition literature and the concerns of more structural approaches. A good example is Linz and Stepan's latest contribution, *Problems of Democratic Transition and Consolidation* (1996). This book argues that the nature of antecedent authoritarian regimes shapes the strategies of actors during democratic transitions and the prospects for successful transition. In doing so, it illustrates the relevance of Linz's typology of authoritarian regimes to the explanation of democracy. Thus, Linz and Stepan show how different kinds of nondemocratic regimes (e.g., authoritarian, totalitarian, and sultanistic regimes) are characterized by different institutional properties, and how these institutional differences in turn provide distinct obstacles and opportunities for authoritarian regime incumbents and prodemocratic challengers. Several of these ideas have been formalized

[17] Diamond's (1999) book is primarily concerned with democratic consolidation and thus falls outside of the issues considered here.

[18] Haggard and Kaufman also show that "crisis transitions" versus "noncrisis transitions" are associated with the quality of the subsequent democratic regime that emerges.

and tested further in Geddes's (1999) important work on the demise of different kinds of authoritarian regimes.

The new Linz–Stepan book is part of a broader effort by scholars to "bring the old regime back in" to the study of regime change (e.g., Roeder 1993; Bratton and Van de Walle 1997; see also Snyder and Mahoney 1999). As a result of this renewed focus, we now know more about the causal effects of political institutional variables than we did just a few years ago.[19] For example, we have good reason to believe that the transition to democracy in sultanistic regimes will be especially difficult because prodemocratic actors must build a civil society, the rule of law, and political and electoral institutions almost completely from scratch (Linz and Stepan 1996, pp. 56–8). Likewise, we know that the degree to which social protest accompanies democratization processes depends on the nature of the antecedent regime. In particular, sultanistic regimes are especially susceptible to violent overthrow, whereas B-A regimes will rarely meet such a demise (e.g., Bratton and Van de Walle 1997). As for totalitarian regimes, we have good evidence that they tend to break down into a kind of "posttotalitarian regime" before democracy can be established. Transitions from such posttotalitarian regimes to democracy will then often require a lapse in the ability of incumbents to employ the option of repression (Linz and Stepan 1996, pp. 57–61).

To recapitulate, O'Donnell's work on bureaucratic-authoritarianism stimulated a focused program of iterated hypothesis testing and hypothesis elaboration in the 1970s and 1980s. In addition, O'Donnell's research made major theoretical and methodological contributions to the dependency theory of the 1970s, and to more recent work on critical junctures and path dependence. Although the worldwide spread of democratic regimes has shifted some attention away from the further elaboration of O'Donnell's explanation of authoritarianism, his work remains a fundamental point of departure for scholars who work on the topic. In contrast to O'Donnell's concern with causal analysis, the Linz–Stepan program was focused more on description and classification, and as a result did not immediately stimulate a cumulative research program based on causal findings. However,

[19] Recently, many scholars – especially in political science – have emphasized the importance of institutional variables such as constitutional laws and electoral rules in their explanations of political outcomes (e.g., Shugart and Carey 1992; Mainwaring and Shugart 1997). These kinds of institutional variables are gradually making their way into the study of regime change.

recent works more centrally located in the comparative historical tradition have fruitfully drawn on important aspects of Linz and Stepan's work to develop exciting new agendas for the study of democracy and authoritarianism, including the challenge of bridging voluntarist and structural meta-theoretical orientations and incorporating work inspired by rational choice theory into the field of comparative historical analysis.

Conclusion

Most social scientists believe that knowledge accumulation is an important measure of the success of a research program. Yet, the meaning of knowledge accumulation is often unclear or understood only implicitly. In this essay, I have argued that accumulation occurs when the generation of new knowledge is dependent on the existence of prior knowledge. And I have argued that knowledge in a research tradition such as comparative historical analysis consists of descriptive findings, causal findings, methodologies, and meta-theoretical formulations. In offering this definition of knowledge accumulation, I have sought to initiate a larger discussion about the nature of knowledge accumulation in social science research.

The essay presented evidence suggesting that knowledge accumulation has taken place in the comparative historical study of democracy and authoritarianism. Three research programs were examined at length: the Moore, O'Donnell, and Linz–Stepan programs. Each of these programs has been characterized by multiple scholars building on one another's work to arrive at conclusions about the sources of democracy and authoritarianism. The Moore program has been especially notable at sustaining an iterated research agenda focused on causal analysis and a structuralist meta-theory, but the O'Donnell and Linz–Stepan traditions have made many valuable contributions in their own right, including in the important areas of concept formation and methodology.

Before exploring the findings of this literature, I would like to reflect on the question of why social scientists should care about knowledge accumulation. What concretely is gained by a research community that produces cumulative knowledge as opposed to an alternative research community that offers noncumulative knowledge? The answer must be that the cumulative research program offers knowledge that is more valid and more substantively enlightening than the noncumulative program. Indeed, the production of such knowledge can be considered the ultimate criterion for evaluating scholarly progress in the social sciences (Coser 1975).

There are clear reasons to believe that the total amount of substantive enlightenment produced by a cumulative research program will surpass that generated by many independent scholars working in a noncumulative program. This is true in part because social science findings are always uncertain, and a cumulative program helps relieve some (but not all) of this uncertainty through replication and retesting. More important, a cumulative research program allows for consciously using the knowledge that others have developed and thereby learning from previous researchers. To the degree that one believes scholars can learn from one another and that learning facilitates knowledge generation, cumulative research communities have an inherent advantage over their noncumulative rivals.

Building on Coser's work, James Rule (1997) provides an interesting thought experiment to measure the extent of substantive enlightenment produced by any individual work in a research community. He asks: "What would be lost, in the broadest assessment, should this line of inquiry simply be stricken from the intellectual record?" (p. 15). Cumulative research programs fare much better than noncumulative programs with respect to Rule's question. In cumulative programs, each piece of research is important not only for the findings it presents, but also because the conclusions of subsequent research depend on these findings. Thus, to remove a single important piece of research from the intellectual record of a cumulative program would entail a huge loss of knowledge, since a great deal of subsequent research would also be lost. For example, to strike the work of Barrington Moore from the intellectual record would not only entail the loss of Moore's findings, but also the loss of countless other works on democracy and authoritarianism. By contrast, in a noncumulative program, the removal of a given piece of research entails only a loss of the findings offered in that particular work.

In the field of comparative historical analysis, many scholars have sought to learn about the origins and workings of democratic and authoritarian regimes. To evaluate their success, one can apply Rule's standard to the field as a whole: What would be lost if one were to strike *all* comparative historical work from the record? Based on the preceding evidence, the answer appears to be much of what we currently know about democracy and authoritarianism. For one thing, in terms of descriptive findings, we would lose many of the basic concepts and conceptual typologies that permit scholarly communication. Scholars are able to have meaningful discussions about democratic and authoritarian regimes – and their various subtypes – in part because comparative historical researchers formulated these concepts and applied them more or less consistently over time. A basic consensus now exists about the classification of countries into democratic and authoritarian regimes; subsequent findings about the causal origins of these regimes have been dependent on this conceptual development.

Without the comparative historical literature, we would also know far less about the origins of democratic and authoritarian regimes. True, we might still have valuable statistical findings concerning the relationship between democracy and readily quantifiable variables such as economic development and education. However, we would have much less knowledge about other kinds of explanatory variables such as social classes, the state, and international structures. And the information we did have about these variables would often be highly misleading, if not simply wrong. For example, we might still suppose that the bourgeoisie or the middle class is the main agent behind democratization. Or we might still erroneously imagine that democratization is fundamentally an urban process in which rural classes have little role to play. We might not have even considered that factors such as the autonomy of the state from the dominant class can influence the democratization process.

In terms of positive claims, we now have many solid findings that are far more reliable than our findings of the past. We have good evidence that the working class played a major role in pushing forward democracy, especially in the historical transitions of Northern Europe and the contemporary transitions of Southern Europe, Latin America, and Africa. Our existing knowledge indicates that, as a general proposition, working-class strength is positively associated with democracy. Yet, we also have good hypotheses about the conditions under which working-class strength will not be positively associated with democracy. These conditions include an inability of the working class to form coalitions with other class actors through instruments such as political parties, the inclusion of labor in the governing coalition of an authoritarian regime, and the existence of a labor movement that enjoys a privileged status position within the society of a country with an authoritarian regime. Furthermore, we know that working-class mobilization in developing countries often immediately precedes a regime change, whether it is a transition to democracy or authoritarianism. While workers' strikes and protests do not guarantee a regime transition in the Third World, we have good evidence to believe that they make it more likely.

Substantial evidence also exists that the presence of powerful landlords who control significant peasant labor is negatively related to democracy. In fact, before the recent wave of democratization, the absence of this condition acted as an almost always necessary condition for the creation and endurance of democracy (or, said differently, the presence of powerful labor-controlling landlords was an almost always sufficient condition for an authoritarian outcome). This finding is currently the most plausible interpretation of the statistical association suggesting that democratic regimes with a high level of economic development rarely become authoritarian regimes. That is, democracies with high levels of economic development tend to have weak landed elites, which reduces the likelihood of any authoritarian breakdown.

Analysis of the impact of state structures on democracy and authoritarianism has been a fruitful site of substantive findings. Comparative historical researchers who work on Latin American regimes have suggested that the development of the military is negatively related to democracy. Recently, this finding has been confirmed in careful work that combines qualitative and quantitative analysis (see Bowman 2002), though it has not been tested for other regions of the Third World as far as I know. Much research suggests that alliances between the bourgeoisie and the military can be a recipe for authoritarianism in developing countries, including in the context of rapid economic development. Current findings also suggest that the lack of bureaucratic development of the state apparatus is closely tied to the persistence of personalistic regimes in certain areas of the Third World (e.g., nineteenth-century Latin America and contemporary Africa). Although some state autonomy from dominant classes is necessary for democracy, we have good reason to believe that such autonomy may actually promote personalistic-authoritarian regimes if other conditions are not favorable to democratization. For example, going back to Marx's work on Bonapartism, comparative historical researchers have found that personalistic regimes often appear in countries where dominant classes are divided among themselves.

The comparative historical literature has made us more sensitive to the potential effects of international conditions on regime outcomes. While international events may sometimes directly force a regime change (e.g., postwar Japan), they are often mediated by domestic conditions, in particular the kinds of class and state structures that comparative historical researchers explore. For example, international events are more likely to promote democracy if they weaken landed elites, strengthen working classes, weaken the military, and/or undermine alliances between dominant classes and the military (opposite values on these variables make authoritarianism more likely). World-historical changes also influence the onset of democracy and authoritarianism, and comparative historical researchers have contributed to our knowledge about the effects of these changes. For instance, they have set the current agenda of analyzing democratic "waves," defined as periods during which the number of transitions from authoritarian regimes to democratic regimes greatly exceeds the number of transitions in the other direction.[20] Moreover, they have developed crucial insights about how the very processes that constitute a transition to democracy shift over time. For example, whereas in the nineteenth and early twentieth century democratization was often an incremental and slow-moving process in which decades of reforms accumulated to produce a democratic regime, by the late twentieth century democratization was often a fast-moving and dramatic process in which a full-blown authoritarian regime was converted into a democracy in a matter of months. Existing knowledge suggests that this difference in the process of democratization itself is closely linked to the spread of knowledge about democratic institutions, norms supportive of democracy, and actors and institutions in society capable of sustaining democratic behavior.

Most comparative historical studies of democracy and authoritarianism seek to identify causal patterns for carefully selected domains of cases; they do not offer general arguments that apply to all cases and times. Hence, a full appreciation of the contribution of comparative historical analysis would require asking about the origins of democracy and authoritarianism in specific countries and assessing what this research tradition has taught us about these specific countries. Although this exercise cannot be pursued here, the preceding analysis suggests that comparative historical researchers have fundamentally shaped the way we think about the origins of democracy and authoritarianism in many countries of the world. Indeed, if asked about the causes of democracy in France (or in Costa Rica, Sweden, India, or just about any other individual country), most scholars who work on regime change would probably answer by drawing heavily on the findings of comparative historical analysis.

Thanks to the work of comparative historical researchers, then, we now know a good deal about the origins of democracy and authoritarianism.

[20] See, for example, Huntington (1991), Markoff (1996), Diamond (1999), and Doorenspleet (2000). In addition to systematically organizing descriptive information about democratic waves, comparative historical researchers have formulated several plausible hypotheses to account for the recent wave of democratization, highlighting factors such as new information technology, pressures from the United States for democratization in the aftermath of the Cold War, and global isomorphism as a single world culture expands.

Much more work remains to be done, but the prospects for future insight are promising: A large number of comparative historical researchers continue to anchor their studies of democracy and authoritarianism in the research programs previously described. These scholars are often younger individuals, not uncommonly a generation or more in age removed from early path breakers like Moore, O'Donnell, and Linz (e.g., Downing 1992; Ekiert 1996; Yashar 1997; Snyder 1998; Gould 1999; Grzymala-Busse 2002; Angrist 2000; Brownlee 2001; Mahoney 2001; Bowman 2002; Luong 2002). The work of these younger scholars, I believe, will go well beyond that of their teachers – not because of the failings of earlier work, but because the new generation can build directly on existing knowledge without having to retrace previous steps. Those founders of the modern comparative historical research tradition who explored questions of democracy and authoritarianism could scarcely have hoped to accomplish anything more.

References

Angrist, Michele. 2000. "Political Parties and Regime Formation in the Middle East: Turkish Democratization in Comparative Perspective." Ph.D. dissertation, Princeton University.

Baloyra, Enrique, ed. 1987. *Comparing New Democracies: Transition and Consolidation in Mediterranean Europe and the Southern Cone*. Boulder, CO: Westview Press.

Bellin, Eva. 2000. "Contingent Democrats: Industrialists, Labor, and Democratization in Late-Developing Countries." *World Politics* 52: 175–205.

Bensel, Richard Franklin. 1990. *Yankee Leviathan: The Origins of Central State Authority in America, 1859–1877*. New York: Cambridge University Press.

Bermeo, Nancy. 1990. "Rethinking Regime Change." *Comparative Politics* 22: 359–77.

1997. "Myths of Moderation: Confrontation and Conflict during Democratic Transitions." *Comparative Politics* 29: 305–22.

Bernhard, Michael. 2001. "Democratization in Germany: A Reappraisal." *Comparative Politics* 33: 379–400.

Bollen, Kenneth. 1979. "Political Democracy and the Timing of Development." *American Sociological Review* 44: 572–87.

Bova, Russell. 1991. "Political Dynamics of the Post-Communist Transition: A Comparative Perspective." Pp. 113–38 in *Liberalization and Democratization: Change in the Soviet Union and Eastern Europe*, edited by Nancy Bermeo. Baltimore, MD: Johns Hopkins University Press.

Bowman, Kirk. 2002. *Militarization, Democracy, and Development: The Perils of Praetorianism in Latin America*. University Park: Pennsylvania State University Press.

Bratton, Michael and Nicolas Van de Walle. 1997. *Democratic Experiments in Africa: Regime Transition in Comparative Perspective*. Cambridge: Cambridge University Press.

Democracy and Authoritarianism

Brownlee, Jason M. 2001. "And Yet They Persist: Explaining Survival and Transitions in Patrimonial Regimes." Manuscript, Princeton University.

Bunce, Valerie. 2000. "Comparative Democratization: Big and Bounded Generalizations." *Comparative Political Studies* 33: 703–34.

Cammack, Paul. 1985. "The Political Economy of Contemporary Military Regimes in Latin America: From Bureaucratic Authoritarianism to Restructuring." Pp. 1–36 in *Generals in Retreat*, edited by Philip O'Brien and Paul Cammack. Manchester: Manchester University Press.

Cardoso, Fernando Henrique. 1977. "The Consumption of Dependency Theory in the United States." *Latin American Research Review* 12: 7–24.

Cardoso, Fernando Henrique and Enzo Faletto. 1979. *Dependency and Development in Latin America*. Berkeley: University of California Press.

Castles, Francis G. 1973. "Barrington Moore's Thesis and Swedish Political Development." *Government and Opposition* 8: 313–31.

Cohen, Bernard P. 1989. *Developing Sociological Knowledge: Theory and Method.* Chicago: Nelson-Hall.

Cohen, Youssef. 1994. *Radicals, Reformers, and Reactionaries: The Prisoner's Dilemma and the Collapse of Democracy in Latin America*. Chicago: University of Chicago Press.

Collier, David, ed. 1979a. *The New Authoritarianism in Latin America*. Princeton, NJ: Princeton University Press.

1979b. "Overview of the Bureaucratic-Authoritarian Model." Pp. 19–32 in *The New Authoritarianism in Latin America*, edited by David Collier. Princeton, NJ: Princeton University Press.

1979c. "The Bureaucratic-Authoritarian Model: Synthesis and Priorities for Future Research." Pp. 363–97 in *The New Authoritarianism in Latin America*, edited by David Collier. Princeton, NJ: Princeton University Press.

Collier, David and Steven Levitsky. 1997. "Democracy with Adjectives: Conceptual Innovation in Comparative Research." *World Politics* 49: 430–51.

Collier, Ruth Berins. 1999. *Paths Toward Democracy: The Working Class and Elites in Western Europe and South America*. New York: Cambridge University Press.

Collier, Ruth Berins and David Collier. 1991. *Shaping the Political Arena: Critical Junctures, the Labor Movement, and Regime Dynamics in Latin America*. Princeton, NJ: Princeton University Press.

Collier, Ruth Berins and James Mahoney. 1997. "Adding Collective Actors to Collective Outcomes: Labor and Recent Democratization in South America and Southern Europe." *Comparative Politics* 29: 285–303.

Colomer, Josep M. 1991. "Transitions by Agreement: Modeling the Spanish Way." *American Political Science Review* 85: 1283–1302.

Coser, Lewis. 1975. "Presidential Address: Two Methods in Search of a Substance." *American Sociological Review* 40: 691–700.

Cutwright, Philips. 1963. "National Political Development: Measurement and Analysis." *American Sociological Review* 28: 42–59.

Dahl, Robert. 1971. *Polyarchy: Participation and Opposition*. New Haven, CT: Yale University Press.

Di Palma, Giuseppe. 1990. *To Craft Democracies: An Essay on Democratic Transitions*. Berkeley: University of California Press.
Diamond, Larry. 1999. *Developing Democracy: Toward Consolidation*. Baltimore, MD: Johns Hopkins University Press.
Diamond, Larry, Juan J. Linz, and Seymour Martin Lipset, eds. 1988–9. *Democracy in Developing Countries*. Four volumes. Boulder, CO: Lynne Rienner.
Doorenspleet, Renske. 2000. "Reassessing the Three Waves of Democratization." *World Politics* 52: 384–406.
Downing, Brian M. 1992. *The Military Revolution and Political Change: Origins of Democracy and Autocracy in Early Modern Europe*. Princeton, NJ: Princeton University Press.
Ekiert, G. 1996. *The State Against Society: Political Crises and Their Aftermath in East Central Europe*. Princeton, NJ: Princeton University Press.
Ertman, Thomas. 1997. *Birth of the Leviathan: Building States and Regimes in Medieval and Early Modern Europe*. Cambridge: Cambridge University Press.
1998. "Democracy and Dictatorship in Interwar Western Europe Revisited." *World Politics* 50: 475–505.
Evans, Peter B. 1979. *Dependent Development: The Alliance of Multinational, State, and Local Capital in Brazil*. Princeton, NJ: Princeton University Press.
Freese, Lee. 1980. "The Problem of Cumulative Knowledge." Pp. 13–69 in *Theoretical Methods in Sociology: Seven Essays*, edited by Lee Freese. Pittsburgh, PA: University of Pittsburgh Press.
Gallie, W. B. 1956. "Essentially Contested Concepts." *Proceedings of the Aristotelian Society* 56. London: Harrison and Sons.
Gasiorowski, Mark and Timothy J. Power. 1998. "The Structural Determinants of Democratic Consolidation: Evidence from the Third World." *Comparative Political Studies* 31: 740–71.
Geddes, Barbara. 1999. "What Do We Know about Democratization after Twenty Years?" *Annual Review of Political Science* 2: 129–48.
Gould, Andrew. 1999. *Origins of Liberal Dominance: State, Church, and Party in Nineteenth Century Europe*. Ann Arbor: University of Michigan Press.
Grzymala-Busse, Anna Maria. 2002. *Redeeming the Communist Past: The Regeneration of Communist Parties in East Central Europe*. New York: Cambridge University Press.
Gudmundson, Lowell. 1995. "Lord and Peasant in the Making of Modern Central America." Pp. 151–76 in *Agrarian Structure and Political Power: Landlord and Peasant in the Making of Latin America*, edited by Evelyne Huber and Frank Safford. Pittsburgh: University of Pittsburgh Press.
Haggard, Stephan and Robert R. Kaufman. 1995. *The Political Economy of Democratic Transitions*. Princeton, NJ: Princeton University Press.
Halperín Donghi, Tulio. 1995. "The Buenos Aires Landed Class and the Shape of Argentine Politics (1820–1930)." Pp. 39–66 in *Agrarian Structure and Political Power: Landlord and Peasant in the Making of Latin America*, edited by Evelyne Huber and Frank Safford. Pittsburgh, PA: University of Pittsburgh Press.

Democracy and Authoritarianism

Higley, John and Richard Gunther, eds. 1992. *Elites and Democratic Consolidation in Latin America and Southern Europe*. Cambridge: Cambridge University Press.

Hirschman, Albert O. 1979. "The Turn Toward Authoritarianism in Latin America and the Search for Its Determinants." Pp. 61–98 in *The New Authoritarianism in Latin America*, edited by David Collier. Princeton, NJ: Princeton University Press.

Huber, Evelyne and Frank Safford, eds. 1995. *Agrarian Structure and Political Power: Landlord and Peasant in the Making of Latin America*. Pittsburgh: University of Pittsburgh Press.

Huber, Evelyne and John D. Stephens. 1995. "Conclusion: Agrarian Structure and Political Power in Comparative Perspective." Pp. 183–232 in *Agrarian Structure and Political Power: Landlord and Peasant in the Making of Latin America*, edited by Evelyne Huber and Frank Safford. Pittsburgh: University of Pittsburgh Press.

Huber Stephens, Evelyne. 1989. "Capitalist Development and Democracy in South America." *Politics and Society* 17: 281–352.

1990. "Democracy in Latin America: Recent Developments in Comparative-Historical Perspective." *Latin American Research Review* 25: 157–76.

Huntington, Samuel P. 1991. *The Third Wave: Democratization in the Late Twentieth Century*. Norman: University of Oklahoma Press.

Im, Hyug Baeg. 1987. "The Rise of Bureaucratic Authoritarianism in South Korea." *World Politics* 39: 231–57.

Karl, Terry Lynn. 1990. "Dilemmas of Democratization in Latin America." *Comparative Politics* 23: 1–21.

Karl, Terry Lynn and Philippe Schmitter. 1991. "Modes of Transition in Latin America, Southern and Eastern Europe." *International Social Science Journal* 128: 269–84.

Kaufman, Robert R. 1979. "Industrial Change and Authoritarian Rule in Latin America: A Concrete Review of the Bureaucratic-Authoritarian Model." Pp. 165–254 in *The New Authoritarianism in Latin America*, edited by David Collier. Princeton, NJ: Princeton University Press.

Kitschelt, Herbert. 1992. "Political Regime Change: Structure and Process-Driven Explanations?" *American Political Science Review* 86: 1028–34.

Kuhn, Thomas. 1970. *The Structure of Scientific Revolutions*, 2nd ed. Chicago: University of Chicago Press.

Lakatos, Imre and Alan Musgrave, eds. 1970. *Criticism and the Growth of Knowledge*. Cambridge: Cambridge University Press.

Linz, Juan J. 1975. "Totalitarian and Authoritarian Regimes." Pp. 175–373 in *Handbook of Political Science*, vol. 3, edited by Nelson Polsby and Fred Greenstein. Reading, MA: Addison-Wesley.

1978. *The Breakdown of Democratic Regimes: Crisis, Breakdown, and Reequilibration*. Baltimore, MD: Johns Hopkins University Press.

1981. "Some Comparative Thoughts on the Transition to Democracy in Portugal and Spain." Pp. 25–46 in *Portugal since the Revolution: Economic and Political*

Perspectives, edited by Jorge Braga de Macedo and Simon Serfaty. Boulder, CO: Westview Press.

Linz, Juan J., and Alfred Stepan, eds. 1978. *The Breakdown of Democratic Regimes*. Baltimore, MD: Johns Hopkins University Press.

1996. *Problems of Democratic Transition and Consolidation: Southern Europe, South America, and Post-Communist Europe*. Baltimore, MD: Johns Hopkins University Press.

Lipset, Seymour Martin. 1959. "Some Social Requisites of Democracy: Economic Development and Political Legitimacy." *American Political Science Review* 53: 245–59.

Londregan, John B. and Keith T. Poole. 1996. "Does High Income Promote Democracy?" *World Politics* 49: 1–30.

Luebbert, Gregory M. 1991. *Liberalism, Fascism, or Social Democracy: Social Classes and the Political Origins of Regimes in Interwar Europe*. New York: Oxford University Press.

Luong, Pauline Jones. 2002. *Institutional Change and Political Continuity in Post-Soviet Central Asia: Power, Perception, and Pacts*. New York: Cambridge University Press.

Mahoney, James. 2001. *The Legacies of Liberalism: Path Dependence and Political Regimes in Central America*. Baltimore, MD: Johns Hopkins University Press.

Mahoney, James and Richard Snyder. 1999. "Rethinking Agency and Structure in the Study of Regime Change." *Studies in Comparative International Development* 34: 3–32.

Mainwaring, Scott and Matthew Soberg Shugart, eds. 1997. *Presidentialism and Democracy in Latin America*. Cambridge: Cambridge University Press.

Markoff, John. 1996. *Waves of Democracy: Social Movements and Political Change*. Thousand Oaks, CA: Pine Forge Press.

Moore, Barrington, Jr. 1966. *Social Origins of Dictatorship and Democracy: Lord and Peasant in the Making of the Modern World*. Boston: Beacon Press.

Mouzelis, Nicos P. 1986. *Politics in the Semi-Periphery: Early Parliamentarism and Late Industrialisation in the Balkans and Latin America*. Pittsburgh, PA: University of Pittsburgh Press.

Munck, Gerardo L. 1994. "Democratic Transitions in Comparative Perspective." *Comparative Politics* 26: 355–75.

1998. *Authoritarianism and Democratization: Soldiers and Workers in Argentina, 1976–1983*. University Park: Pennsylvania State University Press.

O'Donnell, Guillermo. 1973. *Modernization and Bureaucratic-Authoritarianism: Studies in South American Politics*. Berkeley: Institute of International Studies, University of California.

O'Donnell, Guillermo and Philippe Schmitter. 1986. *Tentative Conclusions about Uncertain Democracies*. Baltimore, MD: Johns Hopkins University Press.

Paige, Jeffery M. 1975. *Agrarian Revolution: Social Movements and Export Agriculture in the Underdeveloped World*. New York: Free Press.

1997. *Coffee and Power: Revolution and the Rise of Democracy in Central America*. Cambridge, MA: Harvard University Press.

Palma, Gabriel. 1978. "Dependency: A Formal Theory of Underdevelopment or a Methodology for the Analysis of Concrete Situations of Underdevelopment." *World Development* 6: 881–924.

Pierson, Paul. 2000. "Not Just What, But *When:* Issues of Timing and Sequence in Comparative Politics." *Studies in American Political Development* 14: 72–92.

Plumb, J. H. 1966. "How It Happened." *New York Times Book Review* 71:11.

Przeworski, Adam. 1991. *Democracy and the Market: Political and Economic Reform in Eastern Europe and Latin America*. New York: Cambridge University Press.

Przeworski, Adam, M. Alvarez, J. A. Cheibub, and Fernando Limongi. 1996. "What Makes Democracies Endure?" *Journal of Democracy* 7: 39–55.

Przeworski, Adam and Fernando Limongi. 1997. "Modernization: Theories and Facts." *World Politics* 49: 155–83.

Remmer, Karen L. 1989. *Military Rule in Latin America*. Boston: Unwin Hyman.

1991. "'New Wine or Old Bottlenecks?': The Study of Latin American Democracy." *Comparative Politics* 23: 479–93.

Remmer, Karen L. and Gilbert W. Merkx, 1982. "Bureaucratic-Authoritarianism Revisited." *Latin American Research Review* 17: 3–40.

Richards, Alan and John Waterbury. 1990. *A Political Economy of the Middle East: State, Class, and Economic Development*. Boulder, CO: Westview Press.

Roeder, Philip G. 1993. *Red Sunset: The Failure of the Soviet Union*. Princeton, NJ: Princeton University Press.

Rueschemeyer, Dietrich, Evelyne Huber Stephens, and John D. Stephens. 1992. *Capitalist Development and Democracy*. Chicago: University of Chicago Press.

Rule, James B. 1997. *Theory and Progress in Social Science*. Cambridge: Cambridge University Press.

Schatz, Sara. 2001 "Democracy's Breakdown and the Rise of Fascism: The Case of the Spanish Second Republic, 1931–6." *Social History* 26: 145–65.

Scully, Timothy R. 1992. *Rethinking the Center: Party Politics in Nineteenth and Twentieth Century Chile*. Stanford, CA: Stanford University Press.

Serra, José. 1979. "State and Regime: Comparative Notes on the Southern Cone and the 'Enclave' Societies." Pp. 255–82 in *The New Authoritarianism in Latin America*, edited by David Collier. Princeton, NJ: Princeton University Press.

Share, Donald and Scott Mainwaring. 1986. "Transitions through Transaction: Democratization in Brazil and Spain." Pp. 175–216 in *Political Liberalization in Brazil: Dynamics, Dilemmas, and Future Prospects*. Boulder, CO: Westview Press.

Shugart, Matthew S. and John M. Carey. 1992. *Presidents and Assemblies: Constitutional Design and Electoral Dynamics*. Cambridge: Cambridge University Press.

Skocpol, Theda. 1973. "A Critical Review of Barrington Moore's *Social Origins of Dictatorship and Democracy*." *Politics and Society* 4: 1–35.

1979. *States and Social Revolutions: A Comparative Analysis of France, Russia, and China*. Cambridge: Cambridge University Press.

ed. 1998. *Democracy, Revolution, and History*. Ithaca, NY: Cornell University Press.

Snyder, Richard. 1998. "Paths out of Sultanistic Regimes: Combining Structural and Voluntarist Perspectives." Pp. 49–81 in *Sultanistic Regimes*, edited by H. E. Chehabi and Juan J. Linz. Baltimore, MD: Johns Hopkins University Press.

Snyder, Richard and James Mahoney. 1999. "The Missing Variable: Institutions and the Study of Regime Change." *Comparative Politics* 32: 103–22.

Stepan, Alfred. 1978. "Political Leadership and Regime Breakdown: Brazil." Pp. 110–37 in *The Breakdown of Democratic Regimes*, edited by Juan J. Linz and Alfred Stepan. Baltimore: Johns Hopkins University Press.

1986. "Path Toward Redemocratization." Pp. 64–84 in *Transitions from Authoritarian Rule: Comparative Perspectives*, edited by Guillermo O'Donnell, Philippe C. Schmitter, and Laurence Whitehead. Baltimore: Johns Hopkins University Press.

Stephens, John D. 1989. "Democratic Transition and Breakdown in Western Europe, 1870–1939: A Test of the Moore Thesis." *American Journal of Sociology* 94: 1019–77.

Stokes, Gale. 1989. "The Social Origins of East European Politics." Pp. 210–51 in *The Origins of Backwardness in Eastern Europe: Economics and Politics from the Middle Ages Until the Early Twentieth Century*, edited by Daniel Chirot. Berkeley: University of California Press.

Stone, Lawrence. 1967. "News from Everywhere." *New York Review of Books* 9: 32–4.

Therborn, Göran. 1977. "The Rule of Capital and the Rise of Democracy." *New Left Review* 103: 3–41.

1979. "The Travail of Latin American Democracy." *New Left Review* 113–14: 71–109.

Tilton, Timothy A. 1974. "The Social Origins of Democracy: The Swedish Case." *American Political Science Review* 68: 561–84.

Valenzuela, Arturo. 1978. *The Breakdown of Democratic Regimes: Chile*. Baltimore, MD: Johns Hopkins University Press.

Valenzuela, J. Samuel. 2001. "Class Relations and Democratization: A Reassessment of Barrington Moore's Model." Pp. 240–86 in *The Other Mirror: Grand Theory Through the Lens of Latin America*, edited by Miguel Angel Centeno and Fernando López-Alves. Princeton, NJ: Princeton University Press.

Vanhanen, Tatu. 1997. *Prospects of Democracy: A Study of 172 Countries*. London: Routledge.

Wagner, David G. and Joseph Berger. 1985. "Do Sociological Theories Grow?" *American Journal of Sociology* 90: 697–728.

Wickham-Crowley, Timothy P. 1992. *Guerrillas and Revolution in Latin America: A Comparative Study of Insurgents and Regimes since 1956*. Princeton, NJ: Princeton University Press.

Wiener, Jonathan M. 1976. "Review of Reviews." *History and Theory* 15: 146–75.

1978. *Social Origins of the New South: Alabama, 1860–1885*. Baton Rouge: Louisiana State University Press.

Yashar, Deborah J. 1997. *Demanding Democracy: Reform and Reaction in Costa Rica and Guatemala, 1870s–1950s*. Stanford, CA: Stanford University Press.

PART II

Analytic Tools

5

Big, Slow-Moving, and . . . Invisible

MACROSOCIAL PROCESSES IN THE STUDY OF COMPARATIVE POLITICS

Paul Pierson

> [W]e must question if the particular moment matters. Political science owes much of its origin to political journalism. And like political journalism we have an excessive tendency to concentrate on the here and now, a blindness toward movements on a grander time scale. Processes are not so easily captured, but the postulate on which this work must stand is that they matter more.
>
> – Edward Carmines and James Stimson (1989)

> [R]esearch is a game against nature in which nature counters with a strategy of concealment. . . . Obviously, the effectiveness of a given strategy of discovery will depend on nature's strategy of concealment, and conversely, the effectiveness of the laws of nature as a strategy of concealment will depend on the strategy chosen by research workers. In due course it will be shown that a rather simple strategy of concealment may be quite effective given a certain strategy of discovery. As a first step we may ask, what *is* the favorite strategy of sociologists? It is a marked characteristic of sociological research that it is preoccupied with cross-sectional study of small units, often individuals.
>
> – Gøsta Carlsson (1972)

Thanks to Eric Averion for research assistance. I received helpful comments on earlier versions of this essay from participants at the two conferences on comparative historical analysis held at Brown University and Harvard University, as well as presentations at the American Political Science Association meetings in August 2000 and the Workshop on American Politics at Harvard University. I am especially grateful for extensive feedback from Jim Mahoney, Eileen McDonagh, Dietrich Rueschemeyer, and Allison Stanger. Financial support from the Weatherhead Center for International Affairs and the John Simon Guggenheim Foundation is gratefully acknowledged.

Politics is a strong and slow boring of hard boards.

– Max Weber (1946 [1921])

Many important social processes take a long time – sometimes an extremely long time – to unfold. This is a problematic fact for contemporary social science, particularly in areas of inquiry where individual strategic action has become the central vantage point for framing questions and answers about social life. Especially in economics and political science, the time horizons of most analysts have become increasingly restricted. In choosing what we seek to explain and in searching for explanations, we focus on the immediate; we look for causes and outcomes that are both temporally contiguous and rapidly unfolding. In the process, we miss a lot (Goldstone 1998; Kitschelt 1999). There are important things that we do not see at all, and what we do see we often misunderstand.

It may help to start out by reviewing briefly four examples from the natural sciences. Consider first a tornado. Typically, accounts of these storms suggest that they develop relatively rapidly and that the storm itself lasts for only a short period. This is a "quick/quick" case: the causal process unfolds over a short time period, and so does the outcome of interest.

An examination of earthquakes would ordinarily look different. Like the tornado, the outcome of interest – the earthquake itself – takes place in a very short period, a matter of seconds. The explanation or causal account typically offered, however, invokes a very slow-moving process – the buildup of pressure on a fault line over an extended period of time. We would be very unlikely to focus our explanatory account on what happened in the days or weeks immediately preceding the earthquake – the last, minuscule increment of pressure that triggers the event. In this case we have a "quick" outcome but a very slow-moving, long-term causal process.

A third example is a cataclysmic ecological event, such as the hypothesized meteorite that hit the Earth 65 million years ago, triggering dramatic climatic change and mass extinctions. A standard account would probably treat this as a "quick/slow" case. Here, a cause (meteor impact) takes place over a short time period, followed by a slowly unfolding outcome (climatic change + extinctions). The outcome can be considered even more "slow-moving" if the object of interest is the development of large mammals, which became possible only in the ecological niches vacated by dinosaurs.

A final example is global warming. Models linking the rise in carbon emissions to increased global temperatures suggest that even if emission

Table 5.1. *The Time Horizons of Different Causal Accounts*

		Time Horizon of Outcome	
		Short	Long
Time Horizon of Cause	Short	I Tornado	II Meteorite/Extinction
	Long	III Earthquake	IV Global Warming

increases ceased tomorrow, we would nonetheless see a substantial rise in temperatures during the next century. Much of the increase, it seems, is already "in the pipeline" – stored in the ocean, from which it will gradually be released into the atmosphere (Stevens 2000). Thus the outcome (higher temperatures in the Earth's atmosphere) is slow-moving, with a considerable temporal lag from the key causal force at work. As in the earthquake example, the causal process itself (gradually rising emission levels) is also slow-moving. This, then, is a case of a long-term causal process (increasing emissions) and a long-term outcome (temperature rise).

The "temporal structures" of these explanatory accounts thus reveal substantial diversity, as summarized in Table 5.1. The causal processes claimed to generate outcomes of interest may or may not unfold over a short period. The outcomes themselves are equally subject to variation, with some transpiring over a very short time while others work themselves out completely only over a very extended period. In each case, we may refer to the "time horizon" of a variable or cluster of variables – the period of time over which meaningful change occurs (Abbott 1988). To roughly capture this diversity of the time horizons of causes and outcomes in different explanatory accounts, we can divide the possibilities into four quadrants, with one of the natural science examples occupying each quadrant.

As will be explored in greater depth later in this essay, it is important to stress that the decision to invoke a particular temporal structure depends on how the analyst frames the research question. In the meteorite example, the duration of the outcome depends in part on whether the object of interest is the extinction of dinosaurs or the emergence of large mammals. Similarly, if an analysis treats the meteorite collision as the entire causal process of interest, it unfolds very rapidly. If one also feels a need to explain how that meteorite came to arrive at that particular point in space at that particular moment, the causal process would unfold over a much longer period. Typically, analysts tackling particular kinds of processes will find one or another temporal structure more helpful and convincing for illuminating problems of interest. The key point for the current discussion is that these causal accounts have diverse temporal structures, and these different structures focus the analyst's attention on different phenomena.

The reason to stress this diversity is that so much of contemporary research in political science seems geared toward Quadrant 1. Typically, both causal processes and outcomes are depicted as unfolding entirely over a short period of time. This sort of framework will often be appropriate. There is, however, no reason to think that most political processes, or the most interesting ones, are necessarily best understood by invoking accounts with this kind of temporal structure. In many situations, we will want to extend our temporal field of vision to consider social dynamics that look more like the examples in Quadrants 2–4. In Part I of this essay I discuss causal processes that occur gradually over extended periods of time – reviewing some reasons why certain causes are slow-moving and offering some examples from comparative research. In Part II, I explore the same set of issues for long-term outcomes. Part III moves the discussion beyond the simple framework introduced in Table 5.1. It focuses on two types of processes where there may be significant time lags between the onset of a central cause and the initiation of the outcome of interest.

Throughout this discussion, my emphasis is on distinguishing and outlining different types of processes that might operate over extended periods of time. Such distinctions can help provide the foundation for future efforts to integrate long-term processes into theoretical accounts. That is to say, they provide orientations – sources of both questions and potential hypotheses – for empirical research. They also help to clarify specific methodological challenges facing investigations of long-term processes. Finally, and crucially, the identification of different types of long-term processes can serve as an important bridging device. That is, it may connect research focused on distinct empirical problems, clarifying the extent to which different literatures draw on similar conceptions of causal processes (Hall, this volume) and similar analytical techniques for shaping and assessing explanations (Pierson and Skocpol 2002). In the final section of the essay, I briefly discuss why much contemporary research, at least in political science, seems to gravitate toward Quadrant 1, and I summarize some of the main costs of this preoccupation.

I. Slow-Moving Causal Processes

Social processes take place at different speeds. "Events of equivalent causal importance," as Andrew Abbott has put it, "just don't always take the same amount of time to happen" (Abbott 1988, p. 174). In this part, I focus on causal forces that develop over an extended period of time. There are at least three distinctive types of causal processes that can be described as slow-moving. Slow-moving processes may be cumulative, involve threshold effects, or require the unfolding of extended causal chains. I examine each of these possibilities in turn.

Cumulative Causes

The most straightforward type of slow-moving causal process can be termed "incremental" or "cumulative." Here, change in a variable is continuous but extremely gradual. Aspects of technological change provide good examples. Daniel Bell's analysis of postindustrialism (Bell 1974) presents slow technological shifts as key causes of important political changes – a theme recently incorporated into significant work in comparative political economy (Iversen and Wren 1998). Similarly, a central causal argument in Robert Putnam's recent analysis of declining social capital concerns the impact of television, which gradually became a more pervasive aspect of American popular culture over the past half-century (Putnam 2000). This change stems from two cumulative processes – the gradual spread of television and the gradual replacement of earlier generations with those raised in a context where television was ubiquitous. Another important category of cumulative economic processes is shifts in relative prices, which may have enormous political consequences (Rogowski 1989; North 1990).

Most of the cumulative causes that I have in mind, however, are "sociological" ones – important social conditions that change dramatically over extended periods of time but at a very slow pace. Demography is an excellent example. Migration, suburbanization, literacy rates (Deutsch 1961; Rokkan 1974; Ertman 1996), language and associated conceptions of nationhood (Gellner 1983), and basic cultural outlooks (Tarrow 1992) are all important social variables that typically change very slowly.

For political scientists, cumulative sociological processes are often linked to long-term shifts in electorates, including their partisan attachments. Key, for example, introduced the concept of "secular realignment" – a movement "from party to party that extends over several presidential elections and appears to be independent of the peculiar factors influencing the vote at individual elections" (Key 1959, p. 199). As Edward Carmines and James Stimson argue, secular realignments can be driven by "such essentially non-political forces as differential birthrates between the party coalitions, inter-regional migration patterns, or economic-technological transformations" (Carmines and Stimson 1989, p. 143).

It would be hard to deny that contemporary political scientists typically relegate these types of processes to the background, essentially ignoring their potential impact on outcomes of interest. An analyst investigating a short time frame is likely to treat these incremental or cumulative variables as essentially fixed. If such incremental/cumulative factors are on an analyst's radar screen, however, it is possible to incorporate them in either quantitative or qualitative studies that examine longer time horizons. Thus it is crucial that analysts consider theoretical frames that draw attention to the potential impact of cumulative causes.

Threshold Effects

Theory-generated alertness is even more important with a second, closely related type of slow-moving causal process, one that involves *threshold effects*. In many cases, incremental or cumulative forces may not generate incremental changes in outcomes of interest. Instead, these processes have a modest or negligible impact until they reach some critical level, which triggers major changes. The earthquake example presented in the introduction is a clear instance of this kind of process. Another favorite illustration from the physical sciences is the process leading up to an avalanche – a slow buildup of stress leading to a rapid "state change" once some critical level has been reached.

This is precisely the account that Goldstone (1991) offers in his comparative analysis of revolutions. A slow-moving factor (demographic change) is a principal cause of a rapidly unfolding outcome (revolution). Goldstone notes that social analysts often have a strong bias against explanations with this kind of structure. "[T]hose tied to linear thinking about historical causation may . . . dismiss the role of population increase. Such increases, after all, were gradual and not enormously large. Events such as revolutions and rebellions are both large and sudden; their very nature seems to call for a different kind of explanation" (p. 32).[1]

[1] Goldstone notes another reason for thinking that the impact of slow-moving processes like demographic change often can be very significant. He points out (1991, p. 33) that

There is, however, no reason to exclude the possibility that such slow-moving variables may be tremendously important, even if we are trying to explain outcomes that emerge rapidly. Theorists now suggest that threshold models often make a good deal of sense. Such models have become prominent features in theoretical work on collective action (Granovetter 1978; Marwell and Oliver 1993), including analyses focused on both interest groups (e.g., Baumgartner and Jones 1993) and looser social movements (McAdam 1982) or collectivities such as language communities (Laitin 1998). More generally, threshold dynamics are likely to be prevalent in circumstances where actors face binary choices and where the choices they favor depend in part on their perception of what others are likely to do.

Granovetter's classic article actually invokes a more restricted argument than that suggested here. His focus is on the heterogeneity of *individual* preferences and the resulting differences in their individual thresholds for particular actions (e.g., "I will go to the demonstration if I expect q others to be there with me"). Granovetter's main point is that given significant heterogeneity of individual thresholds, it is possible to generate models in which very small shifts in the thresholds of even a single actor can generate big changes in collective behavior. By contrast, I am interested in collective thresholds, where once a social variable reaches a particular level, it triggers a big effect. The key point is that there are cut points, or tipping points, in many social processes that lead to nonlinearities (Schelling 1978). These processes could, but need not, involve the interplay of heterogeneous preferences that Granovetter has in mind.

Doug McAdam's *Political Process and the Development of Black Insurgency, 1930–1970* (1982) presents a powerful example of a threshold analysis of collective action. Unlike many who present threshold or "critical mass" arguments, however, McAdam is less interested in the striking dynamics that mark a tipping point than in the less dramatic processes that precede

population increases "have a particularly nonlinear effect on *marginal* groups – groups that face some sort of boundary conditions, such as peasants who are seeking to gain new lands, or younger sons of elite families who are seeking new elite positions." The social processes at work here are instances of what Fred Hirsch called "positional competition" – settings where the availability of some valued good is essentially fixed (Hirsch 1977). If the number of seats in a game of musical chairs cannot be increased, adding a few more players may alter the social dynamics dramatically. In Goldstone's demographic account, "increases in total population generally produce a much, much larger increase in marginal populations – that is, in those groups competing for some relatively scarce resource – than in the population as a whole" (1991, p. 33).

it. McAdam places great weight on the role of big, slow-moving processes in establishing the preconditions for successful black mobilization:

> ... the Montgomery bus boycott of 1955–56 ... [and] the 1954 Supreme Court decision in the Brown case ... were landmark events. Nonetheless, to single them out serves ... to obscure the less dramatic but ultimately more significant historical trends that shaped the prospects for later insurgency. Especially critical ... were several broad historical processes in the period from 1933 to 1954 that rendered the political establishment more vulnerable to black protest activity while also affording blacks the institutional strength to launch such a challenge. Later events such as the 1954 decision and the Montgomery bus boycott merely served as dramatic (though hardly insignificant) capstones to these processes. (p. 3)

At the heart of McAdam's analysis is the decline of the cotton economy in the quarter-century after 1925. This decline both decreased the strength of forces opposed to black insurgency and generated patterns of migration that boosted the organizational capacities (e.g., massive expansion of black churches, colleges, and Southern chapters of the National Association for the Advancement of Colored People [NAACP]) of a long-oppressed minority. It was these gradual interconnected social processes that created conditions ripe for a set of triggering events.

Although threshold-style arguments have been particularly prominent in the study of collective action, there are good reasons to expect this type of dynamic to be prevalent when social variables of the slow-moving sort operate in established institutional or organizational settings. Social scientists of various stripes associated with the "new institutionalism" have emphasized the strongly inertial qualities of many existing social arrangements. These tendencies toward persistence imply that pressures will often build up for some time without generating immediate effects. When some critical level is reached, actors reassess their options or expectations about others' likely actions, leading to relatively rapid change. Change in one institution, furthermore, may quickly undermine others. The dynamic at this point is similar to those that Grannovetter and Schelling outline. The analysis emphasizes, however, the long, slow-moving buildup of pressure, rather than the trigger itself or the way in which the ensuing tipping process plays out.[2]

[2] It is worth stressing that path-dependent or self-reinforcing processes, discussed in Part III of this essay, are all based on threshold models – relatively small movements can push above some critical level, triggering a process of positive feedback that leads to much more dramatic (nonlinear) change. It is important to keep the two arguments distinct, because path-dependent processes need not involve the long, slow buildup of pressure suggested in

This kind of claim about threshold effects plays an important role in Huber and Stephens's analysis of the centrality of *long-term* control of government for explaining welfare state outcomes in advanced industrial societies (Huber and Stephens 2001). In outlining the roots of Social Democratic hegemony in Scandinavia, for instance, they stress that a single election result is unlikely to have a big effect on previously well-institutionalized arrangements. On the other hand, electoral success *over an extended period of time* leads to significant changes, including shifts in the expectations of social actors. At some point, these actors adjust their policy preferences to accommodate the new environment. By doing so, they help to propel coordination around these expectations, reinforcing the new regime.

Similar arguments about threshold effects are central to the critical realignment theories that have played such a prominent role in the study of American electoral politics (Burnham 1970; Brady 1988). This line of argument has been summarized by David Mayhew (the quotations in the following passage are from Burnham 1970):

> In brief, what happens is that political "stress" or "tension" builds up over a roughly thirty year period until it reaches a "flash point" or a "boiling point," at which time a "triggering event" brings on an electoral realignment. . . . To put it more elaborately, there exists a "dynamic, even dialectic polarization between long-term inertia and concentrated bursts of change. . . ." Ordinarily, American institutions tend toward "underproduction" of other than currently "normal" policy outputs. They may tend persistently to ignore, and hence not to aggregate, emergent political demand of a mass character until a boiling point of some kind is reached. (Mayhew 2000, p. 8)

Mayhew, I should emphasize, is quite critical of this account of American electoral politics. Indeed, he maintains that short-run processes are often of greater causal significance than realignment theory allows. According to Mayhew, the "genre's model of stress buildup . . . [has] a tendency to elongate political troubles backwards in time without warrant" (Mayhew 2000, p. 24; cf. Bartels 1998). He rightly highlights the need to provide evidence for such a gradual buildup of stress, as well as the need to consider the possibility that short-term processes are adequate to generate such flash points.

Another possible danger of such arguments is that they can present an overly deterministic picture of social processes. References to a boiling

a model like McAdam's. Invoking a path-dependent process implies nothing about the time horizons of the causal factors that initiate positive feedback.

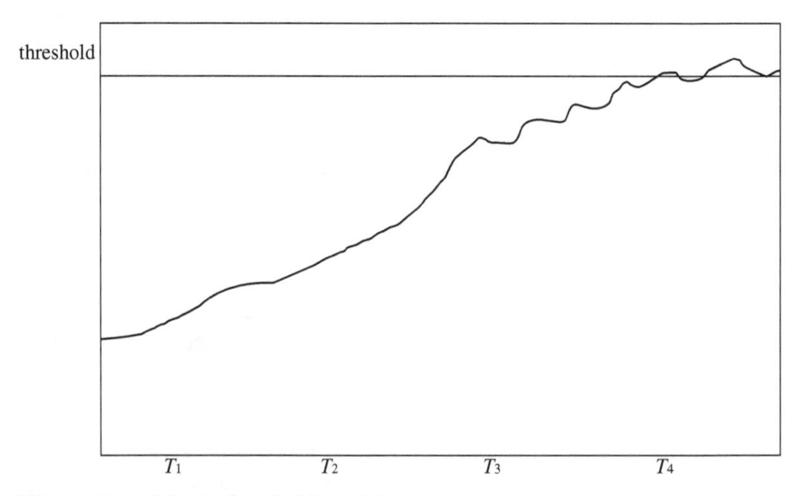

Figure 5.1 A basic threshold model.

point or threshold can suggest, as McAdam notes, that "[m]ovement emergence is... analogous to, and as inexorable as, the process by which water boils" (1982, p. 9). Yet these models can also be substantially more subtle in the way they combine long-term and short-term processes. Consider Figure 5.1, which looks at the movement of a particular social variable (say, the organizational resources of a disadvantaged group) as it approaches a threshold level that triggers a social movement. During time periods T_1 to T_3 there are fluctuations, but there is also a gradual trend, resulting from various slow-moving processes, toward the threshold level that triggers the outcome of interest. As that threshold level is approached in period T_4, particular fluctuations above the trend line become increasingly likely to act as triggers. An analyst could treat the sources of these fluctuations as essentially random (Macy 1990). Alternatively, she could seek to explain these fluctuations as well. What distinguishes a threshold model of this kind, however, is that it does not analyze the sources of fluctuations within period T_4 except in combination with an analysis of the preceding long-term processes that create a context where these fluctuations can have a major impact. This is, for instance, precisely the kind of argument presented in McAdam's analysis of black insurgency.

Particular claims about the role of thresholds in specific contexts must be established with care. Even a critical analyst like Mayhew, however, agrees that such arguments sometimes present a plausible model of reality – one that requires attentiveness to significant stretches of time. In this respect,

Mayhew's views are in line with considerable theoretical work, as well as substantial empirical research on social movements and regime breakdowns.

Causal Chains

We often think of causal processes involving a straightforward connection where *x* directly yields *y*. Yet in many cases the story runs more like the following: "*x* triggers the sequence *a*, *b*, *c*, which yields *y*" (Mahoney 2000; Pierson 2000b). If *a*, *b*, and *c* take some time to work themselves out, there is likely to be a substantial lag between *x* and *y*. Collier and Collier's influential work on labor incorporation in Latin America presents arguments of this kind, in which the ultimate outcomes of interest reflect a sequence of key developments over extended periods of time (Collier and Collier 1991). This type of claim about long-term multistage causal processes is often invoked in work on state-building (Flora 1999a, 1999b) or democratization (Luebbert 1991; Collier 1999).

Swank (2001) offers a particularly instructive recent example. In assessing the impact of political institutions on welfare state retrenchment, he criticizes the conventional view that fragmented institutions will be associated with limited cutbacks in social programs. The standard interpretation holds that institutional fragmentation restricts social policy change by increasing the number of veto points available to defenders of the status quo. Swank accepts that this is true as far as it goes. He notes, however, that the causal chain of long-term indirect effects of institutional fragmentation *runs in the other direction*. Not only does institutional fragmentation limit the initial expansion of the welfare state, but it also reinforces social heterogeneity, inhibits the growth of encompassing interest groups, and weakens cultural commitments to universalism. All of these long-term effects strengthen the welfare state's opponents and weaken its advocates. In short, Swank argues, many of the most important effects of institutional fragmentation work themselves out only indirectly and over extended periods of time. Seeking to analyze the effects of institutions while holding other variables constant, many analysts failed to see that the values of these variables were themselves in part the long-term consequences of institutional structures. Quadrant I investigations are therefore likely to misread systematically the impact of institutional structures on the contemporary politics of the welfare state.

Pierson (1994) makes a similar causal chain argument in an assessment of contemporary processes of welfare state retrenchment. In gauging the impact of conservative governments on the welfare state, it is not sufficient to simply examine their direct efforts to cut social programs ("programmatic retrenchment"). Instead, one has to consider the possibility that reforms (e.g., efforts to curtail the flow of tax revenues) will trigger particular causal chains that facilitate program cutbacks later in a sequence ("systemic retrenchment"). In such a case, a conservative government's main impact on the welfare state might be felt a decade or more after it left office.

Causal chain arguments are often utilized when key institutional, policy, or organizational outcomes lie some distance in time from initial points of crucial political choice. They are often especially promising in contexts where political actions have *multiple* consequences and major long-term outcomes are by-products rather than the principal focus of intended actions. Under such circumstances, analysts are easily misled by a focus on the most immediate, highly visible, and clearly intended consequences (Jervis 1997). Yet as Pierson's analysis of conservative retrenchment initiatives shows, causal chain arguments may also focus on intentional, but indirect, strategies that play out only through a sequence of developments over time.

Causal chain arguments raise some tricky issues. A key challenge is to show that the links in such chains are strong ones ("tightly coupled," as Mahoney 2000 puts it). The persuasiveness of a causal chain argument declines quickly if there are many stages or if the probabilities associated with any particular stage are not very high (Fearon 1996; Lieberson 1997). Even if a chain has only three links, and the probability that each link will hold is 80 percent, there is less than a fifty-fifty chance that the entire chain will operate. Thus these arguments are likely to be persuasive only when the chains invoked have a very small number of links and we have solid theoretical or empirical grounds for believing that the links are quite strong.

As suggested in my discussion of the meteorite example, arguments based on causal chains also face an infinite regress problem: there is always some earlier link in the chain, so what is to keep one from endlessly seeking that earlier stage? There are three reasonable ways to answer this question. First, analysts may choose to break the chain at "critical junctures" that mark a point at which their cases begin to diverge in significant ways. This is the strategy employed by the Colliers, for instance. Second, analysts may break the chain at the point where causal connections become difficult to pin down. If the persuasiveness of arguments about causal chains depends on the demonstration of relatively tight coupling among the links, it makes sense to end the chains where such linkages cannot be established.

The third and perhaps most instructive response for current purposes is to delimit the ends of the causal chain on the basis of the theoretical interests of the analyst. Thus a sociologist interested in demography might deal with long-term processes that overlap with those of interest to a political scientist. Yet each would investigate a somewhat different causal chain. Consider the following example. Iran is currently undergoing significant social turmoil associated with the emergence of a large cohort of underemployed young men. This demographic bulge stems partly from strong pro-natalist policies adopted following the 1979 revolution. One result of the current strains has been the introduction of new policies facilitating family planning and birth control – the most extensive in the Muslim world. This example thus involves a set of developments of considerable interest to both political scientists and demographers. However, the demographer's chain would probably end with the demographic boom itself and might begin with some other sociological variables (e.g., social responses to the initial set of pro-natalist policies). A political scientist would be most likely to begin and/or end with *political* phenomena: the revolution or pro-natalist policies at the outset and the social unrest or new family-planning policies at the end of the chain. This example illustrates how the temporal structure of causal accounts depends to a considerable extent on the intellectual concerns as well as the basic theoretical framework employed by the analyst. These shape the fashioning of key outcomes to be considered, the time frame covered by the analysis, and the hypotheses that are explored.

All three of these classes of argumentation about causal processes – claims about cumulative processes, threshold effects, and causal chains – require the analyst to gravitate away from Quadrant I. Each raises distinct methodological challenges. Each is likely to be visible only if an analyst's research design and methods are open to the possibility that such processes are causally significant. There are strong theoretical grounds for believing that each process characterizes a substantial range of social phenomena. Yet this is only part of the story. When we turn to the consideration of outcomes, we also confront considerable temporal diversity. Many outcomes of great interest to social scientists take a long time to unfold. Processes producing such big, slow-moving outcomes are the subject of the next part.

II. Slow-Moving Outcomes

Slow-moving outcomes are ones with long time horizons – that is, processes where meaningful change in the dependent variable occurs only over the long run. The main category of such processes in the social sciences mirrors that in the earlier discussion of cumulative or incremental causes. Just as causes may have a slow, cumulative quality, the same may be true of the outcomes of interest to social scientists. For instance, if sociologists were seeking to *explain* any of the slow-moving sociological variables discussed in Part I, they would be exploring just such a cumulative outcome. If some factors introduce a shift in, say, birth rates, the impact on population will be realized only over a very extended period of time.

In similar fashion, political outcomes may have a slow-moving, cumulative structure. This will be the case, for example, if the principal causal mechanism involved is one of *replacement*. Because individual partisan attachments reveal considerable inertia, for instance, environmental changes usually have their most powerful effects on new voters. Partisan realignment therefore often works through the extremely gradual replacement of political generations, as old members die off and are replaced with new ones who lack the old attachments. Arguments about generational turnover, for example, focus on the exposure of particular age groups to stimuli that have enduring consequences (Mannheim 1952; Putnam 2000). Slow-moving outcomes result from the changing distribution of these generations in the general population over time.

This mechanism of replacement is applicable in a variety of contexts, suggesting a central reason why many political outcomes have a very slow-moving quality. Consider the case of political elites. If occupants of elite positions possess resources that allow them to defend their positions against challenges, major changes in elite composition will often operate through slow-moving processes of replacement. In the U.S. Congress, for instance, incumbents possess such tremendous advantages that they are rarely voted out of office. The main mechanism of elite-level restructuring is instead replacement: when particular politicians retire or die, they are succeeded by politicians who better match the new social environment. Thus even a major change in the fortunes of particular categories of politicians (e.g., declining prospects for moderate Republicans in the Northeast and for Democrats of all stripes in the South after 1960) may take decades to work itself out.

As this language suggests, one good class of such arguments are those grounded in theories of evolutionary processes, which posit a selection mechanism operating over extended periods of time (Spruyt 1994; Nelson 1995; Kahler 1999). Firms, politicians, and nation-states may pursue many goals and employ many strategies, but social scientists often argue that over time those pursuing particular goals and employing particular strategies are more likely to survive. Similar analyses are very common in sociology, where there is a robust research program in the field of organizational ecology. Such analyses, with their focus on long-term patterns of births and deaths in fairly large populations, have led to the development of distinctive methodological strategies and theoretical propositions (Hannan and Freeman 1989; Carroll and Hannan 2000).

Cumulative outcomes may also be evident in the development of public policy (Rose and Davies 1994). Public expenditure on income transfers, for instance, is an incremental, slowly unfolding outcome of earlier policy choices (Steuerle and Kawai 1996). This is highly relevant for many contemporary studies in political economy, because a great deal of the growth in public expenditure since 1975 reflects these lagged policy commitments rather than the introduction of new, more generous policies. Consider the case of pensions policy (Pierson 2000c; Huber and Stephens 2001). Public pensions account for roughly 40 percent of expenditures on social protection and thus are deeply implicated in the current budgetary stress affecting advanced welfare states. In this policy area there are often *very* long time lags between the enactment of a policy and the realization of its major public expenditure implications. In the case of contributory pensions, it may be *seventy years* – the time it takes for the bulk of the pensioner population to be composed of those who had a full working career under new rules – before policy choices are fully reflected in ongoing expenditures.

Failure to recognize the extent to which public policy outcomes are cumulative and slow-moving can easily lead social scientists astray. Presuming that policy changes are quickly translated into expenditure levels (that is, assuming rapidly unfolding outcomes), analysts may mistakenly construct temporally constricted causal accounts. Notably, they may attribute policy changes (inferred from rising spending levels) to social developments (e.g., globalization) that in fact occurred *after* those policy changes took place.

As in the earlier example of elite turnover, this public policy outcome is slow-moving because it operates through a mechanism of replacement. Only cohorts who enter the labor market after the policy change will work their whole lives under the new rules. Thus it is not until these new workers have completely replaced older workers within the population of pensioners that the new policy's full expenditure implications will be realized. Yet unlike many arguments based on replacement, this one is not evolutionary in the sense of employing a "selection mechanism" that determines "fitness." Like

Table 5.2. *Time Horizons in Different Social Science Accounts*

		Time Horizon of Outcome	
		Short	Long
Time Horizon of Cause	Short	I	II Cumulative Effects
	Long	III Thresholds; Causal Chains	IV Cumulative Causes

the generational turnover arguments discussed earlier, it emphasizes that different cohorts will have been affected by different stimuli. Slow-moving outcomes based on competitive selection are likely to call for quite different theoretical and methodological strategies than those based simply on cohort replacement – differences apparent, for instance, in the distinct analyses of Putnam's study of social capital and generational turnover and the work of Hannan and others on organizational ecology.

Table 5.2 summarizes the argument presented so far by overlaying that analysis on the framework presented in Table 5.1. It suggests that as is the case in the physical sciences, not all processes of interest to social scientists are likely to fit comfortably in Quadrant I. Many causes and outcomes have long time horizons. Causal chain and threshold arguments invoke independent variables with long time horizons. Arguments about cumulative effects, by definition, refer to dependent variables with long time horizons. Arguments about cumulative causes, unlike threshold arguments, involve linear transformations in which a little more of (slow-moving) x produces a little more of (slow-moving) y. Thus cumulative cause arguments imply long time horizons for *both* causes and outcomes.

III. Moving Beyond the Focus on Time Horizons

So far, I have stressed that social scientists may need to look at extended periods of time because they wish to consider the role of factors that change only very gradually. In essence, this argument suggests the need for social scientists to be attentive to the Braudelian focus on the *longue durée*. Yet there are additional aspects of social processes that may also be missed by a focus on the short term – namely, those in which there is a considerable separation in time between the onset of a cause and the development in the main effect. This *temporal separation* is evident in two types of processes that figure prominently in comparative historical analyses: structural explanations and path-dependent explanations.

Structural Determination

Structural accounts constitute a prominent class of arguments about long-term outcomes. Key causal claims are based on the existence of certain broad structures or relationships among structures. Typically, these arguments claim a causal connection between structures and eventual outcomes but are agnostic on issues of timing (Skocpol 1979). Triggering events are seen as essentially random or incidental to the core causal processes at work. In this respect, they resemble the threshold arguments discussed previously. They differ in that structural arguments need not rely on the gradual buildup of pressures over time. In other words, neither causes nor outcomes need be slow-moving. Outcomes, however, may occur at a considerable temporal distance from the appearance of the central cause.

The difference can be seen by contrasting Figure 5.2 with Figure 5.1's summary of threshold arguments. In Figure 5.2, a structural cause (say, the creation of a new institution or the formation of a new alliance) is introduced in Period 3. This moves the pressure on the status quo to a new, much higher level – very close to the threshold level for major political change. From here it is only a matter of time (in this case, until Period 4) before some triggering event precipitates the outcome of interest.

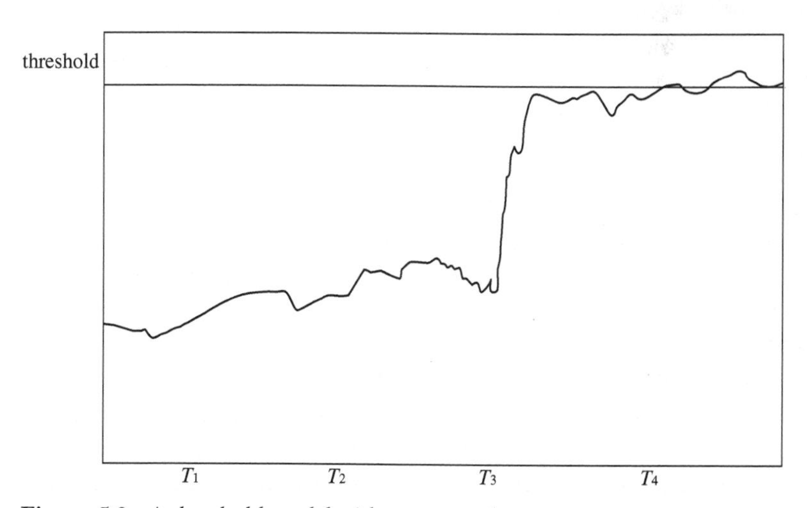

Figure 5.2 A threshold model with a structural cause.

Barrington Moore's account of the origins of dictatorship and democracy offers a classic example of a structural account (Moore 1966). He focuses on macrosocial variables that predispose countries to different regime outcomes. Given particular values on the structural variables, Moore expects certain outcomes to be realized sooner or later. For Moore, triggering events are essentially superficial and should not distract one's attention from the basic causal processes at work.

Structural accounts of social processes can be formalized as instances of "absorbing Markov chains," and a brief explication may clarify the logic of this kind of argument. Over a particular period, there is some probability that particular entities (*X*s) will be transformed into *Y*s (Stinchcombe 1974; Elster 1983). These processes differ from the causal chains discussed previously. In many cases they involve a single transformation ($x \rightarrow y$) rather than a series with several links. In Markov chains, however, the transformations over any particular time period are probabilistic. In fact, the probability of such a shift in any short period may be fairly low. As a result, it is hard to know where things will stand at any particular point in time. There is, however, an *attractor* (in this case *Y*). *X*s turn into *Y*s, but *Y*s don't turn into *X*s. Over the long term, the system in question converges on a single outcome.

Cameron (2000) uses the metaphor of a frog hopping from lily pad to lily pad in a pond where one lily pad is coated with superglue. We do not know when the frog will come to a halt on the superglue pad, and it may take quite a long time, but the eventual outcome is fully determined. Nor do such arguments require the strong claim that *Y*s never turn into *X*s. If the probability of $x \rightarrow y$ transformations is considerably higher than the probability of $y \rightarrow x$ transformations, we will eventually end up with a population made up almost entirely of *Y*s.

While this may seem like a fairly artificial construction, I think it captures the kinds of arguments about causal processes that social scientists often make or should want to make (Lieberson 1985). Przeworski and Limongi (1997), for instance, make an argument of this sort in their analysis of democratization. Once countries reach a certain level of economic development, there is a significant probability that authoritarian governments will turn into democracies but very little chance of transformations in the opposite direction. Over time, we would expect to see fewer and fewer authoritarian governments above that economic threshold level. This structural variable would not, however, explain the timing of particular transitions.

This kind of process suggests the possibility of a substantial temporal lag between the key causal process and the eventual outcome. The "cause" in this case is the structure that generates an absorbing Markov chain dynamic. The chain may take some time to play out, with various quirks influencing the tempo and the particular path taken. The ultimate outcome, however, is not affected by those quirks. The core insight is that temporally constricted analyses may lead to a preoccupation with surface phenomena, while deeper and more fundamental causes are missed.

Path Dependent or Positive Feedback Processes

A frequent claim in comparative historical analysis is that outcomes at a critical juncture induce path-dependent processes. Over time, these processes lead to strikingly divergent outcomes, even from initially similar conditions (see, e.g., Shefter 1977; Collier and Collier 1991; Hacker 1998; Huber and Stephens 2001). Much of this literature implicitly refers to the dynamics of self-reinforcing or positive feedback processes in a political system – what economists call "increasing returns" processes (Pierson 2000a; cf. Mahoney 2000). A fairly modest change induces a feedback loop, which reinforces the initial direction of change. Collective action, for instance, may lead to shifts in expectations and resources that facilitate more collective action; similarly, institutionalization may ease problems of coordination, fostering more than institutionalization.[3]

A path-dependent causal account employs a particular temporal structure. It highlights the role of what Arthur Stinchcombe has termed "historical causation," in which dynamics triggered by an event or process at one point in time reproduce and reinforce themselves even in the absence of the recurrence of the original event or process (Stinchcombe 1968). Thus the full outcome of interest may require substantial time for these self-reinforcing processes to play out, emerging at a considerable distance in time from the critical juncture or "historical cause." One could categorize this type of argument as involving a slow-moving cause (with the self-reinforcing processes constituting part of the cause of the eventual outcome to be considered).[4] Treating this as a long-term process involving temporal separation, however, emphasizes the key point of arguments

[3] This suggests another reason why such processes cannot easily be reduced to the dimensions introduced in Tables 5.1 and 5.2. As feedback loops become central to the process that follows a critical juncture, it becomes impossible to delineate clear causes and effects; instead, a set of factors mutually reinforce each other.

[4] This explains the way in which I categorize the time horizons of path-dependent processes in Table 5.3.

about historical causation. An event or a process may be crucially linked to later outcomes, even if it occurs only once and has ceased to operate long before that final outcome occurs (Lieberson 1985).

As with many of the long-term processes considered here, there are also strong theoretical grounds for believing that path-dependent processes will be prevalent in political life (Pierson 2000a). Once established, specific patterns of political mobilization, the institutional "rules of the game," and even citizens' basic ways of thinking about the political world will often generate self-reinforcing dynamics. Such an argument, for example, underpins Martin Shefter's argument about the impact of initial patterns of party mobilization (Shefter 1977), Douglas North's analysis of the institutional foundations for economic growth (North 1990), and Robert Wuthnow's explanation of the rise of modern ideologies (Wuthnow 1989).

An excellent illustration of a path-dependent account is Thomas Ertman's treatment of the lasting repercussions of the financing methods adopted in those European states that faced military competition before the rise of modern bureaucracies (Ertman 1996). Following predecessors like Hintze and Tilly, Ertman argues in *The Birth of Leviathan* that the onset of military competition constituted a critical juncture for emerging states. What happened at this juncture had a powerful effect on patterns of European state development and, much later, on the prospects for developing parliamentary democracies. Confronting the pivotal problem of generating sufficient revenues to wage prolonged warfare, some monarchs were forced to rely on systems of proprietary officeholding and tax farming "which were much more beneficial to [these officeholders] than to their royal employers." Others could work to construct "proto-modern bureaucracies based upon the separation of office from the person of the officeholder." It is worth noting that a key part of Ertman's explanation for these divergences is a slow-moving variable: literacy rates. The extent of literacy largely determined the bargaining power of monarchs vis-à-vis those capable of handling administrative tasks. Thus the timing of the onset of military competition is crucial – countries facing this challenge later were much more likely to possess an ample supply of potential administrators.

Ertman's argument is one of historical causation. Initial responses to this financial challenge were consequential because they were self-reinforcing. Once a dense network of institutions and interests around tax farming had developed, it was almost impossible to switch over to more modern forms of financing – especially in a context where monarchs often had an immediate need for revenue. And these different paths mattered a great deal,

Ertman argues, because the bureaucratic alternative was both more effective in waging war and more conducive to the development of parliamentary institutions. As noted previously, arguments with a similar structure are now widespread in comparative historical work.

Carmines and Stimson's study of "issue evolution" in the U.S. polity investigates a very different empirical setting, but the analytical structure of their argument is similar (Carmines and Stimson 1989). Carmines and Stimson are seeking to explain a momentous change in postwar American politics – the shift in the "issue environment" from one in which the two major parties (and their supporters) were internally heterogeneous on racial matters to one in which internally homogeneous parties generated far greater partisan polarization around race. Like Mayhew, they criticize critical realignment theory for suggesting a far too rapid "earthquake"-style change in this outcome. Instead, their analysis stresses a critical juncture of elections (especially that of 1964 but also that of 1968), which creates initial partisan differences on race, followed by a protracted period in which differences in recruitment and derecruitment at both the mass and elite levels reinforce that initial difference. The major political outcome they are interested in develops over the long term: "the initial increase in mass issue polarization does not complete the process but only begins it by setting in motion a change that grows over time" (Carmines and Stimson 1989, p. 157).[5]

Thus social processes may not only be slow-moving; they may also require a long time because there is a significant temporal separation between a key cause and the outcome of interest. In either case, the full process may not be visible unless the analysis considers a very substantial stretch of time. My discussion of these different long-term processes is summarized in Table 5.3. It highlights a number of distinct social processes that include at least one of the following features: causal processes with long time horizons, outcomes with long time horizons, or significant temporal separation between key causes and the outcome of ultimate interest.[6] As the scholarly literature reviewed in this essay suggests, the different types of processes

[5] In fact, their study emphasizes generational replacement as well as positive feedback in the growth of partisan differences over time. Thus Carmines and Stimson combine arguments about structural causes and self-reinforcement in explaining their long-term outcome.

[6] It should be emphasized that Table 5.3 highlights features of processes that *logically require* examination of extended stretches of time. Other features of these arguments may or may not also call for attention to long-term processes. Path-dependent arguments, for example, need not rely on a slow-moving cause to explain the initial event (critical juncture) that triggers a process of positive feedback. In actual applications, however, they often do so.

Table 5.3. *Categorizing Long-Term Processes*

Category	Time Horizons	Temporal Separation	Examples
Cumulative Causes	*Long* (causes) *Long* (outcomes)	No	Key 1959; Putnam 2000
Causal Chains	*Long* (causes) Short (outcomes)	No	Collier and Collier 1991; Swank 2001
Threshold Effects	*Long* (causes) Short (outcomes)	No	Burnham 1970; Goldstone 1991; McAdam 1982; Skocpol 1979
Cumulative Outcomes	Short (causes) *Long* (outcomes)	No	Spruyt 1994; Steurle and Kawai 1996
Structural Effects (Markov Chains)	Short (causes) Short (outcomes)	*Yes*	Moore 1996; Przeworski and Limongi 1997
Path Dependence (positive feedback)	Short (for "historical cause") *Long* (for self-reinforcing process)	*Yes* (for "historical cause")	Ertman 1996; Shefter 1977; Carmines and Stimson 1989

Note: Italics indicate a feature that logically implies the need to analyze significant stretches of time.

distinguished in Table 5.3 encompass a range of arguments that can be and have been used to illuminate issues of lasting interest to social scientists.

Packing Politics into Quadrant I

How long a time frame should analysts employ in studying social phenomena? There is no fixed answer to this question. Instead, it depends on the particular problems that analysts hope to tackle, their assumptions about the nature of the most important processes that might be at work in the area they are studying, and judgments about the feasibility of particular ways of proceeding. As David Lake and Robert Powell have argued, "methodological approaches, by their very nature, privilege some forms of explanation over others and are, in effect, bets about what will prove to be fruitful ways to attack certain sets of problems" (Lake and Powell 1999, p. 16). Social scientists are currently placing their bets very heavily on Quadrant I.[7] My

[7] Although I have argued that the key temporal dimensions of social processes cannot be reduced to the simple typology offered in Table 5.1, I use "Quadrant I" as a convenient

argument is not that Quadrant I research is of little value. Rather, it is that we should diversify our bets. Choices about the scope of time covered in a particular analysis have profound effects. They lead to substantial shifts in the kinds of theories we employ, the methods we use, the kinds of causal forces we are likely to see at work, and even the outcomes of interest that we come to identify in the first place. For a social science community largely confined to Quadrant I, a great deal of social life is simply off the radar screen.

Political scientists have not always shown such a decided preference for investigations focused on Quadrant I. From the 1950s through the 1970s, for instance, the field of comparative politics was strongly animated by issues of modernization and state-building that involved the investigation of precisely the kinds of big, long-term processes discussed here (Deutsch 1961; Huntington 1968; Nordlinger 1968; Flora 1999b). As is well known, much of the modernization literature – or at least a caricature of it – came under attack for exhibiting a rather complacent functionalist and teleological bent that suggested eventual convergence on the model of Western democracies. Yet the collapse of the modernization literature is a clear case of throwing out the baby with the bathwater. The discipline jettisoned an undesirable functionalism and teleology (which, ironically, has often reappeared in a new rationalistic form). Along with it went the discipline's most sustained efforts to think about long-term processes of social and political change.

Attention to big, long-term processes has remained alive in fields where comparative historical analysis has gained a strong foothold, including work on democratization, revolutions, and the development of the welfare state.[8] Yet a number of trends seem to have pushed comparative inquiry toward a focus on short-term processes. Quantitative analyses are by no means incompatible with attentiveness to long-term, slow-moving features of social life. Indeed, they can be well suited to identifying the role of such factors. Some structural arguments, for instance, are easily incorporated in large-*N* analyses, and well-designed quantitative studies can test for threshold effects as well. Yet in practice, one often finds that the priority on generating high correlations privileges "shallow" (temporally proximate but often near-tautological) accounts over "deep" ones (Rueschemeyer, Stephens, and Stephens 1992; Kitschelt 1999).

shorthand reference for studies that are not designed to explore processes that unfold over substantial stretches of time.

[8] Of course, the empirical studies cited in this essay provide numerous examples. And various essays in this volume review relevant research traditions at length.

A more fundamental problem is that many of the long-term processes outlined here, such as those invoking threshold arguments or multistage causal chains, are unlikely to be incorporated in quantitative studies unless the theories that analysts employ point them in this direction. The question, after all, is not just what a particular technique is capable of doing in principle, but how it is actually employed in practice – a distinction that is almost always glossed over in general discussions of method and theory. As Ronald Jepperson has noted, when faced with a causal account employing a long-term temporal structure, quantitative scholars (as well as rational choice theorists) might well respond by exclaiming, "I can model that!" This riposte loses much of its bite, however, if the theoretical imageries these analysts employ rarely lead them to identify the outcomes or hypotheses in question (Jepperson n.d.).

Indeed, much in contemporary social science leads precisely to this result. Jon Elster, among others, has drawn on Hume's insistence that there can be "no action at a distance" to argue forcefully that causal analysis should always strive to identify "local" causes – the more micro the better (Elster 1983; Hedström and Swedberg 1998). For Elster, the drive to identify social mechanisms is precisely a matter of bringing causes as close as possible in time to the outcome to be explained: "The role of mechanisms is twofold. First, they enable us to go from the larger to the smaller: from molecules to atoms, from societies to individuals. Second, and more fundamentally, they reduce the time lag between explanans and explanandum. A mechanism provides a continuous and contiguous chain of causal or intentional links . . ." (Elster 1983, p. 24). Yet this reasonable desire to create a contiguous chain of causal links up to the present should be only one priority, and it should not come at the price of pushing important social processes out of the scope of causal argument.

It is in this respect that the increasing prevalence of rational choice accounts in comparative politics exerts its strongest pull toward Quadrant I. Starting from the choices of individuals (or social aggregates treated as strategic actors) strongly encourages the analyst to truncate the investigation in various respects, including the crucial dimension of time. Recent work on transitions to democracy, structured around elite bargaining models, provides a good example of the bias this imparts to causal accounts (Collier 1999). As Charles Tilly puts it, ". . . recent theorists have accelerated the tempo so that at times the transition to democracy looks almost instantaneous: put the pact in gear and go" (Tilly 1995, p. 365). Game-theoretic approaches do not easily stretch over extended spaces (to broad social aggregates) or long time periods without rendering key assumptions of the models implausible.[9]

It is not that rational choice theory, or even game theory, is simply incompatible with the examination of long-term processes (North 1990). "Comparative statics," for instance, offers one way to address some of these liabilities. Here, a game-theoretic model is run with different parameters, allowing the analyst to ask what happens if a structural variable (such as the age distribution of a population) undergoes a major shift (Weingast 1998). While helpful, this seems at best to be a very partial solution. It appears capable of addressing at most a few of the long-term processes discussed in this essay, and even those in a quite restricted manner. And of course, as suggested previously, analysts would need to be thinking along these lines in the first place. Rational choice imagery, focused on the strategic behavior of actors, may not be the most promising way to generate this type of thinking.

Rational choice theory may contribute to the temporal constriction of analyses in comparative politics in a less direct manner as well. Scholars employing this approach typically turn to economics for inspiration. This orientation is likely to make a big difference when it comes to carrying out research. In practice, there appear to be strong elective affinities between the basic theoretical imageries analysts employ and the hypotheses they choose to evaluate. I have argued that many of the strongest candidates for big, slow-moving causal accounts are likely to be sociological. Even if in principle some of these processes could be incorporated into rational choice explanations, they are not the kinds of hypotheses that these analysts typically go looking for.

The pull of Quadrant I is evident not only in quantitative and rational choice investigations. Qualitative analysts are also likely to gravitate to Quadrant I unless they make a conscious effort to explore other possibilities. Writing in a slightly different context, Rueschemeyer et al. (1992, pp. 32–3) summarize the key problem:

> Studying change within the same society implicitly holds constant those structural features of the situation that do not actually change during the period of observation. It is for this reason that process-oriented historical studies – even if they transcend sheer narrative and are conducted with theoretical, explanatory intent – often

[9] See, for instance, Elster's (2000) forceful critique of the stretching entailed in the recent *Analytic Narratives* volume's application of game theory to macrohistorical phenomena. Elster (1989), Scharpf (1998), and Munck (2001) explore related issues.

emphasize the role of voluntary decision and tend to play down – by taking them as givens – structural constraints that limit some options of historical actors and encourage others.

By adding comparative cases, an analyst may be able to overcome some of the blind spots associated with structural factors that concern Rueschemeyer et al. Doing so is unlikely to address the problem of identifying the specific impact of slow-moving causal processes, however, unless the investigation not only covers additional cases but also takes in an extended period of time for each of those cases. As noted previously, this problem appears to mar many recent investigations of transitions to democracy. Even those not grounded in game theory have often advanced highly voluntaristic or nearly tautological explanations (Kitschelt 1999).

Comparative historical analyses will often do a good job of capturing long-term processes, as suggested by the numerous examples cited in this essay. These investigations typically examine considerable stretches of time. Equally important, they draw on theoretical traditions, stretching back to the great works of Marx and Weber, that point to hypotheses with this sort of temporal structure. Yet like other methodologies, comparative historical analyses are likely to miss causes and outcomes that are visible only over the long term unless the investigator is sensitive to the need to consider such possibilities in the first place.[10] And the potential for synergies between small-*N* and quantitative methods for examining such slow-moving processes are likely to be considerable.

Consider Carmines and Stimson's reflections on their efforts to introduce a long-term perspective into the study of American public opinion and elections. Their conclusion provides a telling summary of the core points of this essay and is worth quoting at length:

> For an evolving process one expects gradual but cumulative changes, so slight at any one time as to appear trivial but capable over the long haul of producing profound transformations. That is what we saw. . . . Consider this evidence in another light, not as a pattern of systematic movement over almost fifty years but as one slice in time (or even fifty separate slices). If this same evidence were decomposed in this fashion – if the question, that is, were subtly changed from how much change does this process

[10] Thus my argument here may point to some difficulties for the recent suggestion that improved process tracing represents an important element in more rigorous qualitative analysis (Bennett and George 1998; Hall, this volume). This is an important line of argument, but if process tracing is taken to mean the exploration of more micromechanisms within causal processes, it may have the unintended effect of generating more temporally constricted accounts.

produce? to how much of the observed change in a particular variable in a given year is attributable to the process in question? – then inferences drawn by a reasonable analyst would have a strikingly different character. In few cases would the effects in any given year be notable. Only a few would be statistically significant.... We would have concluded from such a perspective, indeed the literature on American mass behavior has concluded, that racial changes were crucially important for a few years in the mid-1960s, not very much before or since, and that the issue mattered then, not before and not after. That conclusion would be an appropriate reading of the cross-sectional evidence and, we believe, a profoundly mistaken reading of reality. (Carmines and Stimson 1989, p. 196)

The crowding of researchers into Quadrant I comes at a heavy price. In some cases, the price is that important social outcomes fail to attract significant scholarly attention. In others, it is that major social forces do not figure into our causal accounts of political life simply because those forces exert their pressures over extended periods of time. Instead, causality is attributed to those factors that operate as triggers – factors that are temporally proximate to outcomes of interest but of relatively minor significance. In still other settings, analysts can be misled about the very character of the outcomes they investigate because they fail to recognize how slowly those outcomes unfold. In turn, this can lead to mistaken claims about causation. As Swank's research shows, it can even lead analysts to highlight claims about short-term causal effects when the long-term causal processes run exactly counter to them. All of these possibilities suggest the crucial contribution of social research that covers considerable stretches of time. "Macrosociology," as Stinchcombe has said, "has to be a sociology of the long pull" (Stinchcombe 1997, p. 406). Both in theory development and in empirical work, we need to stay attentive to the significance of big, long-term processes.

References

Abbott, Andrew. 1988. "Transcending General Linear Reality." *Sociological Theory* 6: 169–86.

Bartels, Larry M. 1998. "Electoral Continuity and Change, 1868–1996." *Electoral Studies* 17: 301–26.

Baumgartner, Frank R. and Bryan D. Jones. 1993. *Agendas and Instability in American Politics*. Chicago: University of Chicago Press.

Bell, Daniel. 1974. *The Coming of Postindustrial Society*. New York: Basic Books.

Brady, David W. 1988. *Critical Elections and Congressional Policy Making*. Stanford, CA: Stanford University Press.

Burnham, Walter D. 1970. *Critical Elections and the Mainsprings of American Politics*. New York: W. W. Norton.

Cameron, Charles. 2000. "Congress Constructs the Judiciary, 1789–2000." Memo prepared for Russell Sage Foundation Conference on History and Politics, April.

Carlsson, Gøsta. 1972. "Lagged Structures and Cross-Sectional Methods." *Acta Sociologica* 15: 323–41.

Carmines, Edward G. and James A. Stimson. 1989. *Issue Evolution: Race and the Transformation of American Politics*. Princeton, NJ: Princeton University Press.

Carroll, Glenn R. and Michael T. Hannan. 2000. *The Demography of Corporations and Industries*. Princeton, NJ: Princeton University Press.

Collier, Ruth Berins. 1999. *Paths Toward Democracy: The Working Class and Elites in Western Europe and South America*. Cambridge: Cambridge University Press.

Collier, Ruth Berins and David Collier. 1991. *Shaping the Political Arena*. Princeton, NJ: Princeton University Press.

Deutsch, Karl. 1961. "Social Mobilization and Political Development." *American Political Science Review* 55: 493–514.

Elster, Jon. 1983. *Explaining Technical Change*. Cambridge: Cambridge University Press.

1989. *Solomonic Judgments*. Cambridge: Cambridge University Press.

2000. "Rational Choice History: A Case of Excessive Ambition." *American Political Science Review* 94: 685–95.

Ertman, Thomas. 1996. *Birth of Leviathan: Building States and Regimes in Medieval and Early Modern Europe*. Cambridge: Cambridge University Press.

Fearon, James. 1996. "Causes and Counterfactuals in Social Science: Exploring an Analogy between Cellular Automata and Historical Processes." Pp. 39–67 in *Counterfactual Thought Experiments in World Politics: Logical, Methodological, and Psychological Perspectives*, edited by Philip E. Tetlock and Aaron Belkin. Princeton, NJ: Princeton University Press.

Flora, Peter, ed. 1999a. *State Formation, Nation-Building, and Mass Politics in Europe: The Theory of Stein Rokkan*. Oxford: Oxford University Press.

1999b. "Introduction and Interpretation." Pp. 1–91 in *State Formation, Nation-Building, and Mass Politics in Europe: The Theory of Stein Rokkan*, edited by Peter Flora. Oxford: Oxford University Press.

Gellner, Ernst. 1983. *Nations and Nationalism*. Ithaca, NY: Cornell University Press.

Goldstone, Jack A. 1991. *Revolution and Rebellion in the Early Modern World*. Berkeley: University of California Press.

1998. "Initial Conditions, General Laws, Path Dependence and Explanation in Historical Sociology." *American Journal of Sociology* 104: 829–45.

Granovetter, Mark. 1978. "Threshold Models of Collective Behavior." *American Journal of Sociology* 83: 1420–43.

Hacker, Jacob. 1998. "The Historical Logic of National Health Insurance: Structure and Sequence in the Development of British, Canadian, and U.S. Medical Policy." *Studies in American Political Development* 12: 57–130.

Hannan, Michael T. and John Freeman. 1989. *Organizational Ecology*. Cambridge, MA: Harvard University Press.

Hedström, Peter and Richard Swedborg, eds. 1998. *Social Mechanisms: An Analytical Approach to Social Theory*. New York: Cambridge University Press.
Hirsch, Fred. 1977. *The Social Limits to Growth*. Cambridge, MA: Harvard University Press.
Huber, Evelyne and John D. Stephens. 2001. *Development and Crisis of the Welfare State: Parties and Policies in Global Markets*. Chicago: University of Chicago Press.
Huntington, Samuel. 1968. *Political Order in Changing Societies*. New Haven, CT: Yale University Press.
Iversen, Torben and Anne Wren. 1998. "Equality, Employment and Budgetary Restraint: The Trilemma of the Service Economy." *World Politics* 50: 507–46.
Jepperson, Ronald. n.d. "Relations Between Different Theoretical Imageries (with Application to Institutionalism)." Manuscript.
Jervis, Robert. 1997. *System Effects: Complexity in Political and Social Life*. Princeton, NJ: Princeton University Press.
Kahler, Miles. 1999. "Evolution, Choice, and International Change." Pp. 165–96 in *Strategic Choice and International Relations*, edited by David A. Lake and Robert Powell. Princeton, NJ: Princeton University Press.
Key, V. O. 1959. "Secular Realignment and the Party System." *Journal of Politics* 21: 198–210.
Kitschelt, Herbert. 1999. "Accounting for Outcomes of Post-Communist Regime Change: Causal Depth or Shallowness in Rival Explanations." Paper presented at the American Political Science Association meetings, Atlanta, September 1–5.
Laitin, David. 1998. *Identity in Formation: The Russian-Speaking Populations in the Near Abroad*. Ithaca, NY: Cornell University Press.
Lake, David A. and Robert Powell. 1999. "International Relations: A Strategic Choice Approach." Pp. 1–38 in *Strategic Choice and International Relations*, edited by David Lake and Robert Powell. Princeton, NJ: Princeton University Press.
Lieberson, Stanley. 1985. *Making It Count: The Improvement of Social Research and Theory*. Berkeley: University of California Press.
1997. "The Big Broad Issues in Society and Social History: Application of a Probabilistic Perspective." Pp. 359–85 in *Causality in Crisis? Statistical Methods and the Search for Causal Knowledge in the Social Sciences*, edited by Vaughn R. McKim and Stephen P. Turner. Notre Dame, IN: University of Notre Dame Press.
Luebbert, Gregory M. 1991. *Liberalism, Fascism, or Social Democracy: Social Classes and the Political Origins of Regimes in Interwar Europe*. New York: Oxford University Press.
Macy, Michael. 1990. "Learning Theory and the Logic of the Critical Mass." *American Sociological Review* 55: 809–26.
Mahoney, James. 2000. "Path Dependence in Historical Sociology." *Theory and Society* 29: 507–48.

Mannheim, Karl. 1952. "The Problem of Generations." Pp. 276–320 in *Essays on the Sociology of Knowledge*, edited by Paul Kecskemeti. London: Routledge and Kegan Paul.

Marwell, Gerald and Pamela Oliver. 1993. *The Critical Mass in Collective Action: A Micro-Social Theory*. Cambridge: Cambridge University Press.

Mayhew, David R. 2000. "Electoral Realignments: A Critique of the Classical Genre." Unpublished manuscript, Yale University.

McAdam, Douglas. 1982. *Political Process and the Development of Black Insurgency, 1930–1970*. Chicago: University of Chicago Press.

Moore, Barrington. 1966. *Social Origins of Dictatorship and Democracy*. Boston: Beacon Press.

Munck, Gerardo. 2001. "Game Theory and Comparative Politics: New Perspectives and Old Concerns." *World Politics* 23: 173–204.

Nelson, Richard R. 1995. "Recent Evolutionary Theorizing About Economic Change." *Journal of Economic Literature* 33: 48–90.

Nordlinger, Eric A. 1968. "Political Development: Time Sequences and Rates of Change." *World Politics* 20: 494–520.

North, Douglass C. 1990. *Institutions, Institutional Change, and Economic Performance*. Cambridge: Cambridge University Press.

Pierson, Paul. 1994. *Dismantling the Welfare State? Reagan, Thatcher, and the Politics of Retrenchment*. Cambridge: Cambridge University Press.

2000a. "Increasing Returns, Path Dependence, and the Study of Politics." *American Political Science Review* 94: 251–67.

2000b. "Not Just What, but *When*: Timing and Sequence in Political Processes." *Studies in American Political Development* 14: 72–92.

2000c. "Three Worlds of Welfare State Research." *Comparative Political Studies* 33: 791–821.

Pierson, Paul and Theda Skocpol. 2002. "Historical Institutionalism in Contemporary Political Science." In Ira Katznelson and Helen Milner, eds. *The State of the Discipline*. New York: W. W. Norton.

Przeworski, Adam and Fernando Limongi. 1997. "Modernization: Theories and Facts." *World Politics* 49: 155–83.

Putnam, Robert. 2000. *Bowling Alone*. New York: Simon & Schuster.

Rogowski, Ronald. 1989. *Commerce and Coalitions: How Trade Affects Domestic Political Alignments*. Princeton, NJ: Princeton University Press.

Rokkan, Stein. 1974. "Entries, Voices, Exits: Towards a Possible Generalization of the Hirschman Model." *Social Science Information* 13: 39–53.

Rose, Richard and Paul Davies. 1994. *Inheritance in Public Policy: Change without Choice in Britain*. New Haven, CT: Yale University Press.

Rueschemeyer, Dietrich, Evelyne Huber Stephens, and John D. Stephens. 1992. *Capitalist Development and Democracy*. Chicago: University of Chicago Press.

Scharpf, Fritz W. 1998. *Games Real Actors Play: Actor-Centered Institutionalism in Policy Research*. Boulder, CO: Westview Press.

Schelling, Thomas. 1978. *Micromotives and Macrobehavior*. Cambridge, MA: Harvard University Press.

Shefter, Martin. 1977. "Party and Patronage: Germany, England, and Italy." *Politics and Society* 7: 403–52.

Skocpol, Theda. 1979. *States and Social Revolutions*. Cambridge: Cambridge University Press.

Spruyt, Hendrik. 1994. *The Sovereign State and Its Competitors*. Princeton, NJ: Princeton University Press.

Steuerle, Eugene and M. Kawai, eds. 1996. *The New World Fiscal Order*. Washington, DC: Urban Institute Press.

Stevens, William K. 2000. "The Oceans Absorb Much of Global Warming, Study Confirms." *New York Times*, March 24, p. A14.

Stinchcombe, Arthur. 1968. *Constructing Social Theories*. New York: Harcourt, Brace.

1974. "Merton's Theory of Social Structure." Pp. 11–33 in *The Idea of Social Structure: Papers in Honor of Robert Merton*, edited by L. Coser. New York: Harcourt, Brace.

1997. "Tilly on the Past as a Sequence of Futures." Pp. 387–409 in *Roads from Past to Futures*, edited by Charles Tilly. Latham, MA: Rowman & Littlefield.

Swank, Duane. 2001. "Political Institutions and Welfare State Restructuring: The Impact of Institutions on Social Policy Change in Developed Democracies." Pp. 197–237 in *The New Politics of the Welfare State*, edited by Paul Pierson. Oxford: Oxford University Press.

Tilly, Charles. 1995. "Democracy Is a Lake." Pp. 365–87 in *The Social Construction of Democracy*, edited by George Reid Andrews and Hemck Chapman. New York: New York University Press.

Tarrow, Sidney. 1992. "Mentalities, Political Cultures, and Collective Action Frames: Constructing Meanings through Action." Pp. 174–202 in *Frontiers in Social Movement Theory*, edited by Aldon D. Morris and Carol Mueller. New Haven, CT: Yale University Press.

Weber, Max. 1946 [1921]. "Politics as a Vocation." Pp. 77–128 in *From Max Weber: Essays in Sociology*, edited by H. H. Gerth and C. Wright Mills. Oxford: Oxford University Press.

Weingast, Barry R. 1998. "Notes on a Possible Integration of Historical Institutionalism and Rational Choice Theory." Prepared for the Russell Sage Foundation meeting, New York, November.

Wuthnow, Robert. 1989. *Communities of Discourse: Ideology and Social Structure in the Reformation, the Enlightenment, and European Socialism*. Cambridge, MA: Harvard University Press.

6

How Institutions Evolve

INSIGHTS FROM COMPARATIVE HISTORICAL ANALYSIS

Kathleen Thelen

I. Introduction

This essay explores the question of how formal institutions change.[1] Despite the importance assigned by many scholars to the role of institutions in structuring political life, the issue of how these institutions are themselves shaped and reconfigured over time has not received the attention it is due. In the 1970s and 1980s, a good deal of comparative institutionalist work centered on comparative statics and was concerned with demonstrating the ways in which different institutional arrangements drove divergent political and policy outcomes (e.g., Katzenstein 1978). In addition, scholarship in the comparative historical tradition has yielded important insights into the genesis of divergent (usually national) trajectories. Works in this vein include some classics such as Gerschenkron (1962), Moore (1966), and Shefter (1977), but also significant recent contributions such as Collier and Collier (1991), Skocpol (1992), Spruyt (1994), Ertman (1997), Gould (1999), and Huber and Stephens (2001). Finally, we have a number of analyses that address the issue of "feedback mechanisms" that are responsible for the reproduction of various institutional and policy trajectories over time (e.g., Pierson 1993; Skocpol 1992; Weir 1992b).

I am indebted to all of the participants in the project that led to this book for their very helpful input on previous versions of this essay. For written comments and exchanges, I thank Gerard Alexander, Gerda Falkner, Tulia Falleti, Ernst B. Haas, Jacob Hacker, Peter Hall, Evelyne Huber, James Mahoney, Dietrich Rueschemeyer, Ben Schneider, and Steven Vogel. I owe a special debt of gratitude to Paul Pierson for comments on this essay (more than one round), but also and more generally for our ongoing conversation about these issues that has been very important to my own thinking about them.

[1] Following Pierson (2000b), I limit my discussion in this essay to formal political institutions that are the products of conscious design and redesign.

Ongoing theoretical work centering on the concept of path dependence by Mahoney, Pierson, and others has lent greater precision to previous formulations based on the dual notions of "critical junctures" and "historical trajectories" (Mahoney 2000; Pierson 2000a).[2] As these authors have shown, some of the major works in comparative historical analysis can be read as illustrations of path dependence in social and political development. Mahoney has contributed to analytic clarity by specifying various mechanisms of reproduction that may be sustaining different institutions – invoking and distinguishing utilitarian, functionalist, power, and legitimation arguments (Mahoney 2000). His treatment of path dependence returns to insights from Arthur Stinchcombe that note that the factors responsible for the genesis of an institution may not be the same as those that sustain it over time (Stinchcombe 1968).

But path dependence as currently conceptualized tends to encourage a rather strict separation of the issues of institutional innovation and institutional reproduction.[3] Much of the work that invokes this concept is premised on a punctuated equilibrium model that emphasizes moments of "openness" and rapid innovation followed by long periods of institutional stasis or "lock in" (e.g., Krasner 1988). The implication is that institutions, once created, either persist or break down in the face of some kind of exogenous shock. Certainly, this kind of punctuated equilibrium model captures one important mode of change in political life. In my own work (Thelen 1999), I have suggested that the analysis of critical junctures (mostly about institutional innovation) and the study of feedback effects (mostly about institutional reproduction) could be brought into a more sustained dialogue. By examining the specific mechanisms of reproduction behind particular institutional arrangements, we will gain insights into the kinds of exogenous events or trends that would be most likely to bring about institutional breakdown or decay.

But what about institutional changes that fall short of breakdown? It seems to me that one reason we are drawn to the study of institutions is precisely that, frequently, particular institutional arrangements are incredibly resilient and resistant even in the face of huge historic breaks (revolutions, defeat in war); in other words, exogenous shocks of just the sort that one would expect to disrupt previous patterns and give rise to institutional

[2] The work of Collier and Collier (1991) has also been very important in rendering these concepts more rigorous and precise.

[3] For a more extended discussion, see Thelen (1999).

innovation. But this is not what we find empirically, at least not always. One thinks, for example, of how specific institutions facilitating employer coordination reemerged in Germany and Japan after the Second World War, in some cases despite explicit efforts by the Allies to prevent this.[4] Or the way in which the institutional arrangements that developed in Eastern Europe before and under communist rule remain salient even after the disjuncture of 1989 and continue to shape distinctive trajectories in the postcommunist period.[5] Or the persistence of particular modes of interest intermediation ("liberal" in the United States, "corporatist" in some northern European countries, "statist" in France) through major macrohistorical transformations such as industrialization and democratization that completely reconfigured the political and economic landscapes around them.[6]

Conversely, we are also often struck by the cumulative effect of ongoing but often subtle changes in institutional arrangements that persist over long stretches of time. The British House of Lords, for example, has exhibited tremendous staying power and in some ways is a powerful illustration of institutional "stickiness" or "lock in." But it also seems clear that this is a quite different institution today than it was two centuries ago, and political scientists and sociologists are likely to be at least as interested in the way it has changed over time as they are in the forces that have sustained it. The U.S. Supreme Court is another institution that, while preserving many of its core attributes, has nonetheless undergone an enormous transformation over the last several decades. In the nineteenth century, the Court played a very different – much more limited – role in American politics, dealing mostly with federalism cases, disputes over commerce, and occasionally, the issue of presidential power. In the course of the twentieth century, the role and function of the Court within American politics have been substantially transformed, particularly and perhaps most consequentially through its emergence as an important forum for the defense of minority rights and individual freedoms.[7]

[4] See, for example, Shonfield (1969) on cartel legislation in Germany and Aoki (1988) and Aoki and Patrick (1994) on the parallels between postwar *keiretsu* in Japan and prewar *zaibatsu*. Herrigel (2000) also makes an argument about the reconfiguration of prewar political-economic structures in both countries in the postwar period.

[5] See, for example, Stark and Bruszt (1998), Kitschelt et al. (1999b), Grzymala-Busse (2002), and Ekiert and Hanson (in press-b).

[6] For example, Lehmbruch (2001), Levy (1999), and Manow (2001).

[7] Thanks to Ronald Kahn for this example.

In fact, if one thinks about it, there are many political institutions that are interesting precisely because if we look at them today we are struck, simultaneously, by how little *and* how much they have changed over time.[8] Some of the institutions mediating gender relations in the developed democracies come to mind, and further examples could be found in the institutions defining relations between subnational and national governments in many federal systems. From the perspective of a punctuated equilibrium model, there often seems to be too much continuity through putative breakpoints in history, but also often too much change beneath the surface of apparently stable formal institutional arrangements.

The contemporary literature on institutions does not yet offer very good conceptual or theoretical tools for addressing these phenomena. Some of the early literature on diverse national trajectories tended to obscure the issue by conceiving of institutions as the "frozen" residue of critical junctures or as the static, sticky legacies of previous political battles (e.g., Lipset and Rokkan 1968). More recent literature on path dependence and increasing returns effects has pushed the debate forward by specifying the *dynamic* processes that sustain institutions over long periods of time (e.g., Pierson 2000a). But increasing returns arguments tell only part of the story; they are better at articulating the mechanisms of reproduction behind particular institutions than they are at capturing the logic of institutional evolution and change. Moreover, in some cases, explaining institutional persistence itself may require us to look beyond arguments about increasing returns. This is because as we scan the political and political-economic landscapes, we find that institutional survival is often strongly laced with elements of institutional *transformation* to bring institutions in line with changing social, political, and economic conditions.

This essay proceeds as follows. I begin with a brief review of various perspectives on institutions and explore how their different premises lead to divergent views of how institutions emerge and evolve over time. I first consider three prominent approaches – utilitarian-functionalist, power-distributional, and cultural-sociological – that see institutions as brought about and sustained by particular, specified causal factors – whether a set of functional requirements, an underlying balance of societal or political power, or a shared cultural understanding of what organizational forms are

[8] Comments by Peter Katzenstein at a conference in Cologne on the origins of the German and Japanese political-economic "models" prompted me to think about it in this way.

considered legitimate or appropriate.[9] As such, each of these perspectives contains an implicit theory of change: if institutions rest on and reflect a particular foundation (whether efficiency-based, power-based, or cultural) then they should change as a result of shifts in those underlying conditions.

Path dependence perspectives draw on the same causal arguments as the first three perspectives, but where they differ is that they do not necessarily look for "constant causes" through time and space.[10] As Mahoney points out (2000, p. 515), path dependence perspectives posit that the factors responsible for the genesis of an institution may well be different from those that sustain it over time. Such perspectives see institutions as the products of specific historical episodes or turning points that result in configurations that then set constraints on subsequent developments (see especially Collier and Collier 1991, pp. 35–8). In terms of their approach to questions of institutional genesis and change, contemporary arguments about path dependence often emphasize moments of institutional innovation in which agency, choice, and contingency figure prominently. Such moments are then followed by periods of institutional reproduction where the importance of strategy and choice recedes relative to processes of adaptation to institutional incentives and constraints. Institutional change, in this view, is often seen to be a function of exogenous shocks that disrupt previously stable arrangements and open the door again for institutional innovation.

The literature on path dependence and policy feedback has yielded important insights into the ways in which "history matters" and has also produced some compelling accounts of enduring cross-national differences in political trajectories. However, the most precise conceptions tend to yield a somewhat narrow view of how the past weighs on the present. The focus on what Haydu calls "switch points" and "lock-in mechanisms" sometimes suggests an overly contingent view of the "choice points" and a rather deterministic view of institutional reproduction (Thelen 1999).[11] The idea seems to be that institutions either persist and become increasingly entrenched or are abandoned. There are few hints or insights here into the

[9] See also James Mahoney (2000), who develops a similar though not identical typology, in some ways more nuanced than this one.

[10] See Stinchcombe (1968, pp. 101–4) on "historicist" versus "constant cause" explanations. Also see Collier and Collier (1991, pp. 35–7).

[11] This varies across authors, and Mahoney (2000) intentionally embraces a very strong version of the argument in the interest of analytic and conceptual clarity. I return to these issues later.

question of how institutions themselves change and evolve in more subtle and sometimes more interesting ways over time.

In order to appreciate fully the causal weight of the past, we need to complement analyses of path dependence and punctuated equilibrium models with conceptual tools that can capture the logic of institutional evolution and change.[12] Specifically, we need to take account of the way in which crises or turning points can be generated endogenously, including through the working out of the logic of previous switch points. We also need to consider the way in which new problems are conceived and solutions sought are themselves products of the past rather than historical accidents (Haydu 1998). This amounts to a call for introducing somewhat more structure at the "front end" of the analysis of institutional development than most path dependence arguments do – by attending to the way in which historically evolved structures limit the options of political actors even at critical choice points. It also calls for injecting somewhat more agency and strategy at the "back end" of such arguments – by emphasizing the way in which institutions operate not just as constraints but as strategic resources for actors as they respond to changes in the political and economic contexts that present new opportunities or throw up new challenges.

The issue of institutional change is an enormously complicated one, and my aim in this essay is relatively modest. I introduce two ways of conceptualizing the problem of institutional evolution that overcome the current zero-sum view of institutional innovation *versus* institutional reproduction that has been characteristic of much of the literature in this area to date. Arguments about institutional change through *layering* and through *conversion* incorporate elements of increasing returns arguments from the path dependence literature, but they embed these elements in an analysis of ongoing political contestation over institutional outcomes. In doing so, they highlight the processes through which institutional arrangements are renegotiated periodically in ways that alter their form and functions.

What the approach advanced here shares with path-dependence perspectives is that it embraces a strong "historicist" and temporal dimension and provides a way of understanding why, over time, institutional arrangements

[12] For punctuated equilibrium models, of course, "equilibrium" is itself an analytic concept, and how it is defined will vary. What for one scholar is a change in the equilibrium will for another scholar simply be a minor adjustment without an equilibrium shift. But the concept of equilibrium, however defined, suggests a self-reinforcing "resting point" – and as such does not give us much leverage on degrees of change or, more central here, on different modes of change from one such resting point to the next.

may come to serve functions that are quite remote from those originally intended by their designers, how they can affect (rather than simply reflect or reinforce) the prevailing balance of power among societal groups, and how they can become resources for (rather than just constraints on) actors engaged in contests over the types of practices that are coded as appropriate or desirable. But unlike most contemporary path dependence frameworks, the perspective offered here goes beyond the logic of positive reinforcement and increasing returns to address the question of how institutions also continue to evolve and change over time. I provide illustrations of my arguments from the comparative historical and institutionalist literatures, and I close with a brief consideration of the advantages of such a perspective for understanding institutional evolution and change.

II. Approaches to Institutions and Institutional Change

There exist in the literature a number of general approaches to understanding institutions, each of which suggests a somewhat different set of answers to the core questions of how institutions are created, reproduced, and changed. The premises and logic of some of the most prominent perspectives are sketched out briefly in this section. I establish a broad distinction between arguments resting on a logic of "constant causes" and path-dependence explanations of institutional genesis and change. Constant-cause explanations can come in several varieties – functionalist, political, cultural – but all would suggest that the same factors that account for the genesis of an institution will also explain institutional change over time. Path-dependence perspectives, by contrast, suggest that institutions may outlive the forces that brought them into being; that is, the factors responsible for the reproduction of an institution may be quite different from those that account for the existence of the institution in the first place.

Constant-Cause Explanations

Constant-cause perspectives on institutional genesis and change can rely on a variety of causal arguments, including functionalist-utilitarian, power-political, and cultural. *Functionalist/utilitarian perspectives* view political institutions in terms of the functions they perform, particularly their role in solving collective action problems and allowing actors to achieve joint gains through cooperation and exchange. This view is prominent in the work of some social choice theorists, for whom institutions are important in reducing uncertainty, underwriting commitments, providing focal points, facilitating trade-offs, providing enforcement mechanisms, and the like. For example, Weingast and Marshall (1988) see the committee system in the U.S. Congress as having been designed to deal with problems of uncertainty that otherwise make it hard for legislators to negotiate trade-offs and enforce promises they make to one another – something that each of them needs in order to deliver benefits to his or her own constituency. The international relations literature provides further examples – for example, the studies that suggest that international regimes or organizations are set up to allow countries to achieve joint gains through cooperation in an anarchic international system (Keohane 1984).

Regarding institutional evolution, this literature suggests that institutions may evolve as a consequence of repeated interactions and learning effects as individuals "craft tools – including rules – to improve the structure of the repetitive situations they face" (Ostrom 1999, p. 496). This would amount to incremental change within an overall stable institutional context. However, change need not be incremental, and by the logic of utilitarian/functionalist arguments, we might expect institutions to break down as a result of a shift in environmental or other conditions that rendered existing institutions dysfunctional. Such disruptions would presumably drive the search for new solutions to coordination and other problems.

Functionalist and utilitarian explanations can be quite powerful. As Pierson points out, "in a world of purposive actors, it may indeed be the case that the effects of an institution have something to do with an explanation for its emergence and persistence" (Pierson 2000a, pp. 13–14). However, whether the origins of a given institution in fact go back in a straightforward way to efforts by its designers to fulfill certain functions is ultimately an empirical question. As Knight has argued, "one of the most significant mistakes made by proponents of rational choice explanations of institutional change is the practice of working back from identifiable institutional effects to determine the initial preferences of the actors involved in the institutionalization process" (Knight 1999, pp. 33–4). Or as Pierson insists, we cannot assume a connection between effects and intentions; instead, "we have to go back and look" (Pierson 2000a, p. 14).

Power-distributional accounts provide an alternative approach to institutional creation and change, placing the distributive effects of institutions front and center in the analysis. In this view, social institutions emerge not out of a shared concern with achieving joint gains through cooperation, but rather out of political conflict and strategic bargaining among social actors: "institutional development is a contest among actors to establish rules which structure outcomes to those equilibria most favorable for them" (Knight 1999, p. 20). Social institutions, in short, reflect power asymmetries in a society, for it is such asymmetries that allow more powerful actors to impose their institutional preferences on the less powerful actors. Jack Knight's work exemplifies such a perspective within the context of a rational choice approach, but much of the Marxist tradition is also built upon this foundation. To give one example, Walter Korpi traces differences in the welfare state – both cross-national variation and variation within countries over time – to the relative strength of labor and capital (Korpi 1983).

If institutions are forged out of political struggles, and if the particular shape they take on reflects the prevailing balance of power in society, then this perspective suggests that they should change in response *either* to changes in the balance of power among various social actors *or* to changes in the preferences or interests of the most powerful actors. Thus, for instance, many contemporary arguments concerning the effects of globalization on welfare state arrangements hinge on arguments about the relative strength of the working class, for the balance of power between labor and capital (or Left and Right) is what affects the Left's ability to defend previous gains (Garrett 1998; Kurzer 1993; Stephens, Huber, and Ray 1999).

Like functionalist accounts, power-distributional perspectives can be extremely powerful and parsimonious. However, such explanations are subject to the same cautionary critique as that leveled previously against functionalist theories. Contemporary institutions that appear to rest on a particular balance of power may or may not have been created by the constituencies that now benefit from those institutions. In the example of the U.S. Supreme Court cited earlier, the fact that the Court has become a vehicle for defending the rights of women and minorities (admittedly, more under certain courts than others) does not mean that the institution was created with those constituencies or concerns in mind. Sometimes power begets power and institutions reinforce and magnify the position of their creators; but sometimes institutions provide interesting and unintended opportunities for marginal groups to exercise leverage well beyond their apparently meager power resources (e.g., Clemens 1993; Skocpol 1992).

The new institutionalism in sociology has produced a third, *cultural-sociological perspective* on institutional genesis, reproduction, and change. Whereas the utilitarian models cited earlier see institutions as the creation of rational actors pursuing their shared material interests, this perspective sees institutions as embodying collectively defined cultural understandings of the way the world works (Meyer and Rowan 1991; Scott 1995). In this tradition, institutionalization is seen as "the construction over time of a social definition of reality such that certain ways of action are taken for granted as the 'right' if not the only way to do things" (Scott and Meyer 1994, p. 234).

Sociologists in this school emphasize the overarching cultural scripts and see specific organizational forms as generated and sustained by such institutions.[13] In this literature, organizational forms do not reflect solutions to collective action dilemmas (as in functionalist/utilitarian accounts), nor do they reflect the distribution of power in society (as in bargaining and distributive models); rather, they reflect shared cultural understandings of what is efficient or moral or legitimate or "modern." It follows from this that change will occur when a prevailing "script" is replaced or superseded by another. Such processes have been observed in a number of realms. For example, Neil Fligstein has explained changes in corporate practices (e.g., the diffusion of lean production techniques or the new emphasis on shareholder value) as a function of changes in dominant ideas about the modern or rational way to conduct business. These innovations diffuse widely, and their adoption by large numbers of firms, as he shows, proceeds quite independently of their real efficiency effects (Fligstein 1991).

This approach usefully draws attention to the cognitive and normative aspects of social action, and has yielded important insights into sources of institutional continuity that are missed by the other two perspectives outlined previously. However, the notion of institutions as shared scripts tends to obscure strategy and conflict among groups. The most commonly cited mechanisms of change in this literature are imitation and transposition. While these processes are clearly important, they may well work best in concert with more political approaches, since it turns out that in many cases changes in power relations hold the key to creating the openings in which new scripts (or scripts previously only on the margins of an organizational field) can become more central (e.g., Powell 1991, pp. 27, 31).[14]

Path-Dependence Explanations

Each of the perspectives just considered treats institutional origins, persistence, and demise as all derived from a single basic causal process (whether

[13] Just as North, from a rationalist perspective, insists on a strict separation of institutions (the rules of the game) and organizations (the players) (1990, p. 5), institutional sociologists see institutions (scripts) as distinct from organizations.

[14] Powell and Jones (in press) represents an important effort to elaborate mechanisms of institutional change from a sociological perspective.

efficiency-based, power-distributional, or cultural). Less careful applications of these arguments sometimes suggest that the origins of the institutions can be "read backward" off their current functions or features. But this is not inherent in the approaches, and indeed each perspective also contains an implicit theory of change: institutions will evolve in response to (for functionalist theories) changes in the basic purposes around which politics is organized, (for power distributional theorists) a shift in the balance of power or in the goals of the powerful actors, and (for cultural theories) a change in the cultural script that defines what constitutes legitimate or modern organizational forms and routines.

Path-dependence perspectives do not necessarily reject the arguments associated with the first three perspectives, and in fact, they draw on functional, utilitarian, political, and cultural arguments to explain institutional genesis and persistence. However, scholars of path dependence emphasize some contingency at the moment of institutional innovation, and suggest that the forces behind the creation of a particular institution may be quite different from the forces that sustain it over time (see especially Mahoney 2000; also Stinchcombe 1968, pp. 101–29).[15]

While path-dependence theorists as a whole tend toward a "historicist" view (Stinchcombe 1968) of institutional genesis, evolution, and change, there are important differences in how various authors understand and apply the concept of path dependence. William Sewell, for instance, defines path dependence in very broad terms as the idea that "what has happened at an earlier point in time will affect the possible outcomes of a sequence of events occurring at a later point in time" (Sewell 1996, pp. 262–3). This definition is obviously quite open, and unlike most of the other conceptions of path dependence to be discussed, it does not even necessarily suggest a view of development in which an early move in a given direction generates pressures that push further along the same track.[16]

At the other end of the conceptual spectrum, James Mahoney provides a much more precise (and far more restrictive) definition that applies to an interesting but quite rare set of phenomena: "path dependence characterizes specifically those historical sequences in which contingent events set into motion institutional patterns or event chains that have deterministic

[15] Collier and Collier (1991, pp. 35–8) contains a very useful discussion of this difference. See also McDonald (1996).

[16] Again quoting Sewell: "contingent, unexpected, and inherently unpredictable events . . . can undo or alter the most apparently durable trends of history" (1996, p. 264).

properties" (Mahoney 2000, p. 507). For Mahoney and others (see especially Pierson 2000a), this combination of some contingency at the front end and some degree of determinism at the back end of path-dependent processes is what gives rise to the most interesting features of path-dependent social and political processes. These include unpredictability (i.e., outcomes cannot be foreseen ex ante), sensitive dependence on initial conditions (i.e., early events are more important than later events), nonergodicity (i.e., contingent events do not necessarily cancel out), and inertia (i.e., once in motion, processes tend to stay in motion until an equilibrium or final outcome is reached) (Mahoney 2000).[17]

The core ideas behind this conception of path dependence were inspired by the work of economic historians, particularly those interested in technological trajectories. The QWERTY keyboard is the paradigmatic case, but the general argument made by David (1985) and especially by Arthur (1989) holds that certain technologies, for idiosyncratic and unpredictable reasons, can achieve an initial advantage over alternative technologies and prevail despite the fact that in the long run the alternatives would have been more efficient. In this literature, being "first out of the gate" is crucial because once a technology is chosen, it is subject to significant increasing returns effects (Kato 1996; Krasner 1988; North 1990; Pierson 2000a). These processes translate an early (and perhaps idiosyncratically induced) advantage into a stable trajectory of development as firms adapt to the prevailing standard, investing in it in ways that reinforce the initial choice (e.g., people learn to type in a particular way, firms make products that fit the industry standard, and so on). Through these developments, the initial choice gets locked in, making it hard to shift the standard even if a competing technology is revealed to have been the more efficient technology.

What political scientists have taken from this is the intuitively attractive idea that politics, like technology, involves some elements of chance (agency, choice) but that once a path is taken, once-viable alternatives become increasingly remote, as all the relevant actors adjust their strategies to accommodate the prevailing pattern (Levi 1997; Pierson 2000a).[18] North

[17] Pierson's usage is less restrictive, emphasizing mostly that positive feedback processes that set in after some critical juncture make the path not taken ever more remote.

[18] In a way, path dependence arguments reverse the causal logic of the first three perspectives. In functionalist, political-distributional, and cultural accounts, institutions are shaped by their environment and reflect some "deeper" organizing principle. However, path dependence arguments specifically suggest that they do no such thing; in fact, the claim is that the emergence of a particular institution (for whatever reason) prompts shifts in the

has applied the notion of increasing returns to the divergent trajectories of Britain and Spain, suggesting that the early emergence of Parliament in Britain set it on a fundamentally different path (in terms of secure property rights, etc.) from that of Spain. Once in place, the different institutions then developed according to their own internal logic and became entrenched through coordination and learning effects that stabilized expectations and thus contributed to the perpetuation of specific kinds of behaviors and strategies. Institutional development, North emphasizes, is subject to increasing returns; thus, although "specific short-run paths [may be] unforeseeable... the overall direction... is both more predictable and more difficult to reverse" (North 1990, p. 104).

The emphasis in much of the historical-institutional literature on critical junctures and developmental trajectories accounts for the attractiveness of the concept of path dependence, which is being invoked by a growing number of scholars. But, as alluded to earlier, this term has been used in a number of different ways and sometimes has been invoked less carefully than one might hope. Whereas virtually all historical-institutional analyses conform easily (though also somewhat vacuously) to Sewell's expansive definition of path dependence, very few of them in fact fit Mahoney's much more specific version.[19] Empirical analyses in the comparative historical-institutional tradition have certainly shown that institutions forged in particular historical conjunctures may exhibit considerable "staying power" even in the face of developments that alter the set of conditions that originally brought them about. However, it is hard to think of a single case in which institutions are completely "up for grabs" even in what may look like a critical juncture situation, nor one in which they are unalterably locked in in any meaningful sense subsequent to these critical junctures. Rather, most empirical studies in this tradition paint a picture in which politics (and institutions) evolve in ways that – even if not predictable ex ante – nonetheless follow a particular logic that makes sense only against the backdrop of the institutional context in which the "next steps" are inevitably negotiated. Most historical-institutional studies, in other words, are organized around the analysis of what Margaret Weir has called "bounded innovation" (Weir 1992a) and

environment (in the expectations and strategies of key actors, for example) to adjust to the logic of the institution, rather than the other way around.

[19] Thanks to James Mahoney for pointing this out to me. The differing conceptions of path dependence embraced by different authors may also account for why some authors (e.g., Pierson) see path dependence in politics as pervasive, while others (Mahoney, for example) see it as relatively rare (Mahoney 2000, p. 508).

in which developmental pathways are characterized by elements of continuity that channel but do not preclude change (including institutional change).[20]

We do not have very good conceptual tools for characterizing, let alone explaining, such phenomena. The notions of developmental pathways and historical trajectories restate the problem without unpacking exactly what is changing and what is staying the same. One way to deal with this might be to embrace a definition of path dependence that is situated between the expansive and restrictive versions.[21] However, Mahoney makes a strong case that looser definitions simply muddy the conceptual waters (where do we draw the line?) and, in doing so, rob the concept of its analytic "bite." An alternative tack is to focus on specific parts of path-dependent arguments, for example, increasing returns effects, and try to identify the kinds of empirical phenomena that are (and are not) subject to such processes (e.g., Pierson 2000a). A third approach, advocated here,[22] is to distinguish more clearly at both an empirical and an analytic level between the *mechanisms of reproduction* and the *logic of change* at work in particular instances, and to suggest modes of change going beyond the familiar but perhaps ultimately empirically quite rare cases of institutional "breakdown" or wholesale replacement as implied in a punctuated equilibrium model.

For understanding institutional reproduction, increasing returns arguments offer an excellent starting point. As I have argued elsewhere (Thelen 1999), by identifying the feedback mechanisms at work behind particular institutions, we will gain important insights into the specific exogenous events and processes that might disrupt the stable reproduction of these

[20] See also Kitschelt et al. (1999a), where the emphasis is also on the analysis of choice within historically evolved constraints. Ekiert and Hanson (in press-b) usefully distinguish different levels of analysis, such that contingent events at one level of analysis (country-specific) can be related to structural constraints (not necessarily country-specific) at other levels. In other words, there is no need to choose between deterministic models and contingent ones, only a need to frame the analysis and the comparisons so as to draw out each element clearly.

[21] Thus, we could think of path dependence in politics as involving some significant (though not unlimited) openness at the choice points and some degrees of freedom in the subsequent trajectory, but where reversals are unlikely. This is a reasonable position (one that I associate with Pierson, for example) that tries to steer a course between definitions that are so restrictive that they simply don't apply to most of what we are interested in studying and those that are so expansive that they don't provide much guidance in the analysis.

[22] And not incompatible with the second approach; in fact, as I argue later, the two complement one another in important ways.

institutions, and in so doing open up possibilities for change.[23] Since different institutions rest on different foundations, the analysis of the specific feedback processes that sustain them will provide insights into *what aspects* of institutions are renegotiable and *under what conditions*. These kinds of considerations will also help explain why common international trends or events frequently have such diverse domestic consequences, disrupting previously stable patterns in some countries while washing over others seemingly without effect (see also Locke and Thelen 1995).

However, while such an analysis can provide clues as to *when* institutions might be susceptible to change, it needs to be complemented with other lines of analysis that can provide insights into *how* they might change. In other words, to understand the kind of "bounded change" to which North, Weir, and others have directed out attention, we need to weave together insights about institutional reproduction from path dependence perspectives with new tools to understand the modes and mechanisms through which institutional evolution and change occur. Although this second issue has begun to attract more attention, much work remains to be done to lift out the lessons that comparative historical studies yield in terms of general insights.

I begin by sketching out the kinds of empirical puzzles I have in mind, drawing on my own work for concrete examples that can ground this discussion. On this basis, I suggest ways of framing the issues at stake and propose two concepts – institutional layering and institutional conversion – that in my view represent fruitful ways forward in the discussion of institutional evolution and change.[24]

III. A Brief Empirical Example

In the literature on the political economy of the advanced industrial democracies, Germany's vocational training system is commonly held up as an exemplary solution to a number of knotty coordination problems that typically plague private-sector training regimes.[25] The German system encourages

[23] This argument is elaborated in detail, and with empirical examples, in Thelen (1999, esp. pp. 396–9).

[24] The concept of layering comes directly out of the work of Eric Schickler (1999, 2001), and the term "conversion" for the other mode of change described later was suggested to me by Wolfgang Streeck.

[25] This example is drawn from a much more extended analysis of the historical development of vocational training in Germany and elsewhere. See Thelen (2002).

firms to invest in worker training (by protecting them from poaching, for example) and guarantees that apprentices will receive high-quality training (through monitoring and enforcement mechanisms). More generally, vocational training institutions are seen as part of a larger institutional package that, along with centralized collective bargaining, strong bank–industry links, and encompassing employer associations and labor unions, underpins Germany's high-skill, high-wage, high-value-added ("high everything") economy.

This system has been invoked as a classic illustration of each of the first three perspectives sketched out earlier. Thus, for example, from a utilitarian/functionalist perspective, German vocational training institutions are seen as facilitating employer coordination around a "high-skill equilibrium" (Finegold and Soskice 1988). From a power-distributional perspective, it has been assumed to be a reflection of working-class strength (Gillingham 1985). And from a cultural perspective, it has been seen as one of many institutions that embody a distinctively German mode of self-governance that operates through the country's social partners and without much direction from the state (Lehmbruch 2001).

Looking at these institutions from today's vantage point, we can see that each of these characterizations contains an important element of truth. However, historically speaking, they are all somewhat wide of the mark. The core institutional innovation around which the German system came to be built was a piece of legislation passed in 1897 – the so-called Handicraft Protection Law – that was designed to stabilize Germany's large and highly diverse artisanal sector. A key political motive on the part of the authoritarian government of the time was to shore up a reactionary artisanal class that could serve as a political bulwark against the surging and radical working-class movement. Thus, against functionalist arguments, these institutions were not designed with the interests of the industrial sector in mind (indeed, the law bypassed industry altogether); against the power-distributional perspective, labor really played no role in the genesis of these institutions (in fact, the Social Democratic Party opposed the original legislation); and against the cultural perspective, the kind of social partnership of which these institutions are (now) seen to be a part was really nowhere on the horizon.

How did we get from there to here? Not, it seems, through a wholesale breakdown of the old institutions and their replacement with new ones. Indeed, one of the striking features of the system is the resilience of core elements even in the face of enormous disruptions over the twentieth century, including several regime changes, the incorporation of labor, defeat in two world wars, and fascism. These are precisely the kinds of break points that most punctuated equilibrium models might hypothesize to be central.[26] While changes certainly occurred at these junctures, what is in fact remarkable and in need of explanation are some striking continuities in the core features of this system despite these disjunctures. This case, in short, calls for an analysis *both* of the mechanisms of reproduction that sustained these institutions *and* of the mechanisms behind their functional and distributional transformation over time.

For understanding the continuities, the kinds of positive feedback and increasing returns arguments advanced by Pierson and others provide a useful starting point, for these can tell us a great deal about how key actors were constituted and the kinds of strategies they would pursue. The existence in Germany of a system for skill formation centering on the artisanal sector in the early industrial period, for example, shaped the kind of labor movement that would emerge. It did so, among other things, by hastening the demise of skill-based unions by denying them any hope of controlling the market in skills – a function that had been specifically and authoritatively (by the state) delegated to the artisanal associations. However, as the number of skilled workers certified under the artisanal system grew – and especially as these workers joined the social democratic unions – the German labor movement developed a strong interest in democratizing rather than dismantling the system, though this goal would elude them until after World War II.

However, if one told this purely as a tale of positive feedback, one would miss much of what is in fact interesting and important about the way in which these institutions were *transformed* through politics, and specifically through the incorporation of groups whose role in the system was unanticipated at the time of their creation. For example, although the original system covered only the artisanal sector, its existence created pressures among key industrial sectors to develop and seek state recognition for their own training institutions. The 1897 law instituted a system of training for the handicraft sector *with and around which* industry was subsequently forced to work. Key industries such as machine building and metalworking developed their own training practices alongside and in interaction with the artisanal system. The resulting industrial system mimicked some features

[26] Indeed, I see this as a case – like so many others – in which it is not at all obvious how institutions forged at critical junctures in the sometimes very distant past actually *make it* to the present, given the magnitude of some of the intervening events and developments.

of the handicraft system, but without reproducing it precisely. Indeed, the differences and especially the interaction between the two *altered* the trajectory of the system as a whole, driving it away from the decentralized artisanal system toward the centralization, standardization, and uniformity that are now considered defining features of the German system.

Perhaps even more importantly, the function and role of the vocational training system in the German political economy were transformed through the eventual incorporation of labor. Although the Social Democratic Party had opposed the 1897 legislation, as the ranks of social democratic unions filled with workers whose skills had been certified through this system, the labor movement developed a strong interest not in dismantling it, but in comanaging it. The political incorporation of the working class in the early years of the Weimar Republic, and especially the later incorporation of unions into a variety of parapublic "corporatist" institutions – including vocational training institutions – after World War II, recast the purposes of these institutions even as they contributed to institutional reproduction by bringing the system in line with new economic and political conditions. The general point is that institutional survival depended not just on positive feedback, but also on a process of institutional transformation, to accommodate powerful new actors and to adapt the institutions to address new imperatives, both economic and political.

IV. Toward a Specification of Some Common Modes of Institutional Change

This example suggests that it may not be very useful to draw a sharp line between institutional stability and change, for when the context shifts dramatically – as it did (several times) in Germany between the late nineteenth century and the present – institutional stability may involve a major dose of institutional adaptation. We have some useful concepts for making sense of the mechanisms behind institutional reproduction – increasing returns, for example. But we lack similar tools for understanding institutional change. The literature does contain some promising starting points, however, and this section introduces two concepts that may constitute fruitful ways forward in this debate. One is the notion of institutional "layering" which involves the partial renegotiation of some elements of a given set of institutions while leaving others in place (Schickler 2001).[27] The other is what we

[27] See also the discussion of layering in Orren and Skowronek (2000, p. 20).

might call institutional "conversion," as existing institutions are redirected to new purposes, driving changes in the role they perform and/or the functions they serve.[28] Let me say in advance that these two modes of change are but two possibilities among many, and in that sense, the following discussion is but a first foray into a very complex set of issues.[29]

Institutional Layering

The process of institutional evolution through layering figures prominently in the work of Eric Schickler (1999, 2001), whose research on the U.S. Congress illustrates a pattern of institutional change that combines elements of lock-in and innovation. Schickler argues that congressional institutions have evolved through a "tense layering of new arrangements on top of preexisting structures." As he puts it, "new coalitions may design novel institutional arrangements but lack the support, or perhaps the inclination, to replace preexisting institutions established to pursue other ends" (Schickler 1999, p. 13). Some aspects may be locked in in the way that path dependence theorists emphasize, by the power of the constituencies they have created. But in the case of Congress, institution builders "worked around this opposition by adding new institutions rather than dismantling the old" (ibid.). The dynamic is similar to the one described previously in the example of German vocational training – specifically, industry's response to the handicraft training system. In both cases, institutional innovators accommodated and in many ways adapted to the logic of the preexisting system, working around those elements they could not change. However, in both cases – and this is crucial – their actions did not push developments further along the same track, as suggested by increasing returns arguments.

A similar mode of change can be observed in contemporary developments in the welfare state regimes of some developed democracies.[30] As Pierson has suggested, public pension systems (especially pay-as-you-go systems) are subject to significant lock-in effects, creating as they do constituencies and vested interests that pose formidable political obstacles to retrenchment efforts (Pierson 1994). However, even though conservative parties may be incapable of (or uninterested in) dismantling the old

[28] See also a short discussion of related ideas in Thelen and Steinmo (1992).

[29] For example, Steven Vogel reminds me that institutions also evolve through atrophy and drift.

[30] This example was suggested to me by Gerard Alexander, who is writing on this subject.

system, in some cases they can effect changes in the overall trajectory of social security by actively promoting the development of privately funded pensions alongside the public system. The "layering" of an alternative private system onto an existing public system can affect the interests of key constituents, with enormous implications for the overall trajectory of social security in a given country.[31] Rothstein (1998) makes a parallel argument about the potentially transformative effects of individualized private-sector social services that emerge alongside standardized universalistic programs in Scandinavia. The growth of private alternatives can undermine support for universal programs among the middle class, on whose "contingent consent" the whole public system rests.

Elements of layering appear also to be in evidence in transitions to democracy in Eastern Europe. A large number of studies have pointed to significant continuities across the precommunist, communist, and postcommunist periods (e.g., the contributions in Ekiert and Hanson in press-a). Campbell and others have characterized institution building in the post-1989 period in terms of "bricolage" (Campbell 1997), where key actors are not building from scratch but rather "reworking the institutional materials at hand" (Stark and Bruszt 1998, p. 7). As Stark and Bruszt emphasize, institutional innovators in 1989 confronted neither the institutional void that some hoped for nor a landscape completely occupied by the "dead weight of the past" that some feared; innovation was possible, but the innovators had to work with and around existing institutions (Stark and Bruszt 1998, pp. 6–7). Thus, for example, in the case of public administration (especially civil service reform), analysts find such countries continuing to operate "with obsolete organizational structures or government 'machinery' left over from the communist past," with old and new institutions "grafted" together in various ways (Nunberg 1999, pp. 237–8). In the area of social policy as well, many postcommunist countries have constructed new institutions and practices that represent a "blend of old and new structures, institutions, and policy legacies" that "shape opportunities for government action" in the contemporary period (Inglot in press, p. 6).[32]

[31] Myles and Pierson (2001) develop an argument based on cross-national trends that provides a number of empirically verifiable hypotheses concerning the kinds of changes that are possible within particular types of pension systems. They argue that opportunities to shift course in the way described here varies inversely with the maturity of the public pension system.

[32] These arguments bear a family resemblance to arguments made by Jonathan Zeitlin (2000, pp. 34–41) about "hybridization" in the reconstruction of the European and Japanese

Processes of institutional evolution through layering are pervasive, and further examples are not hard to identify. Many constitutions, for example, have evolved over time through a layering process that adapts inherited institutions and practices to emerging new circumstances. In fact, constitutions seem to be a prime case of what many authors have defined as institutional stickiness by design – for example, as amendment processes requiring supermajorities build in a bias against change (Moe 1990; Pollack 1996).[33] But while institutional designers who want their creations to last may do well to make change difficult, they do well *not* to make it impossible. This is because the survival of an institution often depends also on a degree of flexibility and adaptability. Thus, constitutions often evolve through a layering process that preserves much of the core while adding amendments through which rules and structures inherited from the past can be brought into synch with changes in the normative, social, and political environments.

Institutional Conversion

Another way that institutions change is through processes of institutional conversion, as institutions designed with one set of goals in mind are redirected to other ends. These processes can be set in motion by a shift in the environment that confronts actors with new problems that they address by using existing institutions in new ways or in the service of new goals. Or – as in the case of labor's incorporation into corporatist oversight of German vocational training cited earlier – it can be a consequence of the incorporation of groups, previously on the margins, who turn existing or inherited institutions to new ends.

An illustration of institutional evolution through conversion can be found in the history of Argentine federalism (Gibson and Falleti in press). Edward Gibson and Tulia Falleti challenge conventional functionalist accounts that see federalism as a negotiated solution to the need of regional governments for common defense against external threats (e.g., Riker 1964). Instead, their account stresses ongoing contests among regional interests that shaped and reshaped federal institutions in unforeseen ways over time. Argentine federalism was originally created as an institutional infrastructure through which one state – Buenos Aires – was able to dominate the interior. However, once it was in place, the weaker provinces worked

political economies in the wake of the American occupation after World War II. See also Herrigel (2000).

[33] See also the discussion in Pierson (2000b).

with and through federal institutions in ways that allowed them ultimately to bring Buenos Aires itself to heel. As Gibson and Falleti tell it, Buenos Aires had been the architect of a system of "hegemonic federalism" as a means for consolidating its domination over the other states, but by the end, the triumph of "plural federalism" had turned the system on its head. "The federalist provinces which had once seen a strong central authority as the agent of their domination by the union's giant, now embraced it as their deliverer from that domination" (Gibson and Falleti in press, p. 19).[34]

Margaret Weir's characterization of poverty and employment programs in the United States provides another illustration of a similar conversion dynamic, in this case the redirection of existing social policy institutions and instruments to new ends. Weir charts the rise of Lyndon Johnson's Great Society program and shows how its unexpected intersection with the rise of the civil rights movement shaped its political fate. While the poverty program as originally conceived was nonracial in character, its inauguration coincided with an upsurge in racial unrest. As Weir writes, "as riots began to shake northern cities, President Johnson looked to the poverty program as a way to funnel resources into the affected black communities" (Weir 1992a, p. 205). As in the case of private pension "layering" cited in the previous section, the conversion process in this case did not reinforce and in fact undermined the reproduction mechanisms on which previous institutions and policies were based. The more the poverty programs became associated with the plight of African Americans, and the more they became dissociated from economic and employment policies that could link them to broader constituencies, the more vulnerable the programs became to the kind of antigovernment ideology that triumphed later, under Reagan.

Other examples could be culled from the literature on the political economy of the advanced industrial countries. There are many cases, for example, in which institutional arrangements developed under wartime conditions survive through their conversion to peacetime purposes; for example, institutions developed for military production during World War II in some cases were converted to active industrial policy after the war. In a similar vein, Andrew Shonfield characterized some of the institutional arrangements linking state and economy in Italy as "left-overs of Fascism which

[34] Another case of evolved changes in federalism is Canada. Canadian federalism was originally designed as a highly centralized system. Over time, however, it was transformed along more decentralized lines because the founders had delegated to the states functions that were trivial at the time but grew in importance later. This example comes out of Pierson (2000b). For the full analysis, see Watts (1987).

[were] turned to positive purpose" under the postwar democracy (Shonfeld 1969, p. 179). Likewise, Steven Vogel's analysis of changes in many aspects of the political-economic infrastructure in Britain under the Thatcher administration contains many examples of existing institutions being redirected toward goals quite remote from those for which the institutions had originally been created (Vogel 1996).

Finally, the literature on labor provides additional examples of institutions being functionally and politically turned on their heads – as, for example, a system of works councils originating in a few highly paternalistic (and anti-union) companies in imperial Germany was transformed over time into one of the strongest systems for union representation and power in plant decision making in Europe (Thelen 1991), or as the system of job classifications that some large American employers introduced in the 1920s as a tool for exercising unilateral managerial control over internal labor markets later became the key institutional support for union influence over personnel policy on the shop floor (Lichtenstein 1988). Anyone interested in the impact of these kinds of institutions on political and political-economic outcomes can scarcely afford to ignore such changes.

V. Conclusions and Agendas for Further Research

All of these examples combine elements of lock-in with new developments that do not push further in the same direction but rather alter the overall trajectory of policy and politics. Taken together, they do not suggest a world in which institutional form necessarily follows function in any straightforward sense.[35] Moreover, many of them suggest that for almost any institution that survives major socioeconomic transformation (industrialization, democratization) or political disjuncture (revolution, conquest), the story of institutional reproduction is likely to be strongly laced with elements of institutional transformation – through layering, conversion, or some other mechanism. For this reason, formal institutions will often *neither* accurately reflect the "congealed tastes" of their creators (Riker 1980) *nor* simply mirror the present prevailing power distribution (Knight 1992).

[35] But nor do they point to an absolute rejection of utilitarian, functional, political, or cultural arguments. For example, regarding functional accounts, all these examples suggest that one cannot infer origins from current functions, but the idea of conversion nonetheless does describe a process in which actors recast institutions or their strategies within institutions in order to adapt these to new purposes, i.e., to serve new functions. I am grateful to Peter Hall for pointing this aspect out to me.

Moreover, as the foregoing examples make clear, one can make sense of the forms and functions these institutions have taken only by viewing them, as Pierson and Skocpol recommend, in the context of a larger temporal framework that includes the sequence of events and processes that shaped their development (Pierson and Skocpol in press).

Where Do We Go from Here?

What does this mean for how we conduct research on institutional change? Pierson and others emphasize increasing returns, and the preceding examples confirm that this is a promising starting point. But they also suggest the need to go further. Increasing returns arguments focus mostly on the winners and on adaptation effects (after an institution has been "selected") that reinforce a particular trajectory. But this emphasis obscures ongoing political contestation over the form and functions of institutions forged at (often distant and receding) critical junctures. Increasing returns cannot tell the whole story because, in politics, losers do not necessarily disappear and their "adaptation" to prevailing institutions can mean something very different from "embracing and reproducing" those institutions, as in the worlds of technologies and markets. Precisely in the political realm, we should expect institutions to be not just the site but also the object of ongoing contestation (see, for example, Alexander 2001).

Thus, while path dependence models based on increasing returns effects clearly have a place in the analytic "toolbox" we bring to the study of institutional development, we must have a healthy appreciation of the limits of this model and a few other tools to go with it.[36] One analytic task, therefore, may be to distinguish more clearly between cases (such as major entitlement programs like Social Security and associated institutions) where each new constituent added to the system increases the number of stakeholders and thus further entrenches it, and other cases (industrial policy institutions might be an example) where expanding the institution's constituency or "reach" might well open up conflict over the goals and purposes, thus very possibly introducing new pressures for change. In addition, even if particular institutions or policies are subject to increasing returns and lock-in, we need to ask whether or not this "crowds out" the creation of parallel institutions (layering) or prevents the conversion of existing ones.[37]

[36] As Pierson himself (2001) has argued.

[37] I am grateful to Gerard Alexander for this formulation. And this is in fact how Myles and Pierson (2001) frame the question in their analysis of pension reform.

Another, complementary, task will be to distinguish the types of empirical phenomena that are associated with different modes of change. Institutional layering, for example, may be associated with situations in which the context shifts and new challenges emerge but the main actors by and large remain the same – or, as Pierson has put it, where the losers in one round of institutional innovation stay around to contest the next. The U.S. Congress (Schickler's case), for example, is not a place where the winners vanquish the losers in any absolute sense and the latter disappear (Schickler 2001, p. 255).[38] Similarly, but in a very different context, institutional innovators in Eastern Europe often confronted a situation in which former communist parties were transformed but by no means eliminated.

By contrast, it may be that conversion processes are more associated with the incorporation of new or previously excluded groups (pursuing different, perhaps, though not necessarily entirely contradictory goals) into a preexisting institutional framework.[39] This possibility reminds us that studies of institutions and institutional development need to be attuned to processes unfolding on the periphery. As Schneiberg and Clemens point out, institutions do not just generate positive feedback, they also "generate grievance (through political exclusion) . . . [and] actors who are aggrieved but not co-opted are an important source of pressure for institutional change" (Schneiberg and Clemens in press, p. 35). Where the institutions that prevail do not generate significant positive feedback effects among the aggrieved, their later empowerment is likely to spell institutional breakdown.[40] However, as the previous vocational training and federalism examples show, it is also important to look at whether actors who are initially on the periphery themselves become invested in the prevailing institutions and if so, in what ways. In such cases, shifts in the balance of power that go their way may result in institutional conversion rather than breakdown.

The general point is that we need to develop a somewhat more differentiated set of conceptual tools to understand processes of institutional evolution and change. The notions of critical junctures and developmental

[38] Schickler thus suggests that his model of layering may apply best to cases such as these where there is considerable continuity in terms of core constituencies but where members have diverse goals and can each influence the organization's rules and structure – for example, universities or professional associations (Schickler 2001, pp. 255, 268).

[39] I thank Gerda Falkner for her insights on this point.

[40] In the case of Weir's analysis (earlier), for example, the failure to link poverty programs to broader economic and employment policies narrowed their base of support and left them more vulnerable to political attack.

pathways around which a good deal of historical-institutional work has been organized capture something important about institutional development over long stretches of time. However, at the highly aggregated level at which they are often invoked, these concepts also sometimes obscure some of the most interesting questions of all, regarding surprising institutional continuities through apparent break points, as well as "subterranean" but highly significant changes in periods of apparent institutional stability.

The preceding discussion and examples take us beyond the prevailing punctuated equilibrium model by suggesting that it may not be so useful to think of institutional development in terms of a sharp dichotomy between periods of institutional innovation and institutional stasis. For these same reasons, it may also be unwise to draw too sharp distinctions in history between "settled" and "unsettled" times (cf. Katznelson, this volume). Instead, to understand how institutions evolve, it may be more fruitful to aim for a more fine-grained analysis that seeks to identify *what aspects* of a specific institutional configuration are (or are not) renegotiable and *under what conditions*. As Ekiert and Hanson point out, this may involve distinguishing continuities and changes at different levels of analysis (Ekiert and Hanson in press-b). As I have emphasized here, it can also build from the analysis of increasing returns effects and feedback mechanisms, to gain insights into the kinds of events and processes that are most likely to disrupt stable institutional reproduction, and, in so doing, open the door for change (Pierson 2001; Thelen 1999). Finally, and especially for the latter, understanding institutional evolution will require us to be on the lookout for modes of change that do not conform to a classic breakdown or replacement model. These include but are not limited to the processes of institutional layering and institutional conversion discussed earlier, and an important analytic task ahead will be to identify the factors or conditions that facilitate different modes of change along the lines of the hypotheses previously suggested.

Summing up

There has been a great deal of talk recently about the search for "mechanisms" in political analysis, defined by Elster as "frequently recurring ways in which things happen" (Elster 1989; see also Scharpf 1997). Paul Pierson has usefully adapted and applied the notion of increasing returns to politics, and this certainly qualifies as a mechanism (in Elster's sense) that can be quite useful in the analysis of institutional reproduction.

We have fewer tools, however, for making sense of institutional evolution and change. The dual ideas of institutional evolution through layering and through conversion may provide a starting point for making sense of the kinds of incremental or bounded changes that appear to constitute a common way that institutions change in politics. Both of these conceptions open the door for a more nuanced analysis of *when and how* particular institutional arrangements can be expected to change and why some aspects may be more amenable to change than others. As such, these conceptualizations provide a way of thinking about institutional reproduction and change that steers a course between deterministic lock-in models, on the one hand, and overly fluid "one damn thing after another" models, on the other hand.

The perspective offered here has several advantages. First, it avoids facile functionalist approaches that read the origins of institutions off the functions they currently perform. The notion of institutional conversion, in fact, provides an analytic point of departure for understanding how institutions created for one set of purposes can come, in time, to be turned to new ends. In this sense, the idea provides a framework for a tractable approach to the issue of "unintended consequences." In doing so, it addresses concerns raised by Pierson and others for devising a way to think about this problem that "turns on more than a retrospective judgment that particular actors involved 'screwed up'" (Pierson 2000c).

Second, notions of institutional evolution through layering or conversion are "genuinely historical" in the sense on which Skocpol rightly insists, looking at social processes as they unfold over time and in relation to other processes. Models of path dependence appropriated from economics tend to focus on a single process in isolation, bringing history in only as bookends – at the critical juncture moment and then again at the end of a reproduction sequence. By contrast, the models of institutional change suggested here overcome the sharp distinction that is commonly drawn between the analysis of institutional creation and institutional reproduction. They do so by specifically drawing attention to the ways in which adaptation to *other* ongoing processes (and not just positive feedbacks generated by the process itself) contributes to institutional and political continuities over very long periods of time.[41]

[41] In a way, the notion of institutional conversion as elaborated here might help to ground the otherwise extremely abstract argument of Orren and Skowronek concerning the way in which "change along one time line affects order along the other" (Orren and Skowronek 1994, p. 321).

Third, such a perspective provides some insights into why it is that societies seem indeed to exhibit some cohesion across organizational domains and over time. There is an apparently deep contradiction between the view of societies that institutional sociologists like Dobbin (1994) represent (where culture and isomorphism encourage convergence across organizational domains) and the highly fluid view of society embraced by other theorists such as Orren and Skowronek (1994) (where institutions created at different historical conjunctures embodying very different political settlements coexist and continually collide and abrade). I think that there is something to both of these views, and perhaps one reason that the kinds of collisions and contradictions that Orren and Skowronek's view predicts are not, in fact, as pervasive and debilitating as one might suppose is that the process of conversion brings organizational forms that were created in the past broadly into synch with currently prevailing power relations and cultural norms.

References

Alexander, Gerard. 2001. "Institutions, Path Dependence, and Democratic Consolidation." *Journal of Theoretical Politics* 13: 249–70.

Aoki, Masahiko. 1988. *Information, Incentives, and Bargaining in the Japanese Economy*. New York: Cambridge University Press.

Aoki, Masahiko and Hugh Patrick, eds. 1994. *The Japanese Main Bank System*. Oxford: Oxford University Press.

Arthur, W. Brian. 1989. "Competing Technologies, Increasing Returns, and Lock-in by Historical Events." *Economic Journal* 99: 116–31.

Campbell, John. 1997. "Mechanisms of Evolutionary Change in Economic Governance: Interaction, Interpretation and Bricolage." Pp. 10–32 in *Evolutionary Economics and Path Dependence*, edited by L. Magnusson and J. Ottosson. Cheltenham, UK: Edward Elgar.

Clemens, Elisabeth. 1993. "Organizational Repertoires and Institutional Change: Women's Groups and the Transformation of U.S. Politics, 1890–1920." *American Journal of Sociology* 98: 755–98.

Collier, Ruth B. and David Collier. 1991. *Shaping the Political Arena*. Princeton, NJ: Princeton University Press.

David, Paul. 1985. "Clio and the Economics of QWERTY." *American Economic Review* 75: 332–7.

Dobbin, Frank. 1994. *Forging Industrial Policy: The United States, Britain and France in the Railway Age*. New York: Cambridge University Press.

Ekiert, Grzegorz and Stephen Hanson, eds. in press-a. *Capitalism and Democracy in Central and Eastern Europe: Assessing the Legacy of Communist Rule*. New York: Cambridge University Press.

in press-b. "Time, Space, and Institutional Change in Central and Eastern Europe." In *Capitalism and Democracy in Central and Eastern Europe: Assessing the Legacy of Communist Rule*, edited by G. Ekiert and S. Hanson. New York: Cambridge University Press.

Elster, Jon. 1989. *The Cement of Society: A Study of Social Order*. New York: Cambridge University Press.

Ertman, Thomas. 1997. *Birth of the Leviathan: Building States and Regimes in Medieval and Early Modern Europe*. New York: Cambridge University Press.

Finegold, David and David Soskice. 1988. "The Failure of Training in Britain: Analysis and Prescription." *Oxford Review of Economic Policy* 4: 21–53.

Fligstein, Neil. 1991. "The Structural Transformation of American Industry." Pp. 311–36 in *The New Institutionalism in Organizational Analysis*, edited by W. W. Powell and P. DiMaggio. Chicago: University of Chicago Press.

Garrett, Geoffrey. 1998. *Partisan Politics in the Global Economy*. New York: Cambridge University Press.

Gerschenkron, Alexander. 1962. *Economic Backwardness in Historical Perspective*. Cambridge, MA: Harvard University Press.

Gibson, Edward L. and Tulia Falleti. in press. "Unity by the Stick: Regional Conflict and the Origins of Argentine Federalism." In *Federalism: Latin America in Comparative Perspective*, edited by E. L. Gibson. Baltimore: Johns Hopkins University Press.

Gillingham, John. 1985. "The 'Deproletarization' of German Society: Vocational Training in the Third Reich." *Journal of Social History* 19: 423–32.

Gould, Andrew. 1999. *Origins of Liberal Dominance*. Ann Arbor: University of Michigan Press.

Grzymala-Busse, Anna. 2002. *Redeeming the Past: The Regeneration of the Communist Successor Parties in East Central Europe after 1989*. New York: Cambridge University Press.

Haydu, Jeffrey. 1998. "Making Use of the Past: Time Periods as Cases to Compare and as Sequences of Problem-Solving." *American Journal of Sociology* 104: 339–71.

Herrigel, Gary. 2000. "American Occupation, Market Order, and Democracy: Reconfiguring the Steel Industry in Japan and Germany after the Second World War." Pp. 340–99 in *Americanization and Its Limits: Reworking U.S. Technology and Management in Post-War Europe and Japan*, edited by J. Zeitlin and G. Herrigel. New York: Oxford University Press.

Huber, Evelyne and John D. Stephens. 2001. *Development and Crisis of the Welfare States: Parties and Policies in Global Markets*. Chicago: University of Chicago Press.

Inglot, Tomasz. in press. "Historical Legacies, Institutions, and the Politics of Social Policy in Hungary and Poland, 1989–1999." In *Capitalism and Democracy in Central and Eastern Europe*, edited by G. Ekiert and S. Hanson. New York: Cambridge University Press.

Kato, J. 1996. "Path Dependency as a Logic of Comparative Studies: Theorization and Application." Paper read at the 92nd annual meeting of the American Political Science Association, at San Francisco, August 29 to September 1.

Katzenstein, Peter J., ed. 1978. *Beyond Power and Plenty*. Madison: University of Wisconsin Press.
Keohane, Robert. 1984. *After Hegemony: Cooperation and Discord in the World Political Economy*. Princeton, NJ: Princeton University Press.
Kitschelt, Herbert, Peter Lange, Gary Marks, and John D. Stephens, eds. 1999a. *Continuity and Change in Contemporary Capitalism*. New York: Cambridge University Press.
Kitschelt, Herbert, Zdenka Mansfeldova, Radoslaw Markowski, and Gabor Toka, eds. 1999b. *Post-Communist Party Systems: Competition, Representation, and Inter-Party Cooperation*. New York: Cambridge University Press.
Knight, Jack. 1992. *Institutions and Social Conflict*. New York: Cambridge University Press.
1999. "Explaining the Rise of Neo-Liberalism: The Mechanisms of Institutional Change." Unpublished manuscript, Washington University in St. Louis.
Korpi, Walter. 1983. *The Democratic Class Struggle*. London: Routledge and Kegan Paul.
Krasner, Stephen D. 1988. "Sovereignty: An Institutional Perspective." *Comparative Political Studies* 21: 66–94.
Kurzer, Paulette. 1993. *Business and Banking*. Ithaca, NY: Cornell University Press.
Lehmbruch, Gerhard. 2001. "The Institutional Embedding of Market Economies: The German 'Model' and Its Impact on Japan." Pp. 39–93 in *The Origins of Nonliberal Capitalism: Germany and Japan*, edited by W. Streeck and K. Yamamura. Ithaca, NY: Cornell University Press.
Levi, Margaret. 1997. "A Model, a Method, and a Map: Rational Choice in Comparative and Historical Analysis." Pp. 19–41 in *Comparative Politics: Rationality, Culture, and Structure*, edited by M. I. Lichbach and A. S. Zuckerman. New York: Cambridge University Press.
Levy, Jonah. 1999. *Tocqueville's Revenge*. Cambridge, MA: Harvard University Press.
Lichtenstein, Nelson. 1988. "The Union's Early Days: Shop Stewards and Seniority Rights." Pp. 65–74 in *Choosing Sides: Unions and the Team Concept*, edited by Mike Parker and Jane Slaughter. Boston: South End Books.
Lipset, Seymour Martin and Stein Rokkan. 1968. "Cleavage Structures, Party Systems, and Voter Alignments." Pp. 1–64 in *Party System and Voter Alignments: Cross-National Perspectives*, edited by S. M. Lipset and S. Rokkan. New York: Free Press.
Locke, Richard M. and Kathleen Thelen. 1995. "Apples and Oranges Revisited: Contextualized Comparisons and the Study of Comparative Labor Politics." *Politics and Society* 23: 337–67.
Mahoney, James. 2000. "Path Dependence in Historical Sociology." *Theory and Society* 29: 507–48.
Manow, Philip. 2001. "Social Protection, Capitalist Production: The Bismarckian Welfare State and the German Political Economy from the 1880s to the 1990s." Habilitätionsschrift, University of Konstanz, Konstanz.
McDonald, Terrance J., ed. 1996. *The Historic Turn in the Human Sciences*. Ann Arbor: University of Michigan Press.

Meyer, J. W. and B. Rowan. 1991. "Institutionalized Organizations: Formal Structure as Myth and Ceremony." Pp. 41–62 in *The New Institutionalism in Organizational Analysis*, edited by W. W. Powell and P. DiMaggio. Chicago: University of Chicago Press.

Moe, Terry. 1990. "The Politics of Structural Choice: Toward a Theory of Public Bureaucracy." Pp. 116–53 in *Organizational Theory*, edited by O. Williamson. Oxford: Oxford University Press.

Moore, Barrington. 1966. *Social Origins of Dictatorship and Democracy*. Boston: Beacon Press.

Myles, John and Paul Pierson. 2001. "The Comparative Political Economy of Pension Reform." Pp. 305–33 in *The New Politics of the Welfare State*, edited by P. Pierson. New York: Oxford University Press.

North, Douglass C. 1990. *Institutions, Institutional Change and Economic Performance*. New York: Cambridge University Press.

Nunberg, Barbara. 1999. *The State After Communism, World Bank Regional and Sectoral Studies*. Washington, DC: The World Bank.

Orren, K., and S. Skowronek. 1994. "Beyond the Iconography of Order: Notes for a 'New' Institutionalism." Pp. 311–30 in *The Dynamics of American Politics*, edited by L. C. Dodd and C. Jillson. Boulder, CO: Westview.

2000. "History and Governance in the Study of American Political Development." Paper presented at the annual meeting of the American Political Science Association, Washington DC.

Ostrom, Elinor. 1999. "Coping with Tragedies of the Commons." *Annual Review of Political Science* 2: 493–537.

Pierson, Paul. 1993. "When Effect Becomes Cause: Policy Feedback and Political Change." *World Politics* 45: 595–628.

1994. *Dismantling the Welfare State? Reagan, Thatcher, and the Politics of Retrenchment*. Cambridge: Cambridge University Press.

2000a. "Increasing Returns, Path Dependence, and the Study of Politics." *American Political Science Review* 94: 251–68.

2000b. "The Limits of Design: Explaining Institutional Origins and Change." *Governance* 13: 475–99.

2000c. "Not Just What, but *When*: Timing and Sequences in Political Processes." *Studies in American Political Development* 14: 72–92.

2001. "Explaining Institutional Origins and Change." Manuscript, Harvard University.

Pierson, Paul and Theda Skocpol. in press. "Historical Institutionalism in Contemporary Political Science." In *Political Science: The State of the Discipline*, edited by H. Milner and I. Katznelson. New York and Washington, DC: W. W. Norton and the American Political Science Association.

Pollack, Mark. 1996. "The New Institutionalism and EC Governance: Promise and Limits of Institutional Analysis." *Governance* 9: 429–58.

Powell, Walter W. 1991. "Expanding the Scope of Institutional Analysis." Pp. 183–203 in *The New Institutionalism in Organizational Analysis*, edited by W. W. Powell and P. DiMaggio. Chicago: University of Chicago Press.

Powell, Walter W. and Daniel L. Jones, eds. in press. *How Institutions Change.* Chicago: University of Chicago Press.
Riker, William H. 1964. *Federalism: Origin, Operation, Significance.* Boston: Little, Brown.
1980. "Implications from the Disequilibrium of Majority Rule for the Study of Institutions." *American Political Science Review* 74: 432–46.
Rothstein, Bo. 1998. *Just Institutions Matter: The Moral and Political Logic of the Universal Welfare State.* New York: Cambridge University Press.
Scharpf, Fritz. 1997. *Games Real Actors Play.* Boulder, CO: Westview.
Schickler, Eric. 1999. "Disjointed Pluralism and Congressional Development: An Overview." Paper read at the 95th annual meeting of the American Political Science Association, Atlanta, September 2–5.
2001. *Disjointed Pluralism: Institutional Innovation and the Development of the U.S. Congress.* Princeton, NJ: Princeton University Press.
Schneiberg, Marc and Elisabeth Clemens. in press. "The Typical Tools for the Job: Research Strategies in Institutional Analysis." In *How Institutions Change*, edited by W. W. Powell and D. L. Jones. Chicago: Chicago University Press.
Scott, W. R. 1995. *Institutions and Organizations.* Thousand Oaks, CA: Sage.
Scott, W. Richard and John W. Meyer. 1994. "The Rise of Training Programs in Firms and Agencies." Pp. 228–54 in *Institutional Environments and Organizations: Structural Complexity and Individualism*, edited by W. R. Scott and J. W. Meyer. Thousand Oaks, CA: Sage.
Sewell, William H. 1996. "Three Temporalities: Toward an Eventful Sociology." Pp. 245–80 in *The Historic Turn in the Human Sciences*, edited by T. J. McDonald. Ann Arbor: University of Michigan Press.
Shefter, Martin. 1977. "Party and Patronage: Germany, England, and Italy." *Politics and Society* 7: 403–51.
Shonfeld, Andrew. 1969. *Modern Capitalism: The Changing Balance of Public and Private Power.* London: Oxford University Press.
Skocpol, Theda. 1992. *Protecting Soldiers and Mothers: The Political Origins of Social Policy in the United States.* Cambridge, MA: Belknap.
Spruyt, Hendrik. 1994. *The Sovereign State and Its Competitors.* Princeton, NJ: Princeton University Press.
Stark, David and László Bruszt. 1998. *Postsocialist Pathways: Transforming Politics and Property in East Central Europe.* New York: Cambridge University Press.
Stephens, John D., Evelyne Huber, and Leonard Ray. 1999. "Welfare State in Hard Times." Pp. 164–93 in *Continuity and Change in Contemporary Capitalism*, edited by H. Kitschelt, P. Lange, G. Marks, and J. D. Stephens. New York: Cambridge University Press.
Stinchcombe, Arthur. 1968. *Constructing Social Theories.* New York: Harcourt, Brace and World.
Thelen, Kathleen. 1991. *Union of Parts: Labor Politics in Postwar Germany.* Ithaca, NY: Cornell University Press.
1999. "Historical Institutionalism in Comparative Politics." *The Annual Review of Political Science* 2: 369–404.

2002. *How Institutions Evolve: The Political Economy of Skills in Comparative-Historical Perspective*. Book manuscript, Northwestern University. Evanston.

Thelen, Kathleen and Sven Steinmo. 1992. "Historical Institutionalism in Comparative Politics." Pp. 1–32 in *Structuring Politics: Historical Institutionalism in Comparative Analysis*, edited by S. Steinmo, K. Thelen, and F. Longstreth. New York: Cambridge University Press.

Vogel, Steven K. 1996. *Freer Markets, More Rules: Regulatory Reform in Advanced Industrial Countries*. Ithaca, NY: Cornell University Press.

Watts, Ronald L. 1987. "The American Constitution in Comparative Perspective: A Comparison of Canada and the United States." *Journal of American History* 74: 769–91.

Weingast, Barry R. and William J. Marshall. 1988. "The Industrial Organization of Congress; or, Why Legislatures, Like Firms, Are Not Organized as Markets." *Journal of Political Economy* 96: 132–63.

Weir, Margaret. 1992a. "Ideas and the Politics of Bounded Innovation." Pp. 188–216 in *Structuring Politics: Historical Institutionalism in Comparative Analysis*, edited by S. Steinmo, K. Thelen, and F. Longstreth. New York: Cambridge University Press.

1992b. *Politics and Jobs: The Boundaries of Employment Policy in the United States*. Princeton, NJ: University Press.

Zeitlin, Jonathan. 2000. "Introduction: Americanization and Its Limits: Reworking U.S. Technology and Management in Post-War Europe and Japan." Pp. 1–50 in *Americanization and Its Limits: Reworking U.S. Technology and Management in Post-War Europe and Japan*, edited by J. Zeitlin and G. Herrigel. New York: Oxford University Press.

7

Uses of Network Tools in Comparative Historical Research

Roger V. Gould

On first principles, one would not expect a strong elective affinity between network analysis and historical sociology. Social scientists who are drawn to structural analysis typically have a taste for abstraction and formalization and see themselves as engaged in a scientific enterprise. Those drawn to history, even if they are not professional historians, are more attracted to particularity and substance, and are (nowadays) more likely to see their projects as humanistic rather than scientific.[1] In such circumstances, one ought to expect little research applying algebraic or graph-theoretic network methods to historical data.

Quantitatively speaking, this expectation seems to be correct: small as the network analysis community is, the historical network community is smaller still – whether expressed as a proportion of social science history or as a proportion of the network analysis community. Yet I would suggest, at the risk of being accused of self-promotion, that the contribution of network-oriented historical research is more substantial than its quantity alone might suggest. And I would claim, further, that the disproportionate interest of historical network research is more than a matter of novelty or surprise (as it might be, for instance, when the American Sociological Association conference session featuring a jazz ensemble drains people out of the paper sessions nearby). I would suggest, instead, that the enterprise of employing structural analysis in historical research is a

[1] It would be easy enough to think that this generalization fails to apply to the cliometricians or to the quantitative side of *Annales* history. In fact, I would suggest that it applies all the more strongly to these groups: the quantifiers within history have adopted a principled opposition to abstraction and theoretical formalism. They tabulate calories, bushels of wheat, marriages, births, and deaths – not relations of production, social organization, or group identities.

particularly fruitful way to generate new insights and questions and to reframe or resolve old ones. The aim of this essay is to offer some examples of the sort of contribution network analysis can make, but at the same time to suggest that the overenthusiastic application of network methods in some circumstances poses risks that are just as distinctive as the potential advantages. Those risks appear to be greatest when the metatheoretical rationale for network analysis, according to which the world is made up of relations first and individual entities second, is used to justify exotic applications of the method in the absence of strong substantive theory for such applications.

Although it may not appear to be the current fashion, such assertions are in my view better defended with concrete examples than through a priori, programmatic argument. I shall begin with a brief overview of the network tradition, sketch a typology of network analysis methods, and then move to the mercifully slender portfolio of network-analytic historical research. In what follows, I shall for the most part define the category of historical network analysis narrowly, giving only brief consideration to studies that invoke the network concept without offering a systematic examination of relational data. At the same time, I shall include in my discussion research that applies formal network methods to data that do not reflect concrete social relations but rather relations among concepts or discursive elements (for instance, Ansell 1997; Mohr 1994; Mohr and Duquenne 1997). The reason for my relative lack of attention to informal network analyses is simple: investigations that employ network imagery metaphorically but not analytically – say, by referring to an emerging intellectual community as a "network" without analyzing it as one – have had a harder time yielding insights that distinguish them from nonnetwork studies. They may add to the prestige of network research by providing advertising (although I find it more probable that casual use of this kind will have the contrary effect), but they will not add to knowledge in the same way. My reason for including networklike analyses of nonnetwork data will, I trust, become clear presently.

The Social Network Tradition

Although network methods first developed as an approach to analyzing data on social relations, the network tradition has evolved into the relational analysis of data. What began in the 1950s and 1960s as a set of tools for describing or summarizing data on concrete social ties evolved into an approach – promoters like Leinhardt (1977), Berkowitz (1982), and Wellman and Berkowitz (1988) were apt to call it a "paradigm" – that licensed the application of network methods to data that common sense would not view as having anything to do with social networks.

To be more precise, early work in the network tradition, most notably that of Moreno (1953) and his followers, focused unambiguously on social relationships: researchers in sociometry, whether it was directed at schools, fishing villages, gangs, or air force flight crews, generated "sociograms" depicting informants' reports (or independent observations) of friendship, esteem, admiration, animosity, acquaintance, or play (see also Coleman 1961; Hunter 1957; Newcomb 1961; Roethlisberger and Dickson 1939). Early network *analysis*, while more formal and systematic than sociometry, nonetheless followed it faithfully with respect to data sources: while moving from hand-drawn visual portrayals, which were the hallmark of sociometry, to quantitative or algebraic techniques for uncovering patterns in networks, the first efforts at systematic network analysis employed exactly the same sorts of data. This statement holds regardless of whether one looks at connectivity-oriented analyses, which concentrated on identifying cliques, locating central actors, following chains of social ties to trace information flows or discover who was close to whom, and so forth (Granovetter 1974; Kemeny et al. 1962; Laumann and Pappi 1976; Milgram 1967) or at "positional" analyses, whose focus was the identification of structurally similar actors as a means of observing "roles" (Lorrain and White 1971; White 1963; White, Boorman, and Breiger 1976).

Almost as soon as there was a metatheory supporting the network approach, its devotees began to explore its extension to data that, while not recognizably relational, could nevertheless be transformed into a relational data structure. The idea was that if relations among nodes were ontologically prior to, or at least more important than, the nodes they tied together, then naturally all sorts of phenomena that were not self-evidently networklike might be better analyzed as if they were. So joint occurrence in a newspaper article could be treated as a "tie" (Burt 1980), as could joint membership in a club, copresence at an event (Breiger 1974), or even simultaneous possession of an attribute, like age or race. If individuals or their traits could be reframed, through a theoretical Gestalt switch, as the products rather than the agents of interlocking relations, then it was reasonable to treat all sorts of phenomena as if they were networks, regardless of what intuition or mainstream social science might say to the contrary.

As with many metatheoretical positions, the network-structuralist position began early on to divide into two varieties: one weak (i.e., moderate), the other strong (i.e., radical). The weak version consisted of claiming that network representations could reveal interesting patterns not easily recovered by individualist or variable-based approaches (see, e.g., Marsden 1990). The latter approaches, and their attendant methods, were seen as useful for some purposes but not so useful for others. The strong version, sometimes described as "network imperialism," maintained that network methods were the *correct* way to talk about social phenomena. Researchers who believed that there was such a thing as a person independent of his or her structural position were at times portrayed as naive and misguided (Berkowitz 1982; Wellman and Berkowitz 1988). Defenders of the strong position suggested that network analysis should replace, rather than complement, existing methods and their attendant theoretical frameworks.

My aim is not to pass judgment – not yet, anyway – on the reframing of network analysis as a perspective or paradigm rather than as a collection of techniques (not that I don't have an opinion on the matter). It is simply to adumbrate a general point I will make later on, namely, that comparative historical researchers need to be sensitive to the theoretical apparatus to which they are implicitly committing themselves if and when they decide to employ network tools. Naturally, accepting the proposition that all social phenomena are network phenomena licenses the application of structural analysis to a much broader range of substantive problems and data forms. I would suggest that structural thinking does indeed have a great deal to offer in the form of new ways to theorize about both macro- and microprocesses of interest to comparative historical scholars.

At the same time, the broader the range of application, the more conscious one needs to be of what is being assumed. Accordingly, I begin my overview with the more circumscribed body of historical research focusing specifically on concrete social networks. Before describing these empirical studies, though, it may be worthwhile to provide a brief guide to the flora and fauna of network methodology.

Types of Network Analysis

Connectivity Methods

A frequently invoked distinction in the structural tradition – one to which I have already alluded – classifies most network techniques either as "connectivity" methods or as "positional" methods. Connectivity-oriented methods correspond to the commonsense notion of social networks, in which people employ "connections" in the pursuit of various aims. Much as real-world actors do when they pursue contacts with "friends of friends," analysts interested in connectivity trace the paths in a graph (a synonym for network) that link nodes both directly and indirectly, looking, for example, for signs that some actors are centrally or strategically located while others are marginal or dependent. Above the level of individuals, connectivity methods identify cohesive subgroups or divisions among subgroups – for instance, by drawing boundaries around sets of nodes that are densely interconnected but sparsely connected to nodes outside the boundary. A limiting case is a "clique," or a set of actors in which every node is tied to every other; but more expansive definitions are possible; for instance, a k-clique is a set of nodes in which every node is tied to at least k other nodes inside the set. K-cliques can be identified by starting with a small number of nodes that collectively satisfy the criterion and then adding nodes that can join the set without violating the criterion – that is, nodes whose addition does not reduce to less than k the number of nodes in the set to which every node in the set is tied. Inasmuch as completely connected cliques are empirically rare, and typically draw boundaries too narrowly, the more expansive definitions do a better job of identifying groups in real-world contexts. As an illustration, Figure 7.1 depicts two slightly different graphs. In the first, there is a fully connected clique involving five nodes; in the second, two ties are removed, leaving a 3-clique of size 5 (i.e., a subset in which every node is tied to at least three of the four other nodes in the set), but no cliques of size 4 or greater. (Note, however, that the 3-clique itself contains four cliques of size 3 – illustrating the tendency for the strong clique criterion to identify smaller groups.)

This is probably the place to insert a brief word about the sometimes intricate formalism in network analysis. Doubtless the people who are drawn to structural analysis are attracted to logical and mathematical reasoning, but that is not the main reason network techniques are as formal as they are. Identifying cohesive subsets in a graph in the way just described might sound simple enough in principle, but in fact, for all but the simplest network structures, it is a fairly technical matter. The reason is that the rule determining whether a given boundary defines a cohesive subset is a recursive function. One must first posit a boundary before deciding whether a given node belongs inside it or outside it. Yet it is the boundary that one is

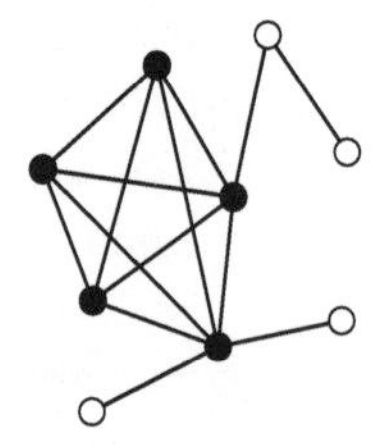

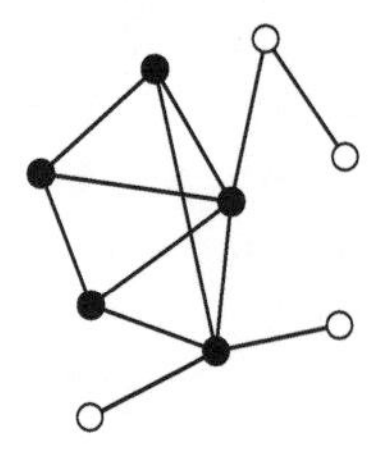

Figure 7.1 Cohesive subgroups: top: clique of size 5 (black nodes); bottom: 3-clique of size 5 (black nodes).

after. Algorithms for identifying cohesive subgroups therefore compare *all possible partitions* of a graph with respect to the cohesion criterion.[2] Similarly, tracing the shortest path between every pair of nodes, a crucial step in measuring some versions of centrality, depends on a graph-theoretic procedure that if done by hand would require hours of work even for graphs with a handful of nodes. If the task is formalized, computers can do it.

Positional Methods

A concise way to summarize connectivity methods, then, is to say that their point of departure is the degree to which any two nodes are *close to* or *far from* each other in the sense of the number of steps through other nodes. Positional methods, in contrast, look for *similarity*, or "structural equivalence," in the patterns of ties nodes have with other nodes. Analyses of position are also sometimes called "algebraic" because they permit the investigation of interlocks in multiple relations: having identified a set of positions involving workplace and neighbor relations, or involving various

[2] Not surprisingly, this can be a computationally intensive procedure, especially for large graphs.

types of kin relations, one can ask whether ego's neighbor's boss is typically also ego's boss's neighbor, or whether ego's father's sister's son is also likely to be ego's husband. In the most general sense, a "position" in this context is a stylized profile of ties (both direct ties, like "neighbor," or compound ties, like "neighbor's boss's husband") that more than one actor might have. Simple, commonsense examples of positions include "leader," "follower," "broker," and "isolate." These terms refer to culturally recognizable roles that have a natural structural interpretation because they are defined with reference to other roles. (Compare roles that do not explicitly presuppose ties to other roles, like "artist," "idler," or "zealot.")

Positional methods, however, are often agnostic about what kinds of positions they will find; that is, they generate assignments of nodes to positions by inductively searching for sets of nodes whose profiles of ties resemble each other, rather than by testing for the existence of positions hypothesized in advance. In the version of positional analysis called "blockmodelling," this usually means partitioning a graph with many nodes into a manageable number of classes (blocks) of structurally similar nodes. A block is a group of actors in a network who are relatively similar in their patterns of ties to others; a "blockmodel" therefore reduces the complexity of the whole network by representing each block as a single node. Ties among blocks (or from a block to itself) then reflect patterns that are typical of each block's members, where "typical" means that some reasonably large percentage of block members have a tie to some percentage of some other block (or to others within the same block).

The result is a simplified graph that nonetheless captures something about the structure of the original network. For instance, if the members of block A are typically tied to members of B, then block A is depicted as having a tie to block B. If members of block A are typically tied to other members of A, then block A is depicted as having a tie to itself. In a marriage system, for example, a reflexive tie of this sort, coupled with absence of ties across blocks, would reflect endogamy. An exogamous system, say of the Aranda type, would be expressed with four blocks, with men in A marrying women in B, men in B marrying women in C, C men marrying D women, and D men marrying A women.

Figure 7.2 gives stylized examples of a variety of such systems. The first involves pure endogamy, in which lineages A and B marry (or, to broaden the range of application, groups A and B exchange goods) internally. In the second system, A and B mutually exchange marriage partners. In the third, women and men (or, as in Kula exchange, complementary goods such as

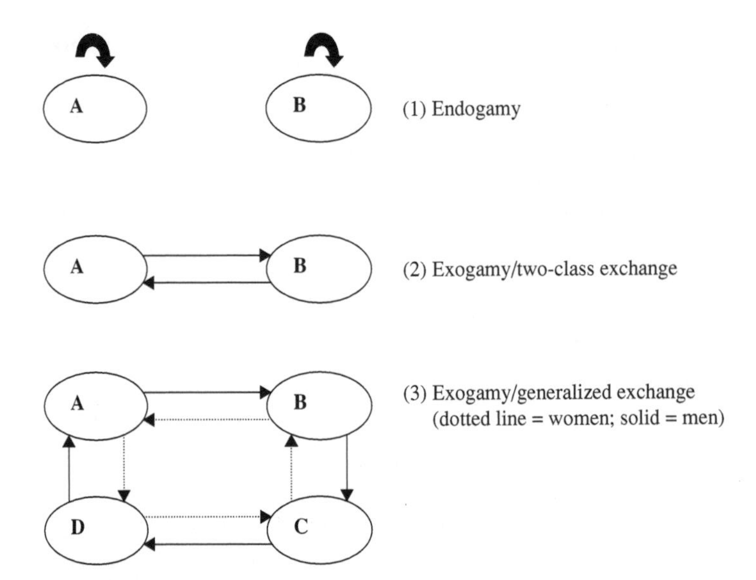

Figure 7.2 Block structures characterizing marriage/exchange systems.

cowry-shell necklaces and spondylus armbands) flow in opposite directions, inducing a system of generalized exchange. Blockmodel analysis permits the representation of complex networks in stylized forms like these. Naturally, empirically observed social networks are always messier than the images in Figure 7.2 indicate, but that is precisely the reason models can be useful. Blockmodel images express the central tendencies in such networks and are viewed by network analysts as the underlying structure of which the observed network is an imperfect realization.[3]

Once again, therefore, analysis of equivalence in empirical networks can be a very technical issue. To begin with, one rarely finds that two real-world actors are identical in their patterns of ties to third parties. Consequently, as with cohesive subgroups, the definition of equivalence needs to be loosened in practice if one wishes to identify anything besides idiosyncratic positions. More significantly, positional methods also depend (usually) on another recursive function: structural similarity between two actors implies that they have similar patterns of ties to *similar* others, not to the *same* others.

[3] The reason network analysts are frequently called structuralists ought to be obvious. The inspiration for this way of thinking was Levi-Strauss's ([1949] 1969) classic, *Les structures élémentaires de la parenté*, and in particular a formal appendix to that work by the mathematician André Weil. See White (1963) and Bearman (1997).

One schoolteacher might be classified as structurally similar to another because they teach the same set of pupils or simply because they both teach classrooms full of pupils. In the latter instance, equivalence among teachers is derived from the recognition of the two sets of pupils as equivalent – but pupils from different classes are, in turn, equivalent because they are tied to teachers who are classified as equivalent.

Both families of network techniques share the following property: they are, as I have indicated, designed to *describe network structure in simplified form*. Graph-theoretic or connectivity methods do this by characterizing graphs in terms of a small number of quantitative dimensions: "closeness," "betweenness," and other sorts of centrality at the level of nodes, or centralization, connectedness, and "vulnerability," for instance, at the level of whole networks. Positional methods offer simplified descriptions by mapping many actors into a small number of structurally defined roles and sometimes by depicting the relations among these roles in equation form. Earlier, for instance, I suggested that positional analysis might reveal that, on average, the compound relation "boss's neighbor" = "neighbor's boss" – which would constitute a structuralist rendering of class-based residential segregation. In organizations, a blockmodel analysis could reveal that "superior's subordinate" = "rival" (note that "superior's subordinate" also equals "self," but there are typically many others also occupying this role). In the Whiskey Rebellion case I cite later, in which political notables appear to have competed for the loyalty of their clients, a full-fledged positional analysis might show, if the proper data were available, that "client's patron" = "rival."

Measuring Network Effects

The forms of network analysis I have described are essentially data-reduction techniques: they summarize network data very much in the way statistics like the mean, median, variance, and covariance give concise summaries of distributions and relationships in variable-based data. But I do not wish to give the impression that these techniques are therefore purely empirical, in the sense of bringing no presuppositions to the encounter with data.[4] It is essential to note that applying any of these techniques – even inductive versions of blockmodel analysis, in which positions are "discovered"

[4] Network types like to point out that statistical methods applied to variable-based data are also theory-laden. The so-called general linear model assumes that the world is composed of individuals, and that these individuals can be adequately summarized as points in a k-dimensional space, where k is the number of variables and coordinates on each dimension

in rather than imposed upon the data – entails an impressive collection of substantive assumptions. Graph-theoretic analyses, for example, assume that *something* – influence, knowledge, opinion, wealth, affection – flows through social ties. Otherwise, concepts like "path distance," "brokerage," and" "network vulnerability" (the dependence of a graph's connectedness on a few nodes whose elimination would break it into pieces) would not mean much. Positional analyses depend on the assumption that there is something called a "role" that does not exist unless multiple nodes can be observed to fill it. (It had better not, because positional analysis requires that multiple nodes be collapsed into roles on the basis of equivalence. Unique network positions are an embarrassment to blockmodel analysis.) It is no accident that the phrase "network analysis" is often used interchangeably with "network theory."

As a result, the data-reduction family of network methods, with its two branches, can in turn be juxtaposed with another, equally important family, yielding another basic distinction – that between *simplified descriptions* of social network structure and analyses that model the impact of social networks, *as observed*, on other social behavior. The most obvious examples of network analysis of the latter kind involve studies of social diffusion: some social behavior, say adoption of a technical or cultural innovation, is observed in a population, and the analyst asks whether social ties act as a conduit for its diffusion. In comparative historical research, the principal area in which this approach has appeared is the study of large-scale protest.

In network analysis of this kind, it is not necessary to offer an interpretation or a description of the structure of relational data. Instead, data on social ties are employed as direct inputs to an empirical analysis that could in principle be conducted without any network data whatever. The aim of such analyses, most of the time, is to test for the impact of social ties without invoking any particular ideas about what aspects of network structure are important. To put it crudely, network data enter the scene on an equal footing with data in variable form: any factor can be found to have a measurable impact on some outcome of interest, or it may be found to have no measurable impact. Data-reduction versions of network

reflecting values on the relevant variable. It would be going too far to say that devotees of variable-based methods believe this as an account of the world (they believe, rather, that it is a useful way to talk about the world); but it is important to remember that the many formal assumptions made in inferential statistics, like the independent observation assumption, are substantively meaningful.

analysis are thus considerably more theory-laden than are analyses of the impact of networks on other phenomena.[5] As a general rule, the more transformations applied to the network data in the course of the analysis, the heavier the influence, acknowledged or not, of substantive theoretical assumptions.

As I shall show in the remainder of this essay, each of these styles of network analysis has been employed more than once in comparative and historical research. The benefits and costs of doing so vary with the method used, the context studied, and the questions asked. These benefits and costs will, I hope, become apparent in the following pages. But it is a good idea to remain mindful of the theory-heavy nature of many network methods. When the background theory is plausible in a given case, the results can be powerful. In particular, the abstraction of network methods can help to reveal commonalities across diverse contexts – an enormously valuable feature for comparativists interested in uncovering regularities. In addition, the practice of deriving substantive implications from formal patterns offers a way out – admittedly, a way lighted by a set of theoretical assumptions – of a perennial problem historical researchers face, namely, that the subjective experience of actors from the past is very difficult to recover.[6] But when the theory is not plausible, or plausible but not articulated, the results can be in the worst case nothing so much as puzzling – or, in the best case, no better than what might be had with a more pedestrian approach.

Network Analysis in Comparative Historical Research

Perhaps the most attractive and frequently visited area for historical network analysis is the study of various kinds of collective action. On the level of elite collective action, such studies concentrate principally on patron–client relations. When the topic is popular mobilization or collective conflict more generally, other types of social ties enter the picture. I will consider the more narrowly circumscribed case of elite politics and revisit the somewhat

[5] Naturally, one can combine these strategies, as in Barkey and Van Rossem's analysis, cited later, of rural contention in the Ottoman Empire. Imagine, for instance, that a blockmodel analysis has identified distinct positions in some group. Membership in the empirically defined subgroups can then be correlated with some other variable – say, opposition to authority. In fact, a network analyst would say that this is precisely what Sulloway (1996) did in documenting an association between birth order and rebellion.

[6] I am indebted to James Mahoney for suggesting that I emphasize this point.

trickier case of network studies of popular mobilization at the end of the essay.

Patron–Client Relations and Elite Political Contention

Network analysts did not, of course, invent research on patron–client relations. It had already been a stock topic for ancient, medieval, and early modern historians of Europe since at least the 1950s (Badian 1958; Brucker 1977; Kettering 1986; Namier 1957; Zagorin 1970) and for students of non-Western political arrangements for even longer. But these earlier studies were necessarily limited to the identification of fairly crude patterns at the macroscopic level – such as factionalization, explicit and widely recognized alliances, and so forth – and to piecemeal tracing of individual careers and the formation or dissolution of well-defined cliques at the microscopic level. Statements about patterns more subtle than Catholic–Protestant, crown–cross, or Guelph–Ghibelline sorts of divisions depended heavily on hunch, ingenuity, luck, and, usually, agonized debate. For every scholar who finds that Cardinal Mazarin had a loyal and cohesive following, there is another whose reading of the documents suggests dissension and mistrust.

Given a reliable and fairly complete data source (and I am the first to admit that that is hardly an easy requirement to meet), network methods offer a way out of the pendulum-swing revisionism so characteristic of historiography. In this respect, network analysis is just like any other set of systematic methods. Not that any methodology, formal or informal, can ever magically put an end to scholarly squabbles; I am suggesting only that, given a reasonably clear research question, the availability of a conventional method makes it possible for opponents in a debate to agree ex ante on which position will be strengthened and which weakened by a given empirical result. If they respond to the evidence in good faith (rather than rephrasing their positions ex post, as is more common), they might actually resolve the debate and move on to a new issue. Only in this way is cumulation feasible.

Consider Peter Bearman's (1993) study of the Norfolk gentry in the period leading up to the English Civil War. Historians of the period have never doubted that noble and gentry control over the appointment of rectors, vicars, seats in the Commons, and justices of the peace was a key ingredient in the building of political clienteles by county notables, and that these clienteles were important collective actors in struggles between the crown and Parliament. But they differ sharply over the best way to explain the shift in the relationship between notables and the monarchy that eventually led to the execution of the English king and to Cromwell's protectorate. (Let us leave aside the perennial "blundering king" line of explanation still favored by many [see Morrill 1984]; inasmuch as the presence or absence of a blundering king is most likely uncorrelated with broader social changes, its causal influence can be disregarded analytically without affecting the sociological issues.) As is often the case, one major axis of disagreement pits materialists, for whom the Protestant challenge to the Stuart dynasty was an expression of a new class interest, against idealists, for whom the Civil War was very much about confessional conflict.

Bearman follows in the path blazed by Stone's (1965) interpretation of the Civil War as the outcome of the English nobility's century-long political decline – a decline having more to do with processes internal to the aristocracy than with the rise of any other group or actor. But rather than accept Stone's portrait of a social category's self-destruction, Bearman is interested in showing that the very existence of broad social categories like "nobility," "gentry," or "urban bourgeoisie" rested on an underlying structure of social relationships. He suggests that individuals and families recognize and act on their membership in such categories with reference to concrete social relationships. Only by noticing their own comparability with others in similar (or distinct) network positions can social actors decide that they plausibly belong to some collectivity. Social categories – classes, religious groups, lineages, and so forth – are not so much the basis on which social life is organized as they are the language people use to describe that organization. And the organization in question is that of social relationships: in this instance, relations of kinship and patronage.

Examining data on (1) genealogical ties among elite families, or at any rate claims of such ties, and (2) patronage ties among elite actors expressed as joint sponsorship of local clergy, Bearman tells the following story about the Norfolk gentry. Until the late sixteenth century, status orderings and mobilization during conflict among Norfolk families could be reckoned straightforwardly through kinship. Families achieved status recognition and built alliances by successfully claiming descent from or intermarriage with illustrious lineages, whose illustriousness could in turn be demonstrated, recursively, by the same means. (One of the elegant achievements of formal network analysis is that patterns in social ties can be used to infer such status orderings *even if the analyst is completely uninformed at the outset about who has status and who does not*. If you give me a list of 100 people who know each other, and tell me who on the list claims to be friends with whom, I can give you back a status ranking that will predict very precisely the prestige ordering native informants will provide if asked. Asymmetric ties will point consistently toward those of high status and away from those of low status. Now this trick might not be of great use when informants are available for direct questioning about who has status. But in historical contexts, they are not.) Locally produced kin relations provided the rhetoric within which ambitious elites acquired and reproduced their status positions. Locally defined allegiances were the stable by-product.

By 1600, however, kinship relations no longer served as the currency in which social rank was traded. Bearman's evidence for this assertion comes directly from a demonstration, using blockmodel analysis (Bearman 1993, p. 80), that the well-behaved structure arraying gentry into a stable status order in the mid-1500s can no longer be found in the genealogical data for the early 1600s.[7] Kin relations for the early period obeyed a straightforward status ordering placing blocks that turn out to be "major gentry" at the top; but for the period 1615–40, this pattern dissolves. It reappears only when patronage relations – specifically, appointments of rectors and advowsons – are examined in place of kin ties.

The interpretation Bearman proposes reflects a theory of group formation that is distinctively the product of structural thinking. In Bearman's account, monarchical state-building efforts undermined local autonomy and persuaded ambitious gentry that their future lay in building clienteles locally and attaching themselves to national elites. They employed their control over religious benefices to this end, attaching themselves to patrons by commending their rectors upward – only to discover that the resulting clientage system they had themselves built organized them (as a second blockmodel analysis shows) into new, rival collectivities that, given their structure, could plausibly be termed only "Catholic" and "Protestant." Bearman's boldest claim is that the abstract confessional rhetoric for the wrenching civil war that followed was utterly a by-product of the shift from kinship to patronage as the organizing principle for status competition.

[7] As I noted earlier, a blockmodel infers the existence of groups directly from the relational data. More traditional historiography also posits the existence of groups, but does so using an a priori scheme based on size of landholding, religious affiliation, or occupation. Naturally, inspection of a blockmodel can reveal – as Bearman's analysis does for some time periods – that occupants of the same block are also similar on these dimensions. But such correspondences are contingent, not necessary. When block memberships do not correspond to classes or confessional groups, the network data are telling us that social relations are not structured by these venerable dimensions of social difference.

I have necessarily offered a schematic account of both the empirical details and the argument in Bearman's book. It is in fact a difficult and at times forbidding monograph, and for that reason few sociologists and even fewer historians have engaged with it, let alone attempted to replicate or refute its conclusions. But for the present purpose, the details of the empirical findings and the interpretation Bearman offers are less relevant than the methodological innovation employed and the theoretical insight that goes with it. To be sure, a structurally oriented and insightful historian could in principle have woven a similar account and illustrated it with anecdotal evidence. But without a method for wrestling literally thousands of social relationships, spread over a whole century, into a pliable form, it is unlikely. It is also unlikely that a researcher not already accustomed to thinking in terms of collections of structurally equivalent actors would have arrived at such an argument in the first place.

More importantly, perhaps, the systematic mapping of a vastly complex set of network ties into an interpretable and reproducible relational model is what makes it reasonable to claim that the patterns in the evidence occur independently of the interpretation. Even if it is the case that hunches and working hypotheses worm their way into coding decisions, density cutoff points, and choices about when partitioning into blocks should stop, that still leaves far fewer wormholes as compared with the impressionistic use of documentary evidence, justified by appeals to expertise and good judgment, of which professional historians are so fond. Future researchers, attempting to replicate Bearman's analysis using related methods, might well find patterns that diverge from his findings. But they will be able to state in precise terms just where the divergences arise and what they consist of. Having done so, they can then work out what critical tests might decide the case in favor of one position or the other.

Another instance of the systematic analysis of patronage networks can be found in my own research on elite mobilization in the Whiskey Rebellion of 1794, which briefly threatened federalism in the United States. In that study (Gould 1996), I set up and addressed a puzzle having to do with the determinants of elite participation in a rural uprising against the first federal excise tax. Western Pennsylvania farmers opposed a tax on whiskey production on the ground that most of their output was consumed locally (by distillers themselves) rather than sold. Not surprisingly, this argument applied primarily to small landholders whose production did not yield a marketable surplus; elite producers, who did market much of their output, were more apt to couch their opposition in terms of democratic principles, decrying Alexander Hamilton's federalist project as a return to the tyranny of the British. The historiography of this challenge to U.S. state-building has, in parallel fashion to the materialist–idealist split over the English Civil War, divided on whether it was genuinely a struggle over principles of self-government or a more instrumental bid for political influence on the part of an ambitious subset of local elites.

Because politically ambitious rabble-rousers are just as likely as true believers to report deep commitments to lofty principles, it is not easy to settle this issue by examining the public pronouncements of rebel leaders or their opponents. Nor, my analysis showed, is it possible to distinguish rebel elites in a reliable way from supporters of the federal government on the basis of such attributes as wealth, participation in whiskey production, or even active participation in the federal apparatus. (The three federal officeholders in southwestern Pennsylvania of course opposed the tax revolt, but so did several dozen elite members who were *not* federal officeholders. Statistically speaking, therefore, federal officeholding was not a predictor of rebel participation.)

Systematic analysis of the network structure of client relations provided the answer. Records of surety bonds, through which political elites vouched for the performance of new appointees or elected officials, furnished the raw material for a structural analysis of the southwestern Pennsylvania political elite. Define an actor's clientele recursively as those officeholders for whom he has posted a surety together with the clienteles of the latter. (In other words, my clientele consists of my protégés together with their protégés, my protégés' protégés' protégés, and so on to the end of the tree; most chains were three steps or fewer in length.) By this definition, it is possible to have multiple patrons because officeholders could have had surety posted for them by different people at different times. Clienteles could therefore overlap. My analysis showed that two aspects of position in this network predicted elite participation in the uprising. They were (1) nonmembership in a federal officer's clientele and (2) possession of a clientele that overlapped with a federal officer's clientele.

It is not hard to see why these characteristics of network position should be related to rebel participation. In the face of an expanding federal apparatus, of which federal taxation was a first crucial element, local elites could look forward to three possible outcomes. First, they might benefit substantially through preexisting connections to newly powerful others; second, they might experience only relative deprivation, as their own positions remained stable while others saw theirs enhanced; third, their own positions might decline absolutely as their clients abandoned them. Federal officers and their clients could look forward to the first of these. Elites without ties to federal officeholders could expect the second, but elites lacking federal patrons whose clients did have federal patrons could expect the third. Those of their clients who saw enhanced opportunities through connections with federalism would naturally be tempted to transfer their loyalties in that direction, eroding the base of support on which elites lacking federal patronage could draw. Elites without ties to federal officeholders, but whose protégés possessed such ties, therefore faced the greatest threat to their influence – and it was just these elites who led the rebellion against the whiskey excise.

As with the Norfolk elite, it would be easy enough to read this account as a sort of exposé of cynical leaders exploiting the rhetoric of radical democracy for careerist ends. This is not the only reading, however. Another interpretation of the structural account is that, just as Catholic versus Protestant became a compelling dimension of elite conflict when the structure of patronage ties made this identification possible, Jeffersonian democracy became a normatively persuasive political cause for elite actors who directly perceived the impact of state centralization on their standing. No cynicism is necessary for the mechanism to operate: from the viewpoint of their threatened network position, political elites without ties to federal patrons may have justifiably perceived their cause as a defense of a genuine public good (whose stewards, as locally based political notables, they happened to be).

The parallel with Bearman's study should be transparent. In each case, something like the argument advanced was already present in inchoate form in the extant literature. But in each case as well, not only was systematic evidence that could reinforce the argument lacking, it was not even clear in the absence of network techniques how such evidence could be marshaled. Moreover, the particular mechanisms invoked – religious identifications emerging from secular uses of church patronage and anticentralist sentiment emerging from the differential impact of federalism on elite clienteles – were not already articulated and awaiting empirical support. Rather, I would suggest that the joint possibility of proposing and of testing for the operation of these mechanisms was an outgrowth of the structural thinking implicit in network analysis. Finally, in these two cases at least, some progress is made toward bridging the gap between materialist accounts that focus on actors' individual and collective interests in wealth and status, and idealist accounts focusing on the clash of religious, ethical, or cultural systems.

Another frequently cited investigation of elite networks is Padgett and Ansell's (1993) simultaneous analysis of kin, finance, and neighborhood relations among powerful Florentine families during the early Renaissance. Although Padgett and Ansell examine a range of different themes, they too are interested in the way patterns of social ties influence the formation of groups. In this instance, the outcome of interest is the rise of the Medici clan from a position of modest distinction to a seemingly paramount place in Florentine politics. Padgett and Ansell again apply blockmodel analysis, this time to marriage, residential, and financial ties. Mapping the relations among several dozen "families," Padgett and Ansell suggest that the Medici clan located themselves, without the intention of doing so, in a delicate but significant broker position in the highly charged post-Ciompi political arena. In an atmosphere of extraordinary political distrust, the broker position occupied by Cosimo di Medici and his clan furnished the only opportunity for political actors to perceive someone as representing collective rather than particular interests. It is not that the Medici actually did so; rather, the authors argue, their structural position made it appear that they could, an appearance from which they were able to reap substantial political benefits.

The same overall point could be made concerning Padgett and Ansell's study that I have already made about Bearman's and my own: the empirical patterns they describe and the interpretations they offer, while again following historians of the period in some respects, are nevertheless distinctive in ways that structural analysis makes possible. One way to state the point is to say that it is the idea of "structural position," in the sense of a network location that is distinguishable in principle from its occupant, that runs through network analyses of historical processes. Network analysts have something in common, in this respect, with materialists who see people as servants of historical forces they did not themselves create. At the same time, structural analysis is open to a wider range of possible roles, and a richer variety of structures, with which to make sense of such forces. One might say that class analysis is a special case of structural analysis, suitable when social structure is shaped principally by relationship to the means of production – but likely to fail when that condition does not hold. Indeed, I hope I have shown that network analysis has the potential to explain why class forces express themselves in some cases, fail to manifest themselves in others, and coexist or compete with religious or ethnic group identities in still others. Network structures are the common ground on which various forms of group definition and contention are free to encounter one another.

Structural Analysis of Nonnetwork Data

As I pointed out earlier, the strong version of the network approach maintains that individual actors, represented formally as network nodes, cannot reasonably be said to exist independently of the relational webs that enclose them. It is a small step from this pronouncement to the proposition that even phenomena that seem at first blush to have nothing to do with social ties ought nonetheless to be studied as if they were networks. In addition, there is an illustrious precedent for this tactic in the form of Claude Lévi-Strauss, whose formal examination of concrete kinship systems (Lévi-Strauss [1949] 1969) slipped almost seamlessly into the structural analysis of myth (Lévi-Strauss 1963). In Lévi-Strauss's deft hands, myths changed from mere stories to tabular representations of "mythemes" whose relations to one another revealed the inner workings of the human mind. Historical network analysts have attempted to do no less by applying structural thinking and methodology to actions, events, utterances, and even (I am only half-joking) train schedules.

Take, for example, John Mohr's study of charitable organizations in New York City during the Progressive Era (Mohr 1994; Mohr and Duquenne 1997). People operating settlement houses, foundling homes, soup kitchens, and refuges for "fallen women" most likely saw their various activities as independent and distinctive, even if they sometimes recognized that they belonged to a broader community of good works. But Mohr's approach to the topic starts from the supposition, familiar to network analysts, that each such organization could be what it was only in relation to others in its organizational field. Examining hundreds of such bodies over several decades, Mohr's research dismantles each organization's self-description into component elements: targeted populations (the hungry, the desperate, the orphaned, the sick, drunken men, wayward girls, delinquent boys, women in distress), types of service (aid, care, succor, betterment, correction), background motivation (charity, Christianity, fraternity, humanity), and so forth. You can guess the next step: Mohr graphs the population of organizations with respect to whether they share a service, a client base, a motivation, or any combination of these. Galois lattice representations (I hesitate to call them "analyses," inasmuch as Galois lattices, unlike the methods described earlier, do not do much in the way of data reduction) simultaneously depict overlaps as (1) relations among services that (for instance) are delivered to the same population and (2) relations among populations offered the same kinds of services. (The hungry and the fallen might, for example, be related insofar as both receive succor. Simultaneously, succor could be related to relief because both are administered to the hungry.) Mohr can show that graphs representing the pattern of such overlaps shift over time, indicating changes in something like the structure of social service.

Whatever story Mohr tells about these shifts – it is not yet clear what this story is, in fact – it will depend for its plausibility on our willingness to believe that these patterns of overlaps are in some way meaningful. If we accept that they are, then studies of this kind have the potential (like the studies of concrete social ties I discussed earlier) to tell us something that conventional history has not told us. Mohr's study might reveal, for instance, that at a crucial moment Christian organizations moved from a niche as teachers of moral rectitude to one of pure charity. The more gradual or diffuse this shift, the more difficulty conventional historical methods would have in identifying it.

The challenge to historical network research of this kind, however, stems from the fact that *by hypothesis* the network ties involved are not subjectively available to social actors. Network studies of clientelism take for granted that patron–client ties are understood as such by patrons and clients; it is the aggregation of these ties into larger systems, and the effects of such aggregation, that are thought to be discoverable by us even if participants are not aware of them. But in cases like the network of shared services/clients/motivations in early-twentieth-century New York, even the basic relations are analytical constructs. While it may be the case that some pairs of organizations recognized their relatedness because they both offered soup to the hungry, this could not be the case in general – particularly when any number of kinds of people might have been in distress or in need of aid. Network analysis already yields unorthodox outputs; research following the dictates of "strong structuralism" combines this fact with unfamiliar inputs.

A second instance of this class of research strikes more of a balance between network imperialism and the surface plausibility of the relations examined. Barkey and Van Rossem (1997) transformed court records from the Ottoman Empire in the 1600s (more precisely, from western Anatolia in the 1650s) into a network of relations among villages. They used the following procedure to effect this transformation: if residents of two different communities testified or litigated against each other in a trial, the communities were coded as having an oppositional tie. If they were on the same side of the case, the communities were assigned a cooperative tie. The same coding was applied when two individuals came from the same village, generating an intravillage relation that could similarly be cooperative or conflictual. (Across multiple trials, of course, these ties became counts: a pair of communities might have a handful of cooperative interactions with each other alongside a large number of conflictual relations, or both counts could be high, both low, and so on; likewise, a single village could have large numbers of internal "conflictual relations" or could be knit by large numbers of internal "cooperative relations." Finally, other kinds of ties – weak social ties, strong social ties, and instrumental ties – were derived from narrative details given in each trial.)

Barkey and Van Rossem use a blockmodel algorithm to collapse villages into blocks and to summarize the pattern of inter- and intravillage relations at the block level. Their analysis suggests, essentially, that villages located between market centers and remote communities occupied similar positions in the network of conflictual and cooperative relations. These villages had high levels of intercommunity conflict, primarily with centrally located communities, and a disproportionate share of these conflictual ties, compared with villages in other blocks, involved what they call "contention," which is defined as challenges to "state or market intervention." Barkey and Van Rossem interpret their evidence as showing that state formation and marketization had little impact on marginal communities, generally positive effects on central communities, and disruptive effects on "intermediate" villages. The differential impact of these political and economic trends, they argue, manifested itself in higher levels of contention directed at state and market actors, typically located in central communities. By way of theoretical conclusion, they suggest – in a way that would presumably please most structuralists – that position in the network of intervillage relations, independent of village attributes, drives contention levels.

The contribution of network thinking, then, lies in the invocation of the concept "position in the network of intervillage relations." Yet in their interpretation of complex empirical results (derived from a discriminant analysis for which the inputs are block memberships and a variety of graph-theoretic measures), Barkey and Van Rossem are reluctant to take the blockmodel literally. They suggest, rather, that the block assignments of villages derive from a set of underlying village attributes, not from the structure of village relations. The structure of village relations is a function of these attributes, not their origin. In fact, the two intermediate blocks are intermediate in different ways. We can recognize one block as intermediate because it was at a medium distance from the market center, and thus had many contentious interactions with it because of its incomplete integration; the second intermediate block's villages were wealthy and geographically farther from the market town, evidently necessitating increased monitoring by the central authorities. Contention resulted in one set of cases from disruptive economic change, in the other set from the centrifugal effects of distance and prosperity along with the state's response to these effects.

In other words, the argument is not about the network of inter- and intravillage interactions as such; rather, these interactions, and the block memberships derived from them, are best interpreted as *expressions* of the underlying processes associated with commercialization and state-building. Barkey and Van Rossem's interpretation of the analysis brings us back to the same mechanisms a traditional social historian would invoke: competing economic actors, uneven development, monitoring and enforcement problems stemming from geographic remoteness, and so on. If they are right (and it bears noting that their historiographic evidence is persuasive), a more conventional statistical analysis, regressing contention levels on a set of independent variables – distance from commercial centers, wealth, mixed forms of agricultural production, and so forth – would have revealed precisely the same patterns. This convergence indicates that, even if the empirical analysis is structuralist, the theoretical argument the authors' historiographic knowledge leads them to defend is not.[8] The analysis might therefore be better described as a replication using network techniques of empirical propositions already derived using conventional historical methods. It is reassuring that network analysis confirms findings established

[8] An important feature of this study, and one that it shares with Mohr's, is the use of an experience-distant definition of what "relations" are. No doubt peasants appearing at the same trial, on the same side or on opposing sides, viewed their participation as interaction of some kind – more so, at any rate, than would two organizations whose mission statements both mentioned "hobos." At the same time, it is unlikely that they viewed such interactions as relations. Aggregating these peasant-level acts of litigation into village-level relations, and then aggregating them again into relations within and among blocks, requires considerable faith in the structuralist program. To be concrete about it, it is only a slight stretch to classify court testimony with or against someone in court as a social tie. It is more of a stretch to call the sum of such court interactions over a period of four years a tie between villages. In the end, of course, Barkey and Van Rossem do not need to make a case for the validity of these coding decisions, because they prefer a nonrelational interpretation of their relational analysis.

through other methods, but structuralists might have been more pleased to learn that their methods had disclosed previously unknown patterns that were nonetheless interesting and plausible.[9]

Network Diffusion and Large-Scale Mobilization

Another area in which comparative historical researchers have applied network methods without explicitly committing to the structuralist worldview is the study of protest mobilization, specifically with reference to the role of social ties in the diffusion of activism. The relative absence of structural theorizing in this research is no accident: I observed earlier that analyses of "network effects," as distinct from analyses of networks, require a research design in which standard variables like class composition and unemployment coexist with social ties as candidates for explanatory relevance.

As in the case of clientelism, sociological and historical studies of social protest had begun to talk about the role of social ties in personal decisions to join protest movements well before formal network analysis entered the picture (Gerlach and Hine 1970; McAdam 1986; Snow, Zurcher, and Ekland-Olson 1980); but later studies pushed the general ideas in this literature several steps further, with efforts to document the diffusion of mobilization through large-scale networks (Hedström 1994; Hedström, Sandell, and Stern 2000); the impact of formal and informal network overlaps, as opposed to the mere presence of "dense networks" (Gould 1991); and the link between social network patterns in mass collective identity formation (Ansell 1997; Gould 1995). Hedström's research has documented a diffusion effect among towns, mediated by both geographical proximity and social contacts, in the founding rates of Swedish trade unions and chapters of the Social Democratic Party. My own research on the Paris Commune of 1871 (Gould 1991) suggested that levels of insurgency diffused through cross-neighborhood contacts induced by militia recruitment patterns. An extension of this work (Gould 1995) showed that the dominance of community-based appeals to solidarity depended on the existence of residential neighborhoods in which social contacts cut across class boundaries: these neighborhoods, located in outlying areas of Paris, contributed

[9] In her conclusion to this volume, Theda Skocpol expresses support for such uses of network methods. I support them as well; my point here is only that the use of structural methods for triangulation, as opposed to investigation of specifically structural propositions, is less likely to generate novel theoretical insights.

more heavily to the mass mobilization of May 1871 than did the artisan neighborhoods of the center, the historic cradle of Parisian insurrections. In an extension of such analyses to "symbolic networks," Ansell's (1997) examination of the crystallization of syndicalism in late-nineteenth-century France suggested that the ideological centrality of the general strike to the French syndicalist movement grew out of the organizational linkage of unions to labor parties inside the labor exchanges that sprang up in certain French cities in the 1880s.

What these studies share is the combination of an interest in social networks with a mainstream methodology modified to incorporate network effects. All three studies employ adaptations of variable-based analytic techniques – event-history models in Hedström's case, autocorrelation regression in the other two – in a way that explicitly permits statistical tests of the relative impact of network ties. Event-history models of founding rates permit the estimation of the likelihood of a founding occurring, conditional on a town's ties to other communities where founding has already occurred. This effect is estimated net of the impact of other factors, like the size of a town's industrial workforce. Similarly, autocorrelation regression estimates the degree to which an outcome variable (mobilization level or support for the general strike) flows through network ties in such a way that the cases (neighborhoods or cities) reciprocally influence each other's outcome – again, net of the impact of other variables.

Unlike the other styles of network research cited in this essay, this approach does not offer reduced-form representations of network data, but rather submits them in relatively undigested form to a variable-based analysis. The net result to date is the demonstration that network ties do indeed matter in the diffusion of mobilization; but, because the network data are taken literally, rather than represented in reduced form, we know little about just what kinds of network *structures* are associated with diffusion of this kind. The work of asking such questions in a precise way has so far been restricted to formal modeling or simulation, at a level of abstraction too high to be immediately useful for comparative historical scholars.

Yet this is precisely the sort of work that, it seems to me, network analysts ought to be doing. Reduced-form images of social structure, of either the positional or the connectivity variety, free the researcher from complete enumeration of network ties. This freedom simultaneously allows bolder theoretical formulations in the structuralist spirit, as my earlier discussion showed, and, just as importantly, makes research on a larger scale more feasible. As research on network effects becomes less dependent on complete network data, it will be easier to contemplate large-scale structural analysis.

It follows that research bridging the gap between analysis of social networks and analysis of network effects has the potential to broaden substantially the range of historical phenomena that are simultaneously amenable to network approaches and significant for comparativists. To take just one example, the "slow-moving" social processes that Paul Pierson, in this volume, sees as crucial for macroscopic change – literacy, commercialization, urbanization, and others – are almost certain to depend on diffusion through social relationships. The more we learn about the ways different network structures shape diffusion processes, the more likely it is that we will be able to study such processes without having to collect complete network data on a complete set of units.

Conclusion

I would suggest that it is not accidental that the more frequently replicated applications of network analysis to problems in historical sociology are those that have, in the first place, addressed theoretical problems with a pedigree outside of network analysis, and in the second place, applied network methods to data that correspond to an experience-near definition of what a network is.

What seems to have made progress possible in this area is the joint presence of a preexisting body of theory from which to derive further questions and a relatively constant focus on networks that self-evidently involve concrete social interaction. In some cases (e.g., Ansell 1997), the "relations" subjected to structural analysis tend in the direction I discussed in the preceding section; but in these cases, the abstraction of the network concept has typically been offset by a firm anchoring in a substantive theoretical agenda.

In contrast, the studies that have been hard to absorb into ongoing debates are those that have applied a strongly theory-centric coding procedure – as any network analysis of nonnetwork data entails – without a self-consciously structuralist theoretical agenda. We can be more confident that we will get somewhere with a nontrivial operation on our raw data if we have a specific reason, in the form of a theoretically derived proposition we wish to test, for performing that operation. Alternatively, we need at least to believe that our data are robust indicators of the phenomenon we care about before we can legitimately impose major transformations on them.

This is all the more important when the availability of thick descriptive material is diminished, as it necessarily is when our principal data sources are archival documents. For this reason, I will offer the prediction that the benefit of major reworkings of nonnetwork data into relational form will be inversely related to how historical the data are.

I trust that the skeptical tone I adopted in describing strong structuralism earlier makes more sense in light of this point. Network analysis is frequently described as a "powerful" tool for describing social structure. This might mean one of two things. First, it might mean that the use of network methods allows us to discover important phenomena not identifiable, or at any rate not easily identifiable, through other means. Second, it might mean that it can be applied to a broad range of phenomena, with neutral implications for how much insight is gained thereby. Metaphorically speaking, we might distinguish between "powerful" in the sense of a strong beam of light and "powerful" in the sense of a steam hammer. The first metaphor tells us that, if we use the tool, we will see more, or further, without distorting the world too much; the second tells us that we can, with enough force, stamp any pattern onto empirical data that we choose to.[10]

The concern I have tried to highlight is that it may be tempting to apply a tool because it has a lot of power_2 but that we are better off if we restrict ourselves to relying on power_1. In the present context, in my judgment, the latter aim is served best when network tools are applied *either* to data that are self-evidently data on social networks *or* to nonnetwork data when we are reasonably confident that we have a good theory – not a metatheory, like structuralism, but a substantively relevant theory – to guide us through the sometimes messy output our analytic procedures generate. Network analysis is good at reducing data complexity, but it does not always do so in a truly straightforward way. In fact, it rarely does so, except in trivial cases. (For example, if one were to apply blockmodel or connectivity analysis to data on friendships in a multiracial classroom, one would probably find – still, in the twenty-first century – that both blocks and cliques were homogeneous with respect to race. But careful observers would not need network analysis to tell them that.) As a consequence, research that forces nonrelational data into a relational form without a strong substantive reason to do so will be unlikely to yield meaningful results.

[10] It is dangerous to argue with metaphors. A critic might say that a powerful beam of light can cast shadows, degrade delicate molecules, cause us to see spots, and the like. All true. But I trust I have made my point clear without going into all the hidden implications of the metaphor.

Uses of Network Tools

I inserted the word "meaningful" deliberately as an entrée to a closing point about the importance of cultural frameworks. The lack of meaningful results I am talking about is not a matter of the subjective meaning the actors we study assign to their actions, their social relations, or the "structures" in which they see themselves as acting. It is, rather, a matter of the meanings we as social scientists assign to our findings. And those meanings have to do with the specific debates that engage us, the connections our findings have to other people's findings, or hypotheses, or middle-range theories. They may or may not have to do with the subjective, or culturally informed, or structurally constrained experiences social actors have when they do or do not do the things that interest us. For that reason, I have said little about the criticism occasionally leveled at network analysts for "ignoring" culture, or the cultural frameworks that may or may not constitute networks (Emirbayer and Goodwin 1994). Extant network methods are not very good at either incorporating or modeling subjective experience, meaning, or symbolic structures – as the example of Mohr's ambitious but inconclusive project shows. But to see that fact as a basis for criticism is rather like seeing a circle as flawed because it is too round. Different methods are good at different things – and for the moment, at least, until someone figures out how to make structural analysis good at modeling meaning, we had better be content with the thought that network methods are meaningful for modeling social networks.

References

Ansell, Christopher K. 1997. "Symbolic Networks: The Realignment of the French Working Class, 1887–94." *American Journal of Sociology* 103: 359–90.

Badian, E. 1958. *Foreign Clientelae, 264–70 B.C.* Oxford: Clarendon Press.

Barkey, Karen and Ronan Van Rossem. 1997. "Networks of Contention: Villages and Regional Structure in the Seventeenth-Century Ottoman Empire." *American Journal of Sociology* 102: 1345–82.

Bearman, Peter S. 1991. "Desertion as Localism: Army Unit Solidarity and Group Norms in the U.S. Civil War." *Social Forces* 70: 321–42.

1993. *Relations into Rhetorics: Local Elite Social Structure in Norfolk, England, 1540–1640.* New Brunswick, NJ: Rutgers University Press.

1997. "Generalized Exchange." *American Journal of Sociology* 102: 1383–1415.

Berkowitz, S. D. 1982. *An Introduction to Structural Analysis.* Toronto: Butterworths.

Breiger, Ronald L. 1974. "The Duality of Persons and Groups." *Social Forces* 53: 181–90.

Brucker, Gene A. 1977. *The Civic World of Early Renaissance Florence.* Princeton, NJ: Princeton University Press.

Burt, Ronald S. 1980. "Models of Network Structure." *Annual Review of Sociology* 6: 79–141.

Coleman, James S. 1961. *The Adolescent Society*. New York: Free Press of Glencoe.

Emirbayer, Mustafa and Jeff Goodwin. 1994. "Network Analysis, Culture, and the Problem of Agency." *American Journal of Sociology* 99: 1411–54.

Gerlach, Luther P. and Virginia H. Hine. 1970. *People, Power, Change: Movements of Social Transformation*. Indianapolis: Bobbs-Merrill.

Gould, Roger V. 1991. "Multiple Networks and Mobilization in the Paris Commune, 1871." *American Sociological Review* 56: 716–29.

1995. *Insurgent Identities: Class, Community, and Protest in Paris from 1848 to the Commune*. Chicago: University of Chicago Press.

1996. "Patron–Client Ties, State Centralization, and the Whiskey Rebellion." *American Journal of Sociology* 102: 400–29.

Granovetter, Mark. 1974. *Getting a Job: A Study of Contacts and Careers*. Cambridge, MA: Harvard University Press.

Hedström, Peter. 1994. "Contagious Collectivities: On the Spatial Diffusion of Swedish Trade Unions, 1890–1940." *American Journal of Sociology* 99: 1157–79.

Hedström, Peter, Rickard Sandell, and Charlotta Stern. 2000. "Mesolevel Networks and the Diffusion of Social Movements: The Case of the Swedish Social Democratic Party." *American Journal of Sociology* 106: 145–72.

Hunter, Floyd. 1957. *Community Power Structure*. Chapel Hill: University of North Carolina Press.

Kemeny, John, Arthur Schleifer, Jr., J. Laurie Snell, and Gerald L. Thompson. 1962. *Finite Mathematics with Business Applications*. Englewood Cliffs, NJ: Prentice-Hall.

Kettering, Sharon. 1986. *Patrons, Brokers, and Clients in Seventeenth-Century France*. Oxford: Oxford University Press.

Laumann, Edward O. and Franz U. Pappi. 1976. *Networks of Collective Action: A Perspective on Community Influence Systems*. New York: Academic Press.

Leinhardt, Samuel, ed. 1977. *Social Networks: A Developing Paradigm*. New York: Academic Press.

Lévi-Strauss, Claude. [1949] 1969. *The Elementary Structures of Kinship*. Boston: Beacon Press.

1963. *Structural Anthropology*. 2 vols. New York: Basic Books.

Lorrain, François and Harrison C. White. 1971. "Structural Equivalence of Individuals in Social Networks." *Journal of Mathematical Sociology* 1: 49–80.

Marsden, Peter V. 1990. "Network Data and Measurement." *Annual Review of Sociology* 16: 435–63.

McAdam, Doug. 1986. "Recruitment to High-Risk Activism: The Case of Freedom Summer." *American Journal of Sociology* 92: 64–90.

Milgram, Stanley. 1967. "The Small-World Problem." *Psychology Today* 2: 60–7.

Mohr, John W. 1994. "Soldiers, Mothers, Tramps, and Others: Discourse Roles in the 1907 New York Charity Directory." *Poetics* 22: 325–57.

Mohr, John W. and Vincent Duquenne. 1997. "The Duality of Culture and Practice: Poverty Relief in New York City, 1888–1917." *Theory and Society* 26: 305–56.

Moreno, J. L. 1953. *Who Shall Survive?* Beacon, NY: Beacon House.

Morrill, John. 1984. "The Stuarts." Pp. 327–98 in *The Oxford History of Britain*, edited by Kenneth O. Morgan. Oxford: Oxford University Press.

Namier, Lewis. 1957. *The Structure of Politics at the Accession of George III*, 2nd ed. London: Macmillan.

Newcomb, Theodore. 1961. *The Acquaintance Process*. New York: Holt, Rinehart, and Winston.

Padgett, John F. and Christopher K. Ansell. 1993. "Robust Action and the Rise of the Medici, 1400–1434." *American Journal of Sociology* 98: 1259–1319.

Roethlisberger, Felix J. and William J. Dickson. 1939. *Management and the Worker: An Account of a Research Program Conducted by the Western Electric Company, Hawthorne Works, Chicago*. Cambridge, MA: Harvard University Press.

Snow, David A., Louis A. Zurcher, and Sheldon Ekland-Olson. 1980. "Social Networks and Social Movements: A Microstructural Approach to Differential Recruitment." *American Sociological Review* 45: 787–801.

Stone, Lawrence. 1965. *The Crisis of the Aristocracy, 1558–1641*. Oxford: Clarendon Press.

Sulloway, Frank J. 1996. *Born to Rebel: Birth Order, Family Dynamics, and Creative Lives*. New York: Pantheon Books.

Wellman, Barry and S. D. Berkowitz, eds. 1988. *Social Structures: The Network Approach*. New York: Cambridge University Press.

White, Harrison C. 1963. *An Anatomy of Kinship*. Englewood Cliffs, NJ: Prentice-Hall.

White, Harrison C., Scott A. Boorman, and Ronald L. Breiger. 1976. "Social Structure from Multiple Networks. I. Blockmodels of Roles and Positions." *American Journal of Sociology* 81: 730–80.

Zagorin, Perez. 1970. *The Court and the County*. New York: Atheneum.

8

Periodization and Preferences

REFLECTIONS ON PURPOSIVE ACTION IN COMPARATIVE HISTORICAL SOCIAL SCIENCE

Ira Katznelson

The Garden of Eden with the Fall of Man, a remarkable painting jointly executed circa 1615 by two painters with very different styles, hangs in the Mauritshuis in The Hague. A standing Eve, offering the apple, and a seated Adam, receiving it, both in the left foreground, were portrayed figuratively by Peter Paul Rubens. The lush garden in which they are placed, an overwhelming background filled with dense flora and the prolific animal kingdom against which the protagonists and their act of exchange stand out, was painted by Jan Breughel the Elder, Pieter Breughel the Elder's second son and friend to Rubens.[1] This collaboration, the best example I know in the visual arts of an oscillation and combination of perspectives and methodologies in a single work, is a performance of analytical history. Marking the critical moment when a single exchange disenchanted the world and transformed the status of humankind inside nature, it is, like the best historical social science, a work about a particular time, setting, and choice, a perceptible narrative constituted by a story of periodization and an account of preferences.

This version of the essay has profited quite a lot from the variety of comments, especially those geared to help me clarify my argument, offered by colleagues in this venture, at the April 2000 conference at Brown University, the project's American Political Science Association panel in Washington, D.C., in September 2000, and the November 2000 conference at Harvard University. I also have had the benefit of two workshop discussions at the Departments of Political Science at Rutgers University and the Graduate Faculty of the New School. I am especially indebted to the counsel provided by David Collier, Marshall Ganz, Jeff Goodwin, Peter Hall, James Mahoney, and Dietrich Rueschemeyer.

[1] Rubens and Breughel worked together on other canvasses, including *Madonna and Child Surrounded by a Flower Garland and Putti*, *Allegory of Sight and Smell*, *Allegory of Feeling, Hearing, and Taste*, and *Landscape with Pan and Syrinx*, the last the most similar in style and execution to their joint depiction of Adam and Eve.

Periodization and Preferences

What I wish to say about the vitality and possibility of comparative historical scholarship is contained in this canvass, or at least suggested by it. Macrohistorical scholarship tilts in the direction of periodization. This rich vein of learning, with a lineage in Marx's story of epochal transformations and class-based agency and in Weber's combination of "objective probability" with sequences and patterns of purposeful action composing what he called sources of "adequate causation," primarily offers large structure analyses of long-term processes marked by titanic transformations.[2] At the heart of this venture lie efforts to discern temporal dynamics systematically within history's inexhaustible complexity. No work of this character can do without a project of periodization that rests on (implicit or explicit) assumptions about broad, structurally inscribed, historical dynamics. These historicist claims define the kinds of moments actors find themselves within.

This genre's concern with temporality divides in two. Comparative historical scholars have been concerned to apprehend both the origins and the character of moments marked by massive change and to assay the secular dynamics of intervening periods that take their impetus from the outcomes produced during critical eras of historical inflection. These quests in the lineage of comparative historical social science have been marked by a strong predilection for structure and a fair amount of silence about agency. Less a condition than a prominent feature is the manner in which periodization habitually has trumped attention to preferences, the act, or fact, of esteeming and preferring objects of choice arrayed in an order of priorities. The analysis of both aspects of temporality, I believe, would profit, by contrast, from more systematic attention to preferences. How, I wish to ask, can human preferences be incorporated, as essential components of purposive action, as periodization's partner? How might the predilections of individuals sited in spatial and temporal contexts (the quality of an interest, desire, value, or belief as being preferable can make sense only in such specific intersubjective situations and relationships) fruitfully join, complement, and inform historical social science with periodization at its core? The goal of such an engagement is a more balanced partnership between the macrofoundations of microdynamics and the microfoundations of macrodynamics.

By contrast to the ways preferences have been treated as unconstrained or as givens by many methodological individualists and in contraposition

[2] I discuss Marx's historical projects in *Marxism and the City* (Katznelson 1992, ch. 2). For Weber, the best recent treatment of these themes is Fritz Ringer, *Max Weber's Methodology: The Unification of the Cultural and Social Sciences* (1997).

to the tendency of methodological holists to unduly constrain their scope, I indicate how the systematic study of institutions, at the junction of agency and structure, can afford means to better connect the study of periodization and preferences. This essay thus considers each type of historical moment in turn, based on the conviction, discussed later, that holism and individualism are not necessary opponents but potential partners when linked to understand history as mediated by an institutional imagination. Microbehavior, we must continue to remember, requires historical macrofoundations. Yet equally, large-scale comparative analysis is underspecified and incomplete when its microfoundations are left implicit, ad hoc, or undertheorized.

By locating actors, as well as categories and networks of actors, in time, originators of periodization stories provide macrofoundations for human action. Comparative historical social science has gauged history by transitions and epochs produced by concatenations of decisive processes and events. As a social science of beginnings grounded mainly in problems, concepts, methods, and categories oriented to large-scale change, it has been disposed toward a language of crisis, passage, and sequence. Not just history but theories of history that probe relations among concepts, cases, and moments have defined its very center. Abjuring simple linearity, this work takes durations, discontinuities, branchings, and trajectories very seriously. But what of the preferences of actors engaged in determined activity during, or between, critical junctures? What part should their hierarchies of estimation play in scholarship that privileges temporality?

Building an effective tandem relationship linking periodization and preferences for comparative historical social science requires more than inserting tools from other research traditions such as rational choice (based on an economic analogy concerning individual utilities) or sociological institutionalism (stressing the social qualities of shared beliefs and values) whose conceptions of agency, respectively, either are too thin or too thick to work well as partners unless prior intervening steps are taken. Without wishing to set aside in advance any implement in the tool kit of the social sciences,[3] I propose that we turn in the first instance to instruments and mechanisms generated from within the ambit of historically oriented social science itself. By distinguishing two partially overlapping but still distinct genres of work in this tradition – comparative historical social science on a grand scale and smaller-scale historical institutionalism (and by discerning differences

[3] I strongly argue against too strong an antinomy of historical and rational choice institutionalism in Katznelson (1998).

between earlier and recent comparative historical social science) – it is possible, I suggest, to see how key features of a more developed historical institutionalism can provide productive means with which to construct a compelling approach to preferences.[4]

Comparative historical social science – understood as the enterprise of apprehending, understanding, and accounting for tremendous change and sharp shifts in the direction of human affairs at key junctures – has begun to enjoy a welcome revival. Important new work including scholarship on the medieval and early modern origins of liberal representative regimes, the extension of public responsibility for social welfare broadly understood, variations to the properties and bureaucratic development of sovereign states, and the role both elite and mass actors have played in shaping race, nation, class, and democracy (Collier 1999; Collier and Collier 1991; de Swaan 1998; Downing 1992; Ertman 1997; Marx 1998; Rueschemeyer, Stephens, and Stephens 1992; Silberman 1993; Skocpol 1992) has been assuming a pride of place in the past decade, after a hiatus caused in part by the exhaustion of Marx-inspired historical materialism, alongside an earlier generation of work associated with such scholars as Barrington Moore (1966), Perry Anderson (1974), Reinhard Bendix (1964), Charles Tilly (1964), Immanuel Wallerstein (1974), and Theda Skocpol (1979). Likewise, work gathered under the rubric of historical institutionalism[5] geared to understand how specific constellations of institutional legacies and patterns shape interactions among states, economies, and citizens joined and vied with other "new institutionalisms" in the 1990s to revivify institutional analysis. My main goal is to suggest how, in partnership with this undertaking, comparative historical social science can make human preferences a more constitutive feature of its endeavors.

I proceed by taking the following steps. First, I revisit and celebrate the powerful structural and configurative impulses of the generation of work that followed the publication of Moore's *Social Origins of Dictatorship and Democracy* while taking note of the relative absence of attention to preferences in this body of scholarship. Focusing, as exemplary, on the deeply structural account of the origins of postfeudal state formation by Perry Anderson, I distinguish when such an approach seems most

[4] This approach also can help clarify the terms on which other "new institutionalisms" might contribute to this research program.

[5] The term first appears, I believe (following a colloquy with Theda Skocpol, Sven Steinmo, and Kathleen Thelen), in Steinmo and Thelen (1992).

compelling and when it is seriously wanting, and I show why the structural holism at the heart of such studies of grand historical change need not vie with a preference-oriented individualism if both holism and individualism are understood in a particular fashion. Noting, second, how recent comparative historical scholarship focusing on regime formation and the development of liberal polities has been able to tilt more in the direction of a systematic incorporation of preferences when dealing with conjunctures of massive change, I probe the paradox that structurally induced unsettled times can provoke possibilities for particularly consequential purposive action. Then personal preferences, choices, and transformative visions can profoundly reshape structures that control human social possibilities. Third, turning to more settled periods that intervene between change on a mega-scale, I register how historical institutionalist scholarship on temporality and sequencing under the rubric of path dependence has opened up fresh questions about how to link periodization and preferences. Building on this impulse, yet concerned that work in this vein tends to overrate contingency at the outset of a path while overstating mechanisms that lock a particular historical trajectory in place, I turn in the conclusion to diverse literatures concerning institutional boundaries, cognition, distribution, and problem solving that lie just outside the usual ken of historical institutionalism in order to specify a conception of "restricted agency" as a helpmate to the project of periodization.

I

Following a discussion of state formation by Moore and Anderson, among others, a strong advocate of historical sociology, Philip Abrams, commented reasonably that "a noticeable feature of the studies I have discussed so far has been their relative indifference to the intentions, dispositions, and purposes of the individuals whose lives made up the historical processes in which the authors were interested." Not absolute indifference, of course, just relative inattention. These books, he observed, underscore the "structural conditions [and] . . . the institutional consequences of relationships" rather than "the *actual* intentions of the parties to the relationships," which tend to be "treated as a factor of quite minor explanatory importance" (Abrams 1982, pp. 177–8).[6]

[6] In a similar, though less sympathetic, vein, commenting on what Theda Skocpol called her "structural perspective" (Skocpol 1979, p. 14) in *States and Social Revolutions*, David Laitin

Periodization and Preferences

Characteristic of the major works of this founding period for modern macrohistorical analysis, a structurally oriented approach to periodization is especially prominent in Anderson's *Lineages of the Absolutist State*. This stunning text lies at the resolute end of a continuum privileging how big results are consequences of the temporal conjoining of large structures and processes. In explaining that "what rendered the unique passage to capitalism possible in Europe was *the concatenation of antiquity and feudalism*" (Anderson 1974, p. 420; italics in text), he developed an account that made virtually no room for an understanding of the social world as the result of decisions taken by particular actors with preferences. What matters in such circumstances, as Susan James puts it in her defense of holism as a particular type of social explanation, are "the social regularities which control classes of people." In this approach to social explanation, "by isolating these features, . . . we can arrive at explanations which either elucidate the relations between large-scale social phenomena, or relate these to individual actions and attitudes" (James 1984, p. 177).

Precisely the promise of the second of these openings offered by a structural, holist, macrohistorical social science has been redeemed too rarely, thus reducing the power of the enterprise to work creatively with the irreducible tensions of structure and the agency of actual persons. There is, for example, no shortage of collective actors with preferences in Anderson's consideration of the absolutist state as the irony-laden last gasp of feudal elites aiming to stave off the disintegration of their social order. In what arguably is the book's pivotal formulation explaining the syncretic character of the new form of sovereign state, a hybrid of the feudal and the modern, he writes, "The threat of peasant unrest, unspokenly constitutive of the Absolutist State, was thus always conjoined with the pressure of mercantile or manufacturing capital within the Western economies as a whole, in moulding the contours of aristocratic class power in the new age. The peculiar form of the Absolutist State in the West derives from this double determination" (Anderson 1974, pp. 23–4). Powerfully, Anderson thus develops a causal argument at a remove from the preferences of individuals,

and Carolyn Warner observed that she had written a brilliant book about revolutions while analytically moving, in their words, "to limit the realm of voluntary action as much as is scientifically possible" (Laitin and Warner 1992, pp. 147–8). Even when elite actors like Robespierre, Trotsky, and Mao or mass actors like peasants and bureaucrats come on the scene, as Skocpol herself put the point, it is "the objective relationships and conflicts among variously situated groups and nations, rather than the interests, outlooks, or ideologies of particular social actors" that are of main causal interest (Skocpol 1979, p. 291).

except in their roles within preformed categories. The causal work is performed not by specific people but by a historically uneven juxtaposition of big social forces defining roles: "Immensely magnified and reorganized, the feudal State of Absolutism was nevertheless constantly and profoundly over-determined by the growth of capitalism within the composite social formations of the early period. These formations were, of course, a combination of different modes of production under the – waning – dominance of one of them: feudalism" (Anderson 1974, p. 39).

Here, there are actors with interests, to be sure. Absolutism "fundamentally represented an apparatus for the protection of aristocratic property and privileges," and it simultaneously promoted "the basic interests of the nascent mercantile and manufacturing classes" (Anderson 1974, pp. 39–40). Yet what is striking is how these preferences swiftly collapse into periodization. "It may be argued," he wrote, "that the real *periodization* of Absolutism in the West is at bottom to be found precisely in the changing rapport between the nobility and the monarchy, and the multiple attendant shifts which were correlated with it" (Anderson 1974, p. 43; italics in text). A similar move is made by Barrington Moore's account of the "three main historical routes from the preindustrial to the modern world," which he sums up this way: "we seek to understand the role of the landed upper classes and the peasants in the bourgeois revolutions leading to capitalist democracy, the abortive bourgeois revolutions leading to fascism, and the peasant revolutions leading to communism. The ways in which the landed upper classes and the peasants reacted to the challenge of commercial agriculture were decisive factors in determining the political outcome" (Moore 1966, pp. xiv–xv, xvii). Here, too, agency at the high level of collective roles is subsumed into and contained within distinctive temporal historical pathways marked by decisive junctures. Both Anderson and Moore advance quickly from a statement of their general propositions to specific cases characterized by variation peopled by many proper names whose action does not so much test as illustrate their role categories in action to produce the expected result. Lineages and origins command preferences.

The many gains achieved by working audaciously in this manner at a high level of erudition and command certainly should not to be sacrificed to a principled individualism. But there are also many analytical hazards inherent in this muscular imposition of theory on history. Complexity is modeled and cases are constructed for comparison. In particularly talented and learned accounts most of us cannot hope to duplicate, remarkable feats can ensue. Anderson's combination of historicism and structuralism produced richly tiered comparisons: between town and country; between states within Western Europe, including England, France, Spain, Italy, and Sweden; between Western and Eastern Europe; between Europe and the Ottoman Empire and Japan. Moore likewise brought into his comparative ambit cases as far-reaching as India and the United States, England and China. These configurative studies are as much works of art as science. When these projects advance well, they recall the bravura performances of theoretical employment by Tocqueville, Marx, and Weber.

Put strongly, the risks of such grand historical macroanalysis and its powerful tilt in the direction of periodization and structure are worth running because there is no substitute for them if we are to understand big moments of large historical change. Yet even with craftsmanship as expert as Anderson's, such enterprises court the linkage of overweening theory to secondary history. It is in this respect, I believe, that systematic attention to preferences inside the elephantine moments of change identified by comparative historical social science can advance understanding of how the multiple possibilities inside unsettled moments of uncommon choice were resolved. The very character of critical junctures as relatively open times produced by concatenations of structural processes invite elucidations of the preferences and choices of the actors – grand to ordinary – placed inside such situations when the potentiality of alternatives explodes as previous constraints on belief and action erode.

The uneasy relationship between treatments of periodization that inscribe history as defined by oscillations between moments of continuity and times of fundamental change and considerations of preferences that focus on the agency of historical actors hardly is new. It certainly appears vibrantly in the work of both Marx and Weber. Writing in *The Holy Family*, Marx (1956) observed that "history is nothing but the activity of men in pursuit of their aims," but most interpreters usually concur with G. A. Cohen's (1982) view that "Marxism is *fundamentally* concerned not with behavior, but with the forces and relations constraining and directing it . . . historical materialism is governed by a dialectic of forces and relations of production that is background to class behavior, and not explicable in terms of it" (Przeworski 1990, pp. 91, 90). Treating class struggle as the centerpiece of human history did not resolve this tension between agent- and structure-centered explanations (the failure to do so, it is worth recalling, weakened Marxism as social theory and convened a cacophonous politics inside the Left that ultimately proved enervating or an excuse for despotism).

Weber, too, wrestled with these concerns, moving back and forth from an explanatory focus on structural variables to a subjectivist quest for individual-level understanding (Brubaker 1984; Löwith 1982; Oakes 1988; Ringer 1997).

This field of tension cannot be eliminated. But it can be navigated, I argue, with the assistance of an institutionalist research program. In an earlier essay, I lamented aspects of the conceptual and substantive retrenchment that marked the movement from macroanalysis in the 1960s and 1970s to historical institutionalism in the 1980s and 1990s, arguing that the often illuminating treatments of public policy, political economy, and the representation of interests in more recent work had "shortened their time horizons, contracted their regime questions, and narrowed the range of considered outcomes" (Katznelson 1997, p. 85). Here, by contrast, I should like to indicate how taking institutions seriously by concentrating on what John Padgett (1990) has called an "institutional topology" and what Perry Anderson (1986) has identified as precise institutional infrastructures can fruitfully link periodization and preferences. By stressing the formation of institutions at critical junctures, by designating the substantive choices they embody, and by highlighting their distributive qualities, networks, flows of information, and framing capacities, we can productively bridge these too often separate zones of inquiry.

Even some of the most structurally oriented macrohistorical works contain such invitations (if too rarely taken up by their authors) to combine chronicles of structural antecedents of critical junctures with accounts of agent-centered possibility. Philip Abrams's review, for example, of *Social Origins* shrewdly observed that by the time the book concludes, an important change of manner and analysis appears characterized by "the shift that occurs within it from a deterministic to a probabilistic tone and mode of argument" (1982, p. 173). Without sacrificing his unremitting focus on his central causal factors, Moore found room for a wide array of local variation based on intentional action often marked by constellations of division within the categories of lord and peasant located inside particular institutional venues. On this reading, what is not claimed is that the configuration of key variables produced invariable effects but that it vastly altered and increased the probabilities for results of a certain kind. As Fritz Ringer has put the point in writing about the character of Weber's methodology (commenting here on the impact of Johannes von Kries), the variety of human subjectivities helps make "the whole conception . . . dynamic; it deals in sequences and processes rather than in successive but unconnected events"

(1997, p. 66). Particular antecedents increase the likelihood of particular results, multiplying their objective probability, not certainty, in historical development. It is on this field of structured probabilities that human agents possessing preferences play.

Not that this can be an engagement without unease. Such collective categories as military officers or working classes or local government officials who inhabit the texts of macrohistorical scholarship tend to skip over the aggregation problems inherent in the fact that human endowments, interests, predilections, and preferences are held by individuals. One does not have to be a methodological individualist pushing (too) hard, often to the point of vacuousness, for a reduction of the social realm to individual-level action and choice to acknowledge that with regard to preferences as outcomes and as motivations, the eventual unit of analysis is individuals established inside networks, power asymmetries, the distribution of information, and the naturalized categories that institutions bestow. Irrespective of where one comes out in the field of tension most commonly thought to be defined as the ontological divide distinguishing holism from individualism (an antinomy I think to be misleading, as I argue momentarily), it seems clear enough that people's intentions, reasons, desires, emotions, dispositions, and decisions compose the heart of any analysis of preferences. Of course, so long as one does not turn social categories into fictional collective actors, it is permissible to assign preferences to collectivities, but only with great care, with self-conscious provisionality, and with the recognition that, ultimately, all preferences are held by persons, not roles.

This individualist dimension of inquiry has not been easy for macrohistorical social scientists to put into play. Its practitioners, myself included, rightly are nervous when preferences are deployed as givens without accounts of their embeddedness or origins. We are drawn particularly to interactive behavior over long periods of time that can entail shifts of preferences rather than to short-term fixed preferences usually announced as existing as the result of some unexamined exogenous process. But skepticism about the pitfalls of hyperindividualism or an understandable partiality to structural explanations and endogenous accounts of motivation in accounting for change on a vast scale are not good enough as reasons to push the study of preferences to the side or abandon the subject to others. Nor is it sufficient, though sometimes legitimate, to aggregate choices by individuals behaviorally or impute the preferences of individuals from collective categories or post-dict preferences of actors by their structural locations in historical circumstances, all common moves that court fallacies of composition.

Unusually large moments of decisive change, the comparative historical literature effectively claims, are products of the configuration of big processes that constrain individuals by placing them in situations where their identities, values, beliefs, intentions, and strategies are compressed into gelatinous sets of preferences based on how they are positioned in the social, political, and economic orders. The social whole binds and confines the formation of preferences. The presence of regularities conferred by position constitutes subjects so powerfully that any portrait we might have of individuals as intentional agents is compromised. What matters first, and most, is the particular constellation of circumstances shaping, defining, and limiting thought and behavior. Yet without such agency, of course, however determined, these objective probabilities could not have been transformed into outcomes.

This type of holism is not an option but a central (and, I believe) wholly defensible feature of comparative historical scholarship. It claims that history cannot be explicated without theory, that social wholes are not reducible to the sum of individual parts, and that the properties and features of individuals are deeply shaped by their situations inside large-scale structures and processes. Understood this way, holism does not vie with individualism as such. Rather, what is at stake are the conditions under which recourse to this particular kind of causal analysis "that appeals to the properties of social wholes to account for features of individuals" makes sense rather than the sort that explains "the characteristics of social wholes as the outcome of individual traits" (James 1984, p. 7). Though holist and individualist explanations cannot either be reduced one to the other or simply amalgamated, there are specific purposes for which each can find its place and its due. The issue that must be considered is when and how they might be linked into coherent accounts of periodization and preferences whose arrangement of elements might vary considerably from one type of historical moment to another.

What seems clear in pursuing this theme is that the familiar antinomy of holism and individualism is much too constricted and misleading. Individualism, Philip Pettit usefully has shown, is best opposed not to holism but to collectivism, the view that aggregate regularities so constrain individual behavior as to make human subjectivity and individual psychology chimerical. In parallel fashion, he demonstrates that holism is best opposed not to individualism but to atomism, a position that treats individuals without sufficient attention to how they are shaped by one another (Pettit 1993, chs. 3, 4). From this perspective, a social ontology marked by the combination, or at least the oscillation, of holism and individualism is possible, even desirable.[7]

If designated without a historical specification of when and how the goal-oriented actions of individuals make history – that is, without sufficient attention to periodization – such a program would cant too far in the direction of agency. Yet in the absence of marking out moments and sites where agency does matter, comparative historical social science runs the reciprocal risk of underspecifying the significance of preferences: where they come from; how they get provisionally fixed; the extent to which they are stable; the number of preference rankings actors possess; the existence of meta-preferences; the extent to which they are based on self-reflection and normative aspiration; and the manner in which they can become strategic (Carling 1990; Gerber and Jackson 1993; Jervis 1988; Quattrone and Tversky 1988; Sen 1977; Waldron 1990; Wildavsky 1987).

II

Two moments analyzed by macrohistorical scholarship beckon the analysis of preferences: epochs of massive change and eras when outcomes fashioned during key historical periods remain constitutive and formative. The place we might accord to preferences is distinct in what William Sewell and Ann Swidler have called "unsettled" and "settled" times (Sewell 1992; Swidler 1986). Yet at both moments, comparative historical social science has tended to downplay individual preferences, albeit differently, favoring

[7] A similar claim from the side of individualism has been advanced by Adam Przeworski. He finds the programmatic intent announced in the statement "that all social phenomena (their structure and their change) are in principle explicable in terms of individuals" to be "barren," with minimal explanatory power. After all, he observes, history and social relations "endow individuals with objectives and possibilities of action," so an atomistic individualism courts either banality or absurdity. Further, there is no direct line between action and result since these so often are unanticipated or indirect. "The conditions we face today constitute consequences of actions undertaken yesterday, but yesterday we acted in pursuit of other goals than producing conditions for tomorrow." The interaction of actors with preferences, he thus observes, cannot replace history and periodization. He thus counsels a constructive interaction between the two modes of working. "If successful, this interaction will lead to: treating preference formation as an endogenous, continuous outcome of social processes; distinguishing categories of actors by their strategic situations; using historically specific concepts of equilibrium; while explaining history, including the origins of conditions, in terms of the goal-oriented actions of individuals" (Przeworski 1990, pp. 91–2).

a largely structural holism as a preferred mode of explanation for critical junctures and a search for mechanisms of lock-in as the main means to explain persistence at times of continuity. In both instances, periodization bests preferences as a focus on structural causes and mechanisms tends to overwhelm their interplay.

To begin to consider an alternative, we might better think about their mutual constitution in the manner recommended by Margaret Archer. She counsels an

> approach which is capable of *linking* structure and agency rather than *sinking* one into the other. The central argument is that structure and agency can only be linked by examining the *interplay between them over time*, and that without the proper incorporation of time the problem of structure and agency can never be solved. (Archer 1995, p. 65)

Though analytically distinct, periodization and preferences are deeply intertwined, with each, ultimately, making no sense without the other and with neither claiming ontological superiority over the other precisely because human societies are "both structured and peopled" (Archer 1995, p. 75). In much methodologically individualist scholarship the agency of preference-holding actors tends to press down on, and thus obscure, the claims of structural and temporal properties to causal status. The obverse has been the case for the orientation that tends to absorb agents and action into various large-scale, long-term, mainly structural stories of determination.

Importantly, this familiar apportioning of the intellectual terrain darkens our view of an absolutely critical feature characteristic of periods of large-scale change. These, after all, are times when the advantages of the status quo are broken, thus conducing an uncommon range of choice. Here, an emphasis on the structural conditions producing points of historical transformation inherently identifies unusual moments when the space for human agency opens wide and the play of preferences can come to possess an unusual capacity to determine outcomes. Of course, even at such times, the conditions under which preferences and agency operate are not simply of their own making. Even at such moments, moreover, the actual existence of competing possibilities, "the universe of possible discourse," occupies more constrained space than the full universe of hypothetical options (Bourdieu 1977, p. 169). The actual field of opinion, debate, and plausibility always is narrower than the range of options the basic structure of the situation might allow. Still, at critical junctures, the gap between the hypothetical and the optional is reduced, often dramatically, because what Arthur Stinchcombe calls "the moral value of the status quo" (1978, p. 17) has been called into question and when, to borrow a phrase from E. E. Schattschneider, the fundamental "scope and bias" of the political order comes to be at stake (1960, ch. 2).

In such circumstances, many constraints on agency are broken or relaxed and opportunities expand so that purposive action may be especially consequential. Not just at revolutionary "moments of madness" "when human beings living in society believe that 'all is possible'" (Zolberg 1972, p. 183), but at longer points of massive transformation, preferences – whether fundamental or strategic – matter quite a lot because they operate to help shape particular institutional outcomes. This plasticity and openness, moreover, characterizes both preferences about goals, purposes, and values (ends) and preferences about strategies and tactics (means), as well as their relationship. Indeed, at such moments, familiar links between ends and means themselves may break down, promoting and deepening uncertainty. With outcomes unpredictable, actors experiment, test, learn, and explore divergent alternatives. Not surprisingly, such times often incubate remarkable advances in political theory (think of Locke on toleration or Constant on constitutionalism) and convene a process of institutional innovation, often the result of multifaceted and contradictory innovations. Often, actors who are most competent and successful when means–ends relations are more predictable founder, and new actors, with distinctive preferences, skills, ideas, and visions of alternative futures, emerge to redefine situations, provide solutions, and create institutional results, some of which then endure for extended periods to reshape boundaries, naturalize outcomes, redistribute power, and provide new contexts for solving problems. It is thus not just agency and preferences that matter at such times, but particular kinds of innovative competence and patterns of discovery.[8]

Though comparative historical scholarship has yet to move systematically and purposefully in these directions when considering critical junctures, we can observe a welcome and beckoning shift in recent scholarship focusing on the making and character of modern states from state formation understood in terms of the strength of their organizational endowments to a concern with the particularities of regimes and patterns of governance, including the lineage of liberal and democratic patterns of rule and alternative types of state capacity. Whereas their precursors had tended to go

[8] I am especially indebted to Marshall Ganz for the formulations in this paragraph.

as far as their holist and structural accounts of origins took them, often holding the preferences of collective actors as role categories constant (and thus unexamined directly) while varying structures and circumstances, the newer body of work is more apt to identify sets of choices and decisions taken both by elite and mass actors whose preferences themselves are key variables *inside* these critical junctures, thus making these predilections a more cardinal part of their analyses. These writings are not less macroscopic in style and reach than the prior generation, but differently so; it is this variance that I wish to underscore.

This modification – in part a self-conscious return to the agenda of Moore, in part a new emphasis in harness with recent scholarship on transitions to democracy and on the global status of liberalism – especially identifies and privileges the distinct role played under certain conditions by representative institutions, notably parliaments, that link state and society. This set of subjects necessarily invites attention to a two-way interaction of preferences. Moreover, by pointing to the importance of substantive ideas about regimes, this recent macroanalysis about large-scale times of inflection also potentially connects to political theory (extending its reach from social and economic theory) and to the preferences held by producers of systematic knowledge about how political orders should be organized, showing that not just the form but the substance of rule matters.

In past comparative historical scholarship, work on early modern European states tended to focus on how "centralized monarchies... represented a decisive rupture with the pyramidical, parcellized sovereignty of the mediaeval social formations, with their estates and liege-systems" (Anderson 1974, p. 17). The centralization and militarization of sovereignty marked by the growing discretionary powers of the monarch, the separation of property from political authority, a distinction between the ruler as a person and the executive as an institution, and the development of state finance, administrative bureaucracies, policing capacities, and professional armies with heightened destructive capacities composed centerpiece themes in this significant body of work. Such scholarship was disposed to treat parliaments merely, as Charles Tilly put the point, as one of a number of "groups which resisted state-making" (1975, p. 22). With the exception of this single mention, for example, representative institutions play no role in the analytical introduction and conclusion he penned for *The Formation of National States in Western Europe.*

This executive-centered treatment of stateness by macrohistorical scholarship in the 1960s and 1970s proved influential at the expense of the type of concern Barrington Moore had expressed for variations in types of regime, a theme that echoed centerpiece issues in Western political thought that largely was neglected in subsequent scholarship in the 1960s and 1970s on "big structures, large processes, and huge comparisons" (Tilly 1984). In consequence, key qualitative substantive and normative issues concerned with stateness dropped almost entirely from view. Form and structure triumphed over a focus on representative mediations between state and society and on the meaning of state capacity.

Clearly, these subjects evoke a concern with preferences that previously had either been absent or dormant. The most recent wave of large-scale historical social science has shifted focus to this subject matter. Returning to Moore's master theme, Brian Downing, for example, put his "focus on the long-run conditions favoring the rise of democracy and dictatorship." Limiting his empirical gaze to Europe and its variations, he distinguished absolutism with and without parliaments as key outcomes on the path to either democracy or dictatorship. At the heart of this variation, he argued, were conditions either facilitating or impeding the reproduction of political representation associated with medieval constitutionalism. "To put the argument in barest form," he wrote,

> medieval European states had numerous institutions, procedures, and arrangements that, if combined with light amounts of domestic mobilization of human and economic resources for war, provided the basis for democracy in ensuing centuries. Conversely, constitutional countries confronted by a dangerous international situation mandating extensive domestic resource mobilization suffered the destruction of constitutionalism and the rise of military-bureaucratic absolutism. (Downing 1992, p. 9)

If Downing thus placed the robustness of parliaments on a continuum of outcomes shaped by particular configurations of threat, resource extraction, and mobilization, Thomas Ertman positioned at the heart of his analysis "the role played by different kinds of representative institutions in the failure or triumph of royal plans to introduce absolutism and in the subsequent development of state infrastructures" (1997, pp. 4–5). Together with the timing of geopolitical competition and the robustness of local medieval governments during the period of absolutist state formation, he identified "an independent influence of strong representative assemblies on administrative and financial institutions" (Ertman 1997, p. 6).

By stretching the number and range of issues they consider in their empirical cases and by extending their understanding of variation, Downing and Ertman importantly have changed the accentuation subjects for the macrohistorical analysis of early modern European statebuilding. Whereas Anderson had sought to answer Weber's "why Europe" question by focusing on the concatenation of antiquity and modernity and had attempted to understand the absolutist state as the last gasp of feudalism, serving as a hinge institution to a capitalist modernity behind its own back; whereas Tilly and his collaborators had tried to understand the lineaments of state capacity by contrast to earlier, more decentralized, forms of rule; and whereas Moore, who had raised these questions about the branching of regimes scrutinized class configurations to understand causation, Downing and Ertman have looked hard inside political Europe to (re)discover the importance of representation and consent broadly in tandem with the central themes of liberal political theory since Locke.

Perforce, this institutionalized location of transactions between state and society is a key site for the formation, articulation, and contestation of preferences. If, as Wim Blockmans puts it, "representation means literally to make present an absent" (1998), the key questions become not only how representative institutions were initiated, sustained, and expanded or contracted in scope and responsibility, but who was represented by whom with what content. The bifurcation of Europe into sites for liberal democracy and dictatorship, from this vantage, pivoted on whether monarchies were limited or unlimited in their exercise of sovereignty, that is, whether it could be legally overridden or had to accommodate to local and national representative bodies (Brewer 1988; Finer 1997, p. 6; Morgan 1988). Where such bodies existed based on consent, and in the context of a large-scale pattern of differentiation that distinguished the sovereign state from the economy, from civil society, and from other states in the global order, key outcomes at critical moments turned on how kings and parliaments together constructed institutional transactions linking the state to each of these other zones. Not just the predilections of monarchs but those of representatives determined these outcomes. Periphery and center; a plurality of centers of power; multiple, heterogeneous, and discontinuous coalitions; diverse theories of sovereignty and just rule; and new forms of association and identity appeared and contended. Preferences mattered in entirely fresh ways as choices were made about how and whom to rule and about the scope of governance (Levi 1998).

Preferences have also begun to appear as a collaborator with periodization in other significant recent macroanalytical contributions. Among others, Tony Marx offers a comparative strategic analysis of white elite bargaining to account for the twentieth-century racialized democracies of South Africa and the United States as compared with the absence of legal racial discrimination in Brazil. Bernard Silberman distinguishes patterns of bureaucratic formation in the nineteenth century by decisions taken with respect to rules for leadership succession under conditions of high uncertainty. Ruth Collier produces an analysis that "distinguishes patterns of democratization according to which actors pushed for regime change or democratic reform." And Abram de Swaan, standing on the shoulders of Norbert Elias ([1939] 1994), crafts a beautiful account of the extension of governmental responsibilities for the provision of public goods by placing a strategic model of growing interdependence in which actors with hierarchies of both common and clashing preferences turn to the state to provide education, health care, and welfare to growing numbers (Collier 1999; de Swann 1998; Marx 1998; Silberman 1993). In accounting for institutional outcomes, each thus provides an exposition of preferences and periodization without collapsing one into the other.

By giving a more central pride of place to preferences and agency, this welcome scholarly turn also brings matters of power, inequality, and the formation of institutions together as themes. Critical junctures close with determinate bursts of institutional creativity that prove durable. These, as Jack Knight has observed, are not the results of some abstract hidden hand working "to constrain groups or societies in an effort to avoid suboptimal outcomes," the preferred way of thinking about institutional innovation by many rational choice institutionalists. Rather, he advances a conception of social institutions focusing on distributional powers and consequences. Institutions fashioned at moments of historical opportunity, in this view,

> are the by-products of substantive conflicts over the distributions inherent in social outcomes. According to this conception, the main goal of those who develop institutional rules is to gain strategic advantage vis-à-vis other actors, and therefore, the substantive content of those rules should generally reflect distributional concerns. The resulting institutions may or may not be socially efficient: It depends on whether or not the institutional form that favors the actors capable of asserting their strategic advantage is socially efficient. Note that the inefficiency need not arise from any incapacity of the actors (due to either lack of information or faulty understanding) but, rather, from their self-interest, their pursuit of a less efficient alternative that gives them greater individual gain. (Knight 1992, p. 40)

This perspective places bargaining between actors under determinate conditions at the heart of institutional innovation without making any a priori assumptions of a functional character. It invites issues of power into the house of institutions rather than seeing this guest as an intruder. And while opening a wide door to the formative impact of institutional legacies, it also makes clear that these constraints never are all-determining. Inside the probabilities they offer, actors with different perspectives, capacities, information, and expectations seek to achieve outcomes that possess a maximum degree of homology between their own interests and those of society as a whole. Even though the results may lower costs of coordination, reduce uncertainty, and perform other services, they rarely can be characterized accurately in the bland and usually substanceless language of efficiency. Above all, the way power and substance entwine matters.

By rendering the contours of liberal political regimes institutional in this manner, recent macroanalysis also provides the means with which to link still largely structural analyses of large-scale change to central themes of preference and decision in normative political theory, especially as they concern the identification and evaluation of alternative political regimes with respect to how they construct linkages between the sovereign state and the economy, civil society, and the international arena. In this way, comparative historical analysis can come full circle to deploy its analytical tools to consider and advance the concluding plea of Barrington Moore: "Whether the ancient Western dream of a free and rational society will always remain a chimera, no one can know for sure. But if the men of the future are ever to break the chains of the present, they will have to understand the forces that forged them" (1966, p. 508).

III

The challenge of preferences also raises important issues about how moments of origin to transformations of state, economy, and society should be joined to assessments of their aftermath and persistent effects. The reproduction of the consequences that come in the wake of historical big displacements is a subject that clearly would benefit from the specification of how they shape human preferences that, in turn, under certain conditions, sustain their outcomes. This is a theme that has been taken up within the ambit of economics, for example, in a famous article by Timur Kuran on "collective conservatism" (1987) seeking to explain how the status quo can get reproduced even when it is at odds with the private preferences of nonactivists. By contrast, the intense focus on the sources of long and enduring patterns and moments (how the sovereign state was made; how particular regime types were forged; why particular kinds of bureaucracies were fashioned; why the scope of governmental responsibilities dramatically altered) in comparative historical social science has tended to make subsequent sequences and behaviors seem rather too automatic and derivative. A telling indicator, as Kathleen Thelen notes, is the familiar use of such metaphoric language as "filling political space" or the "crystallization" or "freezing" of options that serves as a substitute for the characterization of mechanisms that make the legacies of key historical moments endure (Thelen 1999, pp. 390–1). The propensity in comparative historical work has been to do what Karl Polanyi stated as his intention: "we shall make detailed analyses of critical periods and almost completely disregard connecting stretches of time" (Polanyi 1944, p. 4). The dominant strategy has been to identify a particularly challenging and vexing outcome and then look back as far as necessary to identify the juncture when the elements constituting the relevant moment of "origins" first appeared (Katznelson 1981).

Seen in tandem with this tendency to focus primarily on critical junctures, recent scholarship on sequences and path dependence has a breakthrough quality because it connects these periods to subsequent times. As Ruth and David Collier caution, the "importance or lack of a critical juncture cannot be established in general, but only with reference to a specific historical legacy" (1991, p. 33). Without a designation both of outcomes and of the manner in which they are reproduced as constitutive and formative features of social reality, it is impossible either to answer questions about the duration of the formative moment or to distinguish between the production and reproduction of its results. These concerns have been at the center of historical institutionalism's important attempt to grapple with historical temporality and legacies of change under the banner of path dependence.

No periodization scheme is innocent, of course. Each makes assumptions about how to read the past and is animated, self-consciously or not, by a theory of how to organize causal and sequential models of history. Whereas conventional narratives almost always leave such matters implicit, the application of path-dependent insights from evolutionary economics to political subjects has been methodologically self-conscious, pushing to systematize our understanding of historical sequencing to better understand the relations connecting clusters of events to subsequent clusters. Endeavoring "to break the narrative form from its naïve epistemological moorings, from the impression that the narrative is a causal theory because the tone of the language of narrative is causal" (Stinchcombe 1978, p. 14), this orientation to temporality – which, alongside the new focus on regimes in historical macroanalysis, is the second major site of analytical innovation in comparative historical social science – seeks to discover a standpoint located between theoretically reclusive description and efforts to subsume past cases under the umbrella of covering laws.

Path dependency approaches possess a simple, and appealing, causal structure. Key decisions at choice points produce outcomes that set history on a course whose mechanisms of reproduction make the initial selection unstoppable.[9] Moving beyond a tendency to employ evolutionary language, such as punctuated equilibria, adapted from Darwinian biology in quite general and metaphorical terms to underscore how, at critical historical junctures, choices are made that put history on a course from which it is difficult, even impossible, to return,[10] scholars inclined to historical institutionalism have sought to specify the concept more precisely. Dissatisfied with vague claims about how developments at historical turning points leave no room for alternatives, they have explored the positive feedback, self-reinforcing processes stressed by some evolutionary economists under

[9] Paul Krugman, for example, illustrates path dependence in economic geography in his account of the persistent location of the manufacturing belt in the United States in a relatively small part of the Northeast and the eastern part of the Midwest. There is the initial puzzle of why these particular locations were selected and an even more vexing question about persistence. Despite the extraordinary shift westward in the century spanning 1870 to 1970, the dominance of this location continued (between 1900 and 1960, its share of manufacturing employment had dropped only from three in four to two in three jobs). Krugman tells this as a story of how initial advantages too small to triumph without a good deal of luck before economies of scale increased, transportation costs fell, and the share of the population outside agriculture rose in the second half of the nineteenth century when these developments were parlayed into a story of persistence by the process of increasing returns. "Given sufficiently strong economies of scale," he writes, "each manufacturer wants to serve the national market from a single location. To minimize transportation costs, she chooses a location with large local demand. But local demand will be large precisely where the majority of manufacturers choose to locate. Thus there is a circularity that tends to keep a manufacturing core in existence once it is established." What the case explains by example, he concluded, is that "Nicholas Kaldor (1972), Paul David (1985), and Brian Arthur (1989) were right – that increasing returns and cumulative processes are pervasive and give an often decisive role to historical accident" (Krugman 1991a, pp. 80–1; Krugman 1991b; Kaldor 1972; David 1985; Arthur 1989).

[10] "Historical developments," political scientist Steven Krasner wrote in an influential example of this genre, "are path dependent; once certain choices are made, they constrain future possibilities. The range of options available to policymakers at any given point in time is a function of institutional capabilities that were put in place at some earlier period, possibly in response to very different environmental pressures" (Krasner 1988, p. 67).

the heading of increasing returns.[11] Summarizing this orientation's implications for political analysis, Paul Pierson has underscored its elements of *contingency* ("relatively small events, if occurring at the right moment, can have large and enduring consequences"), *timing and sequencing* ("*when* an event occurs may be crucial. Because earlier parts of a sequence matter much more than later parts, an event that happens 'too late' may have no effect, although it might have been of great consequence if the timing had been different"), and *inertia* ("once an increasing returns process has been established, positive feedback may lead to a single equilibrium. This equilibrium in turn will be resistant to change") (Pierson 2000, p. 263). Likewise, James Mahoney suggests that "all path-dependent analyses minimally have three defining features." These, he identifies as a high sensitivity to initial conditions, the idea that "initial events in the sequence are characterized by 'contingency,'" and that "once in motion, path-dependent sequences are marked by relatively predictable or 'deterministic' causal patterns."[12] In this way, a set of initial conditions with multiple possibilities is reduced to a single self-reinforcing trajectory. Irrespective of how an institution was first brought about, distinctive mechanisms of reproduction can be identified.

This path-dependent perspective divides the question of origins in two. The causes of decision making inside a given critical juncture, it counsels, should be conceptualized independently of those that reproduce outcomes. Path dependence comes into play only, as it were, after critical junctures have performed their work. Once this (relative) autonomy is acknowledged, specific mechanisms of persistence that lock in the results of prior developments can be identified. Though the leading candidate for the specification of confinement to the path is the imported notion

[11] Path dependence in economics developed out of a fundamental challenge to Walrasian general economic equilibrium analysis. Price theory, from Smith, through Walras and Marshall, to Debreau, has assumed constant returns to scale, making the absence of increasing returns one of its core axioms. Hand in hand has been the difficulty equilibrium economists have had in treating change because of an inability to specify mechanisms of shift from one equilibrium to another. "Once, however, we allow for increasing returns," Kaldor wrote, "the forces for continuous change are *endogenous*... and the actual state of the economy during any one 'period' cannot be predicted except as a result of the sequence of events in previous periods which led up to it" (Kaldor 1972, p. 1244; Magnusson and Ottosson 1997).

[12] Mahoney importantly distinguishes self-reinforcing sequences, "characterized by processes of reproduction that *reinforce* early events," from reactive sequences in which "initial events trigger subsequent development not by reproducing a given pattern, but by setting in motion a chain of tightly linked reactions and counterreactions." (Mahoney 2000, pp. 510, 526–7).

of increasing returns, that need not exhaust the list of candidates. James Mahoney and Kathleen Thelen thus have proposed broadening the inventory of such mechanisms to include other positive feedback instruments such as incentive structures, conventions, normative appeals, or elite power (Mahoney 2000, pp. 10–17; Thelen 1999, pp. 392–4). What is striking overall, however, is how little we currently know about the range of possible trajectories or about mechanisms sustaining path dependence ranging from those reaching into persons at the level of cognition, to socially shared norms and expectations, to the working of institutional arrangements that structure rules about choice.

A heuristic distinction between critical juncture and path dependence and an expansion of instruments of reproduction beyond the currently dominant mechanism of increasing returns are persuasive. Coherent efforts to specify how the institutional results of large-scale moments of change have played a constitutive role in shaping subsequent developments clearly must depend on specifications broadly similar to those produced by the path-dependent approach. But not, I suggest, without considerable modification.

For fruitful as the path-dependent approach has been, it is marked by a number of limitations. Its break with historical macroanalysis (one gets the sense that this breach has been unintentional) has been much too radical. By underscoring the impact of small, random events at the point of origin of a given path, a view of the world marked even more by luck than by other forms of contingency, path dependency commits itself to a particular, highly partial, view of institutional genesis, a haphazard mixture of chance and opportunism deeply at odds with the comparative historical tradition I have been assaying. By privileging contingency, systematic accounts of large-scale change central to the tradition of macrohistorical scholarship in effect are ruled out of bounds. As a result, points of departure tend to remain veiled in mystery. Such historical minimalism is not so much wrong as radically insufficient.

As in the macrohistorical scholarship of the 1960s and 1970s, in path-dependent approaches periodization tends to command preferences. Its distinction between crossroads where choices are made behind people's backs and roads without exits oversimplifies and narrows what it means to say that an outcome persists. Understating how persistence itself may be a product of the character of the choices taken at the historical juncture, path dependence "leaves unappreciated," Jeffrey Haydu shrewdly observes, "the many ways that history's switchmen come along for the ride. Choices in one period not only limit future options, they may also precipitate later crises, structure available options, and shape the choices made at those junctures" (Haydu 1998, p. 353). To meet a test of influence, the claim of origins, outcomes need not persist unchanged. The very image of a path risks constraining the notion of a sequence to a linear, confined route, thus risking the disappearance of agency as an instrument for identifying the scope of choice and possibility.[13]

If preferences, in this rendering of persistence, hazard a collapse into periodization, more sustained attention to institutions can provide tools to instate a better balance. The sequences of most interest within the ambit of comparative historical social science are arrangements not simply of events, crises, or decisions, but all of these as they converge on configurations of institutions. The sequences we attend to are sequences of institutional design and persistence. The zone of attainable institutional outcomes – with institutions understood as "the constraints that human beings impose on human interaction" consisting "of formal rules (constitutions, statute law, common law, and regulations) and informal constraints (conventions, norms, and self-enforced codes of conduct) and their enforcement characteristics" (North 1995, p. 15) – varies, of course, from time to time and place to place. If critical junctures are marked by the multiplicity of such choices and the range of alternatives they put on offer, their fulfillment and close are defined by the contraction of this temporarily feasible set into a reasonably durable institutional configuration. It is characteristic of such switching moments, whether initiated by external shocks or endogenous processes (or more commonly by a combination of both), that they are marked by a transition from initially very high uncertainty and possibility to less, from a wide array of policy options to fewer, and by institutional innovation that reduces uncertainty and inscribes content and limits to policy.

Far less so, however, when critical junctures come to an end. Because institutional outcomes mold and authorize subsequent developments, they establish new legacies, in the language of the Colliers,[14] by producing macrofoundations for subsequent action, an approach that entails identifying analytically as well as historically when a critical point of inflection occurs, how long it lasts, what legacies it produces, and how long they last (Collier and Collier 1991, pp. 31–4). In considering, as they do, the

[13] For a discussion of this minimalism, see Douglas and Ney (1998, pp. 169–73).

[14] "A critical juncture may be defined as a period of significant change, which typically occurs in distinct ways in different countries (or in other units of analysis) and which is hypothesized to produce distinct legacies" (Collier and Collier 1991, p. 29).

long-term playing out of the legacies of critical junctures, we would do well to treat the uncertainty-reducing properties of institutions as particular distributive arrangements, and to emphasize how institutions create categories and "realities" that seem natural, thus how they compose actors with particular identities, values, interests, and strategies – that is, preferences – who seek to manage and solve problems. Features vital to the very character of institutions shape the place for such agency under determinate conditions. Their naturalizing powers both confer advantages on particular kinds of definitions of identity and change lines of demarcation between noise and silence, probability and improbability, even possibility and impossibility. They produce maps of the social order that include categories for partitioning people. They also transform distributions of valued goods ranging from money to information to access to networks. And they are sites for problem solving by particular agents with specific horizons and prospects.

Approaching linkages connecting periodization and preferences via institutions thus invites movement toward controlled interpretation that could incorporate insights about boundaries, categories, and meanings with accounts of power and problem solving. An engagement by historical institutionalists with literatures that take up these issues in anthropology, sociology, and cognitive psychology could illuminate the character of institutions as rules, framing devices, and formal organizations and fix a more balanced relationship between periodization and preferences by advancing an understanding of what might be called "restricted agency."

These bodies of work do not represent a comprehensive elucidation of relevant mechanisms; after all, the range of historically sensitive theories about the generation of needs and wants, about cognitive frames, normative orientations, access to information, and changes in beliefs and values is as wide and broad as modern social theory. Rather, I single out these literatures because they constitute plausible alternatives to the kind of formalism that is rather too prevalent both in rational choice approaches to agency and the lock-in proclivities of path-dependent approaches to sequence and persistence. They also can help clarify when and how agency operates not quite on its own making, and how the pursuit of preferences underpins continuity without closing off prospects for new moments of large-scale change.[15]

[15] Like the Colliers, I, too, am partial to what Stinchcombe identified as historical as opposed to constant causes. But historical causation need not be reduced to discursive narration (Collier and Collier 1991, pp. 35–6; Stinchcombe 1968, pp. 103, 108–18).

Periodization and Preferences

The first literature is concerned with borders and with the way institutions, in defining boundaries, shape the character and content of preferences. I mainly have in mind the path-breaking contribution to the literature on ethnic conflict in which the anthropologist Frederik Barth broke with the notion that groups are defined a priori by their culture, that is, by internal values and intragroup interactions. He cautions that such groups cannot be identified one at a time by reference to itemized characteristics like language and territory. There are no separate peoples who constitute social actors or their beliefs, utilities, and values. Rather, Barth asks us to focus on "the ethnic *boundary* that defines the group, not the cultural stuff that it encloses." It is the boundary, which he understands as a set of rules and as a structuring of interactions, that "canalizes social life – it entails a frequently quite complex organization of behaviour and social relations." It is the boundaries themselves that are the core of an institutional order whose arrangements of "articulation and separation at the macro-level corresponds to systematic sets of role constraints on the micro-level." By looking at the boundary as a system of institutionalized connections, we then can look at agents to ask, "what strategies are open and attractive to them, and what are the organizational implications of different choices on their part?" (Barth 1969, pp. 15, 16, 17, 33). Institutions, on this view, by organizing the location of distinctions, help define the horizons of actors, situating them in practical and moral space. In this way, institutions within the public sphere help solve collective action problems, making joint activity possible by putting pressure on individuals to identify with specific corporate identities marked by hierarchies of preference (Taylor 2001). Thus the institutional outcomes produced during unsettled times define axes of conflict that themselves are instruments of persistence that delimit and shape content and directions for purposive action.

Increasingly, students of choice have come to treat institutions as constraints on the horizons and mental constructs of actors with motivations, beliefs, and utility functions (Mantzavinos 2001). Yet institutions have an even more fundamental constitutive impact on actors' cognitions. It is not just, as Douglass North (1995), among others, argues that cognitive theory is required to remedy limitations of institutional analysis, but that as the anthropologist Mary Douglas argues, "a theory of institutions that will amend the current unsociological view of human cognition is needed" (1986, p. ix).

Though institutions do not have minds of their own, institutional categories and commitments powerfully shape the divisions individuals possess as categories of thought. Mary Douglas provides a suggestive theory of how they do so by showing that institutions are configurations of ideas; hence "the entrenching of an institution is an intellectual process as much as an economic and political one." Institutions embody formulas that justify "rightness in reason and nature." Such formulas make it possible for institutions to "encode expectations" and "put uncertainty under control" by helping to coordinate behavior within the matrix of institutions. The key to this not entirely unfamiliar line of argument, for Douglas, lies in the propensity of institutions to naturalize social classifications. Institutions become both durable and effective to the extent that they are grounded in analogies to the physical or biological worlds that make them seem like givens rather than as what they are, "socially contrived arrangements." The stronger this process of building analogies, the more enduring the institution. Institutions, on this view, "survive the stage of being fragile conventions: they are founded in nature and, therefore, in reason. Being naturalized, they are part of the order of the universe and so are ready to stand as the grounds of the argument" (Douglas 1986, pp. 45, 48, 52).[16]

The degree of security institutions acquire depends in part on their capacity to shape not just individual cognitions but social identities within which they are implanted. Institutions as boundary formulas confer sameness and sort people out into different groups and classes. "Constructing sameness," Douglas, echoing Barth, goes on to observe, "is to polarize and to exclude. . . . It involves drawing boundaries, a very different activity from grading. To move from recognizing degrees of difference to creating a similarity class is a big jump" (1986, p. 60). Once people are arrayed in categories by institutions, they can offer the solidarities based on identity that in turn reproduce the institution. Institution building and cognition, from this perspective, mutually constitute each other. People make institutions that classify; the classifications entail behavior that, in turn, but only under some conditions, reproduces the classifications that sustain the institution (Douglas 1986, pp. 101–2). Such are the microfoundations of institutional stability.[17]

[16] This is the form the controversial and much-amended claim took that Louis Hartz offered about liberalism in America. The doctrine and its institutions had become so natural, he argued, that it could not be accessed as a category for debate or contestation (Hartz 1955). Such assertions have to be treated not as givens but as variables. That is, institutional outcomes may, or may not, instantiate themselves in the manner identified by Douglas and Hartz. We have to look at the evidence, bearing in mind the powers of categorical naturalization that institutions possess.

[17] For an account of how individuals classify under determinate cultural and institutional conditions, see the suggestive lecture by Amartya Sen (1999).

Periodization and Preferences

Institutions do more, however, than confer categories and organize classifications. They are enormously powerful instruments of distribution and power, an insight at the center, as we have seen, of Knight's *Institutions and Social Conflict*. Institutions embody asymmetries that assert a new structure for the distribution of money, information, access, and other key assets of power in tandem with the naturalization of categories. Making institutions thus helps constitute, organize, and coordinate choices about identities, the construction of boundaries, and the distribution of assets. Such, as the products of times of large-scale change, provide macrofoundations for preference-based behavior and choice.

This pattern of mutual constitution, in short, defines an institutional and historical comparative social science with active but restricted agents. Taken together, these various attributes of institutions create what Karl Popper called a "logic of situation" by making quite durable, though not immutable, dispositions, expectations, and beliefs, that is, by shaping context-bound rationalities that serve as resources for solving problems (Popper 1964, pp. 147–50). Big institutional outcomes alter the states actors can be in, including the identities and roles they can take and the relationships they can enter. Inside these arrangements, the preferences, purposes, attributes, and capabilities of these actors matter (Hernes 1998, pp. 92–5) not in the vacuous sense that all action ultimately reduces to the level of the person (after all, individual agency is best considered a hypothesis, not an assumption) but on the understanding that the identities and preferences of people are products and motivators in a continuous social process of problem solving by actors situated in specific institutional settings. To the extent that paths are reproduced, they extend as a result of what Haydu calls "reiterated problem solving" by actors in possession of preferences (1998, pp. 357–8). We do well to understand the elongation of such sequences within circumstances of institutional persistence not as the result of abstract processes like the satisfaction of functional requisites or increasing returns but as the consequence of how social actors diagnose and seek to address their problems as private troubles linked to public issues with the tools they have at hand (Mills 1959, ch. 1).

There are always losers as well as winners in institutional games, and a variety of understandings of what it means to lose. Thus patterns of continuance always are marked by resistance – even, at times, jumbo change when actors seize the chances structural conditions permit. Since such critical junctures do not appear often, we must take care not to treat diverse patterns of constancy and change all in one register. Together, both major and minor keys produce history's sounds. And at some points in history's temporality, preferences shape periodization rather than the other way around.

References

Abrams, Philip. 1982. *Historical Sociology*. Ithaca, NY: Cornell University Press.

Anderson, Perry. 1974. *Lineages of the Absolutist State*. London: New Left Books.

1986. "Those in Authority." *Times Literary Supplement*, December 12.

Archer, Margaret S. 1995. *Realist Social Theory: The Morphogenetic Approach*. Cambridge: Cambridge University Press.

Arthur, Brian. 1989. "Positive Feedbacks in the Economy." *Scientific American* 262: 92–9.

Barth, Frederik. 1969. "Introduction." Pp. 9–38 in *Ethnic Groups and Boundaries: The Social Organization of Cultural Difference*. Oslo: Universitetsforlaget.

Bendix, Reinhard. 1964. *Nation-Building and Citizenship: Studies of Our Changing Social Order*. New York: Wiley.

Blockmans, Wim. 1998. "Representation (Since the Thirteenth Century)." Pp. 29–64 in *The New Cambridge Medieval History, Vol. 7: c.1415–c.1500*, edited by Christopher Allmand. Cambridge: Cambridge University Press.

Bourdieu, Pierre. 1977. *Outline of a Theory of Practice*. Cambridge: Cambridge University Press.

Brewer, John. 1988. *The Sinews of Power: War, Money, and the English State, 1688–1783*. New York: Knopf.

Brubaker, Rogers. 1984. *The Limits of Rationality: An Essay on the Social and Moral Thought of Max Weber*. London: George Allen and Unwin.

Carling, Alan. 1990. "In Defense of Rational Choice: A Reply to Ellen Meiksins Wood." *New Left Review* 184: 97–109.

Cohen, G. A. 1982. "Reply to Elster on Marxism, Functionalism, and Game Theory," *Theory and Society* 11: 483–95.

Collier, Ruth Berins. 1999. *Paths Toward Democracy: The Working Class and Elites in Western Europe and South America*. New York: Cambridge University Press.

Collier, Ruth Berins and David Collier. 1991. *Shaping the Political Arena: Critical Junctures, the Labor Movement, and Regime Dynamics in Latin America*. Princeton, NJ: Princeton University Press.

David, Paul. 1985. "Clio and the Economics of QWERTY." *American Economic Review* 75: 332–7.

de Swaan, Abram. 1998. *In Care of the State: Health Care, Education, and Welfare in Europe and the USA in the Modern Era*. New York: Oxford University Press.

Douglas, Mary. 1986. *How Institutions Think*. Syracuse, NY: University of Syracuse Press.

Douglas, Mary and Steven Ney. 1998. *Missing Persons: A Critique of Personhood in the Social Sciences*. Berkeley and New York: University of California Press and the Russell Sage Foundation.

Downing, Brian M. 1992. *The Military Revolution and Political Change: Origins of Democracy and Autocracy in Early Modern* Europe. Princeton, NJ: Princeton University Press.
Elias, Norbert. [1939] 1994. *The Civilizing Process: The History of Manners and State Formation and Civilization*. Oxford: Blackwell.
Ertman, Thomas. 1997. *Birth of the Leviathan: Building States and Regimes in Medieval and Early Modern Europe*. New York: Cambridge University Press.
Finer, S. E. 1997. *The History of Government, III: Empires, Monarchies, and the Modern State*. Oxford: Oxford University Press.
Gerber, Elizabeth and John E. Jackson. 1993. "Endogenous Preferences and the Study of Institutions." *American Political Science Review* 87: 639–58.
Hartz, Louis. 1955. *The Liberal Tradition in America*. New York: Harcourt, Brace and World.
Haydu, Jeffrey. 1998. "Making Use of the Past: Time Periods as Cases to Compare and as Sequences of Problem-Solving." *American Journal of Sociology* 104: 339–71.
Hernes, Gudmund. 1998. "Real Virtuality." Pp. 74–101 in *Social Mechanisms: An Analytical Approach to Social Theory*, edited by Peter Hedström and Richard Swedberg. New York: Cambridge University Press.
James, Susan. 1984. *The Content of Social Explanation*. Cambridge: Cambridge University Press.
Jervis, Robert. 1988. "Realism, Game Theory, and Cooperation." *World Politics* 40: 317–49.
Kaldor, Nicholas. 1972. "The Irrelevance of Equilibrium Economics." *Economic Journal* 82: 1237–55.
Katznelson, Ira. 1981. *City Trenches: Urban Politics and the Patterning of Class in the United States*. New York: Pantheon Books.
1992. *Marxism and the City*. Oxford: Clarendon Press.
1997. "Structure and Configuration in Comparative Politics." Pp. 81–112 in *Comparative Politics: Rationality, Culture, and Structure*, edited by Mark Irving Lichbach and Alan S. Zuckerman. New York: Cambridge University Press.
1998. "The Doleful Dance of Politics and Policy: Can Historical Institutionalism Make a Difference?" *American Political Science Review* 92: 191–7.
Knight, Jack. 1992. *Institutions and Social Conflict*. New York: Cambridge University Press.
Krasner, Stephen D. 1988. "Sovereignty: An Institutional Perspective." *Comparative Political Studies* 21: 66–94.
Krugman, Paul. 1991a. "History and Industry Location: The Case of the Manufacturing Belt." *American Economic Review* 81: 80–3.
1991b."Increasing Returns and Economic Geography." *Journal of Political Economy* 99: 483–99.
Kuran, Timor. 1987. "Preference Falsification, Policy Continuity and Collective Conservatism." *The Economic Journal* 97: 642–65.
Laitin, David D. and Carolyn M. Warner. 1992. "Structure and Irony in Social Revolutions." *Political Theory* 20: 147–51.

Levi, Giovanni. 1998. "The Origins of the Modern State and the Microhistorical Perspective." Pp. 58–82 in *Mikrogeschichte, Makrogeschichte: Komplementär oder inkommensurabel?*, edited by Jürgen Schlumbohm. Göttingen: Wallstein Verlag.

Löwith, Karl. 1982. *Max Weber and Karl Marx*. London: George Allen and Unwin.

Magnusson, Lars and Jan Ottosson, eds. 1997. *Evolutionary Economics and Path Dependence*. Cheltenham, UK: Elgar.

Mahoney, James. 2000. "Path Dependence in Historical Sociology." *Theory and Society* 29: 507–48.

Mantzavinos, C. 2001. *Individuals, Institutions, and Markets*. Cambridge: Cambridge University Press.

Marx, Anthony W. 1998. *Making Race and Nation: A Comparison of the United States, South Africa, and Brazil*. New York: Cambridge University Press.

Marx, Karl. 1956. *The Holy Family*. Moscow: Progress.

Mills, C. Wright. 1959. *The Sociological Imagination*. New York: Oxford University Press.

Moore, Barrington, Jr. 1966. *Social Origins of Dictatorship and Democracy: Lord and Peasant in the Making of the Modern World*. Boston: Beacon Press.

Morgan, Edmund S. 1988. *Inventing the People: The Rise of Popular Sovereignty in England and America*. New York: W. W. Norton.

North, Douglass C. 1995. "Five Propositions about Institutional Change." Pp. 15–26 in *Explaining Social Institutions*, edited by Jack Knight and Itai Sened. Ann Arbor: University of Michigan Press.

Oakes, Guy. 1988. *Weber and Rickert: Concept Formation in the Cultural Sciences*. Cambridge, MA: MIT Press.

Padgett, John. 1990. "Networks and Identities in Political Party Formation: The Case of the Medici in Renaissance Italy." Unpublished manuscript.

Pettit, Philip. 1993. *The Common Mind: An Essay on Psychology, Society, and Politics*. New York: Oxford University Press.

Pierson, Paul. 2000. "Increasing Returns, Path Dependence, and the Study of Politics." *American Political Science Review* 94: 251–68.

Polanyi, Karl. 1944. *The Great Transformation*. New York: Rinehart and Company.

Popper, Karl. 1964. *The Poverty of Historicism*. New York: Harper & Row.

Przeworski, Adam. 1990. "Marxism and Rational Choice." Pp. 62–92 in *Individualism: Theories and Methods*, edited by Pierre Birnbaum and Jean Leca. Oxford: Clarendon Press.

Quattrone, George A. and Amos Tversky. 1988. "Contrasting Rational and Psychological Analyses of Political Choice." *American Political Science Review* 82: 719–36.

Ringer, Fritz. 1997. *Max Weber's Methodology: The Unification of the Cultural and Social Sciences*. Cambridge, MA: Harvard University Press.

Rueschemeyer, Dietrich, Evelyn H. Stephens, and John D. Stephens. 1992. *Capitalist Development and Democracy*. Chicago: University of Chicago Press.

Schattschneider, E. E. 1960. *The Semisovereign People: A Realist's View of Democracy in America*. New York: Holt, Rinehart, and Winston.

Sen, Amartya. 1977. "Rational Fools: A Critique of the Behavioral Foundations of Economic Theory." *Philosophy and Public Affairs* 6: 317–44.

1999. *Reason before Identity: The Romanes Lecture for 1998.* Oxford: Oxford University Press.

Sewell, William, Jr. 1992. "A Theory of Structure: Duality, Agency, and Transformation." *American Journal of Sociology* 98: 1–29.

Silberman, Bernard S. 1993. *Cages of Reason: The Rise of the Rational State in France, Japan, the United States, and Great Britain.* Chicago: University of Chicago Press.

Skocpol, Theda. 1979. *States and Social Revolutions: A Comparative Analysis of France, Russia, and China.* Cambridge: Cambridge University Press.

1992. *Protecting Soldiers and Mothers: The Political Origins of Social Policy in the United States.* Cambridge, MA: Harvard University Press.

Steinmo, Sven and Kathleen Thelen, eds. 1992. *Structuring Politics: Historical Institutionalism in Comparative Analysis.* New York: Cambridge University Press.

Stinchcombe, Arthur L. 1968. *Constructing Social Theories.* New York: Harcourt, Brace, and World.

1978. *Theoretical Methods in Social History.* New York: Academic Press.

Swidler, Ann. 1986. "Culture in Action: Symbols and Strategies." *American Sociological Review* 51: 273–86.

Taylor, Charles. 2001. "Modernity and Identity." Pp. 139–53 in *Schools of Thought: Twenty-Five Years of Interpretive Social Science*, edited by Joan W. Scott and Debra Keates. Princeton, NJ: Princeton University Press.

Thelen, Kathleen. 1999. "Historical Institutionalism in Comparative Politics." *Annual Review of Political Science* 2: 369–404.

Tilly, Charles. 1964. *The Vendée.* Cambridge, MA: Harvard University Press.

1975."Reflections on the History of European State-Making." Pp. 3–83 in *The Formation of National States in Western Europe*, edited by Charles Tilly. Princeton, NJ: Princeton University Press.

1984. *Big Structures, Large Processes, Huge Comparisons.* New York: Russell Sage Foundation.

Waldron, Jeremy. 1990. "How We Learn to Be Good." *Times Literary Supplement* (March): 23–9.

Wallerstein, Immanuel. 1974. *The Modern World-System: Capitalist Agriculture and the Origins of the European World Economy in the Sixteenth Century.* New York: Academic Press.

Wildavsky, Aaron. 1987. "Choosing Preferences by Constituting Institutions: A Cultural Theory of Preference Formation." *American Political Science Review* 81: 3–22.

Zolberg, Aristide. 1972. "Moments of Madness." *Politics and Society* 2: 183–207.

PART III

Issues of Method

9

Can One or a Few Cases Yield Theoretical Gains?

Dietrich Rueschemeyer

I. The Issue

The crux of skepticism about comparative historical analysis is the "small-N problem" – the combination of many factors assumed to be causally relevant with evidence from only a small number of comparable cases. Exploring the impact of a large number of relevant factors and conditions in only a few cases seems to run into insuperable obstacles for learning anything that is theoretically relevant. In this essay, I will turn a skeptical eye on these skeptical objections. I go deliberately to the extreme and ask what can be learned theoretically from the study of a single historical case and from comparative analyses of two or very few more cases, a kind of research that permits close attention to the complexities of historical developments.

I begin with two opposite positions that I consider problematic and in their starkest form mistaken. One of these is the most conventional view, taught in countless classes on the methodology of social research. It holds that studying a single case yields only one reasonable theoretical outcome, the generation of hypotheses that may be tested in other, more numerous cases. And conventional methodological wisdom holds the same

I wish to thank several people for their help and support in writing this essay. The many conversations about the methodology of small-N research I had with Jim Mahoney were both enlightening and encouraging. I also learned much from discussions with the other contributors to this volume. Spending a semester at the Swedish Collegium for Advanced Study in the Social Sciences (SCASSS) was helpful for giving this essay its final shape, and I am grateful to Björn Wittrock, one of the directors of SCASSS, for his comments and suggestions. I dedicate this essay to three historians from whom I learned much over the years: Anthony Molho, Jürgen Kocka, and Hans-Ulrich Wehler.

for single comparisons unless they offer by near-miraculous chance a naturally occurring experiment.[1]

The other position is implied in innumerable assertive historical explanations of singular processes. E. P. Thompson's essay "The Poverty of Theory" offers sophisticated, explicit formulations of such views, though I will argue that its overall argument must be understood in a less historicist way than it at first appears. Thompson develops an extended polemic against "both Popper . . . and Althusser . . . [who] affirm the unknowability of history as a process inscribed with its own causation" (Thompson 1978, p. 34). Taken literally, the claim that history is a process "inscribed with its own causation" represents the exact counterposition to the conventional view of social science methodology. Yet Thompson's argument is more nuanced. Disciplined historical discourse consists, in his view, "in a dialogue between concept and evidence, a dialogue conducted by successive hypotheses on the one hand, and empirical research on the other." This dialogue is focused on a past social development in all its particularity. While it is open to *expectations* that derive from other, similar processes and from neighboring disciplines, "history is not rule-governed."[2]

[1] See for instance the following statements, which Campbell recalls in an article (1975, pp. 179–81) that actually revises his earlier position: "Much research . . . today conforms to a design in which a single group is studied only once, subsequent to some agent or treatment presumed to cause change. . . . such studies have such a total absence of control as to be of almost no scientific value. . . . Any appearance of absolute knowledge, or intrinsic knowledge about singular isolated objects, is found to be illusory upon analysis. Securing scientific evidence involves making at least one comparison" (Campbell and Stanley 1966, pp. 6–7). But comparison with just one other real case will not do either: ". . . while there is a crying need for verifying and extending Malinowski's evidence of Tobriand intrafamilial attitudes, such a replication is of minor importance for testing the Freudian hypothesis. We who are interested in using such data for delineating process rather than describing single instances must accept this rule: *No comparison of a single pair of natural objects is interpretable*" (Campbell 1961, pp. 344–5; *emphasis* in the original). For more sympathetic but ultimately similar views of case studies, see Lijphart (1975) and Smelser (1976).

[2] See Thompson (1978, pp. 39, 49). Thompson elaborates the idea of explanatory *expectations*, to which we will return: "These concepts, which are generalized by logic from many examples, are brought to bear upon the evidence, not so much as 'models' but rather as 'expectations.' They do not impose a rule, but they hasten and facilitate the interrogation of the evidence, even though it is often found that each case departs, in this or that particular, from the rule. The evidence . . . is not rule-governed, and yet it could not be understood without the rule, to which it offers its own irregularities. This provokes impatience in some philosophers (and even sociologists) who consider that a concept with such elasticity is not a true concept, and a rule is not a rule unless the evidence conforms to it, and stands to attention in one place" (Thompson 1978, pp. 45–6). His overall conception of "historical

I will argue in this essay that while any explanation requires theoretical premises, the study of single historical cases can do much more than merely generate initial hypotheses. It not only can develop new theoretical ideas, but it can also put them to the test and use the results in the explanation of outcomes. Moving beyond the first case yields often particularly powerful new insights. At the same time, cross-case variation presents difficult methodological problems for macrosocial analysis, both quantitative and qualitative. In response to these difficulties, I argue that testable and tested explanatory propositions are not the only gains we can derive from the analysis of a limited number of cases. More modest results still constitute worthwhile cognitive advances.

II. Some First Considerations

A prima facie case against the conventional view that little can be learned from single cases is easily made. Quite a few single-case studies rank among the most powerful and influential works in social and political analysis.

A first example is E. P. Thompson's own classic work *The Making of the English Working Class* (1963). In offering its rich and thoroughly argued account, the book refuted certain Marxist accounts of class formation, call them vulgar or naive, and it did so in the historical case that was central to thinking in the Marxian theoretical tradition. As a consequence, it changed the way many scholars thought about class formation. Theory challenge led to new theoretical formulations that focused on variable experiences of deprivation and conflict in similar structural locations and on memories of the past that shaped these experiences as well as the actions that arose from them. The theoretical orientation of class analysis – what was considered the most reasonable and fruitful approach – turned in a less objectivist direction. Thompson's historical account strengthened the view that class formation is a process that cannot be read off from objective conditions, not even in the long run; it is, rather, subject to social construction and cultural circumstance.

Another example is Robert Michels's *Political Parties: A Sociological Study of the Oligarchical Tendencies of Modern Democracy*, one of the big success

logic" is spelled out in colorful polemic language, often full of suggestive ambiguities, in Section vii of the essay *The Poverty of Theory* (Thompson 1978, pp. 37–50).

stories of sociological research.[3] This work took off from the encounter of Michels, a young academic and the son of a Catholic millionaire from Cologne, with the German Social Democratic Party (SPD) before the First World War, a party that represented milieus and interests radically set apart from the bourgeois world of his family and of higher education. True, Michels referred to other European parties as well, focusing on socialist parties as the most prodemocratic, and he developed his ideas within a theoretical frame that was indebted to Max Weber's political and organizational sociology; but the core empirical referent of his analyses was the SPD. Yet the results of this research go far beyond a complex account of structures and processes in the SPD. Michels's central claim, the "iron law of oligarchy," is stated as a universal proposition:

> It is organization which gives birth to the domination of the elected over the electors, of the mandataries over the mandators, of the delegates over the delegators. Who says organization says oligarchy.[4]

This central proposition is supplemented with an explication of the mechanisms that seem to underlie it. *Political Parties*, then, develops and makes plausible a theoretical account of oligarchic tendencies in politically relevant associations. Published before the First World War, it proved to be an accurate prediction of countless processes in political parties and voluntary organizations, it cast doubt on the realism of democratic aspirations, it foreshadowed a critique of the Russian Revolution of 1917, and it anticipated Milovan Djilas's claims in *The New Class: An Analysis of the Communist System* (Djilas 1957).

My third exhibit is a book that responded to Michels's thesis with the analysis of a deviant case. Seymour Martin Lipset, Martin Trow, and James Coleman, having seen Michels's proposition confirmed in many cases, chose to examine a union in which democratic processes led repeatedly to

[3] First published in Germany in 1911, it was soon translated into English as well as French, Italian, Japanese, and other languages. Most recently, it was republished yet another time in English (Michels 1999). Seymour Martin Lipset traces in his introduction the substantive impact of "one of the twentieth century's most influential books" (Michels 1999, p. 20).

[4] This is S. M. Lipset's rendering, opening his introduction. Michels's own words speak of a *tendency toward oligarchy*. This difference in formulation does not, however, transform his claim into a probabilistic one; the tendency is claimed to be present universally, but it may have different strengths; see *Soziologie des Parteiwesens in der modernen Demokratie. Untersuchungen über die oligarchischen Tendenzen des Gruppenlebens*, 2nd ed. (Stuttgart: Alfred Kröner, 1925, p. 25) (italics in the original); the other part of Lipset's summary formulation is found on pp. 370–1 of the German text.

leadership turnover. The title of their book, another of the great empirical classics of sociology, is worth quoting in full: *Union Democracy: The Internal Politics of the International Typographical Union. What Makes Democracy Work in Labor Unions and Other Organizations?* (Lipset, Trow, and Coleman 1956). Against the background of the breakdown of democracy in Europe, the rise and fall of Nazism, and the turn of the Russian Revolution into Stalinism, *Union Democracy* used theoretical arguments that derived from analyses of the breakdown and stability of democracy in national regimes to explore the limits of Michels's iron law about oligarchy in parties and voluntary associations. The new propositions included prominently claims about the critical role of autonomous intermediary groups, claims that have in the last ten to fifteen years found renewed attention under the heading of "civil society." *Union Democracy* challenged an established theory and formulated a new theoretical account that could explain both conforming and deviant cases. It thus embraced as well as transcended Michels's theory, and the detailed analysis of the International Typographical Union (ITU) gave it considerable credibility.

Yet, while even a brief reminder of books such as *The Making of the English Working Class*, *Political Parties*, and *Union Democracy* casts doubt on the proposition that little can be learned theoretically from single-case studies, the conventional view has strong arguments on its side as well and cannot be dismissed by reference to a few extraordinarily successful case studies.

Any explanation, the argument runs, requires propositions with a broader range of application than the phenomena to be explained. Ideally, these propositions should hold – under specified conditions, of course – universally. To be persuasive, the explanatory propositions must be subject to some discipline if one of the many possible explanations is to be chosen over others – that is, if one really cares about one's explanation. Arthur Stinchcombe has suggested that graduate students who cannot think of three explanations when confronted with a correlation that interests them should choose another career (Stinchcombe 1968, p. 13); and one might invoke a similar belief in the cornucopia of reason when dealing with the explanation of historical sequences. Explanatory propositions, then, have to be explicitly developed *and tested* before they can claim the credibility that warrants their use rather than that of competing accounts.

The conventional view distinguishes sharply between the "context of discovery" and the "context of validation" of explanatory propositions. Discovering an idea is seen as a methodologically irrelevant psychological process that may indeed involve one instance of the phenomena to be explained or may be only as tangentially related to the issues at hand as the falling apple that supposedly inspired Isaac Newton in his work on gravity. Even if the explanatory idea is developed in work on one instance of the explanandum, it has to be put to the test in different cases. Discussing the problems of "testing the theory on the body of data that suggested it," one formulation of the conventional view held: "These problems are as real and as defeating for the qualitative essays of the knowledgeable political scientist or historian as for the multivariate statistician. . . . the scholar has an unexplicit but very large number of potential 'considerations' which he has, or could have, brought to bear on one instance or another. This, rather than its pattern-recognition characteristics is the crux of the problems of the *Verstehen* approach – one source of its exquisitely satisfactory fit to particular instances, and its unsatisfactoriness as a reality-testing process" (Raser, Campbell, and Chadwick 1970, pp. 186–7, parentheses omitted).

These arguments make a strong case against taking E. P. Thompson's formulation of "history as a process as inscribed with its own causation" literally. Yet I will show that single cases can indeed do more than inspire new hypotheses and insights. They can serve the purpose of theory testing as well. And even the explanatory use of theory in the same case in which it was developed is not as unreasonable as it first seems.

III. Theory Development, Theory Testing, and Explanatory Use of Theory in a Single Case

Clearly, a single case can force the rejection of a hypothesis or its modification, provided that the proposition in question was not formulated in probabilistic terms. This is not as rare in social analysis as one might think. *Union Democracy* broke the iron cast of Michels's "Who says organization says oligarchy." And a theory of class formation that insists on predicting the collective organization of workers as a class, as well as the goals of their actions as a class from the class members' "objective" relation to the means of production in conjunction with a few further conditions such as urbanization, factory work, and repeated conflicts over pay and work conditions, was rendered untenable by the far more complex, contingent, and constructivist account Thompson offered in *The Making of the English Working Class*.

That single cases can – aside from inspiring theoretical ideas – falsify nonprobabilistic propositions will be readily granted by any neopositivist methodologist. But can a single case history have theoretical implications that go beyond that? This rhetorical question overlooks, first of all, that such falsification may be more complex than the rejection of a single proposition. A long sequence of historical development offers, provided that it is approached with sufficiently specified theoretical expectations, a large number of theoretically relevant observations that may rule out or suggest the revision of a whole series of propositions. Any demonstration of path dependence, dealing for instance with the persistence of a structure of domination that remains stable under conditions that differ substantially from the conditions of its origin, can invalidate – or force the modification of – quite a few claims about the conditions of stable domination. Many hypotheses about the stability of rule are, after all, formulated in a "presentist" way that disregards the interaction of changing current conditions with factors that account for a path-dependent character of the phenomenon.

Aside from falsification, there is also a positive contribution of single cases to theory that many will accept. This is based on the theoretical implications of "least likely" cases, least likely in terms of a widely accepted theory or an implicit theoretical expectation. Such cases, for which Michels's demonstration of oligarchic tendencies in social democratic organizations (i.e., in the very prime promoters of democracy) is a good example, will greatly increase the plausibility of the alternative theoretical understanding they suggest.[5]

That hypotheses, which are developed (or refined) in one case, can be tested and used as explanations in the same case is more counterintuitive. However, good historical explanations, and especially analytically oriented historical studies, do precisely this. Thompson clearly refers inter alia to his own analysis of class formation between 1790 and 1830 in England, when he talks about the dialogue, in which historical practice is characteristically engaged:

> with an argument between received, inadequate, or ideologically-informed concepts or hypotheses on the one hand, and fresh or inconvenient evidence on the other; with the elaboration of new hypotheses; with the testing of these hypotheses against the evidence, which may involve interrogating existing evidence in new ways, or renewed research to confirm or disprove the new notions, with discarding those hypotheses which fail new tests, or refining or revising those which do, in the light of this engagement. (Thompson 1978, p. 43)

[5] The powerful theoretical implications of deviant and least likely cases have long been explicitly recognized (see Eckstein 1975; Lijphart 1971, 1975; Smelser 1976); for a sophisticated recent discussion of what she calls "negative case methodology" see Emigh (1997).

This is precisely what fills the pages of *The Making of the English Working Class*. And the same can be said about Michels's examination of the implications and corollaries of his main claim in *Political Parties*. Part of this multiple creation, testing, revising, and retesting of hypotheses may go unrecorded, but it is this complex process that lies behind the assurance of the authors' claims and the confidence their arguments inspire in the reader. It is above all this dialogue between theory and evidence that constitutes the comparative advantage of comparative historical analysis.

One source of this ever-renewed questioning and testing of hypotheses may be surprising: intense political interest. Given that the standard advice for social and historical analysts urges neutral objectivity, this may be worth a moment's reflection. It is almost certainly true that the authors of all three books I chose here as exemplars were continuously involved in passionate political discussions, with endless iterations of confronting claims with evidence and counterevidence. Political interest can, of course, encourage wishful thinking and lead to blind spots in perceiving social reality. Yet political interest can also create a very strong urge to know, to understand the conditions under which one's aims can be realized, what the major obstacles are, which goals must be considered utopian, what compromises will likely impose themselves, what the consequences of the routinization of passionate commitment will be, and so on. The powerful theoretical results of these three works seem testimony to the realism of this second possibility.

Would it be worthwhile to make the complex dialogue between theoretical imagination and empirical evidence that characterizes so much of comparative historical work explicit? From a methodological point of view, the answer must be an unqualified yes. But insisting on full explication is unlikely to meet with resounding success, because it is at odds with the way many, if not most, historical analysts work. For many, the "context of discovery" is intellectually more closely interrelated with the "context of validation" than the textbooks assume. Many also share Max Weber's distaste for methodological reflection and a bookkeeping of the research process, feeling that it would hamper their work, detract from substantive concerns, and cramp imaginative intuition as well as interesting presentation. Yet, it turns out that authors such as E. P. Thompson – much like Max Weber – are quite capable of methodological argument when controversy requires it, and that in the face of contention about their findings, much of the iterative analytic interrogation of the evidence can be recovered.

Thompson – other than Michels or Lipset, Trow, and Coleman – was only in a limited way interested in making theoretical claims beyond an elucidation and explanation of the particular historical developments he studied. True, he sought to reject an "economistic" theory of class formation; but that aside, his theory–evidence dialogue remained confined to component developments in the rise of working-class consciousness in four decades of English history, seeking to establish, for instance, that and how earlier cultural patterns (and not only new employment relations or the distribution of economic resources) shaped the experience and the meaning of exploitation in different groups of workers.

The distinction between analytically oriented history, which focuses on the explanation of particular developments, and a history-conscious social science primarily interested in the propositions usable in various historical explanations marks important differences in intellectual style; but one must not overestimate its significance. The theoretical core of both kinds of work consists in the development and validation of explanatory causal hypotheses. Yet in order to bridge the gap that separates the self-understanding of many historians from that of other social scientists, it may be worthwhile to focus a little longer on the more implicit analytic work of the historian than on the self-conscious theorizing of historical social scientists.

Thompson's focus on a bundle of historical explanations, which together account for the emergence of a coherent working class with a particular consciousness and organization, has been understood as a general hostility toward theory. And since he was very much concerned with people's *experience* of changing objective conditions and their understanding of that experience, his work has been construed as interpretive rather than causal analysis.[6] Neither reading takes sufficient notice of Thompson's abiding interest in developing, testing, and using causal and structural hypotheses. A footnote to the text quoted earlier explains:

> By "concepts" (or notions) I mean general categories – of class, ideology, the nation-state, feudalism, &c., or specific historical forms and sequences, as crisis of subsistence, familial development cycle, &c. – and by "hypotheses" I mean the conceptual organization of the evidence to explain particular episodes of causation and relationship. (Thompson 1978, p. 43)

His choice of words makes it clear that he wishes to stay close to the actual process of historical analysis and keep his distance from the formal prescriptions of social science methodology; but there is no ambiguity about his interest in explanatory propositions.

[6] See Trimberger (1984, pp. 225–30), who reports on the first critique and argues the second.

Even if confined to microexplanations within the overall historical account of the "making of the English working class," these propositions are different from sheer narrative, and they are so distinguished by Thompson. Here is how he describes the construction of narrative by historians:

> The discrete facts may be interrogated . . . as *links in a linear series* of occurrences, or contingent events – that is, history "as it actually happened" (but as it can never be fully known) – in the construction of a narrative account; such a reconstruction (however much it may be despised by philosophers, by sociologists, and by an increasing number of contemporary historians who have been frightened by the first two) being *an essential constituent of the historical discipline*, a pre-requisite and premise of all historical knowledge, the ground of any objective (as distinct from theoretic) notion of causation, and the indispensable preliminary to the construction of an analytic or structured account (which identifies structural and causal relations), even though in the course of such an analysis the primitive sequential narration will itself undergo radical transformation.[7]

Yet Thompson remains skeptical about full-scale causal accounts: "History is not rule governed, and it knows no sufficient causes." It can learn "*how* things turned out . . . not why they *had* to turn out that way" (Thompson 1978, p. 49). This reservation about sufficient causes may at first surprise. Yet it seems often – though not always – reasonable, and this on two grounds. First, it corresponds to the sense of historical actors that the future is open. To recover this sense about historical processes, even though we know the outcome, is critical for the historical imagination. Whether such a sense of openness is actually realistic depends, of course, on the processes in question. Some outcomes may be quite determined – reasonable

[7] Thompson (1978, p. 29). Looking at the same issue with a primary interest in explanatory theory, Arthur Stinchcombe comes to a very similar view: "All the books I choose to analyze are narratives of a sequence of events, and this choice is central to my argument. I believe that the test of any theory of social change is its ability to analyze such narrative sequences, and that the poverty of the theory of social change is due to paying no attention to that narrative detail. . . . for the purpose of advancing causal understanding, the unique sequence . . . has to be broken up into theoretically understandable bits. When those bits get back into the narrative, having been theoretically interpreted, the narrative will also be improved by being grounded in general ideas" (Stinchcombe 1978, p. 15). John Stephens and I discussed the same point more recently: "Causation is a matter of sequence. One needs diachronic evidence, evidence about historical sequences, to explore and test ideas about causation directly. This remains true even if it is also true that simple historical narrative is not the same as causal explanation. *Post hoc* does not any more translate directly into *propter hoc* than correlation demonstrates causation. Explanation can indeed not proceed without analytic hypotheses; but causal explanation ordinarily needs hypotheses about sequence which can best be tested against evidence about sequences" (Rueschemeyer and Stephens 1997, pp. 55–72).

examples are the reproduction of institutions such as marriage or private property in many known societies – while others, such as the outcomes of wars or such achievements "against the odds" as large-scale working-class organization or the unification of independent political units, are or were indeed open. Close historical examination can often yield some reasonable estimate on these alternatives. It appears, however, that many outcomes are not just determined but overdetermined. The continuation of private property rights over large sections of productive capital in most Western political economies and the persistence of many lines of ethnic division are probably good instances of such overdetermination. So many phenomena seem, in fact, to fall into this category that a functionalist might be tempted to draw the mistaken conclusion that all really important outcomes tend to be overdetermined. Ironically, this phenomenon of overdetermination offers another reason for reserve about claims of sufficient causes: if more than one condition is sufficient to account for an outcome, it becomes clearly more difficult (though not impossible in principle) to identify different singly sufficient causes.

Whether the primary interest is in historical explanation or in the generation of theoretical propositions, detailed case analyses often entail the generation, testing, revising, and retesting of explanatory propositions within the same complex material. The discipline that in such endeavors is imposed on willful interpretation and speculation derives from the often large number of theoretically relevant observations and from the fact that, for each of these, analytic intent and empirical evidence can be fairly closely matched, more closely than is possible in many studies with large *N*s. This is also the gist of Donald Campbell's "revisionist" article on the value of anthropological case studies:

> In a case study done by an alert social scientist who has thorough local acquaintance, the theory he uses to explain the focal difference also generates predictions or expectations on dozens of other aspects of the culture, and he does not retain the theory unless most of these are confirmed. In some sense, he has tested the theory with degrees of freedom coming from the multiple implications of any one theory. The process is a kind of pattern-matching . . . in which there are many aspects of the patterns demanded by theory that are available for matching with his observations on the local setting.

Campbell likens this mode of analysis to knowledge construction in everyday life, and he concludes his article with an observation that hints at the evolutionary basis of human cognitive efficiency: "after all, man is, in his ordinary way, a very competent knower, and qualitative common sense is not replaced by quantitative knowing."[8]

To claim that anthropological interpretations of cultural patterns and the explanations of historical processes involve a complex interrelation of theory development, theory testing, and the explanatory use of theoretical propositions runs counter to a standard maxim of conventional methodology: disregard confirming observations that were known at the time the proposition was formulated. Some such "peaking" is unavoidable in historical sociology. It is after all less than likely that people who are truly ignorant of the history to be analyzed will do a worthwhile job. Small wonder that Arthur Stinchcombe opens his argument in *Theoretical Methods in Social History* with an invective "... against the fashion of discussing the relation of theory to facts, sired by Kant, foaled by the Vienna School, and raced past us in our statistics textbooks.... the whole Kantian idea contradicts our everyday experience of research. We do not form a historical interpretation before finding out what was going on. Only respect for philosophical appearances could generate such an outcome" (Stinchcombe 1978, p. 4). It is also common knowledge that the maxim is routinely violated in quantitative research as well. Yet unavoidable and common in normal research experience or not, does peaking make confirmation too easy? That may be a danger in relatively simple studies. In much historical work of quality, however, an explanatory or structural proposition has, together with its various corollaries and implications, to meet a very large number of diverse "data points," so that it is often not easy to settle on any one account, no matter how much of the evidence was – in some sense – known in advance. Arthur Stinchcombe may be right that any intelligent person can respond to isolated correlations (as well as simple sequences of events) with three, four, or five accounts, but that view does not apply to more complex patterns of evidence.[9]

[8] Campbell (1975, pp. 181–2, 191). Substantively, Campbell's article is somewhat awkward testimony for the case I am making. His central example is E. H. Erikson's interpretation of Yurok culture and personality in terms of psychoanalytic notions of fixation, a mode of analysis that is perhaps less plausible today than it was in 1943, when the study was published, or in 1975, when Campbell referred to it ("... its initial implausibility is made worse in the following oversimplification: rather than an oral or anal fixation, the Yurok were fixated on the whole alimentary canal" [p. 184]). Yet surely the rejection of this example would not invalidate the revised methodological argument.

[9] Campbell notes: "Even in a single qualitative case study the conscientious social scientist often finds no explanation that seems satisfactory" (1975, p. 182). In our discussion with John Goldthorpe, John Stephens and I took a certain pleasure in pointing out that Goldthorpe himself was unable to offer an adequate theoretical account for his very impressive comparative quantitative findings about social mobility (Rueschemeyer and Stephens 1997, p. 69).

Can One or a Few Cases Yield Theoretical Gains?

If it is true that historical research often involves theory development as well as theory testing and explanatory theory use, it is also true that the studies that have yielded the most analytic insight were informed by intensive advance theoretical reflection. The results of this reflection may have remained largely implicit or they may have been stated as an explicit theoretical framework of questions, concepts, orienting ideas, and central hypotheses.[10] Such reflection not only shapes the questions and the premises of the case analysis, it also links them to earlier scholarship and thus to analytic work on other instances of the issues under investigation. It therefore increases – if indirectly – the number of cases on which conclusions are built.

> As in everyday life we can gain powerful insights from a few encounters because these are assessed against the experience of a lifetime, so the theoretical framework – when informed by previous thought and research – provides the background against which the picture of the cases studied yields more telling results. (Rueschemeyer et al. 1992, p. 38)

The role of such a theoretical framework must be clarified a little further, and Arthur Stinchcombe offers a good foil. He opens his book on *Theoretical Methods in Social History* with the assertion that what is usually called "theory" is irrelevant for analytically oriented historical investigation: "When it comes down to analysis of specific cases, I would argue that when they do a good job of historical interpretation, Marx and Weber and Parsons and Trotsky and Smelser all operate the same way" (Stinchcombe 1978, p. 2). He rejects grand meta-theories as "dross" and looks for propositions that actually can explain historical processes. Does this mean that the theoretical frameworks I just referred to are in Stinchcombe's judgment also just dross? The theoretical frameworks I have in mind are not empirical theories; they are not primarily ensembles of testable propositions, though they may contain some of those. To a large extent, they consist of problem formulations, conceptualizations, and reasons given for these. These reasons, which prepare causal analysis by pointing to factors likely to

[10] In Barrington Moore's *The Social Origins of Dictatorship and Democracy* (1966), this remained largely implicit. By contrast, Theda Skocpol opened her *States and Social Revolutions* (1979) with a review of the literature and a formulation of her structuralist approach. In *Capitalist Development and Democracy*, Evelyne Huber Stephens, John Stephens, and I made the formulation of a theoretical framework an explicit part of our procedure that informed the country analyses, which of course allowed for additional hypotheses and which could – and did – lead to a partial reformulation of the framework (Rueschemeyer, Stephens, and Stephens 1992).

be relevant for different outcomes, often constitute what Thompson calls "theoretical expectations."[11] In a formal sense, theoretical frameworks are largely meta-theoretical in character, as they contain few directly testable hypotheses; but – and this is critical – these frameworks are meta-theory that is problem-specific, dealing with class formation, organizational democracy, or the growth of welfare state policies. As *focused meta-theory*, theoretical frameworks are in their specificity very different from the grand theoretical schemes of, say, functionalist systems theory or historical and dialectical materialism. They are immediately preparatory to what Stinchcombe looks for, testable explanatory propositions, and I believe that they greatly advance the cause of such explanatory theory.

The result of these reflections about inquiries into single historical cases can be summed up simply. Such case studies can do more than generate theoretical ideas. They can test theoretical propositions as well, and they can offer persuasive causal explanations. Skepticism about this claim rests ultimately on the mistaken identification of a single case with a single observation. Good historical analysis that is analytically oriented goes through frequent iterations of confronting explanatory propositions with many data points. If this confrontation does not proceed with the quantitative use of standardized items but typically works in a qualitative way, examining many different implications of the explanatory propositions entertained, it nevertheless involves many such empirical checks. And it gains its credibility precisely from the fit between theoretical ideas and their complex implications, on the one hand, and the best empirical evidence, on the other. In this confrontation of theoretical claims with empirical evidence, analytical history enjoys two significant advantages compared to all but the most exceptional quantitative research: it permits a much more direct and frequently repeated interplay between theoretical development and data, and it allows for a closer matching of conceptual intent and empirical evidence.

Before I move to some consideration of the analytic gains to be made by going beyond a single case, one implication of the argument developed up to this point should be made explicit. A good deal of the extant quantitative research is confined to a single country or a single community. This research, though proceeding with different techniques of data collection and analysis, is as much confined to a single case as is good analytic historical work that deals with, say, the emergence of a partially organized working class in one country.

[11] See footnote 3.

IV. Going beyond a Single Case

When exploring what can be gained from going beyond the confines of a single case, we must confront two deceptively simple questions: What is a case? And where are its boundaries?[12] The claim that analytically oriented historical case studies develop and test many explanatory hypotheses and in the process make use of large numbers of theoretically relevant observations might be countered with the objection that it is deceptive to speak here of a single case. In reality, it might be argued, these studies agglomerate congeries of explained phenomena into what is then presented as one case.

This argument has an apparent justification when applied to Michels's *Political Parties*. Not only did Michels include references to socialist parties other than the SPD or to organizations other than parties, such as unions, but his central argument is also demonstrated in local and regional organizations as well as in the national party. This is in fact the way his analysis was taken by Lipset, Trow, and Coleman, when they studied the ITU in New York as a deviant case. Yet in another sense, Michels's empirical study did aim primarily at the SPD – possibly, by extension, at the continental European socialist movement – since it represented the political force with the strongest claim to truly democratic goals. In this broader sense, the "case" here is an ensemble of socialist parties and related organizations in neighboring countries. It thus transcends national borders; but while nation-states are frequently chosen as units of analysis in comparative historical studies (for the good reason that many important factors are associated with national-state organization), aggregates of interrelated organizations that cut across national boundaries can surely constitute a case as well.

To say that we deal here not just with many observations but many cases does not even have face plausibility when applied to Thompson's *Making of the English Working Class* or to *Union Democracy*. In both works there are indeed many separate explanatory arguments based on numerous observations, but the aim is clearly to give an account of the formation of an organized and self-conscious national class and the functioning of a democratic electoral system in the ITU.

[12] I do not mean to enter here into all the fundamental questions that are raised by the contributors to the symposium edited by Charles Ragin and Howard Becker, *What Is a Case?* (Ragin and Becker 1992), though a fuller treatment than is possible in this essay would have to do so.

The upshot of these mere glances at our three initial examples is an answer to the questions that is simple in principle yet quite complex in actual use: What is a case? and Where are its boundaries? are questions whose answer depends on the theoretical problem posed. Even E. P. Thompson's work can be taken as a number of cases in which past cultural patterns shape the work and life experiences of different working-class groups, and these repeated causal accounts within the overall story give the analysis much of its credibility. Or it can be read as what it presents itself as: the account of one complex historical development. Whether we deal with one case or a complex of instances, then, is another issue to be decided by the theoretical framework that defines problems, proposes conceptualizations, and gives reasons for these decisions, whether that framework is only implied by the analysis or made explicit, and even whether the framing is offered by the original author or is later imposed by a secondary analyst.

Anybody who has ever engaged in macrocomparative research knows of the impressive gains that can be reaped when one moves across boundaries within which causally important but theoretically perhaps unrecognized factors are held constant. This is quite often the case when we move across societal, national, and/or cultural boundaries. One can conceptualize this move as a shift from within-system analysis to system-level analysis (cf. Przeworski and Teune 1970; Schriewer 1999, pp. 56–8), though I would prefer not to put it in the terms of system theory language. The critical point here is simple: only by going beyond the first case does the impact of factors on the outcomes of interest come into view that does not show up in within-case analyses because these factors are – completely or largely – held constant.

A recent example is found in Robert Putnam's attempts to explain his findings about a decline of civic engagement in the United States since the 1970s. Putnam first emphasized the increased labor force participation of women, while later giving greater weight to the impact of television. The second explanation was made plausible with a complex analysis of the development of television viewing and the generational aspects of the decline in social participation in the United States (Putnam 1995a, 1995b, 1998). Though not uncontested in the light of American evidence (e.g., Norris 1996), these explanations run into much more potent problems when viewed in the light of elementary cross-national comparison. Norway and Sweden have higher women's labor force participation rates than the United States, yet they have experienced no significant decline in social and political participation. Similar and equally strong objections arise from even a superficial cross-national comparison linking increasing television viewing to a decline in civic engagement.

At a minimum, these comparisons suggest further research questions about contextual factors that appear salient when Northwestern European patterns and developments are contrasted with those in the United States. Institutions and regulations supporting women's labor force participation are more developed in Scandinavia, and these may well support both work outside the house and civic engagement. More broadly, contrasts in the associations and parties appealing to the public as well as in the overall pattern of political opportunities may be as important for civic engagement as aggregate changes in individual needs and interests. In Scandinavia, unions and political parties are organizationally stronger and more involving than they have been in the post–New Deal United States, and a wide range of associations are more closely interrelated with public institutions and public resources than all their counterparts in the United States. It is quite possible that the major explanations for the differences in social and political participation are found at the mesolevel of associations and parties and at the macrolevel of national political opportunities rather than at the aggregate micro level of changed individual preoccupations (Rueschemeyer, Rueschemeyer, and Wittrock 1998).

Max Weber's work on law and the rise of capitalism provides another example of the striking effect of moving the analysis beyond a single case. Weber developed a pure type of "formally rational" law that guarantees a maximum of the calculability that he considered necessary for the sustained development of a capitalist order. In his formally rational formula, the formal character of a legal order refers to its differentiation from the substantive concerns of religion, morality, and political interest, while rationality means in Weber's sociology of law the universal and systematic character of legal rules. If the "ideal type" of formally rational law is in the first place a complex pure construct, to which the multiplicity of historical phenomena can be compared, it represents at the same time an embryonic theory, because it is joined to the claim that economic calculability is the greater the more closely a particular legal order approximates the pure type. This claim appeared to be substantiated by the character of continental legal systems, especially the German legal system, which became highly rationalized, even before unification, in the course of capitalist development. However, the case of England presented a challenge. The English legal order exhibited a much lower degree of both formalism and rationality. Yet England was the first country to develop vibrant capitalist growth.

Weber never came to a firm solution of this "English problem"; but he considered a series of alternative hypotheses, which demonstrate the powerful effect of moving comparatively beyond the macrocontext in which the original proposition was developed:

> (1) The English legal system offered a low degree of calculability but assisted capitalism by denying justice to the lower classes. (2) England was unique in that it achieved capitalism "not because but rather in spite of its judicial system." The conditions allowing this, however, did not prevail anywhere else. (3) The English legal system, while far from the model of logically formal rationality, was sufficiently calculable to support capitalism since judges were favorable to capitalists and adhered to precedent....
>
> [Another hypothesis was developed later:]... the English judiciary was to a significant degree independent of the state, so that autonomy in this sense remains part of the model. Because of this latter aspect of English legal life, some observers have argued that England did develop a truly "rational" legal system before the rise of capitalism, and that the major flaw of Weber's analysis was the false distinction he drew between English and continental law. (Trubek 1972, pp. 747–8, notes omitted)

Going beyond boundaries within which causally relevant factors may be held constant, then, brings substantial gain. Both Putnam's explanation of the decline of civic engagement in the United States and Weber's account of the relation between the character of the legal system and the chances of capitalist development can be substantially improved by examining intensively one more case that seems to challenge the first version. (In the interest of space, we have to leave the substantive questions raised by the two examples behind; such is the annoying disregard of methodological discussions for the real world.)

The contrast in the explanandum may sometimes be due to a major new factor not previously considered, as in one combination of Weber's alternative hypotheses about England: what made capitalist development possible was not predictable law, but the more direct favors of the judicial system to capitalist entrepreneurs. At other times, an empirically substantiated explanation of the different outcome in the second case may not so much reveal new factors as a different interaction among otherwise well-known factors that are equally visible in both cases; our conjecture about the differences in the impact of labor force participation of women on civic engagement between the United States and Scandinavia offers an – as yet unsubstantiated – example of this.

Of course, dual case studies very rarely can settle questions about the impact of factors that differ across cases. This would be possible only in the rare constellation where theoretical predictions come to definite stipulations that are contradicted by the second case – the second-case equivalent of the falsification of nonprobabilistic claims by a single case. Considerable increases in the plausibility of theoretical claims can be gained if the second case is in light of theory and for specified reasons least likely to confirm it – the second-case equivalent of Michels's choice of a social democratic party as least likely to be undemocratic.

Beyond this, increasing the number of cross-case comparisons without losing the advantage of close familiarity with the complexity of cases becomes imperative. Hypotheses about factors that differ across large-case boundaries – that is, all hypotheses about macrosocial phenomena – require testing against a larger, though not necessarily a very large number of cases. Increasing the number of macrocomparative cases raises complex questions of case selection and of defining the most appropriate total set of comparable cases. For both, full-scale hypotheses and the expectations embodied in focused theoretical frameworks are of critical importance, though extensions of the analysis beyond a single case often operate with a great deal of ignorance about the dynamics of the phenomenon under study outside the first context of analysis. In this essay, I will not go further into these matters of case selection and domain definition.[13]

The issues of macrocomparative analysis are normally discussed in an order that I reversed in this essay. The usual starting points are cross-case comparisons and the problems of such comparisons raised by the small number of cases. I will not rehearse here again the considerable methodological refinements that have been achieved in dealing with these problems, since they are treated in the essay by Mahoney in this volume. But I do wish to emphasize that the perspective gained by focusing first on the theoretical gains achieved through within-case analysis puts the problems of cross-case analyses in a different light. As Mahoney (2000 and in this volume) makes clear, within-case analyses complement in important ways different modes of cross-case exploration. In particular, a procedure he calls "causal narrative" directly combines within-case causal sequences with cross-case identification of likely causal factors.[14]

[13] For an excellent treatment see Collier and Mahoney (1996).

[14] "A good example of the use of causal narrative to compare event structures is found in Skocpol's (1979) work on social revolutions. Many of Skocpol's key explanatory variables are actually made up of numerous causally linked processes. Likewise, the outcome of social revolutions is itself composed of a series of causally connected events. These constituent processes represent an event-structure pattern that could be formally diagrammed and compared across cases (see Mahoney 1999). Although Skocpol does not carry out a formal

A final point about comparative advantages that analytically oriented historical work on a small number of closely understood cases enjoys over quantitative cross-national studies employing multiple regression for its causal inferences should at least be adumbrated. Even though the procedures used in analytic historical research have remained until recently largely implicit, comparative historical analysis has shown itself better able to deal with certain problems that cause trouble for multiple regression analysis when it deals with macrocausal issues and therefore relatively small numbers of cases. Thus, comparative historical work that uses both within-case and cross-case analysis can explore more complex interactions among causal factors, it can better trace multiple paths of causation, and it does not make the assumption of a linear relation between independent and dependent variables that – in the absence of historical information suggesting other relations between causal factors and outcomes – multiple regression analyses often adopt.[15]

V. And Yet There Are Limits to the Theoretical Results of Single and Small-N Case Studies

It is one thing to dispel myths about single-case and comparative historical analysis; it is quite another to claim that qualitative macroanalyses encounter few or no serious methodological problems. Despite considerable advances in making explicit what shrewd and careful comparative historical scholars have practiced for a long time, there is little reason for a triumphalist assertion of the value of small-*N*/close-acquaintance studies.

Comparative historical analysis does not and cannot follow a radically different logic from other investigations of reality, be it in the social or the natural sciences. The two major recent publications on the methodology of qualitative research rightly insist on this point: both *The Comparative Method*

mapping of event structures, she does implicitly compare the event structures of her cases to judge whether they follow a similar causal logic at a disaggregated level. According to Sewell (1996), Skocpol's ability to show [that] a similar event structure is at work in each case of social revolutions greatly contributes to the persuasiveness of her argument" (Mahoney 2000, p. 416).

[15] I learned much on these issues from an article on limits of multiple regression in comparative research on advanced welfare states that Michael Shalev made available to me, even though he does not yet want to have it cited in any detail (Shalev 1998–9). I should note, however, that the alternatives Shalev favors are not comparative historical analyses but simpler forms of quantitative analysis that frankly acknowledge the consequences of the limited number of cases, which are at the disposal of comparative studies of welfare states.

by Charles Ragin (1987) and *Designing Social Inquiry* by Gary King, Robert Keohane, and Sidney Verba (1994) hold that qualitative and quantitative research follow in principle the same underlying logic.[16] This means above all that the hypotheses developed and used in analytic historical work must be checked systematically and in complex multiple ways against empirical evidence. I have argued that this testing in fact takes place in many historical case analyses, though both the raw fact of massive empirical testing and the various sophisticated modes of hypothetically identifying, tracing, and comparing causal sequences have often remained implicit.

Yet comparative historical macroanalysis of cross-case similarities and differences does run into difficulties that are related to the small number of cases available for study. The point is not only the immediate issue of too few cases chasing too many causal factors. This is a disabling problem for many cross-case analyses, though it may not loom as large as many critics assert. Combinations of within-case and cross-case comparison can alleviate it, at least to some extent. Furthermore, nominal comparisons based on deterministic assumptions about the underlying causes do not require large numbers of cases to acquire statistical significance (Mahoney 2000, pp. 395–6, citing Dion 1998). And under some circumstances, it is possible to examine a fairly large number of cases without losing a close acquaintance with each of the histories (see Rueschemeyer et al. 1992). Still, the small number of cases is a serious handicap of macrocomparative research.

Some are inclined to argue that with various assumptions about the underlying structures of reality and thus about causality (see Hall, this volume) and with much increased methodological refinement, small-*N* historical studies have reached a level of validity comparable to that of the larger-*N* model of mainstream methodology. Thus, comparative historical analysis should be granted the same standing as quantitative research. The main problem I see here concerns precisely the different underlying assumptions about causal patterns in social reality. While we have guesses about these "ontological" patterns, it is difficult to find out more about the realism of

[16] Ragin's book is largely a defense of qualitative methods and an attempt to upgrade the level of methodological reflection and practice among qualitative researchers. King, Keohane, and Verba take methodological reflections on quantitative research as their starting point and draw from these conclusions for qualitative research. It is true that greater methodological reflection is one of the strengths of the quantitative research tradition. Yet as indicated, methodological reflection has greatly advanced in comparative historical analysis. A review of King et al.'s book that acknowledges both, yet points out that much can be gained by a more equal dialogue, is Munck (1998).

such causal models because of the limitations of the evidence, including very importantly the numerical limitations of cross-case analysis. At the same time, it is worth noting that these limitations are ultimately shared by quantitative work as well, because multiple regression analysis also presupposes models of causality that may very well not be realistic.[17]

When, for example, and on what grounds can we make the assumption that a set of causes can reasonably be conceived of as deterministic, thus making nominal comparison the procedure of choice? In nominal comparisons, a single deviation leads to the rejection of a hypothesis, but a quite limited number of strategic confirmations increases the credibility of the analysis dramatically. Similar questions arise from any other set of assumptions about causal patterns. It is in this broader sense that we also have to view the age-old arguments that derive from a causal logic embodied in experimental designs, that in macrocausal analysis it is not only impossible to "rerun history" but also extremely difficult to approximate the experimental causal logic with randomization. I consider the limitations an inevitably small number of cases imposes on our exploration of these underlying assumptions ultimately as the most serious of the different small-*N* problems.

I will conclude these reservations about the theoretical claims that can be derived from historical macrocausal comparisons with an even broader reflection. The revival of comparative historical analysis a generation ago was largely a rebellion against the vacuous conceptual schemes of grand theory, of functionalist modernization theory, and of a neo-Marxism that had turned highly scholastic. This rebellion was also a retreat from the ideal standard for comparative social inquiry that demands replacement of *proper names* of phenomena that are located in a particular time and space with *variables* that are specified independently of a particular time and place (Przeworski and Teune 1970, pp. 24–6). In the ideal world of logic this is a persuasive standard. It was not attained by the grand research programs that dominated the first long generation after the Second World War. But if we had to give up on it in order to gain the advantage of nontrivial substantive explanations of important outcomes, it may be useful to be clear about the loss. Historically delimited explanations – historically

[17] Another, more trivial but no less telling reason why quantitative macrostudies often share the limitations of small-*N* comparative historical research is that for many issues a large number of comparable cases simply does not exist. These limitations are accentuated when, as is often the case, quantitative cross-case analyses confine themselves to the examination of standardized case features and are not complemented by within-case causal tracing.

delimited in the causal patterns they claim and in the domains within which the causal relations are said to hold – inevitably involve an endless number of unspecified conditions because unique historical phenomena are inherently related to everything under the sun. Measured against the ideal standard, this is a truly unsatisfactory state of affairs for which no solution is in sight.

VI. Tested Empirical Hypotheses and Persuasive Explanations Are Not the Only Worthwhile Products of Comparative Research

The inherent difficulties of macrocomparative research suggest not very optimistic conclusions. On the one hand, we can make plausible that variations in the macrocontext have causally relevant consequences for many important phenomena and processes. On the other, we clearly have trouble even envisioning a state of knowledge that conforms to positivist idealizations of how valid knowledge is gained. Even by much more modest standards, it must be said that sociology and political science are generally not rich in powerful explanatory hypotheses that are not already put into question by known evidence. Eckstein (1975, p. 99) spoke a generation ago about an "*embarras de pauvreté*," and the situation has hardly been turned around substantially since then. One response to this has been a theoretical nihilism that underlies the more extreme versions of postmodern relativism.

Given the dearth of tested theoretical propositions about nontrivial issues, not to mention coherent bundles of them worthy of the more elevated conceptions of theory, it seems that the sophistication of our methodological discourse has outrun our theoretical achievements. Furthermore, since some fields of inquiry are more suited than others for implementing methodological rules that are in principle sound, these (partial) successes are all too often used to legitimate attacks on the actual procedures used in other fields. This is in spite of the fact that the research questions pursued in these other fields may well be – and are in fact likely to be – relevant for comprehensive answers in the methodologically more advanced fields as well. All social science explanations are, after all, partial, leaving a substantial amount of the variation in the explananda unaccounted for. That partial accounts can be thoroughly misleading is captured in the old saying "A little learning is a dangerous thing." The same point is made more drastically in the joke about the drunk who, when asked why he looks for his keys under the street lamp, answers: "Because here I can see."

What I have in mind is, however, more than a plea for an armistice in the fights between quantitative and qualitative inquiry. I wish to argue that while we should not lose sight of the desirability of fully specified and tested hypotheses, we have to come to appreciate a much less impressive but also more subtle and nuanced learning as well. Comparative historical analysis has yielded some powerful theoretical propositions, as well as many plausible explanations of interesting historical developments that use more specific, albeit often historically circumscribed, explanatory hypotheses. Yet it has also contributed much more to our understanding of large and important processes of change. These contributions range from specifying *conceptual equivalencies* across political, social, and cultural boundaries through the *identification of universal or quite general problems* that occur in varied historical contexts to the development of highly *focused theoretical frameworks* that are indispensable for analytic historical research even if they themselves are not (yet) testable theories. I will discuss briefly some of these more limited theoretical advances. In each, comparative historical analysis has been of great importance, and it was so primarily for two reasons: because of its insistence on pursuing important issues comparatively even against the odds of methodological difficulties and because of the lively theoretical engagement with the evidence that is characteristic of this work.

Half a century ago, Robert Merton argued for "middle range theories" against the grand conceptual constructions of Talcott Parsons (Merton [1949] 1968), and T. H. Marshall made a similar plea for what he called "stepping stone theories." Yet if we inspect more closely a paradigmatic specimen of middle range theory, namely, reference group theory, we make an interesting discovery. Both in its version that deals with cognitive estimates, explaining for instance the perceived chances for promotion in different branches of the military, and in its application to normative orientations, pointing for instance to the role of anticipatory socialization in the course of career advancement, reference group theory instills a good sense of explanation but it is not able to predict. The reason is clear: it does not specify sufficiently *what* is "referred" to, *by whom*, and *under which conditions*. It represents a causal hypothesis, but one whose conditions are insufficiently specified. Such underspecification is characteristic of many theoretical propositions that have recently found much attention under the label of "mechanisms." These are often, in the ironic formulation of James Coleman and Arthur Stinchcombe, "bits of sometimes true theory."[18]

[18] For the recent revival of interest in mechanisms see Hedström and Swedberg (1998) and, earlier, Stinchcombe (1991). For the ironic formulation see Stinchcombe (1998, p. 267) and Coleman (1964, pp. 516–19).

Incomplete theoretical propositions of this kind are commonplace in contemporary social science. Most models of rational action theory have the same character, as they make underspecified assumptions about what people or organizations are after, how they understand their situation, and by which norms and values they are guided and constrained. And many of the – implied or explicated – propositions that analytically oriented historians deploy in their causal accounts are similarly underspecified.

And yet, it is hard to deny that such bits of sometimes true theory constitute real advances in knowledge. Reference group theory, arguing that cognitive assessments tend to be informed by references to certain kinds of experience, prevents the naive substitution of the observer's estimate of the "objective" situation for the understandings and assessments of the people observed. The rational choice analysis that identified the "collective action problem" prevents us from assuming that interests shared by a large number of people or organizations will inevitably or almost always lead to coordinated action. If neither is sufficiently specific to be tested directly, they do give a useful new orientation to the study of common problems.[19]

A second category of theoretical results that are easily underestimated if our attention centers exclusively on testable and tested hypotheses are the *focused theoretical frameworks* for the study of particular substantive problem areas to which I have referred a number of times. These are of profound importance. Theoretical frameworks that identify research problems and offer useful conceptualizations, as well as give reasons for problem choice and the conceptual identification of relevant factors, shape the analysis of a given set of problems and are in turn reformulated in light of the results. They are in one sense meta-theories, but in contrast to traditional grand social theory, they are subject- and problem-specific meta-theories. I characterize them as meta-theories, because they are not directly testable but seek to establish the most fruitful intellectual framework for the investigation. As such, however, they have been of critical importance in comparative historical

[19] On reference group theory see Merton (1968). Ironically, Merton had, in the opening chapters of the same seminal volume of essays on sociological theory, distinguished between "theoretical orientations" of a meta-theoretical character and theoretical propositions in the narrower sense. My earlier comments suggest that the theories of the middle range, on which he placed his bets for the future of social analysis, are actually best understood as instances of the former rather than the latter. As such, they can become important components of the next category of underestimated theoretical results, focused theoretical frameworks.

research. Thompson (1978, pp. 45–6) speaks of the same thing when he characterizes the use of explanatory *expectations* in historical investigation:

> They do not impose a rule, but they hasten and facilitate the interrogation of the evidence, even though it is often found that each case departs, in this or that particular, from the rule. The evidence . . . is not rule-governed, and yet it could not be understood without the rule, to which it offers its own irregularities.

Thompson's own reformulation of Marxist ways of framing class formation, emphasizing the lasting effect of socially grounded cultural patterns and the important element of social construction in the formation of class organization and class goals, is a good example of such a subject-specific meta-theory.[20] The most important advances in social and political theory, I submit, are not found in empirically testable and tested specific propositions of universal applicability but in theoretical frameworks of *tested usefulness* for the study of particular areas of analysis, say of class formation, of revolutions, or of constitutional change.

A much less accomplished and yet cognitively very respectable advance that may result from the dialogue between theoretical expectations and evidence in historical case studies is the identification of *universal or quite general problems*, the variable responses to which are still poorly understood. The collective action problem offers one of many examples: both its severity and the variety of successful and unsuccessful responses by different actors in historical specific situations are ill understood in spite of the significant advances in theoretically framing the problem in such different areas as the analysis of social movements or state–society relations.[21] Another, more specific problem of this kind that has been examined in a number of varied comparative historical investigations is the social organization of expert services that deploy superior knowledge to the solution of urgent and important problems of a clientele that is less informed and thus limited in its ability to control the experts.[22] Jürgen Schriewer (1999)

[20] We benefited from this reorientation of class analysis in our work on *Capitalist Development and Democracy* (Rueschemeyer et al. 1992, pp. 53–7 passim).

[21] For a systematic consideration of a large variety of mechanisms involved in collective action see the important pair of books by Mark Lichbach (1995, 1996).

[22] Comparative research broadened these studies from a market-based understanding of the delivery of expert services to a more comprehensive understanding that included state-based and other forms of social control (Rueschemeyer 1986, ch. vi). Of the extended literature I cite here only Freidson (1970), Johnson (1972), Rueschemeyer (1973), and Larson (1977).

offers other examples from comparative research on education. Schriewer makes the variability of responses to common problems (together with the interrelations of all social phenomena in a global system) the basis for a proposal to reorient comparative research that diverges much more radically than the ideas I present here from the positivist vision of social analysis. I am not inclined to follow his line of argument, but I do wish to argue that the identification of common and perhaps universal problems should be ranked among the major achievements of comparative case research.[23]

Finally, there is a gain from comparative historical work, even from dual case studies, that is much more modest and yet of critical importance for future comparative studies. Any comparison of similar phenomena in two different societal, national, or cultural settings has to determine *conceptual equivalences* that cut across the two contexts. This is a far more daunting task than it may appear to the majority of sociologists who either work empirically within their own society or argue theoretically at a level of abstraction that leaves all historical particularity out of view. Yet this astounding dualism in the work of a discipline that claims to study societies and the paucity of comparative work on many of the most common subjects of sociological investigation may be due precisely to the elementary difficulties of establishing such conceptual equivalencies that do justice to two or more macrosocial and cultural contexts and at the same time represent faithfully the analytic intent of the hypotheses and theoretical frameworks involved. Even concepts as simple as medical or legal work require translating local understandings and conceptualizations into a more universal conceptual lingua franca. And this can be done only with a painstaking examination of two or more social and cultural contexts. Such research may actually go beyond isolated conceptual equivalencies and also lead to subject-specific meta-theory or the identification of common problems, but the conceptual equivalencies by themselves are certainly a nontrivial gain.[24]

[23] See Schriewer (1999, pp. 63–83). I should add that I was far more inclined toward a dismissive criticism of such research results when some time ago I reviewed the comparative historical work of Reinhard Bendix (Rueschemeyer 1984).

[24] In *Lawyers and Their Society* (Rueschemeyer 1973), I had to deal with the specific conceptual equivalencies concerning legal work. In a later article I focused specifically on the equivalence issues concerning legal work but now ranging across many more countries (Rueschemeyer 1989).

VII. What Can Be Learned from One or a Few Cases?

Comparative historical analysis can do much more than its detractors allow. Yet it falls short – as does its cousin, macrocomparative quantitative research – of the ideal inspired by neopositivism: the standard of a universally applicable social theory whose propositions are substantively meaningful and hold under specified conditions independent of time and place. It is quite possible that the distance between this ideal and actual macrosocial analysis cannot be closed.

Even analytically oriented analysis of single historical cases, however, can yield significant theoretical gains. These gains go far beyond the rejection of determinist propositions from which the case deviates and the increased credibility a proposition receives from a confirmation under least likely conditions. They include the generation of new hypotheses, as well as their testing and retesting against the multiple data points a thoroughly analyzed historical case offers. Much of the skepticism about the theoretical value of single historical case studies derives from the mistaken equation of a single case with a single observation.

Yet single historical processes are not literally "inscribed with their own causation." The sheer inductivism suggested by this formulation is as impossible in analytically oriented history as it is in other modes of inquiry. In fact, the best analytic history is characterized by a high degree of theoretical reflection that embodies a wide range of previous observations and analyses in theoretical frameworks. The expectations derived from these frameworks focus and guide the inquiry, whether it aims primarily at causal explanation of particular developments or is interested foremost in the formulation and testing of the theoretical propositions used in such explanations.

Analyses that are confined to single cases – whether they are qualitative historical or quantitative and present-oriented in character – cannot deal effectively with factors that are largely or completely held constant within the boundaries of the case (or are simply less visible in that structural or cultural context). This is the reason why going beyond the boundaries of a single case can put into question seemingly well-established causal accounts and generate new problems and new insights. Cross-case analyses are critical for understanding variations in macrophenomena, which frequently modify the dynamics of meso- and microphenomena.

While methodological reflection and the refinement of practices in comparative historical analysis have made great strides in recent years, the limitations of an inevitably small number of cases remain a serious problem.

This does not only – or even primarily – relate to the fact that cross-case comparisons involve often too many relevant factors; an equally or more important problem is that a limited number of large cases does not allow us to come to reasonable conclusions about our assumptions regarding underlying causal patterns. It is here that I see virtually insurmountable obstacles blocking the ability to come close to the ideal of a universally applicable social theory that is at the same time of substantive interest.

Yet reading the best comparative historical work or being involved in such research gives us a sense of insight and understanding that seems at odds with this negative conclusion. In the closing paragraphs, I tried to explicate this sense of intellectual accomplishment. I argued that side by side with convincing causal explanations and the partially generalized propositions these involve, comparative historical analyses yield also other results that constitute real theoretical gains, even if they do not constitute directly testable and substantively powerful propositions. Perhaps the most important of these are the theoretical frameworks that guide analytic historical work and are in turn revised by it.

References

Campbell, Donald T. 1961. "The Mutual Methodological Relevance of Anthropology and Psychology." Pp. 333–52 in *Psychological Anthropology: Approaches to Culture and Personality*, edited by F. L. K. Hsu. Homewood, IL: Dorsey Press.

1975. "'Degrees of Freedom' and the Case Study." *Comparative Political Studies* 8: 178–93.

Campbell, Donald T. and J. C. Stanley. 1966. *Experimental and Quasi-Experimental Design for Research*. Chicago: Rand McNally.

Coleman, James S. 1964. *Introduction to Mathematical Sociology*. New York: Free Press of Glencoe.

Collier, David and James Mahoney. 1996. "Insights and Pitfalls: Selection Bias in Qualitative Research." *World Politics* 49: 56–91.

Dion, Douglas. 1998. "Evidence and Inference in the Comparative Case Study." *Comparative Politics* 30: 127–46.

Djilas, Milovan. 1957. *The New Class: An Analysis of the Communist System*. New York: Praeger.

Eckstein, Harry. 1975. "Case Studies and Theory in Political Science." Pp. 79–138 in *Handbook of Political Science* 7, edited by Fred Greenstein and Nelson W. Polsby. Reading, MA: Addison-Wesley.

Emigh, Rebecca Jean. 1997. "The Power of Negative Thinking: The Use of Negative Case Methodology in the Development of Sociological Theory. *Theory and Society* 26: 649–84.

Freidson, Eliot. 1970. *Profession of Medicine: A Study of the Sociology of Applied Knowledge*. New York: Dodd, Mead.

Hedström, Peter and Richard Swedberg. 1998. *Social Mechanisms: An Analytical Approach to Social Theory*. Cambridge: Cambridge University Press.

Johnson, T. J. 1972. *Professions and Power.* London: Macmillan.

King, Gary, Robert O. Keohane, and Sidney Verba. 1994. *Designing Social Inquiry: Scientific Inference in Qualitative Research*. Princeton, NJ: Princeton University Press.

Larson, Magali Sarfatti. 1977. *The Rise of Professionalism: A Sociological Analysis.* Berkeley: University of California Press.

Lichbach, Mark. 1995. *The Rebel's Dilemma*. Ann Arbor: University of Michigan Press.

1996. *The Cooperator's Dilemma*. Ann Arbor: University of Michigan Press.

Lijphart, Arend. 1971. "Comparative Politics and the Comparative Method." *American Political Science Review* 65: 682–93.

1975. "The Comparable Cases Strategy in Comparative Research." *Comparative Political Studies* 8: 158–77.

Lipset, Seymour M., Martin Trow, and James Coleman. 1956. *Union Democracy: The Internal Politics of the International Typographical Union. What Makes Democracy Work in Labor Unions and Other Organizations?* Glencoe, IL: The Free Press.

Mahoney, James. 1999. "Nominal, Ordinal, and Narrative Appraisal in Macrocausal Analysis." *American Journal of Sociology* 104: 1154–96.

2000. "Strategies of Causal Inference in Small-*N* Analysis." *Sociological Methods and Research* 28: 387–424.

Merton, Robert K. [1949] 1968. *Social Theory and Social Structure*, 3rd ed. New York: Free Press.

Michels, Robert. [1911] 1999. *Political Parties: A Sociological Study of the Oligarchical Tendencies of Modern Democracy*. New Brunswick, NJ: Transaction Publishers.

Moore, Barrington, Jr. 1966. *The Social Origins of Dictatorship and Democracy*. Boston: Beacon Press.

Munck, Gerardo L. 1998. "Canons of Research Design in Qualitative Analysis." *Studies in Comparative International Development* 33: 18–45.

Norris, Pippa. 1996. "Does Television Erode Social Capital? A Reply to Putnam." *PS: Political Science and Politics* 29: 474–80.

Przeworski, Adam and Henry Teune. 1970. *The Logic of Comparative Social Inquiry.* New York: Wiley-Interscience.

Putnam, Robert D. 1995a. "Bowling Alone." *Journal of Democracy* 6: 65–78.

1995b. "Tuning In, Tuning Out: The Strange Disappearance of Social Capital in America." *PS: Political Science and Politics* 28: 664–83.

1998. "Democracy in America at the End of the Twentieth Century." Pp. 233–65 in *Participation and Democracy East and West: Comparisons and Interpretations,* edited by D. Rueschemeyer, M. Rueschemeyer, and B. Wittrock. Armonk, NY: M. E. Sharpe.

Ragin, Charles C. 1987. *The Comparative Method: Moving Beyond Qualitative and Quantitative Strategies.* Berkeley: University of California Press.

Ragin, Charles C. and Howard S. Becker, eds. 1992. *What Is a Case? Exploring the Foundations of Social Inquiry*. Cambridge: Cambridge University Press.

Raser, J. R., D. T. Campbell, and R. W. Chadwick. 1970. "Gaming and Simulation for Developing Theory Relevant to International Relations." *General Systems* 15: 183–204.

Rueschemeyer, Dietrich. 1973. *Lawyers and Their Societies: A Comparative Study of the Legal Profession in Germany and the United States*. Cambridge, MA: Harvard University Press.

1984. "Theoretical Generalization and Historical Particularity in the Comparative Sociology of Reinhard Bendix." Pp. 129–69 in *Vision and Method in Historical Sociology*, edited by Theda Skocpol. Cambridge: Cambridge University Press.

1986. *Power and the Division of Labour*. Stanford, CA: Stanford University Press.

1989. "Comparing Legal Professions Cross-Nationally: From a Professions-Centered Approach to a State-Centered Approach." Pp. 289–321 in *Lawyers in Society*, vol. III: *Comparative Theories*, edited by Richard L. Abel and Philip S. Lewis. Berkeley: University of California Press.

Rueschemeyer, Dietrich, Marilyn Rueschemeyer, and Björn Wittrock. 1998. "Conclusion: Contrasting Patterns of Participation and Democracy." Pp. 266–84 in *Participation and Democracy East and West: Comparisons and Interpretations*, edited by D. Rueschemeyer, M. Rueschemeyer, and B. Wittrock. Armonk, NY: M. E. Sharpe.

Rueschemeyer, Dietrich, Evelyne Huber Stephens, and John D. Stephens. 1992. *Capitalist Development and Democracy*. Chicago: University of Chicago Press.

Rueschemeyer, Dietrich and John D. Stephens. 1997. "Comparing Historical Sequences – A Powerful Tool for Causal Analysis. A Reply to John Goldthorpe's 'Current Issues in Comparative Macrosociology'." *Comparative Social Research* 16: 55–72.

Schriewer, Jürgen. 1999. "Vergleich und Erklärung zwischen Kausalität und Komplexität." Pp. 53–102 in *Diskurse und Entwicklungspfade: Der Gesellschaftsvergleich in den Geschichts- und Sozialwissenschaften*, edited by Hartmut Kaelble and Jürgen Schriewer. Frankfurt: Campus.

Sewell, William H., Jr. 1996. "Three Temporalities: Toward an Eventful Sociology." Pp. 245–80 in *The Historic Turn in the Human Sciences*, edited by Terrence J. McDonald. Ann Arbor: University of Michigan Press.

Shalev, Michael. 1998–9. "Limits of and Alternatives to Multiple Regression in Macro-Comparative Research." Paper presented at the second conference on "The Welfare State at the Crossroads," Stockholm, June 1998.

Skocpol, Theda. 1979. *States and Social Revolutions: A Comparative Analysis of France, Russia and China*. Cambridge: Cambridge University Press.

Smelser, Neil J. 1976. *Comparative Methods in the Social Sciences*. Englewood Cliffs, NJ: Prentice-Hall.

Stinchcombe, Arthur L. 1968. *Constructing Sociological Theories*. New York: Harcourt, Brace & World.

1978. *Theoretical Methods in Social History*. New York: Academic Press.
1991. "The Conditions of Fruitfulness of Theorizing about Mechanisms in Social Science." *Philosophy of the Social Sciences* 21: 367–87.
1998. "Monopolistic Competition as a Mechanism: Corporations, Universities, and Nation-States in Competitive Fields." Pp. 267–305 in *Social Mechanisms: An Analytical Approach to Social Theory*, edited by P. Hedström and R. Swedberg. Cambridge: Cambridge University Press.
Thompson, E. P. 1963. *The Making of the English Working Class*. London: Gollancz.
1978. *The Poverty of Theory and Other Essays*. New York: Monthly Review Press.
Trimberger, Ellen Kay. 1984. "E. P. Thompson: Understanding the Process of History." Pp. 211–43 in *Vision and Method in Historical Sociology*, edited by Theda Skocpol. Cambridge: Cambridge University Press.
Trubek, David M. 1972. "Max Weber on Law and the Rise of Capitalism." *Wisconsin Law Review* 3: 720–53.

10

Strategies of Causal Assessment in Comparative Historical Analysis

James Mahoney

Scholars who write about comparative historical methods sometimes make it appear that the research tradition has a single basic approach for identifying patterns of causation. Yet, in fact, comparative historical analysts employ a wide range of strategies of causal assessment in their substantive research. These strategies encompass both methodologies for juxtaposing cases with one another and methodologies for analyzing processes that take place within individual cases. And they include both techniques of causal assessment designed to identify the necessary or sufficient causes of an outcome and tools for locating causal factors that covary with outcomes in linear patterns. Rather than narrowly limiting themselves to any one approach, then, comparative historical researchers are eclectic in their use of methods.

In this essay, I attempt to analyze systematically these different strategies of causal analysis. My main objectives are to specify the concrete procedures entailed in the strategies, discuss their underlying assumptions about causality, and assess their comparative strengths and weaknesses. Along the way, I engage the long-standing debate about small-*N* versus large-*N* research.[1] I devote particular attention to the ways in which different comparative historical methods are or are not compatible with the assumptions that guide

Portions of the discussions of ordinal analysis and within-case analysis are adapted from James Mahoney, "Strategies of Causal Inference in Small-*N* Analysis," *Sociological Methods and Research* 28: 4 (May 2000), pp. 387–424. Dietrich Rueschemeyer provided many helpful comments. This material is based upon work supported by the National Science Foundation under Grant No. 0093754.

[1] See Lijphart (1971, 1975), Smelser (1976), Lieberson (1991, 1994, 1998), Collier (1993), Goldthorpe (1997), Goldstone (1997), Rueschemeyer and Stephens (1997), Ragin (1997), Munck (1998).

Table 10.1. *Strategies of Causal Inference in Small-N Analysis*

		Level of Measurement		
		Nominal	Ordinal	Interval
Level of Aggregation	Aggregated	Nominal Strategy	Ordinal Strategy	Not Typically Used
	Disaggregated	Within-Case Analysis		

causal inference in conventional statistical methodologies. My hope is that this discussion will help clear up some of the misunderstandings that have developed between advocates of small-*N* and large-*N* research and refocus attention on the real points of contention between the traditions.

The essay identifies three basic strategies of causal analysis that are often combined in particular pieces of comparative historical research: nominal, ordinal, and within-case strategies. Each of these strategies may entail a number of more specific methodologies that differ in important respects. Nevertheless, for the purposes of classification, the strategies can be defined along two dimensions: level of measurement and level of aggregation (see Table 10.1). Both ordinal and nominal strategies make comparisons across highly aggregated units (e.g., nation-states), but the two differ in level of measurement. A nominal strategy makes comparisons using nominal measurement; an ordinal strategy employs ordinal measurement. By contrast, a within-case strategy differs from these two alternatives along the dimension of level of aggregation. Whereas nominal and ordinal strategies involve comparisons across cases, a within-case strategy entails a shift toward disaggregation and a focus on comparisons within particular cases. A within-case strategy does not contrast with ordinal and nominal strategies in terms of level of measurement. In fact, as we shall see, a within-case strategy can be used in conjunction with multiple levels of measurement, including nominal, ordinal, and interval measurement.

Important contrasts in the logic of causal inference underlie nominal and ordinal strategies. A nominal strategy implicitly or explicitly assumes a nonlinear understanding of causation built around the ideas of necessary and sufficient conditions. This understanding of causation is quite different from that employed by most large-*N* researchers, who often analyze linear causation and who rarely test for necessary and sufficient conditions. By contrast, an ordinal strategy is more compatible with the linear and correlational assumptions that guide much large-N research. At the same time, however, some comparative historical researchers argue that ordinal analysis (and perhaps even most statistical research) is itself best understood in terms of necessary and sufficient conditions. Finally, different variants of a within-case strategy can be used in conjunction with different understandings of causation. In some instances, within-case analysis may replicate the procedures underlying nominal or ordinal strategies; in other cases, this kind of analysis may involve the statistical evaluation of a large number of observations.

Nominal Comparison and the Question of Determinism

Nominal (or categorical) comparison entails the use of categories that are mutually exclusive (cases cannot be classified in terms of more than one category) and collectively exhaustive (one of the categories applies to each case).[2] Examples of these categories in comparative historical research include various regime classifications (e.g., democratic, authoritarian, and totalitarian regimes), typologies of different states (e.g., conservative, liberal, and social-democratic welfare states), and countless dichotomous variables (e.g., revolution versus nonrevolution). Because vivid labels can be attached to nominal categories, comparative historical analysts often summarize their arguments with this kind of comparison. In addition, as a first step in research, they may employ nominal comparison to measure independent and dependent variables and to develop an initial sense of whether potential explanations and outcomes are roughly matched.

My concern in this section, however, is with the use of nominal comparison to evaluate systematically the validity of alternative explanations. In the discussion that follows, I consider how both deterministic and probabilistic nominal methods are used for this task.

What Is a Deterministic Explanation?

Although comparative historical analysts are often criticized for presenting "deterministic" explanations, the concept of determinism itself is often not clearly defined. For some scholars, determinism entails focusing on

[2] With respect to different levels of measurement, nominal categorization is sometimes considered unsophisticated because it does not involve rank ordering cases, much less quantifying the degree to which particular cases differ from one another. Yet, for conceptualizing certain kinds of phenomena, nominal categories are highly appropriate (Sartori 1987, pp. 182–5; see also Collier and Adcock 1999).

structural variables at the expense of agency (see Giddens 1979). For example, analysts who view Theda Skocpol's *States and Social Revolutions* (1979) as suffering from determinism often are really concerned with its emphasis on structure relative to agency (e.g., Colburn 1994; Selbin 1993; see also Skocpol 1994). In this essay, I am not concerned with this kind of determinism, although I do believe many comparative historical researchers effectively combine agency and structure in their studies (Mahoney and Snyder 1999).

For other scholars, determinism represents a particular understanding of the nature of the world that can be contrasted with probabilism. In this view, a fully deterministic approach assumes that all occurrences in the world are the product of nonrandom prior occurrences; given the right variables, methods, and measurement devices, the world is completely predictable. By contrast, a fully probabilistic approach assumes that all occurrences in the world are at least in part the product of inherently stochastic processes that cannot even in principle be identified. As a result, full prediction is impossible under all circumstances. These two approaches pose a sharp dichotomy, and scholars who employ deterministic and probabilistic explanations in social science research need not fully embrace one side or the other. For example, scholars who adopt deterministic explanations may assume that much of the world conforms to the probabilistic understanding and that only selected cases can be modeled deterministically. Likewise, scholars who employ probabilistic explanations may assume that the world really is deterministic, but that our inability to identify and correctly measure all relevant variables forces us to act as if it were probabilistic (see Goldthorpe 2000, pp. 137–8; King, Keohane, and Verba 1994, pp. 59–60).

In actual research, a deterministic explanation assumes the existence of causes that exhibit, in at least certain respects, invariant relationships with outcomes within a specified domain of cases. For example, in most statistical research, a deterministic explanation assumes that values on an explanatory variable fully predict values on an outcome variable without error within a specified population. As a result, at least for every case within that population, one can predict the exact causal effect on an outcome variable of a given change on an explanatory variable. The inability of statistical researchers to formulate successful deterministic models has meant that nearly all research in this field adopts probabilistic explanations that assume such prediction is impossible.

In comparative historical studies, a deterministic explanation usually involves modeling conditions (or combinations of conditions) that are necessary or sufficient for the occurrence of an outcome within a specified population of cases. This kind of analysis also makes certain predictive assumptions. For example, with a *necessary* cause, the absence of this cause is always associated with the absence of the outcome in question, at least within the relevant population of cases. However, if a necessary cause is present, the outcome could be either present or absent. With a *sufficient* cause, the presence of this cause is always associated with the occurrence of the outcome in question (again, within the relevant population). Only when a given factor is a necessary *and* sufficient cause will the outcome *always* be present when the cause is present and *always* absent when the cause is absent.

Comparative historical researchers often implicitly understand a probabilistic explanation as one in which explanatory variables (or combinations of variables) are treated as to some specified degree necessary or sufficient for the occurrence of an outcome. For example, a probabilistic explanation may treat explanatory variables (or combinations of variables) as *almost always* necessary or *almost always* sufficient conditions. With this kind of explanation, the analyst may assume that an inherently stochastic process explains why a condition is not always necessary or always sufficient for an outcome of interest. Alternatively, the analyst may assume that the world really is fully deterministic and that measurement error accounts for the probabilistic relationship. In either case, however, the researcher is not committed to a deterministic explanation.

Deterministic Methods

Some nominal techniques are used deterministically by comparative historical researchers, including, most notably, J. S. Mill's method of agreement[3] and method of difference.[4] Although these Millian methods do not permit the analysis of multiple explanatory factors or interaction effects, they provide a sound logical basis for *eliminating* potential necessary and

[3] With the method of agreement, the analyst attempts to establish that cases that share a common outcome also share common hypothesized causal factors, despite varying in other significant ways (see Skocpol and Somers 1980).

[4] The analyst using the method of difference contrasts cases in which an outcome under investigation and hypothesized causal factors are present to other cases in which both the outcome and the hypothesized causes are absent, even though the cases may be similar in many other respects (see Skocpol and Somers 1980).

sufficient causes.[5] Specifically, the method of agreement can be used to eliminate potential *necessary* causes, whereas the method of difference can be used to eliminate potential *sufficient* causes. Thus, with the method of agreement, the outcome of interest is present in all cases. Consequently, it is logically impossible for any hypothesized cause that is not shared by the cases to be individually necessary for the outcome's occurrence, since some cases possess the outcome but not the cause. By contrast, with the method of difference, the outcome is present in some cases and not present in others. Hence, any hypothesized cause that is shared by all the cases cannot by itself be sufficient for the outcome, since not all cases with the hypothesized cause experience the outcome of interest.

With these deterministic methods, a single deviation from a hypothesized pattern of necessary or sufficient causation is enough to eliminate a given factor as a potential cause. As a result, the methods provide a powerful basis for systematically eliminating rival causal hypotheses, even when only a small number of cases are selected. For instance, in her explanation of contrasts in the national electoral systems of three post-Soviet Central Asian countries, Pauline Jones Luong (2002) uses the method of difference to eliminate plausible causal factors that do not vary across the countries. She shows that, given their similar levels of socioeconomic development, one cannot argue that level of development was by itself sufficient for an inclusive and populist electoral system in Kyrgyzstan, a restrictive and centralist electoral system in Uzbekistan, and a hybrid electoral system in Kazakhstan. Likewise, in *Making Race and Nation: A Comparison of the United States, South Africa, and Brazil*, Anthony W. Marx (1998) uses the elimination procedures of the method of agreement to assess explanations of the major similarities in racial domination in the United States and South Africa. He eliminates factors that do not vary systematically between the countries, such as the presence of an African or African-descendant majority population, because they are not by themselves necessary conditions in accounting for the major

[5] It bears emphasis that causal factors eliminated using these methods might, in conjunction with other factors, represent part of a larger combination that is itself necessary or sufficient for an outcome of interest. The methods of agreement and difference do not provide a basis for analyzing such combinations of variables, except insofar as the combinations are treated as a single factor. For example, Skocpol (1979) uses the methods in this fashion (see Mahoney 1999, p. 1158). It is also worth noting that the "most similar systems design" and the "most different systems design" have the same logical structure as the method of difference and the method of agreement, respectively, except that Przeworski and Teune's (1970) original formulation of these designs was based on the premise that the scholar is combining two levels of analysis.

similarity of interest. At the same time, Marx uses the method of difference to eliminate possible explanations of the contrast between repressive racial domination in these countries, on the one hand, and significant racial tolerance in Brazil, on the other. For instance, the presence of early labor coercion and colonial discrimination are eliminated because these factors do not vary across the three countries.

Against the backdrop of having eliminated initially plausible explanations using the methods of agreement and difference, comparative historical researchers frequently hold up their favored argument as the one that can survive the deterministic tests. When this takes place, the analytic logic of comparative historical analysis can be strikingly convincing. For example, Loung's explanation, which highlights the perceptions of central and regional leaders in Central Asia concerning their relative power vis-à-vis one another, seems remarkably persuasive in light of the failure of many other plausible explanations. Also compelling is Marx's explanation of major similarities between the United States and South Africa, which emphasizes the existence of significant divisions among whites following the Boer War and the Civil War. Ultimately, in these two countries, white unity and nationalist loyalty to the state were forged through the construction of systems of racial domination that systematically excluded blacks. By contrast, in Brazil, the absence of a similar intrawhite cleavage obviated the need for similar policies of racial domination to ensure white unification.

Boolean algebra is distinct from other nominal methods because it allows the analyst to treat several different *combinations* of variables as the causes of an outcome (Ragin 1987). In particular, this methodology provides a logical basis for identifying combinations of causal factors that are *sufficient* for the occurrence of an outcome.[6] Analysts who use this method may identify several different combinations of factors, each of which is sufficient for an outcome. In this way, Boolean procedures enable researchers to recognize that multiple causal combinations may produce the same outcome, what Ragin (1987) calls "multiple conjunctural causation."

A nice illustration of Boolean analysis is Wickham-Crowley's (1992) work on the origins of peasant support for guerrilla movements in Latin America. Wickham-Crowley focuses on twenty cases, and he looks at

[6] The Boolean minimization procedure through which causal combinations are reduced eliminates potential *necessary* causes among cases that share the same outcome. Final combinations of causal factors are understood to be *sufficient* for the occurrence of the outcome. In addition, by looking at final combinations of explanatory variables, it is possible to state whether any single factor is a necessary or sufficient cause.

four different explanatory variables: agrarian structure (A), agrarian disruption (B), rebellious cultures (C), and peasant linkages (D). He first pools cases in which the outcome of peasant support for guerrillas is present and identifies all combinations of scores on explanatory variables that are associated with this outcome. Next, he reduces the number of these combinations by assuming that if two combinations of explanatory variables differ in their scores for a single variable, then that variable can be eliminated from the combination. The implicit rationale behind this Boolean reduction procedure is that the variable is not *necessary* for the combination to have a causal effect since it is both present and absent in combinations associated with the outcome. For example, all four of Wickham-Crowley's explanatory variables are present in one combination with peasant support for guerrillas (expressed as ABCD), while the explanatory variables A, B, and C, but not variable D, are present in another combination with peasant support for guerrillas (expressed as ABCd). Hence, Wickham-Crowley assumes that variable D is irrelevant to the combination and eliminates it, reducing the causal expression to ABC.

Through this Boolean reduction procedure, Wickham-Crowley narrows the range of explanations down to four possible combinations of variables under which peasants have supported guerrillas: ABD, AC, CD, and abD. Although Wickham-Crowley does not identify any *individual* causal factor that is necessary or sufficient to produce strong support for guerrillas, the final four expressions are each understood to represent a *combination of factors* that are *sufficient* for peasant support. For example, the combination of a rebellious culture (C) and peasant linkages (D) is understood to be sufficient for strong support for guerrillas in modern Latin America.

Probabilistic Methods

Other methods that rely on nominal comparison are probabilistic in the sense that they relax standards to permit causes that are "usually" or "almost always" necessary or sufficient. Comparative historical researchers who draw on these methods readily acknowledge that inherent randomness or measurement error may make it difficult to locate patterns of association that are fully necessary or fully sufficient for an outcome. At the same time, however, these methods make it somewhat more difficult to eliminate rival explanations. For example, a single deviation often does not provide a basis for eliminating an explanation when causation is assumed to be probabilistic. As a rule, comparative historical researchers need to select more than just a few cases to use probabilistic nominal methods as a basis for systematically eliminating rival explanations.

A nice example of how a probabilistic nominal approach can be effectively used in practice is Thomas Ertman's (1997) magisterial work *Birth of the Leviathan: Building States and Regimes in Medieval and Early Modern Europe*. Ertman's goal is to explain why particular European countries developed one of four major types of early modern regime-states, each defined in terms of constitutionalism versus absolutism and patrimonialism versus bureaucracy. Ertman first systematically eliminates rival explanations derived from the theories of state development formulated by Otto Hintze, Charles Tilly, Perry Anderson, and Michael Mann. He does so by showing how, within a population of fourteen cases, these theories lead to predictions about regime-state outcomes that are contradicted by at least four cases. Based on the failings of these theories, Ertman offers his own explanation, which emphasizes three dichotomously measured variables – administrative versus participatory government, pre-1450 versus post-1450 geopolitical competition, and existence versus nonexistence of powerful representative associations. Together these variables are understood to represent an explanation that "can account for most of the variation" in early modern state building in Europe (Ertman 1997, p. 6). In particular, the explanation is consistent with twelve of the fourteen cases, failing to explain state outcomes only in Sweden and Denmark, where "powerful contingent events conspired to confound expected paths of development" (p. 33). Because of these two exception cases, Ertman cannot treat his explanatory variables as *always* sufficient for the occurrence of outcomes. Instead, he must adopt a probabilistic approach in which his explanation is *usually* sufficient.

The decision of analysts to employ a probabilistic approach raises important issues regarding the benchmark for determining degrees of sufficiency or necessity. In his most recent methodological work, Ragin (2000) offers precise terminology and benchmark proportions for discussing causes with different degrees of necessity and sufficiency. For instance, a cause that is usually necessary or usually sufficient must meet a .65 benchmark (i.e., the cause must be necessary or sufficient at least 65 percent of the time), while a cause that is almost always necessary or sufficient must meet a .80 benchmark. These benchmarks can be applied to all of the nominal techniques discussed previously, including Boolean approaches that focus on combinations of factors.

In the case of Ertman, we saw how he found that twelve out of fourteen cases are consistent with his explanation, which yields a percentage of

.86 and is thus higher than the benchmark for an almost always sufficient cause. However, given the relatively small number of cases, he can achieve statistical significance at a .10 level only by treating his explanation as usually sufficient for the regime-state outcomes.[7] By contrast, the explanations eliminated by Ertman can explain at best ten out of the fourteen cases (.71), thus falling below the benchmark of almost always sufficient. Moreover, these alternatives cannot meet any reasonable level of statistical significance even if they are evaluated at the lower benchmark of usually sufficient. In short, Ertman has a logical and statistical basis for rejecting alternative explanations by scholars such as Hintze, Tilly, Anderson, and Mann while preserving his own explanation as identifying a set of factors that are usually sufficient for producing regime-state outcomes in early modern Europe.

A major new probabilistic technique is found in Ragin's (2000) discussion of fuzzy-set methods.[8] Fuzzy-set measurement defies easy classification along standard scales of measurement (i.e., nominal, ordinal, interval, and ratio measurement), though it parallels the nominal concern with set membership. To use fuzzy sets, the analyst must score cases from 0 to 1 based on their degree of membership in a category. Some cases will be "full" instances of a category and thus receive a score of 1, even if these cases have different scores on an interval scale. For example, with respect to the category of "wealthy country," both the United States and England are full members, and thus both receive the same score of 1, despite the fact that these countries have different levels of wealth on an interval scale.[9] Other countries receive scores based on the extent to which they overlap with the category "wealthy country." For example, a country that is "mostly in" the category will receive a score only slightly less than 1 (e.g., .83), while a country that is "mostly out of" the category will receive a score closer to 0 (e.g., .17).

[7] I have applied the significance test identified by Ragin (2000, p. 112) with some liberty here, given that Ertman actually offers an explanation for four different outcomes. In this sense, he does not have a total of fourteen cases for each of his outcomes. However, since he uses the same set of explanatory variables to account for each of these outcomes, there is a logical basis for using the binomial test as if Ertman's variables successfully explained twelve of fourteen cases on the same outcome. The conclusion I reach here addresses a concern with Ertman's work I raised but did not resolve in an earlier article (see Mahoney 1999, p. 1175).

[8] I discuss fuzzy-set methods in greater depth in Mahoney (2001).

[9] Although the decision to ignore variation at the extreme ends of continuous variables is a source of bias in conventional statistical research, this problem does not arise in the analysis of necessary and sufficient conditions. In fact, error might arise if the additional variation were included.

The decision to assign fuzzy-set membership scores must be grounded in the analyst's substantive knowledge of actual cases.

Fuzzy-set measurement is highly appropriate for the analysis of necessary and sufficient conditions, including under probabilistic assumptions where different degrees of necessary or sufficient causation are considered. To employ the technique, the analyst must apply the fuzzy-set measures just described to all potential causal factors and outcomes and then assess the relationship between their values. With a *necessary* cause, fuzzy membership scores on the *outcome* will be less than or equal to fuzzy membership scores on the *cause*. By contrast, with a *sufficient* cause, fuzzy membership scores on the *cause* will be less than or equal to fuzzy membership scores on the *outcome*. To incorporate considerations of probabilistic causation, the researcher might argue that if no case's score on the outcome (or cause) exceeds its score on the cause (or outcome) by more than a small portion of a fuzzy membership unit, then the pattern is still consistent with the interpretation of causal necessity (or sufficiency). Likewise, the probabilistic benchmarks and significance tests mentioned earlier can be applied when using fuzzy measures of variables. Although the procedures involved become especially complicated when *combinations* of variables are considered using probabilistic criteria, a free software package that performs the operations is already available (Drass and Ragin 1999).

Although Ragin offers interesting examples of how these methods might be applied to substantive questions such as the onset of International Monetary Fund protest and the establishment of generous welfare states, the techniques are still too new (at the time of this writing) to have been used by other researchers. Some comparative historical researchers may resist the formal constraints of this methodology, preferring instead the flexibility of alternative strategies of causal inference. Nevertheless, several comparative historical researchers already have sought to apply rudimentary versions of fuzzy-set logic through analyses that combine nominal and ordinal comparison (discussed later). These works suggest that at least some comparative historical researchers will welcome the formal application of Ragin's latest innovation.

Evaluating Criticisms of Methods That Use Nominal Comparison

The sharpest criticisms of comparative historical methods have focused specifically on nominal techniques. Most of these concerns have been raised by scholars working in the tradition of statistical analysis who argue that comparative historical researchers violate standard rules for conducting valid research. In this section, I evaluate the five most important of these criticisms, suggesting that they are often unfounded concerns based on the misapplication of conventional statistical reasoning to the study of necessary and sufficient causation.

Criticism 1: Necessary and Sufficient Conditions Are Not a Useful Way to Think About Causation Even if logical methods exist for identifying necessary or sufficient causation, some analysts contend that it is still not a productive way to think about causation. A common concern is that many necessary or sufficient causes are not analytically helpful. For example, regarding specifically the *necessary* causes of an outcome, there are potentially an infinite number of such causes for any outcome, most of which are unimportant or trivial (e.g., the existence of human beings is a necessary cause of a social revolution). Likewise, many *sufficient* causes of an outcome are obvious or tautological (e.g., war is a sufficient cause of large-scale death).

However, examples of trivial necessary conditions and tautological sufficient conditions found in the literature are hypothetical ones offered by critics who seek to dismiss the study of these conditions (see Braumoeller and Goertz 2000). The literature offers few or no examples of real researchers who use nominal methods to analyze trivial necessary conditions or tautological sufficient conditions. In fact, critics of the study of necessary and sufficient conditions seem unaware that *empirical* criteria – as opposed to normative or political criteria – exist for differentiating trivial necessary causes from nontrivial ones and tautological sufficient causes from nontautological ones. *Trivial necessary causes* are those in which the cause is present in all cases, irrespective of the value of the dependent variable (Braumoeller and Goertz 2000; Dion 1998). For example, the existence of human beings is trivially necessary for social revolutions, because this condition is present in all cases of revolution and nonrevolution alike. Braumoeller and Goertz (2000) show through an evaluation of more than a dozen published studies that actual social researchers who make claims about necessary conditions do not refer to trivial ones. Dion (1998) reaches the same conclusion in his evaluation of the use of necessary conditions in comparative politics.

With *tautological sufficient conditions*, the analyst identifies a set of factors that are contained within the very definition of the outcome being considered. When this happens, there is no temporal separation between the cause and outcome (or the outcome may actually occur *before* the cause). For instance, the claim that war is a sufficient cause of death is tautological because there is no definitional distinction or temporal separation between the occurrence of war and death (or the outcome of death may actually occur before full-scale war breaks out). Again, comparative historical researchers who make claims about sufficient causes are not referring to these kinds of tautological conditions. For example, it is not tautological to assert that a high level of domestic financing for military modernization in the sixteenth and seventeenth centuries was sufficient for an autocratic regime outcome in early modern Europe (Downing 1992), or that large group size and growth are together sufficient for ethnic political mobilization (Ragin 2000, p. 138), or that the combination of state structures conducive to breakdown in the face of international pressures and peasant agrarian structures that facilitate revolt are sufficient for social revolutions in agrarian bureaucratic societies (Skocpol 1979).

A somewhat different concern involves the fact that many causal factors are not necessary or sufficient conditions, but rather follow a linear pattern of causation like that assumed in many probabilistic regression models. As a consequence, the analyst using nominal methods might erroneously dismiss these kinds of linear causal factors as unimportant. Lieberson's (1991) well-known example of drunk driving and automobile accidents illustrates this criticism for deterministic versions of the methods of agreement and difference. Thus, with the method of agreement, an analyst who examines three cases of automobile accidents will eliminate drunk driving as a cause if it is present in only two of the three cases. Similarly, with the method of difference, the analyst will eliminate drunk driving as a cause of automobile accidents if it is present in cases of both accidents and nonaccidents. It is essential to recognize that this example does not call into question the ability of nominal methods to evaluate necessary and sufficient causation. These methods correctly show that drunk driving by itself is neither a necessary nor a sufficient condition for an automobile accident (i.e., some automobile accidents occur in the absence of drunk driving, and not all instances of drunk driving produce automobile accidents). Rather, the example suggests the problems that can arise if one thinks about causation in terms of necessary and sufficient conditions when more conventional linear causation likely is at work.

In response to Lieberson, one might point out that actual researchers who sought to use nominal methods to analyze the effect of drunk driving on automobile accidents would doubtless explore whether drunk driving *in combination with* other variables is a sufficient (or usually sufficient) cause of auto accidents *in a specific population of cases*. Moreover, they would arrive at final conclusions using other techniques of causal assessment, including within-case evaluation. Nevertheless, it is worth noting that nominal methods generally will have difficulty assessing the net effect of any single factor of special interest – such as drunk driving on automobile accidents or cigarette smoking on lung cancer – that follows a roughly linear pattern of causation similar to that assumed in conventional statistical research. By the same token, of course, linear regression models will have difficulty identifying necessary and sufficient conditions, whether individually or in combination. As a general rule, analysts must rely on theory and common sense to decide whether a given factor should be tested as a necessary or sufficient condition or as a linear cause that increases or decreases values on an outcome.

Criticism 2: Achieving Statistical Significance Is Impossible with These Methods This criticism grows out of the belief that comparative historical studies suffer from a "degrees of freedom" problem equivalent to that which arises in quantitative analysis.[10] In fact, however, the criticism is an example of an inappropriate application of conventional statistical assumptions to studies designed to analyze necessary and sufficient conditions. It is true that comparative historical studies that examine a very small number of cases (e.g., fewer than five) cannot achieve statistical significance when nominal methods are used in isolation. However, studies with a very small *N* do not necessarily use only nominal methods, but instead may rely extensively on other strategies of causal assessment. Moreover, in contrast to conventional quantitative research, a relatively small number of cases is often enough to achieve statistical confidence when assessing necessary and sufficient conditions. Using Bayesian assumptions, for example, Dion (1998) shows that only five cases will be enough to yield 95 percent confidence about necessary causes. Using a simple binomial probability test, Ragin (2000, pp. 113–15) shows that if one works with usually necessary or usually sufficient causes, seven consistent cases are enough to meet this level of significance. Braumoeller and Goertz (2000) offer many examples of case-oriented studies that pass such significance tests. In short, scholars need to rethink how appropriate the idea of a degrees of freedom problem

[10] As Rueschemeyer (this volume) notes, the degrees of freedom problem is probably the most common criticism of small-*N* analysis. For different perspectives, see Campbell (1975), Lijphart (1971, 1975), Nichols (1986), Collier (1993), Lieberson (1991), King et al. (1994), and Goldthorpe (1997).

really is for comparative historical analysts who adopt an understanding of causality built around necessary and sufficient causes. When this understanding of causality is employed, a relatively small number of cases will often meet the confidence demands of standard statistical analyses.

Criticism 3: Because These Methods Select on the Dependent Variable, They Suffer from Selection Bias Drawing on insights from ordinary least squares regression, Geddes (1990) and King et al. (1994) have criticized studies that select cases based on their score on the dependent variable because this selection procedure can lead to truncation on the dependent variable and thus biased estimates of causal effects (see also Collier and Mahoney 1996). In the worst case scenario, analysts may select cases with no variation on the dependent variable, which, according to King et al. (1994, p. 129), makes it impossible to learn anything about the causes of that variable.

Notwithstanding the rules for valid research in ordinary least squares (OLS) regression analysis, selection on the dependent variable – including the selection of cases that do not vary at all on the dependent variable – is *not* a source of bias when nominal methods are used to identify necessary conditions. Selection on the dependent variable is *highly appropriate* for the study of necessary causation (see Braumoeller and Goertz 2000; Dion 1998; Most and Starr 1989; Ragin 2000). In fact, when analyzing necessary conditions, a standard design is to intentionally permit no variation on the dependent variable. The statistical concern about selection bias undermining valid research simply cannot be extended to comparative historical studies that use nominal techniques.

One might raise the more general concern that the particular sample of cases included for analysis in comparative historical work is not representative of the larger population of cases, and that therefore findings about necessary and sufficient causes in the sample analyzed are not consistent with the findings that would have emerged if a more representative sample was selected. However, comparative historical analysts are in fact among the most self-conscious researchers in terms of defining populations of cases that can be understood as homogeneous (Ragin 2000). Whereas cross-national statistical researchers commonly risk violating assumptions of causal homogeneity by arbitrarily selecting large samples of nations, comparative historical analysts assess necessary and sufficient conditions in carefully formulated populations of cases where these assumptions are more sustainable. Furthermore, to the degree that a nonarbitrary definition of the population cannot be established in this kind of research, the whole idea of bias deriving from an unrepresentative sample becomes problematic (Collier and Mahoney 1996).

Criticism 4: The Deterministic Versions of These Methods Do Not Allow for Measurement Error As suggested earlier, measurement error does not pose special problems for probabilistic nominal methods that relax assumptions about necessary and sufficient causation. However, the fully deterministic versions of these methods assume that the analyst is able to measure all variables correctly, since a change in the scoring of a variable for a single case could lead to opposite conclusions about that variable's causal relevance. In this sense, deterministic nominal methods do not permit any notion of measurement error (see Lieberson 1991).

It is not clear how important a criticism is raised by this objection, however. Comparative historical researchers are typically experts on each of their cases, and given that with this strategy they conceptualize variables as nominal – not continuous – categories, they may indeed be able to avoid measurement error for all of their variables. For example, Skocpol (1979) may well have correctly scored all major dichotomous variables for all of her cases of social revolution and nonsocial revolution. Moreover, if comparative historical researchers like Skocpol do score a particular variable incorrectly for even one case, it is likely that other case experts or comparative historical analysts will identify this error, since much debate in this kind of research entails arguments about the scoring of particular variables for specific cases.

Criticism 5: The Results Generated by These Methods Might Change Substantially if Omitted Explanatory Variables Were Included in the Model This objection holds that variables not included in a nominal assessment might have avoided elimination if they had been included. Likewise, with techniques such as Boolean algebra and fuzzy-set analysis, variables that were eliminated might have been causally important if other relevant variables were included in the model. This criticism is correct, and it has been discussed by comparative historical methodologists at some length (e.g., Amenta and Poulsen 1994; Ragin 1987).

Yet, it is essential to recognize that the problem addressed here is one of correctly specifying a causal model, an issue that arises with *all* methods of causal assessment, including the most sophisticated statistical analyses. For example, in quantitative research, omitting an important variable can entail misunderstanding the causal effects of the other variables that are included in the analysis (Lieberson 1985). Thus, like all other researchers using all other methodologies of causal assessment, comparative historical investigators who employ nominal methods can never know for certain whether they have correctly specified their models and thus proven the existence of causation.

To conclude this section, I would like to underline three points. First, it is sometimes useful to think about causation in terms of (probabilistic or deterministic) necessary and sufficient conditions. Second, comparative historical researchers have nominal methods that contain logical rules for locating necessary and sufficient conditions. Third, existing criticisms of comparative historical methods fail to call into question their capacity to identify successfully necessary and sufficient conditions.

Ordinal Comparison and the Question of Linear Causation

A second major strategy of causal assessment in comparative historical research – ordinal comparison across cases – relies on techniques more familiar to scholars working in the tradition of large-N statistical research. Ordinal analysis is in fact the strategy of inference that comparative historical researchers turn to when they seek to identify linear correlations across a small number of cases. Although the technique has important limitations when employed in isolation and with only a small number of cases, it can be combined in creative ways with other strategies of causal assessment.

Identifying and Interpreting Ordinal Associations

Ordinal analysis involves rank ordering cases using variables with three or more values based on the degree to which a phenomenon is present. This kind of analysis facilitates the use of J. S. Mill's method of concomitant variation, in which the analyst tries to establish causation by looking at the relationship between scores on an ordinally measured explanatory variable and scores on an ordinally measured outcome variable (DeFelice 1986; Mill 1974). For example, if values on an explanatory variable and an outcome variable are measured as high, medium, and low, then cases are compared to see if there is an association (possibly an inverse association) between the two variables. If there appears to be a strong association, the analyst may infer that the relationship is causal.

What, however, constitutes a strong association for the comparative historical researcher who uses the method of concomitant variation? Some scholars committed to a deterministic understanding of causation may argue that anything less than a perfect match between values on the explanatory variable and on the outcome variable will fail to indicate causation. However, Mill himself (1974, pp. 402–6) argued that, when using the method of concomitant variation, a perfect match between cause and outcome is not required to infer causality. Rather, associations in which the values on explanatory and outcome variables do not always match may still indicate causation. As a general rule, comparative historical researchers who follow Mill's standard should not infer causation unless they can establish statistical confidence that the relationship is not simply a product of pure chance. As we will see, this can be achieved by having a moderate number of cases and by systematically combining ordinal analysis with other strategies of causal assessment.

The discovery that an explanatory variable is related to an outcome variable in an ordinal assessment does not indicate how one should interpret the nature of the association. One possibility is to assume a linear pattern of causation like that analyzed in much conventional statistical research. Even though ordinal comparison does not strictly speaking permit the assessment of linear causation, it is not uncommon for qualitative and quantitative researchers to interpret ordinal results in this fashion. In doing so, the goal of analysis becomes estimating the proportion of an outcome that can be attributed to a particular value on an explanatory variable (see King et al. 1994, pp. 76–82).

Comparative historical researchers who use ordinal comparison to assess linear causation and estimate the causal effects of variables in this fashion face obvious disadvantages when compared to researchers who have a large number of cases at their disposal. When an ordinal strategy is used in comparative historical analysis, one can meaningfully speak of a degrees of freedom problem that inhibits the use of all but the most simple bivariate statistical methods. Furthermore, insights from statistical research about case selection, measurement error, and the construction of causal theories are often highly appropriate when applied to comparative historical works that seek to use the method of concomitant variation to identify patterns of linear causation. Yet, it must be emphasized that comparative historical researchers usually do not rely on ordinal analysis in isolation, instead combining it with nominal and within-case analysis. In this sense, one cannot mechanically extend advice from large-*N* analysis to even those comparative historical studies that do rely extensively on ordinal analysis.[11]

Special problems can arise when comparative historical researchers attempt to combine an ordinal strategy with a nominal strategy in comparative historical research. In particular, the practice of first assessing a variable as a necessary or sufficient condition and then reassessing this variable at the same level of aggregation using ordinal comparison raises concerns. The problem is that necessary or sufficient causes do not typically follow a linear pattern when plotted against an outcome. Yet, when researchers use ordinal analysis to assess hypotheses, they do generally test to see whether variable scores can be matched in a pattern that resembles linear change. One would therefore not necessarily expect a necessary or sufficient condition to appear causally important when evaluated through ordinal comparison.

In light of this problem, some comparative historical researchers may reject the very idea that ordinal findings should be interpreted as modeling linear causation or representing a correlational pattern. Instead, they may argue that ordinal associations should be viewed as reflecting necessary *and* sufficient causation. For example, an explanatory factor that reveals a very strong association with an outcome variable in an ordinal analysis could be meaningfully interpreted as a (probabilistic) necessary *and* sufficient condition. In other words, the bivariate scatter plot for a variable that is usually necessary *and* sufficient typically will appear as a very strong correlation in an ordinal analysis.

This discussion raises two general points of relevance to both statistical researchers and comparative historical researchers. First, conventional methods used by statistical researchers could potentially be recast as tools that seek to identify necessary and sufficient conditions. For example, additive linear models might be seen as tools designed to locate causal factors that are probabilistically sufficient but not necessary for an outcome.[12] These models compute the effects of each explanatory variable net of all other variables under the assumption that an increase on an explanatory variable leads (probabilistically) to an increase (or decrease) on an outcome variable all by itself. This notion that individual causes are capable of producing an effect by themselves within some probability is consistent with the

[11] In addition, some comparative historical researchers who use ordinal analysis extensively to study linear causation may select a rather large number of cases similar in size to that of much cross-national research (e.g., Rueschemeyer, Stephens, and Stephens 1992).

[12] Thanks to Charles Ragin for pointing this out to me.

understanding of a probabilistic sufficient cause (but not a probabilistic necessary cause). An additive linear equation that fully explained the variation on the outcome could be seen as having identified all of the individual variables that are sufficient for values on the dependent variable. A key priority for methodologists should be to explore the extent to which various statistical methods can be reframed in terms of necessary or sufficient conditions.

Second, comparative historical researchers who combine nominal and ordinal analysis should be explicit if they believe the explanatory variable under consideration operates as a condition that is necessary and sufficient, a condition that is necessary but not sufficient, a condition that is sufficient but not necessary, or a linear cause that increases or decreases values on an outcome. In general, logical problems will arise if the variable is treated as either a necessary but not sufficient condition or a sufficient but not necessary condition in a nominal evaluation and then is reassessed as either a necessary and sufficient condition or as a probabilistic linear cause in the ordinal analysis. The exception to this rule is scholars who disaggregate the variable when shifting from nominal to ordinal analysis (e.g., Skocpol 1979). When this takes place, the analyst can meaningfully assume that the disaggregated variables used in the ordinal assessment follow a linear pattern or a pattern of necessary and sufficient causation, whereas the aggregated nominal variable follows a pattern of necessary but not sufficient or sufficient but not necessary causation.

Examples of Ordinal Analysis in Comparative Historical Research

In some cases, comparative historical analysts may use ordinal analysis to strengthen an argument that is developed primarily through nominal comparison. In other cases, they may employ ordinal comparison as the central strategy of investigation. It is instructive to consider examples of both uses here.

Luebbert's (1987, 1991) work on interwar regimes in Europe employs ordinal analysis to strengthen a primarily nominal argument. In his overarching nominal assessment, Luebbert argues that the presence or absence of "lib-labism" (i.e., a liberal party–labor alliance) before World War I explains liberal versus nonliberal regime outcomes during the interwar period (see Table 10.2). Thus, when lib-labism was present before World War I, as in England, Switzerland, and France, a liberal regime developed in the interwar period. By contrast, when lib-labism was absent, as in Norway, Sweden, Denmark, Germany, Italy, and Spain, a nonliberal regime

Table 10.2. *Nominal Comparison in Luebbert's Analysis of Interwar Regimes*

	Prewar Lib-Labism	Interwar Liberalism
Switzerland	Yes	Yes
England	Yes	Yes
France	Yes	Yes
Belgium	No	No
Netherlands	No	No
Denmark	No	No
Italy	No	No
Norway	No	No
Spain	No	No
Sweden	No	No
Germany	No	No

developed. Hence, the dichotomous explanatory variable of lib-labism is perfectly matched with interwar liberalism.

Although his main explanation relies on nominal comparison, Luebbert reconceptualizes lib-labism and interwar liberalism as variables that are ranked across cases. Table 10.3 presents estimates of this ranking for the main countries considered by Luebbert. If the two ordinal variables are compared across cases, it is apparent that there is substantial, but not perfect, matching. Among the eleven cases, six of them (France, Belgium, the Netherlands, Denmark, Spain, and Germany) maintain their rank order; three cases (Switzerland, England, and Norway) move only one rank order or less; and two cases (Italy and Sweden) move about three rank orders. Lib-labism thus emerges as strongly, but not perfectly, associated with liberalism (the Spearman rank order correlation for the data in the Table is .92; the correlation is significant at a .01 level).

The use of ordinal comparison allows Luebbert to state certain findings in a more nuanced way than is possible when nominal categories are strictly employed. For example, he points out that among the countries where lib-labism failed before World War I, Belgium and the Netherlands "most closely approximated the British-French-Swiss pattern of liberal hegemony" (Luebbert 1991, p. 56). That is, these two countries were borderline success cases vis-à-vis the dichotomous explanatory variable of lib-labism. In turn, Belgium and the Netherlands established interwar regimes in which significant liberal elements were present, making them a subtype of liberal regimes (Luebbert 1991, pp. 248, 250). It appears that

Table 10.3. *Ordinal Comparison in Luebbert's Analysis of Interwar Regimes**

	Prewar Lib-Labism† (1 = least; 11 = most)	Interwar Liberalism (1 = least; 11 = most)
Switzerland	11	10
England	10	11
France	9	9
Belgium	7.5	7.5
Netherlands	7.5	7.5
Denmark	6	6
Italy	5	2
Norway	4	4.5
Spain	3	3
Sweden	2	4.5
Germany	1	1

* I have rank ordered cases based primarily on passages on the following pages of Luebbert's 1987 ("Social Origins") and 1991 (*Liberalism, Fascism, or Social Democracy*) works: England: (1987, p. 452), (1991, pp. 37–48, 166); Switzerland: (1991, pp. 49, 166); France: (1987, pp. 455–6), (1991, pp. 37–48, 166); Belgium and the Netherlands: (1987, p. 451), (1991, pp. 56–7, 248, 250); Denmark: (1987, p. 451), (1991, pp. 57–8, 236–7, 270–1); Sweden and Norway: (1991, pp. 57–8, 239–42, 270); Italy: (1991, pp. 57–8, 272–7); Spain: (1991, pp. 151–3, 272–7); and Germany: (1991, pp. 272–7).

† Luebbert measures lib-labism as the "degree of liberal hegemony" present before World War I.

Luebbert believes lib-labism is an almost always necessary and sufficient cause of interwar liberalism in Europe. In fact, his combined nominal-ordinal analysis could be seen as a rudimentary attempt to use fuzzy-set methods to assess this kind of causation.

In her work on social revolutions, Skocpol (1979) also uses ordinal comparison to supplement what is primarily a nominal argument. She does so by disaggregating nominal variables into constituent subvariables that are evaluated through ordinal comparison (see Mahoney 1999). Hence, while Skocpol's (1979, pp. 154–7) explanatory variable of "conditions for state breakdown" is treated as a dichotomous variable for the purpose of using the methods of agreement and difference, this variable is disaggregated into three constituent subvariables (international pressure, state autonomy, and agrarian backwardness) when evaluated through ordinal comparison. These constituent variables are ranked across all cases of revolution and nonrevolution. Likewise, Skocpol's dichotomous outcome variable of social revolution is reassessed in terms of ordinal constituent processes. Social revolution is defined in part as "rapid, basic transformations of a society's state and class structures" (Skocpol 1979, p. 4), and Skocpol notes ordinal differences among cases along these dimensions. For example, social revolution unfolded most rapidly in Russia, least rapidly in China, and at an intermediate pace in France. These differences are explained in part by ordinal contrasts on key explanatory variables, including the extent of international pressure that marked the revolutionary process (Skocpol 1979, p. 172). In sum, even though Skocpol's book is famous for its use of nominal comparison through the methods of agreement and difference, ordinal analysis plays a major role in underpinning the nominal argument.

While Luebbert and Skocpol use ordinal analysis to strengthen and support their overall nominal arguments, other scholars use ordinal comparison as the principal cross-case method of investigation. One example is Collier and Collier's (1991) work on labor incorporation in eight Latin American countries. Collier and Collier identify four types of labor incorporation periods, and they seek to explain ordinal differences in the "scope of mobilization" that characterized these periods. They first eliminate certain explanatory factors that lack any consistent relation to the scope of mobilization. For example, the authors reject explanations centered on the strength of the labor movement because there is "no systematic relationship between labor movement strength and type of incorporation period" (p. 750). The authors then show how their main explanatory variable – the political strength of the oligarchy – does reveal a clear pattern with mobilization during the incorporation period. In particular, the authors show that there is "an inverse relation between the political strength of the oligarchy . . . and the degree to which . . . mobilization was pursued in the incorporation period" (p. 748). Although there is a clear inverse relationship for six of Collier and Collier's eight cases, two cases deviate from this pattern. In Peru and Argentina, the oligarchy was in many spheres quite powerful, yet these cases exhibited relatively high levels of labor mobilization during the reform period, thus seemingly violating the hypothesized inverse pattern. The authors explain these deviations based on crucial "flaws" in the strength of the Peruvian and Argentine oligarchies (pp. 748–9). Once these flaws are taken into account, the inverse relationship at work for the other six cases also makes sense for Peru and Argentina. In this way, the authors show how what initially appears to be a deviation in fact reflects the general inverse pattern once more appropriate measures are introduced.

Another work that relies extensively on ordinal comparison is Orloff's (1993) comparative historical analysis of social provision for the elderly in Britain, Canada, and the United States. Orloff not only conceptualizes her own central explanatory variables as ordinal categories, but also evaluates rival explanations using this type of assessment. For example, she (pp. 47–8) uses ordinal comparison to reject explanations of the relative timing of social provision that focus on changes in the number of aged persons present in society. She argues that the expected relationship between age distribution and the timing of pension legislation is not supported by her cases. For example, Britain witnessed only a marginal increase in the number of elderly citizens but nevertheless enacted pensions at an early date. By contrast, Canada saw a very substantial increase in the elderly population but adopted old age insurance at a relatively late date. For the United States, the elderly population exhibited intermediate to high levels, yet pensions were adopted at a very late date. Hence, there is no apparent relationship between the two variables, and Orloff eliminates size of the elderly population as a potential explanatory factor.

Within-Case Analysis

In addition to comparing cases with one another, most comparative historical analysts also compare processes drawn from within particular cases. This strategy of within-case analysis entails examining multiple features of what was originally considered only a single case to assess hypotheses developed through cross-case analysis. In making within-case evaluations, analysts will often rely on nominal and ordinal measurement. However, whereas the nominal and ordinal strategies discussed previously entail highly aggregated comparisons across cases, the procedures discussed in this section involve disaggregated comparisons within cases. Hence, a within-case strategy is distinguished from nominal and ordinal strategies in terms of level of aggregation.

Within-case analysis is a tool specifically designed to compensate for limitations associated with cross-case methods. The most general type of within-case analysis is "pattern matching," a procedure in which the analyst assesses cross-case associations in light of multiple within-case hypotheses. An important subtype of this procedure is "process tracing," a technique in which the analyst attempts to locate the causal mechanisms linking a hypothesized explanatory variable to an outcome. Finally, a third technique – "causal narrative" – combines cross-case and within-case analysis by comparing cases in terms of highly disaggregated sequences of processes and events that lead to outcomes.

Pattern Matching

Causal patterns derived from cross-case comparison often suggest additional hypotheses about aspects of specific cases. Following a procedure that Campbell (1975) calls "pattern matching," comparative historical analysts test these additional hypotheses, evaluating whether patterns derived from cross-case analysis can be matched with observations from within specific cases.[13] Campbell (1975, p. 182) points out that pattern matching provides a powerful tool for theory falsification in small-*N* research: investigators routinely find that their arguments cannot be sustained when within-case hypotheses are assessed. Alternatively, if within-case observations are repeatedly consistent with a cross-case finding, researchers have stronger grounds for believing the cross-case finding is valid.

Comparative historical analysts pursue pattern matching using different levels of measurement. Both nominal and ordinal measurement can be used in conjunction with pattern matching. Researchers may also use interval measurement when assessing within-case hypotheses. Indeed, if a large number of within-case observations are measured at an interval level, researchers may employ statistical methods with the pattern-matching procedure.

A nice example of the use of statistical research for the purpose of pattern matching is Goldstone's (1991) work on revolutions during the early modern period. Goldstone's cross-case nominal argument suggests that demographic growth leads to revolutions by triggering structural crises (i.e., fiscal crises, elite–state and intraelite conflict, and mass opposition). To bolster this cross-case, small-*N* argument, he conceptualizes explanatory variables in terms of a large number of within-case quantitative measures and combines these measures into an overall "political stress indicator" that is evaluated statistically. These statistical evaluations are used as supplementary evidence to assess hypotheses that apply to a small number of cases, offering powerful confirmatory evidence in support of Goldstone's small-*N* argument.

In contrast to Goldstone's statistical analysis of within-case patterns, Luebbert (1991) uses ordinal and nominal comparison when employing

[13] See also Collier (1993), Eckstein (1975), and George (1979).

pattern matching. For example, his argument that an alliance between the socialist party and the middle peasantry (a "red–green" alliance) caused social democracy in interwar Europe has multiple within-case implications. Some of these within-case implications entail ordinal propositions – for example, the governing social coalition will lack a high level of stability; the working class will exercise a high degree of autonomy from the state; and high levels of strikes and labor activism will develop (Luebbert 1991, pp. 234–6). Other within-case implications entail nominal propositions – for example, socialists will not challenge the distribution of wealth in the countryside or try to mobilize the rural proletariat; and the middle peasantry will not provide a viable social base for the socialists (Luebbert, 1991, pp. 268–9, 272, 286–8). Luebbert's within-case analysis finds support for these hypotheses, significantly enhancing one's confidence that the cross-case argument is correct.

Regardless of the level of measurement (nominal, ordinal, interval) employed, the additional leverage offered by pattern matching helps compensate for the weaknesses of cross-case strategies. For example, one of the limitations of cross-case nominal methods is that several explanations may be supported by the data, leaving the analyst without a clear basis for deciding which explanatory factor is the most important. Pattern matching helps narrow the range of potential explanations by offering an additional means of eliminating variables. After variables are eliminated through pattern matching, analysts are often left with much more parsimonious explanations.

Pattern matching is also a key tool for those comparative historical researchers who seek to avoid the determinism of nominal methods but who lack enough cases to employ these methods probabilistically. Analysts can use pattern matching to show that a relationship is causal despite the fact that a cross-case nominal comparison reveals one or more cases in which scores on the explanatory and outcome variables deviate from a general pattern of matching. For example, if only three out of four cases reflect a general pattern of matching on nominal explanatory and outcome variables, scholars may conclude that the pattern reflects causation if they find significant within-case support. Likewise, analysts may use pattern matching to argue that a relationship is *not* causal even though scores on an explanatory variable are perfectly matched with scores on an outcome variable in a cross-case nominal assessment. They can do so by showing how the cross-case pattern is not supported when assessed against multiple within-case patterns. Hence, comparative historical analysts who choose to think about causation in probabilistic terms may use pattern matching as a basis for retaining explanatory variables that do not withstand deterministic cross-case nominal tests while rejecting other explanatory variables even though they do withstand such tests.

Finally, pattern matching can be a valuable supplement to cross-case ordinal comparison. Pattern matching can help analysts make a better judgment about the causal status of a relationship that is ambiguous when evaluated through cross-case ordinal analysis. Likewise, pattern matching can call into question the findings of ordinal comparison, showing how an apparently causal relationship is in fact not causal when viewed in light of multiple within-case implications.

Process Tracing

An important part of causal analysis involves establishing that there is some association between explanatory variables and an outcome variable. Yet, for many comparative historical analysts, an equally important part involves identifying the causal mechanisms that link explanatory variables with the outcome variable (Blalock 1961, p. 9; Elster 1989, pp. 4–7; Goldthorpe 1997; Hedström and Swedberg 1998; Salmon 1984, ch. 5). Causal mechanisms can be defined as the processes and intervening variables through which an explanatory variable exerts a causal effect on an outcome variable (Bennett 1997). Following George and McKeown (1985), the effort to infer causality through the identification of causal mechanisms can be called "process tracing."[14]

Process tracing is often used to help the analyst who works with a small number of cases avoid mistaking a spurious correlation for a causal association. The problem of spuriousness arises when two correlated variables appear to be causally related but in fact are the product of an antecedent variable. In small-*N* research, cross-case comparative methods are often vulnerable to this problem. For example, when three temporally ordered variables are correlated in a sequence, small-*N* analysts have difficulty using cross-case methods to determine if the sequence represents a causal path or a spurious correlation. The first variable in such a sequence is often perfectly correlated with both the second and third variables. Small-*N* cross-case methods do not provide a strong basis for judging whether this first variable represents an antecedent cause that "explains away" the presumed

[14] Because causal mechanisms are within-case implications of cross-case patterns, process tracing is actually a particular application of pattern matching.

causal relationship between the second and third variables, or whether the first and third variables are correlated because of the presence of the second variable, in which case the idea of causal path makes sense. Process tracing can help the analyst distinguish between these two possibilities by showing whether causal mechanisms link the variables together. Thus, if hypothesized causal mechanisms can be identified between the second and third variables through process tracing, the analyst has a basis for believing that the sequence is a causal path; that is, the second variable has a real causal effect on the third variable. Alternatively, if causal mechanisms cannot be identified between the second and third variables, the analyst has grounds for believing that the sequence may be a spurious correlation; that is, the second and third variables are correlated only because of the presence of the first antecedent variable.

Comparative historical analysts frequently argue that a correlation identified through cross-case analysis is not causal because mechanisms linking the presumed explanatory variable and the outcome variable cannot be identified. For example, Skocpol's (1979, pp. 170–1) work on the origins of revolutions uses process tracing to reject causal variables – such as ideologically motivated vanguard movements – that were not eliminated through cross-case methods. Although ideologically motivated vanguard movements were present in her three cases of social revolution, she argues that they did not exert an important causal effect in bringing about revolutions. In particular, in contrast to what other scholars have hypothesized, she argues that vanguard movements were not responsible for triggering widespread revolts against landlords and state agents. Rather, according to Skocpol, vanguard movements were marginal to the central political processes that defined social revolutions, emerging on the scene only very late to take advantage of situations they did not create. Hence, she concludes that these movements were not a crucial cause of social revolutions in France, Russia, and China.

Likewise, Luebbert uses process tracing to eliminate the "Moore–Gerschenkron thesis," which holds that fascist regimes result from the presence of a labor-repressive landed elite that is able to draw substantial lower-class rural support for fascism (Luebbert 1991, pp. 308–9). Although there is a matching between the presence/absence of a repressive landed elite and the presence/absence of fascism, Luebbert suggests that the mechanisms through which this specific factor supposedly produces fascism are not supported by the historical record of the fascist cases. Thus, rural support for fascism was generally not present in areas where a landed elite predominated. Likewise, the evidence shows that the landed elites who could deliver large numbers of votes did not usually support fascism (Luebbert 1991, pp. 308–9). In short, despite the matching, Luebbert rejects the Moore–Gerschenkron hypothesis because it is not validated by process tracing.

Other scholars use process tracing not to eliminate causal factors but to support their own explanations. For example, Collier and Collier (1991) identify mechanisms linking different types of labor incorporation periods with different types of party systems. In their analysis of Colombia and Uruguay, Collier and Collier systematically identify the processes and events through which the incorporation pattern of "electoral mobilization by a traditional party" led to the party system outcome of "electoral stability and social conflict." These processes included a period in which the party that oversaw incorporation briefly maintained power, the gradual emergence of conservative opposition, a period of intense political polarization, a military coup, and, finally, the creation of a party system marked by stable electoral politics and social conflict. Each of these events acts as a mechanism linking labor incorporation with a particular party system outcome. The ability of the authors to show how these and other processes connected explanatory and outcome variables is crucial to the success of their argument. Indeed, although any work can potentially benefit from process tracing, it is an especially important tool for those studies such as Collier and Collier's in which explanatory and outcome variables are separated by long periods of time.

Causal Narrative

A final procedure illustrates how comparative historical researchers use cross-case comparisons of within-case chronologies as a basis for making causal inferences. With this technique of "causal narrative," to use Sewell's (1996) terminology, the analyst attempts to validate aggregated cross-case associations by "breaking apart" variables into constituent sequences of disaggregated events and comparing these disaggregated sequences across cases. The purpose of unpacking aggregated variables through narrative is not only to provide a contextualized description of cases; rather, the goal is to support a cross-case argument at a more disaggregated level.

This technique relies on historical narrative, which has received significant attention in recent methodological discussions (e.g., Abbott 1990, 1992; Aminzade 1992; Franzosi 1998; Griffin 1992, 1993; Haydu 1998; Isaac 1997; Mahoney 1999; Somers 1992; Stryker 1996). However, the procedures through which analysts decide whether a narrative account lends support to a cross-case causal pattern have not been well specified. Griffin's (1993; see also Heise 1989) discussion of event-structure analysis is the most well developed statement on how narrative can be wedded to causal inference. Event-structure analysis provides a formal apparatus for unpacking events and reconstituting their constituent parts as a causal interpretation of historical processes. This procedure can underpin causal narrative by identifying the causally linked processes that constitute highly aggregated variables in cross-case analysis (Mahoney 1999, pp. 1165–7). With causal narrative, the analyst compares event sequences across cases to determine if the cases can reasonably be seen as following aggregated causal patterns at a more fine-grained level. In this sense, causal narrative entails the matching of event structures across cases (see Griffin and Ragin 1994, pp. 14–15; Sewell 1996, p. 262).[15] In addition, causal narrative can be used to show how two or more cases that are marked by important differences in causal processes at an aggregated level of analysis are also characterized by substantially different event structures at a disaggregated level.

A good example of the use of causal narrative to compare event structures is found in Skocpol's (1979) work on social revolutions. Many of Skocpol's key explanatory variables are actually made up of numerous causally linked processes. Likewise, the outcome of social revolution is itself composed of a series of causally connected events. These constituent processes represent an event-structure pattern that could be formally diagrammed and compared across cases (see Mahoney 1999). Although Skocpol does not carry out a formal mapping of event structures, she does implicitly compare the event structure of her cases to judge whether they follow a similar causal logic at a disaggregated level. According to Sewell (1996), Skocpol's ability to show that a similar event sequence is at work in each case of social revolution greatly contributes to the persuasiveness of her argument.

An interesting example of a work that uses causal narrative to contrast event-structure sequences is Yashar's (1997) excellent analysis of the origins of democracy in Costa Rica in 1949 and authoritarianism in Guatemala in 1954. Yashar notes that both Costa Rica and Guatemala experienced major democratic and social reform periods in the 1940s and 1950s. However, her narrative shows that these reform periods were actually composed of quite different event processes, and these different processes were highly

[15] Causal narrative cannot be used to assess cases that arrive at a given outcome through different causal processes. When this is true, one would expect the cases to be characterized by different – not similar – event-structure sequences.

consequential for the development of contrasting regimes. Thus, Yashar's narrative shows how particular actor choices about coalitional allies triggered differing reform efforts, reactions, and counterreactions. These differences in event sequences lend support to Yashar's overarching argument, which stresses the importance of political coalitions and alliance patterns.

Most comparative historical analysts use causal narrative as an informal technique presented through "stories" of event processes. It remains to be seen whether causal narrative can be more formally employed through event-structure diagrams that explicitly map each step and logical connection in a narrative argument. Griffin's (1993) work on event-structure analysis suggests that formally diagramming narratives can be complicated when a large number of events are considered. Yet, without such formal diagramming, the procedures through which analysts compare and contrast event-structure sequences across cases cannot be easily evaluated. The complex trade-offs between the clarity of informal narrative presentations and the rigor of explicitly diagrammed narrative accounts warrant further attention from methodologists.

Conclusion

Methodological recipes for producing successful research are neither possible nor desirable. Nevertheless, an awareness of the different tools available can help analysts improve the quality of their work and better present their findings to scholars from other traditions. Toward this end, this essay has identified and discussed three basic strategies of causal assessment used in comparative historical research: nominal comparison, ordinal comparison, and within-case analysis. By way of conclusion, I would like to bring together some of the unresolved questions and future methodological agendas suggested by the discussion of these strategies.

First, with respect to nominal methods, the study of necessary and sufficient conditions (including *probabilistic* necessary and sufficient conditions) deserves more attention from methodologists, including especially quantitative methodologists who do not ordinarily think about causation in this way. Comparative historical researchers have productively studied these conditions, and their work provides a valuable point of departure for those who are interested in learning more. It is indeed unfortunate that graduate students often lack the training to meaningfully evaluate arguments about necessary and sufficient causation. I would encourage both quantitative and qualitative methodologists to learn more about these methods, include them as a basic component of their courses on research methods, and let students make up their own minds about potential applications in comparative research.

Second, the fact that many comparative historical researchers combine an ordinal strategy with a nominal strategy suggests that they may think about ordinal relationships in terms of necessary and sufficient conditions. Yet, other comparative historical researchers believe ordinal relationships reflect a linear pattern of causation similar to that studied in much statistical research. These two alternatives need to be sorted out in future work. In general, questions about the extent to which linear statistical findings can or should be translated into the language of necessary and sufficient conditions will not be resolved until methodologists give more attention to nominal methods.

Finally, more methodological work needs to be done on the relationship between cross-case and within-case analysis. Part of the problem in understanding this relationship is that comparative historical researchers often do not say enough about how they use within-case analysis in their substantive studies. For example, we still do not have many systematic discussions of within-case analysis informing the selection of categories and cases *before* formal nominal tools are applied. Moreover, once initial nominal associations are established, more needs to be said about the application of particular types of within-case analysis. With pattern matching, researchers need to consider the special issues that may arise when a given study uses both nominal and statistical methods to evaluate the same within-case observations. Likewise, when using process tracing, methodologists need to explore more seriously the extent to which it is really possible to specify causal mechanisms as empirical hypotheses with directly testable implications. Regarding causal narrative, the overall debate between using words versus formally diagramming event structures as a means of representing disaggregated patterns of within-case causation needs to be sorted out.

These agendas will likely be at the forefront of the next generation of work on comparative historical methods.

References

Abbott, Andrew. 1990. "Conceptions of Time and Events in Social Science Methods: Causal and Narrative Approaches." *Historical Methods* 23: 140–50.

1992. "From Causes to Events: Notes on Narrative Positivism." *Sociological Methods and Research* 20: 428–55.

Strategies of Causal Assessment

Amenta, Edwin and Jane D. Poulsen. 1994. "Where to Begin: A Survey of Five Approaches to Selecting Independent Variables for Qualitative Comparative Analysis." *Sociological Methods and Research* 23: 22–53.

Aminzade, Ronald. 1992. "Historical Sociology and Time." *Sociological Methods and Research* 20: 456–80.

Bennett, Andrew. 1997. "Lost in the Translation: Big (*N*) Misinterpretations of Case Study Research." Paper Presented at the 38th annual convention of the International Studies Association, Toronto, March 18–22.

Blalock, Hubert M. 1961. *Causal Inferences in Nonexperimental Research*. Chapel Hill: University of North Carolina Press.

Braumoeller, Bear F. and Gary Goertz. 2000. "The Methodology of Necessary Conditions." *American Journal of Political Science* 44: 844–58.

Campbell, Donald T. 1975. "'Degrees of Freedom' and the Case Study." *Comparative Political Studies* 8: 178–93.

Colburn, Forest D. 1994. *The Vogue of Revolution in Poor Countries*. Princeton, NJ: Princeton University Press.

Collier, David. 1993. "The Comparative Method." Pp. 105–19 in *Political Science: The State of the Discipline II*, edited by Ada Finifter. Washington, DC: American Political Science Association.

Collier, David and Robert Adcock. 1999. "Democracy and Dichotomies: A Pragmatic Approach to Choices about Concepts." *Annual Review of Political Science* 2: 537–65.

Collier, David and James Mahoney. 1996. "Insights and Pitfalls: Selection Bias in Qualitative Research." *World Politics* 49: 56–91.

Collier, Ruth Berins and David Collier. 1991. *Shaping the Political Arena: Critical Junctures, the Labor Movement, and Regime Dynamics in Latin America*. Princeton, NJ: Princeton University Press.

DeFelice, E. Gene. 1986. "Causal Inference and Comparative Methods." *Comparative Political Studies* 19: 415–37.

Dion, Douglas. 1998. "Evidence and Inference in the Comparative Case Study." *Comparative Politics* 30: 127–46.

Downing, Brian M. 1992. *The Military Revolution and Political Change: Origins of Democracy and Autocracy in Early Modern Europe*. Princeton, NJ: Princeton University Press.

Drass, Kriss and Charles C. Ragin. 1999. *QC/FSA: Qualitative Comparative/Fuzzy-Set Analysis*. Evanston, IL: Institute for Policy Research, Northwestern University.

Eckstein, Harry. 1975. "Case Studies and Theory in Political Science." Pp. 79–138 in *Handbook of Political Science* 7, edited by Fred Greenstein and Nelson W. Polsby. Reading, MA: Addison-Wesley.

Elster, Jon. 1989. *Nuts and Bolts for the Social Sciences*. Cambridge: Cambridge University Press.

Ertman, Thomas. 1997. *Birth of the Leviathan: Building States and Regimes in Medieval and Early Modern Europe*. Cambridge: Cambridge University Press.

Franzosi, Roberto. 1998. "Narrative as Data: Linguistic and Statistical Tools for the Qualitative Study of Historical Events." *International Review of Social History* 43: 81–104.

Geddes, Barbara. 1990. "How the Cases You Choose Affect the Answers You Get: Selection Bias in Comparative Politics." Pp. 131–50 in *Political Analysis*, vol. 2, edited by James A. Stimson. Ann Arbor: University of Michigan Press.

George, Alexander L. 1979. "Case Studies and Theory Development: The Method of Structured, Focused Comparison." Pp. 43–68 in *Diplomacy: New Approaches in History, Theory, and Policy*, edited by P. G. Lauren. New York: Free Press.

George, Alexander L. and Timothy J. McKeown. 1985. "Case Studies and Theories of Organizational Decision Making." *Advances in Information Processing in Organizations* 2: 21–58.

Giddens, Anthony. 1979. *Central Problems in Social Theory: Action, Structure and Contradiction in Social Analysis*. Berkeley: University of California Press.

Goldstone, Jack A. 1991. *Revolution and Rebellion in the Early Modern World*. Berkeley: University of California Press.

1997. "Methodological Issues in Comparative Macrosociology." *Comparative Social Research* 16: 107–20.

Goldthorpe, John H. 1997. "Current Issues in Comparative Macrosociology: A Debate on Methodological Issues." *Comparative Social Research* 16: 1–26.

2000. *On Sociology: Numbers, Narratives, and the Integration of Research and Theory*. Oxford: Oxford University Press.

Griffin, Larry J. 1992. "Temporality, Events, and Explanation in Historical Sociology: An Introduction." *Sociological Methods and Research* 20: 403–27.

1993. "Narrative, Event-Structure, and Causal Interpretation in Historical Sociology." *American Journal of Sociology* 98: 1094–133.

Griffin, Larry and Charles C. Ragin. 1994. "Some Observations on Formal Methods of Qualitative Analysis." *Sociological Methods and Research* 23: 4–21.

Haydu, Jeffrey. 1998. "Making Use of the Past: Time Periods as Cases to Compare and as Sequences of Problem Solving." *American Journal of Sociology* 104: 339–71.

Hedström, Peter and Richard Swedberg, eds. 1998. *Social Mechanisms: An Analytical Approach to Social Theory*. New York: Cambridge University Press.

Heise, David. 1989. "Modeling Event Structures." *Journal of Mathematical Sociology* 14: 139–69.

Isaac, Larry W. 1997. "Transforming Localities: Reflections on Time, Causality, and Narrative in Contemporary Historical Sociology." *Historical Methods* 30: 4–12.

King, Gary, Robert O. Keohane, and Sidney Verba. 1994. *Designing Social Inquiry: Scientific Inference in Qualitative Research*. Princeton, NJ: Princeton University Press.

Lieberson, Stanley. 1985. *Making It Count: The Improvement of Social Research and Theory*. Berkeley: University of California Press.

1991. "Small *N*'s and Big Conclusions: An Examination of the Reasoning in Comparative Studies Based on a Small Number of Cases." *Social Forces* 70: 307–20.

1994. "More on the Uneasy Case for Using Mill-*Type* Methods in Small-*N* Comparative Studies." *Social Forces* 72: 1225–37.
1998. "Causal Analysis and Comparative Research: What Can We Learn from Studies Based on a Small Number of Cases?" Pp. 129–45 in *Rational Choice Theory and Large-Scale Data Analysis*, edited by Hans-Peter Blossfeld and Gerald Prein. Boulder, CO: Westview.
Lijphart, Arend. 1971. "Comparative Politics and the Comparative Method." *American Political Science Review* 65: 682–93.
1975. "The Comparable Cases Strategy in Comparative Research." *Comparative Political Studies* 8: 158–77.
Loung, Pauline Jones. 2002. *Institutional Change and Political Continuity in Post-Soviet Central Asia: Power, Perceptions, and Pacts.* New York: Cambridge University Press.
Luebbert, Gregory M. 1987. "Social Foundations of Political Order in Interwar Europe." *World Politics* 39: 449–78.
1991. *Liberalism, Fascism, or Social Democracy: Social Classes and the Political Origins of Regimes in Interwar Europe.* New York: Oxford University Press.
Mahoney, James. 1999. "Nominal, Ordinal, and Narrative Appraisal in Macro-causal Analysis." *American Journal of Sociology* 104: 1154–96.
2001. "Beyond Correlational Analysis: Recent Innovations in Theory and Method." *Sociological Forum* 16: 575–93.
Mahoney, James and Richard Snyder. 1999. "Rethinking Agency and Structure in the Study of Regime Change." *Studies in Comparative International Development* 34: 3–32.
Marx, Anthony W. 1998. *Making Race and Nation: A Comparison of the United States, South Africa, and Brazil.* Cambridge: Cambridge University Press.
Mill, John Stuart. [1843] 1974. *A System of Logic.* Toronto: University of Toronto Press.
Most, Benjamin and Harvey Starr. 1989. *Inquiry, Logic, and International Politics.* Columbia: University of South Carolina Press.
Munck, Gerardo L. 1998. "Canons of Research Design in Qualitative Analysis." *Studies in Comparative International Development* 33: 18–45.
Nichols, Elizabeth. 1986. "Skocpol on Revolution: Comparative Analysis vs. Historical Conjuncture." *Comparative Social Research* 9: 163–86.
Orloff, Ann Shola. 1993. *The Politics of Pensions: A Comparative Analysis of Britain, Canada, and the United States, 1880–1940.* Madison: University of Wisconsin Press.
Przeworski, Adam and Henry Teune. 1970. *The Logic of Comparative Social Inquiry.* New York: Wiley.
Ragin, Charles C. 1987. *The Comparative Method: Moving Beyond Qualitative and Quantitative Strategies.* Berkeley: University of California Press.
1997. "Turning the Tables: How Case-Oriented Research Challenges Variable-Oriented Research." *Comparative Social Research* 16: 27–42.
2000. *Fuzzy-Set Social Science.* Chicago: University of Chicago Press.

Rueschemeyer, Dietrich and John D. Stephens. 1997. "Comparing Historical Sequences – A Powerful Tool for Causal Analysis." *Comparative Social Research* 17: 55–72.

Rueschemeyer, Dietrich, Evelyne Huber Stephens, and John D. Stephens. 1992. *Capitalist Development and Democracy*. Chicago: University of Chicago Press.

Salmon, Wesley. 1984. *Scientific Explanation and the Causal Structure of the World.* Princeton, NJ: Princeton University Press.

Sartori, Giovanni. 1987. *Theory of Democracy Revisited.* Chatham, NJ: Chatham House.

Selbin, Eric. 1993. *Modern Latin American Revolutions.* Boulder, CO: Westview.

Sewell, William H., Jr. 1996. "Three Temporalities: Toward an Eventful Sociology." Pp. 245–80 in *The Historic Turn in the Human Sciences*, edited by Terrence J. McDonald. Ann Arbor: University of Michigan Press.

Skocpol, Theda. 1979. *States and Social Revolutions: A Comparative Analysis of France, Russia, and China.* Cambridge: Cambridge University Press.

1994. "Reflections on Recent Scholarship about Social Revolutions and How to Study Them." Pp. 301–44 in *Social Revolutions in the Modern World*, edited by Theda Skocpol. Cambridge: Cambridge University Press.

Skocpol, Theda and Margaret Somers. 1980. "The Uses of Comparative History in Macrosocial Inquiry." *Comparative Studies in Society and History* 22: 174–97.

Smelser, Neil. 1976. *Comparative Methods in the Social Sciences.* Englewood Cliffs, NJ: Prentice-Hall.

Somers, Margaret R. 1992. "Narrativity, Narrative Identity, and Social Action: Rethinking English Working-Class Formation." *Social Science History* 16: 591–630.

Stryker, Robin. 1996. "Beyond History versus Theory: Strategic Narrative and Sociological Explanation." *Sociological Methods and Research* 24: 304–52.

Wickham-Crowley, Timothy. 1992. *Guerrillas and Revolution in Latin America: A Comparative Study of Insurgents and Regimes Since 1956.* Princeton, NJ: Princeton University Press.

Yashar, Deborah J. 1997. *Demanding Democracy: Reform and Reaction in Costa Rica and Guatemala, 1870s–1950s.* Stanford, CA: Stanford University Press.

11

Aligning Ontology and Methodology in Comparative Research

Peter A. Hall

Some of the liveliest debates about methodology in the social sciences center on comparative research. This essay concentrates on comparative politics, a field often defined by reference to the use of a particular "comparative method," but it also bears on sociology, where there is active controversy about methodological issues. I use the term "methodology" to refer to the means scholars employ to increase confidence that the inferences they make about the social and political world are valid.[1] The most important of these are inferences about causal relationships, where the object of a methodology is to increase confidence in assertions that one variable or event (x) exerts a causal effect on another (y).

One of the curious features of contemporary debates is that they pay more attention to methodology than to issues of ontology.[2] "Ontology"

I am grateful to Samuel Beer, Suzanne Berger, Bear Braumoeller, Tim Büthe, David Collier, Peter Gourevitch, Lars Mjøset, Paul Pierson, Jim Shoch, Allison Stanger, Paul Steinberg, Christian Toft, Laurence Whitehead, and the editors of this volume for comments on earlier versions of this essay, and to Grzegorz Ekiert for many discussions.

[1] I refer to both "internal" and "external" validity, where the former refers to confidence that the relationship the researcher posits between x and y actually exists in the case at hand and the latter refers to confidence that, ceteris paribus, the same relationship exists in other cases as well (see Cook and Campbell 1979). Although a mainstream formulation, this definition of methodology is deliberately oriented to the issues on which the essay concentrates and so is somewhat restrictive. Social science also involves other tasks, such as the development of theory and the establishment of limiting cases, to which a set of methodological issues not covered here apply.

[2] There are a few exceptions to this assertion, including the pioneering work of Ragin (1987, 2000). In sociology, there is also a lively debate about epistemology, which I define as the study of what we can know. It is inspired by interest in scientific realism and postmodernism and touches, at points, on issues of ontology (cf. McDonald 1996; Goldthorpe 1997; Archer et al. 1998).

refers to the character of the world as it actually is. Accordingly, I use the term to refer to the fundamental assumptions scholars make about the nature of the social and political world and especially about the nature of causal relationships within that world. If a methodology consists of techniques for making observations about causal relations, an ontology consists of premises about the deep causal structures of the world from which analysis begins and without which theories about the social world would not make sense. At a fundamental level, it is how we imagine the social world to be.

Used as it is here to refer to a set of assumptions, of course, an ontology is a theoretical construct, and the line between it and the "theories" of social science is a fine one. However, I use the term to refer to especially fundamental assumptions about the causal structures of the social or political world that may or may not be explicit in a theory but are always implicit in the "middle-range" theories on which most comparativists concentrate. In this respect, ontologies are analogous to the "socioeconomic machines" that Cartwright (1997) posits as the indispensable antecedent for more specific causal statements. Many theories about a phenomenon, such as stable democracy, neocorporatist arrangements, or political tolerance, share the same overarching ontology, but different theories can also reference different ontologies.

Ontology is ultimately crucial to methodology because the appropriateness of a particular set of methods for a given problem turns on assumptions about the nature of the causal relations they are meant to discover. It makes little sense to apply methods designed to establish the presence of functional relationships, for instance, if we confront a world in which causal relationships are not functional. To be valid, the methodologies used in a field must be congruent with its prevailing ontologies. To some this will seem obvious.

However, my analysis is motivated by the observation that a substantial gap has opened up between the methodologies popular in comparative politics and the ontologies the field embraces. Comparative politics is a river with many currents but, as Lijphart (1975, p. 165) notes, there has been "a postwar trend in comparative politics" toward statistical methods, based preeminently on the standard regression model.[3] Influential texts now give priority to such approaches, and many scholars have become critical of other methods (Geddes 1990; King, Keohane, and Verba 1994;

[3] The current popularity of pooled cross-sectional time series regressions is one manifestation of this trend.

Goldthorpe 1997). Over the same period, the ontologies of the field have moved in a different direction: toward theories, such as those based on path dependence or strategic interaction, whose conceptions of the causal structures underlying outcomes are at odds with the assumptions required for standard regression techniques and conventional comparative method to provide valid causal inferences (cf. Bates, Greif, Levi, Rosenthal, and Weingast 1998; Pierson 2000a). The ontologies of comparative politics have substantially outrun its methodologies.

The purpose of this essay is to reexamine the alignment of ontology and methodology in comparative politics with a view to establishing the magnitude of the problem and potential solutions for it. It begins with a brief account of the development of the field in order to show how ontologies and methodologies developed in tandem. I then examine the contemporary divergence between ontology and methodology in more detail. After reviewing several responses to that divergence, I argue that small-*N* research designs based on systematic process analysis offer considerable potential for resolving the dilemmas posed by this divergence. I conclude by noting the implications of these developments for conventional understandings of case studies and the comparative method.

The Development of Ontology and Methodology in Comparative Politics

A complete survey of how the intricate relationships between ontology and methodology developed in comparative politics is beyond the scope of this essay. However, a synoptic review will illustrate how these two sides of scholarship developed in tandem. At the cost of some simplification, we can see how the field has moved to its current crossroads.[4]

The Initial Institutionalism

As Eckstein (1963) points out, the modern field of comparative politics originated with the study of constitutions and legal systems. This was the original "institutionalism." The approach focused on the formal institutions of governance and, while appropriately cynical about their more ceremonial features, tended to assume that one could say most of what needed to be

[4] For more extensive reviews of theoretical developments in the field of comparative politics see Eckstein and Apter (1963), Bill and Hardgrave (1973), Chilcote (1981), and Lichbach and Zuckerman (1997).

said about the politics of a nation by describing its legal system and national history (cf. Bagehot 1867; Wilson 1890; Friedrich 1950; Eckstein and Apter 1963). From the perspective of causality, the ontology underlying the field was circumscribed. Although the natural world was said to be governed by lawlike regularities, the institutions of the political world were seen primarily as the product of national histories. In this respect, the incipient field of comparative politics was less developed than those of sociology or economics, where Marx, Weber, Durkheim, Marshall, and others had begun to posit general causal forces driving social and political outcomes.

The methods adopted by the pioneers in this field were appropriate to such an ontology. Their analyses were largely descriptive, often idiographic in the sense that they sought a complete understanding of one case rather than generalizations that could travel across cases, and their orientation was frequently normative. Where the early comparativists engaged in causal explanation, they adopted the methods of historians focused on detailed narrative about the chain of events leading up to a phenomenon. Cross-national comparison concentrated primarily on formal institutions. Although the study of American politics became more sophisticated in the interwar years, following the paths blazed by Bentley (1908), Lasswell (1936), and Schattschneider (1935), the ambitions of comparative politics remained circumspect. Its methods were appropriate to its ontology, but the latter militated against systematic cross-national generalization.

The Comparative Revolution

In this context, developments in the field during the 1950s and 1960s were genuinely revolutionary. Although often construed as methodological, they were initially ontological. Following American studies that found whole new dimensions to politics hidden beneath the formal governmental system, in the clash of social interests and the operation of political machines, the field expanded its conception of what lay within the purview of political inquiry. Seeking terms with which to characterize the broader ambit of this new politics, Easton (1953, 1965) and Almond (1956; Almond and Powell 1966) turned for inspiration to Parsons's (1951) view of social relations as structured patterns of roles and beliefs fostered by an overarching social system (cf. Merton 1949). They emerged with a concept of the "political system" whose operation was structured not only by governmental institutions, but by a wide range of formal and informal relationships among individuals, rooted in the secondary associations of a nation or its political culture, understood as a set of values or attitudes often affective or normative in nature (Almond and Verba 1963). This expansion in the scope of political inquiry was the first key postwar development revolutionizing the study of comparative politics.

The second was a movement toward views that saw the political world in terms normally applied to the natural world, namely, as a sphere governed by causal relationships that take the form of lawlike regularities operative across space and time. With this ontological shift, the new political science became a nomological inquiry, oriented to the discovery of causal generalizations expected to hold across a diverse range of cases. Explanation was construed as a process of identifying "covering laws" under which specific cases could be subsumed; and causation was usually understood, in conventionalist terms, to imply something like logical necessity or, in empiricist terms, as constant conjunction, that is, to denote the fact that wherever one finds *x* one finds *y* (Hume 1748; Hempel 1965; Nagel 1961; Moon 1975). Comparative politics found a new mission.

The third development central to ontological shifts of the 1950s and 1960s, drawing on biology rather than physics for inspiration and not entirely compatible with the others, was the growing popularity of functionalist conceptions of causation. Generally speaking, a functionalist view assumes that the presence of a phenomenon can be explained by its consequences (Elster 1983). The presence of a specific set of political institutions, for instance, might be explained by the contribution it makes to the efficient functioning of a social or political system. The holism characteristic of postwar views of the political system encouraged functionalist perspectives. If the polity forms a coherent whole of interrelated parts, it is but a short step to see the relationships among these parts as functional ones.

These ontological shifts encouraged a set of methodological developments that continue to influence the discipline today. They led many to attach new importance to comparative inquiry. If the character of political institutions or endeavor is to be explained as the requisite of an overarching political system, one needs general knowledge about how such systems operate that cannot be based entirely on a single national case. The new emphasis on finding causal laws valid across time and space sent scholars in search of diverse cases from other venues in which to test their propositions. For more than a decade, some of the most exciting work in the discipline was sponsored by the SSRC Committee on Comparative Politics that developed a famous set of propositions about modernization based on the transformation of "traditional" societies into "modern" ones (Lerner 1958; Apter 1965; Binder et al. 1971; Chilcote 1981, ch. 7). Scholars soon produced a large literature on political regimes (Almond and Powell 1966; Greenstein and Polsby 1975). Characteristically, these works tied political science closely to sociology by linking political developments to a range of other social phenomena. The drive was to characterize phenomena around that world that were once seen as distinctive in terms that were genuinely comparable so that national cases could be subsumed under general theories of modernization, revolution, democracy, or political stability.

In methodological terms, this project attached high value to effective concept formation and the development of cross-national taxonomies (Holt and Turner 1970; Frey 1976; cf. Collier and Adcock 1999). Eckstein (1965) argued that the formation of effective typologies is a central methodology of comparative politics, and lively debate ensued about the level of abstraction at which one's concepts and typologies should be pitched (cf. Sartori 1970; MacIntyre 1978).

Contemporary interest in functionalism reinforced the taxonomic emphasis of the field. Scholars attempted to specify the functions a polity had to perform in order to be effective and the institutions that performed such functions. Political development was often approached as a problem of specifying the processes any nation would experience en route to stable democracy and of comparing such conceptions with the paths nations actually followed. Lively debate ensued about whether the timing of a process, such as industrialization, would affect its impact (Gerschenkron 1962; Binder et al. 1971; Grew 1978).

In one of the most influential methodological statements of the time, Verba (1967) described the methodology appropriate to comparative politics as one of "disciplined, configurative inquiry," construed as a search for systematic patterns of similarity and difference in the features of political systems transcending idiographic studies that privilege full description of the distinctive features of a polity. Comparative inquiry was distinguished by efforts to relate the features of each nation to a set of categories and causal mechanisms designed to apply across nations. The key challenge, as Verba identified it, was one of characterizing the relevant developments in terms that do not do distort their contextual character but still locate them within the categories of an overarching theory (cf. Verba 1971). This challenge remains a touchstone for comparative politics, one amplified by George's (1979) call for "structured, focused comparison."

However, the field was bedeviled by problems intrinsic to functional analysis. It is easy to posit functional relationships but difficult to establish their causal force relative to other factors. Visions of the polity as a system in equilibrium foundered on fuzziness about how equilibrium is distinguished from disequlibrium and on the apparent ease with which new equilibria could be attained. Where some saw stability, others saw flux. Functional equivalence became a major problem for explanation: if several institutions can perform the same function, it is difficult to explain the presence of any one of them by reference to those functions (Merton 1949). To cope with such problems, the categories of functional analysis became increasingly abstract, and, faced with their growing elasticity, scholars began to demand that the field move down the conceptual "ladder of abstraction" to focus on middle-range categories with limited fields of denotation that were more closely connected to actual events (Sartori 1970).

The Comparative Method

In the face of withering critiques, functionalist analysis was discredited during the 1960s and 1970s, and the ontology of the field shifted again. Political scientists began to move away from holistic conceptions of the polity and from the previous focus on complex interaction effects among its parts. More of them began to embrace the view that the ultimate causes for political outcomes lie in individual behavior. Structural-functionalist images of the causal structures in the political world gave way to "variables-oriented" images in which variation in a "dependent" variable is said to be caused by variation in another set of variables construed as ones that vary independently of the variable to be explained and of each other. The search remained a nomothetic one, focused on discovering causal regularities, but those regularities were now construed in new terms.

The methodologies of comparative politics changed in tandem with these shifts in ontology. The influential textbook by Przeworski and Teune (1970) exemplifies the methodological emphasis of the era. It reflected growing interest in the methods of agreement and difference devised by Mill (1872) that establish the existence of a causal relationship between two variables by comparing cases that are similar in all respects except for the values taken by the two variables of interest or that differ in all relevant respects but the correspondence among such variables. Reflecting the interest in political explanations rooted in individual-level behavior popular at that time, Przeworski and Teune evinced a preference for the latter, which they termed a "most different systems" design, because it allows one to examine relationships among variables below the level of the nation or system in a diverse range of contexts. Building on the work of Smelser (1966, 1976), this book substantially advanced the practice of what became known as the "comparative method" – the method normally applied when a small number of cases are being examined, namely, in small-*N* research designs.

The quintessential expression of the comparative method was provided by Lijphart (1971, 1975), whose views exemplify what became the dominant understanding in the field. Lijphart defined the comparative method by contrasting it to two other methods. The "experimental" method is one in which investigators actively alter the variables with which they expect to explain an outcome in cases randomly assigned to a treatment group, comparing the outcomes there with those in cases randomly assigned to a control group where the relevant variables have not been altered. This is a powerful method for testing causal inferences, but it is rarely practical in the sphere of comparative politics, where Lijphart suggested that the best substitute would be the "statistical" method. Practitioners of the statistical method inspect a large number of cases showing various combinations of values on a number of explanatory variables and calculate the partial correlations between them and a dependent variable, using the rules of probability to establish the likelihood that each potential explanatory variable has an effect on the dependent variable as well as the magnitude of each effect.

Lijphart's conception of the comparative method was deeply influenced by his framing of it. This framework led him to see the comparative method as one analogous to the statistical method and different from it largely because only a small number of cases are inspected. Again, the bases for that inspection are Mill's methods of agreement and difference.[5] The investigator looks across a range of cases for the similarities in explanatory variables that would explain similarities in outcomes or for difference on one or two explanatory variables that would explain corresponding differences in outcomes. The key point is that, as portrayed by Lijphart and most others, the comparative method is essentially correlational. It bases inference about causal relations on covariation between a dependent variable and a small set of independent variables, and inspection of the cases is used primarily to determine the presence or value of such variables in them.

[5] Lijphart (1971, p. 688) notes, as have many others (cf. Smelser 1976, pp. 62, 141), that neither Mill nor Durkheim believed these methods could be applied in the social sciences, but he rejects their objections for being "founded on too exacting a scientific standard."

This conception of how small-N comparison should be conducted and of the comparative method became highly influential. It conditioned both the character of debate and the gradual methodological movement in the field. Construed in these terms, the comparative method is a distinctly fragile one for establishing causal inferences, fraught with problems of "omitted variable bias" that arise when one has many variables and few cases to consider (Lieberson 1985). The method yields strong inferences only if the explanatory variables can be seen as "necessary" or "sufficient" causes of the relevant outcome and causal relations as deterministic, even though scholars now tend to view many such relations as probabilistic.[6] Lijphart (1971, 1975) responded heroically to these concerns, suggesting several ways to improve comparative research designs, essentially by increasing the number of cases, reframing the variables to reduce their number, or focusing on cases that provide "critical" tests for a theory. But it is not difficult to see why he and many others concluded that "because the comparative method must be considered the weaker method, it is usually advisable to shift to the statistical method if sufficient cases are available for investigation" (1975, p. 165).

This stance set the tone for much of the subsequent debate. Some scholars have suggested important refinements to the comparative method, and many continue to rely on it (Campbell 1975; George 1979; Skocpol and Somers 1980; Collier 1991). But there is a growing tendency to regard statistical methods as superior for establishing causal inferences (Geddes 1990; King et al. 1994; Goldthorpe 1997). In practice, this means a heavy emphasis on regression analysis. The vast majority of studies in comparative politics employing statistical techniques use some form of regression analysis, whether probit, logit, generalized, or ordinary least squares. The drive to secure enough cases to employ such methods now leads many scholars to privilege studies based on pooled cross-sectional time-series data.

The Contemporary Dilemma

What then is the contemporary dilemma facing the field? Standard regression analysis and the comparative method understood in conventional terms

[6] This follows whether causal relations are ontologically probabilistic, i.e. operative only in a certain proportion of the cases, or deterministic but observable only in a proportion of the observations because of errors in measurement or research design. The problem arises because, if x causes y in only 80 percent of the cases, when we find one or two cases of y without x, we do not know whether x does not cause y or whether these cases are part of the exceptional 20 percent.

provide strong bases for causal inferences only when the causal structures in the world to which they are applied conform to an exacting set of assumptions. Both methods imply specific ontologies.

The comparative method requires especially demanding assumptions. It provides effective tests only where the world conforms to a Humean ontology that associates causation with constant conjunction or where the causal variables being sought are necessary causes of an outcome, that is, so important to it that they must be present for that outcome to occur (see Braumoeller 2000).

Regression analysis is more flexible. It is well adapted to an ontology that envisions probabilistic causation and, given enough cases, it can cope with some interaction effects (cf. Jackson 1996). However, the types of regression analyses commonly used to study comparative politics provide valid support for causal inferences only if the causal relations they are examining meet a rigorous set of assumptions (see Wallerstein 2000). In general, this method assumes unit homogeneity, which is to say that, other things being equal, a change in the value of a causal variable x will produce a corresponding change in the value of the outcome variable y of the same magnitude across all the cases. It assumes no systematic correlation between the causal variables included in the analysis and other causal variables omitted from it but correlated with the dependent variable. It assumes that all the relevant interaction effects among the causal variables have been captured by interaction terms in the regression. It assumes that the cases are fully independent, such that the values of the causal variables in one case are unaffected by the value of the causal variables or outcomes in other cases.[7] Although instrumental variables can sometimes be used, most regression analyses assume that there is no reciprocal causation, that is, that the causal variables are unaffected by the dependent variable.

In short, the comparative method, as it is usually understood, and the standard regression models employed in comparative politics make strong sets of assumptions about the nature of the causal relations they are being used to examine. They do not assess causal relationships well if the world does not conform to that ontology.

The problem is that the world may not have this causal structure. Even when the standard regression model was on the rise, some argued that it did

[7] In other words, most such analyses assume no "diffusion effects" of the sort to which Galton drew our attention. Although there are techniques for assessing such effects, they are used rarely in comparative political inquiry.

not (Macridis 1968; Wolin 1969; Richter 1970). In recent years, however, more and more of the models embraced by comparative politics violate the assumptions about causal structures that must be valid if methods based on the standard regression model or conventional comparison are to be valid. Consider how different the complex models now advanced to explain transitions to democracy are from the parsimonious generalizations of an older literature about the conditions for stable democracy (cf. Lipset 1959; O'Donnell and Schmitter 1986). The causal relationships on which scholars now focus are different from those posited two decades ago, and many acknowledge forms of multicausality that previous work ignored.

Ragin's (1987) pioneering work identifies many of these causal complexities under the rubric of "multiple conjunctural causation" (see also Lieberson 1985). In most cases, the problems arise from *interaction effects* among causal or contextual variables that standard analyses tend to assume away.[8] Traditional methods focused on identifying a set of independent variables ($x_1 \ldots x_n$) that exert consistent causal effects on an outcome (y) tend to miss the following types of causal relationships:

i. We find instances in which an increase in x (level of economic development) causes an increase in y (movement toward democracy) in some cases but does not have this effect in others, where y is caused by an entirely different set of variables, w.
ii. We find cases in which an increase in x (social democratic governance) is associated with an increase in y (social spending) at one point in time, t_i, but not at another point in time, t_{ii}.
iii. We find instances in which an increase in x (social protest) causes an outcome y (government turnover) in some cases but an entirely different outcome (repression) in other cases.
iv. We find instances in which an outcome y (successful wage coordination) depends on the value of many other variables – v (union density), w (social democratic governance), and x (social policy regime) – whose values are in turn jointly dependent on each other.
v. We find cases in which increases in x (support for democracy) increase y (the stability of democracy) and in which increases in y also tend to increase x.

[8] Here as elsewhere in this essay, I adopt a variables-oriented approach to causation both to relate recent approaches to older ones and because I believe it remains the most fruitful perspective on causation. But readers should note the literature that rejects this approach in favor of others, including case-oriented approaches (cf. Ragin 1987, 2000).

If causal structures of this sort were unusual, it might be feasible to relegate them to the realm of the unknowable in order to concentrate on simpler relationships that can be assessed. But growing numbers of scholars have concluded that these types of causal structures are common features of the political world. Some of the most prominent theories in comparative politics now understand the world in terms that do not conform to the assumptions required by standard regression analysis. Two major lines of theorizing are especially important. Each is distinctive and influential among a different group of scholars, but both advance ontologies that pose singular problems for conventional methods of analysis.

The first of these two lines of theoretical development regards political outcomes as the result of strategic interaction among actors of a sort that can often be modeled by noncooperative game theory. Now applied to many issues, this perspective sees political outcomes as the result of chains of choices that the actors make in response to each other through iterated rounds of interaction. At each point in time, the choices of the actors may be influenced by the presence of specific types of institutions, but the latter rarely specify a unique equilibrium. As a result, the outcome usually depends on a further set of conditions – social, economic, or cultural – that can be complex or evanescent. In the tree diagrams of games presented in extensive form, there are many branches. A shift in the conditions underpinning strategic choice at one juncture can have radical effects on later outcomes. As a result, although some elements of these theories, including conjectures about the equilibrium impact of various types of institutions, can be tested using standard comparative analysis, it is usually difficult to reduce the chains of causation envisioned by such theories to a simple set of independent variables (cf. Knight and Sened 1995; Milner 1998; Bates et al. 1998).

The second line of theory that is transforming our understanding of causal structures is advanced by an influential literature about path dependence (Collier and Collier 1991; Thelen 1999, 2000; Mahoney 2000a; Pierson 2000a). Although their views about how path dependence should be defined and what propels a unit along a path vary, analysts taking this perspective tend to agree on two points with serious implications for causal analysis. First, they agree that causal developments of great import for the character of an ultimate outcome often occur early in the long causal chain that leads to that outcome, perhaps even in the distant past. If the impact of subsequent developments in all the relevant cases were homogeneous across them, this observation would not be a major problem for

conventional methods: variables representing early developments could be incorporated into a standard regression analysis. However, path-dependent approaches to politics usually advance a second contention. They suggest that a key development in the distant past (whether a fateful choice or a crucial event) often affects a case so deeply that it alters the impact of subsequent developments there, thereby vitiating the assumption that such developments x, y, z can be expected to have the same impact across cases. In effect, this is a contention that interaction effects occur over time and can multiply.

Among analysts of path dependence, there is debate about whether the key developments are typically contingent or predictable and whether they occur mainly at critical junctures that are broadly transformative in character or at multiple points in time, with effects that are initially incremental but increase over time. However, path-dependent images of the world challenge traditional methods because they contend that early developments can change the context of a case so radically that subsequent developments will have different effects in each of the cases. Interaction effects build up over time, carrying cases down such different paths that it becomes unreasonable to suppose that an x occurring today has the same effect, y, across all settings.

In short, theories of strategic interaction and of path dependence both see the world not as a terrain marked by the operation of timeless causal regularities, but as a branching tree whose tips represent the outcomes of events that unfold over time (cf. Sewell 1996). If this is true, the timing of a particular development can matter a great deal to its effect. The sequence in which developments occur becomes important to the effects that they generate (Pierson 2000b; Thelen 2000; cf. Binder et al. 1971). The prototypical contention is that the impact of x will depend on whether it occurs before or after w. The effect of industrialization depends on whether it occurs in the late eighteenth or nineteenth century (Gerschenkron 1962). The overarching premise is that context matters: the impact of x will rarely be independent of the value of other variables (u, v, w), and contextual heterogeneity is a function of events unfolding over time.

Theories of path dependence explicitly draw our attention to the importance of history. They imply that current outcomes can rarely be explained by reference only to the present or the immediate past. But theories of strategic interaction also reference a chain of iterated choices, often extending into the distant past. Both approaches militate against analyses into which past developments are simply imported as an independent variable because they imply that the causal impact of such developments depends on where they are located within the historical chain.

Although claims of this sort pose profound challenges to mainstream analysis, they have a great deal of intuitive plausibility. Six years of social democratic governance in the 1930s had a lasting impact on policy regimes, but it almost certainly did not have the same impact as six years of social democratic governance in the 1980s. Moreover, because the impact of social democratic governance can be conditioned by other factors, it may not be the same across cases even at one point in time.[9] When the effects of a few variables are very strong and measurable in a substantial number of cases, regression analyses can assess some of these types of interaction effects. In practice, however, the interaction effects are often so complex and the data so limited that regression analysis cannot test the relevant propositions. Many analysts simply assume them away.

The new theories in comparative politics based on strategic interaction or path-dependent models of the world also carry implications for what can be said to constitute adequate explanations for a given political outcome. This is an issue about which social scientists can disagree. Weber (1949), for instance, argued that an explanation for a particular set of events is adequate only if it can account for the views that contemporary participants had of those events. Friedman (1968) argued just the opposite: that an explanation is adequate if it predicts subsequent occurrences of the events regardless of whether it portrays the beliefs and motivations of the actors accurately. One of the principal divisions in such debates falls between those who believe explanation requires a relatively full account of the developments leading up to an outcome and those who believe that a good explanation is parsimonious, that is, one that cites only a few causal variables (Shively 1974, p. 15; Abbott 1988; cf. Bennett and George 2001). Historians are closely associated with the first view, and political scientists are often associated with the second.[10]

For many years, a substantial number of scholars of comparative politics have seen explanation as a matter of attaching weights to a small set of

[9] See the observation of Donald Winch (1989) that the economic policies of the Swedish social democrats were deeply conditioned by the conclusions they drew from watching the efforts of a British Labour government that preceded them.

[10] For illuminating discussions that explore some of the similarities between explanation in history and social science, see Bennett and George (in press).

causal variables seen as consistent predictors of a given outcome. Ontologies that saw the political world as a sphere governed by immutable causal regularities based on a few forceful causal variables, often socioeconomic in nature, were conducive to such views. Methods based on regression analysis and conventional forms of comparison reinforced this stance because they produced precisely these kinds of results. During the formative moment in the field that occurred during the 1960s and 1970s, scholarly views about ontology, methodology, and appropriate modes of explanation converged into a cohesive package with continuing influence.

Because they advance new ontologies, however, theories of path dependence and strategic interaction are also shifting conventional conceptions of what constitutes adequate explanation in the field of comparative politics. If important political outcomes depend not on a few socioeconomic conditions but on complex chains of strategic interaction, they cannot be explained except by reference to that chain. If contemporary outcomes reflect the outermost tips of a branching tree of historical developments, allusions to one or two causal variables of putative importance will not constitute an adequate explanation for them. Accordingly, parsimony is no longer seen as a key feature of explanation in political science, and views about what constitutes an acceptable mode of explanation have shifted toward the historical (cf. Shiveley 1974; King et al. 1994, p. 20; Bates et al. 1998).

In sum, our ontologies have outrun both our methodologies and standard views of explanation. Comparative politics has moved away from ontologies that assume causal variables with strong, consistent, and independent effects across space and time toward ones that acknowledge more extensive endogeneity and the ubiquity of complex interaction effects. Many scholars now see the world in terms that do not conform to the assumptions required if standard regression methods are to provide valid tests of causal contentions. Many substantive problems now seem to involve reciprocal causation. Scholars are positing interaction effects too complex to model fully in regressions. Some argue that the impact of causal variables is so context dependent that it is meaningless to assume unit homogeneity, and that multicausality is so important that it does not makes sense to focus causal analysis on the identification of individual independent variables (cf. Ragin 1987, 2000).

Given these developments, scholars of comparative politics must now search for new methods. But which ones should they adopt? It is to this problem that I now turn.

Toward Solutions

There is no single solution to the methodological quandaries posed by contemporary ontologies. That they pose genuine dilemmas is reflected in the growing range of responses from thoughtful scholars. A full review of these responses is beyond the scope of this essay, but I will survey a few of the most prominent ones.

Some Recent Proposals

Some eminent analysts of major social and political processes have reacted to such problems by proposing a shift in the focus of inquiry away from the search for direct explanations of macropolitical outcomes such as revolutions, modernization, and regime change that were once the subjects of grand theory in the field and toward a lower level of analysis where the effort is to identify recurrent microlevel processes that contribute to many such outcomes (Tilly 1995). Although the rationale for this move is multifaceted, many argue that major political events are generated by causal processes that are so complex or context dependent that they cannot be explicated in general terms. Instead, analysis should concentrate on "social mechanisms" construed as basic forms of human behavior or recurrent forms of collective action that are constitutive components of the causal chains leading to broader political outcomes (Elster 1998; Hedström and Swedberg 1998; cf. Mahoney 2001). The premise is that such mechanisms appear with sufficient frequency to be feasible objects of generalization and carry enough causal significance to merit the interest shown in them. There are advantages and disadvantages to this approach. The new focus promises useful analyses of collective action, but it is difficult to greet a retreat from the search for direct explanations of such important outcomes without regret (cf. Katznelson 1997).

Others are attempting to improve statistical analyses in order to cope with the problems afflicting standard regression approaches. Some are exploring new ways in which to estimate interaction effects, using structural equation models, for instance, to overcome problems of endogeneity (Jackson 1996; Franzese 2001). Others suggest that scholars in the field of comparative politics should draw from a wider statistical repertoire, either making more use of familiar techniques, such as discriminant analysis, or devising new ones, such as agent-based modeling (Braumoeller 2000; Cederman 1997). Some argue that statistical analysis should invariably be combined with in-depth investigation of the cases, careful attention to how cases distribute themselves across the relevant cells in a tabular analysis, and greater effort to account for the residuals (Shalev 1998). Statistical analysis that is attentive to such matters certainly has a role to play in the understanding of causal complexities.

A third approach to the types of ontological issues identified here has been devised by Ragin (1987), who was one of the first to draw attention to such problems. He is especially concerned about "multiple conjunctural causation," broadly speaking, the possibility that an outcome may be caused not by the same one or two variables operating in all cases independently of other variables, but by diverse combinations of factors, each operative in some of the cases. Noting that the parameter estimates of regression models do not normally identify such effects, he has sought techniques to specify which combinations of factors constitute necessary and/or sufficient conditions for the occurrence of a particular outcome. Ragin has devised techniques in which the researcher divides the cases into sets according to their values on the outcome of interest and the values taken by potential explanatory variables, with a view to identifying the frequency with which particular combinations of explanatory variables are associated with a given outcome. He elaborates a Boolean algebra for reducing these comparisons to manageable summaries and, in a recent advance, increases the level of information that can be included in such analyses by adopting a "fuzzy-set" approach to the construction of categories that allows the variables to take on continuous values (Ragin 2000).

This approach offers many insights. It is especially effective for revealing how conditions combine to generate particular outcomes and for assessing which conditions are necessary or sufficient for these outcomes. Standing between the conventional comparative method and regression analysis, Ragin's approach draws strengths from each. The fuzzy-set approach, for instance, demands deeper knowledge of the cases than standard regression analysis does but offers conclusions that are often richer. From the perspective of this essay, however, it should be noted that these methods retain a key feature of regression analysis and of the comparative method conventionally understood: they test causal inferences largely through inspection of covariance across cases between a few explanatory variables of theoretical interest and the outcomes to be explained.[11]

[11] Although Ragin (1987) contrasts his case-oriented approach to a variables-oriented approach, to draw out some of its distinctive features, I use the language of variables here to describe the basic features of the approach.

At its edges, Ragin's (1987) analysis can be interpreted in radical terms, as one that rejects the concept of causal *variables* in favor of seeing social science as an enterprise that compares *cases* by building up accounts of the cases whose generality lies in the categories the analysis generates and the grouping of the cases into sets that represent distinctive causal trajectories. Movement in this direction takes the field back toward the "disciplined, configurative analysis" characteristic of the best work of the 1960s. Those who criticized the studies of this era for being "merely descriptive" missed the generalizing power of works that identified new types of political phenomena and created general concepts for them that could be applied across nations.[12]

In the face of these ontological shifts, some scholars would go even further to press fundamental critiques of positivism that view the search for variables with consistent causal force across national settings as a fruitless enterprise. Influenced by "critical realism' and "constructivist" approaches to the social world, many have become skeptical about the categories of political analysis, sensitive to how the objectives of the analyst influence them, and more interested in explanations that focus on the interpretations actors develop of their own world (Somers 1996; Archer et al. 1998; Wendt 1999; cf. Abbott 2001). There is much to be said for such views.

Even this brief survey shows that there is no easy consensus about the methods available to the field of comparative politics today. Issues that have long lain just below the surface of the field have become prominent again, partly because new ontologies have come to the fore. Rather than conclude with a statement about dilemmas, however, I want to take some steps in the direction of solutions. In essence, I will argue for the usefulness of a method, based on small-N comparison, that has long been available to the field but underappreciated because small-N comparison has too often been seen as a terrain for the application of "weak" versions of the statistical method rather than as one on which a robust but different kind of method can be practiced.

My claim is not that this method is superior to all others, even for coping with the structures of causality implied by recent theoretical shifts in the field. To justify such a claim would require an extended discussion that is not

[12] Stanley Hoffmann's (1963) magisterial analysis of Third Republic France is a case in point. Although focused on a single case, his account of how a "stalemate society" was constituted and how that regime worked offers insights that reorganized thinking about many other nations and categories that can be applied to many regimes.

possible here, and, as I have indicated, one can make several methodological moves in response to the new ontologies. However, this method has the advantage that it does not depart radically from the mainstream positivism of contemporary political science. It retains a "variables-oriented" approach to causal relationships, and it can readily be embraced by the mainstream of the field, even if others will prefer a different route. However, this method also offers advantages over the standard regression model or the conventional comparative method for assessing the types of causal relationships posited by the new ontologies of comparative politics. Indeed, I suggest that we reframe our understanding of the "comparative method" applied to comparison across a small number of cases in order to place this method at its center.

Systematic Process Analysis

I term the method I have in mind "systematic process analysis." It bears some resemblance to the approaches described by Campbell (1975) as "pattern matching" and by George and McKeown (1985) as "process tracing" (Collier 1991, p. 23; Mahoney 2000b; Bennett and George in press). Because I want to outline the requisites of the method in highly specific terms, with which some of these scholars might disagree, however, I adopt a distinctive label for it. The method is far from new: with some variations, it has long been practiced to great effect by more than a few analysts (cf. Moore 1966; Skocpol 1979; Collier and Collier 1991). But it is undervalued by a field mesmerized by a standard regression model whose limitations are now becoming clear.

To understand what systematic process analysis entails and to appreciate its value, it is useful to recall the fundamental character of (social) scientific inquiry, as specified by the mainstream positivism that dominates the field. From this perspective, social science is an effort to identify the causal factors (or variables) that tend to produce a particular kind of outcome. One begins such an inquiry by formulating a set of theories that identify the relevant causal factors and how they operate, along with a rationale for their operation generally couched as deductions from more general contentions about the world based both on previous observations and on axiomatic premises. From each theory, the investigator then derives predictions about the patterns that will appear in observations of the world if the causal theory is valid and if it is false, with special attention to predictions that are consistent with one theory but inconsistent with its principal rivals so as to discern which among a set of competing theories is more likely to be valid.[13] Relevant observations are then made of the world (past or present) using a range of technologies and the specialized body of advice associated with their use. By general agreement, the investigator should seek as many and as diverse a set of observations as possible (cf. King et al. 1994, ch. 6). The patterns present in these observations are then inspected for consistency with the predictions of each of the relevant theories with a view to reaching a judgment about which causal theory is superior to the others.

Because observations are never fully independent of the theories they are being used to test, as Lakatos (1970; Kuhn 1970) reminds us, this judgment entails drawing simultaneous conclusions about the accuracy of the observations and the value of the theory. A theory with substantial deductive power that has survived many anterior observations might not be rejected simply because it is inconsistent with recent observations. Instead, the adequacy of the observations (in terms of measurement, sampling, and the like) must be weighed against the attractiveness and plausibility of the theory.[14] The theories may be refined and further observations made before one theory is declared superior to another. Progress in social science is ultimately a matter of drawing fine judgments based on a three-cornered comparison among a theory, its principal rivals, and sets of observations.

Although this is a very brief synopsis of the social scientific enterprise, missing some nuances and open to challenge from those with radically different conceptions of science, it should be uncontroversial for the mainstream positivist. Therefore, it is important to note that nothing in this account implies that the only observations relevant to testing a theory are ones drawn on the values of the outcome (or "dependent" variable) and on a small set of variables designated the ultimate "causes" of that outcome (often termed "independent" variables).[15] Observations on the latter will be

[13] Note that when I use the term "predictions," I refer not only (or even primarily) to future developments but to predictions about patterns observable in data gathered about past events.

[14] This point raises the important issue of what criteria should be used for judging the adequacy of a theory, especially when the observations are not congruent with it, as well as issues about what criteria should be used for judging observations. But discussion of these issues is beyond the scope of this essay.

[15] It can be argued that if the purpose of social science is primarily to generate predictions about the future, it may be useful to focus on the association between a small set of (independent) variables and an outcome. However, this is a rationale based on contentions about the *purpose*, rather than the *nature*, of social science; and many argue that the principal objective of social science is to understand the world, with prediction a secondary exercise

valuable, but a viable theory should also generate predictions about many other facets of the case on which observations can be drawn to test the theory. In particular, good theories specify a set of causal processes associated with the operation of particular variables. These include predictions about the events that can be expected to occur, the sequence of those events, and the public and private positions actors are likely to take, as well as many other features of the relevant causal chain.

The basic point should be clear: observations bearing on a theory's predictions about the process whereby an outcome is caused provide as relevant a test of that theory as predictions about the correspondence between a small number of causal variables and the outcomes they are said to produce. This is true even when the main object of the theory is to identify a small number of "causal variables" because even such an argument about causes must specify a process whereby these ultimate causes generate the outcome.[16] The explanatory power of a theory rests, in large measure, on the specification of such a process. Given the movement in comparative politics toward ontologies that envision multiple interaction effects, this point becomes especially significant. The validity of arguments about path dependence or strategic interaction can often be assessed only by comparing predictions about process to observations of process in the cases at hand (cf. Bates et al. 1998).[17]

In short, systematic process analysis examines the processes unfolding in the cases at hand as well as the outcomes in those cases. The causal theories to be tested are interrogated for the predictions they contain about how

at best. Others argue that even if the purpose of social science is prediction, that objective is best served by developing theories that comprehend complexity and can withstand tests that extend beyond inspection of the correlations between a putative set of causal variables and an outcome.

[16] It is not enough, for instance, to say that the "presence of social democrats in government" explains the "development of neocorporatist arrangements." To have explanatory power, any theory to this effect must contain some account of the causal chain whereby one leads to the other. As Waltz (1979) points out, a theory consists of substantially more than a set of hypotheses.

[17] I take this to be the fundamental point of Bates et al. (1998), which is another example of the search now underway in the discipline for methods appropriate to the new ontologies. There are many respects in which their account parallels mine, although my conception of systematic process analysis puts more emphasis on ensuring an even confrontation among rival theories deliberately rendered as brittle as possible and on searching for observations that test the full range of a theory's postulates, including assumptions about attitude and motivation that form part of the (untested) core heuristic of the rational choice theories in which Bates et al. are primarily interested (cf. Lakatos 1970; Elster 2000).

events will unfold. The point is to compare these predictions with observations drawn from data about the world. The theory should be rendered as "brittle" as possible against observations and other theories, that is, it should be formed so as to yield predictions that could be shown to be false by available data and that are distinguishable from the predictions of rival theories. As usual, the analyst should seek as many and as diverse a set of predictions and observations as possible. In general, this means predictions not only about ultimate outcomes and the general shape of processes but about the specific actions expected from various types of actors, statements that might reveal their motivation, and the sequences in which actions should occur.[18] When other things are equal, a theory that survives tests against more observations and more observations of different kinds is more likely to be valid than one that is tested on a smaller or more homogeneous set of observations (cf. King et al. 1994).

The systematic process analyst then draws observations from the empirical cases, not only about the value of the principal causal variables, but about the processes linking these variables to the outcomes. Because each theory is being tested against others, the investigator should focus special attention on phenomena about which the predictions of the theories diverge. This is not simply a search for "intervening" variables. The point is to see if the multiple actions and statements of the actors at each stage of the causal process are consistent with the image of the world implied by each theory.[19]

In the final stages of the investigation, the observations drawn from the cases are compared with the predictions of the theories and a judgment about the superiority of one theory over the others is made, largely on the basis of congruence between predictions and observations. If there are

[18] This injunction runs counter to the argument of Friedman (1968) that theories should be judged primarily by the adequacy of their predictions about ultimate outcomes without inspecting the realism of a theory's assumptions about the actors' motivations. Although systematic process analysis leaves open the possibility that a theory might be accepted because of the superiority of its predictions about outcomes, even if its assumptions about motivation are untested or apparently unrealistic, I argue that the realism of a theory's assumptions should be assessed on the grounds that it is difficult enough to test one theory against another without denying the investigator this basis for comparison. Testing in social science should make full use of available information.

[19] Although systematic process analysis does not necessarily entail it, the perspective suggests some sympathy for Weber's (1949) argument that the researcher should ask whether the theory is consistent with evidence about the meanings the historical actors themselves attributed to their actions..

reasons to doubt the adequacy of the data or to attach high value to a theory that seems contraindicated, further observations can be made in existing cases or new cases examined to improve the judgment.

Although process tracing has sometimes been denigrated as a simple injunction to "study history," it should be apparent that systematic process analysis is a very different project from the one in which most historians engage. It demands examination of the histories behind outcomes but one guided more extensively by theory than are most of those undertaken by historians. Although every researcher should remain open to serendipitous discovery, this enterprise is not an inductive one. It is focused on the testing of propositions derived from a deductive process of theory formation. Moreover, the results yielded by this kind of investigation are quite different from those sought by most historians. If they seek explanations, historians generally seek relatively complete accounts for a particular set of events, usually couched in the form of detailed narratives that spell out all the antecedent events relevant to the one they want to explain within a richly embroidered context. Systematic process analysis, by contrast, is an effort to elaborate and assess the validity of theories capable of explaining a broad class of events or outcomes. It seeks generalizations that are both more simple and more portable than those at which historians typically aim. Despite points of tangency between the two enterprises, they are distinct (cf. Roberts 1996; Bennett and George in press).

Reconsidering Case Studies and the Comparative Method

This analysis contains important implications about the value of case studies and about how the comparative method should be understood. The role of the case study has been obscured for years by pervasive confusion about what constitutes a case and what constitutes an observation pertinent to the testing of theory. The origins of this uncertainty go back to the pioneering articles of Eckstein (1975) and Lijphart (1971) when it was often assumed that the only observations pertinent to the testing of a theory were those based on observations of a dependent variable and a few independent variables cited to explain it. From this perspective, where the outcome of interest was a system-level variable, the concept of a case could be assimilated to a single observation.

From such formulations, many scholars concluded that research based on a single case study has no role to play in causal inference: after all, there is little basis for causal inference when one can make only a single observation.

Eckstein (1975) argued that one could use a single case to falsify a theory by identifying a "crucial case" in which a theory is "most likely" to hold if it is valid anywhere; but others pointed out that this is viable only when causes are deterministic, rather than probabilistic, and when testing claims about "necessary" causes (Lieberson 1992, p. 117). Many retreated to the claim that single case studies are useful for generating new hypotheses or refining theories, by virtue of their inductive richness, but not for testing causal propositions. The result has been pervasive skepticism about the value of case studies, despite a revival of interest in them (cf. Ragin and Becker 1992).

To dispel the confusion surrounding these issues, a sharp distinction must be drawn between the concept of a *case* understood as a single unit where the outcome being investigated is unit-level variation and the concept of an *observation* understood as a piece of data drawn from that unit and pertinent to the theories being examined.[20] A single unit may provide only one observation on the principal outcome of interest, but it can yield a diverse array of other observations pertinent to the testing of a theory, including ones bearing on the causal processes specified by the theory. In other words, when systematic process analysis is applied to them, single case studies have an important role to play in the testing of causal theories. As Campbell (1975) noted some years ago, because they allow for more careful measurement and the tracing of causal processes, which statistical methods cannot normally accommodate, single case studies can be superior to aggregate analysis for testing some theories.

The implications of this analysis for small-*N* comparison are equally striking. They suggest that small-*N* comparison is far more useful for assessing causal theories than conventional understandings of the "comparative method" imply. As I have noted, the comparative method is often treated as a subsidiary version of statistical analysis, in which the only important observations to be drawn from the cases are taken on the values of the dependent variable and a few explanatory variables (cf. Lijphart 1971, 1975). From this perspective, because the number of pertinent observations available from small-*N* comparison is seriously limited, the analyst lacks the degrees of freedom to consider more than a few explanatory variables, and the value of small-*N* comparison for causal inference seems distinctly limited.

[20] King et al. (1994) are attentive to this distinction. In general, the concept of a case study should be used to refer to the study of a single case as defined here, although some use the term loosely to refer to a study of a nation, region, organization, or other unit that may encompass many cases.

However, we need not see small-N comparisons or the comparative method exclusively in these terms. Instead of viewing comparison primarily as an exercise in correlating a few independent variables with a dependent variable, we should understand the comparative method as a technique in which inspection of this kind is combined with systematic process analysis of the cases. Precisely because such research designs cover small numbers of cases, the researcher can investigate causal processes in each of them in detail, thereby assessing the relevant theories against especially diverse kinds of observations. Reconceptualized in these terms, the comparative method emerges not as a poor substitute for statistical analysis, but as a distinctive approach that offers a much richer set of observations, especially about causal processes, than statistical analyses normally allow. As a method, it is especially appropriate to the ontologies of comparative politics in recent years.

My point is not to denigrate statistical analysis but to suggest that research based on small-N comparison can be substantially more useful than many acknowledge. The emphasis in systematic process analysis on considering multiple types of observations builds fruitfully on practices in the natural sciences. Few biologists would consider their theories adequately tested if they examined only macrolevel correlations between ultimate outcomes and a few causal factors. Even when they cannot apply experimental methods, natural scientists normally seek many kinds of observations pertinent to the causal processes they are studying.[21] So should social scientists.

When should scholars apply systematic process analysis and when should they use regression analysis? Much will depend on the character of the theories to be tested and the ontologies they imply. Standard regression methods will be especially useful when the cases available are large in number and genuinely independent of each other, the relevant outcomes heavily dependent enough on a small set of causal variables that are independent of each other and so powerful that their impact shows up consistently across cases, and the relevant interaction effects limited enough to be modeled within the available degrees of freedom. In many studies, statistical techniques may be useful for assessing some aspects of the causal relations specified by a theory, while systematic process analysis is employed to test other aspects of those relations.

As Abbott (1988) observes, however, the conditions required for effective regression analysis are often not met. In such contexts, systematic

[21] I owe this point to a comment of Paul Steinberg.

process analysis can have distinctive value. It allows scholars to assess more complex causal processes and to move beyond modes of explanations that turn on statistically significant coefficients and relatively thin causal theories toward ones that contain more extensive specifications of causal processes (cf. Archer et al. 1998; Mahoney 2001). In these respects among others, small-*N* comparison based on systematic process analysis offers substantial potential for resolving the methodological dilemmas posed by the new ontologies of comparative politics.

Conclusion

This essay considers the relationship between ontology and methodology in comparative research. Although the relationship is always a crucial one, I have argued that the dilemmas facing comparative politics today are especially intense because its ontologies have outrun its methodologies. Many important theories in the field are now based on ontological views that see political outcomes as the result of causal processes in which distant events, sequencing, and complex interaction effects play important roles. However, the most prominent methodologies in the field are still based on a standard regression model that was more appropriate to the ontologies of thirty years ago, when many theories implied that political phenomena are caused by a few powerful factors operating independently of context and with roughly similar force everywhere. Modernization theories built on socioeconomic determinants provide a classic example.

I have reviewed several responses to this dilemma, each with some promise and some with radical implications for how we do research. But I have also argued that the field has long had available a methodology appropriate to the new ontologies, which I label systematic process analysis. Taking seriously the principle that "correlation is not causation," this methodology assesses the adequacy of a theory not only by inspecting key causal variables and outcomes but by comparing a theory's predictions about causal processes with multiple observations about such processes in the cases at hand. The method puts substantial demands on theories, asking that they do more than specify a few causal variables, and distinctive requirements on empirical research, asking investigators to make multiple kinds of observations about how events unfold over time.

This perspective emphasizes the value of research designs based on case studies and small-*N* comparison. For too long, such research designs have been seen as weak variants of statistical analysis. When used as a site for systematic process analysis, however, intensive comparison of a small number of cases can provide rigorous assessments of any kind of theory, and such research designs are indispensable for assessing theories of comparative politics whose ontologies specify complex causal structures incompatible with the assumptions required by regression analysis. I have also suggested that it is time to reconceptualize the comparative method. We should see it not as another version of the statistical method, but as a form of comparison that entails systematic process analysis. Seen in this light, the comparative method emerges as a powerful technique, and one used by scholars for some time with excellent results.

Although I have emphasized the limitations of regression analysis, especially in the face of new ontologies, I am not suggesting that it should be abandoned. For some types of problems, statistical methods have great value. The point of this essay is not to narrow the range of methods used in comparative politics but to argue that we should expand them. Social science is a difficult endeavor. We perceive the world only dimly, and all techniques for testing causal theories are imperfect. In this context, we need more, not fewer, weapons in our methodological arsenal, including those based on case studies, small-*N* comparison, and historical analysis.

My ultimate objective is to suggest that, when choosing research designs in comparative inquiry, we should pay as much attention to what I have called ontology as we normally do to methodology. The value of a method will depend on its congruence with causal structures in the world. The field of comparative politics will be stronger if those who work within it can transcend the separation that often occurs between discussions of methodology and ontology to give careful consideration to issues of ontology before deciding what method is appropriate for the problems at hand.

References

Abbott, Andrew. 1988. "Transcending General Linear Reality." *Sociological Theory* 6: 169–86.

1993. "Sequences of Social Events: Concepts and Methods for the Analysis of Order in Social Processes." *Historical Methods* 16: 129–47.

2001. *Chaos of Disciplines*. Chicago: University of Chicago Press.

Almond, Gabriel A. 1956. "Comparative Political Systems." *Journal of Politics* 17: 391–409.

Almond, Gabriel and G. Bingham Powell, Jr. 1966. *Comparative Politics: A Developmental Approach*. Boston: Little, Brown.

Almond, Gabriel and Sidney Verba. 1963. *The Civic Culture*. Princeton, NJ: Princeton University Press.

Apter, David E. 1965. *The Politics of Modernization*. Chicago: University of Chicago Press.

Archer, Margaret, Roy Bhaskar, Andrew Collier, Tony Lawson, and Alan Norrie, eds. 1998. *Critical Realism: Essential Readings*. London: Routledge.

Bagehot, William. 1867. *The English Constitution*. London: Chapman and Hall.

Bates, Robert, Avner Greif, Margaret Levi, Jean-Laurent Rosenthal, and Barry Weingast. 1998. *Analytical Narratives*. Princeton, NJ: Princeton University Press.

Bennett, Andrew and Alexander George. 2001. "Case Studies and Process Tracing in History and Political Science: Similar Strokes for Different Foci." Unpublished manuscript.

in press. *Case Studies and Theory Development*. Cambridge, MA: MIT Press.

Bentley, Arthur. 1908. *The Process of Government*. Cambridge, MA: Belknap.

Bill, James A. and Robert Hardgrave. 1973. *Comparative Politics: The Quest for Theory*. Columbus, OH: Charles Merrill.

Binder, Leonard, James S. Coleman, Joseph LaPalombara, Lucian W. Pye, Sidney Verba, and Myron Weiner. 1971. *Crises and Sequences in Political Development*. Princeton, NJ: Princeton University Press.

Braumoeller, Bear. 2000. "Modeling Multiple Causal Paths: Logic, Derivation and Implementation." Unpublished manuscript.

Campbell, Donald T. 1975. "Degrees of Freedom and the Case Study." *Comparative Political Studies* 8: 178–93.

Cartwright, Nancy. 1997. "What Is a Causal Structure?" Pp. 342–58 in *Causality in Crisis? Statistical Methods and the Search for Causal Knowledge in the Social Sciences*, edited by Vaughtn R. McKim and Stephen P. Turner. Notre Dame, IN: Notre Dame University Press.

Cederman, Lars-Enik. 1997. *Emergent Actors in World Politics*. Princeton, NJ: Princeton University Press.

Chilcote, Ronald H. 1981. *Theories of Comparative Politics*. Boulder, CO: Westview.

Collier, David, 1991. "The Comparative Method: Two Decades of Change." Pp. 7–31 in *Comparative Political Dynamics*, edited by Dankwart Rustow and Kenneth Erickson. New York: HarperCollins.

Collier, David and Robert Adcock. 1999. "Democracy and Dichotomies: A Pragmatic Approach to Choice about Concepts." *Annual Review of Political Science* 2: 537–65.

Collier, Ruth Berins and David Collier. 1991. *Shaping the Political Arena*. Princeton, NJ: Princeton University Press.

Cook, T. D. and Donald T. Campbell. 1979. *Quasi-Experimentation*. New York: Houghton Mifflin.

Easton, David. 1953. *The Political System: An Inquiry into the State of Political Science*. New York: Alfred A. Knopf.

1965. *A Framework for Political Analysis*. Englewood Cliffs, NJ: Prentice-Hall.

Eckstein, Harry. 1963. "A Perspective on Comparative Politics." Pp. 3–33 in *Comparative Politics*, edited by Harry Eckstein and David Apter. New York: The Free Press.

1965. "On the Etiology of Internal Wars." *History and Theory* 4: 133–63.
1975. "Case Study and Theory in Macro-Politics." Pp. 79–139 in *Handbook of Political Science I*, edited by Fred Greenstein and Nelson Polsby. Reading, MA: Addison-Wesley.
Eckstein, Harry and David Apter, eds. 1963. *Comparative Politics: A Reader*. New York: Free Press.
Elster, Jon. 1983. *Explaining Technical Change*. New York: Cambridge University Press.
1998. "A Plea for Mechanisms." Pp. 45–73 in *Social Mechanisms: An Analytical Approach to Social Theory*, edited by Peter Hedström and Richard Swedberg. New York: Cambridge University Press.
2000. "Review Essay: 'Analytical Narratives.'" *American Political Science Review* 94: 685–95.
Franzese, Robert. J., Jr. 2001. *Macroeconomic Policies of Developed Democracies*. New York: Cambridge University Press.
Frey, Fredrick. 1985. "The Problem of Actor Designation in Comparative Politics." *Comparative Politics* 17: 127–52.
Friedman, Milton. 1968. "The Methodology of Positive Economics." Pp. 508–29 in *Readings in the Philosophy of Social Science*, edited by May Brodbeck. New York: Macmillan.
Friedrich, Carl J. 1950. *Constitutional Government and Democracy*, rev. edition. Boston: Ginn.
Geddes, Barbara. 1990. "How the Cases You Choose Affect the Answers You Get." *Political Analysis* 2: 131–49.
George, Alexander. 1979. "Case Studies and Theory: The Method of Structured, Focused Comparison." Pp. 43–68 in *Diplomacy: New Approaches to History, Theory and Policy*, edited by Paul Larson. New York: Free Press.
Gerschenkron, Alexander. 1962. *Economic Backwardness in Historical Perspective*. Cambridge, MA: Harvard University Press.
Goldthorpe, John A. 1997. "Current Issues in Comparative Macrosociology: A Debate on Methodological Issues." *Comparative Social Research* 16: 1–26.
Greenstein, Fred I. and Nelson Polsby, eds. 1975. *Handbook of Political Science*. Reading, MA: Addison-Wesley.
Grew, Raymond. 1978. *Crises of Political Development in Europe and the United States*. Princeton, NJ: Princeton University Press.
Hedström, Peter and Richard Swedberg, eds. 1998. *Social Mechanisms: An Analytical Approach to Social Theory*. New York: Cambridge University Press.
Hempel, Carl. 1965. *Aspects of Scientific Explanation*. New York: Free Press.
Hoffmann, Stanley. 1963. "Paradoxes of the French Political Community." Pp. 1–117 in *In Search of France*, edited by Stanley Hoffmann et al. New York: Harper.
Holt, Robert T. and John E. Turner, eds. 1970. *The Methodology of Comparative Research*. New York: Free Press.
Hume, David. [1748] 1955. *An Enquiry Concerning Human Understanding*. Indianapolis: Bobbs-Merrill.

Jackson, John E. 1996. "Political Methodology: An Overview." Pp. 717–48 in *A New Handbook of Political Science*, edited by Robert Goodin and Hans-Dieter Klingemann. Oxford: Oxford University Press.

Katznelson, Ira. 1997. "Structure and Configuration in Comparative Politics." Pp. 81–112 in *Comparative Politics: Rationality, Culture, and Structure*, edited by Mark Lichbach and Alan Zuckerman. New York: Cambridge University Press.

King, Gary, Robert Keohane, and Sidney Verba. 1994. *Designing Social Inquiry*. Princeton, NJ: Princeton University Press.

Knight, Jack and Itai Sened, eds. 1995. *Explaining Social Institutions*. Ann Arbor: University of Michigan Press.

Kuhn, Thomas. 1970. *The Structure of Scientific Revolutions*. Chicago: University of Chicago Press.

Lakatos, Imre. 1970. "Falsification and the Methodology of Scientific Research Programs." Pp. 91–196 in *Criticism and the Growth of Knowledge*, edited by Imre Lakatos and Alan Musgrave. Cambridge: Cambridge University Press.

Lasswell, Harold. 1936. *Politics: Who Gets What, When, Where, How?* New York: McGraw-Hill.

Lerner, Daniel. 1958. *The Passing of Traditional Society*. Glencoe, IL: Free Press.

Lichbach, Mark and Alan Zuckerman. eds. 1997. *Comparative Politics: Rationality, Culture and Structure*. New York: Cambridge University Press.

Lieberson, Stanley. 1985. *Making It Count: The Improvement of Social Research and Theory*. Berkeley: University of California Press.

1992. "Small *N*'s and Big Conclusions." Pp. 105–18 in *What Is a Case*?, edited by Charles C. Ragin and Howard S. Becker. New York: Cambridge University Press.

Lijphart, Arend. 1971. "Comparative Politics and the Comparative Method." *American Political Science Review* 64: 682–93.

1975. "The Comparable-Cases Strategy in Comparative Research." *Comparative Political Studies* 8: 158–77.

Lipset, Seymour Martin. 1959. "Some Social Requisites of Democracy: Economic Development and Political Legitimacy." *American Political Science Review* 53: 69–105.

MacIntyre, Alasdair. 1978. "Is a Science of Comparative Politics Possible?" Pp. 226–84 in *The Practice of Comparative Politics*, edited by Paul Lewis, David Potler, and Francis Castles. New York: Longman.

Macridis, Roy. 1968. "Comparative Politics and the Study of Governments: The Search for Focus." *Comparative Politics* 1: 79–90.

Mahoney, James. 2000a. "Path Dependence in Historical Sociology." *Theory and Society* 29: 507–48.

2000b. "Strategies of Causal Inference in Small-*N* Analysis." *Sociological Methods and Research* 28: 387–424.

2001. "Beyond Correlational Analysis: Recent Innovations in Theory and Method." *Sociological Forum* 16: 575–93.

McDonald, Terrence J., ed. 1996. *The Historic Turn in the Human Sciences*. Ann Arbor: University of Michigan Press.
Merton, Robert K. 1949. *Social Theory and Social Structure*. Glencoe, IL: Free Press.
Mill, John Stuart. 1872. *A System of Logic*. New York: Harper.
Milner, Helen. 1998. *Interests, Institutions and Information*. Princeton, NJ: Princeton University Press.
Moon, Donald. 1975. "The Logic of Political Inquiry." Pp. 131–95 in *Handbook of Political Science*, edited by Fred Greenstein and Nelson Polsby. Reading, MA: Addison-Wesley.
Nagel, Ernest. 1961. *The Structure of Science*. New York: Harcourt, Brace and World.
O'Donnell, Guillermo and Philippe Schmitter. 1986. *Transitions from Authoritarian Rule: Tentative Conclusions about Uncertain Democracies*. Baltimore, MD: Johns Hopkins University Press.
Parsons, Talcott. 1951. *The Social System*. Glencoe, IL: Free Press.
Pierson, Paul. 2000a. "Increasing Returns, Path Dependence and the Study of Politics." *American Political Science Review* 94: 251–67.
2000b. "Not Just What but *When*: Timing and Sequence in Political Development." *Studies in American Political Development* 14: 72–92.
Przeworski, Adam and Henry Teune. 1970. *The Logic of Comparative Social Inquiry*. New York: Wiley.
Ragin, Charles C. 1987. *The Comparative Method*. Berkeley: University of California Press.
2000. *Fuzzy-Set Social Science*. Chicago: University of Chicago Press.
Ragin, Charles C. and Howard S. Becker, eds. 1992. *What Is a Case? Exploring the Foundations of Social Inquiry*. New York: Cambridge University Press.
Richter, Melvin. 1970. *Essays in Theory and History: An Approach to the Social Sciences*. Cambridge, MA: Harvard University Press.
Roberts, Clayton. 1996. *The Logic of Historical Explanation*. University Park: Pennsylvania State University Press.
Sartori, Giovanni. 1970. "Concept Misformation in Comparative Politics." *American Political Science Review* 64: 1033–53.
Schattschneider, E. E. 1935. *Politics, Pressures and the Tariff*. New York: Prentice-Hall.
Sewell, William. 1996. "Three Temporalities: Toward an Eventful Sociology." Pp. 245–80 in *The Historic Turn in the Human Sciences*, edited by Terrence J. McDonald. Ann Arbor: University of Michigan Press.
Shalev, Michael. 1998. "Limits of and Alternatives to Multiple Regression in Macro-Comparative Research." Paper presented at a conference on "The Welfare State at the Crossroads," Stockholm.
Shively, W. Phillips. 1974. *The Craft of Political Research*. Englewood Cliffs, NJ: Prentice-Hall.
Skocpol, Theda. 1979. *States and Social Revolutions*. New York: Cambridge University Press.
Skocpol, Theda and Margaret Somers. 1980. "The Uses of Comparative History in Macrosocial Inquiry." *Comparative Studies in Society and History* 22: 174–97.

Smelser, Neil. 1966."Notes on the Methodology of Comparative Analysis of Economic Activity." *Transactions of the Sixth World Congress of Sociology*. Evian: International Sociological Association.

1976. *Comparative Methods in the Social Sciences*. Englewood Cliffs, NJ: Prentice-Hall.

Somers, Margaret R. 1996. "Where Is Sociology after the Historic Turn? Knowledge, Cultures, Narrativity, and Historical Epistemologies." Pp. 53–90 in *The Historic Turn in the Human Sciences*, edited by Terrence J. McDonald. Ann Arbor: University of Michigan Press.

Thelen, Kathleen 1984. *Big Structures, Large Processes, Huge Comparisons*. New York: Russell Sage.

1999. "Historical Institutionalism in Comparative Politics," *Annual Review of Political Science* 2: 369–404.

2000. "Time and Temporality in the Analysis of Institutional Evolution and Change." *Studies in American Political Development* 14: 102–9.

Tilly, Charles 1995. "To Explain Political Processes." *American Journal of Sociology* 100: 1594–610.

Verba, Sidney. 1967. "Some Dilemmas of Comparative Research." *World Politics* 20: 111–28.

1971. "Cross-National Survey Research: The Problem of Credibility." Pp. 309–56 in *Comparative Methods in Sociology*, edited by Ivan Vallier. Berkeley: University of California Press.

Wallerstein, Michael. 2000. "Trying to Navigate between Scylla and Charybdis: Misspecified and Unidentified Models in Comparative Politics." *APSA-CP: Newsletter for the Organized Section in Comparative Politics of the American Political Science Association* 11: 1–21.

Waltz, Kenneth. 1979. *A Theory of International Relations*. Reading, MA: Addison-Wesley.

Weber, Max. 1949. *The Methodology of the Social Sciences*. New York: Free Press.

Wendt, Alexander. 1999. *Social Theory of International Politics*. New York: Cambridge University Press.

Wilson, Woodrow. 1890. *The State*. Boston: Heath.

Winch, Donald. 1989. "Keynes, Keynesianism and State Intervention." Pp. 107–28 in *The Political Power of Economic Ideas*, edited by Peter A. Hall. Princeton, NJ: Princeton University Press.

Wolin, Sheldon. 1969. "Political Theory as a Vocation." *American Political Science Review* 63: 1062–82.

12

Doubly Engaged Social Science

THE PROMISE OF COMPARATIVE HISTORICAL ANALYSIS

Theda Skocpol

Social science achieves its potential and proves its worth as a human enterprise when it offers "substantive enlightenment . . . about the social structures in which we are enmeshed and which largely condition the course of our lives," declared Lewis Coser (1975, p. 698) in his 1975 presidential address to the American Sociological Association. As Coser articulated this demanding standard, U.S. social science was not only caught up in the social upheavals triggered by "the sixties." It was also in the early stages of what was to become a remarkable renascence of comparative and historical scholarship engaging big questions about social change and politics.

To be sure, Coser's vision was in tension with reigning academic paradigms of the 1960s and 1970s. Economists were committed to abstract equilibrium models almost entirely detached from empirical trends, while most sociologists and political scientists practiced what C. Wright Mills (1959) decried as "abstracted empiricism" tempered with flights of artificially generalized "grand theory." Enamored of advances in survey research and statistical analysis, most postwar U.S. sociologists and political scientists produced atemporal studies of contemporary social problems, voting behavior, or processes of individual status attainment, while a minority of macroscopically focused scholars attempted to fit all the nations of the world along a single evolutionary path toward the "modern social (or political) system" – a construct that looked suspiciously like an idealized version of the United States circa 1960.

Yet new stirrings were underway as scholarly insurgencies in sociology and political science questioned atemporal and overly abstracted approaches. Soon there would be cumulating comparative historical literatures about democratic and authoritarian regimes; the roots and outcomes of modern revolutions; the development of major kinds of modern welfare states; the dynamics of social movements and identities in politics; and the possible roles of national states in promoting (or undercutting) economic development – to name only a few of the many important matters analysts would address.

Barrington Moore, Jr.'s *Social Origins of Dictatorship and Democracy* appeared in 1966 and was soon accompanied by a flood of additional agenda-setting opuses – works such *Political Order in Changing Societies* by Samuel P. Huntington (1968); *The Modern World System* by Immanuel Wallerstein (1974); *Modern Social Politics in Britain and Sweden* by Hugh Heclo (1974); *The Formation of National States in Western Europe* edited by Charles Tilly (1975); *The Breakdown of Democratic Regimes* by Juan Linz (1978); *States and Social Revolutions* by Theda Skocpol (1979); *Dependent Development: The Alliance of Multinational, State, and Local Capital in Brazil* by Peter B. Evans (1979); *City Trenches: Urban Politics and the Patterning of Class in the United States* by Ira Katznelson (1981); and *Political Process and the Development of Black Insurgency, 1930–1970* by Doug McAdam (1982). Taken together, such agenda-setting works – macroscopic in scope and grounded in contextualized case comparisons and careful process tracing – inspired remarkable accumulations of findings and hypotheses.

Not that all these works agreed with one another. Far from it: their authors and readers engaged in lively debates about alternative causal explanations and ways to frame problems. Should nations be compared across or within eras of world history? Did the emergence of the "modern world system" mean that cross-national studies no longer made sense? How valid were Marxian, Weberian, or modernizing hypotheses about the roots and characteristics of sociopolitical transformations? All these issues, and many more, were up for grabs – and the discussions made for lively social science. As much because of the debates and further investigations they sparked as because of any issues they "settled," early agenda-setting works both inspired and provoked younger scholars entering the social science disciplines from the late 1970s to the 1990s. They, in turn, built comparative historical analysis into a major approach within contemporary social science – an approach that has gone far toward meeting Coser's hopes for substantively enlightening social science.

Most of the contributors to this volume are from the ranks of those who heard the siren call of comparative historical analysis and went on to make breakthrough contributions of their own. Along with many compatriots whose writings are cited throughout this volume, these now mid-career scholars have moved theoretical discussions and research methods far beyond the starting points of the 1960s and early 1970s. They are therefore ideally placed to take stock of knowledge accumulated over the past generation. Stepping back from particular topics and explanatory debates, they offer new perspectives on how comparative historical research at its best has been done. They update and sharpen the rationale for comparative historical analysis, identify new theoretical and methodological challenges, and suggest fresh research agendas. In this brief conclusion, I offer my own comments on these matters, building on the central insights proffered in this remarkable collection.

Doubly Engaged Social Science

To understand the accomplishments of recent decades, it is important to realize that comparative historical social science is a *doubly engaged* enterprise. Aiming to understand real-world transformations, its practitioners are simultaneously enmeshed in scholarly debates about causal hypotheses, theoretical frameworks, and optimal methods of empirical investigation. Such double engagement is what makes comparative historical social science so challenging and attractive.

Comparative historical analysts are passionately engaged with "first-order questions" – to invoke the felicitous term coined by James Rule (1997, p. 46) to refer to "questions that draw people to study social life in the first place, and that are constantly raised anew in the minds of nonspecialists." We do not live in settled times, and the global and national transformations of the past half century have obviously focused inquiring minds on first-order questions. The dissolution of colonial empires and the proliferation of a bewildering variety of new nations; the eruption of the civil rights revolution in the United States and the spread of rights and environmental movements across the globe; the travails of national efforts to cope with an ever-changing world economy; the eruption of revolutions, wars, international terrorism, and ethnic conflicts; the global spread of democracy; transformations in gender and family roles; and the maturation and restructuring of modern welfare states – all these developments and more raise challenging questions of great import to educated publics and policymakers as well as to academics. Again and again, momentous real-world occurrences have prompted scholars, especially the young, to raise bold new questions about the dynamics – and interrelationships – of societal transformations, political development, and contentious politics. Comparative historical scholars have certainly not been the only social scientists to wonder about such matters, but they have been, and remain, at the forefront. Explanatory studies framed in comparative historical terms are ambitious and offer richly contextualized and long-term perspectives on exactly the sorts of questions of most concern to broad audiences in an era of momentous social and political transformations.

Yet preoccupation with the real world has not been the only mark of comparative historical social science. After all, social change and politics can be addressed in many ways, even from inside academia. Scholars who care about public issues can focus on current events, offering normative commentaries or interpretive studies. But comparative historical analysts take a longer and broader perspective and do not just preach or interpret. They aim to further scientific knowledge by adapting *social science theories and methods* to develop new causal propositions about society and politics. Engaged as much with debates in university-based social science as with developments beyond the academy, comparative historical scholars justify their findings and explicate their approaches in long-running and periodically refocused discussions with other scholars who do social science differently.

Arguments about theory and method are central to contemporary comparative historical analysis because this approach has never been at the core of any disciplinary "establishment." To be sure, the nineteenth-century founders of modern social science developed contextualized comparisons and analyzed historical processes. How else could pioneers like Alexis de Tocqueville, Karl Marx, or Max Weber grasp the dynamics of emergent industrial society or probe the variety of social structures, governments, and polities they aspired to comprehend? But in due course, early political economy divided into separate academic disciplines that became formally institutionalized in U.S. universities after World War II. Ever since, there have been powerful pulls toward purely academic theorizing and research. So populous and proliferated are American academic disciplines – and indeed subdisciplines – that they can support encapsulated subcommunities focused on, say, a single theoretical paradigm or a particular set of research techniques. Whether they be quantitatively or qualitatively oriented, no matter: if specialized sets of scholars gain sufficient leverage over academic appointments and research funding, they can start speaking in their own jargon and begin to define scholarly "progress" in strictly intramural terms. Good research can be defined as applying a specific set of techniques or relying on a certain kind of data, regardless of the research question. The puzzles specialists address can be derived deductively from a single theoretical paradigm (such as rational choice or postmodernism) rather than formulated with reference to important real-world concerns.

Comparative historical social scientists have never accepted such tendencies toward academic introversion, and so they repeatedly find themselves making the case for broad-minded and pluralistic scholarly agendas. In debates with more intramurally oriented colleagues of many flavors, comparative historical scholars press for substantively rich research informed by historical process and variety. And they remain resolutely committed to methodological and theoretical eclecticism as the best way for social science to proceed toward genuinely cumulative "substantive enlightenment." As Coser (1975, p. 698) put it – in a sentence alluding to the abstracted "grand theorizing" and the atemporal abstracted empiricism regnant within the academic social science in his day – "if we refuse the challenge" of doing macroscopic, historically informed social science, "we shall forfeit our birthright and degenerate into a congeries of rival sects and specialized researchers who will learn more and more about less and less."

Who Are They Arguing with?

Recognition of the double engagement of comparative historical social science entails a clear implication: to understand the preoccupations of comparative historical scholarship, we must notice not only the worldly transformations that throw up new questions for scholars to address, but also the academic orthodoxies with which comparative historical scholars are contending at any given point. We can trace these arguments from the emergence of modern comparative historical analysis to the recent debates embodied in this volume.

Debates are central to comparative historical scholarship for a number of reasons. For one thing, these analysts regularly define their projects as challenges to accepted wisdom. As both Jack Goldstone and Dietrich Rueschemeyer spell out in their contributions to this book, particular studies are often launched as case studies or comparisons deliberately chosen to test and question reigning theoretical orthodoxies. This is a powerful way to do scholarship. It is also an intrinsically argumentative way to proceed – which is why comparative historical books usually open by declaring: here's what scholars – or people in general – tend to believe, but here are some cases that, if properly explored, may force us to change our views in important ways.

More generally, comparative historical analysis has evolved in critical dialogue with other approaches to social research. When modern comparative historical analysis first took shape back in the 1960s and 1970s, early agenda-setting books took sharp issue with structure-functionalist systems theories and with modernization models of sociopolitical development. Charles Tilly (1975, 1984), Samuel Huntington (1968), Immanuel Wallerstein (1974), Theda Skocpol (1979), and others all set out new analytic frames of reference as alternatives to established grand theories. Other innovators, meanwhile, defined their studies in critical dialogue with cross-sectional statistical studies. In the third essay in this volume, Edwin Amenta explains how comparative historical studies of the modern welfare state stepped into the lacunae and unresolved puzzles apparent in early cross-national, large-*N* statistical studies of national welfare programs. Pioneering studies relied on atemporal data, but scholars soon discovered that the origins of social insurance programs prior to the 1930s did not fit the logics proposed in cross-sectional, large-*N* studies. Deploying systematic historical evidence and tracing processes in smaller sets of cases (ranging from one to a dozen or so), comparative historical scholars reset agendas of scholarly investigation and theoretical debate. They created a lively new research community – both for themselves and for statistical researchers who have, ever since the commencement of comparative historical research on welfare states, continually adapted their quantitative hypotheses and research designs to take account of case-based findings.

That modern comparative historical research originally took shape in critical dialogue with modernization theory and large-*N* cross-sectional research is not surprising, because these approaches dominated sociology and political science in the 1960s and 1970s. Yet the original comparative historical resurgence also challenged Marxist grand theorizing and relatively atheoretical "area studies" scholarship. Understandably, skepticism about grand theory of any kind made most comparative historical analysts as unwilling to accept Marxist worldviews as they were to accept modernization theory. Hypotheses about class factors were certainly welcome, along with hypotheses from modernization theory and Weberian institutionalism. Despite its radical cachet among many young social scientists of the 1960s and 1970s, Marxism was no more acceptable as an a priori grand paradigm than the establishment social science theories its proponents attacked.

Yet as skeptical as they are of grand theories, comparative historical analysts remain interested in generalizing across multiple instances of a phenomenon under investigation – whenever this can be done with fidelity to conceptually defined contexts and with due attention to the causal complexities of historically embedded conjunctures and processes. In important respects, therefore, contemporary comparative historical analysis developed as an alternative to atheoretical area studies, specialties in which social scientists trained in languages and devoted to understanding particular cultures tended to define objects of research confined to single countries or particular regions of the world. Research in comparative politics or macrosociology has obviously always been intertwined with specialized historical and regional scholarship. Yet virtually all of the agenda-setting books listed at the start of this essay came as something of a shock to area specialists, who often dismissed their efforts at causal generalization on the grounds that their authors did not know all the relevant languages or cultures in enough depth. To the chagrin of such critics, comparative historical analysts use secondary as well as primary sources – and they always aim for generalizations defined in theoretical terms, creating what may seem (to area specialists) jarring juxtapositions of cases from different regions or eras.

A final reason for argumentativeness in comparative historical research brings us closer to what this volume specifically has to offer. As comparative historical analysis came of age over the past quarter of a century, it was subjected to tough scrutiny and criticism from practitioners of other styles of social science (for a range of instances, see Geddes 1990; King, Keohane, and Verba 1994; Lieberson 1991; Sewell 1996). Criticism is, in fact, a high form of flattery – and statistical methodologists, rational choice true believers, and culturally oriented interpretivists have all jumped into the fray to point out methodological flaws in comparative historical analysis precisely because they recognize the visibility and challenging nature of research in this genre. There are good answers to all the critiques, as so many of the essays in this book demonstrate. But that is the point. We cannot understand why the contributors to this volume have chosen to spell out metatheoretical and methodological principles without understanding that they are responding to debates within today's social science that prompt comparative historical scholars to justify and explicate the distinctive value of their enterprise. It is not incidental, I would argue, that many essays in this book make metatheoretical and methodological arguments, even as others reflect on the mix of theories and methods responsible for the accumulation of knowledge in established comparative historical literatures. As this volume appeared at a moment when comparative historical analysis has already accomplished so much in substantive terms, its contributors seek to explicate the premises of this genre and spell out its most fruitful methods and theoretical insights, responding to critics in the process.

Clarifying the Mission, Defending the Method

One critique of empirical comparative historical scholarship comes from culturally oriented scholars who believe that interpretation rather than causal generalization should be the goal of contextually sensitive scholarship on human affairs (cf. Sewell 1996). Contributors to this volume respond mainly by showing that comparative historical research has successfully developed valid generalizations about many phenomena of great importance without ignoring contextual particularities. What is more, culture and ideology can themselves be analyzed causally, not just assessed for their meanings (cf. Clemens 1997; Skocpol 1982). Still, interpretivist critiques receive relatively little attention here, because this volume grapples much more closely with criticisms from other explanatory camps.

Especially in political science, a new generation of sophisticated statistical empiricists have arrayed themselves behind the banner of *Designing Social Inquiry*, a methodological treatise by Gary King, Robert Keohane, and Sidney Verba (1994) that aims to extend the logic of multivariate statistical hypothesis testing to all realms of empirical research. "KKV," as this ambitious work is called for short, challenges key aspects of the research strategies used by case-oriented comparative historical analysts. To maximize the possibilities for statistical tests of causal relationships, KKV encourages investigators to rely on large quantitative data sets, even if such data are often relatively "thin" in terms of the hypotheses they can operationalize. For establishing causal propositions, moreover, KKV questions the value of the in-depth case explorations and comparisons of small numbers of cases that figure so centrally in much comparative historical scholarship.

Comparative historical analysis is also challenged by a new cadre of grand theorists, rational choice modelers who seek to reconceptualize virtually all sociopolitical processes as strategic games among goal-seeking actors (for a critical discussion, see Green and Shapiro 1996). Rational choice may be compatible with the use of historical case studies for selective applications of favored models (cf. Bates et al. 1998). Taken to an extreme, however, this approach questions the theoretical value of most macroscopic, comparative historical research. In rational choice analysis, "theory" becomes synonymous with the application of strategic models to maneuvers among actors, usually individuals, situated within taken-for-granted institutional and cultural contexts. Rational choice explanations are ideally derived mathematically; thus historical process and macroscopic configurations of institutions usually fade from view. Among rational choice purists, comparative historical studies are easily dismissed as mere narrative storytelling, as attempts to do "thick description" of contexts rather than to theorize about human behavior in general terms.

Contributors to this volume answer challenges from statistical methodologists and rational choice theorists. One response stresses the unique strengths of the comparative historical approach for building causal generalizations through contextualized comparisons and process tracing. A second rejoinder underlines the causally relevant temporal processes that fade from view in the synchronic and microlevel studies to which survey researchers and game theorists usually confine themselves.

The distinctive approaches comparative historical analysts use to establish theoretically informed causal generalizations are, we learn, especially well suited to untangling the complex and often recursive causal configurations we actually see in world history. In a vivid analogy, Jack Goldstone suggests that comparative historical analysts are like bands of explorers who spread out over disparate zones to map the varied contours of poorly understood territories. A large-*N* statistical approach makes little sense for such an endeavor, because the territory is unlikely to be homogeneous; truly random samples of locales are impossible; and the explorers – and the audiences to whom they report – are as interested in the specific locales as they are in the overall contours. Generalizations can still be developed, however, if each explorer investigates locales that seem puzzling or interesting in the light of available knowledge. Locales are explored in depth, with careful assessments of preconceived wisdom. Each explorer reports significant findings, which are then developed or modified by kindred explorers who move into new terrains. Gradually, maps of locales are modified and linked together. According to Goldstone, comparative historical generalizations about the causes, processes, and outcomes of revolutions – and other complex macroscopic phenomena – have been built up in exactly this manner (see, for example, Goldstone 1991; Goodwin 2001; Skocpol 1979, 1982; Snyder 1998; and Wickham-Crowley 1992). Understood thus, comparative historical analysis is a much more effective way to develop theoretically general and empirically rich causal knowledge than large-*N* studies that rely on unrealistic assumptions about the "homogeneity of the territory," in other words, that presume the random distribution of cases and the constancy of simple causal relationships. "By starting from the premise that specific cases first need to be thoroughly understood before advancing to general patterns," comparative historical analysis "never assumes an identity or equivalence or representativeness of specific cases; instead the extent of similarity or difference between cases is considered a crucial part of the investigation."

Goldstone's argument is echoed and amplified in the essays by Peter Hall and James Mahoney. In-depth case explorations, or comparisons of a similar phenomenon across a small to medium-sized number of contexts, should *not* be considered a mere second-best way to establish simple correlations among generally framed "dependent" and "independent" variables. Comparative historical analysts, Hall and Mahoney each point out, use close comparisons and process tracing within cases to examine sophisticated and up-to-date ideas about causation. Current theories of sociopolitical causation and statistically derived research techniques are not always well "aligned," Hall argues. The "standard regression model" toward which statistical reasoning has pushed most large-*N* comparativists makes unrealistic assumptions about case independence and the homogeneous operation of variables – not to mention the fact that variables are usually operationalized in relatively thin (or even arbitrary) ways with cross-national data sets that happen to be available. Lost in the rush to apply statistical techniques can be theoretical ideas about reciprocal causation, path dependence, and alternative causal paths to similar outcomes (Ragin 1987).

Comparative historical analysis, by contrast, embraces such hypotheses about how the social and political world is structured, about how processes of social change and political conflict actually play out. Detailed case investigations and careful, theoretically defined comparisons allow investigators to go far beyond establishing simple correlations – and these research approaches are often more suited to available data than are statistical methods that, in principle, allow tests of interaction effects but in practice make unrealistic demands on available sources of evidence. To render certain theoretical claims plausible or implausible, comparative historical analysts use focused, modest-*N* comparisons across nations, time periods (e.g., Ikenberry 2001), or policy areas (e.g., Hacker 2002). In addition, they make multiple observations within each case, to "provide serious tests of theories" about precise causal mechanisms and complex causal configurations. Because comparative historical analysis allows "careful measurement and close investigation of causal processes," Peter Hall argues, "it may sometimes even be better than aggregate analysis" for testing ideas about causal mechanisms (see also Bennett and George 1997). Furthermore, as Mahoney shows, comparativists have developed rigorous research designs that *combine* nominal comparisons, ordinal comparisons, and within-case analyses to develop or test theoretical inferences.

Using such techniques, each "explorer" – in Goldstone's terms – can substantially advance the process of knowledge accumulation. In comparative historical analysis, as in all other modes of research, no one investigator does it all. The question is whether the research methods employed push the *shared* scholarly enterprise of knowledge accumulation steadily forward. Hall, Mahoney, and Goldstone make a compelling case that comparative historical methods do just that, avoiding many of the pitfalls of unrealistic assumptions and superficial correlation to which large-*N* techniques may be prone when they are misapplied to issues of macroscopic social change and political development.

Temporal Process to the Fore

If a number of the contributors to this volume elaborate the rationale for case studies and contextualized case comparisons, others develop theoretical justifications for *over-time analysis* – taking issue with the push toward atemporal correlation that we see in many survey-based statistical studies and questioning the nearly exclusive focus on deliberate, short-term individual maneuvers encouraged by game-theoretic approaches. Theoretical as well as practical arguments about over-time analysis figure most centrally in the essays by Paul Pierson and Kathleen Thelen – who, interestingly enough, do not entirely agree with one another (for additional arguments by these authors, see Pierson 2000a, 2000b, 2000c; Thelen 1999, 2000). A close reading of their arguments suggests a rich menu of analytic possibilities for comparative historical researchers inclined to explore temporally protracted causal chains.

Too much social science today, declares Paul Pierson, focuses on "causes and outcomes that are both temporally contiguous and rapidly unfolding." Because so many fundamental social and political phenomena are "slow-moving," either as outcomes or in their causal roots, "we miss a lot. There are important things that we do not see at all, and what we do see we may misunderstand." Giving many concrete examples, Pierson shows that slow-moving causes, or slow-moving outcomes, or both, are often important in social change and politics. Mass or elite outcomes, for example, can be shaped by generational replacement. Social movements or policy shifts may be attributable, in significant part, to long-term cumulative processes that reach a certain threshold or flashpoint. Furthermore, many phenomena of interest may be attributable to interrelated chains of events or causes that play out over long stretches of time. Pierson's taxonomic aim is to "clarify specific methodological challenges facing investigators of long-term processes," whether they be causes or outcomes in any given investigation. More generally, he offers a brief for the long-term temporal purview featured in comparative historical analysis as a basic approach in the social sciences. Maybe other approaches can, in principle, accommodate long-term causes or slow-moving outcomes, but in practice they often ignore them, especially at the macro level. By definition, comparative historical studies examine stretches of time. Consequently, research communities in which such practitioners are central will be more likely to notice and theorize about the many slow-moving causes and outcomes that influence society and politics.

As he offers a general framework, Pierson especially hones in on one way to understand "positive feedback" processes – in which a "critical juncture" of change sets in motion a tightly recursive series of reinforcements of one possible causal chain among the many that might have been conceivable at the moment of the original critical happenings. Adapting arguments from economic history, Pierson believes that relatively determinist positive feedback processes should be at the heart of comparative historical theorizing about historical causation as such. He questions looser notions that suggest more open trajectories in which institutions or policies may well have considerable staying power – because of cultural understandings or the vested interests of powerful actors – but can nevertheless be disrupted or shifted at later points in the sequence of events analyzed.

In contrast, Kathleen Thelen argues for a more open-ended approach to policy feedbacks in her essay. Choices of institutions or policies are not always rigidly "locked in," she suggests. Political struggles are often involved in shaping and reshaping outcomes, and the losers may not disappear from history after one critical juncture. They may remain on the scene in a subordinate, parallel location, ready to modify institutional or policy trajectories. Persistent institutions or policies, moreover, may subtly change their functions or meanings, even as they persist in form and certain core functions. Thus, comparative historical analysts must keep in mind a wider range of theoretical possibilities (than locked-in, positive feedback processes) as they go about describing, comparing, and explaining patterns of institutional evolution.

Of course, Pierson and Thelen agree that long-term analysis is not just descriptively entertaining – not just an occasion for writing rich descriptive narratives – but is also theoretically central and innovative. They differ only about the most promising ways to conceptualize and explain instances of institutional persistence and change. This is exactly the sort of friendly disagreement that will enliven further rounds of comparative historical research, where an important theoretical frontier for the next generation will be to clarify further the conditions under which positive feedback effects lock in, making institutions or policies impervious to all but major shocks, versus the conditions under which continual small adjustments are more likely. Untangling conditions for continuity versus varieties of grounded change – that is, change from a starting place, whose effects continue to be felt even as adjustments occur – is where much comparative historical research will focus. This is a challenging theoretical goal that can be pursued as comparative historical scholars go about making sense of many important substantive phenomena while keeping an eye on the general issues Pierson and Thelen have raised. As they pursue a stronger theory of institutional persistence and change, comparative historical analysts can be confident that they are highlighting for all social scientists fundamental processes that might otherwise fade from view.

Methodological Pluralism and New Research Frontiers

As we have seen, this volume enters the fray of contemporary "paradigm disputes" to make a strong case for the special capacities of comparative historical analysis – an approach that aligns ontology and methodology to better explain outcomes, explore contexts, and assess causes that unfold over long stretches of time. Methodological and metatheoretical issues have been highlighted for good reason. Not only are contemporary comparative historical scholars responding to challenges posed by statistical methodologists and game theorists. They are also "telling it like it is" about comparative historical analysis, which is properly understood as a *research approach* rather than as a single overarching theory or technique of data collection or analysis. Comparative historical analysis is not committed to any single theory or technique – and thus it is splendidly open to synergy and innovation in both areas.

Descent into theoretical monism or methodological rigidity is always a risk in academia – and it can easily lead to sterile dead ends (cf. Shapiro 2001). But areas of scholarship where comparative historical analysts are prominent will not fall into this trap. Scholars in this genre consistently commit themselves to asking big questions of real-world relevance, exploring cases in context, and analyzing processes over time. Within such confines, they are happy to argue with, or use, any and all available theories; and they are opportunistically on the lookout for fresh data and techniques for exploring contexts and causal processes. Such methodological openness helps to explain why many comparative historical scholars have moved from doing "secondary" syntheses of primary historical studies completed by others to doing their own primary data gathering (compare, for example, Skocpol 1979 with Skocpol 1992 and Skocpol, Ganz, and Munson 2000). Openness also explains why so many comparative historical analysts are eager to learn new techniques and, when useful, to combine apparently disparate approaches to data analysis or theory building.

For example, Roger Gould's essay in this volume rehearses rationales and models for using quantitative network techniques in conjunction with historical case studies or dynamic process tracing. As he presents previous studies that have used network techniques to array and analyze data, Gould distinguishes between applications that use individual-level relational data and approaches that use network ideas somewhat more metaphorically to explore interactions at the organizational, community, or institutional level. Something of a micropurist himself, Gould has a clear preference for the former approach, and he gives several wonderful examples of the effective use of network techniques to explore changes in patterns of elite interaction. Once rigorously mapped, shifting elite interactions can both signify and help to explain broader institutional and political shifts in locales ranging from medieval Italy (Padgett and Ansell 1993) to modernizing England (Bearman 1993) to nineteenth-century Paris (Gould 1995). Gould is much more skeptical of the structural applications of network analysis in works by the historian John Mohr (1994) and sociologists Karen Barkey and Ronan Van Rossem (1997). My own conclusion, however, is that these scholars may well have made worthwhile use of network techniques to reinforce causal arguments also supported by other kinds of empirical analysis in their historical accounts. At this early stage of the adaptation of network techniques to comparative historical research, a multiplicity of models and attempts are instructive. In the future, comparative historical analysts will increasingly use network methods as one technique among others for identifying structural patterns or assessing causal hypotheses (for a readable introduction to network techniques, see Scott 2000). Without buying into any fixed theoretical or methodological program, comparative historical analysts will add network techniques to their eclectic armature.

Beyond this volume as well as within its pages, we see many instances of theoretical and methodological synergy in comparative historical scholarship as scholars synthesize ideas and techniques from this genre with contributions from other research approaches. In the literature on modern welfare states, for example, long-established synergies between statistical and case-based research continue apace, with investigations of the impact of globalization on varied patterns of national welfare-state "retrenchment" taking center stage in some of the latest major works (cf. Huber and Stephens 2001; Swank 2000). "Globalization" is a hot topic today, yet comparative historical scholars are demonstrating that it is not best understood as a massive, synchronic shock that wipes out all previous sociopolitical variations. Nations, regions, and sectors respond variously to similar transnational shocks and opportunities, and the variation can be explained through close case comparisons supplemented, where suitable data are available, by statistical hypothesis testing.

At a very different intersection of approaches, scholars studying gender rights and social programs affecting women have adapted ideas from largely interpretivist feminist writings and used them to devise testable hypotheses about variations across nations, regimes, time periods, and policy areas. In this way, Julia O'Connor, Ann Shola Orloff, and Sheila Shaver (1999) explain the gendered aspects of social programs in Australia, Canada, Britain, and the United States. Similarly, Mounira Charrad (2001) shows how trajectories of nation-state formation facilitated, and were furthered by, varied legal measures affecting women's rights in Tunisia, Algeria, and Morocco. And Mala Htun (in press) analyzes the evolution of women's rights under authoritarian and democratic regimes in Argentina, Chile, and Brazil. Previous studies of women's rights have usually used feminist concepts to interpret single cases. Comparative historical scholars show us that much richer explanations of conditions favoring – or impeding – women's rights can be developed through studies that use process tracing and careful comparisons to test and develop explicit causal hypotheses. Gender studies are one of the most exciting new frontiers in comparative historical scholarship, as are comparative explorations of the dynamics of ethnic conflict (e.g., Lustick 1993; Varshney 2001) and racial domination (e.g., Marx 1998).

In the literature on civic engagement in democratic polities, meanwhile, innovative investigators combine behavioralist survey research with arguments about historical roots and feedback processes. Thus Andrea Campbell (in press) combines process tracing and survey research to show that universal U.S. social programs for the elderly have had the effect of boosting political interest and involvement among lower-income elderly citizens. Because of "policy feedbacks" from two major government programs, Social Security and Medicare, political participation is less class-stratified among contemporary elderly Americans than it is among nonelderly adults. Campbell could not have arrived at this important finding without supplementing survey techniques with sophisticated ideas from historical and institutional analysis. Her study shows what a difference it makes to explore the interplay of macrocontexts and aggregate behaviors while taking feedback effects and temporal causation seriously.

To look at a final set of examples, studies of representative institutions are yet another frontier for comparative historical analysis – building on the cumulative studies of democracy and authoritarianism surveyed in this volume. In this area of scholarship, synergies of game theory and comparative history often prove fruitful. One fine example is Eric Schickler's (2001) study of twentieth-century institutional innovations in the U.S. House of Representatives. In two respects, Schickler's analysis synthesizes contributions from major research approaches. Theoretically, he tests various functional hypotheses about institutional design drawn from rational choice scholarship, sorting them out and combining them with the aid of insights (from Orren and Skowronek 1994) about the layering of institutional arrangements over time and about institutional choices that are the result of interacting processes. Methodologically, Schickler combines the quantitative analysis of roll-call votes typical of congressional studies with sophisticated process tracing of a large number of institutional innovations drawn from four time periods (each lasting a decade or more). The result is the most serious effort yet to test the strength of a number of prominent theories of institutional choice. Developing a nuanced explanation of the conjunctures of interests that shape institutional change, Schickler demonstrates that previous atemporal game-theoretic analyses have captured only parts of the overall dynamic of institutional evolution.

Another young scholar who effectively blends theoretical ideas from both rational choice and comparative historical institutionalism is Pauline Jones Luong. Across the globe, new democracies are emerging from previously entrenched authoritarian polities. Explaining variations in new institutional rules, and in the processes by which they take shape, represents a major challenge for students of comparative politics. In her new book, *Institutional Change and Political Continuity in Post-Soviet Central Asia*, Luong (2002) compares the establishment of electoral systems in Kazakhstan, Kyrgyzstan, and Uzbekistan – and, in the process, develops a new and potentially generalizable theory of "institutions designed under transitional circumstances." Although comparative historical scholars have directed our attention to persistent legacies from the past, new "rules of the game" can and do emerge from strategic bargains among elites, especially in a period of crisis and uncertainty. Yet rational choice approaches too easily fall into the trap of assuming that elite bargaining over new arrangements occurs on a tabula rasa, without regard to entrenched understandings and power relationships. In Jones Luong's model, actors change goals and perceptions in response to uncertainty and bargain in a dynamic way – producing different outcomes in three Central Asian polities with many prior structural similarities. But elites work from power positions and understandings embedded in inherited arrangements; indeed, they try to encode those older meanings and power relationships into seemingly new structures.

Jones Luong's work would not have been possible without prior breakthroughs in game theory. At the same time, she is inspired by the theoretical agendas set out by such comparative students of institutional development as Kathleen Thelen, who, as we have seen, calls for careful analyses not just of institutional outcomes but of the temporally and structurally embedded *processes* by which actors entrenched in previous institutions maneuver to create modified arrangements that retain many continuities from the past. Methodologically, moreover, Luong makes a powerful case for close comparison of kindred polities within a geocultural region, as a valuable "laboratory" for working out explanations of institutional change that may have much broader theoretical application. Her work splendidly combines area studies, strategic modeling, and explicit comparative historical analysis with generalizing pretensions. In his contribution to this volume, Ira Katznelson argues that comparative historical research can effectively bridge micro, mezo, and macro levels of analysis to incorporate choices by individuals and organizations into explanations of institutional transformations. Jones Luong's work can be considered a case in point for Katznelson's brief.

In concluding the reflections offered in this essay, I have mentioned but a few of many possible examples of cutting-edge comparative historical analysis. Looking back over the past quarter of a century, one can only be pleasantly amazed at the cumulation and creativity of literatures involving scholars who use this approach. Long-standing puzzles have been fruitfully revisited and important new questions tackled. As the essays by Edwin Amenta, James Mahoney, and Jack Goldstone show, in some literatures comparative historical analysts have accumulated knowledge primarily by extending investigations to new sets of cases, developing fresh hypotheses in the process, while in other areas comparative historical analysts have cooperated closely with large-*N* statistical researchers to establish findings that neither case-based analysts nor statistical researchers could likely have arrived at in isolation. Across the board, as they have pursued answers to substantive questions, comparative historical scholars have listened and responded to critics, clarifying not just the arguments they make about various topics, but the basic premises and methods of their shared research approach.

Fortunately, I am inclined to say, comparative historical analysis is no more an establishment within academic social science today than it was back in 1975, when Lewis Coser called for a renewal of the classical tradition. Never hegemonic, comparative historical analysis retains its critical edge, its daring, and its capacity to challenge self-satisfied orthodoxies and overweening scientisms. Yet comparative historical analysis certainly has come of age over the past quarter century. By now, comparative historical analysis has claimed its proud place as one of the most fruitful research approaches in modern social science, side by side with behaviorialism, rational choice, and interpretivist genres.

Of all the major approaches flourishing today, moreover, comparative historical analysis remains truest to the double mission of scholarship. As comparative historical scholars develop and argue about scientifically sound explanations of social change and politics, they invariably tackle issues that matter to more than just fellow scholars. Comparative historical studies speak to all those outside as well as within academia who yearn to better understand "the social structures in which we are enmeshed and which largely condition the course of our lives." This persistent double engagement bodes well for the future, for history and evolving human perspectives continually throw up new questions, concerns, and angles of vision. Social science done effectively may well be cumulative, but it is never complete. Thus, for those prepared to take up the double challenge of comparative historical scholarship – to do academically sound research while speaking to ever-changing worldly issues – the future is sure to be just as bright and challenging as the recent past. And that means the future will be very bright indeed.

References

Barkey, Karen and Ronan Van Rossem. 1997. "Networks of Contention: Villages and Regional Structure in the Seventeenth-Century Ottoman Empire." *American Journal of Sociology* 102: 1345–82.

Bates, Robert H., Avner Greif, Margaret Levi, Jean-Laurent Rosenthal, and Barry R. Weingast. 1998. *Analytic Narratives*. Princeton, NJ: Princeton University Press.

Bearman, Peter S. 1993. *Relations into Rhetorics: Local Elite Social Structure in Norfolk, England, 1540–1640*. New Brunswick, NJ: Rutgers University Press.

Bennett, Andrew and Alexander George. 1997. "Process Tracing in Case Study Methods." Paper presented at the MacArthur Workshop, Harvard University, October.

Campbell, Andrea Louise. In press. *Shaping Policy, Shaping Citizens: Senior Citizen Activism and the American Welfare State*. Princeton, NJ: Princeton University Press.

Charrad, Mounira. 2001. *States and Women's Rights: The Making of Postcolonial Tunisia, Algeria, and Morocco*. Berkeley: University of California Press.

Clemens, Elisabeth S. 1997. *The People's Lobby: Organizational Innovation and the Rise of Interest Group Politics, 1890–1925*. Chicago: University of Chicago Press.

Coser, Lewis. 1975. "Presidential Address: Two Methods in Search of a Substance." *American Sociological Review* 40: 691–700.

Evans, Peter B. 1979. *Dependent Development: The Alliance of Multinational, State, and Local Capital in Brazil.* Princeton, NJ: Princeton University Press.

Geddes, Barbara. 1990. "How the Cases You Choose Affect the Answers You Get." *Political Analysis* 2: 131–49.

Goldstone, Jack A. 1991. *Revolution and Rebellion in the Early Modern World.* Berkeley: University of California Press.

Goodwin, Jeff. 2001. *No Other Way Out: States and Revolutionary Movements, 1945–1991*. Cambridge and New York: Cambridge University Press.

Gould, Roger V. 1995. *Insurgent Identities: Class, Community, and Protest in Paris from 1848 to the Commune*. Chicago: University of Chicago Press.

Green, Donald P. and Ian Shapiro. 1996. *Pathologies of Rational Choice: A Critique of Applications in Political Science*. New Haven, CT: Yale University Press.

Hacker, Jacob. 2002. *Boundary Wars: The Political Struggle over Public and Private Social Benefits in the United States*. Cambridge and New York: Cambridge University Press.

Heclo, Hugh. 1974. *Modern Social Politics in Britain and Sweden*. New Haven, CT: Yale University Press.

Htun, Mala. In press. *Democracy, Dictatorship, and Gendered Rights*. Cambridge and New York: Cambridge University Press.

Huber, Evelyn and John D. Stephens. 2001. *Development and Crises of the Welfare State: Parties and Policies in Global Markets.* Chicago: University of Chicago Press.

Huntington, Samuel P. 1968. *Political Order in Changing Societies.* New Haven, CT: Yale University Press.

Ikenberry, G. John. 2001. *After Victory: Institutions, Strategic Restraint, and the Rebuilding of Order after Major Wars.* Princeton, NJ: Princeton University Press.

Katznelson, Ira. 1981. *City Trenches: Urban Politics and the Patterning of Class in the United States.* New York: Pantheon Books.

King, Gary, Robert O. Keohane, and Sidney Verba. 1994. *Designing Social Inquiry: Scientific Inference in Qualitative Research.* Princeton, NJ: Princeton University Press.

Lieberson, Stanley. 1991. "Small *N*'s and Big Conclusions: An Examination of the Reasoning in Comparative Studies Based on a Small Number of Cases." *Social Forces* 70: 307–20.

Linz, Juan J. 1978. *The Breakdown of Democratic Regimes.* Baltimore: Johns Hopkins University Press.

Luong, Pauline Jones. 2002. *Institutional Change and Political Continuity in Post-Soviet Central Asia: Power, Perceptions, and Pacts.* Cambridge and New York: Cambridge University Press.

Lustick, Ian. 1993. *Unsettled States, Disputed Lands: Britain and Ireland, France and Algeria, Israel and West Bank–Gaza.* Ithaca, NY: Cornell University Press.

Marx, Anthony. 1998. *Making Race and Nation: A Comparison of South Africa, the United States, and Brazil.* Cambridge and New York: Cambridge University Press, 1998.

McAdam, Doug. 1982. *Political Process and the Development of Black Insurgency, 1930–1970.* Chicago: University of Chicago Press.

Mills, C. Wright. 1959. *The Sociological Imagination.* New York: Oxford University Press.

Mohr, John W. 1994. "Soldiers, Mothers, Tramps, and Others: Discourse Roles in the 1907 New York Charity Directory." *Poetics* 22: 325–57.

Moore, Barrington, Jr. 1966. *Social Origins of Dictatorship and Democracy: Lord and Peasant in the Making of the Modern World.* Boston: Beacon Press.

O'Connor, Julia S., Ann Shola Orloff, and Sheila Shaver. 1999. *States, Markets, Families: Gender, Liberalism and Social Policy in Australia, Canada, Great Britain and the United States.* Cambridge and New York: Cambridge University Press.

Orren, Karen and Stephen Skowronek. 1994. "Beyond the Iconography of Order: Notes for a New Institutionalism." Pp. 311–30 in *The Dynamics of American Politics*, edited by Lawrence Dodd and Calvin Jillson. Boulder, CO: Westview Press.

Padgett, John F. and Christopher K. Ansell. 1993. "Robust Action and the Rise of the Medici, 1400–1434." *American Journal of Sociology* 98: 1259–319.

Pierson, Paul. 2000a. "Increasing Returns, Path Dependence, and the Study of Politics." *American Political Science Review* 94: 251–67.

2000b. "Not Just What, But *When*: Timing and Sequence in Political Processes." *Studies in American Political Development* 14: 72–92.

2000c. "The Limits of Design: Explaining Institutional Origins and Change." *Governance* 13: 475–99.

Ragin, Charles C. 1987. *The Comparative Method: Moving Beyond Qualitative and Quantitative Strategies*. Berkeley: University of California Press.

Rule, James B. 1997. *Theory and Progress in Social Science*. Cambridge and New York: Cambridge University Press.

Schickler, Eric. 2001. *Disjointed Pluralism: Institutional Innovation and the Development of the U.S. Congress*. Princeton, NJ: Princeton University Press.

Scott, John. 2000. *Social Network Analysis: A Handbook*, 2nd ed. London and Thousand Oaks, CA: Sage.

Sewell, William H. 1996. "Three Temporalities: Toward an Eventful Sociology." Pp. 245–80 in *The Historic Turn in the Human Sciences*, edited by Terrence J. McDonald. Ann Arbor: University of Michigan Press.

Shapiro, Ian. 2001. "Problems, Methods, and Theories in the Study of Politics, or: What's Wrong with Political Science and What to Do About It." Typescript of the Charles E. Lindblom Lecture in Public Policy, delivered on February 14 at the Institution for Social and Policy Studies, Yale University.

Skocpol, Theda. 1979. *States and Social Revolutions: A Comparative Analysis of France, Russia, and China*. Cambridge and New York: Cambridge University Press.

1982. "Rentier State and Shi'a Islam in the Iranian Revolution." *Theory and Society* 11: 265–303.

1992. *Protecting Soldiers and Mothers: The Political Origins of Social Policy in the United States*. Cambridge, MA: Belknap Press of Harvard University Press.

Skocpol, Theda, Marshall Ganz, and Ziad Munson. 2000. "A Nation of Organizers: The Institutional Origins of Civic Voluntarism in the United States." *American Political Science Review* 94: 527–46.

Snyder, Richard. 1998. "Paths Out of Sultanistic Regimes: Combining Structural and Voluntarist Perspectives." Pp. 49–81 in *Sultanistic Regimes*, edited by H. E. Chehabi and J. J. Linz. Baltimore, MD: Johns Hopkins University Press.

Swank, Duane. 2000. "Political Institutions and Welfare State Restructuring: The Impact of Institutions on Social Policy Change in Developed Democracies." Pp. 197–237 in *The New Politics of the Welfare State*, edited by Paul Pierson. Oxford: Oxford University Press.

Thelen, Kathleen. 1999. "Historical Institutionalism in Comparative Politics." *Annual Review of Political Science* 2: 369–404.

2000. "Time and Temporality in the Analysis of Institutional Evolution and Change." *Studies in American Political Development* 14: 102–9.

Tilly, Charles, ed. 1975. *The Formation of National States in Western Europe*. Princeton, NJ: Princeton University Press.

1984. *Big Structures, Large Processes, Huge Comparisons*. New York: Russell Sage Foundation.

Varshney, Ashutosh. 2001. *Ethnic Conflict and Civic Life: Hindus and Muslims in India*. New Haven, CT: Yale University Press.

Wallerstein, Immanuel. 1974. *The Modern World System: Capitalist Agriculture and the Origins of the European World-Economy in the Sixteenth Century*. New York: Academic Press.

Wickham-Crowley, Timothy. 1992. *Guerrillas and Revolutions in Latin America: A Comparative Study of Insurgents and Regimes since 1956*. Princeton, NJ: Princeton University Press.

Conclusion

Index

Abbott, Andrew, 181, 397
Abrams, Philip, 274, 278
absorbing Markov chains, 194–5
abstracted empiricism, 407
Africa, 4, 8, 155, 165
agency: and collective actors, 276; and lack of attention in comparative historical analysis, 271; and path dependence, 212, 213, 219; restricted version of, 274, 294; and tension with structuralism, 157, 272, 275, 277, 279–81, 282–3, 340
agricultural commercialization, 139
Alber, Jens, 99
Algeria, 421
Almond, Gabriel, 376
Althusser, Louis, 306
Amenta, Edwin, 412, 424
America. *See* United States
American Political Science Association (APSA), 3
American Revolution (1776), 53, 55
American Sociological Association (ASA), 3, 241, 407
analytic tools, 26
Anderson, Perry, 273, 274–8, 286, 345, 346
Ansell, Christopher K., 258, 264
Aquino, Corazon, 83
Archer, Margaret, 282
area studies, 11, 15, 412, 413
Argentina, 359, 421; and authoritarianism, 153–4; and democratization, 144, 147, 161; and institutional evolution, 228–9
Aristotle, 53, 55
armed forces. *See* military
Arthur, W. Brian, 219
Asia, 4, 8, 68, 69
atomism, 280–1
Austria: and democratization, 143
authoritarianism, 4; and Barrington Moore research program, 137–52; class-based origins of, 147–9, 165–6; and conclusions about knowledge accumulation, 164–7; and data collection, 16; and the Guillermo O'Donnell research program, 152–6; and international causes, 149–51, 166; and statistical research, 134; *see also* bureaucratic authoritarianism, military authoritarianism, sultanism, totalitarianism
autocorrelation regression, 264

Baltic states, 67
Barkey, Karen, 251n. 5, 260–2, 420
Barth, Fredrick, 295, 296
Bates, Robert H., 24, 393n. 17
Bayesian analysis, 44–7, 51
Bearman, Peter, 252–5, 257–8

Index

Becker, Howard, 319n. 12
Belgium: and democratization, 143–4, 149, 357
Bendix, Reinhard, 273
Bennett, Andrew, 19, 386n. 10
Bentley, Arthur, 376
Berkowitz, Edward, 113, 243
Bermeo, Nancy, 160
Beveridge, William, 98
big questions, 11, 92, 93, 97, 105, 112, 407, 420; defined, 7; *see also* first-order questions
Bloch, Marc, 3
block modeling, 247–8, 254, 261, 266
Blockmans, Wim, 286
Bolivia, 73; and authoritarianism, 147; and democracy, 161
Bonnell, Victoria E., 23, 24
Bonapartism, 166
Boolean algebra, 6, 111, 112, 113, 136, 352, 389; example of, 343–4
bounded innovation, 220
bourgeoisie: and democracy and authoritarianism, 138–9, 142–4, 146, 148, 165; and revolution, 45, 60–1; and social policy, 102
Braudel, Fernand, 192
Brazil, 421; and authoritarianism, 144, 147, 153–4, 156; and democracy, 161; and racial tolerance, 342
Breughel, Jan, 270
Breughel, Pieter, 270
Brinton, Crane, 41
Britain, 8, 12, 13, 49–50, 53, 63, 79, 220, 230, 277, 346; class formation in, 307, 311, 313; democracy in, 138, 139, 356–7; legal system in, 321–2; social policy in, 100, 104, 112, 360; *see also* English Civil War; English Revolution
Braumoeller, Bear F., 348, 350
Bruszt, László, 227
bureaucratic-authoritarianism, 152–5, 158, 162
Burundi, 43
Calhoun, Craig, 73
Cambodia, 43, 62
Cameron, Charles, 194
Campbell, Andrea, 422
Campbell, Donald T., 306n. 1, 315–16, 361, 391, 396
Canada, 8, 104, 229n. 34, 360
capitalist class. *See* bourgeoisie
capitalist democracy, 110
capitalist development, 7, 50, 60–1, 146, 152–3, 276, 321–2
Caribbean, 13
Carmines, Edward, 182, 197, 202
Cartwright, Nancy, 374
cases: and constituting populations, 8, 20, 42–3, 63, 323, 351–2; independence of, 13, 382; jarring juxtapositions of, 413; "least likely" version of, 311; number of 13, 14–15, 16, 19, 21, 42, 44, 45, 50, 51, 65, 93, 110, 112, 150, 315, 319–20, 323, 332, 342, 350, 380, 381, 416; and probabilistic explanation, 345; versus observations, 318, 319–20, 332, 395–6, 416; similarities and differences of, 8, 10, 13, 44, 65, 305; single instances of, 305, 307, 310–8; types of, 14; *see also* causal homogeneity; degrees of freedom problem; sampling; selection bias; small-*N* analysis
Castles, Francis G., 142–3
Catholic Church, 54
causal homogeneity, 8–10, 18, 20, 42, 43, 351, 382, 387, 415, 416
causal inference: approaches to, 5, 11–12, 26, 42–44; as component of comparative historical analysis, 6, 11–12, 17–18, 23, 46, 94, 337, 410; and complexity, 44, 76, 81, 84, 112, 271, 315, 389, 413, 415; and context dependence, 388; and correctly specifying a model, 352–3; and correlational assumptions, 380, 398, 416; and covering laws, 377; and

Index

critical cases, 46, 396; and critical tests, 381; and cultural approaches, 24, 414; and deterministic views, 47, 51, 339–44, 381; and functionalist conceptions of, 377, 379; and history as a process inscribed with causation, 306, 310; and a Humean ontology, 382; and knowledge accumulation, 134–5; and linear models, 337, 338–9, 349–50, 353–6; as the foundation of methodology, 134, 373–4; and partial explanation, 327; and prior beliefs, 45–47, 51; and probabilistic explanation, 18, 42, 340–1, 344–7, 381, 382; *see also* Bayesian analysis; congruence testing; iterated hypothesis testing; necessary conditions; nominal analysis; ordinal analysis; process tracing; small-*N* analysis; sufficient conditions; within-case analysis
causal chain arguments, 376, 417; defined, 187; examples of, 187–9; methodlogical issues surrounding, 188
causal mechanisms. *See* mechanisms
causal narrative, 323, 365–7, 368
Charles XI, 142
Charrad, Mounira, 421
Chile, 421; and authoritarianism, 153–4; and democratization, 144, 147, 161
China, 49–50, 63, 64, 69, 79, 277, 359, 364; *see also* Chinese Revolution
Chinese Revolution, 50, 60, 61, 63, 82
civil society, 309
class analysis, 22, 277, 330, 412; and cultural conditions, 307, 313, 320; and the study of revolutions, 58, 60–1, 64; and the study of democracy and authoritarianism, 147–50
Clemens, Elisabeth, 232
clique (network analysis), 245
Cloward, Richard A., 113
Cohen, G. A., 277
Coleman, James, 308–9, 312, 319, 328
collective action problem, 21, 71, 329, 330
Collier, David, 12, 91, 117, 154–5, 156, 187, 188, 208, 289, 293, 359, 365
Collier, Ruth Berins, 12, 147, 156, 187, 188, 208, 287, 289, 293, 359, 365
Colombia, 59, 365; and authoritarianism, 145
Committee on Concepts and Methods, 4n.9
communism, 137, 158, 232
comparative historical analysis, paradigm of: and big questions 7–9, 407, 409; controversies surrounding, 5, 16–25, 131, 411–17; decline of, 3; definition of, 5, 10–15, 93–4; and delimited theorizing 8–10, 326; and double engagement, 409–11, 424–5; and historians 15, 18n. 40, 97; inferential goals of, 42–4; and institutionalization in the social sciences, 4, 407–8; and insights into divergent trajectories, 208; and meta-theory, 136, 413; and policy advice, 9; revival of, 3–5, 26; and strengths and weaknesses, 103–5, 414–17
comparative method, 373, 375, 380, 391, 396–7, 398; and necessary and sufficient conditions, 381; relationship to comparative historical analysis, 15; and omitted variable bias, 381
comparison: contextualized and systematic, 6, 13, 15, 21, 51, 408, 410, 415, 417; individualizing, 94n. 3; structured, focused, 378
concepts: and dialogue with evidence, 306, 318; formation of, 6, 13, 20, 21, 92, 163, 331, 378; and knowledge accumulation, 134, 158, 159; level of generality of, 9, 10, 52, 379, 390;

concepts: (*cont.*)
refinement of, 52–5, 100, 102, 105, 154–5; validity of, 13, 111; *see also* generalization; particularity
conceptual equivalences, 328, 331
Congo, Democratic Republic of, 62, 75
congruence testing, 50–2, 65, 84
conjunctures, 80–2, 102, 274, 413
connectivity methods, 243, 244–6, 264, 266
Constant, Benjamin, 283
constant causes: and explanations of institutional genesis and change, 214–17
constant conjunction, 382
constructivist, 390
context of discovery, 309, 312
context of validation, 309, 312
contingency, 51, 152, 221n. 20, 310; and path dependence, 212, 218–19, 274, 292
contrast of contexts, 11n. 27; 94n. 3
corporatist welfare regime, 108
Coser, Lewis, 407, 408, 411, 424
Costa Rica: and democracy, 144, 147, 167, 366
covering laws, 290
critical junctures, 156, 188, 195, 209, 211, 220, 231, 232, 272, 276, 277, 278, 282, 283–4, 287, 289, 290–2, 294, 385, 418; examples of 196–7
Crowell, Oliver, 253
Cuba, 43, 62, 73, 74, 75, 82
cultural approaches, 5, 22–4, 151, 267, 376–7, 414; and class analysis, 307; *see also* interpretive analysis; postmodern theory
cultural scripts, 217
cultural-sociological mechanisms of institutional reproduction, 211; defined, 216–17; example of, 217, 223; critique of, 217, 223
cumulative causes, 190; defined, 181; examples of, 181–2; importance of, 182
cumulative outcomes, 191
Czechoslovakia, 76

Dahl, Robert, 149, 158
Darwin, Charles, 133n. 1
David, Paul, 219
decommodification, 108, 109
deduction, 20, 48, 49, 392, 395
deepening hypothesis, 153–4
degrees of freedom problem, 350–1, 354, 396
democracy, 4, 61, 78; and associational life, 150; and the Barrington Moore research program, 137–52; and causal chain arguments, 187; and class-based origins of 147–9, 165–6; and conclusions about knowledge accumulation, 164–7; and data collection, 16; definition of, 158–9; and international causes, 149–51, 166; and the Linz-Stepan research program, 156–62; measurement of, 134; Moore's argument about, 137–8; and statistical research, 134, 146, 150–1, 165, 166; subtypes of, 159, 164; waves of, 167
Denmark, 345; and democratization, 143, 149, 356–7
dependency theory, 153, 162
descriptive inference, 6, 23, 155, 376; and studies of democracy and authoritarianism, 157, 162; and knowledge accumulation, 133–4
De Swaan, Abram, 287
determinism, 157, 219, 221n.20, 314–15, 325, 332, 339–44, 349, 352, 354, 362, 381, 418; definitions of, 339–41; *see also* contingency
Diamond, Larry, 161
Diaz, Porfirio, 83
Dion, Douglas, 348, 350
"disciplined, configurative inquiry," 378, 390
Djilas, Milovan, 308
Dobbin, Frank, 235

Douglas, Mary, 295–6
Downing, Brian M., 149, 285
Durkheim, Emile, 376, 380n. 5

Easton, David, 376
Eckstein, Harry, 327, 375, 395, 396
economic development, 4
Ecuador: and authoritarianism, 145, 147
Ekiert, Grzegorz, 221n. 20, 233
El Salvador, 54; and authoritarianism, 144, 147
Elias, Norbert, 287
Elster, Jon, 200, 233
endogamy, 247–8
England. *See* Britain
English Civil War, 252–5
English Revolution (1640), 47, 54, 55, 60, 61, 62, 63, 82, 138, 139
Enlightenment, 53
environment: and lack of attention in comparative historical studies, 5
Erikson, E. H., 316n.8
Ertman, Thomas, 9, 148n.13, 150, 196–7, 208, 285–6, 345–6
Esping-Andersen, Gφsta, 108, 118, 121, 122
ethnicity: *see* racial relations
Europe, Eastern, 4, 9, 12, 62, 102, 210, 277, 285; anticommunist revolutions in, 41, 53, 66, 67, 70, 72, 76; and democracy and authoritarianism, 143n.8, 356–8; and institutional persistence, 227, 232
Europe, Western, 4, 7, 9, 12, 69, 132, 277, 285; democracy and authoritarianism in, 150, 286, 309, 356–8; social policy in, 106, 108
European revolutions of 1848, 54
exogamy, 247–8
experimental designs, 326, 380, 397
Evans, Peter B., 408
event history models, 264
event structure analysis, 366–7
evolutionary theory, 190–1, 289

Falleti, Tulia, 228, 229
Farabundo Marti National Liberation Front, 54
farmers. *See* peasants
fascism, 9, 61, 224; and Moore's argument, 137, 142, 149
feedback processes: and institutional reproduction, 208, 209, 212, 221–2, 224, 233; and social policy, 106, 107, 122; see also increasing returns
feminist theory, 52, 109
Finland: and democratization, 149
first-order questions, 131–2, 409
Fligstein, Neil, 217
Flora, Peter, 98, 99
focused meta-theory, 318
focused theoretical frameworks, 323, 328, 329–30
Foran, John, 41, 71, 73
formalization, 241, 245
France, 49–50, 63, 64, 138, 167, 210, 277, 359, 364; democratization in, 138, 141, 356–7; *see also* French Revolution
Franco, Francisco, 158
Freese, Lee, 133n.1
French Revolution (1789), 41, 45, 50, 53, 54, 55, 61, 62, 63, 66, 67, 80, 82, 83, 141
Friedman, Milton, 386, 394n.18
functionalism, 9, 151, 199, 209, 315, 326, 412, 422; as an ontology, 374, 377–9
functionalist-utilitarian perspectives. *See* utilitarian-functionalist mechanisms of reproduction
fuzzy-set analysis, 6, 136, 346–7, 352, 389

Galois lattice representations, 259
game theory, 9, 70, 384, 419, 422–3; short time horizon of, 200–1, 415, 417
Geddes, Barbara, 162, 351
Geertz, Clifford, 22, 23

Index

gender, 4, 80, 421
gender-based policy regimes, 109
general linear model, 249n.4
general theory, 20
generalization, 5, 10, 11n.27, 19–20, 22, 43–4, 45, 47, 49, 50, 51, 58, 63, 65, 76, 77, 91, 92, 94, 135, 149, 150, 160, 309, 376, 383, 388, 395, 412, 415; *see also* particularity
George, Alexander L., 19, 363, 378, 386n.10, 391
German Revolution (1848), 47, 63
German Social Democratic Party (SDP), 308, 319
Germany, 13, 60, 61, 63, 79, 138, 142, 210, 230, 321, 356–7; vocational system in, 222–5; *see also* German Revolution
Germany, East, 76
Gerschenkron, Alexander, 208
Gibson, Edward, 228, 229
globalization, 8, 216, 421
Goertz, Gary, 348, 350
Goldstone, Jack A., 182, 182–3n.1, 361, 411, 415–17, 424
Goldthorpe, John, 19, 316n.9
Goodwin, Jeff, 41, 71, 73, 76
Gorbachev, Mikhail, 75, 76
Gould, Andrew, 208
Gould, Roger V., 71, 420
grand theory, 407, 412
Granovetter, Mark, 183, 184
graph-theoretic analyses, 250
Greece: and democratization, 149
Grenada, 73
Griffin, Larry J., 366, 367
Guatemala: and authoritarianism, 144, 147, 366
Gurr, Ted Robert, 41, 42, 57, 58, 59
Gustav III, 142

Haggard, Stephan, 161
Hall, Peter A., 416, 417
Hamilton, Alexander, 256
Hannan, Michael T., 192
Hanson, Stephen, 221n.20, 233
Hartz, Louis, 296n.16
Haydu, Jeffrey, 212, 292–3, 297
Hechter, Michael, 19
Heclo, Hugh, 91, 94, 101, 408
Hedström, Peter, 263, 264
Hicks, Alexander, 111
Hintze, Otto, 3, 196, 345, 346
Hirschman, Albert O., 154
historical causation, 195
historical institutionalism: and new institutionalisms, 273; relationship to comparative historical analysis 11, 15, 272–3
historical logic, 306–7n.2
historical sociology: relationship to comparative historical analysis, 11
historicism, 277
Hoffman, Stanley, 390n. 12
holism, 272, 274, 275, 280–1, 282, 377
Honduras: and authoritarianism, 144
Htun, Mala, 421
Huber, Evelyne, 13, 110, 111, 112, 118, 185, 208, 317n. 10
Hume, David, 200, 382
Hunt, Lynn, 23, 24
Huntington, Samuel P., 41, 57, 58, 59, 160–1, 408, 412
hybridization, 227n. 32
hypothesis elaboration: definition of, 135; and the study of democracy and authoritarianism, 146–50

ideal type, 321
identity formation, 4, 73; *see also* ideology
identity theory, 22, 102
ideology, 56, 66, 69, 70, 73, 79, 82, 83, 414
Immergut, Ellen, 101
inclusionary authoritarian regime, 155

Index

increasing returns, 195, 291–2, 418; and institutional persistence, 211, 213, 214, 220, 221, 225, 226, 231, 233
India: and democratization, 167; and Moore's theory, 144n. 9
individualism: and agency, 282; and relationship to holism, 272, 274, 276, 280–1; and treatment of preferences, 271, 279
Indonesia, 75
induction, 19–20, 395
industrialization, 7, 61, 65, 100, 110, 153–4, 230, 378, 385
inequality, 42, 98
infinite regress problem: strategies for overcoming, 188–9
information technology, 8
institutional conversion, 222, 230, 231, 234; compared to functionalist approaches, 234; defined, 226; examples of, 228–30; phenomena associated with, 232; and relationship to increasing returns, 213
institutional evolution, 211, 213, 215, 225–30; and the German vocational system, 222–5; lack of attention devoted to, 208; *see also* institutional conversion; institutional layering
institutionalism, original, 375–6; *see also* historical institutionalism
institutional layering, 222, 230, 231, 234, 422; defined, 225; examples of, 226–8; phenomena associated with, 232; and relationship to increasing returns, 213; ubiquity of, 228
institutional persistence: examples of, 210, 220; and flexibility, 228; and historicist view, 218; and "lock-in," 209, 212, 226, 230, 231, 282, 294, 418; and "losers," 231; and mechanisms of reproduction, 209, 211–12, 214–17, 225, 291–2
institutional typology, 278
institutional variables, 162
institutions: breakdown of, 209, 221; fragmentation of, 187; innovation of, 209, 213, 220, 226; and combining periodization and preferences, 278, 295–7; *see also* institutional evolution; institutional persistence
interaction effects: and comparative historical analysis, 416; and new ontologies, 385, 393; and statistical analysis, 382, 383, 386, 388; ubiquity of, 387
international relations theory, 22
International Typographical Union (ITU), 309, 319
interpretive analysis, 11, 15, 22–5, 310, 313, 390, 413, 414
interval measurement, 338, 361
intervening variables, 394
Iranian Revolution (1979), 53, 56, 59, 66, 67, 73, 74, 75, 77, 189
iron law of oligarchy, 308–9, 311
Italy, 53, 60, 61, 277, 356–7; and democratization, 143
iterated hypothesis testing: and Collier and Collier's argument, 156; definition of, 135; and Linz and Stepan's argument, 158; and Moore's argument, 138–45, 163; and O'Donnell's argument, 154–5, 162; and the transitions literature, 160

James, Susan, 275
Japan, 60, 61, 63, 138, 142, 166, 210, 277
Jepperson, Ronald, 200
Johnson, Chalmers, 57, 58
Johnson, Lyndon B., 229

Kant, Immanuel, 316
Katz, Michael, 95
Katznelson, Ira, 408, 423
Kaufman, Robert R., 154, 161
Kazakhstan, 342, 423
Keohane, Robert O., 17, 24, 111, 325, 414

Key, V. O., 181
Khomeini, Ayattolah, 83
King, Gary, 17, 24, 111, 325, 351, 414
Kiser, Edgar, 19
Knight, Jack, 215, 216, 287, 297
knowledge: definition of, 133–6, 163; universal forms of, 8, 9, 13, 20; validity of, 22, 24; *see also* knowledge accumulation
knowledge accumulation, 25; causes of, 92–3, 114–20, 132, 392; and conclusions about revolutions, 80–4; and conclusions about social policy, 114–20; definitions of, 95–6, 132–7, 163, 410; importance of, 131, 163–4; and network analysis, 252, 265; process of, 43–4, 95–6; versus knowledge generation, 132–3
Korpi, Walter, 216
Kuran, Timur, 288
Kyrgyzstan, 342, 423

labor. *See* working class, urban
Laitin, David, 274–5n.6
Lakatos, Imre, 392
Lake, David, 198
landed elites, 60; and democracy and authoritarianism, 138–49, 165; and revolutions 61
Lasswell, Harold, 376
Latin America, 4, 8, 12, 62, 67, 132, 155, 156, 165, 187, 343
law, 5
lawlike propositions, 20, 22, 376, 377
leadership, 69, 70, 73, 77, 78, 79, 81, 82, 83, 152, 159
legitimacy, 157–8
legitimation arguments, 209, 216–17
Leinhardt, Samuel, 243
Lenin, Vladimir, 60, 70, 77, 84
level of aggregation, 338, 360
Lévi-Strauss, Claude, 259
liberal welfare regime, 109
liberalism, 9
Lichbach, Mark, 42, 71
Lijphart, Arend, 374, 380, 381, 395
Limongi, Fernando, 194
Linz, Juan J., 132, 134, 152, 156–9, 161–3, 168, 408
Lipset, Seymour Martin, 151, 308–9, 312, 319
Locke, John, 283, 286
Locke, Richard, 13
Lowi, Theodore, 107
Luebbert, Gregory M., 9, 142, 149, 356–8, 359, 361, 364–5
Luong, Pauline Jones, 342, 343, 422–3

Machiavelli, 55
macrocausal analysis, 11n.27
Madero, Francisco, 83
Mahoney, James, 209, 212, 218–19, 220, 221, 291, 292, 323, 416, 417, 424
Mandela, Nelson, 83
Mann, Michael, 345, 346
Marcos, Ferdinand, 53, 66
Markoff, John, 67
Marshall, T. H., 104, 328, 376
Marshall, William J., 215
Marx, Anthony W., 286–7, 342–3
Marx, Karl, 3, 55, 58, 60, 166, 202, 271, 277, 317, 376, 410
Marxist theory, 45–6, 52, 60–1, 101, 115, 148, 151, 216, 273, 277, 307, 326, 330, 408, 412
Mayhew, David, 185, 186–7, 197
McAdam, Doug, 116, 183–4, 185n.2, 186, 408
McCarthy, John D., 116
McKeown, Timothy J., 18, 363, 391
McQuaid, Kim, 113
measurement, 6, 13, 113, 136, 338, 346–7, 359, 361, 362, 416
measurement error, 344, 352, 354
mechanisms, 19, 44, 58, 84, 103, 378, 417; definitions of, 233, 328, 363, 388; replacement as an example of, 190; and contiguous causation, 200;

and local causes, 200; and process tracing, 363–5
Meiji Restoration (Japan, 1868), 47, 63, 83
Merton, Robert, 328, 329n.19
Messick, Richard, 91, 117
meta-theory: and Barrington Moore, 151–2; as a component of knowledge accumulation, 136, 163; as "dross," 317; definitions of 136, 318; and focused theoretical frameworks, 329; and Linz and Stepan, 152, 159; versus methodology, 136; and network analysis, 242, 243, 266; and O'Donnell, 155; subject-specific version of, 330, 331; *see also* focused meta-theory; structural approach to structural analysis; voluntarism
method of agreement, 93, 104, 136, 341–2, 349, 358–9, 379, 380
method of concomitant variation, 353, 354
method of difference, 93, 104, 136, 341–2, 349, 358–9, 379, 380
methodological individualism. *See* individualism
Mexican Revolution (1911), 59, 82, 83
Mexico: and authoritarianism, 145
Michels, Robert, 307–8, 310–12, 319, 323
microfoundations, 272, 296
micro–macro levels, 5, 21, 272, 388, 423
middle classes: and democracy and authoritarianism, 146, 148, 165
Middle East, 4, 68
middle-range theory, 20, 96, 100, 102, 104, 114, 115, 267, 328, 329n. 19, 374
military: and democracy and authoritarianism, 143, 149, 154, 166
military authoritarianism, 158
Mill, John Stuart, 136, 341, 353, 379, 380
Mill's methods. *See* method of agreement; method of concomitant variation; method of difference
Mills, C. Wright, 407
Mishra, Ramesh, 111
mobilization theory, 60, 64
modernization theory, 52, 57–62, 63, 91, 92, 100, 103, 110, 115, 117, 148, 199, 326, 377–8, 407, 412
Mohr, John, 259–60, 262n. 8, 267, 420
moments of madness, 283
Montesquieu, 55
Moore, Barrington Jr., 41, 64, 65, 132, 157, 158, 160, 163, 164, 168, 194, 208, 284, 285, 286, 288, 317n. 10, 408; extensions of his argument, 146–50; falsification of his argument, 145; and lack of focus on preferences, 273, 274, 276–8; and sequence analysis, 152; and structuralism, 151–2; summary of his argument, 137; tests of his hypotheses, 138–45; and theory of revolutionary consequences, 60–2
Moore–Gerschenkron thesis, 364–5
Morocco, 421
Mosca, 64
most different systems design, 342n. 5, 380
most similar systems design, 104, 342n. 5
multiple conjunctural causation, 343, 383, 389
multiple regression analysis. *See* regression analysis
Munck, Gerardo L., 155, 160
Myles, John, 112

narrative analysis, 6, 20, 50–1, 63, 72, 94, 146, 395; and causal analysis, 289, 314, 365–7
natural history approach, 151
Nazism, 309

necessary conditions, 18, 44, 337, 389; and Boolean algebra, 344; and causes of revolutions, 65, 80; criticisms of, 348–53; defined, 341, 382; and deterministic explanation, 341–2, 381, 396; examples of, 166, 348, 342–3, 358; and fuzzy-set analysis, 347; versus linear causation, 349–50, 355–6; and nominal analysis, 338, 344–5, 352; and probabilistic explanation, 344–5, 347, 352; and selection bias, 351; and trivial causes, 348
negative case methodology, 311n. 5
neopatrimonial dictatorships, 74, 78
neopositivism, 310, 332
Netherlands, 357: and democratization, 143–4, 357
network analysis, 22, 26, 420; and cultural frameworks, 267; descriptive uses of, 250; as data reduction tool, 250, 266; theoretical assumptions of, 242, 243–4, 251; examples of using network data, 252–8; examples of using nonnetwork data, 259–63; and historical research, 241; as a "powerful" tool, 266; strong versus weak varieties of, 244; and "symbolic networks," 264; types of, 244–9
New Deal (United States), 55, 108
new institutionalism: and the study of persistence, 184
Newton, Isaac, 310
Nicaragua: and authoritarianism, 144
Nicaraguan Revolution (1979), 66, 67, 73, 74, 75, 82
nominal analysis, 339; combined with oridinal analysis, 355–9, 368, 417; and deterministic explanation, 339–44, 349, 352, 362–3; examples of, 342–4, 356–9; and probabilistic explanation, 344–6, 352, 362; and relationship to within-case analysis, 338, 360, 362; as a strategy of causal inference, 325, 326, 338–9, 341–7, 367–8; and vivid labels, 339; and within-case analysis, 362–3, 368, 417; *see also* necessary conditions; sufficient conditions
North, Douglass, 196, 219–20, 222, 295
Norway, 320, 356–7

Obershall, Anthony, 71
objectivity, 312
O'Connor, Julia S., 122, 421
O'Donnell, Guillermo, 132, 152–6, 157, 158, 160, 162, 163, 168
ontology, 26, 282, 325, 419; and the comparative method, 379–81; and the comparative revolution, 376–9; defined, 373–4; and the initial institutionalism, 375–6; and lack of fit with existing methodology, 374–5, 382–3, 398; versus methodology, 373–4; and need for greater attention to, 399; and recent methodological advances, 388–91; and recent theoretical developments, 384–7; versus theory, 374
Opp, Karl-Dieter, 71
ordinal analysis: combined with nominal analysis, 355–9, 368, 417; examples of, 356–60; interpreting associations based on, 354–6, 368; and necessary and sufficient conditions, 355–6, 368; and relationship to within-case analysis, 338, 360, 362; as a strategy of causal inference, 338–9, 353–6; and within-case analysis, 363, 417
Orloff, Ann Shola, 8, 13, 101, 109, 122, 360, 421
Orren, Karen, 235
Ottoman Empire, 69, 260–1, 277
outcomes: consensus regarding in the study of social provision, 92, 97–8, 114, 116; large-scale, 4; substantively important, 4, 6

Index

Padgett, John F., 258, 278
Paige, Jeffery M., 145
Paine, Thomas, 53
paradigms: and academic communities, 410–11; defined, 15; disputes between, 15–25, 407, 419; and knowledge accumulation, 136; and network analysis, 243; synergies between, 25, 419, 421
Paraguay: and authoritarianism, 145
parallel demonstration of theory, 11n. 27
Pareto, Vilfredo, 64
Paris Commune (1871), 263–4
Parsa, Misagh, 71, 73
parsimony, 386, 387
Parsons, Talcott, 317, 328, 376
particularity, 5, 9, 10, 19–20, 50, 108, 241, 306
path dependence, 6, 26, 51, 61, 107, 193, 209, 289–94, 375, 387, 416; and adequate explanation, 386, 393; and contingency, 51, 212, 213, 218–19, 292, 385; definitions of, 195, 218–19, 220, 221, 384–5; and economics, 291n.11; examples of, 196–7; and institutional genesis, 212, 213, 218–20, 234; and institutional persistence, 211, 212, 213, 214, 218–21, 226, 231, 234; and legacies, 289; and reactive sequences, 291n.12; structure of, 195–6, 290; and theory testing, 311; ubiquity of in politics, 196
pattern matching, 360–3, 368
Patterson, James, 95
peasants, 60; and democracy and authoritarianism, 138–40, 142, 144, 146, 149; and revolutions, 49, 61, 66
periodization, 99, 270; and bias toward in macrohistorical research, 271, 273–8; and macrofoundations, 272; and preferences, 271–2, 276–82, 298
personalistic authoritarianism. *See* sultanism
Peru, 54, 359; and authoritarianism, 145, 147; and democracy, 161
Pettit, Philip, 280
Philippines, 53, 59, 66, 67, 74, 75, 83, 161
Pierson, Paul, 12, 106, 117, 187–8, 209, 224, 226, 231, 233, 234, 265, 291, 417–9
Piven, Frances Fox, 113
Piven–Cloward hypothesis, 101
Plato, 53, 55
Polanyi, Karl, 289
policy feedback. *See* feedback processes
Popper, Karl, 297, 306
positional methods, 243, 246–9, 250, 264
positive feedback. *See* increasing returns
positivism, 327, 390, 391–2; *see also* neopositivism
postindustrialism, 181
postmodern theory, 11, 22–5, 52, 133, 327
Powell, Robert, 198
power, 23, 287–8, 423
power arguments, 209
power-distributional mechanisms of institutional reproduction, 211; defined, 215–16, 287, 297; examples of, 216, 223; critique of, 216, 223
preferences: and collective actors, 279, 284; defined, 279; and moments of change, 280–1; neglect of in comparative historical research, 271–3, 275–8; and periodization, 271–2, 276–82, 298
primary data sources, 18n. 40, 97, 99, 420
process tracing, 6, 47–50, 65, 75, 84, 363–5, 368, 395, 408; *see also* systematic process analysis
Prussian Reform Movement, 54, 63
Przeworski, Adam, 194, 281n. 7, 342n. 5, 379

public policy: economic, 4, 107, 108; *see also* social provision
punctuated equilibrium model, 211, 213, 221, 224, 290
Putnam, Robert, 181, 192, 320, 322

qualitative data, 6, 113, 134
quantitative data, 16, 41, 49, 110, 111, 117, 134, 243, 249, 318, 414, 420
quantitative research. *See* statistical research

racial relations, 4, 183–5, 342–3, 409
Ragin, Charles C., 18, 44, 110, 319n. 12, 325, 343, 345, 346–7, 350, 383, 389–90
rational action theory. *See* rational choice theory
rational choice theory: and agency, 294; and dispute with comparative historical analysis, 19–22, 413, 414–15; empirical contribution of, 19; and empirically underspecified propositions, 329; "pragmatic" forms of, 19, 21; short time horizon of, 201; and synergy with comparative historical analysis, 421, 422–3; and the study of democracy and authoritarianism, 160; and the study of revolutions, 70–1, 72, 80
realism, critical, 390
realism, philosophical, 12n. 28
reference group theory, 328–9
regression analysis, 12, 324, 326; assumptions of, 375, 383–4; and importance in statistical research, 381, 391, 416; and necessary and sufficient conditions, 349–51; limitations of, 386–9, 399, 416; and trends toward in the social sciences, 374
reiterated problem solving, 297
relations, network, 265; definition of, 262n. 8
relative deprivation, 57
Remmer, Karen, 155, 160
replacement mechanism, 190
revolutions: 4; anticommunist type of, 53, 66; challenges to structural theories of, 71–6; and class coalitions, 75, 81; communist type of, 47, 50, 60, 82; definitions of, 41, 52–5, 359; and dual power, 60; and elite divisions, 48, 49, 63–4, 67, 69, 74–5, 80; and inflation, 48–9, 69; and international pressures, 63–4, 66–7, 68, 69, 70, 74, 80, 81, 358; liberal type of, 47, 50, 60; and modernization, 57–62; nationalist type of, 60; number of, 41; natural history approach to, 55–6; and population growth, 48, 68–9, 79, 81. 361; outcomes of, 65, 66–7, 69, 73, 83–4; and social-structural theory, 62–70
Rimlinger, Gaston, 94, 118
Ringer, Fritz, 278
roles, 249, 250
Romania, 76
Roosevelt, Franklin D., 55
Rothstein, Bo, 227
Rubens, Peter Paul, 270
Rueschemeyer, Dietrich, 13, 143–7, 150–1, 201–2, 411
Ruggie, Mary, 117
Rule, James, 164, 409
Russia, 64, 76, 77, 359, 364; *see also* Russian Revolution; Soviet Union
Russian Revolution (1917), 41, 50, 53, 54, 55, 59, 60, 61, 63, 66, 70, 82, 83, 84, 308, 309

Sainsbury, Diane, 109
sampling, 42–3, 52, 105
Scandinavia, 185, 227, 321, 322
Schattschneider, E. E., 283, 376
Schelling, Thomas, 184
Schickler, Eric, 226, 232, 422
Schmitter, Philippe, 160

Index

Schneiberg, Marc, 232
Schriewer, Jürgen, 330–1
scope conditions, 10, 92, 110, 135, 139n. 5, 155
secondary data sources, 18, 94, 97, 99, 420
Selbin, Eric, 73
selection bias, 18, 23, 42, 105, 351–2
selection mechanism, 190, 191
sequence analysis, 94, 95n. 4, 104, 113, 146, 147, 152, 363–4, 393, 398; and causal chains, 187–9, 418; and causation, 314, 325, 385; *see also* path dependence; temporal processes
Serra, José, 154
Sewell, William Jr., 218, 220, 281, 365, 366
Shah of Iran, 66
Shalev, Michael, 324n. 15
Shaver, Sheila, 421
Shefter, Martin, 196, 208
Shining Path (Peru), 54
Shonfield, Andrew, 229
Silberman, Bernard, 287
Skocpol, Theda, 5, 13, 26, 41, 46–7, 50, 79, 95, 99, 101, 118, 141, 208, 231, 234, 263n.9, 273, 317n.10, 358–9, 364, 366, 408, 412; and structural theories of revolutions, 62–70, 274–5n.6
Skowronek, Stephen, 235
small-*N* analysis: advantages of, 13–14, 18, 315, 318, 375, 390, 398–9; and the comparative method, 380, 397; and the generation of hypotheses, 305, 307; and pattern matching, 361; and relationship to large-*N* analysis, 16–18, 41–4, 103–5, 110, 325, 337–8, 390, 398; skepticism about, 17–18, 42, 105, 145, 305, 324–6; and systematic process analysis, 397; and temporality, 112; *see also* cases; causal inference
Smelser, Neil J., 317, 380
Smith, Adam, 3
social democracy, 9, 108, 149; and a model, 106
socialism: origins of, 61, 84; fall of, 8
social mechanisms. *See* mechanisms
social movements, 14, 72, 111, 114, 115–16; defined, 115
social movement theory, 22, 72, 114–15, 119–20
social provision, 4, 8; amount of, 92, 98, 110; and "big five" programs, 103; and consensus on, 92, 97–8, 102, 120–1; and data availability, 97–9, 117, 119; defined, 97–8, 107–9, 116; and political organization theories, 101; and political party coalitions, 102; and qualitative–quantitative synergies, 92, 93, 100, 102, 109–12, 117–20, 422; reasons for progress in the study of, 114–20; retrenchment of, 92, 99, 106–7, 109, 117, 122; stages of development of, 92, 102, 106–7; and state-centered theories, 101–2, 103; types of, 97–8, 107–9, 121–2
Social Science History Association (SSHA), 3, 4n.9
Social Science Research Council (SSRC), 377
Social Security Administration (U.S.), 98
sociometry, 243
South Africa, 59, 83, 342, 343
Southern Europe, 155, 165
South Korea, 155, 161
Soviet Union, 43, 53, 66, 67, 70, 75, 79, 80, 82, 158
Spain, 158, 220, 277, 356–7; and democratization, 143
Spruyt, Hendrik, 208
spurious correlation, 363–4
Stalin, Joseph, 54, 84, 309
Stark, David, 227
state-centric theory, 6, 22; and causal chain arguments, 187; and

state-centric theory (*cont.*)
democratization, 141, 151; and revolutionary theory, 63–4; and theories of social policy, 101–2, 110, 115
states: as cases, 14; and democratization, 141, 165, 166; origins and growth of, 9, 98, 196–7; and relations with elites, 64, 67, 68; revolutionary reconstruction of, 67, 73, 79; sources of stability of, 78–80; *see also* welfare states
statistical research: accomplishments of, 16–17, 41–2; and advice for comparative historical analysis, 354–5, 419; assumptions of, 18, 44–5, 337–9, 355–6; and criticisms of comparative historical methods, 17–18, 347–53, 413; and deterministic explanation, 340; and focus on short-term processes, 199–200, 417; inferential goals of, 42–4, 380, 382; innovations in, 388–9; methodological problems of, 18–19, 307, 386–9, 396–7, 399, 415; and necessary and sufficient conditions, 339, 349–51, 355–6, 367–8, 389; and probabilistic explanation, 340; rise of, 16, 407; and single case studies, 318; and the study of democracy and authoritarianism, 134, 146, 150–1, 165, 166; and the study of revolutions, 41–3, 45, 120; and the study of social provision, 91, 92, 93, 100, 102, 109–12, 117–20, 412; and synergy with comparative historical research, 17, 92, 93, 100, 102, 109–12, 117–20, 150–1, 166, 202, 325, 327, 361, 412, 421; and within-case analysis, 361; *see also* Bayesian analysis, regression analysis
statistical significance, 18, 49, 346, 350–1, 354
Steinmo, Sven, 101
Stepan, Alfred, 132, 152, 156–9, 161–3
Stephens, Evelyne Huber. *See* Huber, Evelyne
Stephens, John D., 13, 95, 101, 110, 112, 118, 142, 147, 185, 208, 314n.7, 317n.10
Stimson, James, 182, 197, 202
Stinchcombe, Arthur, 195, 203, 209, 283, 309, 314n.7, 316, 317, 318, 328
Stone, Lawrence, 253
structural approach, 62–70, 102; and cultural analysis, 5; definitions of, 151, 193; and historicism, 277; and network theory, 241–5, 254–5, 259–64; and relationship to comparative historical analysis, 6, 21–2, 271–9, 340; and statistical analysis, 199; and the study of democracy and authoritarianism, 136, 151–2, 157, 160–1, 163; *see also* agency
structural equivalence, 246–9
structural functionalism. *See* functionalism
structural position, 258; *see also* roles
Stryker, Robin, 50
subjective beliefs, 21, 151, 251, 267, 278, 280, 313
substantive enlightenment, 407, 411
Sudanese civil wars, 62
sufficient conditions, 18, 44, 314–15, 337, 389; and Boolean algebra, 343–4; and causes of revolutions, 65, 78, 80; and combinations of variables, 343, 344; criticisms of, 348–53; defined, 341; and deterministic explanation, 340–2; and fuzzy-set analysis, 347; versus linear causation, 349–50, 355–6; and a nominal strategy, 338, 344, 345, 352; and probabilistic explanation, 344–5, 347; and selection bias, 351–2; and tautological causes, 348–9
Sulloway, Frank J., 251n.5

sultanism, 158, 161, 162, 166
Swank, Duane, 187, 203
Sweden, 277, 320, 345; and democratization, 142–3, 149, 167, 356–7
Swidler, Ann, 281
Switzerland: and democratization, 143, 149, 356–7
systematic process analysis, 375, 391–5, 397, 398
system-level analysis, 320
systems theory, 9

temporal processes: brief textual references to, 6, 7, 12, 26, 43, 61, 77, 94, 100, 271, 272, 415, 420; and cases, 14, 41; and conjunctural causation, 80–2; and duration, 91; and large structures, 275; and process tracing, 47, 51; and "quick" or rapidly unfolding causes, 178–80; and "quick" or rapidly unfolding outcomes, 178–80, 182; and relative timing, 12, 13, 26, 61, 111, 112, 152, 291, 360, 385; and the separation of cause and effect, 192–5, 197, 365; and slow-moving causes 178–80, 182, 195, 417; and slow-moving outcomes, 178–80, 189–92, 417; and speed of events, 167, 181; and statistical methods, 16; and tautological causes, 348–9; and testing hypotheses, 103–4, 383; and time lags, 180, 191, 194, 200; *see also* critical junctures; path dependence; process tracing; sequence analysis
temporal structure, 179; and dependence on theoretical framework, 189; in natural science examples, 178–80
Teune, Henry, 342n.5, 379
Thailand, 161
Thatcher administration, 230
Thelen, Kathleen, 13, 289, 292, 417–19, 423
theoretical expectations, 318
theoretical framework, 5, 8n.24, 26, 96, 308, 318, 333; and formulation of cases, 320; and implications for temporal structure of explanation, 179, 180, 200, 201–2; and the infinite regress problem, 188–9; and network analysis, 244, 249–50; *see also* focused theoretical framework
theory, 6, 20–2, 266, 350, 394; and anomalies, 45–6, 50, 96, 100, 105, 115; and case selection, 13, 14, 43, 46, 411; and dialogue with evidence, 13, 20, 312–13, 318; development versus testing of, 316–17, 394n.18, 396–7; generation of, 310, 354; and history, 280; and narrative construction, 50–1; pluralistic approach to, 21; and ontology, 374; rejection of, 45–7, 52, 313, 392; refinement of, 96, 307, 411; and single cases, 310–18; and statistical methods, 249–50n.4; *see also* metatheory; middle-range theory; theoretical framework
thick description, 415
Thompson, E. P., 306, 307, 310, 311–14, 318, 319, 320, 330
threshold effects: and boiling points, 185–6; defined, 182; examples of, 182–7; individual versus collective thresholds, 183; and tipping points, 183
Tilly, Charles, 12, 59–60, 62, 64, 71, 196, 200, 273, 284, 285, 345, 346, 408, 412
Tilton, Timothy A., 142
time horizon: defined, 179; restriction of in economics and political science, 178
Tocqueville, Alexis de, 3, 55, 64, 101, 150, 277, 410
totalitarianism, 158, 161, 162
transitions literature, 160–1; short time horizon of, 200

Trotsky, Leon, 55, 59, 77, 317
Trow, Martin, 308–9, 312, 319
Tunisia, 421
Turkey, 49–50, 155, 161
typologies: and authoritarianism, 158, 161, 164; and conceptual development, 134, 158, 378; and democracy, 164

uncertainty, 137, 215
unit homogeneity. *See* causal homogeneity
United States, 4, 8, 12, 13, 66, 74, 77, 210, 277, 342, 343, 346, 409; and civic engagement, 320–2; and democratization, 138, 139–40; Civil War in, 61, 138, 139, 140; and social policy, 91, 95, 99, 104, 106, 108, 112, 113, 360, 422; *see also* American Revolution
universal problems, 328, 330–1
Uruguay, 365; and authoritarianism, 153–4; and democratization, 144, 161
utilitarian arguments, 209
utilitarian-functionalist mechanisms of reproduction, 211; critique of, 215, 223; defined 214; examples of, 215, 223
Uzbekistan, 342, 423

validity, 13, 111, 373n. 1
values, 53, 54, 58
Van Rossem, Ronan, 251n. 5, 260–2, 420
Venezuela, 156
Verba, Sydney, 17, 24, 111, 325, 378, 414
violence, 42, 53, 54, 56, 58, 59
Vogel, Steven, 230
voluntarism: and the study of democracy and authoritarianism, 136, 157, 159, 160–1, 163, 202

Wallerstein, Immanuel, 63, 273, 412
Waltz, Kenneth, 393n. 16
Warner, Carolyn, 275n. 6
Weber, Max, 3, 79, 101, 202, 271, 277, 278, 286, 308, 312, 317, 321–2, 376, 386, 394n. 19, 410
Weberian theory, 408, 412
Weingast, Barry R., 215
Weir, Margaret, 220, 222, 229
welfare states: development of, 4, 92, 98; reconstruction of, 8; retrenchment of, 106–7, 109, 187–8; *see also* social policy
Wellman, Barry, 243
Whiskey Rebellion, 249, 255–7
Wickham-Crowley, Timothy, 71, 73, 343–4
Wilensky, Harold, 91, 113
Winch, Donald, 386n. 9
within-case analysis: and causal inference, 18, 324, 325, 337, 338, 350, 360–7, 417; defined, 360; and narrative, 323; and quantitative analysis, 49, 111; types of, 360–7; *see also* causal narrative; pattern matching; process tracing
within-system analysis, 320
women. *See* gender
working class, urban, 60; and democracy and authoritarianism, 146–9, 165; and social policy, 216; *see also* working-class movements
working-class movements, 8, 49, 111, 149
world-historical changes, 166–7
world system theory, 63
World War I, 65, 77, 149, 308, 356, 357
World War II, 224, 225, 229, 326, 410
Wuthnow, Robert, 196

Yashar, Deborah J., 366–7
Yeltsin, Boris, 76

Zaire. *See* Congo, Democratic Republic of
Zald, Mayer, 116
Zeitlin, Jonathan, 227n. 32

Other Books in the Series (*continued from front of book*)

Roberto Franzosi, *The Puzzle of Strikes: Class and State Strategies in Postwar Italy*
Geoffrey Garrett, *Partisan Politics in the Global Economy*
Miriam Golden, *Heroic Defeats: The Politics of Job Loss*
Jeff Goodwin, *No Other Way Out: States and Revolutionary Movements, 1945–1991*
Merilee Serrill Grindle, *Changing the State*
Anna M. Grzymala-Busse, *Redeeming the Communist Past: The Regeneration of Communist Parties in East Central Europe*
Frances Hagopian, *Traditional Politics and Regime Change in Brazil*
J. Rogers Hollingsworth and Robert Boyer, eds., *Contemporary Capitalism: The Embeddedness of Institutions*
Ellen Immergut, *Health Politics: Interests and Institutions in Western Europe*
Torben Iversen, *Contested Economic Institutions*
Torben Iversen, Jonas Pontusson, and David Soskice, eds., *Unions, Employers, and Central Banks: Macroeconomic Coordination and Institutional Change in Social Market Economies*
Thomas Janoski and Alexander M. Hicks, eds., *The Comparative Political Economy of the Welfare State*
David C. Kang, *Crony Capitalism: Corruption and Development in South Korea and the Philippines*
Robert O. Keohane and Helen B. Milner, eds., *Internationalization and Domestic Politics*
Herbert Kitschelt, *The Transformation of European Social Democracy*
Herbert Kitschelt, Peter Lange, Gary Marks, and John D. Stephens, eds., *Continuity and Change in Contemporary Capitalism*
Herbert Kitschelt, Zdenka Mansfeldova, Radek Markowski, and Gabor Toka, *Post-Communist Party Systems*
David Knoke, Franz Urban Pappi, Jeffrey Broadbent, and Yutaka Tsujinaka, eds., *Comparing Policy Networks*
Allan Kornberg and Harold D. Clarke, *Citizens and Community: Political Support in a Representative Democracy*
Amie Kreppel, *The European Parliament and the Supranational Party System*
David D. Laitin, *Language Repertories and State Construction in Africa*
Fabrice E. Lehoucq and Ivan Molina, *Stuffing the Ballot Box: Electoral Reform and Democratization in Costa Rica*
Mark Irving Lichbach and Alan S. Zuckerman, eds., *Comparative Politics: Rationality, Culture, and Structure*

Pauline Jones Luong, *Institutional Change and Political Continuity in Post-Soviet Central Asia*
Doug McAdam, John McCarthy, and Mayer Zald, eds., *Comparative Perspectives on Social Movements*
Scott Mainwaring and Matthew Soberg Shugart, eds., *Presidentialism and Democracy in Latin America*
Anthony W. Marx, *Making Race, Making Nations: A Comparison of South Africa, the United States and Brazil*
Joel S. Migdal, *State in Society: Studying How States and Societies Constitute One Another*
Joel S. Migdal, Atul Kohli, and Vivienne Shue, eds., *State Power and Social Forces: Domination and Transformation in the Third World*
Scott Morgenstern and Benito Nacif, eds., *Legislative Politics in Latin America*
Wolfgang C. Muller and Kaare Strom, *Policy, Office, or Votes?*
Maria Victoria Murillo, *Labor Unions, Partisan Coalitions, and Market Reforms in Latin America*
Ton Notermans, *Money, Markets, and the State: Social Democratic Economic Policies since 1918*
Roger Peterson, *Understanding Ethnic Violence: Fear, Hatred, and Resentment in Twentieth-Century Eastern Europe*
Paul Pierson, *Dismantling the Welfare State?: Reagan, Thatcher and the Politics of Retrenchment*
Simona Piattoni, ed., *Clientelism, Interests, and Democratic Representation*
Marino Regini, *Uncertain Boundaries: The Social and Political Construction of European Economies*
Jefferey M. Sellers, *Governing from Below: Urban Regions and the Global Economy*
Yossi Shain and Juan Linz, eds., *Interim Governments and Democratic Transitions*
Theda Skocpol, *Social Revolutions in the Modern World*
Richard Snyder, *Politics after Neoliberalism: Reregulation in Mexico*
David Stark and László Bruszt, *Postsocialist Pathways: Transforming Politics and Property in East Central Europe*
Sven Steinmo, Kathleen Thelen, and Frank Longstreth, eds., *Structuring Politics: Historical Institutionalism in Comparative Analysis*
Susan C. Stokes, *Mandates and Democracy: Neoliberalism by Surprise in Latin America*
Susan C. Stokes, ed., *Public Support for Market Reforms in New Democracies*

Duane Swank, *Global Capital, Political Institutions, and Policy Change in Developed Welfare States*
Sidney Tarrow, *Power in Movement: Social Movements and Contentious Politics*
Ashutosh Varshney, *Democracy, Development, and the Countryside*
Elisabeth Jean Wood, *Forging Democracy from Below: Insurgent Transitions in South Africa and El Salvador*

Made in the USA
Lexington, KY
12 January 2013